"MY BRAVE MECHANICS"

D1104687

GREAT LAKES BOOKS

A complete listing of the books in this series can be found online at
wsupress.wayne.edu

Editors

PHILIP P. MASON
Wayne State University

CHARLES K. HYDE
Wayne State University

Advisory Editors

JEFFREY ABT
Wayne State University

LAURIE HARRIS
Pleasant Ridge, Michigan

SIDNEY BOLKOSKY
University of Michigan–Dearborn

SUSAN HIGMAN LARSEN
Detroit Institute of Arts

SANDRA SAGESER CLARK
Michigan Historical Center

NORMAN McRAE
Detroit, Michigan

JOHN C. DANN
University of Michigan

WILLIAM H. MULLIGAN, JR.
Murray State University

DE WITT DYKES
Oakland University

ERIK C. NORDBERG
Michigan Technological University

JOE GRIMM
Detroit Free Press

GORDON L. OLSON
Grand Rapids, Michigan

DAVID HALKOLA
Hancock, Michigan

MICHAEL D. STAFFORD
Cranbrook Institute of Science

RICHARD H. HARMS
Calvin College

JOHN VAN HECKE
Wayne State University

ARTHUR M. WOODFORD
Harsen's Island, Michigan

"MY BRAVE MECHANICS"

The First Michigan Engineers and Their Civil War

MARK HOFFMAN

Foreword by William M. Anderson

W WAYNE STATE UNIVERSITY PRESS   DETROIT

© 2007 by Wayne State University Press, Detroit, Michigan 48201.

Manufactured in the United States of America.

11   10   09   08   07   5   4   3   2   1

Library of Congress Cataloging-in-Publication Data

Hoffman, Mark.

My brave Mechanics : the First Michigan Engineers and their
Civil War / Mark Hoffman ; foreword by William M. Anderson.

p. cm. — (Great Lakes books)

Includes bibliographical references and index.

ISBN-13: 978-0-8143-3292-4 (hardcover : alk. paper)
ISBN-10: 0-8143-3292-7 (hardcover : alk. paper)

1. United States. Army. Michigan Engineers and Mechanics Regiment,
1st (1861–1865) 2. Michigan—History—Civil War, 1861–1865—Regimental
histories. 3. United States—History—Civil War, 1861–1865—Regimental
histories. 4. Military engineers—Michigan—History—19th century.
5. United States—History—Civil War, 1861–1865—Engineering
and construction. 6. United States—History—Civil War,
1861–1865—Campaigns. I. Title.

E514.9.H64 2007
973.7'474—dc22
2006036379

• To •

HENRY HOFFMAN,
36th Iowa, and Connor Been, 117th Illinois,
my ancestral links to the Civil War;

to

ANN, PATRICK, AND ALICE HOFFMAN,
my living links to the future they fought to ensure;

and to

HOWARD AND PAULINE HOFFMAN,
who first understood and supported my interest in the Civil War.

Contents

CONTENTS

Illustrations

Maps

Tables

Foreword

Mark Hoffman makes a significant contribution to the growing literature of Michigan's role in the Civil War with his story of the First Michigan Engineers and Mechanics. In a larger sense, this study reflects the strong current interest in regimental histories and the life of ordinary soldiers.

Like most Civil War soldiers, engineers were volunteers, yet they were different from the common soldiers who made up the ranks of other military units, bringing applied mechanical skills crucial to their new occupation. As Hoffman observes, a majority of the men who made up the First Michigan Engineers and Mechanics were craftsmen and had experience in various construction and mechanical trades.

Hoffman is especially effective in introducing the main characters and profiling the rank and file in this regimental history. Certainly his deep background as a genealogist aided his penetrating research and analysis.

Given their different backgrounds, it seems easy to differentiate engineers and infantrymen as skilled and unskilled laborers. Given the mission of engineers, a similar distinction seems accurate concerning officers, where the "bridge builders" were often highly trained compared to infantry leaders, who frequently won their position based on successful recruitment of soldiers and political influence.

There were also pronounced differences in the field. Like other similar units, the members of the First Michigan were combat engineers required to ward off attackers bent on disrupting vital communication and supply lines. Infantry commanders always longed for a stand-up fight, a situation rarely realized by engineers. Instead they contended with an enemy that sometimes struck at night, was often highly mobile, and exploited the isolation and vulnerability of workmen with surprise and ambush tactics. In sharp contrast, most army commanders ensured that infantry supported artillery, pickets were posted around the perimeter, and cavalry protected the flanks. Just as color bearers, officers on horseback and artillerymen were special targets; engineers constructing a bridge or repairing a railroad were in the crosshairs for elimination. Different than infantrymen, they were almost never dug in and truly ready for an attack.

And their common adversary was formidable. Guerillas and bushwhackers were not governed by the usual rules but engaged their foes in a mean and ugly kind of warfare. To U. S. Grant's chief of staff, Gen. William T. Sherman wrote, "I have little confidence in railroads running through a country where every house is a nest of secret, bitter enemies." Similarly, Gen. Don Carlos Buell reported that his "communications, 500 miles long, are swarming with an immense cavalry force of the enemy, regular and irregular, which renders it almost impossible to keep them open."

Particularly during the early years of the war, historians agree that cavalry represented the best dimension of the Confederacy military capability and exceeded the effectiveness of Union horse soldiers by a considerable margin. Thus, engineers doubling as combat soldiers defended against the best Confederate forces. Cavalry leaders like Nathan Bedford Forest, John Hunt Morgan, Jeb Stuart, John Mosby, and Joe Wheeler were legendary and among the very best Confederate commanders. As exasperated General Sherman reported to Secretary of War Edwin Stanton, "I will order them to make up a force and go out and follow Forest to the death if it costs 10,000 lives and breaks the Treasury." In a raid of a little more than two weeks in December 1862, Morgan's cavalry tore up many miles of track and destroyed fifty trestle bridges.

Yet despite overwhelming odds, this Michigan engineer unit, and many others, performed great service constructing bridges, blockhouses, fortifications, railroads, and telegraph lines. They also knew how to destroy all of these assets when a retreating federal army needed to buy some time or deny resources to the enemy.

This account of the First Michigan Engineers provides wonderful descriptions of trestle bridges and blockhouses as well as great detail about recruiting soldiers, both initially and after the Union imposed a draft, the regiment's experiences with the civilian population, and how the men behaved away from home. Hoffman's story is contextual, allowing the reader an opportunity to appreciate the experiences of the ranks while understanding the larger perspective of the war. There are many welcomed human interest stories here, none better than the long struggle over engineers' premium pay that had been promised.

Mark Hoffman is a researcher of the first rank and could have easily produced the first ever multiple-volume regimental history. This work is a great start at telling the story of Michigan's only engineer regiment, and we will look forward to subsequent publications surely to come from the author's exhaustive research.

William M. Anderson

Acknowledgments

I have spent more than twenty years researching and writing this book. It was a long journey, but along the way I met many great people who took the time and energy to encourage and assist me. In many ways, discovering them and sharing their passion for the story was the best part of the trip.

First, there are two people without whom this book would not have been written or published. Nancy Obermayer began researching the regiment several decades ago, intrigued by the service of her great-great-grandfather Capt. John W. Williamson, one of the original members of the First Michigan Engineers. She was very generous in guiding my early research and then turned over all her materials and great advice. It was Nancy who first opened my eyes to the wealth of primary source materials found in the National Archives and tipped me off to many of the surviving letters and diaries. My boss and mentor Dr. Bill Anderson provided the constant example, encouragement, and friendship that made this book possible. He patiently read the first manuscript, and his positive comments gave me hope that it was publishable. Bill also generously wrote the foreword and coached me through the publishing process.

Second, there are four institutions without which this story could not have been written. Though I've used materials from many others, the largest amount of information came from these four, their rich collections made accessible and enjoyable by knowledgeable and professional staff: the Archives of Michigan (especially Le Roy Barnett, Mary Zimmeth, Dave Johnson, and Mark Harvey), the Library of Michigan (especially Bernadette Bartlett, Arlean Crenshaw, and the late Carole Callard), the National Archives (especially DeAnne Blanton), and the Bentley Historical Library (especially Nancy Bartlett). Every researcher should be as fortunate as I in finding so much material in such great hands.

I have no ancestral link to the Michigan Engineers, but I met many who do. They generously shared surviving letters, diaries, photos, and family stories. In addition to Nancy Obermayer, these include Tom Lowry (descendant of William Simms), Norm and Dale Rolison (John L. Rolison), Sharon Patton (Nathan Robinson), Jeannette Studley (James D. Robinson), Jane Damon and Margaret Parker

(Francis D. Adams), Jane Tripodi (several), Dee Harris (Willard and William Gitchell), Virginia Beck (James M. Beck), Timothy Cook (George A. Cook), Orrin Watkins and Bonnie Pierce Hartnett (Levi Watkins), and Fran Woods (Henry Lampman).

In addition, I want to recognize several established historians and scholars who said the right things at the right time to a novice researcher. The impact of their patient advice went well beyond the issues we discussed at the time and was instrumental in this book. As an undergraduate student at Michigan State University, I had the great luck to have Dr. Frederick Williams for several history courses, and he patiently took time during his office hours to feed my enthusiasm for the Civil War. In every sense, the seeds of this book were first planted during those discussions in his office in Morrill Hall, when he told me to quit talking about writing a book and get started. During the same time period, the late Dr. Justin L. Kestenbaum hammered home the obligation I had as a student of Michigan history to conduct original research and add chapters to its story. He was also the first to point me in the direction of the rich collection of Michigan newspapers on microfilm at the Library of Michigan.

In a similar vein, a chance encounter with the late John Collins of Marshall in 1987 opened my eyes to the rich local archival resources found throughout our state. Since the Michigan Engineers rendez-voused at Marshall, it was a particularly fortunate chance encounter on my part, but his kind urging and patience with my questions would have been helpful regardless. Years later he provided valuable infor-mation on the location of 1861 Camp Owen. John was a true leader in state and local history, serving for almost twenty years on the Michi-gan Historical Commission and sharing generously with all. Tom and Beverly Lowry took time from their own research during my visits to the National Archives to answer questions and point me in the direc-tion of seldom-used primary sources. They also shared very gener-ously with me their findings in Civil War court-martial records. As a descendant, Tom also provided me with family materials related to the service of his great-grandfather William Simms of Company L.

I had the good fortune very early to be introduced to the tremen-dous materials of the Archives of Michigan by former reference archi-vist Le Roy Barnett and then benefit from his enthusiasm in the final years of this project. His passion for preserving and telling Michigan's story is legendary and much appreciated. I also want to publicly ac-knowledge the valuable assistance over many years from the late Car-ole Callard of the Library of Michigan. As I tried to research and tell the story of the men who served in this regiment, I kept falling back on the genealogical research skills that she taught me. All of us who knew Carole are richer for it, and this story can be better told because of her generosity of time and talent.

As I finished work on this manuscript, I had the great fortune to meet John Gelderloos. He generously shared with me important materials from his collection. He also kindly granted permission to quote from the letters of Perrin and Newton Fox, which he had purchased from fellow collector Tom Jones. Tom had previously shared the content of these letters when they were in his collection. Collectors the caliber of John and Tom have been careful stewards of the rich legacy of the paper and artifacts left by those who served. The story is much richer because of them.

Wayne State University Press was willing to take a chance on this unpublished author. I'm particularly grateful to acquiring editor Kathryn Wildfong, who patiently guided me through the process of manuscript submission and review and then handed me off to the very capable hands of others.

I also wish to acknowledge the excellent maps that were prepared by Sherman Hollander. He came highly recommended by Le Roy Barnett and lived up to the endorsement.

At the risk of omitting anyone, I'd like to acknowledge the many other individuals and institutions that aided my efforts during this long journey: Albion Historical Society (Frank Passic), University of Detroit Mercy (Margaret Auer), Robert Beasecker, Byron Brown, Chattanooga-Hamilton County Bicentennial Library, Chicago Historical Society, University of Cincinnati Library, Clarke Historical Library, William L. Clements Library, Detroit Public Library, Duke University Library, Richard L. Edwards, the Grand Lodge of Free and Accepted Masons–Michigan (Richard Amon), the Filson Club, Flint Public Library, Dale E. Floyd, John H. Graham and the Stevenson Railroad Museum Depot, Grand Rapids Public Library, Pete Hannah, Richard Harms, Hillsdale County Historical Society, Illinois State Historical Library, University of Iowa Library, Jackson District Library, Randal Jelks, Kalamazoo College Library, Kansas State Historical Society, Kentucky Department for Libraries and Archives, Knox College, Knoxville Public Library, Constance Larson, Marion Loyd, Louisville and Nashville Railroad Historical Society (Charles Bogart), University of Louisville Elkstrom Library (Charles B. Castner), Marshall Historical Society (Richard Carver and Roger Graves), Michigan State University Archives, University of Minnesota Library, Minnesota Historical Society, University of Missouri–Rolla Archives, Montana Historical Society, Public Library of Nashville and Davidson County,

Oberlin College Archives, Ohio Historical Society, Delores Richardson, Historical Society of Pennsylvania, Railroad Historical Research Center (Thomas T. Taber, III), Richard M. Rupley, Linda B. Rye, Philip L. Shiman, Steve Soper, Ron Thinnes, Leland W. Thornton, Matthew VanAcker, Geoff Walden, Western Michigan University Archives and Regional History Collections, and the Western Reserve Historical Society.

Finally, and most important, my love and thanks to Ann. In 1985 she married "the dead guys," this project, and me. She has put up with us all ever since. She neither hears the guns nor feels the tug from a distant past, yet she understands that I do and always will. Thank you, my dear.

· 1 ·

Volunteer Engineers

On a small scale, engineer troops were part of the American military experience as far back as the Revolutionary War, and in 1802 a permanent and separate Corps of Engineers was established within the U.S. Army. Expanded in 1812, the Corps of Engineers saw service against the British during the War of 1812 but was reduced again after 1821. For twenty-five years it remained a handful of specially trained officers scattered along the nation's coasts and frontiers. Facing war with Mexico, Congress expanded the corps in 1846 to include a company of enlisted men to work alongside the engineer officers. The new company organization proved its worth during active campaigning in Mexico and remained a part of the regular army after the war ended.[1]

On August 3, 1861, the wartime Congress authorized a small expansion of the Corps of Engineers. Several senior officers argued for a substantial engineer organization of regulars, but Congress added only three engineer companies to the existing one. The Corps of Engineers never grew beyond these four companies during the Civil War, and it was not until March 1863 that any additional officers were added. As late as January 1865, the Corps of Engineers numbered fewer than six hundred enlisted men, and the eighty-six officers actually on duty were seven fewer than at the outbreak of the war.[2]

As a result, the North had to rely on volunteer engineers to preserve the Union, just as it did in the other branches of the military. Of the estimated twenty-five thousand men who eventually served as Union engineers, virtually all were volunteers. This development was the result of a slow evolution of military policy, prompted not by foresight but rather by the embarrassing fact of necessity. Volunteer engineers came to form an important part of Union efforts, first as companies and eventually as entire regiments and brigades.[3]

Union volunteer engineers were part of the same jumbled process as their infantry, cavalry, and artillery counterparts in the summer of 1861. Many of the embryonic engineer units never completed their formation. For example, a group of Illinois Central Railroad employees who tried to form a company of sappers in May 1861 failed to obtain official authorization and lost interest or drifted into infantry regiments. Another company, Abram J. David's Chicago sappers and miners, found themselves converted to infantry upon reaching the field, much to the consternation of the men. Many more companies appear only briefly in the historical record and then promptly disappear for unknown reasons. This was the case with two Michigan companies in 1861: P. Morey tried to raise a company in Adrian, and Thomas W. Collins made a similar attempt in Marquette.[4]

In addition to the generally chaotic nature of Union military mobilization in 1861, several unique problems plagued volunteer engineer units. First, the law made no provision for volunteer engineer units because none had been raised since the last days of the Revolutionary War. Even though the War Department and President Lincoln authorized several men to raise volunteer engineer regiments, there was no specific congressional action in 1861 to back them up. Nor was it very likely, given the strong feelings many members of Congress had against the Corps of Engineers and its "exclusive elite." Though these strong views were not shared by all, they were "enough to make any legislative action concerning the engineers difficult." The case for volunteer engineers also received little support from much of the regular army engineer establishment, which instead focused efforts on gaining more pay and rank for their own organizations. Instead of official sanction in 1861, volunteer engineer units generally had to rely on War Department promises that they would be assigned engineering duty, even though they organized as infantry regiments.[5]

There also was no standard on what the volunteer engineer troops should be paid. Recruiting officers for engineer companies and regiments in 1861 were consistent only in offering higher levels of pay than for infantry service. Most made the inflated offers in good faith, relying on communications from War Department officials or President Lincoln. In fact, there was no congressional authorization to pay volunteer engineers more than the infantry arm. This would create tremendous problems after volunteer engineers took to the field.[6]

In addition, there was little agreement on how the troops should be used. Existing army regulations directed that regular army "sappers, miners, and pontoniers" aid in the training of cadets at West Point, oversee the erection of fortifications while serving as "fort-keepers," and "open the way or repair the road" while assigned to an active army in the field. It was suggested that this latter function could best be performed if the men were mounted to allow them to regain the advance after repairing the road. Maj. Gen. John C. Fremont's grandiose plans in Missouri—encompassing companies of men in gaudy uniforms serving as telegraph operators and guards, pontoniers, sappers, and miners—were shelved upon his dismissal. Others argued that volunteer engineers could provide a source of skilled labor on fortifications but did not distinguish between their labors and those of hired civilian workers. Few suggested the repair and operation of captured rebel railroads as a suitable task, yet this proved to be one of the most important roles volunteer engineers played in the West.[7]

Even fewer foresaw the tremendous future demand for trained engineer troops in units as large as regiments and brigades. West Point–trained Henry Halleck, major general in the California militia but soon to be called East for higher command, was an exception. He wrote regular army chief engineer Joseph G. Totten before Bull Run that it was a serious mistake not to form at least two regiments of regular army engineers and entire brigades of volunteer engineers. Three months later, Lt. Col. Barton S. Alexander of the Corps of Engineers emphasized his belief that the small engineer establishment was a "drop in the bucket" and that entire regiments of volunteers should be converted to engineer duty. Alexander pointed out what should have been obvious to more: "Our country is full of practical bridge-builders. We must secure their services. It is full of instructed labor so nearly akin to that which we require in engineer troops, that we must, if possible, embark it in that channel."[8]

All of these problems were eventually resolved, but they significantly complicated the raising of volunteer engineer regiments in 1861. The relative ability, or inability, of each regiment's officers and men to overcome these uncertainties determined in large measure if their unit was to be successful. A notable casualty of the early difficulties was James W. Wilson's regiment at Chicago. Wilson received permission to raise a regiment of engineers in the summer of 1861, and efforts were quickly under way in several states. Throughout the fall, however, the regiment remained camped near Chicago. Wilson was soon gone, and officials at Camp Douglas were unable to contain the mutinous recruits. In February 1862 the War Department recognized the inevitable and dissolved the regiment. Though it never joined the army, Wilson's regiment spurred the recruitment and eventual formation of other engineer units, particularly the First Michigan Engineers and Mechanics.[9]

Notices and advertisements for Wilson's regiment appeared in regional newspapers throughout the late summer of 1861. Because there were more companies being raised in Michigan than the War Department had authorized Governor Austin Blair to accept, regiments like Wilson's offered a chance for enterprising captains to gain official status and a regimental assignment. The advertisements for Wilson's regiment also offered a higher rate of pay than that of other arms, making it an appealing regiment to join.[10]

By early September 1861 there were Michigan companies being raised for Wilson's regiment in Ionia, Marshall, Albion, Grand Rapids, and possibly Kalamazoo. On the morning of September 10, two men raising the Grand Rapids company, surveyor Wright Coffinberry and master carpenter Baker Borden, met with merchant James W. Sligh and contractor Perrin V. Fox to discuss this new endeavor. The four decided that it would be better to raise an entire engineer regiment within the state and "thereby give Michigan the credit" than to send companies elsewhere. After discussing several options on how to proceed, the four men decided to urge William Power Innes to "take hold of the matter." Innes was a respected railroad surveyor and civil engineer from Grand Rapids whose labors had taken him throughout the state. The men also conveyed to Innes their opinion that he should command such a regiment if accepted by the War Department. Innes readily agreed.[11]

Following their discussion, Innes sent a telegram to Secretary of War Simon Cameron, asking, "Will the War Department accept a regiment from Michigan on the same terms as Colonel Wilson's of Chicago?" Cameron approved the offer, pending the endorsement of Governor Blair. Innes telegraphed Governor Blair, who agreed to take a train that night for Grand Rapids.[12]

Blair met with Innes, Coffinberry, Sligh, Borden, Fox, and former mayor Wilder D. Foster on the morning of September 12. After a thorough discussion, Governor Blair authorized Innes to raise the regiment and serve as colonel. The regiment was to be officered and equipped as infantry and provided with implements for engineer service. Blair gave Innes the authority to designate his officers, who in turn would be issued commissions by the governor. Blair also instructed that the regiment be designated as the First Michigan Engineers and Mechanics. Coffinberry, Sligh, Borden, and Fox would each command a company.[13]

On September 13 Blair wired Cameron that he had "cheerfully authorized" the formation of a regiment of mechanics, "finding that several companies have already been formed for this purpose." He also pledged to "assist it to the utmost of [his] ability." That same day, Michigan adjutant general John Robertson issued General Order No. 76 announcing the formation of the regiment. The order included the direction that "captains of companies desiring assignment to this regiment will transmit certified rolls of their companies to this office,

A meeting of Wright L. Coffinberry, James W. Sligh, Baker Borden, and Perrin V. Fox in Grand Rapids on September 10, 1861, started the movement that led to the formation of the Michigan Engineers and Mechanics. Each commanded one of the original companies. Sligh, *Michigan Engineers.*

signed by each member respectively, and entering thereon their occupation. . . . None but mechanics or engineers will be received." Three days later the order was modified to allow up to one quarter of each company to "consist of laborers, but in no case shall they exceed that proportion." Despite the exception, the order directed that "it [is] desirable, so far as practical [that] none but practical engineers and mechanics shall be accepted to complete this organization."[14]

Within four days, the concept of a regiment of volunteer engineers from Michigan had gained official recognition and encouragement. The speed with which Blair and the others acted on Innes's proposal was a good example of the competence and energy of the nation's governors as well as the degree to which authority devolved upon them to raise and equip the Union army. For example, Cameron directed that new units be organized and made ready for service by state governors "in the manner they may judge most advantageous for the interests of the General Government." In turn, state authorities relied upon the new regimental commanders to solve a wide range of challenges. Michigan was not an exception.[15]

The first decision facing Innes was to select a point at which the various companies could rendezvous and train before leaving for the South. In May the War Department had issued a circular that specified what was needed for a rendezvous or camp of instruction: "A rolling surface or porous soil should be chosen. Other conditions are proximity to wood, water, abundant subsistence for men and horses and railroad or water transportation." There were also obvious advantages if the rendezvous site was located in the region of the state where most of the men were from.[16]

Grand Rapids was the hometown of the regiment's founders and would have been an obvious choice, but its facilities were already in use by two new cavalry regiments. Instead, Marshall was selected as the point of rendezvous for the Michigan Engineers. Marshall was a city of about four thousand people astride the Michigan Central Railroad. As the seat of Calhoun County government, it boasted a bustling business district and large fairgrounds suitable for a military camp. There was a significant economic advantage to Marshall in having upward of one thousand men in town plus the visitors the regiment could be expected to draw. In exchange, the citizens of Marshall were expected to provide housing, use of the fairgrounds, new offices for the regiment's headquarters, one thousand blankets and pillows, marsh hay, ice for water, and other necessary items.[17]

The selection of Marshall was convenient for the first men to arrive at the regimental rendezvous. Within days, two Calhoun County companies were ordered to the engineer camp: Marshall's own Tyler Fusileers, commanded by Emery O. Crittenton, and John B. Yates's men from neighboring Albion. Both had intended to join Wilson's Illinois regiment but were ordered by Robertson to Marshall instead. Within days other companies began to arrive in Marshall. The last to arrive, the men from Jackson, reached Marshall on October 1. Recruits continued to trickle in as officers sought to fill out the rosters of their commands.[18]

· 2 ·

The Sinews of War

The regiment was the basic unit of Civil War armies, and its colonel was critical for the success of arms. Yet, to command these regiments the War Department was forced to rely heavily upon civilians. The colonels in turn could rely on very few experienced company commanders and field officers to support them. How well Colonel Innes and his officers performed their unfamiliar duties would to a large degree determine how well the Michigan Engineers performed during its service.[1]

Two months before the Bull Run disaster, the War Department cautioned governors "to commission no one of doubtful morals or patriotism and not of sound health." Furthermore, it was emphasized that "moral character and general intelligence of the officers" were critical qualifications for any appointment. The governors were also given recommendations on the appropriate maximum ages for officers, beginning with lieutenants at twenty-two and ranging to colonels at forty-five. These commissions, which the governors had the authority to appoint, were for the regiments of militia being raised for ninety days' service. In July Congress decreed that the enlisted men would elect their company officers, who in turn would select the field grade officers. A month later, governors were again given the sole authority over all regimental volunteer officer commissions below the rank of brigadier general. Governor Blair would make the decisions on the officers in the engineer regiment forming at Marshall.[2]

The pool of experienced military men for governors to choose from was much too small to meet the need. By the end of 1861, about 27,000 officers were holding commissions in the Union army volunteer units. At the outbreak of war, the entire U.S. regular army had only 1,098 commissioned officers, of which 313 resigned to serve in the Confederate army. The Lincoln administration's decision to keep most of the prewar regular army together as a reliable reserve prevented the wholesale redistribution of the loyal officers into volunteer regiments. Even counting all who had graduated from West Point or any private military academy or had served as officers against the Mexican army or Indian tribes, the total numbered no more than 3,000 men to fill the 27,000 positions. General and staff positions would also place a heavy demand on this same small pool.[3]

Given the scarce supply of experienced military officers, the Michigan Engineers were fairly typical for regiments raised in the summer and fall of 1861. None of the original officers were graduates of West Point or other military academies. Nor had any held a commission in the regular army. Innes probably served a short six weeks as a private during the Mexican War. If so, he was one of only two original officers with active military experience before the war. The other, Lt. Elias Broadwell of Company G, had served as an enlisted man in the regular army's Eighth Infantry from 1840 to 1845.[4]

Of the original thirty-eight commissioned officers, only a few had any military experience in the fall of 1861 and none had commanded men under fire. Capt. Marcus Grant and his cousin Lt. Solon E. Grant served in the enlisted ranks of the First Michigan Infantry (three months) and might have fought at Bull Run. Capt. Baker Borden briefly commanded a company in the Third Michigan Infantry during the summer of 1861 but did not see any action. Lt. William S. Nevius had been a sergeant in the Michigan-raised Company K, First New York (Lincoln) Cavalry, for four months without facing enemy fire. A handful of others had experience of mixed value in prewar militia companies.[5]

What the Michigan Engineers' officers lacked in military experience, however, they made up for in engineering and mechanical experience. In fact, the prewar experience of most of the officers might have made this regiment better prepared for its contemplated war assignment than most infantry or cavalry regiments being raised on either side.

That experience started at the top. Though Innes was younger than most of his company commanders, he already had almost twenty years' experience in engineering and railroads. Born in 1826 in New York City, Innes left home at age thirteen to support his widowed mother and younger sister and brother. By age sixteen, he was employed on the construction of the Erie Railway and learned engineering in a variety of jobs. In 1853 he left New York for Grand Rapids to work as a civil engineer on the Oakland and Ottawa Railroad. This company was attempting to extend the existing Detroit and Pontiac line of track to Lake Michigan via Grand Rapids. Innes had charge of the route from Ada westward to the lake at Grand Haven. Eventually reorganized as the Detroit and Milwaukee, the line was completed to Lake Michigan in November 1858. During this time Innes also served as chief engineer for the prospective Grand Rapids and Northern Railroad Company and reported on the feasibility of opening the Muskegon River to steamboat navigation as far upriver as Newaygo.[6]

William P. Innes served as colonel of the Michigan Engineers and Mechanics from its formation in 1861 until the fall of 1864. He deserves much of the credit for its success, though he often found himself in the center of controversy. This is a postwar image. Sligh, *Michigan Engineers.*

After the success of the Detroit and Milwaukee, Innes contracted with the Amboy, Lansing, and Traverse Bay firm to build a twenty-mile stretch of railroad running south from Owosso to Lansing, the state's capital. The work was the first step in an effort to construct a railroad from Amboy in southern Hillsdale County to northern Michigan via Albion, Lansing, and Saginaw, a circuitous route that earned the line the nickname of the "Ram's Horn Road." Innes was also expected to take charge of operating the line between Jonesville and Saginaw when construction was completed. Work began in Owosso, a connection with the existing Detroit and Milwaukee, and progressed quickly toward Lansing through the fall and winter. In March 1860, however, work came to a grinding halt a few miles from Lansing, near the hamlet of Bath.[7]

A large swamp, centered around a sinkhole 640 feet long, blocked the road's surveyed route, and Innes had apparently underestimated the efforts necessary to cross it. The company poured its resources into spanning the terrain but managed only to drain its coffers instead of the swamp. Appeals to Lansing businessmen for more capital were

Kinsman Hunton was Innes's right hand man as the regiment's lieutenant colonel from 1861 to 1864. With Innes frequently detached on railroad and other duties, command often fell upon Hunton, and he performed well. Sligh, *Michigan Engineers*.

unsuccessful, and work was suspended. Under Innes's direction, the company operated the track that was in place, connecting the last few miles with Lansing by wagon road. The board of directors fired Innes in March 1861, seeking to cut costs and at odds with him over management of the short distance of line in operation. In retaliation, he threatened to take all the company's survey records with him. His efforts were frustrated when company officials secured the records and locked them up. Innes returned to Grand Rapids and other opportunities.[8]

Innes's second-in-command also brought practical and professional competence to the regiment, as well as a smattering of military experience. Born in 1826, Lt. Col. Kinsman Hunton worked on railroads in his native New Hampshire and Massachusetts before moving west to Michigan. By 1858 he was a master mechanic in the Marshall workshop of the Michigan Central Railroad and also worked as an engineer in the middle division of that road. Hunton briefly served as first lieutenant in the Marshall Light Guard militia company until it disbanded in the fall of 1859.[9]

John B. Yates organized Company A and moved through the ranks to replace Innes in the fall of 1864. Yates often commanded detachments of the regiment and won high praise for his service. Though only twenty-seven years old in 1861, Yates already had extensive experience in railroad construction in New York and Michigan. Sligh, *Michigan Engineers.*

Though not an engineer, Maj. Enos Hopkins was a successful manufacturer and businessman from Jackson, Michigan. He first had a successful career in Naugatuck, Connecticut, as a prominent leader in the development of cutlery, button, and malleable iron firms. By 1858 he was in Michigan, serving as the executor for a Jackson-area estate worth three hundred thousand dollars. Even after the estate's holdings, consisting primarily of a farm implements manufacture, were settled a year later, Hopkins retained ties to both his Connecticut holdings and business in Jackson. Hopkins was promoted to major over all the other captains upon his arrival at Camp Owen. Perhaps this was a tribute to the confidence Innes had in his abilities but was likely also the result of his prewar friendship with fellow Jackson resident Governor Blair. Upon the promotion, Hopkins's place commanding the Jackson company was taken by Lt. Marcus Grant.[10]

Innes would also increasingly rely on the services of John B. Yates, senior among the original captains and eventually Innes's replacement as colonel. Though only twenty-seven, Yates was an excellent choice to lead an engineer company. A New York native, Yates earned an engineering degree from prestigious Union College and worked for the

Marcus Grant was another young company commander, being selected to lead Company H while he was still twenty-two years old. As a veteran of the First Michigan Infantry (three months' service), Grant was one of only a few men at the regimental rendezvous with any previous military experience. He ended the war as the regiment's senior major. Archives of Michigan.

Utica and Schenectady Railroad before moving west. In Michigan he continued as a railroad engineer, working on the construction of the Detroit and Milwaukee line to Lake Michigan. At the war's outbreak, he was a practicing civil engineer and surveyor in Albion and was also employed by the Amboy, Lansing, and Traverse Bay Railroad. He carried strong recommendations from Chief Engineer John Higham of the Detroit and Milwaukee Railroad and Republican U.S. senator Zachariah Chandler.[11]

Innes was also able to assemble a team of staff officers with important and relevant prewar experience. Regimental quartermaster Lt. Robert S. Innes, Colonel Innes's younger brother, was a civil engineer and cartographer in Grand Rapids and had also operated a dry goods business and steam sawmill in Muskegon County. Surgeon William H. DeCamp and Asst. Surgeon Willoughby O'Donoughue both had college medical degrees and established practices. Adjutant Clement F. Miller was an accomplished civil engineer and surveyor. Chaplain

David B. Tracy had served six Michigan churches as a Methodist Episcopal minister, most recently in the rough-and-tumble mining town of Houghton.[12]

The depth of relevant experience extended to most of the company commanders. Baker Borden, Emery O. Crittenton, Perrin V. Fox, and Garrett Hannings were all experienced skilled tradesmen. Wright Coffinberry was a prominent surveyor. Yates had been a railroad engineer for almost a decade. Silas Canfield was a millwright. There was also a high level of experience in the engineering and skilled trades among the junior commissioned officers. Of the twenty original company lieutenants, thirteen were skilled artisans, two were engineers, and another was working for a railroad at the outbreak of the war. The others were businessmen, teachers, or farmers. Overall, the

Table 1. Original field and staff officers and company commanders

Officer	Age	Primary occupation
Col. William P. Innes	35	Civil Engineer
Lt. Col. Kinsman A. Hunton	35	Railroad Master Mechanic
Maj. Enos Hopkins	40	Manufacturer
Q.M. Robert S. Innes	26	Civil Engineer
Surg. William H. DeCamp	35	Physician
Asst. Surg. Willoughby O'Donoughue	33	Physician
Adj. Clement F. Miller	31	Civil Engineer
Chaplain David B. Tracy	32	Minister
Capt. John B. Yates (A)	27	Civil Engineer
Capt. Baker Borden (B)	47	Carpenter
Capt. Wright L. Coffinberry (C)	54	Surveyor
Capt. Perrin V. Fox (D)	39	Surveyor, Builder
Capt. Silas Canfield (E)	37	Millwright
Capt. James W. Sligh (F)	39	Merchant
Capt. Garrett Hannings (G)	39	Joiner
Capt. Marcus Grant (H)	22	Farmer
Capt. Heman Palmerlee (I)	40	Farmer
Capt. Emery O. Crittenton (K)	50	Building Contractor

One of the original lieutenants, Albert Culver led his company in the fight at Lavergne and remained in the service until failing health forced his departure in late 1863. Archives of Michigan.

vast majority of Innes's officers had significant prewar experience in relevant occupations.[13]

Innes was also able to call upon proven prewar professional ties in the selection of his officers. Yates had worked closely with Innes on the construction of the Detroit and Milwaukee, serving as his assistant during the completion of the line from Ada to Grand Haven. Later, while Innes struggled to complete the first section of the Amboy, Lansing, and Traverse Bay from Owosso to Lansing, Yates was supervising the design of the route further south. Among other future original officers also working on the Amboy were Lts. Robert Innes, Rodney Mann, and Horace Gilson. When Yates recruited his company in Albion, Mann and Gilson were among the first to join, and many of the enlisted men bear the same surnames as his workers in surviving Amboy Road records. Likewise, the Michigan Central employed Hunton when war broke out, a position that undoubtedly brought him into professional contact with Innes and the others. The Grand Rapids officers also were a tight-knit group with existing personal and business relationships even before the war began. This was particularly true for Innes, James W. Sligh, Coffinberry, and DeCamp.[14]

Innes's corps of officers was also bound together by strong ties within the Masonic fraternity. Tracy, Innes, Sligh, and Lt. Joseph J. Rhodes were all active in the order on a state level. Other commissioned officers active in their local Masonic lodges at the outbreak of the war included O'Donoughue, Lt. Lorenzo D. Mason, Coffinberry, Fox, DeCamp, Lt. William T. Hess, and Lt. Albert H. Kimball. At the war's outbreak, Hunton and Innes were also both leaders in the related Knights Templar, Innes as state deputy grand commander for Michigan and Hunton as head of Commandery No. 8 in Kalamazoo.[15]

Whatever their background or ties, these original officers provided a steady core of leadership for the regiment throughout its four years of service. Over half of the original thirty-eight remained with the regiment for at least three years, and almost one-quarter stayed through the entire war. Most important, of the nine men to hold a field grade commission in the Michigan Engineers, every one was first commissioned in the regiment in September 1861.[16]

As with the officers, the enlisted ranks included only a small handful with any military experience, but there was a great depth of experience in the trades and professions most valuable for an engineer regiment. Engineering units had a special role to play and required men with specific skills: artisans with the ability and experience to construct wooden bridges and buildings, mechanics with the technical experience to repair and run trains, sawmills, and forges, and men experienced in turning the abundant timber into the wood needed for all of the above. In all areas, the regiment was well prepared, with a significantly greater concentration of relevant occupations within its ranks than in the Michigan male population as a whole.

Overall, at least half of the original recruits were skilled craftsmen or artisans. Almost one in every three original recruits was a carpenter, joiner, or cabinetmaker, more than nine times the state rate. The enlisted men in the Michigan Engineers were six times more likely to be a carriage or wagon maker or wheelwright than adult males in the Michigan population, three times more likely to be a blacksmith, and almost eight times more likely to be working on the railroad at the start of the war.[17]

William C. Swaddle is one of the Michigan Engineers who gave his life for the Union. Swaddle enlisted in September 1861 and was discharged thirteen months later by the surgeons. Health recovered, he again enlisted in the Michigan Engineers, only to die of disease in a Nashville hospital on July 31, 1864. Archives of Michigan.

One-third of the original recruits were farmers, and many of those were familiar with clearing forests. During the first few years in the wilderness, pioneer farmers were forced to fashion their own homes, furniture, and many of their tools. Along the way they developed at least a rudimentary understanding of many of the skilled crafts and became no less than functional at turning standing timber into building materials. Many of the balance were the sons of farmers, raised in central and western Michigan amid the clearing of native forests for farms.[18]

Because the Michigan Engineers drew more heavily on established skilled artisans and mechanics, the recruits were an older group than those joining other new Union regiments. The average age at enlistment for an 1861 Michigan Engineer was 28.75 years, about three full years older than original members of other regiments raised in the North. They were typical of early regiments in the wide range of age as well as in the frequency with which rules were ignored.[19]

Army regulations prohibited the enlistment of boys younger than eighteen (unless as musicians) or men older than forty-five, but many

Benjamin Edwards was a typical member of the Michigan Engineers. A thirty-two-year-old moulder from Litchfield, he enlisted in the fall of 1861 and served three years as a regimental musician. He fought at Perryville and Lavergne and was still alive forty years later. Archives of Michigan.

of the original Michigan Engineers were outside of this range. At least 29 enlisted men who gave their ages as forty-six or older were allowed to join. Another 9 boys were added to the regimental rolls with official ages of seventeen or younger, and regimental records include letters of consent for most. Many others simply lied. Counting both those who listed ages outside the eighteen to forty-five range and research-based projections on others, it is likely that at least 150, or about 15 percent, of the original Michigan Engineers were officially too old or too young to be in the ranks. The oldest was probably Isaac Howell, born in the previous century but recorded as a forty-four-year-old recruit. Another "forty-four-year-old" contender for the honor of oldest recruit was his neighbor, Jonathan Cudney, who was at least sixty and enlisted with his thirty-three-year-old son, Charles. Another father and son duo were Peter Passenger and his son William, who were actually about fifty-four and thirteen but who claimed to be forty-five and eighteen.[20]

Regulations about medical inspections were also frequently ignored. Even though DeCamp performed at least some inspections, something not done in many 1861 regiments, there were many men in poor health who were allowed to enlist. Two examples are illustrative: Pvt. Norwin C. Johnson was "unsound in one eye . . . and . . . it was the subject of remark at the time he was mustered, but the officers concluded that it would not incapacitate him." The officers apparently also discounted the fact he was lame. He was discharged six months later, half of his service having been spent in the hospital. Bugler Albert Sivey was discharged in May 1862 after surgeons discovered a preenlistment fractured arm made it impossible for him to serve further. He had been able to hide this injury from examining physicians.[21]

Like the officers, the men who served in the ranks of the Michigan Engineers also had strong prewar ties. Many of the companies were raised within a single community or county, and many of the recruits enlisted alongside family and friends. Clearly, Grand Rapids sent large numbers of men into the regiment, but the concentrations of recruitment were even greater in some of the smaller hamlets and farm communities across the state. For example, Waverly Township in Van Buren County had about 120 men of military age in 1861. That fall 14 men were enlisted as a group for Hannings's company. Later recruits followed, and by war's end about one in five men of military age in this township served in the Michigan Engineers, mostly in Company G.[22]

Such concentrations also included large numbers of relatives. At least 160 of the original Michigan Engineers joined with another family member. Among the largest family groupings to enlist in 1861 were Thomas White and his sons James and Henry, who all joined Company A, and Company E brothers Chauncy and Gerard Brink and their kinsman Eli. There were at least twenty-five pairs of fathers and sons and probably twice as many groups of brothers or cousins.[23]

Writing about enlistment during the Civil War, historian J. Matthew Gallman has observed, "The war did bring men of disparate backgrounds together to fight side by side, but when new recruits paraded out of town they often marched with the same men with whom they had celebrated the most recent holiday."[24]

Over one thousand men joined the First Michigan Engineers and Mechanics in 1861. They were well trained by life and work for their assignment in the war but were novices at the regime of military service and the cruel truth of combat. In the short period of time between recruitment and departure for Kentucky, Innes and his green officers had to mold these men into a cohesive military unit, install military discipline, provide rudimentary instruction in military service, and equip and train the men.

· 3 ·

Camp Owen

Colonel Innes's first priority at Marshall was to create a proper military environment for the care and training of his new recruits. For the first few days after their arrival, the men gathering at Marshall were accommodated in temporary quarters. Floral Hall was quickly renovated by the addition of bunks for nearly three hundred men, enough to accommodate the Marshall, Albion, and Kalamazoo companies. As additional companies arrived, the other men were housed in tents and put to work building new barracks and bunks. When the Jackson company finally arrived in early October, they were temporarily housed in an old circus tent until the men could build their own bunks. The men cleared a drill ground on the north side of the county fairgrounds.[1]

The regiment was fed cooked rations by local merchants at a cost to the state of twenty-six cents per man per day. Though the specifics of this contract are unknown, a contemporaneous bid issued by state military authorities for a new regiment being organized at Grand Rapids provides some detail on what they were probably fed. Michigan quartermaster general Jabez H. Fountain expected the men to be fed each day with one pound of bacon or one and one-quarter pounds of salt beef; eighteen ounces of bread or flour, twelve ounces of corn bread, or one and one-quarter pounds of corn meal; and eight quarts of peas or beans or ten pounds of rice per one hundred men, along with sufficient coffee, sugar, vinegar, candles, soap, and salt.[2]

The makeshift quarters at Floral Hall were soon insufficient for the growing number of recruits in Marshall. In early October the regiment moved into more proper military quarters on the county fairgrounds. The men pitched tents on the inside of the racetrack and formed a military camp. Each tent was made of sailcloth with a center pole and was capable of holding twelve to fifteen men sleeping with their feet in the center. A floor of straw made the accommodations more comfortable. The camp was christened Camp Owen, in honor of John Owen, a successful Detroit banker and the newly elected state treasurer.[3]

A regular schedule of drill and camp work had been established just before the move to Camp Owen and was continued thereafter.

Table 2. Arrival of companies at regimental rendezvous, 1861

Company	Captain	Counties of major recruitment	Arrived in camp
A	John B. Yates	Calhoun, Jackson, Washtenaw	Before September 25
B	Baker Borden	Kent, Genesee	September 27
C	Wright L. Coffinberry	Kent, Barry	September 26
D	Perrin V. Fox	Kent, Ottawa	After September 27
E	Silas Canfield	Ionia, Clinton	September 25
F	James W. Sligh	Wayne, Monroe, Genesee, Kent	After September 27
G	Garrett Hannings	Kalamazoo, Van Buren, Genesee	September 25
H	Enos Hopkins Marcus Grant	"Withington Rifles" Jackson	October 1
I	Heman Palmerlee	Lapeer, Wayne, Washtenaw, Oakland	After September 27
K	Emery O. Crittenton	"Tyler Fusileers" Calhoun, Ionia	Before September 25

The daily orders for October 3 were typical: Waking at 6 A.M., the men ate thirty minutes later. After time for sick call, they drilled from 8 to 11 A.M. and 1 to 5 P.M., with a break for dinner. Officers attended military school in the afternoon. Retreat was sounded at 5 P.M., with supper following at 5:30. The evening was spent in camp until taps at 9 P.M. One company was assigned fatigue duty each day. A camp guard of thirty men was detailed to maintain the camp's discipline under the direction of the officer of the day.[4]

The time for drill was especially important. Though raised as an engineer unit, the men were expected to give a good account in combat. Military tactics during the Civil War required the ability to move men into and out of linear formations, often under fire and with a minimum of shouted commands. Drill also developed the esprit de

corps and discipline necessary to triumph in combat. The men began with individual and squad drill, learning to handle their weapons
and mastering the basic commands for facing and deportment. From
there they graduated to company drill and then to regimental drill,
which was important as the officers learned to maneuver the regiment
through the various formations.[5]

The process of drilling the men at Camp Owen evolved slowly,
as one would expect of green soldiers led by inexperienced officers.
Though Captain Crittenton's Marshall men were frequently the targets
of jokes, most of the officers and men had many of the same problems.
Pvt. William H. Kimball admitted that while training in the double
quick, most of the Jackson company stumbled and fell, "causing considerable merriment." Eventually the officers and men became competent. Ezra Stearns noted, "the majority of the boys took the drill very
easily and bid fair to make efficient soldiers," while the *Detroit Daily
Advertiser* claimed the men were "said to have metamorphosed, from
engineers and hard-fisted artisans, into quite respectable soldiers."[6]

Since most of the commissioned and noncommissioned officers
had little military experience, time was set aside every afternoon for
"school call." At this session, the regimental leaders first had to learn the
lessons they would in turn teach to the recruits. Historian T. Harry Williams describes this process in new regiments with green officers: "And
so the regiment became a huge school, with faculty members teaching
each other and each trying to stay a lesson ahead of his students."[7]

The men also had time to relax. As a general rule, recruits were
free from work and drill on weekday evenings and Sundays. They used
their free time at Camp Owen to play cards, sing, write letters home, or
just sit and talk with one another. Some organized Bible classes, and the
soldiers were regular participants at prayer meetings. This emphasis on
religion by many of the soldiers was not unusual. Because the army was
generally viewed as a breeding ground for sin, vice, and immorality, the
men with stronger religious beliefs strove even harder to maintain their
faith. In early October a Bible class was organized and regularly attended
by the more devout engineers. In addition, frequent prayer meetings
were held, so, as Stearns found to his relief, "it did not necessarily follow
that a man would leave his religion at home to become a soldier." The
meetings continued throughout the regiment's stay at Camp Owen.[8]

Despite accounts of religious meetings and cerebral discussions,
the reports of the camp guards reflect the usual independent streak
found in volunteers of this era, and new officers demonstrated a re-
luctance to strictly enforce the rules. Much of the reason for this dis-
ciplinary restraint was that officers and men had been neighbors and

equals just weeks before. Albert Graves reported that the regiment was a "sociable democratic crowd, no one assuming any consequential airs from the Captain down." Officers were reluctant to be rigid disciplinarians with the very men they had recruited. For example, two men who snuck out of camp on October 12 were merely reprimanded, since "they seem very sorry and promise to never do it again."[9]

One incident in particular demonstrates the independent streak of these volunteers and the sympathetic views of their officers. During the first weeks in camp, the letters of the recruits gave generally high marks to the rations provided by area contractors. Near the end of October, however, the quality of the food took a marked turn for the worse. The men complained of rancid butter, greasy pork, and the absence of sugar for coffee. Taking matters into their own hands, several of the men in Captain Borden's company picked up a table loaded with the offensive food, carried it outside, and turned it onto its side, spilling the contents all over the ground. Members of Captain Yates's company joined in but did not even take their tables outside before tipping them over. There was little reaction from the officers, and Borden, for one, "didn't scold very hard." A quick conference between the officers and the contractors resulted in a spread deemed "excellent" by the men.[10]

Most of the infractions committed at Camp Owen were minor in nature and involved slipping the camp guard, drunkenness, and being out after hours. The offenders were sentenced to twenty-four hours to a few days in the guardhouse or extra duty. Some, however, committed the more serious offense of desertion, a crime punishable in the field by death. Many were apparently never caught or enlisted in other units without penalty. Those who returned voluntarily or were captured were usually confined to the guardhouse for a week. Of those who were returned to Camp Owen and subsequently punished, many later gave good service.[11]

The case of George Waldo reflects the attitude of many of the men toward the deserters at Camp Owen. Captain Grant returned to Camp Owen on November 2 after a fruitless search for deserter Waldo. In camp he discovered that Waldo had returned voluntarily to Marshall the day before. Waldo claimed that he had left camp only because his wife was sick. He was given a trial and fined the fifty-seven dollars it cost to chase him. The men of the company were sympathetic to Waldo's plight and offered to pay fifty dollars of the fine. They were never called upon for the money since the fine was never imposed.[12]

It was the men's pay, not desertion, that proved to be the most serious challenge to discipline at Camp Owen. By early October there was significant grumbling among the men over the question of their rate of pay. Many of the men had been drawn to this particular regiment because the advertised pay for engineer troops was higher than for the other branches. In addition, many had signed up to serve in James W. Wilson's regiment or other independent engineer companies with varying advertised pay levels. For example, early recruits in the Marshall company had responded to an advertisement in area papers for Wilson's regiment that promised twenty-six dollars per month—double the pay of infantrymen. Lieutenant Kimball's recruiting in Detroit for Company F promised pay of one dollar per day "with everything found." Others had signed up expecting to receive eighteen dollars per month or more, and Capt. Loren Chadwick's independent engineer company was being recruited in nearby Battle Creek with advertised compensation of seventeen dollars per month and double rations, or "the highest pay of any branch."[13]

The confusion over the regiment's pay and status was not limited to the ranks. Innes based the authorization for the regiment on telegrams from the War Department, accepting his regiment on the same terms as Wilson's. This was understood to be as an engineer regiment, both in service and pay. On September 19 Innes received a note from Michigan Adjutant General Robertson accompanying a dispatch sent by Capt. George D. Ruggles, assistant adjutant general in the War Department. Ruggles notified Robertson that "Engineers and Mechanics regiments receive extra pay only when employed on extra duty of a mechanical nature" but did not elaborate on the base monthly rate. Robertson added to Innes, "What the pay is you will be able to get from the Army Regulations." Army engineer regulations at this time authorized seventeen dollars per month for first class sapper, miner, and pontonier privates ("artificers") and thirteen dollars per month for unskilled privates. At the same time, army pay regulations for the infantry stated that soldiers employed on working parties be paid forty cents per day extra if skilled and twenty-five cents if laborers or teamsters.[14]

The regiment was assembled into parade formation on October 3. Innes informed the men that official word had been received from the War Department that skilled privates would receive seventeen dollars per month and an extra forty cents per day and detailed and unskilled privates would receive thirteen dollars per month and twenty-five cents per day. Innes offered the men twenty-four hours to think it over and promised that any man who was still dissatisfied could leave the regiment without penalty. A number did. Crittenton's company lost twenty of its earliest recruits in this fashion, many in the Kalamazoo company left, and in Borden's another seven or eight departed. The balance of the regiment lost a handful more. Though the pay was less than the men had expected, the vast majority remained. Sergeant Graves wrote his wife about the incident and told her he "could send [her] enough to keep [her] tolerably comfortable even at $17 per month."[15]

Though the immediate crisis had been defused, Innes left within days to meet with authorities in Washington, D.C. He hoped to finalize the arrangements for the regiment's departure for the front and to resolve any remaining questions about the regiment's status and the men's level of pay. Upon his arrival at the War Department, officials informed him that there was no authorization for a regiment of volunteer engineers but that the president could grant the authority if he so chose. Innes then personally met with President Lincoln, who directed the War Department to provide Innes with proper papers for the regiment.[16]

Innes was back in Camp Owen by October 20 with the written authorization, issued "by direction of the President." The document authorized "a regiment of volunteer engineer officers and soldiers to act as sappers and miners and pontoniers." Governor Blair was given the final authority to accept or deny the organization, and his support was already on record. Federal quartermasters were directed to provide clothing and equipment, and Innes was instructed to report for duty to the War Department when the regiment was ready to leave for the war, which was optimistically expected to be in about twenty days. There was no specific mention in the order, however, of what pay the men would receive.[17]

In addition, the same order granted Innes permission to raise a battery of artillery to be attached to his regiment. Wilson's engineer regiment had also been authorized to have a battery to protect it, and Innes's similar authorization reinforced the belief that the Michigan Engineers were being organized under that precedent. Edward Serrell had also been authorized to raise a company of artillery for his New York engineer regiment, a fact widely reported in New York newspapers and known to the men at Camp Owen.[18]

Blair commissioned Grand Rapids native John J. Dennis as battery commander, and recruiting began at Marshall, Grand Rapids, Detroit, and other towns. Dennis had previously commanded a company in the Third Michigan. His battery rendezvoused at Marshall alongside the engineers, and by November 7 two brass field pieces were in camp.[19]

On October 10, the Michigan Engineers were assembled to receive the regiment's stand of colors while Innes was in Washington. A regiment's colors represented the honor of the regiment, and the importance of their formal presentation was evident by the attention given it. The *Detroit Free Press* reported ten thousand people in attendance as Governor Blair personally reviewed the regiment. Prominent educator and editor Francis W. Shearman represented John Owen, the camp's namesake. Shearman presented the national banner and declared in his remarks that the mission of the regiment was to "participate in the salvation of our country from the armed attacks of rebellion, to aid in the maintenance of our free institutions, and our glorious constitution, and in the preservation of our national union." Echoing the Spartan mothers, he challenged the engineers to "come to us with it, when the battle is done, or in it from the field" of battle. With Innes absent, the responsibility for accepting the flag and Shearman's challenge fell to Lieutenant Colonel Hunton. He pledged that the regiment would "defend it with their heart's blood" and would return at war's end "under the broad folds of our victorious national banner."[20]

Within days a special sermon reinforced the grim admonition of the color presentation. Rev. Seth S. Chapin, rector of Marshall's Trinity Church sternly reminded the men that each "go forth because you believe our country is in danger, stand by her; fight her battles courageously; vindicate her rights; sustain her government, or perish in the attempt."[21]

The first death in the regiment a few days later also emphasized the seriousness of the task before them. In early October a regimental hospital had been established at the Marshall House and usually contained ten to fifteen patients with a variety of illnesses. The most common were measles, ague, typhoid fever, and colds. Private Mitchell of Borden's company died on October 15. In a moving ceremony, his body was "taken by hearse to the [railroad] cars, escorted by the company, with slow and measured tread, the martial music playing the subdued strains of 'Pleyel's Hymn.'" On November 11 Mitchell was followed to the grave by eighteen-year-old Dwight Hunt of the Jackson company, who succumbed to typhoid fever. In December at least three more men died at Camp Owen.[22]

While the regimental hospital saw a steady of flow of sick men, as a whole the regiment enjoyed good health at Camp Owen. On October 10 only ten men out of some seven hundred in camp were reported on the sick list. The men were vaccinated on November 1. As of November 21 there were only about twenty men in the regimental hospital, and all were reported as "doing well under the skillful treatment of Surgeons DeCamp and O'Donoughue."[23]

By the end of October plans were under way to muster the men at Camp Owen into federal service. Up until this time, the regiment was considered to be in state service, governed by state military regulations and subject only to service within the confines of the state. After the men were mustered in they would belong to the War Department, subject to all its regulations and requirements. They would be held to their enlistment until death, discharge, or the expiration of their term.[24]

On October 29 Capt. Henry R. Mizner of the regular army arrived from Detroit to muster the men into federal service. They were drawn up in a line of battle upon the parade ground and mustered in one company at a time. The first 791 men were sworn in without incident. Crittenton's company was held for last because of indications that at least some of the men would refuse to be sworn in. When Mizner asked if there were any who refused from Crittenton's company, 1 stepped forward and was followed by about 30 more. They stated that they were unwilling to serve under Crittenton because they had little confidence in his ability as an officer to lead them and wanted to serve in a different company. This request was refused, and they were marched off to the guardhouse. The procession, however, took on comic proportions when the untried regimental band substituted an alternate lighter air for "The Rogue's March." To complete the fiasco, the band led the procession instead of playing from a standing position. As observer Graves noted, it appeared that the mutineers "went out under an escort" instead of a mark of shame. The balance of Crittenton's company, some 40 men, was sworn into the service, and the regiment marched back to camp.[25]

Few were surprised by the controversy in Crittenton's company, which had been embroiled in internecine disputes since its formation in August and election of officers on September 10. There had been bad blood between Crittenton and some of the other early organizers of the company, escalating when Crittenton dismissed harsh critic 1st Lt. Horace Phelps. Many complained about Crittenton's lack of military knowledge, especially when contrasted with Phelps, who had commanded a local militia company. Several of the more vocal critics took up Innes's offer to leave on October 3, citing the pay issue, but problems continued. With Innes absent, Hunton was in a difficult spot as a Marshall resident and former comrade of Phelps. When Crittenton was offered several hundred dollars as reimbursement for recruitment expenses if he would resign, his supporters characterized it as an attempted bribe.[26]

The reaction of the press to the October 29 muster-in incident was as divided as the men of Crittenton's company. The *Detroit Free Press* was critical of those who refused to muster in. Their conduct was described as "so unbecoming and unpatriotic" as to disqualify them for service in other units being formed. Caught in the middle were the two papers from Marshall, the hometown of most of the company. The *Statesman* was of the opinion that "generally, the Marshall boys had the sympathy of our citizens." The *Democratic Expounder* believed that the only fault of the refusals was an unwillingness to go into battle under a leader they had no confidence in and that they should be allowed to serve under different officers in another regiment. The position of Michigan's military establishment was unambiguous, issuing a strong admonition that "under the circumstances it is not considered desirable that [the men who refused] should be enrolled in any state regiment." At this point in the war, service was still considered a privilege, reserved only for those deemed worthy, though eventually the majority of the October 29 protesters were able to sign up with other Michigan units.[27]

Innes could return his attention to equipping his men. In the first year of the war, regimental commanders were often responsible to obtain the necessary arms and equipment before the men could move to the front. Federal depots lacked enough material to equip all of the regiments organizing, and the state authorities were often locked in competition with one another for the limited stocks. Innes insisted that as much of the regiment's equipment as possible be produced or purchased within the state and was able to convince federal authorities to that effect during his trip to Washington. This probably made the task of supplying the regiment more difficult but won him praise from at least one local newspaper: "This is better than any other regiment has done that the state has sent out, and will secure a large amount of money to be distributed among our citizens, that would have otherwise been paid out elsewhere. Colonel Innes is deserving of credit."[28]

Throughout October Innes and his officers directed the manufacture and purchasing of all the necessary equipment. A large quantity of the regiment's equipment was made in Jackson, much of it using convict labor at the Michigan State Prison. Major Hopkins directed much of the regiment's purchasing effort, using his prewar business ties. The Jackson firm of Sprague, Withington, and Cooley produced the entrenching tools, while the firm of Austin and Tomlinson provided the wagons. Hopkins had ties to both firms, which operated using both convict and free labor. Shoemaker Walter Fish's firm manufactured boots and shoes at the prison and contracted for the regiment's footwear, though half of the first two hundred shoes produced by Fish were rejected as shoddy work and returned. Other contracts were probably let to Jackson firms.[29]

Some of the remainder of the clothing and equipment came from Detroit. Innes received many inquiries from that city's leading firms, including Sykes and Company, Buhl and Company, and Charles Trow-bridge. All of these companies were involved in clothing and equipping new Michigan regiments in 1861, though it is not clear which ones supplied what for the Michigan Engineers. The harnesses for the wagon horses were also made in Detroit, though the firm is not identified. Like many other new officers, Innes purchased his sword, sash, and belt from the Detroit firm of Morrison and Conklin.[30]

In mid-October Quartermaster General Fountain published a notice of sealed bids for the outfitting of one of the new regiments being formed in the state. Though the unit is not identified, Innes's regiment was to be equipped as infantry and probably was similarly outfitted with one thousand overcoats, blouses, pairs of pants, cloth caps, canteens, haversacks, knives, forks, spoons, and tin plates; two thousand flannel shirts and pairs of drawers; three hundred mess pans; 120 kettles; ten mess chests; twelve company desks; ten drums and bugles; fifty-five axes; fifty hatchets; and twenty-five spades and pickaxes.[31]

Innes also had a hand in the purchasing of items being provided by the federal government, pushing to make sure deliveries were as prompt as possible. On October 31, for example, he wrote Capt. E. G. Owen, U.S. quartermaster in Detroit, that it was important not to allow horse contractors the full thirty days for delivery. This delay would set back the regiment's departure and force it into barracks because of the approach of winter. As it turned out, it took a lot longer than thirty days for the regiment to receive all the horses it needed.[32]

Though Innes hoped to have most of the regiment's equipment in hand by November 10, numerous delays meant that two weeks after the deadline the regiment was still not able to take the field because of a lack of equipment. Innes even wrote Brig. Gen. Don Carlos Buell, to whom they were to report, asking if equipment could be obtained after arriving in the field. In particular, Innes had a difficult time obtaining arms, accouterments, and mathematical and engineering instruments for the regiment. His appeals to officials in Washington, D.C., were redirected to U.S. quartermaster officers in Detroit, who did not have the equipment and sent Innes back to War Department officials.[33]

Arms were especially difficult to obtain. In early October and again in late November, Adjutant General Robertson ordered Quartermaster General Fountain to send state arms to Innes's regiment, but there were few to send. State authorities were still struggling to fill the void that had been created by shortages in federal depots and fierce competition among the various states. By the end of November, there were only enough arms in camp to equip the camp guard and allow one company to drill with weapons.[34]

One of the original company commanders, Wright L. Coffinberry is pictured in the original dress uniform issued to the Michigan Engineers at Camp Owen. The hats and plumes soon disappeared when the regiment entered active operations. Bentley Historical Library, University of Michigan.

Companies A and B were eventually issued modern English Enfield rifles since they were the flank companies and expected to serve as skirmishers. The other eight companies had to be content with obsolete foreign muskets. A late December inspection reported the latter to be of Belgian manufacture and "serviceable but clumsy." The heavy Belgian muskets, of .69 and .71 caliber, were commonly used in the beginning of the war and were plagued with problems of "uneven caliber and crooked barrels." Even the flank companies were later forced to trade their rifles for U.S. Harper's Ferry muskets upon reaching Kentucky. In early January Innes was still reporting that the regiment lacked its full complement of small arms, and the men were not issued ammunition for live fire until reaching Kentucky.[35]

Clothing and uniforms reached Camp Owen over a period of several weeks, not beginning until early November and concluding just as the regiment was preparing to leave for Kentucky. The delay prompted critical comments from throughout the regiment. In mid-November a soldier wrote the *Jackson American Citizen* that they were still waiting for their uniforms that had "been coming for two months now." Without heavy blankets, the colder nights were hard on the men. One wrote home on November 8, "If we don't get a blanket to-night we will tear down the tents before tomorrow morning." Though such an action would have done little to provide warmth, it illustrates the frustration of the men in Camp Owen.[36]

A large supply of shirts, drawers, and shoes arrived on November 21, with most of the balance a few days later. The hats reached camp about the same time and were quickly the subject of much admiration. Unlike standard infantry hats, these were similar to those issued to regular army soldiers, with a brass eagle insignia and worn with the right side pinned up. A small brass castle was affixed to the front, and a yellow cord and plume completed the trimmings. One private wrote that the hats were "all trimmed to death covered with brass and feathers." The balance of the uniforms reached camp during the last few days of November and first week of December, arriving in small quantities and immediately distributed throughout the companies.[37]

Other important items continued to trickle in, though not everything was on hand when the regiment left Michigan. The night before the men left Michigan, the noncommissioned officers were labeling just-arrived knapsacks, and some companies did not receive any camp kettles and the last of the clothing until they had been in Kentucky for a week.[38]

Though about eighty wagon horses went to Kentucky with the regiment, the final group of two hundred did not leave Camp Owen until January 8, 1862. These had originally been purchased at Coldwater for the Chandler Horse Guard, but the organization was disbanded before leaving the state. The detachment escorting the horses was under the command of Adj. William Richards of the Lancer Regiment, another unit that was disbanded by federal authorities without seeing any service.[39]

Not only did Innes have to find the equipment to supply the regiment, it was also his responsibility to get the regiment to Kentucky. Starting in late November, Innes wrote letters to Superintendent Reuben N. Rice of the Michigan Central Railroad and other railroad officials. He asked for details about the different routes the regiment could take, "hoping to avail ourselves of the nearest and best route."[40]

Many in the regiment tried to get furloughs to visit their families one last time. Though they often complained about the bureaucracy involved, many of the men received permission. One of these was Ezra Stearns. He obtained his furlough on November 24 and so was able to be home for Thanksgiving. He did not expect to see his family and friends again before leaving Michigan, and after making his farewells, he returned to camp "with many regrets."[41]

Some soldiers, already pressed for money due to the lack of pay, decided to stay in camp for reasons of economy. Others were convinced that any advantages of a visit with their families would be more than offset by the difficulty of another emotional parting. Cpl. David Noble wrote his wife, "I should like to come home but . . . it would be hard to part again. I could not leave again without drowning you in a flood of tears." It is doubtful that he ever saw his wife again; he died in the service on June 22, 1862.[42]

While some spent Thanksgiving at home, the citizens of Marshall treated those still in camp to a feast. The men who were still in camp jauntily displayed their new uniform hats, wearing them to the dinner. The entire town turned to the task of preparing the massive feast, which included seven hundred chickens, six roasted pigs, 430 loaves of bread, twelve hundred pies, and much more—so much, in fact, that there was a great deal left over, which the men gladly took back to camp.[43]

By early December the regiment was making arrangements to leave for the South. Amid the rush of final preparations for the regiment's departure, however, there were again rumblings among the men over the pay question. They expected to be paid up to date before leaving for Kentucky. On November 4 Innes had written to Governor Blair, asking for his "best endeavors" to get the regiment paid before it left Michigan. Innes included a resolution signed by the regiment's officers. The paymaster visited Camp Owen in early December but did not have enough money to pay the men the seventeen dollars per month that they had been promised. Innes ordered the paymaster to go get enough money and return to Marshall. The paymaster was unable to get authorization to pay the men at the seventeen-dollar rate, and the men refused to accept the thirteen dollars per month infantry pay that was offered. In fact, there was some talk among the men of refusing to move until they were fully paid. A few even took to wearing their hats backward as a sign of their solidarity, but the officers were able to defuse the situation once again. Captain Grant, for example, allayed the fears of Company H by telling them that he thought their pay awaited them in Louisville, though it is unclear if he believed this to be true. Most likely, the men were willing to go because they believed their service was important and because they understood. Graves wrote to his wife that confidence in the regiment's officers was "not on the increase just at present" but that "patience is a jewel and charity requires us to consider that there is a great many formalities to be complied with before everything is got into working order in a new regiment and green hands are liable to [make] mistakes." Graves's patience, and that of the entire command, would be sternly tested before the matter of pay was ever resolved.[44]

On December 4 Innes ordered Major Hopkins to Louisville, where he was to report to General Buell. Hopkins was to obtain orders for the regiment and attempt to locate needed equipment. That same evening all men on furlough were due back in camp. Official orders were issued by Adjutant General Robertson on the fifteenth to "proceed with as little delay" as possible for Kentucky.[45]

By December 15 the regiment was nearly ready to leave. A special service was held for the soldiers at the Presbyterian church, while others attended the Baptist church by special invitation. Even though it was the Sabbath, the camp was very busy as newly arrived equipment was sorted out, labeled, and finally distributed. Some still managed to get a pass to visit friends in the area for one last time.[46]

Preparations continued on the sixteenth, and the men received orders to be ready to move the next day. The men were busy all day packing their equipment. In anticipation of the soldiers' desire to celebrate their last night in Michigan, a heavier guard was posted by Innes but to little avail. About half of the men managed to sneak out, "the guards not being desirous of keeping anyone in against their will." At least some men were engaged in helping the sutler in "closing out his goods."[47]

One final activity before the regiment left for Louisville was the transferring of men around the regiment to fill up the understrength companies. In all, seventeen were transferred, mostly from Yates's and Heman Palmerlee's to Crittenton's and Silas Canfield's companies. In addition, several men transferred to the battery, mostly from Company F. Though still well short of full strength, the battery prepared to leave with the engineers for Kentucky.[48]

Reveille was beaten at 5 A.M. on the morning of the seventeenth. The men were quickly up, breakfasting and completing the job of packing up the regiment's equipment. By 8 A.M. the regiment and battery were formed and marching to the railroad depot. It was an inspiring sight for the citizens of Marshall and the gathered friends and families of the men. The column moved down State Street, wheeled left onto Eagle Street, and headed toward the depot amid the cheers of the crowd. The proud *Marshall Democrat Expounder* boasted that the men, "uniformed and equipped, . . . their guns glittering in the sunlight, presented a fine military appearance."[49]

At the station, the men waited while railroad officials finished the last details. It was a time for difficult good-byes. The *Marshall Statesman* reported, "The convulsive heave of the strong man's breast and the spasmodic, agonizing sob of the weaker sex testified to a pardonable weakness." Young William H. Kimball confided in his diary, "Some of the boys appeared sad and dejected, others serious and thoughtful, while some who had imbibed too freely were rather boisterous. As for myself I could not help wondering how long we would be obliged to be gone and how many of us would return again to our homes and friends and what changes would take place among them during our absence."[50]

Many of the engineers were the recipients of last-minute gifts and mementos, and one had money pressed into his hand when it was discovered that the regiment had not received any pay. By 10 A.M. the twenty-seven cars, pulled by the Michigan Central Railroad's two best engines, were under way amid the "cheers and applause of the masses."[51]

The route along the railroad took many of the men through, or near, their own communities. Battle Creek and Kalamazoo were both along the route, and some of the men were able to catch a last glimpse of a loved one. At each station there were cheering crowds. After 120 miles the men switched onto the line of the New Albany and Salem Railroad at Michigan City, Indiana. The receptions continued on through Indiana southward toward the Ohio River. One Michigan Engineer reported, "Everybody came out to see us from the aged to the infant . . . and in several instances [I] could discover banners waving away off across the prairie." Another wrote home, "Men, women, and children came to their doors, to the road and waved their hats, bonnets and handkerchiefs and everything else you could think of and we had a good time generally."[52]

The train reached Lafayette, Indiana, late that night to a mighty Hoosier welcome. Local ladies served the grateful engineers more than three hundred gallons of coffee. The bolder soldiers were able to get a little more than just coffee—a comrade told one man that the ladies of Lafayette had been especially generous with their kisses. Another noted in his diary, "There are lots of handsome girls there too, which is nothing against the place." On leaving Lafayette the train was split into two and rolled through the dark Indiana countryside into Indianapolis and then southward.[53]

About noon on the eighteenth, the train reached Jeffersonville, Indiana, across the Ohio River from Louisville, and they ate their first soldiers' meal. The regiment was given a rousing welcome by the citizens, particularly on their march through town to the river landing. By late afternoon, they were crossing the Ohio River with Louisville in clear view. Perhaps inspired by the reception that they had received in Jeffersonville, the men called out the officers for another round of speeches, which "were repeatedly interrupted by vociferous cheering."[54]

The march through Louisville was the final triumph of the trip. James M. Sligh (son of Captain Sligh) wrote his mother, "All the way from the river to the camp the streets were crowded with spectators who cheered us on our way by the waving of handkerchiefs and cheering for the Union and Michigan." After a meal of pilot bread, the exhausted men slept their first night in the South on the bare ground.[55]

There was also a somber side to the trip from Marshall to Louisville. The regimental teamsters and baggage train left Marshall on the night of the sixteenth under the command of Lt. Joseph Rhodes. Joel Detterow of Company H stepped on a broken step while the train was in motion, just two miles from Jeffersonville. He was thrown from the train and run over by the cars. Detterow died from his injuries on December 22, leaving a widow and two small children. There could have been many other deaths on the trip: several men on the troop train were able to smuggle liquor aboard and promptly got drunk; fortunately, none of these fell from the moving train.[56]

On December 19 the regiment straightened out the confusion caused by a night encampment and then moved to a camp further away from the railroad. The next few days were spent resting, drilling, and firing with blanks for practice. The men took advantage of the opportunity to play tourist in Louisville, though at least fifteen were caught in the city without a pass and spent Christmas in the guardhouse. Capt. Charles C. Gilbert of the regular army inspected the men on December 20 and pronounced them "more mature and uniform in size and appearance than usual." While in Louisville, the Jackson company lost another man. Jacob Shafer had been unwell before leaving Camp Owen and died on the twentieth from "congestion of the brain." The forty-one-year-old Shafer left a wife and several children. His death, and that of Detterow two days later from his injuries, "cast a gloom over the company."[57]

As Christmas drew near, the officers worked on an orderly division of the regiment. The understrength battery was ordered away, never to rejoin the regiment. Eventually, any administrative responsibility for the battery passed to other hands, consistent with efforts by army officials to consolidate management of the artillery.[58]

Lieutenant Colonel Hunton and Companies D, F, and G left on Christmas Day for Lebanon to join Brig. Gen. George H. Thomas's First Division. Major Hopkins and Companies C and H left the following day, with orders to join Brig. Gen. William "Bull" Nelson's

Fourth Division. Captain Yates and Companies A and K left on the twenty-seventh to join Brig. Gen. Ormsby Mitchel's Third Division at Bacon Creek. Colonel Innes and the remaining three companies left Louisville on the thirtieth, moving by rail to Munfordville, where they would join Brig. Gen. Alexander McCook's Second Division.[59]

South to Kentucky and Tennessee

At the end of 1861 most Union forces between the Appalachian Mountains and the western frontier were part of either the Department of the Ohio or the Department of the Missouri. The former was commanded by Maj. Gen. Don Carlos Buell and included the states of Michigan, Indiana, Ohio, and Tennessee, as well as that part of Kentucky east of the Cumberland River, with headquarters in Louisville. From his headquarters in St. Louis, Maj. Gen. Henry Halleck commanded the balance of Kentucky and the states of Missouri, Iowa, Minnesota, Wisconsin, Illinois, and Arkansas. Opposite Halleck's and Buell's forces was the Confederate Department No. Two, commanded by Gen. Albert Sidney Johnston.[1]

Nashville was the logical target for future Union advances. It was the state capital of Tennessee and an important railroad hub. Factories there produced gunpowder, rifles, swords, and percussion caps, and army depots were filled with large quantities of food and equipment. Its loss, which would also mean the loss of the entire Cumberland River line, might force Confederate troops to retreat behind the Tennessee River, thus surrendering the main east-west rail link along the Memphis and Charleston Railroad. The capture of Nashville would also be a huge moral victory for the North.[2]

Johnston had his forces posted along the Kentucky-Tennessee border, astride the most likely avenues of Union advance. In the east, Brig. Gen. Felix Zollicoffer and four thousand troops guarded the approaches to the Cumberland Gap. In the center, Maj. Gen. William J. Hardee and twenty-five thousand men at Bowling Green blocked any advance along the Louisville and Nashville Railroad, the most direct land route. The left center was concentrated on the point where Confederate Forts Henry and Donelson blocked Union movement up the Tennessee and Cumberland rivers. Johnston's left flank was anchored by the Mississippi River defenses at Columbus, Kentucky.[3]

Union efforts were badly hobbled because Halleck and Buell operated independent commands and cared little for each other. Neither man was willing to subordinate his troops to the other, though they each needed the other to succeed. The easiest way for Buell to take

Louisville to Nashville and eastern Kentucky. Map by Sherman Hollander.

Nashville was using waterborne transport up the Cumberland River, but that route and the Confederate fortifications blocking it at Fort Donelson were in Halleck's area of command. Likewise, if Halleck moved against Fort Donelson, Buell would need to tie down Hardee's men at Bowling Green. Both Halleck and Buell were preoccupied by the effort to gather, train, and equip their green forces. Buell's planning was also hampered by the strategic distraction of East Tennessee, where political and military considerations argued for military activities to protect the majority pro-Union population and secure natural resources.[4]

While Buell organized his forces and debated the next move, Confederate action shifted attention to the right of Johnston's line. Zollicoffer's poorly supplied troops occupied an exposed position on the north bank of the Cumberland River, dug in near Beech Grove. He had been ordered to re-cross to the south bank in late November but had not done so. Opposing Zollicoffer in the region was Brig. Gen. George H. Thomas with the three brigades of his First Division. On December 29, 1861, Buell ordered Thomas to strike the isolated Confederates. Among the troops available to Thomas were Lt. Col. Kinsman Hunton and Companies D, F, and G of the Michigan Engineers. Thomas planned to move out of Lebanon with the bulk of his division toward a junction with Brig. Gen. Albin Schoepf's Second Brigade. Schoepf occupied an advanced observation position at Somerset, closer to Zollicoffer's position. United, they would move against Zollicoffer and crush his force.[5]

Thomas's column left Lebanon on the last day of 1861. This first march was very difficult for Hunton's engineers. Loaded down with knapsacks, haversacks, canteens, arms, and ammunition, the men were exhausted after marching ten dusty miles. Their route took them up and down steep Muldraugh's and Reed's hills and then on to near Campbellsville, about twenty miles from Lebanon, by the evening of the second.[6]

The entire command remained at Campbellsville until January 6 while wagons were sent back to Lebanon for provisions. The men prepared tools, cooked and distributed rations, and drilled. Significantly, the men also held target practice for the first time. The result from the green soldiers was "not creditable to the muskets which were loaded with ball and buck," according to one observer.[7]

The command left Campbellsville early on the seventh for the most difficult part of their march. Leaving camp with Thomas and the advance regiments, the engineers were forced to help struggling wagon teams that broke through the thin ice covering the road. By midday on the eighth, they left the pike near Columbia and moved onto hilly clay roads. Hampered by the chilling rains, the engineers now labored to move the wagons over slippery, rocky roads. While crossing Russell Creek, a wagon from Company D broke, and the men had to manhandle it the rest of the way. On the ninth some of the men remained in camp to fix the wagon, while Captain Fox and sixty men from his company were detailed to repair a footbridge over the troublesome creek. That night the exhausted rear of Thomas's column straggled into camp.[8]

Thomas's column moved out of camp on the tenth, with the engineers delayed by the need to build another crossing over Russell Creek for the division's wagons. The next few days were especially difficult ones for Hunton's battalion. Often the men had to build the road in advance of the column and then move back and help push the wagons and artillery pieces along the new track. Sometimes the engineers had to clear and corduroy as much as four miles of road, laying the cut logs across the muddy route. They also had to repair broken wagons and harnesses and pull stuck wagons out of the mud. When the teams wore out, the engineers pulled the wagons themselves. They performed much of this exhausting work while loaded down with equipment and additional tools and in freezing rain. From the tenth to the seventeenth, the column covered only some forty miserable miles.[9]

Thomas and the advance of his column reached Logan Crossroads, just ten miles from Zollicoffer's position, on January 17. By now, the engineers were marching with the rear of the division, helping to move the wagons and teams, and they did not arrive until January 18. They spent the rest of the day pitching tents, settling into camp, and preparing for a much-needed rest. For Thomas's men, however, the rest would be short-lived. The Confederates were moving to the attack.[10]

On January 3 Maj. Gen. George B. Crittenden, commanding forces in East Tennessee and Zollicoffer's superior, had arrived at Mill Springs to find the command still on the exposed northern bank, kept there by a high river and a lack of boats. Crittenden ordered the command to build rafts and prepare to cross, but work progressed slowly. On January 18 Crittenden received information from a local resident that swollen Fishing Creek separated Schoepf's brigade from the balance of Thomas's command. Unable to withdraw his command to the safety of the south bank, Crittenden decided to attack Thomas before he could unite with Schoepf.[11]

The vanguard of Crittenden's force, under Zollicoffer's personal command, struck the advance Union pickets at about 5:30 A.M. and began to drive them back. The Michigan Engineers, camped near the rear of the Union forces, were not aware of the growing fight until drummers in surrounding regiments called the men into line of battle at about 6:45 A.M.[12]

This was Hunton's first brush with the enemy, so he went to Thomas's headquarters for orders. He was directed to form the engineers into a camp guard, stationing the companies at different points around the perimeter. Another trip to headquarters resulted in orders to stack arms and let the men eat. No sooner had the men done that, however, than the sound of firing became much closer. Hunton ordered the men back into line, and they marched by company to their designated camp guard positions. This was at about 7:30 A.M. Their orders were to serve as a final line of defense for the camps and stop Union stragglers. They remained in position until about noon, after the firing had ceased. While spent balls did reach their positions, no engineers were hit.[13]

As Hunton and his three companies were forming and reforming the camp guard, a confusing battle was fought between Crittenden's men and part of Thomas's command. The Confederates moved to the attack in the rain through rough terrain and woods. They quickly became disorganized. Most of the attacks were carried out piecemeal. Stubborn defense by the advance Union regiments, along with timely ammunition and reinforcements, stopped Crittenden's men. Zollicoffer was killed when he mistook a Union regiment for one of his own. A Union counterattack broke the Confederate left flank, and the entire line disintegrated. For the Confederates it was a crushing defeat. Zollicoffer was dead, and Crittenden's army was scattered, abandoning its artillery and equipment on the north bank of the river in the haste to get to safety on the south bank.[14]

The Michigan Engineers were very proud of the role that they played in the campaign, even though they had not engaged in the fighting. Sgt. Morgan Parker of Company F claimed a "proportionate share [of the glory] for the brave fellows" in the regiment who had struggled so hard to get Thomas's command there. Capt. James W. Sligh pointed out to his wife that "if we had not cut out new roads and made the old ones better than they were, and if they had not got here as soon as they did, those that were here would have been cut to pieces."[15]

The battle also provided the engineers with a valuable lesson on the high cost of war. Though a minor engagement by later standards, the Battle of Mill Springs cost Thomas about 10 percent of the twenty-five hundred men of his command who were actually engaged. Assigned to bury the dead and gather up the wounded, the Michigan Engineers were assailed by the gruesome sights and emotionally moved. Two of the men in Company F assigned to bury the enemy dead in mass unmarked graves wrote home about the carnage. One noted, "It was the most sickening sight I have ever seen, all bloody and some with legs and arms shot off," and the other proclaimed, "how awful is war!" A captain in the Thirty-first Ohio claimed that "as the boys of the 1st Michigan Engineers were burying the dead, one of them found a $5.00 bill in a vest pocket—says he to him: 'my fine fellow I will bury you a little nicer.'"[16]

Fox and eighty men from Companies F and G were assigned to guard forty-five prisoners taken by the Tenth Indiana. The Confederate prisoners were the first enemy the Michigan Engineers had come face to face with, and they were anxious to talk with them about the war and its causes. That night several of the officers stayed up talking with Lt. Col. Fountain B. Carter of the Twentieth Tennessee, the highest ranking Confederate taken in the battle, and Surgeon Daniel B. Cliffe, who had stayed behind with the wounded. Fox's detachment delivered the prisoners to Somerset on the twenty-second and was joined there by the rest of Lieutenant Colonel Hunton's battalion on the twenth-third.[17]

Thomas concentrated his men at Somerset in the days following the battle, awaiting orders from Buell. The engineers repaired the division's wagons and set up their camp. In late January the engineers started to build boats to ferry Thomas's division across the Cumberland to Waitsboro and Jamestown.[18]

Meanwhile, Buell's other forces, including the seven other companies of Michigan Engineers, remained in position while Thomas's command drove the Confederates back into eastern Tennessee. Colonel Innes and Companies B, E, and I arrived at Camp Wood near Munfordville, seventy-three miles south by rail, on December 30. The small village of Munfordville was a strategic point in Union plans because of its location astride the Louisville and Nashville Railroad and the important railroad bridge across the nearby Green River. Completed amid great fanfare in 1859 with five spans of iron superstructure crossing the river at a height of 115 feet, the 1,000-foot-long bridge had been partially destroyed by retreating Confederates.[19]

Innes's men joined the troops of Brig. Gen. Alexander McCook's Second Division, who had been along the Green River since early December. Men from the Thirty-second Indiana had constructed a pontoon bridge across the river, and other detachments were repairing the railroad bridge and constructing defenses on the south bank. Upon arrival, Innes's men were put to work getting out timbers for the railroad bridge and providing work parties to protect the pontoon bridge from rising waters.[20]

Heavy rains soon turned the river into a raging torrent, and floating logs threatened to carry away the pontoon span. Despite the engineers' best efforts, the bridge did break up, and Lieutenant Rhodes supervised its repair. Protecting the pontoon bridge was dangerous and exhausting duty. Forty years later, the danger was still vivid for one Pennsylvania infantryman who had spent "one of the darkest and most disagreeable nights of the winter on that pontoon bridge. The wind was blowing a hurricane, a cold rain was falling, the night was dark, and there was constant danger that some heavy drift-wood might carry the bridge away at any moment."[21]

Once the railroad bridge was finished by civilian working parties, many of the Michigan Engineers were shifted over to clearing and framing timber for several depots and commissary buildings. Others worked on fortifications on the south side of the river and cleared trees for fields of fire. These defenses, reportedly dubbed Fort Innes by McCook, consisted simply of eight or ten acres of ground enclosed by a earth and log wall surrounded by a ditch some ten feet away. It was apparently located west of the railroad near the crossing. By early February details from the three companies were also running a sawmill at nearby Woodsonville. From Woodsonville the engineers sent the cut lumber to the Michigan Engineers who were repairing the pontoon bridge and constructing boats for use on the river. Others laid down lumber planking on the railroad bridge and constructed railings so that it could be used by the wagons of Union troops moving forward. On February 10 Brig. Gen. Ormsby Mitchel's division, including Captain Yates's battalion, crossed on this planking. Meanwhile, details under Captain Palmerlee relaid railroad track.[22]

During this time McCook's force largely outnumbered the small parties of Confederate cavalry assigned to the area, but the green Michigan Engineers expected to have to fight for their lives at any moment. On January 6 a Confederate observation balloon was sighted floating near the Union camp, and twenty rounds of ammunition were issued Innes's men to be used in repelling the expected attack. On the seventeenth a returning party of Union scouts recklessly discharged their guns upon reaching friendly lines. In response, a general alarm was sounded, and several regiments of reinforcements were rushed across the bridge to the south bank, prepared to rescue their beleaguered comrades. They sheepishly returned after the cause of the alarm was determined, none the worse for the practice.[23]

Despite their fears, in several instances men from the regiment wandered beyond the Union pickets armed only with curiosity and naiveté. Albert Graves and others from Company B were cutting wood on the south side of the river when told by sentinels that a rebel party was lurking nearby. The men, armed with only one musket among them and a few axes, "rushed around the picket captain with the eager request to be permitted" to go after the enemy. The request was wisely denied.[24]

Innes's men were not the only new troops lacking military discipline. On January 26 thirty men from each of the Michigan Engineer companies were detailed to gather straw for the camp from locations several miles south of the bridge. Three infantry regiments were sent along to protect them, but the guard failed to maintain any military formation and treated the expedition as a lark. One member of Innes battalion remembered, "We could see them running over the hills like a flock of quails running over plowed ground."[25]

Meanwhile, more than seventy miles by rail to the northeast of Munfordville, Companies C and H under Major Hopkins faced even less danger from rebel cavalry. On December 26 Hopkins's two companies had ridden by rail the forty-five miles from Louisville to New Haven, a station on the Lebanon branch of the Louisville and Nashville Railroad. From New Haven they marched two miles to Knob Creek with guns loaded, moving forward squad by squad to guard against any sudden enemy onslaught. Camp was made in a defensible position along the banks of the creek. Apparently reassured that his men were not going to be slaughtered, Hopkins allowed them to roam throughout the neighboring countryside. Close by camp, and of chief interest to the men, were the birthplace and former schoolhouse of President Lincoln. Others marveled at the beautiful knobs and drank from the cold and clear mountain streams. The men were also allowed to practice firing their muskets at turkeys that Hopkins provided as targets.[26]

After four days at this point, Hopkins marched his men eight miles and reached Camp Wickliffe, a large encampment along the pike on the southwestern slope of Muldraugh's Hill. The camp was the headquarters of Brig. Gen. William "Bull" Nelson, commanding Buell's Fourth Division. A towering man at six feet four inches and over three hundred pounds, Nelson was possessed with a mercurial temperament, alternately genial and consumed with rage. He was also a strict disciplinarian who kept his troops busy by drilling them constantly.[27]

The men's first exposure to Nelson's brand of discipline was immediate and memorable. On December 31 he ordered the two companies to move their tents twenty rods and set them up according to regulations. One soldier's salute was not crisp enough, so he ignored it. Two engineers found along the pike away from camp were ordered returned, and Hopkins was told that the next man caught out of camp would be arrested and punished. At least one member of Company H took comfort in Nelson's soldierly conduct: "General Nelson . . . gave us a going over. He is a cross looking man but may be a good officer. We will have to keep close now and I am glad of it too." The men quickly settled down into the routine of army life, leading the same soldier to note in his diary that "things begin to take a sensible shape and soldiering is alright."[28]

With little work to do, Nelson drilled his men constantly. Much of the drill focused on weapons exercises: bayonet practice, manual of arms, and skirmish drill. There were also dress parades, inspections, and battalion drills. For purposes of training, the two companies were attached to the Forty-first Ohio and drilled together under the direction of Col. William B. Hazen, an 1855 graduate of West Point who proved his mettle in subsequent battles during the war. Within days the Michigan Engineers at Camp Wickliffe were also repairing area roads and bridges and building bunks for hospitals. Captain Coffinberry and most of Company C returned to New Haven to repair a bridge. Lt. Harry J. Chapel and some of his men from Company H were sent to New Buffalo to build a bridge and repair the road.[29]

Despite the drill and Nelson's iron discipline, there were several incidents among the engineers that were typical of new recruits. After dark on January 1, Pvt. Alex Matheson of Company H fired at a stray dog, believing it to be an encroaching rebel. The long roll was sounded, and Nelson's entire division formed into line of battle. Twice within the next week, members of Company C carelessly fired what they thought was an unloaded musket, slightly wounding men in camp. On January 3 a member of the regiment was seriously wounded in the head in a similar incident. On January 12 Pvt. John Courtney fell and accidentally fired his gun, sending a bullet whistling through the camp, though no one was hurt. Problems caused by false alarms continued through the month, and in early February there were several incidents involving drunken members of the battalion.[30]

When not drilling, details from the battalion labored on area construction projects. By late January, most of the men in the two companies were forward of Camp Wickliffe, repairing the pike road leading south toward the Green River. Away from Nelson's strict camp discipline, the men settled into a comfortable existence. Foodstuffs bought or bartered from neighboring farms largely replaced army rations. There was a steady stream of visitors to camp, and many of the men were able to play the tourist in the surrounding country-side. One diarist in Company H declared, "This is the best soldiering I have seen." One of the officers with the detachment, fearing orders to return to camp, wrote, "There is not one of us but what would rather march toward the enemy." The good times came to an abrupt end on February 5, when the men returned to Camp Wickliffe and regular work resumed on nearby roads.[31]

Meanwhile, Captain Yates and Companies A and K had arrived from Louisville at Bacon Creek, just six miles north of the Green River crossing near Munfordville, on December 27 and went into camp alongside the men of Mitchel's Third Division. Mitchel was a West Point graduate, renowned astronomer, and railroad man who led his division aggressively.[32]

Within days of their arrival at Bacon Creek, Yates's men were ordered to march back fourteen miles northward along the Elizabeth-town Road to Nolin River, where a road bridge needed repair. Arriving on January 1 they found the bridge in such poor condition that as the companies crossed over, the officers spread the files six or eight feet apart to avoid collapsing it. The baggage wagons forded between the bridge and the milldam above so as not to risk falling through the floorboards. That night they pitched tents and prepared to work. First, it was necessary to repair two abandoned sawmills and start cutting planks from the timber brought back by regimental details sent into the woods. Then details used the framed timber to rebuild the 295-foot-long bridge by January 18. After a day of rest, the three companies moved out of camp on the twentieth and made the difficult march back south to Bacon Creek. The men were forced to push the heavily loaded wagons most of the way over the fourteen miles of muddy roads. One wagon tipped, and the men scrambled into the mud after its contents. They finally reached Bacon Creek late that night. The following morning Pvt. William L. Clark of Company K reported that there was not "one set of really clean uniforms or accouterments" and that the lieutenant "looked as though his sword had been doing service of the right sort the night before." This was the first hard marching for the men of these companies.[33]

The two companies under Yates remained near Bacon Creek until February 10, gaining more experience in a large number of engineering assignments that would be necessary in the months ahead. Details repaired and operated a nearby sawmill, while others built hospitals at Bacon Creek and Elizabethtown with the finished lumber. Another working party constructed a large platform for the railroad depot at Bacon Creek Station. Others were ordered to work with the artillerymen in planting batteries and target practice. Another detail repaired the pike leading back to Elizabethtown. Most of the men took advantage of any idle time to write letters home, leading Clark to predict that his company would "shed more ink than blood during the war." Clark did both, writing detailed letters home for publication and dying at the hands of guerrillas in 1864.[34]

It is difficult to overstate the importance that Clark and the other men attached to receiving mail from home. Sgt. Edwin R. Osband at Camp Wickliffe recorded the joy of the mail's arrival: "Major Hopkins came from Louisville today and brought a large lot of letters. . . . I tell you I was glad to hear from old Michigan once more." Another soldier, writing from Munfordville, noted the recent arrival of mail and declared, "if I ever felt to rejoice it was last evening. My heart felt to leap for joy."[35]

The men also wrote home frequently, usually commenting on the daily activities of the regiment and often speculating about when they would be able to return home. After detailing his company's activities, Graves wrote home to a worried wife to "have confidence that I shall be home and the war closed before long." He did not return for another year, badly broken in health.[36]

Since most were visiting Kentucky for the first time, much ink was dedicated to a comparison with Michigan. Most of the Michigan Engineers were particularly harsh, criticizing what they viewed as a dramatic lack of education and enterprise among the people of Kentucky. Captain Sligh wrote home that "the inhabitants are the most ignorant I ever met . . . the inhabitants lack enterprise," and another noted, "the people are fifty years behind the times and age of the North." Nathan Robinson, writing home from near Camp Wickliffe, was particularly struck with the lack of any schools and the lack of windows in houses and public buildings. He related a report from Chaplain Tracy that the only minister in the area, though considered a "right smart preacher, powerful smart man," could not write.[37]

Meanwhile, developments were rapidly changing the strategic picture and Buell's deployment of his divisions. Brig. Gen. Ulysses S. Grant had convinced Halleck to give permission for an expedition to capture Forts Henry and Donelson. The fall of both would turn Johnston's left center and open up Middle Tennessee. Halleck remained nervous about the chance of success, a concern shared by the War Department. As a precaution, Buell was ordered to support Grant by advancing his own command. The Michigan Engineer battalions quickly found themselves in motion: Yates with Companies A and K moving with Mitchel; Hopkins and Companies C and H en route by steamer as part of reinforcements for Grant; and Innes and Hunton with the other six companies, part of Buell's effort to gather his forces and send them overland toward Nashville.[38]

In response to orders from the War Department, Buell ordered Mitchel to demonstrate against Bowling Green and prevent the reinforcement of Fort Donelson by Hardee's troops. On February 10 Companies A and K under Yates marched with Mitchel's division from Bacon Creek to Munfordville. They crossed the Green River on the narrow, towering bridge that night and camped near the railroad. For the next two days Union cavalrymen scouted possible routes south from their camp, and early on the thirteenth Mitchel's division left for Bowling Green.[39]

Retreating rebel cavalry tried to slow their advance by felling trees across the road and blocking the advance of wagons and artillery. Yates's two companies were ordered forward from their place in the column and directed to clear the obstructions. Working with axes, picks, spades, and ropes and hooks, the Michigan Engineers labored at the front of the column, "clearing the roads in a remarkably quick time" in the estimation of the cavalry regiment's commander. One of his troopers remembered that "the sappers and miners from Wisconsin [sic] were so active in cutting their way through, that the infantry were never brought to a halt but keep steadily on their march." Clearing roads was hard work, and the thirsty men could not drink from nearby pools, since the retreating Confederates had polluted them with dead livestock. Camp that night was near Rock Hill Station, nearly twenty miles from the Green River.[40]

The next day the rain gave way to a cold blustery wind, and snow fell on the men as they struggled forward, Yates's men with the main body. Retreating Confederates were able to burn the bridges over the Big Barren. Mitchel's command was forced to halt on the north bank, staring across the swollen river at their goal. That night Mitchel reported to Buell that the "engineers and mechanics will soon enable us to cross the river." It would actually be twelve days before Yates's men were across the Big Barren.[41]

While Yates's battalion faced a hard march to Bowling Green, Hopkins and Companies C and H had an easier assignment as part of reinforcements designated for Grant's force. Nelson was ordered to move with part of his division and embark on steamers waiting at the mouth of the Salt River. The boats would take the command to join Grant. Nelson was to travel light, with promises that supplies would be provided by Grant upon his arrival. Their greatest challenge would not be the enemy but indecision and the temper of their division commander.[42]

Companies C and H marched from Camp Wickliffe on February 14 and reached the Salt River at West Point two days later. The following morning the men repaired the road for quartermaster teams and in the afternoon prepared to embark. Nelson had ordered that the engineers be split between two steamers, on the *Autocrat* with the Twenty-fourth Ohio and the *Golden State* with three companies of the Forty-sixth Indiana. When his men arrived at the steamers, Hopkins discovered that the boats were already full. Nelson ordered them to load regardless or be left behind and placed on report with Buell. Hopkins believed that he had a choice and ordered the men to make camp.[43]

Finding the battalion still in camp, Nelson, "in great passion," told the men he had arrested Hopkins and Capt. Marcus Grant and ordered the tents struck immediately. He threatened that if the men were not quick enough in breaking camp and loading onto the steamers, he would send a regiment to march them to the landing at the point of the bayonet. Nelson, now "fairly purple with rage," was quickly able to convince them, and the two companies finished loading onto the *Lancaster No. 4* by 10 P.M. Captain Coffinberry now commanded the battalion with Hopkins and Grant gone. William Kimball reported that the men "felt rather blue as we were well aware we had incurred the displeasure of General Nelson and the Captain and Major were left behind under arrest." Hopkins and Grant were turned over to Maj. Dorus M. Fox of the Ninth Michigan, who was commanding the post, and ordered to Louisville to await trial. Nelson preferred charges against them, "not desiring to have such persons accompany him to the presence of the enemy."[44]

Hunton's battalion, veterans of the Mill Springs campaign, left their camps near Waitsboro on February 10 en route to Lebanon. For six days the companies struggled to move wagons, artillery, and men through mud, freezing rain, and snow. Many of the roads were barely passable. On the evening of the fifteenth, after a grueling six-day march of about fifty-seven miles, the exhausted column reached Danville. Thomas's division was then ordered by Buell to participate in the overland general advance on Bowling Green, and the division left Danville on the seventeenth with Thomas's men.[45]

McCook's long stay at Munfordville ended on February 13, when he received orders from Buell to move to West Point at the mouth of the Salt River and await steamers. After a miserable day's march, new orders were received to reverse course and move back to Munfordville and then overland to Bowling Green. Trudging along with this column were Colonel Innes and Companies B, E, and I.[46]

Innes's detachment worked southward along the Louisville and Nashville Railroad toward Bowling Green for the next several days.

Retreating Confederates had cut the railroad leading south from Louisville, destroying a four-mile stretch of railroad north of Horse Cave and also between Cave City and Bell's Tavern. They had also burned vital railroad buildings and destroyed critical bridges over the Big Barren and Cumberland rivers. Buell wanted the railroad repaired so that his overland march against Nashville could be supplied from the depots at Louisville. Most of Innes's working parties were detailed to cut replacement ties. On the sixteenth McCook reported to Buell that he would "push matters will all possible haste," assigning at least one regiment per day from his division to work with Innes's men.[47]

Railroad repair was a makeshift affair in the early days of the war. Civilian railroad officials were unable to get captured roads back in working order quickly enough for military authorities, forcing the detachment of infantrymen to fill the void. The Michigan Engineers were particularly suited for this assignment because of the number of experienced railroad men within its ranks, especially among the officers. Others were capable of cutting down trees of uniform size and hewing a flat side to which the rail could be attached. At this point in the war the Louisville and Nashville Railroad was not using tie plates but rather attaching railroad iron directly to wood running parallel with the iron, fastened at the joints with devices known as chairs.[48]

Meanwhile, General Grant had captured Forts Henry and Donelson. Johnston with half of the remnant of his command retreated south of the Tennessee River, while the balance concentrated to defend the now-exposed position at Columbus, Kentucky, on the far left flank. The sudden collapse of the Confederate positions meant that Nashville was soon abandoned to the Union. Buell put his scattered commands into motion, all focused on reaching Nashville as soon as possible.[49]

Following Grant's capture of Fort Donelson, news of which reached Nelson's transports on the twentieth or twenty-first, a debate ensued among Halleck, Buell, and Grant about where the division should be sent. In the meantime, the men of Companies C and H enjoyed their journey on the water. The seven transports carrying Nelson's division finally reached Nashville on the twenty-fifth. Nelson landed a small force to take formal possession of the city, and the Sixth Ohio raised the U.S. colors over the capitol building. William Kimball recorded, "It was a day we felt proud of."[50]

The next day they unloaded the boat and marched two miles away from the landing. On the twenty-seventh the battalion marched another mile out from town and settled into camp. Several days were spent resting, cleaning equipment, and preparing the camp for inspection. Since their camp was near Nelson's headquarters, one soldier claimed the battalion was determined "to keep right side up [or] he will swear at us."[51]

By February 20 Companies B, E, and I of Innes's detachment had worked their way down to near Bell's Tavern, repairing broken track. With McCook's division nearing Bowling Green, Innes was ordered to leave a detail behind to finish the work and move with the rest of his command to rejoin the infantry. On the twenty-third Innes's battalion, less Captain Palmerlee and a detail from his company, made the twenty-three-mile march to Bowling Green. They arrived that afternoon. Innes's battalion crossed the Big Barren River on February 25, with assistance from Yates's detachment, and entered Bowling Green. Palmerlee's force followed later.[52]

On February 27 McCook's command left Bowling Green under orders to march southward to Nashville, with Innes's battalion in the column. One member of a Pennsylvania regiment in the division complained that the mud that first day was "indescribable; it rained most of the day and when we turned aside into the woods for the night, we seemed a spectacle for men and angels." The column made twenty-two miles, followed by twenty the next day, and another fifteen on the twenty-ninth. By this time the column was near Nashville, with the engineers finally reaching Edgefield on the north bank of the Cumberland River on March 2. Innes's battalion crossed over on steamers on March 4 and set up camp south of town on the Franklin Pike.[53]

For Yates's men in Companies A and K, the hardest part of the route was just getting across the Big Barren and into Bowling Green. After arriving at the river with Mitchel's division on February 14, the engineers started building ferries to cross the balance of the division. For a week the battalion labored in the cold to cross Mitchel's men. Every technique was tried. A captured flat boat ferried a few regiments across. The engineers completed a footbridge on the sixteenth, built on the ruins of the railroad bridge, and a few more men were pushed across. By the eighteenth, two ferries were in operation as part of a pontoon bridge, after "incredible labor, in rain and mud." Soon, however, rising waters put them out of service. Innes and Companies B, E, and I arrived on the twenty-third with McCook's division but were forced to encamp along the river. There was little they could do to help Yates's men force a crossing. Not until steamboats were brought up the river did the wagons and artillery of the two divisions get across. Innes and his three companies were ferried over on the twenty-fifth, followed the next day by Yates's two companies. Companies A and K finally reached Nashville by March 5.[54]

Since the Confederates were rapidly evacuating Middle Tennessee, Thomas received new orders on February 23. He was to march his men to Louisville, where they would board steamers for Nashville. The men were on the road by 5 A.M. on the twenty-fourth, making twenty-nine miles before camping. The next day the men were again moving early and marched the final seventeen miles by noon. The Michigan Engineer companies marched through Louisville as an escort for the Ninth Ohio and Second Minnesota, heroes of the fight at Mill Springs. That night Hunton and companies D, F, and G slept aboard the steamer *Argonaut*. The *Argonaut* left Louisville on February 26 and arrived at Nashville on March 4. On the fifth they marched west four miles on the Charlotte Pike and set up camp.[55]

Not all of the men in the Michigan Engineers were able to keep up on the march to Nashville. By the end of February at least 175 were scattered across Kentucky and Tennessee, lying in hastily erected hospitals or private buildings taken over for the sick and wounded. Another 39 sick and injured had been able to keep up with the regimental hospital. Captain Grant reported to a soldier's aid society that "a large portion of the men are scattered sick all along the line for 300 miles." Upon reaching Nashville, Army of the Ohio medical director Robert Murray assessed the situation facing the army. He reported, "The Army is encumbered with soldiers who will never be fit for duty."[56]

A month later, disease had caused the death or medical discharge of 50 Michigan Engineers. Another 350 were reported sick in their tents or army hospitals, including 6 officers. When the regiment left the Nashville area in early April, at least 200 sick men were left behind, and by the end of April, over 40 percent of the men who had not already died or been discharged in the regiment were listed as sick. This was the highest monthly percentage sick that the regiment would have during four years of service. Some of the men left behind in Nashville or other hospitals would never rejoin the regiment, and most would remain absent for several months.[57]

Innes and his men were quickly learning two basic facts of nineteenth-century warfare: that disease killed and disabled far more men than battles and that the most common killer diseases were not exotic ones. Diarrhea, dysentery, typhoid fever, and malaria were leading causes of Civil War deaths. The high death rate in the crowded army camps could be largely attributed to the soldiers' diet and hygiene. Although Union soldiers generally had enough to eat, too much of their diet was salted meat, beans, and hardtack. There was a serious lack of vegetables and fruit, especially during the winter months. The men also lacked the experience to prepare food properly. Green soldiers generally preferred to fry all foods and were generally ignorant of basic cooking methods.[58]

At least as deadly to the soldiers as diet was their ignorance of proper sanitation. Latrines were often placed in locations that fouled a camp's drinking water. Some men, placing modesty over common good, refused to use the public latrines and relieved themselves in areas surrounding the camps. Garbage was allowed to collect in rotting piles. The men seldom bathed or washed their hands and were covered with lice and fleas. Many exercised little restraint in what or how much they ate. Officers must bear some responsibility because the regulations of the day, which were specific on these subjects, were not followed. Many officers in turn blamed the men. Captain Sligh wrote home about his enlisted men, complaining that "they must take care of themselves, but lots of them never think of that and drink at every stream or spring they come to and eat everything that a sutler may have to sell and thereby breed disease." Fellow officer Lt. James D. Robinson complained in a letter home about men who get out of work by feigning sick but then stay "in their crowded tents eating all they can stuff down . . . enough to make a well one sick. . . . I am sorry to say that we have some of this stripe."[59]

Hard marching during winter campaigns was also a significant cause of poor health, especially when combined with periods of climate-enforced inactivity and confinement to camp. Hunton's battalion, Companies D, F, and G, made the toughest marches among the Michigan Engineers in early 1862. The marches to the Cumberland River and back to Louisville were made in freezing rain while struggling to move wagons and teams over rutted roads. Their camps in Somerset and along the Cumberland River were primitive even by early 1862 standards. The men were forced to sleep directly on the wet or frozen ground, and it was not always possible to even light fires for warmth. Under these conditions it was inevitable that the men's health would break down. Captain Sligh left Company F on January 26 to obtain building materials for a ferry, and the men were generally in good health. When he returned one week later, however, he found one half of his company in the hospital or confined to tents unable to do any work. When Hunton's battalion left Waitsboro, Kentucky, for Lebanon on February 9, at least thirty men were left behind sick. A similar number were too sick to accompany the three companies when they departed Lebanon for Louisville on February 20. By the time the three companies arrived in Nashville in early March, one-third of their combined strength was absent due to death, discharge, or illness.[60]

Much of the underlying cause for sickness and disability during this time was the army's lack of effective medical screening at the time of enlistment. Surgeon Charles S. Tripler, medical director of the Army of the Potomac, studied the records of the four thousand men discharged from that army in the last three months of 1861. He determined that almost 75 percent of the medical conditions had been present at the time of enlistment and should have been discovered by any examining surgeon. The physical demands of active campaigning quickly felled those men who should not have been allowed to enlist at Camp Owen, especially the older recruits who were physically less able to fight off disease and infection.[61]

These early deaths from disease were difficult for their comrades to bear. They had accepted the possibility of a battlefield death, but to see companions suffer and die in such a lingering manner was painful. Captain Sligh wrote his wife, "It is hard for a man to be killed in battle away from all that he holds dear on earth, but it is still harder according to my conception of the thing to be struck down by disease far from home."[62]

As death in the camps became a more common occurrence, many of the men noted a discouraging pattern. After paying his respects to a deceased soldier in his company, Pvt. William B. Calkins complained about the manner in which his comrades' remains were treated: "They had them both in one box. They had one head one way, the other the other way. Their eyes and mouths were open and it was the hardest sight that I ever saw. A person that is sick and dies in the army ain't thought anything of at all."[63]

Judson W. Carter of Company K died at Bowling Green of disease on March 3. Just two weeks later, his brother George W. Carter died of typhoid fever in a makeshift Union hospital at Murfreesboro. Judson was, according to the *Kalamazoo Telegram*, "another of those loyal hearts that gave up family and all else that he might serve his country in any capacity." After less than three months in the field, the Michigan Engineers permanently lost the services of at least one quarter of its "loyal hearts." The pattern of hard marching, hard work, and attrition from disease would continue in the months ahead.[64]

· 5 ·

On to Corinth

As the Michigan Engineer battalions arrived in Nashville, they camped alongside the army divisions to which they had been attached, doing little work. Colonel Innes and Companies B, E, and I were located at Camp Andy Johnson, three miles south of Nashville on the Franklin Pike. Captain Yates and Companies A and K were at Camp Andrew Jackson, several miles to the southeast on the Murfreesboro Pike. Major Hopkins and Companies C and H were camped near the same place. Lieutenant Colonel Hunton and Companies D, F, and G set up camp four miles west of the city on the Charlotte Pike. For the next ten days, the battalions remained apart though many of the officers and men visited their comrades.[1]

The Union command structure in the West changed during this same period. On March 11, 1862, General Halleck was promoted to command of the newly created Department of the Mississippi, giving him control over the forces under Gens. U. S. Grant, D. C. Buell, and John Pope, among others. While Pope moved against the isolated Confederate strongholds at New Madrid and Island No. 10, Grant and Buell would unite and move against Corinth, Mississippi. Meanwhile, Gen. Pierre G. T. Beauregard and General Johnston were concentrating their scattered Confederate forces at Corinth.[2]

On March 15 Halleck ordered Buell to move his command to Pittsburg Landing and Savannah, located on the Tennessee River thirty miles northeast of Corinth and the point of concentration for Grant's forces. Buell ordered his cavalry forward to take control of the bridges along the pike to Columbia, Tennessee. He would take only five divisions of his Army of the Ohio, leaving about half of his men behind to protect Middle Tennessee and threaten Confederate-held Cumberland Gap in Kentucky. The advance came to a halt at the Duck River crossing. Confederate troopers of the First Louisiana Cavalry had destroyed the bridge there, and Buell's column waited while repairs were made. Other destroyed bridges along the route from Nashville would also have to be repaired to allow for wagons bringing supplies from Nashville.[3]

The ease with which a few hundred men brought five divisions to a grinding halt at the Duck River crossing demonstrated the vulnerability of supply lines relying on wagon and rail transport. A single burned bridge could put an immediate halt to efforts to reinforce or supply the Union columns driving deep into the Confederacy. As Buell was quickly discovering, the maintenance of a reliable supply line depended on the ability of Union authorities to repair and protect bridges and railroad tracks. The problem was clear, but the solution would come only after a long period of trial and error involving the Michigan Engineers and other forces in Buell's command.

As Union armies moved further south in the spring of 1862, railroad company officials and their key trained employees fled with the Confederate armies. The conquering Union commanders were forced to operate the railroad as best as they could, detailing officers with railroad backgrounds to provide the day-to-day management. The railroad was considered to be army property, operated for the benefit of the army, usually in cooperation with quartermaster officials.[4]

In Buell's Department of the Ohio, captured railroad lines had operated under the direction of John Byars Anderson since November 1861. The experienced Anderson was a senior official with the Louisville and Nashville when war broke out. Anderson remained a civilian with no military rank, reported directly to Buell, and contracted with loyal railroad companies with little direction from outside the department.[5]

South of Nashville, however, the railroad had been destroyed by retreating Confederates and was a long way from being operated by any Union authority. Buell tapped Col. William Sooy Smith of the Thirteenth Ohio to personally direct their repair using military resources. Smith was a West Point graduate and a successful prewar civil engineer and bridge builder.[6]

Repair efforts were focused on two major railroad lines. The Nashville and Chattanooga had been completed in 1854. Its route ran south from Nashville to Stevenson and then east to the Tennessee River bridge at Bridgeport. From that point it continued eastward to Chattanooga. The other rail route south, commonly called the Nashville and Decatur, was actually a combination of three separate lines: the Tennessee and Alabama from Nashville to Columbia, the Central Southern from Columbia to the state line, and the Tennessee and Central Alabama from the state line to Decatur on the Tennessee River. Not completed as a through route until November 1860, this line had been completely wrecked by retreating Confederates just eighteen months later as far south as the Elk River crossing.[7]

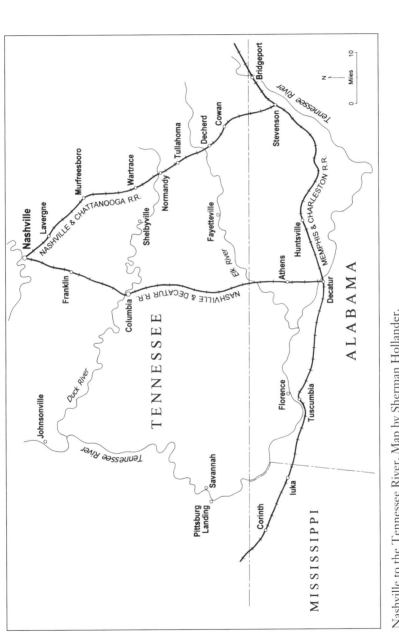

Nashville to the Tennessee River. Map by Sherman Hollander.

Smith's new assignment was a daunting one. Not only had the Confederates and nature destroyed the major bridges leading south from Nashville, rebels had taken or destroyed much of the rolling stock as they retreated. Acquiring locomotives and cars was critical, but any cars transferred from northern lines had to be modified to the narrower gauge used on the Louisville and Nashville and lines further south. Capturing train engines and rolling stock from southern lines quickly became as critical to Buell's supply efforts as rebuilding bridges.[8]

On March 15 Innes and the eight companies with him were ordered to report to Smith. While Hunton and most of the regiment would repair nearby railroad bridges, Innes and a small force were to mount a waterborne expedition from Nashville to near Reynoldsburg (Johnsonville). A partially completed railroad, the Nashville and Northwestern, ran east from Lucas Landing five or six miles toward Waverly. Buell believed that retreating Confederates had left rolling stock along the short line, and these cars, of the narrower gauge favored on Southern roads, would further his plans to use captured railroads.[9]

Innes and about one hundred men from Companies B, E, and I departed Nashville on March 16 aboard the steamer *J. W. Hailman*. At night the sternwheeler tied up downriver along the bank. After an early morning fog burned off, the expedition continued up the river, passing Fort Donelson and stopping for the night at Smithland at the confluence of the Cumberland and Ohio rivers. The next day the expedition steamed down the Ohio to Paducah and, taking a barge in tow, proceeded up the Tennessee. The procession reached the railhead at Lucas Landing on the twentieth, and Innes and his detachment disembarked. Moving east along the railroad, they took possession of the engine *Stranger*, six platform cars, one boxcar, one handcar, and two living cars. The engine and cars were run on the rails back to the landing at the river and loaded onto the barge with no opposition.[10]

The next morning the steamer and barge swung into the river en route for Nashville. Retracing their path, Innes and his men arrived back in Nashville on the twenty-fifth. Upon arrival, the detachment marched through Nashville to the Chattanooga Depot. Major Hopkins, along with Companies C and H and the regimental sick, had moved the regimental headquarters to the depot in Innes's absence.[11]

Detached Companies A and K were also in motion, repairing bridges as General Mitchel's division moved south from Nashville. Mitchel had been left behind by Buell to guard Middle Tennessee, but the aggressive general was on the move. Retreating Confederates had effectively destroyed the pike bridges, denying Yates's men any chance at quick repairs, and Mitchel's men took a circuitous route before reaching Murfreesboro on the twentieth.[12]

The Nashville and Chattanooga Railroad and Nashville Pike both crossed the Stones River in the approach to Murfreesboro, and the bridges had to be repaired before Mitchel's command could move further south. In all, three bridges totaling some 920 feet in length had to be rebuilt—two railroad bridges and one on the pike. Yates and his two companies started work immediately. Mitchel personally oversaw the bridge construction and ordered details from nearby infantry regiments to assist Captain Yates's men. The work progressed quickly, and by March 27 the trestle was nearly half finished. By April 2 the three bridges were nearing completion.[13]

Bridge repair was progressing much slower along the railroad back to Nashville. Mill Creek No. 2 crossing, one of the most important railroad bridges between Nashville and Murfreesboro, had been washed out by high water. Details from Companies C and H were at work on the bridge by the twentieth, reinforced several days later by men from Companies B, E, and I after their return from the expedition to Waverly. The men of the five companies remained camped at the depot in Nashville and took the cars each day to Mill Creek. Despite the importance of the bridge, work proceeded slowly, and large numbers of the men remained in camp at the depot or were allowed to visit the city or surrounding countryside. One Michigan Engineer, writing to a newspaper back home, noted that they were "doing a little work but there does not seem to be much to do."[14]

Southwest of Nashville another battalion of the Michigan Engineers had been ordered to open the second railroad route south from Nashville. Between March 17 and 25, the men in Companies D, F, and G repaired a small culvert near Nashville, a nearby bridge over Brown Creek, and the seventy-four-foot-long bridge over the Little Harpeth River. With Hunton sick in Nashville, Captain Fox led the three companies on to Franklin and the more challenging railroad crossing over the Big Harpeth.[15]

Retreating Confederates had destroyed the crossing at Franklin, and Fox was ordered to build a temporary truss 110 feet long and lay the foundation for a more permanent bridge. His efforts were aided by one of Anderson's civilian work crews, this one from the McCallum Bridge Company of Cincinnati. Additional help was provided by the Thirty-eighth Indiana, which furnished details to work with the teams of animals the engineers used to get out timber. Several of the engineers also repaired and operated a sawmill at the nearby Carnton plantation. Work continued until early on April 2.[16]

With the bridge nearing completion, Captain Sligh received orders on March 31 to move his Company F in advance of the others to Columbia to work on another bridge. Sligh's company finally reached Columbia on the afternoon of April 1, after a long delay caused by the congestion of Buell's wagon trains. They went to work putting the finishing touches on the pike bridge over the Duck River. Hunton and Companies D and G joined them after dark on the second. The next day the railing for the bridge was finished, and the men prepared to move forward.[17]

While the battalions under Yates and Hunton repaired railroads south of Nashville, the remaining five companies stirred themselves into an uproar over the pay issue, and many of the men began to talk openly of mutiny. The controversy over their status and lack of pay had continued to fester after the regiment left Camp Owen. The men expected to get paid, needed the money, and were frustrated it was not forthcoming. While at Camp Wood, Kentucky, on January 12, one engineer reported home ruefully, "I will send you some money just as soon as I get it which I hope will be sometime before you starve or the land is sold for taxes." Seven days later, another updated his wife on prospects for pay and confided, "I think of you every day and have been sorry a great many times that I have ever enlisted on your account."[18]

In early 1862 Innes outlined his assessment of the situation in a letter to his scattered officers. He stated that the War Department apparently did not have congressional authority to pay volunteer engineers anything higher than infantry pay and had so instructed the paymaster at Louisville. While the matter was being resolved in the nation's capital, Innes believed the men in the regiment should accept infantry pay, reserving their future rights to the higher pay after Congress acted. General Buell bolstered Innes's position with an order that "receiving the pay as infantry shall in no way prejudice any claim they may have against the Government." In response to a petition signed by men in Company I, Innes wrote Captain Palmerlee that "this whole matter has been brought to the notice of General Buell . . . and however he may decide will be considered satisfactory to all." Not wanting to leave any stone unturned, at least one hundred men in Companies B, E, and I addressed a letter directly to Buell on February 7, asking for "counsel and advice that will lead to our having justice done us." A committee of men from Companies C and H sent Buell a similar direct appeal that same day, "in the name of all that is sacred to these noble sons of America." They requested to be paid what they had been promised or be discharged from the service.[19]

Buell's suggestion fell on deaf ears. Sgt. William C. Swaddle of Company G wrote home of his conviction that "if every man would protest for his *whole* rights and accept nothing *less*, redress would more speedily be realized" (emphasis in original). While still at Munford-ville some of the men in Innes's battalion were offered thirteen dollars per month infantry pay but refused. There was another unsuccessful attempt to pay the three companies with Innes on February 28 when a paymaster came aboard the steamer *Argonaut*. The men with Hopkins at Camp Wickliffe were offered thirteen dollars per month several times, each time producing "another excitement." Most refused to accept it, as did men in the other battalions. Part of the men's resolve was drawn from the solidarity expressed by the other companies. Kimball reported on February 6 that "a letter was received from Company A saying they had also been offered $13 per month but refused it. It set our camp in commotion again."[20]

Innes and his officers were in a very difficult position. Engineer pay would not be offered to the men until Congress acted, yet the men largely blamed Innes for the situation. Many thought that Innes had been engaged in a fraud and that the regiment was being held in the service because he did not want to lose his rank. One man wrote home, "Our Colonel has used fraud and deception ever since our first enlistment and he has got caught at it. The Colonel never had any orders to get up any such regiment as we are. . . . Thank fortune we have him on the fence and we calculate to keep him there." Even those less cynical of Innes's motivations harbored hard feelings toward the officers of the regiment for the problems. "There is good reason to believe the whole thing is a humbug . . . confidence in the Colonel is a very low ebb so far as sustaining the rank and position of the regiment," wrote one man.[21]

Innes was not the only officer whose motives were questioned. Nathan Robinson, himself a half brother of Lt. James D. Robinson, wrote home, "If this regiment does break up, it will give the commissioned officers fits. James will lose a good deal of money and so will the whole of them and they are getting dreadful uneasy about it. They want us to take [the lower pay] and run the risk of getting [the balance owed], but they don't fool the boys."[22]

For their part, many of the officers were just as frustrated with the men. Captain Sligh did not understand how "some of the men act in all of the companies with regard to the eternal pay question. . . . It is enough to make a man strike his Father, leave alone swear—and all for four dollars per month." He attributed much of the dissent to homesickness.[23]

Compounding the problem was a stubborn refusal by Congress to remedy the problems of volunteer engineers. In February 1862 legislation was introduced by Missouri congressman Francis P. Blair Jr. that would have retroactively recognized the volunteer engineer units already accepted into the service and authorized up to twenty-five thousand in uniform. Despite the pleas of Blair and the support of Congressman Francis W. Kellogg of Grand Rapids, the bill was voted down by a final vote of sixty-six to fifty-seven. The legislation also lacked any vigorous support from the tradition-bound regular army engineer establishment, which remained skeptical of a large volunteer engineer force.[24]

While Congress debated the status of volunteer engineers, Innes insisted that his officers remain firm. His intention was to take his own advice and accept the pay. He made it clear to his subordinates that he expected the officers of the regiment to do likewise. Nor were the officers to encourage the dissension. Innes suggested to Hunton that the surest way for the matter to be resolved to their satisfaction was to "make ourselves as useful throughout as we have been since we started and have no doubt of the ultimate result." If the men, however, were determined not to accept the pay, "they may go without until time is no more. We are here to put down rebellion, not to encourage it and I am determined not to countenance it in any shape."[25]

The officers tried their best in a difficult situation. According to Pvt. William H. Kimball, Major Hopkins was a man who "would sympathize with a private when he was in trouble and in fact his money was the bone and sinew of the regiment for the first six months." Another wrote home that Captain Coffinberry told his men he "would march us back to Michigan" but added "he has not started that way and don't act like going that way." Sligh later wrote his wife that "there is hardly a Captain on the ground but what has loaned money and become security for goods for his men to the amount of $200 and over" with little prospect of getting it back. Lt. James D. Robinson noted that the men in his company who refused pay in early March were those who owed him and the sutler the most.[26]

Despite his best efforts, after the arrival of the companies in Nashville, it became clear to Innes that rebellion was in the offing among his men. He was determined to prevent it, and his words and actions took a harder tone than before. The day he arrived in Nashville, Innes issued an order reducing 1st Sgt. Jerome Gouldsbury to the ranks for writing a letter "containing matter inciting the men to mutinous conduct" in relation to the pay question. The letter had been sent to Hunton's detachment while it was at Somerset, Kentucky, allegedly "advising the men to mutiny and rebellion instead of pursuing the only legitimate cause that could remedy the evil which was to have the matter brought before Congress." On March 6 Innes announced that any man who did not accept infantry pay forfeited it, regardless of the eventual settlement of the controversy. The tactic failed because the men did not believe he had the authority to make such a threat. The next day Innes issued an order forbidding the men or officers of his regiment from presenting any petition of any kind or matter to higher authorities. This method of addressing their grievances was deemed "irregular," and violators were threatened with a general court-martial.[27]

Innes also tried to douse the fire by forbidding communications between his men and newspapers back home. By his actions Innes hoped to stop the storm of criticism produced by certain hostile editors. One of the targets of the ban pointed out the futility of such efforts: "All such orders are silly and futile. We have letters from the regiment in spite of the order, but none speaking any good of the Colonel. Under the order, none but his enemies write to us; whereas, but for this policy, his friends, if he has any, would also be heard."[28]

In addition to disciplining men he accused of inciting mutiny, Innes continued efforts to get the men to accept infantry pay while the whole matter was being resolved. Despite being "groaned and hissed at considerably," he was able to get some fifteen or twenty to sign the payrolls on March 6 and 7. There was another attempt on March 12 to pay the men in the five companies at Nashville, but most of the men refused. A few days later, another attempt was made to pay the companies remaining at the depot. None of the men in Companies B or I accepted their pay, and only four did in Company E. Only in Hopkins's battalion, where sixty of the men in Companies C and H accepted, did large numbers of men take the proffered pay. While the officers apparently all took the pay, large numbers of noncommissioned officers did not.[29]

Discontent grew in the days that followed. The men even engaged in a work slowdown. When Innes's detachment returned to Nashville with the captured rolling stock, the men were slow to unload them: "In unloading the engine the boys, proposing to work according to the pay received, were grunting and tugging at it without moving it when one of the officers proposed they should give one $17 pull. It was done and the engine run off the boat without difficulty. A $13 lift wouldn't move it."[30]

On March 27 men in Company H, and probably others, signed a demand for their pay and presented it to Colonel Innes. The next day, three men in Company C were arrested for refusing to do any work without engineer pay and inciting the men to mutiny.[31]

On April 1 the friction came to a head when the five companies received orders to move in the morning for Columbia. The men prepared another petition outlining their grievances and warned they would not march without pay. On the following morning Innes ordered the company commanders to form their men in front of their quarters and record the names of any men who "intend to refuse to march or disobey any other order." The list must have been very long, since the men held firm and refused to move at the appointed time. Brig. Gen. Ebenezer Dumont, commanding the post of Nashville, told the men that he considered their act as mutiny, that force would be used to move them if necessary, and that the leaders of the mutiny could be shot for their actions. He did, however, postpone the march order for one day to let tempers cool and promised that the men's complaints would receive an impartial hearing.[32]

Most of the men were reluctant to push the action to an actual mutiny and decided to move as directed, leaving Nashville on April 3. Innes arrived at Columbia by rail that evening with the five companies and joined with Hunton and Companies D and G. The next day they marched southward along the pike and joined up with Sligh and Company F. Though the issue over pay had not been resolved, the regiment was at least out of camp and back on active operations. It was an important victory for Innes, albeit an incomplete one.[33]

In the meantime, there was work to be done. The route from Columbia to Savannah was about eighty-two miles, the last sixty-five of which had to be made over a single rough country road that was bad in the plateau region and became progressively worse as it descended into the Tennessee River valley. Captain Fox wrote home that it was a "long bad road to travel." Despite the worsening roads, General Nelson and his Fourth Division set a fast pace, and the column averaged about fifteen miles per day. General Thomas's division, bringing up the army's rear, did not cross until April 2. Innes's men crossed two days later and caught up with Thomas en route.[34]

For most of the march, the engineers were in the army's rear with the wagons, helping the teams over rough spots. The first day's march was along a good pike and passed several of the most prosperous plantations in Middle Tennessee, including those owned by the prominent Pillow and Polk families. The men noted the large white-columned houses and expansive grounds. On the fifth Innes's regiment camped for the night at Summertown, a prewar resort popular with the region's wealthy families. The road and scenery deteriorated, however, with each passing day as the column moved further from Nashville and onto "awful hard roads."[35]

By April 6 the engineers were near Henryville and the Buffalo River crossing. In the distance they could hear the sound of heavy cannonading as Gen. U. S. Grant's surprised command fought for its life near Pittsburg Landing on the Tennessee across from Savannah. Confederate General Johnston had moved his thirty-five thousand men the thirty miles from Corinth and caught Grant's scattered divisions by surprise. That night Grant's men clung to a small perimeter along the river, bolstered by the divisions of "Bull" Nelson, Thomas Crittenden, and Alexander McCook of Buell's command and Lew Wallace's fresh division from Grant's army. The next day, with twenty-four thousand fresh troops, the Union forces drove the Confederates from the field.[36]

The engineers continued their steady advance southwestward to Savannah. Hampered by bad roads and rough terrain, Innes and his men did not reach Savannah until April 11, marching to that point via Waynesboro and across Hardin and Indian creeks. Even then, they had to take a circuitous route to get around the hundreds of army wagons clogging the roads. Part of the regimental wagon train had to be left behind in the interest of movement, and the last of the regiment teams did not arrive at Savannah until the twelfth. Not until the morning of the fifteenth were the men ferried across the river on the sternwheel steamer *Fort Wayne*. They set up camp near Pittsburg Landing.[37]

Though the battle had been over for a week, signs of bloody conflict were everywhere as the Michigan Engineers settled into camp. Sergeant Osband noted, "I have now seen what I never seen before, a battlefield. Indeed I hope I shall never see again." Trying to describe the terrible scenes for those back home, Captain Sligh penned a vivid account for his wife back in Grand Rapids: "The ground so far as I have been over it . . . is literally a grave yard."[38]

On April 15 the men settled into camp about two miles from Pittsburg Landing, southeast of Shiloh Church and near Lick Creek. On the eighteenth their tools arrived from Nashville by steamer and were unloaded and carried to camp. Over the next ten days working parties from the Michigan Engineers constructed steamboat landings on the Tennessee River and built pontoon bridges over the swollen creeks near camp. On several days heavy rains that turned the ground into deep mud and prohibited most movement confined the men to camp. The weather did briefly clear enough on April 23 for the regiment to drill and have a dress parade. Union military authorities, however, had more demanding tasks in store for the Michigan Engineers. The railroad hub of Corinth, Mississippi, beckoned Halleck's growing throng encamped near Pittsburg Landing.[39]

Corinth was an obvious target for advancing Union forces in the spring of 1862. It was the point of intersection for two important rail lines, the Memphis and Charleston and the Mobile and Ohio. The former was the only railroad line still in Confederate control that linked the Mississippi River with the eastern seaboard. The latter was a key route for the movement of men and material to the upper South from the gulf shore. Following the defeat at Shiloh, Beauregard led the remnants of Johnston's force back to Corinth and tried to rebuild the army. Halleck collected together the troops placed under his command in the Department of the Mississippi, and by late April he had over one hundred thousand men in camp ready for the campaign against Corinth.[40]

The advance on Corinth was different from any other that the Michigan Engineers had ever participated in. Unlike the relatively rapid marches made to Bowling Green, Nashville, and Savannah, Halleck's campaign proceeded at a snail's pace. Halleck was concerned about a repeat of the surprise at Shiloh, so the huge army moved forward in small advances, with troops entrenching after every move. Hampered by rough terrain and his self-imposed tactical considerations, Halleck took almost a month to cover the twenty miles. The last six miles took two weeks.[41]

Halleck divided his forces into three wings for the advance. The left wing was to be Pope's Army of the Mississippi, fresh from victories against Confederate forces at Island No. 10 and now camped at Hamburg Landing, a few miles up the Tennessee River from Pittsburg Landing. The center was commanded by Buell and included his divisions of Nelson, Thomas Wood, Crittenden, and McCook. Thomas commanded the right wing with his own division from Buell's Army of the Ohio and four divisions from Grant's command. Grant was designated second-in-command of Halleck's forces but given little actual authority. The Michigan Engineers would move primarily with Buell's forces, their work dictated by the rough terrain and Halleck's desire to be protected by fortifications each step of the way.[42]

The area between Pittsburg Landing and Corinth was rolling ground with forest, occasional clearings, and impassable scrub brush on the low ground. Several flooded streams had to be bridged. The only approaches to Corinth were along narrow dirt roads. Supplies for the large army had to be transported by wagon from Pittsburg Landing. Things did not improve closer to Corinth. Swampy bottomlands bred mosquitoes, making malaria a serious threat, and there was a shortage of potable drinking water.[43]

On April 28 Companies B, D, E, and H of the Michigan Engineers marched from their camp, followed by the balance of the regiment on the next day. For several days the engineers built bridges over Lick Creek and corduroyed the approaches to the crossings near the Greer house and Atkin's Mill. They were assisted by work details drawn from the infantry regiments. These bridges and crossings were to be used by Buell's wing in the first few days of the advance.[44]

When Nelson's division started the advance of Buell's command on May 2, the engineers moved forward with it. After a march of several miles camp was made at Three Chimneys on the Old State Line Road. Innes's men repaired roads on the third while the balance of Buell's center caught up. Heavy rains confined the engineers to camp on May 4.[45]

This period set the pattern for the rest of the advance. Weather permitting, the regiment would set up a new camp and then work in detachments on various projects for several days, only occasionally returning at night. Regimental orders issued May 2 and May 4 laid down the rules for the march. The men would move forward with three days' cooked rations and their blankets rolled and carried over the shoulder. Knapsacks would be left in camp, guarded by the men too sick to work. The regimental train would be limited to four tents for the hospital, one tent for the regimental headquarters, ambulances, and two wagons. Captain Palmerlee remained in command of the camp in the absence of the regiment, making sure that the working parties were properly supplied with cooked rations for their haversacks.[46]

Over the next several days, detachments from the regiment repaired roads and built makeshift bridges for Buell's advancing divisions, including those over Chambers Creek and Seven Mile Creek at Nichol's Ford. Bad weather and confusing orders had the men tramping through flooded countryside and along circuitous routes.[47]

As the engineers worked in advance of the main Union forces, they were exposed to rebel attack with only a screen of pickets to their front. On May 9 Innes was ordered to take Companies B, C, H, and I and corduroy a swamp two miles in advance of McCook's division. A detachment of one hundred men drawn from the Seventy-seventh Pennsylvania and Twenty-ninth Indiana regiments was detailed for fatigue duty with the engineers. Union cavalry pickets to their front soon came under fire from mounted Confederates. Innes quickly formed his men into a line of battle with the infantry and two squadrons of the Third Ohio Cavalry on his left and advanced his men into the woods to their front. When the cavalry suddenly withdrew, however, Innes and the infantry were forced to follow them to the safety of the Union line. Union losses were light, with the Twenty-ninth Indiana's five casualties the heaviest. Only one engineer was wounded, a member of Company I struck in the wrist at long range.[48]

By May 10 the engineers had completed the roads up to the Union lines, but there was no time for rest. The Confederates had tried to destroy the advance brigades of Pope's army at Farmington the day before. Though they were repulsed, a nervous Halleck ordered Buell to close up his left with Pope's right and put his forces within supporting distance.[49]

For the next week, the engineers built the necessary roads in support of these new positions and to prepare for the army's inevitable advance. Much of their work went into constructing bridges across Seven Mile Creek and rebuilding the roads leading to Nichol's and Job's fords. On May 12 the regiment's camp was moved across the Mississippi state line and closer to their work near Seven Mile Creek. Even the light duty men were put to work improving the new camp and loading wagons with food for the working parties. The work details finished repairing the bridges on May 16, and many of the men were able to finally rest on the seventeenth. It was a welcome respite after almost three weeks of backbreaking labor.[50]

Albert Graves of Company B tried to convey to his wife the difficulties of the terrain they were working through: "We have been constantly on detail for opening roads for the army to advance . . . much of the way through swamps and low land full of brooks which had to be bridged . . . you will form some idea of the amount of labor to be performed to open these routes through a wilderness."[51]

While the engineers rested, Halleck's forces moved forward along the entire front, first on the seventeenth and then again the next day. These new positions were within two miles of the main Confederate line. On the eighteenth the Michigan Engineers' camp was moved forward three miles to put the men closer to their new assignments. The work of the engineers now changed to reflect the close proximity of Halleck's command and the entrenched Confederates. While scattered detachments continued to repair roads and bridges, most of the engineers were engaged in erecting fortifications to protect the open ground between Nelson and Crittenden and the area around Bridge Creek and the Serratt house. Others defenses were placed to provide cover for long-range siege guns that Halleck had brought with him.[52]

The engineers also built army hospitals in anticipation of a bloody battle. These were constructed of canvas stretched over a wooden frame, about forty-five by fifteen feet, and were built by the engineers in large numbers, as were the bunks to be occupied by the wounded.

By May 27 Lieutenant Colonel Hunton and six companies of the regiment were at work on the general hospital.[53]

On May 28 the Union line again advanced, Buell's forces taking possession of Serratt's Hill and Bridge Creek. The main Confederate defenses were now within thirteen hundred yards on Buell's front. The following day the engineer camp was moved a final time, this time to near Buell's headquarters. As preparations for a siege continued against light opposition, the men were beginning to worry that Beauregard's army would escape to fight another day. A bitter Sergeant Swaddle wrote his father on the twenty-seventh that he expected Halleck to let Beauregard escape, "thus entailing upon the nation, loss of valuable time, millions of expenses, [and] many lives. Our generals mean to have an awful good ready, and move as gingerly as though they expected to meet the combined forces of the world."[54]

Beauregard and his army evacuated Corinth two nights later, unmolested by the strongly entrenched army Halleck had led from Pittsburg Landing. Pvt. Richard Barker noted in his diary, "They have vacated Corinth and we are thus defeated." The Confederate divisions that escaped with Beauregard would fight again. One man expressed the frustration of many: "I wish they had stayed their ground, I think the war would have been brought to a close."[55]

On May 31 Halleck instructed Buell to have the Michigan Engineers begin repairing the Memphis and Charleston Railroad from Corinth to Decatur, Alabama. The goal was for Buell's army to move across northern Mississippi and Alabama toward Chattanooga, Tennessee, repairing the railroad as it advanced. Events elsewhere were drawing Buell's command, including the Michigan Engineers, eastward to a junction with Mitchel's division and Yates's two-company detachment.[56]

· 6 ·

With Mitchel to the Tennessee

Captain Yates and his two-company battalion remained attached to General Mitchel's Third Division, while Colonel Innes and the other eight companies were moving from Nashville to Corinth. General Buell gave Mitchel general directions on March 27, 1862, for the troops he was leaving behind in Middle Tennessee. Mitchel's division of eight thousand men would take an advanced position at Fayetteville, which could serve as a depot for offensive operations against Confederate forces in northern Alabama. Col. William W. Duffield's Twenty-third and Brig. Gen. James S. Negley's Seventh independent brigades at Murfreesboro and Franklin, respectively, would also be within supporting distance of Mitchel's division. Though only the men in his division would be under Mitchel's immediate command, Buell made it clear that the division commander would take command of all troops in the area if Nashville were threatened.[1]

By April 9 Mitchel's division was at Shelbyville, having arrived there from Nashville with no opposition. Not content with remaining on the defensive, Mitchel decided that after reaching the forward position at Fayetteville he would take the offensive and move his command on into northern Alabama. The advance of Mitchel's division left Shelbyville on April 9 and completed the short march to Fayetteville that same day. Along the route a shocked Mitchel learned from civilians that the rebels had driven Gen. U. S. Grant's army back on April 6 and were claiming a great victory. This was his first news that a battle was being fought at Pittsburg Landing. Mitchel sent couriers back to Shelbyville, where telegraphic communication with Nashville was possible, and the advance of the division went into camp at Fayetteville.[2]

After receiving a welcome dispatch from Buell with news of the second day's victory at Pittsburg Landing, and after the balance of his division came up, Mitchel ordered his men into column midday on the tenth. His objective was Huntsville, Alabama, a prosperous and strategically located city of thirty-six hundred people. Huntsville sat firmly astride the Memphis and Charleston Railroad, the longest east-west railroad still in Confederate hands. If the Memphis and Charleston was cut by Union forces, trains carrying men and supplies would be forced to use a complicated route through Mobile, relying on railroads of several different gauges and even water transportation.[3]

Mitchel's column camped about ten miles north of Huntsville after dark on April 10. Early the next morning an advance force was thrown forward against the town. The surprise was complete, and the few Confederate troops in Huntsville were powerless to stop Mitchel's men. They hastily evacuated their camps, leaving behind large numbers of rail engines and rolling stock, a large quantity of commissary stores, and a number of recently arrived wounded Confederate soldiers. The capture of Huntsville was an immediate blow to Confederate efforts to reinforce General Beauregard at Corinth following the heavy losses at Shiloh. Troops and supplies en route to Corinth had to be held back at Chattanooga or rerouted on a long detour through Mobile.[4]

Mitchel immediately sent out forces from Huntsville to secure all of the rail line north of the Tennessee River. Moving west by rail, Gen. John B. Turchin's Eighth Brigade captured Decatur and the important railroad bridge over the Tennessee. This secured Mitchel's western flank. Yates's Company A was part of this command and pushed forward to repair a small railroad bridge beyond Decatur. Gen. Joshua W. Sill's Ninth Brigade pushed east from Huntsville along the railroad on the twelfth. Mitchel and Sill's men rode the seventy miles to Stevenson by rail and then continued on by foot. They destroyed a bridge over Widow's Creek, just four miles from Bridgeport and the Tennessee crossing. This move secured Mitchel's eastern flank. Sill's men returned to Stevenson and then eventually Huntsville. In just two days, Mitchel had taken control of over one hundred miles of rail line and effectively cut the key Confederate east-west rail artery.[5]

While most of Yates's Company A was with Turchin, Captain Crittenton's Company K was sent back along the wagon road leading to Huntsville from Fayetteville to make repairs. Another detail of engineers was sent to repair the turnpike back from Elkton to Columbia. Until the railroads were repaired and operations along them restored, these roads were the supply lines upon which Mitchel's command relied for survival.[6]

For the balance of April Mitchel consolidated his forces, strengthened his hold on the Memphis and Charleston north of the Tennessee River, and prepared his command for a likely Confederate counterattack. Mitchel also organized an expedition eastward to Stevenson and Bridgeport. Stevenson was the site of a rail junction with the Nashville and Chattanooga, and a critical railroad bridge crossed the Tennessee River at Bridgeport. Possession of the two bridges at Bridgeport, totaling over fifteen hundred feet in length, would serve as a bridgehead for further moves against Chattanooga. Possession of Stevenson also provided greater protection for his left flank and opened up another possible route of railroad supply from Nashville depots.[7]

Moving east along the railroad on April 26, Sill's brigade was delayed at Mud Creek, eight miles west of Stevenson, where Confederates had recently burned a road bridge. Mitchel's artillery could not cross without a bridge, and the Michigan Engineers were ordered to construct a crossing. For use as bridging material, the engineers had bales of cotton that had been captured by the Twenty-fourth Illinois and boards from nearby buildings. The bales were cased in wood and spliced together in pairs, bound end to end, and laid perpendicular to the bank. Thirty-three pairs were thus laid down, ten feet apart, and then connected by boards for the roadway. For added strength, ropes were used to secure the entire serpentine arrangement to remnants of the destroyed bridge and trees along the bank. In just twenty-four hours, a passable pontoon bridge, measuring as much as 315 feet in length, was constructed over Mud Creek by the detail commanded by Sgt. Mark Mason of Company K. The cotton was later taken out of the water and sold by U.S. officials for more than twenty thousand dollars. Mitchel "was highly pleased and pronounced it the best piece of mechanism he had witnessed during the war."[8]

The expedition continued on another seven miles before crossing Crow Creek, using a captured scow this time. Once over Mud and Crow creeks, the Union troops moved the last mile to Stevenson and arrived early on the morning of the twenty-eighth. On the twenty-ninth, they continued on to Bridgeport. Retreating Confederates tried to destroy the critical spans across the Tennessee but were only partially successful. The longer east span, running from an island in the middle of the river to the east bank, was destroyed. The Confederates, however, failed to burn the west bridge from the island to the west bank, and Mitchel's men captured it.[9]

By the end of April Mitchel controlled the railroad on the north bank of the Tennessee from Bridgeport to opposite Decatur. The river provided a defensive shield of sorts to his front, while the major crossing points on his flanks were in Union hands. He confidently wrote Secretary of War Edwin Stanton that "this campaign is ended, and I now occupy Huntsville in perfect security, while all of Alabama north of the Tennessee River floats no flag but that of the Union."[10]

During April Mitchel gathered locomotives and large numbers of rolling stock. They would allow his command to reinforce and supply threatened points from Stevenson to Decatur. As long as the trains could run along the Memphis and Charleston, Mitchel would be able to consolidate his scattered brigades to confront any Confederate threat from Chattanooga or northern Alabama. In addition, repair of the Nashville and Decatur and the Nashville and Chattanooga railroads would provide a much more efficient supply link with Nashville than the road-bound wagon trains from Fayetteville.[11]

In the days following the capture of Huntsville, Mitchel appointed Captain Yates as military superintendent of the Memphis and Charleston Railroad with assistance from Lt. Henry F. Williams of Company K. Yates, operating from the Huntsville Depot, directed all of the trains running between Stevenson and Decatur, as Mitchel consolidated his position astride the railroad. The captured trains were usually crewed by Union soldiers with railroad experience detailed for the task. Among these were several from Yates's own battalion. They were part of an improvised policy occurring along Southern lines coming under Union control.[12]

Civilian John B. Anderson was still in charge of running railroads in Buell's department. In April he also was given the responsibility for repairing the lines south from Nashville, replacing newly promoted Brig. Gen. William S. Smith, who had marched with his brigade in Buell's column. At this point, however, Anderson's control over railroad activities beyond Nashville was limited to the pace with which his men could rebuild the road southward. Mitchel retained responsibility for operating and repairing the Memphis and Charleston Railroad and such portions of the Nashville and Chattanooga and Nashville and Decatur running northward from his position as he could put in working order. Mitchel continued to rely on Captain Yates and his battalion of Michigan Engineers.

Civilian J. Howard Larcombe, a prewar employee of the railroad and a Pennsylvania native, also assisted Yates. Larcombe and his wife operated the telegraph lines and assisted with the running of the line. The isolated positions held by portions of Mitchel's command necessitated the prompt dispatch of regiments and even whole brigades from one threatened point to another during April and May. Yates continued to direct this growing operation with his small staff, now settled into the Huntsville Depot. Pvt. William Clark penned a colorful description of the hustle and bustle surrounding the depot offices of Yates and Capt. Joseph J. Slocum, Mitchel's quartermaster: "This is a business . . . lively enough. The constant ingress and departure from these rooms of officers and others, the comings and goings of cars, and the marching of guards and soldiers as they enter or leave the trains, greatly differs from the comparative monotony of camp life."[13]

One of Yates's most difficult tasks was keeping the captured railroad engines and rolling stock in operation. Though at least 20 locomotives were taken by Mitchel at Huntsville and Stevenson, many were not working, and frequent use and a shortage of parts quickly reduced the available stock even further. Shortly after the capture of Huntsville, Yates reported to Mitchel that there were 9 working engines and 128 cars. Another 7 engines and 80 cars would be ready in eight or ten days. By June 17 Yates was reporting that there were only 10 working engines with the combined pulling capacity of 54 loaded cars. After further repair, another 2 engines would be available with the combined locomotive strength to pull only 15 loaded cars. At the same time, it was not possible to reinforce Yates's dwindling inventory until the railroad connection with Nashville was repaired.[14]

Yates's efforts also faced increasing dangers from the enemy, and attacks soon followed. The first one to affect the Michigan men was in conjunction with an attack by Col. John S. Scott and his Louisiana troopers on the position of the Eighteenth Ohio at Athens on May 1. Scott's troopers were accompanied by a section of artillery. The men of the Eighteenth Ohio were considered good soldiers, but without artillery of their own it would be a one-sided fight. As their commander, Col. Timothy R. Stanley, prepared to pull his men out of the city, Mitchel arrived at Athens on a commandeered small train and took over command. He agreed with Stanley that it was not possible to resist without artillery, and he organized a hasty retreat by rail back to division headquarters at Huntsville. Mitchel's train reached the rail junction at Decatur eleven miles to the south and then steamed east along the Memphis and Charleston. Behind his train followed a second one, with a supply train bringing up the rear. The crew of this final train included at least three detached Michigan Engineers: engineer William Harvey and firemen Thomas Jenkinson and James Bates. Mitchel reached Huntsville without incident. The second train, however, found the bridge over Limestone Creek on fire as it approached. Driving full speed into the flames, the engineer was able to get the train across the flaming span and on toward Huntsville. Harvey, following closely behind, tried to make the same desperate dash, but the weakened bridge timbers collapsed. The locomotive, tender, and several cars fell through them to the creek below, taking Harvey, Jenkinson, and Bates with them. Some of the wreckage quickly caught fire, threatening the trapped survivors on the train. The fire was helped along by some of the attackers.[15]

Charging to their rescue were Captain Crittenton and seventy comrades from Company K camped at nearby Mooresville. Seeing the smoke along the railroad, Crittenton rushed his command to the scene and fired upon the plunderers, driving them off, but it was too late for Jenkinson. He had been trapped in the ruins of the engine, "suffocated by the flames and smoke, while appealing piteously to be got out or shot dead at once." Despite Jenkinson's agony, the bushwhackers refused his pleas for help and threatened blacks who offered to try to extricate him. His body was burned along with the engine, cars, and bridge. Harvey was "dug out of the wreck, crushed and mangled," by Crittenton's men, barely alive. He had been struck by gunshot in the arms and thigh, suffered serious internal injuries from the crash, and been burned by the fire. Bates also survived but suffered a broken leg as the cars were crunched together. A fourth, unnamed member of Company A escaped with just minor injuries. A handful of Union soldiers hitching a ride were able to jump from the train and escape the attackers.[16]

It had been a close call for other members of the regiment. They were part of a telegraph repair party using a small train to carry replacement poles along the railroad. Twice they crossed the bridge over Limestone Creek without incident that same day before Mitchel commandeered their train for the relief of Athens. Back across the bridge they had gone again, probably watched by hidden Confederate raiders.[17]

Most of the early attacks on Mitchel's men were the work of parties of local civilians or small bands of partisans. Beginning with Scott's attack on Athens, however, Confederate cavalry and artillery harassed Union positions along the Memphis and Charleston and supply trains running from Nashville to Stevenson and Decatur. Col. John Hunt Morgan, striking north from Corinth against the Nashville and Decatur, captured Pulaski, Tennessee, on May 2. The 286 prisoners he took included Lt. Edward M. Mitchel, the general's son. Though Morgan was in turn surprised at Lebanon and driven away on May 4, it was clear that Mitchel's hold on northern Alabama was becoming precarious.[18]

By May 5, just one week after asserting "perfect security," Mitchel was reporting to Stanton that "armed citizens fire into the trains, cut the telegraph wires, attack the guards of bridges, [and] cut off and destroy my couriers, while guerrilla bands of cavalry attack whenever there is the slightest chance of success."[19]

The attacks continued, drawing increasingly harsh responses. Col. John Beatty and his Third Ohio were fired upon as they rode a train from Bellefonte to Huntsville. Several of the Ohio volunteers were wounded. Beatty disembarked his command and burned the nearby village of Paint Rock to the ground in retaliation. Beatty believed his action was consistent with Mitchel's policy and suffered no penalty.[20]

Apparently Yates took a similar approach when dealing with another attempted ambush. An Ohio soldier later recounted how "Gates [*sic*] and his Michigan Engineers and Mechanics," after being fired upon while riding on a train, located and burned the house of the man responsible: "While he was talking with the women, a sergeant went upstairs and piling window curtains and other combustibles on a bed, set them on fire, and came down, closing the door. Soon the smell of fire alarmed the women, but the Captain strove hard to quiet their fears, until it could no longer be concealed, when he quietly remarked, 'I guess the house is on fire,' and walked away."[21]

The strongest retaliation, however, was inflicted by Turchin's brigade, which returned to Athens on May 2. For two hours the men sacked the town in retribution for the attack on Stanley's Eighteenth Ohio and the death of Jenkinson at Limestone Bridge. The men did at least fifty-four thousand dollars' damage to the prosperous community, according to claims filed by the citizens. A subsequent investigation criticized Turchin and his regimental commanders, though Turchin was promoted and escaped any lasting punishment for his actions. Though critical of Turchin's excesses, Mitchel tried to explain the brigade's actions to Stanton: "Not that I had any special sympathy with the citizens, for I believed they had led the enemy to the attack upon Athens, and when my troops were driven from town they were cursed, hooted, and spit upon. *Two* [sic] *of their comrades on the day before were burned alive*" (emphasis added).[22]

On May 9 Buell placed Mitchel in charge of all Union troops on the railroads leading from Nashville to Decatur and Stevenson, as well as his division along the Memphis and Charleston. The largest forces added to Mitchel's command were the brigades of Negley and Duffield. He immediately ordered the latter to move against rebel concentrations along the Tennessee River, but attacks on U.S. forces and supply lines continued.[23]

On May 17 a company of Confederates crossed Elk River and attacked a Union railroad guard near Athens. Fortunately, some of the Michigan Engineers were nearby and rushed to their rescue. Joining with the retreating Union soldiers, the combined command struck back at the Confederates and "drove the rebels like sheep into the Elk River, where many of them were drowned."[24]

Mitchel was also finding it harder to keep his lines of communications open. Even though J. Newton Crittenton, son of Captain Crittenton and an experienced telegraph operator from Marshall, had greatly improved the telegraphic ability of Mitchel's command after taking charge of it, the working parties remained exposed to attack, and wires were frequently cut. These telegraph working parties contained both civilian employees and detailed soldiers from Mitchel's command, including several members of the Michigan Engineers.[25]

Under Crittenton's direction, the eighty-some miles of telegraph line between Stevenson and Decatur were quickly repaired, but keeping them in operation was more difficult. In addition, the telegraph lines leading back to Nashville were beset with technical problems and were frequently the target of John Morgan's Confederate cavalry. It was not until May 20 that Mitchel could communicate with Nashville by reliable telegraph via Decatur. In the meantime, Mitchel was forced to send his couriers with a strong mounted escort, and telegraph working parties had to be heavily guarded.[26]

When not heavily guarded, they were easy prey for marauding Confederates and sympathizers. A detail of ten men, drawn equally from the two companies, was gobbled up in May while repairing the telegraph line between Stevenson and Bridgeport. Taken south by their captors, they were held in miserable conditions at Macon, Georgia, and Richmond before being paroled in November. Only four of the ten ever returned to the regiment, the rest dead or discharged for disabilities.[27]

An increasingly desperate Mitchel tried various tactics to keep the Confederate cavalry south of the Tennessee. Yates was ordered to build a gunboat to patrol the river and secured a horse ferry measuring fifty-two by twelve feet that had been captured near Whitesburg. He directed the construction of barricades along its sides, which were then filled with cotton bales since the weight of protective iron would have sunk it. A steam sawmill engine from the nearby Bibb plantation at Indian Creek provided the motive power, coupled with an unreliable reversing gear cast in Huntsville. The improvised gunboat, grandly christened the *Tennessee*, was armed with a Parrott artillery piece borrowed from Loomis's Michigan battery and crewed by infantrymen from Capt. William H. Steele's company of the Tenth Wisconsin. Plagued by mechanical problems, the boat made only one trip up the Tennessee and was fired upon from the banks. It proved so unwieldy that it was later stripped of armaments and used as a ferry at Decatur. Despite its problems, the gunboat worried Maj. Gen. Edmund Kirby Smith enough to order Danville Leadbetter to send a small party to destroy it, though there is no evidence any attempt was ever made.[28]

By early June Mitchel's forces were on the defensive all along the Tennessee River and on the railroads leading back to Nashville. On the ninth he reported to General Halleck, "My force is totally insufficient to do anything more than to guard the extensive region over which they are spread from hostile citizens and small bands of the enemy. I wait your orders with anxiety."[29]

Work and Warfare
along the Tennessee

Following the evacuation of Corinth, General Pope's Army of the Mississippi was reinforced with two of General Buell's divisions and sent in pursuit of the Confederate forces that were retreating southward to Tupelo. On May 31 General Halleck instructed Buell to have the Michigan Engineers begin repairing the railroad line from Corinth to Decatur, and the next day Brig. Gen. Thomas J. Wood's Sixth Division was assigned to help. Halleck then turned his attention to deciding what to do next with his army. He had several options. His army could move west against Vicksburg and complete the division of the Confederacy along the Mississippi River, or he could move south against the main Confederate army in the West that had retreated from Corinth to Tupelo. Halleck could also move part of his army east toward Chattanooga, an option he finally selected.[1]

The move east would have two main objectives. Through Chattanooga ran railroads northeast into East Tennessee and Virginia and also south to Atlanta and the region bounded by the Atlantic and Gulf of Mexico. Possession of Chattanooga and control of the surrounding region was critical for Confederate success in the West. The region around Chattanooga was also the obvious route for Union armies moving south into Georgia. Likewise, Chattanooga could serve as a Union base to fulfill President Lincoln's long-cherished desire to free unionist East Tennessee from the hard yoke of Confederate control.[2]

Halleck hinted to Buell as early as June 2 that his entire Army of the Ohio might be moving eastward along the Memphis and Charleston toward East Tennessee. For the next several days, Halleck and Buell exchanged messages about the opening of communications with General Mitchel's forces at Decatur, though Buell remained with the pursuing forces south of Corinth. By June 9 Halleck concluded that the pursuit was pointless and recalled Buell to Corinth for further discussions. Buell was also instructed to put the divisions of "Bull" Nelson,

Thomas Crittenden, and Alexander McCook in motion toward Decatur, joining Wood. On June 11 Halleck reemphasized to Buell that his destination was to be Chattanooga, leaving the defense of Middle Tennessee and Nashville to Mitchel.[3]

The most direct route from Corinth to Chattanooga was through the Tennessee River valley of northern Alabama, along the route of the Memphis and Charleston Railroad. From Corinth the rail line ran south of the river until Decatur, where it crossed over and followed the river on its north bank until Bridgeport, just twenty-eight miles west of Chattanooga. In early June much of this route, some eighty miles between Decatur and Bridgeport, was already in operation by Mitchel's troops. Any movement along the Memphis and Charleston, however, would require repair of the key bridge at Decatur, destroyed by Mitchel to protect his right flank. Buell's men would also have to rebuild the two spans over the Tennessee River at Bridgeport, whose destruction was started by Confederates and completed by Mitchel. In addition, retreating Confederates and raiding federals burned many of the smaller bridges along the Memphis and Charleston.

Buell had more than fifty thousand men available to repair the railroad, defend Tennessee, and capture Chattanooga. Mitchel and almost ten thousand men were already in northern Alabama, with about fifteen thousand in Middle Tennessee guarding supply lines or near Cumberland Gap. Buell was near Corinth with almost thirty thousand men in four divisions. Directly opposing his campaign against Chattanooga were a few thousand poorly armed Confederates. Chattanooga was the left flank of Maj. Gen. Edmund Kirby Smith's Confederate Department of East Tennessee, spread from Chattanooga to Cumberland Gap. Even after evacuating Cumberland Gap and concentrating the troops of his department at Chattanooga in mid-June, Kirby Smith could muster only about twelve thousand men. In addition, a few regiments of mounted troops were south of the Tennessee River in northern Alabama.[4]

That supply net was Buell's weak point. The route back to Louisville was long and vulnerable to attack by Confederates. From Louisville, the Louisville and Nashville Railroad wound through tunnels and across bridges built over steep ravines. Upon reaching Nashville the supplies could be sent by rail to either Decatur, along the Nashville and Decatur, or to Stevenson via the Nashville and Chattanooga line. In early June, however, neither line was operational south from Nashville because retreating Confederates had destroyed the bridges. Supplies for Mitchel's men had to be brought by wagon to Athens, Huntsville, or another point before they could be distributed. As

Buell's men advanced to Decatur they would have to carry their own supplies from Corinth or be supplied by shallow draft boats that could navigate the rapidly dropping Tennessee River only as far as Eastport. Once Buell's men reached Decatur they would be dependent on the railroads and whatever they could forage from a countryside already picked clean by Mitchel's men during a two-month occupation.[5]

The summer low water levels of the Tennessee River prohibited large-scale water transport beyond Pittsburg Landing. Further downriver, a series of shoals in northern Alabama made the river inaccessible to even small craft. In addition, any waterborne supply route would require constant patrolling by gunboat. To make matters worse, the Cumberland River water level was also dropping and could not be counted on for use by large steamers supplying Nashville. Throughout the campaign, Buell and his men would have to rely on the ability of Union troops to repair and protect the long, exposed rail route from Louisville through Nashville and on to northern Alabama.[6]

The first phase of Buell's advance required the occupation and repair of the Memphis and Charleston from Corinth to Decatur. If the rail line was repaired, engines and cars could be forwarded from those left behind at Corinth by retreating Confederates and some regular communication and minimal supply would be possible between Corinth and Mitchel's division. After the fall of Corinth, Buell turned again to Gen. William Sooy Smith to direct the repair eastward into Alabama. Smith was given direct control of Innes and his eight companies and was authorized to call upon the commanders of Buell's infantry divisions for work details to supplement them.[7]

First, however, Buell had to incorporate his plans into Halleck's preference for a centralized engineer force in the Department of the Mississippi. On June 4 Halleck ordered the formation of an engineer brigade consisting of Josiah Bissell's Engineer Regiment of the West, William P. Innes's Michigan Engineers, and an unnamed regiment from Gen. Stephen A. Hurlbut's division. Halleck selected Brig. Gen. James B. McPherson to command the brigade. McPherson was a member of the Corps of Engineers, a former professor of engineering at West Point, and had recently been chief engineer on General Grant's staff. By the same order Halleck directed that McPherson be appointed "general superintendent of military railroads" in the department, thus centralizing responsibility for their repair and operation. The effect of this order on the Michigan Engineers was to remove Innes's eight companies from Buell's direct control for the next month, though they would continue to labor under Smith's direction and work with infantry detailed from Buell's divisions.[8]

On June 1 and 2 the Michigan Engineers marched to Burnsville. Along the way they repaired bridges over Bridge Creek and at Knowles Mill. Innes's men were the first Union troops to reach Burnsville and were determined to make a strong and positive impression. One of the men in Major Hopkins's advance force wrote home, "We showed off to great advantage being the first Union troops that had passed through. . . . [We] marched into the place in great style."[9]

On the third the regiment continued its movement eastward for eight miles, reaching Bear Creek. The next morning, many of the men started to set up the new camp, while others explored their new surroundings. Suddenly, shots rang out; the long roll was beaten, and the men hastily formed into position. Pvts. Henry Bellamy and Philip Coon of Company E had been shot while fishing along the bank of Bear Creek, the former fatally. In response, Innes and some of his men crossed the creek and scoured the woods for the bushwhackers to no avail. Fearing a general attack, Company D was posted along the creek north of the bridge, with Company F in a similar position south of it. The remainder of the regiment was posted in reserve on the railroad. The Michigan Engineers remained on guard until the afternoon of the fifth, when Wood's division arrived. The attackers were never apprehended, though a number of shots were fired by nervous sentries at what they thought were enemy soldiers. For the companies with Innes, this was their introduction to the guerrilla war that Yates's two companies had been fighting for weeks.[10]

Wood's division remained as guard while the Michigan Engineers started work on the bridge. Two 110-foot spans and almost 500 feet of trestlework had been chopped and burned by a raiding party from Brig. Gen. William T. Sherman's men on April 13 and required rebuilding. Though the Michigan Engineers had repaired several bridges near Nashville in the spring, the work at Bear Creek marked the beginning of an intensive bridge-building effort by Innes and his men, reflective of a greater understanding of the importance of the railroad as a means of supply.[11]

By 1860 engineers had developed several styles of railroad truss bridges in which a series of triangles, "the natural inelasticity of which give it rigidity and strength," were joined together in a horizontal frame that rested on piers of masonry. Such a construction was strong and lasting and, because it required fewer piers for support, less subject to washing out in floods or freshets. First constructed in the 1820s of wood, truss bridges were refined to meet the needs of heavier engines and rolling stock. Many of the newest truss railroad bridges also incorporated iron arcs as another means of distributing the weight. By the war's outbreak, substantial iron truss railroad bridges were being built over major crossings. The Louisville and Nashville Fink truss bridge over the Green River near Munfordville, Kentucky, was representative of the capital and energy put into prewar railroad bridges at critical crossings.[12]

Once these existing prewar bridges were destroyed, however, the opposing commanders were likely to initially sacrifice the permanence of iron and wood truss for the convenience of a trestle style of wooden bridge, which could be built quickly from readily available materials. Civilian railroad employees following in the army's wake could construct a more permanent crossing as time and materials were available. Writing of his pioneer work developing railroad bridges for the U.S. military in Virginia, Herman Haupt noted that "bridges on military railroads are not required to fulfill precisely the conditions as those which are . . . constructed for general railroad business. . . . Its parts should be few and simple." In particular, when the crossing was not threatened by freshets, the elevation not too high, and materials readily on hand, "an ordinary trestle bridge is preferable to any other; one of its advantages being, that material is usually procurable in the vicinity of the proposed structure, and its transportation by rail avoided." They did not convey the sweeping majesty of the new iron truss bridges, but they sufficed for the immediate need. Upon personal inspection of Haupt's 1862 trestle bridge over Potomac Creek, President Lincoln commented, "I have seen the most remarkable structure," noting in exaggeration and wonder that there was "nothing in it but bean-poles and cornstalks." It worked admirably for its intended purpose.[13]

Trestle bridges consisted simply of a "deck held up by a series of relatively closely spaced frame supports called 'trestles,' each of which may be composed of one or more 'bents.'" The bents were driven into the riverbed or rested on platforms. The legs measured five or six inches square and were connected, in varying numbers, to a perpendicular cap. The caps were placed perpendicular to the general direction of the bridge, much as railroad ties are to a railroad line, providing a bridge twelve to sixteen feet in width. For added stability, transoms and braces supported the legs horizontally. Each arrangement of cap, legs, and supporting timbers was called a bent, or sometimes a trestle.[14]

The bents were usually cut from nearby standing timber, preferably pine, spruce, or ash because they were light and stiff. Framed bents rested upon the remains of masonry piers or wooden cribs filled with ballast and were secured on their lower end with horizontal timbers called sills. They were often first framed on a nearby piece of level ground and then hoisted into position, one complete trestle at a time.

Pile bents were secured directly to the riverbank by driving or anchoring the vertical legs. The men often worked from boats or standing in chest-high water for hours at a time during the critical setting of each trestle. Soft or uneven riverbeds required additional labor to ensure that the trestles were firmly planted and that the caps remained level. Successive trestles, either pile or framed, were placed twelve to fifteen feet apart until the creek or ravine was spanned from bank to bank. Perpendicular, or transverse, planking connected the caps and served as bridge flooring or the bed for railroad iron. Side rails were sometimes added if the bridge was to be used for crossing troops, artillery, or wagons. Bridges exceeding twenty-five or thirty feet in height generally included two or more tiers of trestles.[15]

The exact details of each bridge varied with local circumstances. For example, the timbers could be left round if time or lack of sawmills so dictated. The trestles could be formed from two to six legs in several different configurations, again depending on need and urgency. It was even possible to construct a trestle bridge, for at least temporary use, without the benefit of any tools except axes and augers in the hands of inexperienced detailed infantry. The few extant pictures of trestle bridges constructed by the Michigan Engineers show a combination of design structures. In practice, the men probably adapted each bridge to fit the availability of nearby timber and time allowed for its construction or repair.[16]

For ten days beginning on June 6, 1862, details from the Michigan Engineers and working parties from Wood's infantry labored on the Bear Creek crossing. The creek was 16 feet deep at the crossing, and the 316-foot-long bridge was constructed at a height of 44 feet above the water because of the steep banks. The swampy bottomland east of the creek required more than 300 feet of additional trestle. The timber for these structures was cut in the area and sawed by Union soldiers who had repaired and were running the nearby Castleberry and Brothers Mill. Regimental supply wagon trains made the trip to Eastport on the Tennessee River, where shallow draft steamers were tied up. Other details supplemented the rations by foraging in the area.[17]

As the work in the Bear Creek area neared completion, Buell ordered Smith to advance eastward along the railroad and distribute the detachments of the Michigan Engineers. Wood received orders from Buell to cooperate with Smith and the engineer working parties. Innes and companies C, E, and H left Bear Creek on June 13, eventually reaching Town Creek, fifteen miles east of Tuscumbia, on the fifteenth. They camped near the creek and prepared to rebuild a large bridge that had been destroyed by retreating Confederates.[18]

By June 16 work on Bear Creek and nearby bridges was completed, and the five remaining companies left by rail, arriving near Tuscumbia two days later. Small groups of stragglers arrived in camp throughout the following day, some having had been forced to push rail cars up steep grades and then walk the final few miles. These five companies were to rebuild another large bridge over Spring Creek, just east of Tuscumbia.[19]

For the balance of June the Michigan Engineers repaired the railroad bridges necessary to put the line in working order. After Companies C, E, and H finished at Town Creek on June 25, they were sent forward eight miles to work on two small bridges over the Big Nance Creek at Courtland. The other five companies continued to work on the Spring Creek Bridge, not finishing until June 27. A detachment also rebuilt the span over Mallet's Creek between Courtland and Decatur. During this time the divisions of Wood, McCook, and Crittenden leapfrogged each other along the line of the railroad, providing infantry details for bridge repair and guarding the working parties.[20]

Meanwhile, Companies A and K were at work on railroad bridges further east near Stevenson. Captain Crittenton commanded the small battalion, since Yates was still running the Memphis and Charleston Railroad. Crittenton's battalion remained attached to Mitchel's command during June. At the beginning of June, details from companies A and K started rebuilding the important Nashville and Decatur Bridge over the Elk River, about three miles north of the Alabama state line. The bridge spanned 625 feet in length and was 40 feet high. While Anderson's civilians were repairing the railroad south from Nashville to the burned bridge, Mitchel was trying to open the line further south, between the Elk River crossing and the junction with the Memphis and Charleston near Decatur.[21]

On June 12, however, Buell ordered Mitchel to move his railroad repair parties from the Nashville and Decatur road to the Nashville and Chattanooga road running to Stevenson. The latter road was considered to be "the most important because it can be the soonest put in order." Once repaired to Stevenson, this road could supply Huntsville via the Memphis and Charleston that Yates was operating under Mitchel's orders. Crittenton's two companies were pulled off their work on the Nashville and Decatur at Elk River immediately and ordered to repair several smaller bridges near Stevenson. Work began on June 14 on a new three-hundred-foot bridge over Mud Creek eight miles west of Stevenson and continued until its completion on the twentieth. Then Crittenton's working parties moved to the bridge over Crow Creek west of Stevenson, which was completed within days. On the twenty-ninth Crittenton received orders from Mitchel to repair another destroyed bridge over Crow Creek, this one north of Stevenson. That labor completed, Crittenton moved his men to repair the bridge over Widow's Creek, five miles west of Bridgeport.[22]

During this time, several members of the Michigan Engineers were detailed to run the trains over the road as it was made operational. Among them were Sgt. Albert Wells and Pvt. William Walker of Company B, who served as engineers on trains running between Corinth and Decatur. The work was dangerous and demanding. In June Wells was badly injured in the side when the train he was running jumped the sabotaged tracks near Cherokee Station, Alabama. The engine was badly damaged. The hard service wore down both men's health, and Innes spent months trying to get them the extra pay they were entitled to for their service.[23]

In addition to repairing bridges and running trains, the men were again embroiled in controversy over pay. On June 1 Buell appointed Brig. Gen. William S. Smith to investigate charges of fraud and cruelty that had been leveled against Innes. The regiment apparently found out about Smith's appointment a week later, most likely when he started to interview the men.[24]

This round of investigation had been prompted by complaints from Pvt. Franklin Estabrook of Company I, who had been at the center of the controversy surrounding the Michigan Engineers for months. In March he was arrested by Innes and turned over to the Nashville provost guard for his agitation over the pay question. He was still there in June and would not be returned to the regiment for several months, but his involvement had a far-reaching influence. Estabrook's brother Joseph, a prominent educator from Ypsilanti, Michigan, complained to his powerful friend U.S. senator Jacob Howard, who forwarded it to the secretary of war. While at the War Department, Estabrook's missive (with endorsement by Howard) was apparently assigned to Catharinus P. Buckingham for quick resolution.[25]

Buckingham was a West Point graduate, a prominent civil engineer, and adjutant general of Ohio before his assignment as roving trouble-shooter for the War Department. On May 17 he directed Halleck to muster Innes out of the service, citing "reliable representations" that Innes had "practiced great fraud in the organization of his regiment as well as cruelty to his men since they have been in the service." Halleck issued the order on May 26 but suspended it two days later upon receipt of a telegram from Adjutant General Thomas. Innes subsequently claimed that Buell had stopped the attempt to dismiss him, declaring, "I cannot muster out Colonel Innes for he is at present rendering me efficient service and knowing as I do a great part of the accusation is unfounded." Apparently under some pressure on the matter, Buell handed the matter off to Smith for investigation.[26]

Smith's investigation and report, sent to Buell on June 17, cleared Innes of the two charges and was sympathetic to the men's demands for recognition as engineers. Smith documented that the earliest recruits had enlisted with the expectation of receiving fifty cents per day extra when engaged in engineering work and stated that Innes had legitimate reasons to believe this was the case based on Wilson's regiment and communications from the War Department. Smith pointed out the problem that only engineer troops could receive the higher seventeen dollars and that only infantry was eligible for the per-day additional pay while engaged in mechanical work. Since there was no law providing for the raising of volunteer engineer units, the men could not receive engineer pay. They had to accept the infantry pay and hope that the army would retroactively recognize the extra compensation owed them.[27]

Smith dismissed the cruelty charges against Innes. He pointed out that Innes had merely handed over men who refused to follow the orders of their company officers while at Nashville. The provost marshal in Nashville had actually confined the men. While Smith admitted that Innes had made "some harsh, and, it would appear very injudicious, remarks" to his men, he reported that the officers and men he had interviewed all believed that the cruelty charge was false.[28]

During the investigation Smith determined that a wrong had been done to the regiment, not by Innes, but by the lack of proper recognition of their services and special type of organization. His report ended with the following observation: "I cannot conclude this report without calling immediate and special attention to the unfortunate condition of the regiment. . . . It reflects great credit on the men of this useful regiment, who have continued faithful and obedient, that they have been willing to wait so patiently for the settlement of the questions in dispute, and in the meantime labor without pay."[29]

Despite the generally favorable review from Smith, Innes was concerned about his reputation back home and standing with Governor Blair. On June 29 he sent the governor a copy of the report, along with a cover letter with a clear request for support: "Now, Sir, justice to me and honor to you and the state of which you are the commander-in-chief would seem to suggest that it be set right on the matter and I leave it in your hand to do."[30]

On that same date, Innes sent a stinging letter for publication to the Democratic *Detroit Free Press* in which he roundly denounced

Republican Senator Howard and others for their actions. Innes suggested that if Howard had expended half as much effort in passing legislation correcting the problem as he had in organizing an effort to remove Innes, the problem would have already been resolved in the regiment's favor. Employing strong phrases such as "abuse has been heaped upon my head by low vile cowardly rascals" and "low lived mean hits made by sneaking cowards at home," Innes declared that his time and energy must be saved for service in the field and expressed his confidence that an "enlightened public [would do] justice." Just to make sure, he attached a copy of Smith's report to his letter. He also sent a copy of the report to prominent attorney Lucius Patterson of Grand Rapids and suggested that his friends there might use the report to influence the Grand Rapids papers.[31]

This controversy, like many during the war, was rife with partisan politics. Much of the partisan bickering occurred in the hometown newspapers, virtually all of which were financially backed by prominent party leaders and served as party organs. Letters written home excited the efforts of partisan editors, and their columns were in turn widely circulated in camp. Captain Sligh, a Democrat like Innes, placed much of the blame for the controversy in camp squarely on the Republican shoulders of the *Grand Rapids Eagle.* Sligh blamed the *Eagle* for "the great many camp croakers . . . that have the most to say about the pay, do the least work and are sick one half of the time . . . and they find enough at home to echo their croakings without knowing the merits of the case."[32]

The Democratic *Grand Rapids Weekly Enquirer,* a staunch opponent of the *Eagle* and supporter of Innes and Sligh in general, remained confident that Smith's investigation would result in the full payment of the men but had harsh words for the critics: "Let the cowardly miscreants who traduce and vilify the brave men who are fighting our battles be remembered."[33]

Some Republicans, in turn, accused Innes of himself introducing partisan elements into the debate over the regiment's status. The *Allegan Journal* claimed that Innes, when faced with a petition from men refusing to work without engineer pay, taunted them by declaring that "having voted for Lincoln," they should "be willing to work for him for nothing."[34]

Republican Governor Blair's role in the investigation of Innes is uncertain. Republican state senator Solomon S. Withey wrote Adjutant General Robertson on July 2, inquiring if it were true that Innes had been dismissed by the War Department only to be spared through Blair's efforts on his behalf. Withey concluded, "I hope this is not so."

The Republican *Allegan Journal* reported in detail on the enlisted men's complaint of unfair treatment by Innes and assured its partisan readers that "the Governor of the state endorsed the [men's] statements in the main." Perhaps Blair simply thought that Innes was doing a good job under the circumstances. Or maybe Blair was influenced by the fact that 1862 was an election year and Republican fortunes, including his own reelection, were uncertain. Whatever the reason, Innes probably could not have remained in his position without Blair's support.[35]

During all of this very public debate, there was still a lot of confusion over the regiment's proper pay, even among senior commanders. On June 25 Mitchel wrote Buell for permission to pay the Michigan Engineers in his command the extra allowance allotted to men engaged on engineering detail. He considered the money to be due them, "richly earned by hard labor." Within days he notified Captain Crittenton, commanding Companies A and K at Huntsville, that he had received authorization to pay the men the extra per diem, which he would do "immediately with the greatest satisfaction." Within days, however, Mitchel was promoted elsewhere, and there is no evidence that the men in these two companies actually received the extra pay.[36]

Meanwhile, Buell continued efforts to have the Michigan Engineers reassigned to his command from McPherson's brigade. In particular, Buell noted the near completion of repairs on the railroad to Decatur and questioned any continued need for the existing arrangement. On July 1 Halleck ordered that the Michigan Engineers be returned to Buell. Innes was already consolidating Companies B–I of his regiment at Huntsville. He also regained operational command of Companies A and K, though they did not reach Huntsville until finishing work on Widow's Creek Bridge two weeks later.[37]

For most of July Innes and his Michigan Engineers continued to repair and rebuild railroad bridges, primarily the two roads leading back to Nashville. Along the Nashville and Decatur the most important repair projects were the rebuilding of three bridges over meandering Richland Creek and completing reconstruction of a major bridge further south over Elk River. In addition, on the Nashville and Chattanooga, roving Confederates had destroyed several bridges and obstructed the long tunnel near Cowan. Companies of the Michigan Engineers were shifted among these three sites as needed, and infantry regiments often provided fatigue parties to help.[38]

Work on bridges near Reynold's Station and Richland Creek began by July 6. Richland Creek No. 1 was 375 feet long, 28 feet high, and had to be built in about six feet of water. The crossing at nearby Richland Creek No. 2 was 300 feet long and 30 feet high. Another smaller bridge near Reynold's Station, probably also over Richland Creek, was 150 feet long and 30 feet high. In addition, the engineers rebuilt over 1,000 feet of trestles, some over 60 feet high. They also cleared out portions of the quarter-mile tunnel north of Elk River. When heavy rains washed out part of the bridge over the Duck River at Columbia, details of Michigan Engineers were sent to repair it.[39]

The largest and heaviest bridge rebuilding assigned to the engineers in 1862 was that over the Elk River, the southernmost point in the twenty-three-mile-long rupture along the Nashville and Decatur. In late June Buell's commissary staff conferred with Innes, who estimated that it would take a month to repair the bridge. Work started on July 7 and continued until August 3. The men rebuilt a bridge seven hundred feet long, fifty-eight feet high, and located in water up to twenty feet deep. When the Confederates destroyed the bridge they had left only the three stone piers standing in the river and the stone abutments along the banks. Seven bents had to be constructed and raised for each of these four intervals. Hunton personally supervised the work.[40]

Companies B, F, and I left Huntsville on July 6, probably with Colonel Innes. They were taken by rail to Cowan Station on the Nashville and Chattanooga, about twenty-five miles north of Stevenson. By July 12 the 120-foot-long bridge had been repaired, the nearby railroad tunnel had been cleared out, and the men were waiting for transportation back to Stevenson. Once transportation arrived, they were shifted over to help the other engineer companies working on the Nashville and Decatur road. Their train did not arrive until the fifteenth.[41]

The regimental headquarters remained at Huntsville, and the ailing Captain Fox directed the activities of the men there in support of the regiment. Yates was also there, still directing operations of the captured rail lines until they passed into John B. Anderson's civilian operation in mid-August. Yates was also part of the ongoing debate within the Union leadership over which route back to Nashville should be the focal point of efforts.[42]

Huntsville was the scene of one of the regiment's great mysteries. During the night of June 30–July 1, a strongbox containing at least twenty thousand dollars was stolen from Major Hopkins's tent. The paymaster had entrusted the strongbox, or safe, to Hopkins. An extensive search turned up the strongbox in three feet of mud and water at a nearby spring, but the money was gone. Pvt. Edmund N. Hayden was eventually convicted of stealing the box and other things while on guard duty and was sentenced to thirty days. On his deathbed in March 1864,

Hayden admitted his role but would not finger his accomplice who remained unknown. Neither, apparently, was the money ever found.[43]

By July 12 Buell's working parties had put the Nashville and Chattanooga into running order to Stevenson, and the first train loaded with provisions was scheduled to run in the morning. Before the train even left the Nashville Depot, however, Brig. Gen. Nathan Bedford Forrest and his Confederate cavalry struck the Union forces at Murfreesboro. After a spirited fight the federals surrendered, and Forrest and his men destroyed the nearby railroad bridges. A few days later Forrest again struck exposed Nashville and Chattanooga bridges, this time over Mill Creek near Nashville. Buell's supply line remained fractured. On July 14 his men were put on half rations.[44]

Roving bands of Confederates, both regular and irregular, continued to attack all along Buell's line of supply and communication, with many of the Michigan Engineers in harm's way. On June 22 James H. Clark was serving as train conductor when he was fired upon by bushwhackers. The blast left him with seven buckshot wounds on his arm. Samuel S. Glover was sent on July 13 as a mounted courier from Shelbyville south along the pike to Buell's headquarters at Huntsville. While crossing over Elk Ridge near Fayetteville, Glover was shot in the right knee by bushwhackers. In great pain he clung to his horse and barely escaped capture by outdistancing his attackers. His wound never healed properly and was still troubling him thirty-five years later.[45]

The men's attitudes toward Southern civilians changed as the supply situation became more serious as losses mounted from Confederate raids. Upon their arrival in Burnsville six weeks earlier, Major Hopkins had told the assembled soldiers and civilians, "We did not come south to take property but to protect rights and property of loyal citizens." After a summer of hit-and-run guerrilla raids and the frustration of continued failure to deter them, the men's attitudes hardened.[46]

Bitter Union soldiers, including many of the Michigan Engineers, harshly criticized Buell and his policy of being "soft" on rebels and their property. Though Buell's actions were well within the official Union policy and common practice of the war's first year, he was increasingly at odds with those whose views changed in the face of resolute Confederate opposition. An officer of the Michigan Engineers, writing in mid-July to the *Detroit Free Press*, described this evolution of opinion: "My feelings in regard to the conduct of this war have very much changed since I have been South, and especially of late. When I have seen the hardships our army has to endure and the cruelties inflicted on the soldiers by these miserable traitors in the South, wolves in sheep's clothing, I have made up my mind that our government has got to take off its kid's gloves if it ever intends to squash this rebellion."[47]

Having Union troops guard the property of Southerners who were in turn resisting Union efforts was particularly galling. Private Graves deeply resented the "miserable privilege of guarding rebel property while they are scourging the country as guerrillas and bushwhackers." Soldiers were quick to applaud the harsh measures used increasingly by Union troops and their commanders to combat such bushwhackers. Captain Sligh reported approvingly to his wife that Ohio troops had "orders not to bring any more such prisoners [bushwhackers] into camp. They know what that means, and they will carry that out."[48]

Since slaves were legally considered property in 1862, their fate formed part of the debate over the treatment of Southern civilians. Here too opinion in the army was changing. When the Michigan Engineers arrived in Kentucky, their actions were generally ones of noninterference. On December 31, 1861, a runaway slave fled to the Michigan Engineer column. Lieutenant Colonel Hunton and the captains of his three companies refused to shelter the runaway, stating, "We were not here to induce Negroes to run away, to steal them, but to assist to maintain the laws and put down Rebellion." When the slave found refuge with the Tenth Kentucky that same day, Captain Sligh took comfort that "the blame [for violating orders] is with them, not with us, our skirts are clear, and we intend that they will be." Eight months later Sligh was applauding the government's decision to confiscate rebel property, including "using their Negroes for laboring purposes," and noted, "If they had adopted that policy six months ago I think that the war would have been ended."[49]

This change in opinion was recognition by the soldiers of the importance of the slaves to the Confederate war effort. Freedom for the slaves began to be viewed as a tool to end the war and bring the troops home. Some in the regiment took this view further by addressing the question of eventual freedom for those in bondage. Albert Graves wrote his wife in August 1862 that "in the outset a large proportion [of the men] were opposed to meddling with slavery in any manner. Now they think to deprive the rebels of their slaves not only just but the most effective method of suppressing the rebellion and freely admit that if the government takes possession of the slaves they cannot be again returned to bondage."[50]

By the end of July the Nashville and Chattanooga had once again been restored to working order, and supplies were reaching Stevenson by rail. Buell's men were put back on full rations, and Buell prepared to finally move his forces against Chattanooga. The final major obstacle was the Tennessee River. To force a crossing, Buell needed boats for a surprise landing and a pontoon bridge to cross reinforcements over. After troops were across and in firm possession of the southern bank, a replacement railroad bridge could be built to ensure supply for the advancing army from Nashville. First, however, Buell had to have the pontoons, and the Michigan Engineers were to build them.

At the outbreak of the war only one complete pontoon train was in the possession of the U.S. Army, but it had been built for war with Mexico, and the rubber hulls were deteriorated beyond repair. There were various schemes for the construction of pontoon boats, and each had its advantages and disadvantages. None, however, could match the wooden French-style bateaux. These boats were heavier and harder to transport over distances, but the ready supply of wood and their strength and durability for nearby crossings made them the pontoon of choice during the first two years of the war in the western theater.[51]

On July 6 Capt. James St. Clair Morton, recently appointed chief engineer of the Army of the Ohio, prepared plans for a pontoon bridge to be thrown across the Tennessee above Stevenson. Four days later, after being reassigned to direct the construction of railroad defenses along the Nashville and Chattanooga, Morton reported that three mills near Stevenson were in operation, producing the timber that would be used on the two-thousand-foot span. Morton optimistically projected that the plan would "be executed in about a week."[52]

Morton was soon gone, and little was accomplished in his absence. Responsibility for completing the pontoon bridge fell upon Colonel Innes and his regiment. Beginning in late July, scattered companies of the Michigan Engineers received orders to report to Stevenson. All ten companies and the regimental headquarters were there by August 7. When the Michigan men arrived, they discovered that there was little cut timber on hand for the construction of the pontoons and necessary planking.[53]

The shortage was not because of any lack of effort by Captain Yates of Company A, who inherited efforts to put area mills into operation, along with his other duties. He was able to get only two mills into operation: Paint Rock Mill along the creek of the same name near Woodville and Jackson's Mill within one mile of Stevenson. Their exposed locations made it hard to get local civilians to work there, so soldiers and runaway slaves formed the working parties. Innes took control of the two mills in operation after his arrival in Stevenson in early August, but the work on the pontoon boats continued to be delayed by the lack of cut timber.[54]

Innes also lacked other key materials necessary for the completion of the pontoon boats. Nails had disappeared into the maze of supply warehouses at Nashville, and replacements were hard to find. The oakum and pitch to be used as caulking had to be brought forward from Louisville and Cincinnati. On August 8 Buell reprimanded Innes about the lack of activity on the pontoons: "I am surprised and regret very much that you have not commenced work. If the stuff could not be transported you could have been getting out the pieces. Push the boats with might and main and report if anything interferes with your work."[55]

The Michigan Engineers started work on the boats on August 11 as materials for their assembly were being gathered. Buell was optimistic enough about the future to order Innes to immediately repair the railroad between Stevenson and Bridgeport, a final step before attempting to cross the Tennessee. The supply situation had even improved, since, after maddening delays, loaded trains could now be sent to Decatur over the repaired Tennessee and Alabama road and then forwarded from there to the depots at Huntsville and Stevenson.[56]

On August 12, however, Brig. Gen. John H. Morgan and his Confederate cavalry captured the sleeping Union garrison at Gallatin, Kentucky, and ran a train loaded with combustibles into the Louisville and Nashville tunnel south of that point. The fire caused the collapse of the wooden supports, and an avalanche of stone fell into the tunnel, effectively closing it for months. Low water levels ruled out other supply routes for Buell's forces. Any advance toward Chattanooga was out of the question until the supply lines could be reestablished.[57]

Confederates also struck at the Michigan Engineers, who were working long shifts at the two mills near Stevenson. On the night of August 17, six of Innes's men working at Jackson's Mill returned to nearby Stevenson for rations and discovered that two engineers and several runaway slave laborers had been captured in their absence. One of the laborers was able to escape to the main camp. Company A promptly followed the trail of the raiders to the Tennessee River but was unable to rescue the prisoners. The two engineers were quickly paroled, but it is almost certain, given Confederate policies, that the laborers taken with them were killed or returned to slavery.[58]

The raids of Forrest, Morgan, and others on Buell's supply lines had effectively stopped his advance on Chattanooga. In the interim, the Confederates were making plans to force Buell from Alabama and Tennessee. On June 20 General Beauregard was replaced by Braxton Bragg as commander of the Army of Mississippi, which had fallen back from Corinth. Bragg decided to gather his army at Chattanooga to operate against Buell and quickly moved most of his command on the 776-mile route from Tupelo to that point. Generals Bragg and Kirby Smith agreed upon a plan to drive Union troops from Cumberland Gap and all of Middle Tennessee. In the days following, the plan was modified, at Kirby Smith's urging and with Bragg's grudging acceptance, into a much more grandiose one to drive Union troops out of Kentucky entirely and back to the Ohio River. Kirby Smith's column moved out from Knoxville on August 14, with Bragg's last troops crossing at Chattanooga two weeks later.[59]

On August 16 Buell ordered Nelson back to Kentucky to take command of its defense in response to reports of Kirby Smith's move north from Knoxville. A week later Kirby Smith's column was over the mountains and there were reports of Bragg's Confederates crossing the Tennessee at Chattanooga. With his supply line ruptured and rear threatened, Buell began to move his divisions from northern Alabama to positions southeast of Nashville.[60]

By this time, the Michigan Engineers were scattered throughout Buell's command. Innes and Companies A, B, D, G, and H were north of Nashville repairing the railroad from Louisville. The balance of the regiment was still in northern Alabama. Company E had left Stevenson by rail for Huntsville on the nineteenth and remained to help with the defense of the place. Only Companies C, F, K, and I were still near Stevenson.[61]

As long as Stevenson remained in Union hands, trains from along the Memphis and Charleston could utilize the Nashville and Chattanooga as a line of evacuation. On August 21 its defense was placed in the hands of Col. Michael Shoemaker of the Thirteenth Michigan. His small force included only his regiment, an Indiana infantry company and battery, four companies of the Michigan Engineers under Lieutenant Colonel Hunton, and some convalescents.[62]

On August 23 Shoemaker received orders from Buell's headquarters to be prepared to evacuate the post after destroying the pontoons. Orders to prepare the boats for destruction were sent to the engineers. Most, but apparently not all, of the pontoons were burned on the twenty-fourth, and the engineers fell back four miles into Stevenson. They took up defensive positions in two stockades and two brick buildings within the town. That same day water was hauled into the defensive position as the stream of Union troops on their way to Nashville continued to move through Stevenson. Shoemaker received a warning from Buell's chief of staff to "be ready for an obstinate defense." On the twenty-seventh the Ohio infantry and cavalry at exposed Fort McCook east of Stevenson evacuated their position under Confederate artillery fire. The following day Shoemaker was reassured that "a brigade cannot dislodge you . . . hold the place" but was also reminded that "the property must be gotten away."[63]

Shoemaker intended to offer an "obstinate defense" and continued to strengthen his position while losing pieces of his command to the evacuation. On the twenty-eighth Captain Rhodes started the hard march to Decherd with Companies F and I and the Michigan Engineers' regimental wagons. The regiment's sick went by train to Decherd the same day. By this time Shoemaker's command at Stevenson had shrunk to his own Thirteenth Michigan, two companies of the Twenty-ninth Indiana, the Indiana battery, and a provisional force under Lieutenant Colonel Hunton, which included Companies C and K of the Michigan Engineers and convalescents from various units.[64]

Among the many Union troops passing through Stevenson were J. Newton Crittenton and his fellow telegraph operators, withdrawn from exposed positions along the Memphis and Charleston Railroad. Crittenton reported to Capt. Samuel Bruch, in charge of military telegraphs in the region, the status of each of his operators and then closed with a promise: "I am withdrawing everything from my section as quietly and orderly as possible."[65]

On the thirtieth Buell ordered the concentration of his army at Murfreesboro, and it was clear that Huntsville and Stevenson would have to be abandoned. That same day Shoemaker received orders to prepare for evacuation. The men were up all that night, loading baggage and tools onto rail cars and preparing to leave in the morning. Shoemaker was promised that Union cavalry moving south from Decherd would screen his movement.[66]

On the morning of the thirty-first Shoemaker sent out a mounted force toward Bridgeport to scout Confederate troops reported to be moving on Stevenson. The mixed column included mounted infantry, at least one artillery piece, and Hunton with some of the engineers on borrowed horses. The mounted command encountered scattered Confederate cavalry in its front and drove them as far as Bolivar before a large force of Confederate infantry was spotted. In response, the Union force quickly retreated to the prepared positions in Stevenson.[67]

Confederate infantry and artillery advanced from the southeast and began to shell the town. An artillery duel between the Indiana battery and Tennessee and Georgia gunners continued for several hours without significant loss. At 3 P.M. the last train from Huntsville arrived with the Tenth Wisconsin and refugees. Also on the train were sick and wounded Union soldiers evacuated from the hospital at Huntsville. As the train came into Stevenson, sick engineer Pvt. William B.

Calkins of Company K watched the last hour of the artillery fight from his car window.[68]

Shoemaker and his men sent off the last four trains at Stevenson, full of equipment and convalescents, and marched northward by 4 P.M. After a short, sharp exchange with pursuing cavalry, the column marched unmolested to Anderson's Station, which they reached at 3 A.M. on the morning of September 1. The retreat of Shoemaker's column was aided by the destruction of bridges over which they passed. Ironically, unable to rebuild and repair bridges as fast as the enemy could destroy them, Buell's men were able to retreat from northern Alabama only by destroying bridges behind them.[69]

Company E remained in Huntsville until the morning of August 31, when the post was evacuated. After destroying the machinery in the railroad machine shop and burning stores, Lt. Lucius F. Mills and his company evacuated with the Union garrison. They marched northward to Murfreesboro via Shelbyville. At Murfreesboro they scrambled aboard a northbound train and rode the cars until rejoining the regiment a few miles south of Gallatin, Tennessee, on September 5. Some of the most seriously ill Union soldiers in the hospital at Huntsville were in no condition to travel and were left behind.[70]

Yates's battalion of Michigan Engineers had been among the first Union troops to move into northern Alabama, and now the men under Hunton and Mills were among the last federal troops to leave it. Hampered by the need to repair the railroad as he advanced and then to keep it open, Buell had failed to take the critical rail junctions near Chattanooga, and now he was being forced back to prevent the loss of most of Tennessee and Kentucky.[71]

One study of the Army of the Ohio's engineering arm during 1862 has concluded that "Buell's failure was to a large extent a failure of engineering, namely in repairing, maintaining, and defending his railroads." It was not that the troops themselves, even those like the Michigan Engineers specifically assigned the railroad work, had failed the army's commander. Innes and his men "performed valiantly" along with civilian working parties despite the failure to restore and maintain regular rail supply. Rather, the blame rests squarely on Buell's shoulders.[72]

Like all other commands in the West, the Army of the Ohio suffered from a shortage of trained military engineers and equipment. Buell failed to properly use what limited resources he did have. Even if the railroads had been left unmolested by Confederate raiders, Buell lacked the means to cross over the Tennessee and pose any significant threat to Chattanooga or points east or south. This oversight forced

Buell to assign the Michigan Engineers, his largest and most experienced force for railroad repair, to build pontoons instead of bridges. Because the bridges were not fixed fast enough, the boats had to be burned anyway.[73]

The Michigan Engineers trudging northward at the end of August were a dispirited lot. Writing later, even after the sting of humiliation had lessened, Private Clark wrote his hometown paper what he saw as a "disgraceful retreat, and the hardships *then endured*, though great, were increased by mortification at leaving all the ground we had gone over and held so long, to be overrun once more by armed rebels, exulting at our expulsion" (emphasis in original).[74]

Into Battle at Perryville

At the end of August 1862 General Buell's army was scattered across northern Alabama and Middle Tennessee under orders to concentrate at Murfreesboro along the Nashville and Chattanooga. Buell was unsure if Nashville or Kentucky was the real target of General Bragg's flanking movement from Chattanooga and was attempting to protect both. He decided to fall back to Nashville, to which point his army moved shortly after concentrating at Murfreesboro. By conceding the positions south and east of Nashville, Buell placed both Nashville and his supply line with Louisville at risk. He also handed the initiative to Bragg's Confederates and would have to race his army north to expel the gray columns from Kentucky and relieve the threats to Louisville and Cincinnati.[1]

By early September the engineers were spread along a line from Kentucky to the Tennessee-Alabama border. Colonel Innes and Companies A, B, D, G, and H were finishing work on the large Louisville and Nashville Bridge over Manscoe Creek that John H. Morgan's men had destroyed. Their next assignment was to replace the nearby railroad bridge over Station Camp Creek. Detachments of Kentucky and Indiana infantry and the other companies of the Michigan Engineers helped them as they arrived from northern Alabama. By September 7 all ten companies were together finishing the work.[2]

Company E had marched overland from Huntsville to Murfreesboro, where they were able to catch a ride on a northbound train as far as Saundersville. Companies F and I under Captain Rhodes marched north from Stevenson as a wagon guard as far as Decherd and then further north as that point was evacuated. Lieutenant Colonel Hunton and Companies C and K followed the rail line north from Stevenson through rough terrain and caught up with Rhodes's men near Tullahoma on September 2. They completed the movement north together, catching a train from Nashville to near Station Camp Creek.[3]

After completing Station Camp Creek No. 3 Bridge on September 8, the entire regiment moved three miles further north to another railroad bridge that Morgan had burned, almost certainly over the same stream. The bridge was similar in size to the one just completed and was located two miles south of Gallatin. By this time it was apparent to Buell that Bragg's destination was well to the north of Nashville, so the bulk of his command was ordered to concentrate at Bowling Green. The men had barely started repairing the bridge on the eighth when they received orders to stop their work and prepare to move. Most of the night was spent in preparation. Leaving General Thomas and three divisions behind to defend Nashville, Buell marched north with the six other divisions under his command.[4]

The engineers moved north to Bowling Green as a regiment, leaving their camp in the early morning dark of the ninth. After hard marching, Bowling Green was finally reached on the morning of the eleventh, and the weary men camped one mile northwest of town. The men quickly stretched out on the ground and were almost immediately fast asleep.[5]

The men were both tired from the march and angry about forfeiting the gains made since the spring. Sgt. James M. Sligh wrote of these feelings in a letter to his mother: "For six days we subsisted entirely on the enemy, or the citizens, and got nothing but what we could pick up to eat. The boys are nearly all foot sore and depressed to think we have had to retreat so far and in such haste, having come from Stevenson to Bowling Green in ten days over some of the most mountainous country in the west."[6]

After resting on the eleventh, the engineers were put to work on the twelfth. Details from the regiment were assigned to help repair the army's pontoon bridge across the Big Barren River just north of Bowling Green. Work on the bridge continued under the direction of Captain Hannings for several days. Meanwhile, Hunton was in charge of constructing fortifications on College Hill. For three days the men assigned to Hunton gathered timber, constructed gun platforms, and hauled dirt to strengthen the parapet. Lt. Edwin Baxter commanded a detail of thirty men assigned to take the regiment's wagons and secure forage for the horses from the surrounding countryside. On September 16 the men rested and received orders to move northward again, this time to strike against Bragg's column at Glasgow.[7]

While Buell concentrated his command at Bowling Green, Bragg reached Glasgow, located just over thirty miles to the east. Bragg's command was in a good position, between Buell and General Kirby Smith's forces at Lexington, and able to cut off any retreat by Buell along the direct route to Louisville. That changed after a clumsy attempt by Bragg's advance to overrun the small Union force at Munfordville was repulsed. On the fifteenth Bragg gave the order for the balance of his command to move to that point and reduce the position, determined to prevail and avoid a morale-depressing loss.[8]

On September 16 Bragg invested the Union position at Munfordville and demanded the surrender of the post. Hopelessly outnumbered, and convinced that nothing would be accomplished by further fighting, the garrison surrendered the following morning. Among those surrendered were several new recruits for the Michigan Engineers. They were en route from Grand Rapids to join the regiment and had been stopped at Munfordville because of the Confederate offensive. As was the policy at this point in the war, Bragg quickly paroled the men, and they were sent to Union lines, where they would be held until formally exchanged. The long column of paroled prisoners passed through the Union army on September 19, but it was many months before some of the men ever reached the regiment.[9]

Bragg had possession of Munfordville and the bridge over the Green River, but the victory cost him time and position. Though his forces were astride the Louisville and Nashville and could entrench behind the Green River, his move from Glasgow to Munfordville had cost him the use of the best roads to keep his army supplied from Confederate depots in central Kentucky, especially the turnpike from Bardstown.[10]

Unknown to Bragg, Buell had already decided to strike with his force against the Confederate position at Glasgow. He divided his command into three columns, each consisting of two infantry divisions and screened by a cavalry brigade. Lovell H. Rousseau with his division and that of Jacob Ammen were to move north on the Louisville to Dripping Springs and then east and southeast toward Glasgow, as would the column under Alexander McCook, which also included General Mitchel's division. Thomas Crittenden, reinforced with Thomas Wood's division, would turn east off the pike above Bristow on the Merry Oaks Road and move directly upon Glasgow.[11]

The engineers moved from Bowling Green to Louisville in three battalions, each attached to one of the columns. The first to leave Bowling Green was that commanded by Major Hopkins, Companies A, C, and H attached to Rousseau's command. The column marched out of Bowling Green on the afternoon of the sixteenth, a day ahead of the other columns. Innes with Companies B, I, E, and K marched with Crittenden's column and left Bowling Green on the morning of the seventeenth, as did Hunton with Companies D, F, and G attached to McCook. Buell's army moved forward in fits and starts, the trains had trouble negotiating the congested roads, and the men were often without food or shelter.[12]

Buell received word of the fall of Munfordville on September 18 and that night met with the garrison's commander, who had been released by the Confederates on parole. Col. John T. Wilder reinforced

Buell's view that the Confederates were low on supplies and would have to leave Munfordville and move eastward toward Kirby Smith's command and sources of supply. If Bragg did stay in position, Buell's men would have to attempt to evict them from the Green River line by force, an option the army's leaders expected to be costly. Buell, however, was willing to give Bragg a little time before launching a direct attack on Munfordville.[13]

Following the surrender of Wilder's garrison and heady euphoria of victory, Bragg had to face the vulnerability of his position and lack of favorable options. After evaluating his options, he decided the best course was to move his army to a union with Kirby Smith at Bardstown. In doing so, he yielded to Buell the direct route to Louisville without a fight but united the two columns of the Confederate invasion of Kentucky and provided a better source of supply for his troops. His men evacuated Munfordville the afternoon of the twentieth.[14]

Buell's army moved through Munfordville. He decided not to follow Bragg's withdrawing army but rather to march his command directly to Louisville. The columns moved up the Louisville Turnpike, reaching Nolin on the twenty-third. At Elizabethtown, the Union troops turned off the turnpike northwest toward West Point on the junction of the Salt and Ohio rivers, thus avoiding an attack to their right flank from Bragg at Bardstown. At West Point the men received full rations for the first time since leaving the Cumberland Plateau. From West Point most of the men moved on the Salt River Turnpike the last twenty miles to Louisville. The march was very difficult, and many dropped out along the way from exhaustion or arrived in Louisville in tattered uniforms and nearing collapse. By the twenty-seventh Buell's divisions were in Louisville, and the city had become one of the most defended positions in the nation.[15]

It was difficult for the Michigan Engineers accompanying the columns. In addition to moving their own equipment, they were called upon to assist the other troops. On the twenty-second Captain Fox's company was detailed to repair the bridge over Bacon Creek, and a detachment drawn from all three companies in the battalion helped pass wagons over it. Upon arrival at West Point, Hopkins's men were put to work repairing the pontoon bridge over the Salt River. The engineer battalions also suffered a great deal from straggling. On one day Company K ended the march with eighteen men missing out of the forty who started. On September 23 Company H reached camp with only eight men still marching. When the men did finally arrive in Louisville, Pvt. William Clark reported to the *Marshall Statesman*, they were "the dirtiest lot of men your readers ever saw together."[16]

Perhaps the hardest lot fell on those Michigan Engineers who were detailed to move the regiment's wagons. Moving as a part of Buell's two-thousand-wagon supply train, the regiment's teamsters left Bowling Green on September 27 and did not arrive in Louisville until October 4. Their route was via Brownsville, Priceville, Millerstown, Hayesville, and Deep Spring and then on to West Point and Louisville.[17]

The Michigan Engineer battalions reached Louisville with their respective columns and went into camp in different parts of the city without reuniting. The four companies with Innes were the first to arrive, reaching Louisville at about 11 P.M. on the twenty-fifth, ahead of most of the army. Hunton's men were in Portland on the outskirts of the city the morning of the twenty-sixth but had to wait for the rest of McCook's column to come up. They marched and countermarched through the city until finally making camp in a lumberyard along the Ohio River on the eastern edge of the city. Hopkins's men were probably the last to arrive but doubtless had the easiest final leg. They were loaded onto the sternwheeler steamer *Poland* at West Point. After a "splendid ride up the river," the men disembarked at Portland and marched the few miles remaining to Louisville. At Louisville the engineers, like the rest of Buell's men, rested, drew and cooked rations, and otherwise prepared for the active campaigning to come.[18]

On September 29 Buell reorganized his army into three army corps, each with three divisions. George H. Thomas was appointed second-in-command. Maj. Gen. Alexander McCook would command the I Corps, Maj. Gen. Thomas L. Crittenden the II Corps, and command of the III Corps was given to newly promoted Brig. Gen. Charles C. Gilbert. Two more divisions were guarding Nashville, and one division with Buell remained unassigned to any corps. The cavalry was organized into one division. Recognizing their importance to the army, the Michigan Engineers remained split into detachments, assigned to the various columns. Buell planned to leave Louisville with about sixty thousand men, at least twenty thousand of whom were green troops. Though some effort was made to incorporate the new regiments into veteran divisions, at least two divisions were composed almost exclusively of inexperienced troops.[19]

President Lincoln, determined to do some reorganizing of his own, replaced Buell with Thomas, the orders arriving on the twenty-ninth. Thomas immediately protested by telegram to General Halleck that Buell should remain in command since the army was about to move against Bragg. Halleck accepted Thomas's argument and rescinded the order that same day. Thomas remained second-in-command of the army. The men of the army would have preferred Buell's departure regardless of the proximity of the enemy. Alexander Campbell of Company F believed that if the army "had not a coward or a traitor for a leader we would have the rebels cleaned out." The major Union army in the West would go into battle under the command of a man neither the commander-in-chief nor the soldiers had any faith in.[20]

On October 1 Buell's army marched out from Louisville, determined to find and defeat the Confederates. McCook's I Corps marched on the road southeast toward Bardstown about six miles and then turned off east on a route to reach Taylorsville. McCook had divisions of Brig. Gens. James S. Jackson and Lovell H. Rousseau, joined by Hopkins with Companies A, C, and H. Crittenden's II Corps moved on the direct road to Bardstown and included three divisions and Innes with Companies B, E, K, and I. Gilbert's III Corps moved toward the same place but on roads to the south through Shepherdsville. Brig. Gen. Joshua Sill with his division of McCook's corps and the independent division of Brig. Gen. Ebenezer Dumont was sent eastward on the Shelbyville Road toward Frankfort to distract the attention of Kirby Smith's forces in that area. Hunton accompanied Sill with Companies D, F, and G.[21]

While the Union troops were marching toward him, Bragg was attending to political matters and arranging for a prolonged stay in Kentucky as his army rested and resupplied. Confederate scouts sent back word of advancing Union troops, but Bragg misunderstood where the real Union strength was. By the time Maj. Gen. Leonidas Polk received orders to move the main portion of the army northeast from Bardstown toward Frankfort, Union movements had already left him vulnerable to a flank attack. By October 4 Bragg's forces were in full retreat from Bardstown before the army's commander was even aware that Buell's whole army had left Louisville.[22]

Beginning to understand that the main threat from Buell was against Polk and not Kirby Smith, Bragg designated the Lexington-Danville area, where supplies were already being gathered, for the junction of Polk's force with that of Kirby Smith. Bragg ordered Kirby Smith to withdraw his men south to Harrodsburg for the junction with Polk's retreating force but then reversed himself two days later and ordered Kirby Smith to remain near Lexington. Only five days after leaving Louisville, Buell had managed to force back both parts of the Confederate army in Kentucky and threaten each one. Bragg's force was still divided, and he did not understand the dispositions of the Union army facing him.[23]

Sill's column of Buell's advancing army played a role greater than its numbers would have justified, keeping Bragg's attention focused away from Buell's main effort to the south. On the first day out of Louisville the three companies of Michigan Engineers under Hunton worked with the column's rearguard, moving ambulances and wagons forward and camping near Floyd's Fork. The next day Hunton's force was moved to the advance and worked as pioneers until reaching Shelbyville via Simpsonville. The men left camp on the sixth, marching with Sill's column toward Frankfort and reaching the Kentucky River across from Frankfort that evening. The next day, the engineers were put to work replanking the bridge over the river, planks for which the Confederates had hastily dismantled and thrown into the water. On October 7 Buell ordered Sill to move with his division by forced marches and rejoin the rest of the army, which he did at Perryville on the eleventh. Hunton's men marched with the main body.[24]

The detachment under Innes moved forward from Louisville with Crittenden's column. Beginning October 2 the engineers spent four days building a bridge 150 feet long over Floyd's Fork for the passage of Crittenden's corps and wagons on the Louisville to Bardstown Road. In the meantime, most of the corps moved on toward Bardstown and Springfield. On the sixth the engineers left their camp at Floyd's Fork and reached Bardstown on the eighth. By then the rest of Crittenden's corps was in position near Perryville, which Innes's battalion did not reach until the tenth.[25]

Not delayed by bridge building, the detachment under Hopkins was able to keep pace with McCook's corps as it moved southeastward from Louisville. They rested for two days after reaching Taylorsville on October 2, camped near Bloomfield on the fifth, and marched to Chaplinville on the sixth. They reached Mackville on the seventh in response to orders from Buell. That night the men at Mackville heard cannonading to their front.[26]

Moving on a parallel route farther to the south, Gilbert's column marched to within four miles of Perryville on the seventh and came into contact with both Confederate infantry and cavalry in some strength. Buell ordered McCook and Crittenden to move their commands to that point and take position alongside Gilbert. Meanwhile, Bragg responded to requests for reinforcements from General Hardee commanding at Perryville. Bragg ordered Polk to reinforce Hardee, take command at Perryville, and drive the Union troops from their positions west of town on the eighth.[27]

Over fifty thousand men were at, or converging on, Perryville, determined to fight for possession of the town and its water. A severe drought had dried up most of the streams and creeks, and soldiers in both armies suffered during the marching from the lack of fresh water.

Since any place with water was valuable, the thirsty soldiers thought the several streams west of Perryville containing pools of brownish water were worth fighting for.[28]

Early on the morning of the eighth, a brigade of Gilbert's III Corps was thrown forward to take possession of the water in Doctor's Creek and the heights beyond. After driving back the enemy, the brigade was reinforced and defended its position on Peter's Hill. Bragg arrived at 10 A.M. Believing that he faced only a portion of Buell's army, he immediately set about organizing an assault on the Union left. He intended to hit the open Union flank from north to south with the divisions of Maj. Gen. Benjamin F. Cheatham, Maj. Gen. Simon Bolivar Buckner, and Brig. Gen. James P. Anderson.[29]

Cheatham's men moved forward at about 2 P.M., crossed the Chaplin River, and struck the Union troops of McCook's corps. Both sides were surprised. The Union soldiers were startled to find anything but cavalry to their front, while the Confederates were surprised to find any Union troops in position this far north. The Union left had been filled just in time.[30]

The Union soldiers facing Cheatham's attack were the divisions of Jackson and Rousseau of McCook's I Corps. They had been marching on the Mackville Road since early that morning. Nearing Gilbert's position, McCook ordered Rousseau to take up position on the III Corps' left flank and directed Jackson to extend the line further north with his green troops. Companies A, C, and H of the Michigan Engineers under Major Hopkins were placed in reserve.[31]

They were settling into position and scouting nearby streams for possible water when Cheatham's assault crashed into the Union left. After an initial repulse, Cheatham's men were able to flank Jackson's left brigade commanded by Brig. Gen. William R. Terrill. Some of the inexperienced regiments gave way, and Jackson was killed trying to rally his men. Rousseau's division, composed of more veteran material, held firm and provided a rallying point for Terrill's men. Despite heavy losses, the Confederates continued to push forward against McCook's line as Anderson's and Buckner's men were fed into the attack. At 2:45 P.M. McCook sent a staff officer to Gilbert, asking for reinforcements. By 3 P.M. McCook's right, where a gap existed between his line and Gilbert's left, was under pressure. His men fell back from the Widow Bottom's farm about an hour later in the face of determined attacks.[32]

McCook's corps was slowly being compressed into a crescent-shaped line forward of the intersection of the Mackville and Benton roads. Within that position were the remains of the five brigades of Rousseau's and Jackson's divisions. The key to the right flank of

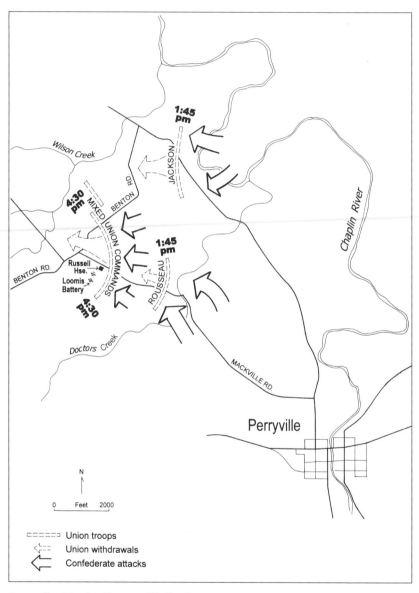

Perryville. Map by Sherman Hollander.

the crescent was the high ground near the Russell house, astride the Mackville-Perryville Road a quarter-mile from the junction with the Benton Road. By 4:30 P.M. McCook was in danger of losing this position. Rousseau arrived at the Russell house to meet with McCook and remained to personally direct its defense. His only infantry were the battered remnants of regiments from the brigades of Cols. William H. Lytle (who had been wounded and captured) and Leonard Harris.[33]

Hopkins and his three companies of the Michigan Engineers had been in the rear of McCook's corps since arriving on the field. At about 4:30 P.M. they were ordered forward to support Loomis's battery, which had been withdrawn to a commanding rise of ground about 150 yards to the rear of the Russell house and hill to replenish its ammunition. Lytle's and Harris's men were under fire from at least three enemy batteries, and a fresh Confederate brigade was advancing toward the Russell house. In short order, three more enemy brigades threw themselves against the Union troops holding McCook's right. Finally, at about 5 P.M. Harris's position across the road from the Russell house began to fall back under tremendous pressure. McCook's weary men were on the verge of being driven back beyond the crossroads by the weight of the Confederate attack.[34]

Desperate to stem the Confederate onslaught, Rousseau rounded up any troops he could. Among those he hastily collected in his immediate rear were Captain Loomis's Michigan battery and Hopkins's three companies of Michigan Engineers. Rousseau rode up to Loomis and ordered him to open fire on the advancing Confederates. Loomis replied that he had been ordered by McCook to reserve his limited ammunition supply for "close work." Rousseau replied that "it was close enough and would be closer in a minute." Rousseau also turned to Hopkins's men, who were lying prone to avoid "the cutting fire of the enemy" directed at Loomis's guns. Rousseau ordered Hopkins to move his command forward to the Russell farm buildings and, according to some reports, personally led them into the maelstrom with his hat on the point of his sword. After ordering his men to load their weapons, Hopkins drew his sword, declaring, "Now my brave mechanics if you work you can fight, follow me," and led them into the storm of Confederate lead.[35]

The desperate leadership of Rousseau and Hopkins's bold gesture were not enough. Within minutes the Union line was being pushed back through the buildings of the Russell farm, hard-pressed by yelling Confederates. Among the Union soldiers falling back before the onslaught were Major Hopkins and his small command. Details are unclear, but the large number of men struck in the torso or thigh suggests that the men were fighting without any cover. Since several of the men were wounded in the back of the torso, it would appear that at least some of Hopkins's men were part of the general stampede to the rear. Likewise, the scattered condition of the battalion that night suggests that unit cohesion broke apart during the swirling withdrawal.[36]

Fortunately for McCook's men, reinforcements were arriving just as they were being pushed back beyond the Russell house and the crossroads. Col. Michael Gooding's brigade of III Corps veterans were nearing the crossroads as Rousseau led what remained of Lytle's brigade off the field and out of the fight. Almost certainly Hopkins's battalion left the field with Rousseau and the remnants of Lytle's command. Gooding's brigade moved forward beyond the Russell house and for the next hour resisted attacks by Wood's and Liddell's Confederate brigades until forced back after dark. Gooding was captured as his command fell back. Brig. Gen. James B. Steedman's III Corps Union brigade did not arrive until the fighting had effectively ceased but was able to relieve some of the exhausted men of Rousseau's division.[37]

The remnants of McCook's corps, reinforced only by Gooding and later Steedman, remained in position that night, northwest of the crossroads. Division and brigade commanders tried to reform their commands, and regimental commanders mustered what was left of their bloodied units. The entire process was made more difficult because of the death or capture of so many senior officers. Losses among the men were heavy. Of the 12,500 men in McCook's two divisions who entered the fight, at least 3,300 had been killed, wounded, or captured in the fighting. Thousands more were stumbling through the dark trying to rejoin their units or escape any further fighting.[38]

The Michigan Engineers were no different. Hopkins led fewer than 150 men into action. At least 14 of his men were wounded, 2 fatally. Another 3 were reported captured, and many more were cut off during the confusion of the withdrawal. Pvt. William H. Kimball and a soldier from Company A stumbled through the dark looking for the battalion. While at a spring they heard the familiar voices of Merrick Chamberlain and Abner Walker of Company H. Together, the four spent the night comparing their experiences. Private Stearns of Company H went looking for water and got lost. He spent the night with the Second Michigan Cavalry camped nearby.[39]

Major Hopkins met in the dark with what was still together of his battalion and told them to get sleep since they would probably have to fight in the morning. Those who could put aside the horror of the day's fighting and their fears for the morrow got what sleep they could. The battalion spent the night in a position behind John C. Starkweather's brigade, which now formed the reserve of McCook's decimated command. That night Bragg, reviewing the reports of his units, realized for the first time that he was facing virtually all of Buell's army. Bragg feared an early morning attack on his position and withdrew his command in the darkness northeast toward Harrodsburg some ten or twelve miles. The fighting at Perryville was over.[40]

Despite the losses and confusion, Hopkins's three companies had done well after being thrown into an impossible situation with only a fraction of the men needed to reverse the Confederate onslaught. This is particularly true since none of Hopkins's men had been engaged in battle before, and many were green recruits. At least one-third of Hopkins's men had just joined their companies, many as recently as October 1. Among the new recruits was at least one who could not face the enemy and deserted as Rousseau led the battalion forward. Musician Benjamin Harris was not apprehended until March 1864. He was tried for desertion and convicted, but the sentence of execution was commuted to a life sentence on the Dry Tortugas.[41]

Many of those who remained in their places with the companies paid a fearful price, their bodies torn apart by the soft lead balls fired by Confederate infantry. Two died of their wounds, and six more were so badly wounded that they were discharged from the service. Eugene Noble's destroyed arm was amputated, and he died a lingering death a month later. Anson Eddy also succumbed to his wounds. Walter Kimball was hit twice in the body, one ball piercing his lung and lodging against his shoulder blade and another striking a rib and glancing into his biceps. He was still carrying the first bullet in his body when he died forty years later. William B. Conley took a bullet in his leg while falling back, fracturing the bone and causing his discharge. William C. Harrison was struck on the left side of his chest, causing a permanent partial paralysis. Ayers Grosevenor of Company H was struck by a minié bullet in the left side of the neck, making a "fistful hole clean through," and laid among those to be hastily buried. The burial detail heard him calling out for water, and he eventually rejoined the regiment after spending six months in Union hospitals.[42]

Dawn finally came on the ninth, and the men fully expected to renew the battle. Union cavalry, however, scouted toward the Confederate positions and reported that the only enemy left was a cavalry screen. Union infantry divisions moved forward with little opposition and took position in and beyond the town of Perryville. Hopkins's men remained in camp while the battalion regained much of its strength with the continuing return of men who had been separated during the battle. New recruit John Weissert scoured the battle's Union position looking for wounded comrade William Goodyear, who had been carried from the field. Weissert came across the gruesome carnage of battle: "There was a corpse with a bullet through his breast. We stood still and I looked at him with tears in my eyes and a prayer for him on my lips."[43]

On the tenth Buell's army marched forward and took position facing Bragg's command near Harrodsburg. Even though his forces had finally been augmented by Kirby Smith's command, Bragg decided not to fight. Facing supply problems, frustrated by the failure of troops under Gens. Earl Van Dorn and Sterling Price to move into western Tennessee, and sorely disappointed by the refusal of Kentucky recruits to flock to his army, Bragg began the long withdrawal from Kentucky.[44]

Hopkins's battalion moved forward two miles on the tenth and then again two more miles on the eleventh. Innes and his four companies joined them that night. The next morning Innes and the seven companies now under his command marched six or eight miles and were joined by Hunton's three companies near Harrodsburg. Hunton's men had arrived with Sill's division. That night of the twelfth was the first time the regiment had been together since leaving Bowling Green a month earlier. They were camped near the headquarters of Generals McCook and Rousseau, serving as guard.[45]

Four men from Hunton's battalion did not make the reunion of the regiment. Pvts. Lorenzo Colby, Jonathan Coomer, Charles Saunders, and Abel C. Smith of Company G were taken prisoner on October 9 near Lawrenceburg while with Sill's diversionary column. Following a spirited clash between his advance and rebel soldiers of Kirby Smith's command, Sill reported to Buell, "I presume they picked off some of our stragglers and I fear they have captured a train of sixteen wagons sent after me unadvisedly." The men might have been among the stragglers and guards that Sill feared for, or they might have been foraging. The four men did not return to the regiment for several months, though they were almost immediately paroled and sent north to await exchange.[46]

The engineers drew rations on the morning of the thirteenth and marched seven miles southward in the direction of Danville. They were now serving as the advance of McCook's corps, to which the entire regiment was attached. On the fourteenth the men marched forward through Danville and then southeast to near Stanford, still with McCook's advance. The next day the regiment moved through Crab Orchard and camped a few miles beyond the town, remaining there through the nineteenth. The welcome rest was spent issuing rations, repairing equipment, and washing clothes. There was even the chance for a rare Sunday inspection on the nineteenth.[47]

On the fourteenth Buell learned that Bragg's army had withdrawn further eastward and ordered his command forward in pursuit. By the seventeenth Buell considered there to be little value in pursuing Bragg's army and informed Halleck that his army was returning to Nashville. He returned to Louisville, leaving Thomas to direct the movement of the army toward Nashville.[48]

The engineers received orders on the night of the nineteenth to march the following morning. They left camp near Crab Orchard and marched northwest to Stanford and then west on the road to Lebanon, which they reached early in the afternoon of the twenty-second. They camped several miles south of that place on Rolling Fork. After one day in camp to receive new clothing and five days' rations, the march continued southwest toward Bowling Green. By the thirty-first, they were camped along Lost River, three miles from Bowling Green, and remained there until November 4.[49]

They were also happy with the news that Buell had been dumped as army commander. Albert Graves wrote home from Bowling Green that despite the difficult marches, the men were cheered "by the knowledge that Buell no longer controls the movements of the army of the Ohio. Neither officers or privates had any confidence in his management and made no bones of saying as much." Lincoln and Halleck wanted action, at least a movement into East Tennessee. Buell was content to return to Nashville. He was soon sent packing and was replaced by Maj. Gen. William S. Rosecrans.[50]

On October 30 Rosecrans arrived at Louisville to assume command of the Department of the Cumberland and Buell's Army of the Ohio, which was merged into it. On November 2 the new commander inspected the Michigan Engineers and met with the field officers, leaving a favorable impression. Rosecrans was a West Point graduate, an engineer, and a successful businessman and came to the command fresh from victories at Iuka and Corinth.[51]

On the fourth the regiment left camp and marched toward Nashville. The next day Hunton and Companies D, I, and K were ordered to halt in Mitchellville just south of the Tennessee state line, while Innes and the balance continued on. The rail from Louisville was intact as far south as Mitchellville Station, which served as a base for wagon trains supplying Nashville and was the scene of "unparalleled activity." More buildings were needed to store the provisions and supplies being trained down from Louisville until they could be loaded on the wagons. For three days Hunton's men built commissary buildings and repaired the depot. Work was completed in the morning of the seventh, and the detachment marched south toward Nashville. They caught up with the rest of the regiment at Edgefield across the Cumberland River from Nashville that day. After eight months of marching, building, and fighting, the regiment was back in Nashville, with the war no closer to a conclusion than it had been in March.[52]

· 9 ·

Mutiny

The War Department offered General Rosecrans two alternative lines of operation: a direct move east and south against General Bragg to capture East Tennessee while covering Middle Tennessee or a concentration at Nashville and then a move across the mountains into East Tennessee. Though he clearly preferred the first, General Halleck did accept that the need to protect Nashville, the difficulty of supply, and the unknown condition of the forces in the field might require the second option. Rosecrans chose the latter.[1]

Rosecrans's first concern was to concentrate his command at Nashville. By November 21, 1862, Braxton Bragg's entire Confederate army was in Middle Tennessee and had established positions at Murfreesboro, Shelbyville, and Manchester. From this position, Bragg would be able to block any advance by Rosecrans along the direct routes southeast from Nashville. Detachments of his command were sent on cavalry raids deep into Kentucky and West Tennessee, and reinforcements were sent to join Lt. Gen. John C. Pemberton's forces in Mississippi.[2]

By November 9 Rosecrans was personally in Nashville, and most of his command was with him or positioned along the railroad back to Gallatin. The army was officially retitled the XIV Corps of the Department of the Cumberland. The nine divisions of infantry and artillery were divided into three wings that functioned in a manner similar to corps, and the three brigades of cavalry constituted another division.[3]

Rosecrans's intention was to secure his supplies before attacking Bragg, and his rail line from Louisville to Nashville required extensive repair. John B. Anderson, retained as department military superintendent of railroads by Rosecrans, would direct civilian working parties along the railroad north of Gallatin, repairing track and bridges as well as clearing out the Gallatin tunnel. Colonel Innes and the Michigan Engineers, helped by infantry details, would repair breaks in the line between Gallatin and Nashville.[4]

Before Colonel Innes and his Michigan men could begin work, however, the regiment erupted into outright mutiny over the pay question. Despite the fact that Congress had recognized them as volunteer engineers, they still had not been paid. The soldiers had been very optimistic following the passage of legislation on July 17, 1862. This act retroactively recognized and authorized the volunteer engineer units already in the service and placed volunteer engineer troops on the same pay structure as the regular army Corps of Engineers. The act specifically provided that these men were to be paid the higher engineer pay for services already performed during their war service. It only remained for the men to wait until the army's pay department received the orders and the money was made available.[5]

Upon reaching Louisville in late September the men expected to be paid in full under the provisions of the new legislation. They were familiar with the act, and copies of it were circulating in camp. General Buell's paymasters had the money on hand for some of the army's regiments, most of which were months behind in their pay. Paymaster Maj. Charles T. Larned, however, refused to pay the Michigan Engineers without specific orders from the War Department. He was uncertain as to the point at which the regiment's status officially changed: with the passage of the act or its actual reorganization as a volunteer engineer unit. Innes was able to convince Larned to at least clarify the situation with the War Department. The men of the regiment left Louisville as ordered without their pay but were "grievously disappointed."[6]

The regiment's officers continued to fight for their men's pay. On October 13 Innes sent a letter to Secretary of War Stanton complaining about Larned's refusal to pay the men. Four weeks later the assembled officers of the regiment sent a petition to General McCook asking that Innes be sent to Washington, D.C., to meet with the War Department and see the matter resolved.[7]

The men also prevailed upon public sentiment for help. Several of them sent a letter to the *Louisville Journal*, explaining the financial needs of their families. The letter also expressed the frustration at not yet being paid despite congressional recognition of their status: "We shall continue to perform the duties of good soldiers, but we are somewhat discouraged that we have been treated in the manner we have been."[8]

The *Journal* article was reprinted in the *Detroit Free Press*, and Captain Sligh, still on recruiting duty in Michigan, referenced it in strong letters to both Governor Blair and Congressman Kellogg. Kellogg forwarded Sligh's letter to the paymaster general's office and was notified in response on November 18 that the regiment would be paid as soon as they completed new muster rolls. The men in the field, however, did not know that progress was finally being made with the War Department.[9]

On November 8 Ezra Stearns recorded in his diary that there was "excitement brewing in camp about pay as the boys think that they have rendered services as long as they wish to without compensation." The next day he noted, "Excitement is increasing . . . the men talk of making a strike." When the regiment received orders to march on November 10, it was the final straw for a large number of the men. At least one hundred men refused to serve any longer without the pay due them. Considering that they had been in the service for almost a year without any pay and that more than three months had elapsed since Congress had authorized engineer pay, the only real surprise is that more men did not step forward and refuse to march. Apparently a majority of the regiment felt that they should not work without pay, but when the confrontation came, only about a quarter of the assembled men held firm. Others in the ranks felt everything was being done that could be done, were unwilling to be branded as mutineers, or were concerned that their action could result in a loss of pay when the matter was finally settled.[10]

The men who refused to march belonged exclusively to Companies B, E, F, G, and I. Three-quarters of the mutineers were in Companies B, E, or I. There were at least thirty-four mutineers from just Company I. These three companies had, nearly en masse, refused to accept infantry pay in early 1862 and had been among the companies that nearly mutinied at Nashville on April 1.[11]

Though there is no direct evidence that their officers handled the pay dispute poorly, Companies B, E, and I had all suffered from high officer turnover. They were the only companies that had already lost their original captains, and there had been controversy surrounding the departure of each. Captain Borden (B) was with the company for only a few weeks in the field, and his successor, George M. Lane, was sick most of his short tenure in command. Captains Canfield (E) and Palmerlee (I) both left only a few months after Borden. There might have also been bitter feelings caused by Innes's refusal to appoint the men's choice to replace Borden in Company B and the efforts by the field officers to force Palmerlee out of the service. Likewise, Lt. Theodore Prall in Company I had been driven from the regiment as a result of his vocal criticism of Innes over the pay issue. There were eighteen of Prall's original recruits still present with the regiment, and eleven of them mutinied.[12]

The men in the five companies that did not mutiny might have been dissuaded from participating by their officers or were less fertile ground for the mutiny's organizers. Captain Fox apparently defused outright mutiny in Company D by meeting with his men on November 9 after hearing rumblings of a refusal to obey orders. He noted in his diary, "After talking to them, showing the affect of such a course, all agreed to go forward in the discharge of their duties." No man from his company mutinied on the tenth. Many, and perhaps the majority, of the men in Companies C and H had already accepted infantry pay as far back as March, signaling a willingness to be patient on the whole matter, and companies A and K had generally been the least contentious on the issue.[13]

The names of the mutineers have been preserved. Some of them, like Franklin Estabrook and at least four others, had been reduced to the ranks in April and were already identified with the agitation over pay. Many others, however, are absent from earlier accounts of trouble.[14]

One of the best measures of the commitment of these men to serve their country once the pay issue was resolved is their subsequent records within the regiment. Three were later commissioned as officers and thirty-one promoted to noncommissioned status before the end of the war. Eleven reenlisted when given the chance a year later, while only two of the mutineers later deserted according to regimental records. Eleven eventually died in the service, were discharged by the surgeons, or were transferred to the Invalid Corps or Veteran Reserve Corps. The balance served out their three-year terms without further incident.[15]

Faced with outright mutiny and the loss of a large portion of his regiment's effective force, an exasperated Innes sent a lengthy letter to General McCook on November 11, recounting the regiment's important service and problems with pay. In closing, Innes put it clearly to the general: "Some permanent disposition [must] be made of the regiment, either put upon a firm basis or disbanded." After over a year of trying to resolve the situation, Innes seemed resigned to the possibility that his command would be disbanded. Final resolution, however, would have to wait yet longer. Despite the grumbling in the ranks and even outright mutiny, the army needed the regiment, even if it was not willing to pay it.[16]

Meanwhile, the work continued by those who were not under arrest. By November 11 trains were running from Louisville to as far south as the blocked tunnel near Gallatin. Two weeks later full through service to Nashville was restored. During those two weeks, the Michigan Engineers rebuilt several bridges constructed by the regiment just two months earlier but destroyed by Confederates during the recent campaign. These included bridges over Manscoe's Creek, Station Camp Creek, and South Drake's Creek. When they were finished, the men returned to camp at Edgefield on November 19.[17]

Though the regiment was in camp at Edgefield only three days, there again was considerable excitement about the pay question. On the twentieth some of the men refused to work and then tied up the orderly sergeant of Company F and locked the camp guard in the guardhouse. The next day Innes had a telegram from the secretary of war read to each company. The telegram was directed to Rosecrans and ordered that the men receive engineer pay in compliance with the War Department's General Order No. 177. On the twenty-second the men of the regiment planned to refuse when ordered to march. Innes swore all would be shot for mutiny if they did not, scaring all but about twenty-five from Companies A and H. Doubting Innes would keep his threat, these men expected to join the others in Nashville confinement. Instead, they were arrested and made to march with full knapsacks. Upon arrival in camp, they were made to police the new camp and all reduced to second-class privates. On the twenty-fifth they were taken before Lieutenant Colonel Hunton, regimental provost marshal, made to take the oath of allegiance, and then were sent back to their companies for regular duties.[18]

On the twenty-second the regiment marched six miles southeast on the Murfreesboro Pike with orders to repair the Mill Creek No. 2 Bridge on the Nashville and Chattanooga Railroad. Mill Creek ran roughly parallel to both the Nashville and Chattanooga and the Murfreesboro Pike before joining the Cumberland River east of Nashville. There were three Nashville and Chattanooga bridges across Mill Creek within nine miles of Nashville. The No. 2 Bridge was a 260-foot span located six miles from Nashville. The men were at work by the twenty-third and completed the bridge on the morning of the twenty-fifth. While at Mill Creek No. 2 the engineers also cut and prepared five hundred railroad ties for use on the nearby line. For most of the next month the regiment remained in camp along the pike a few miles southeast of Nashville and near the Mill Creek crossings.[19]

Most important to the men, they were mustered for pay as engineers on December 1 for pay due through August 31, signed the pay rolls, and then finally received the long-awaited money on the eighth. In accordance with the act of Congress, the first-class privates ("artificers") received seventeen dollars per month, while the other privates received thirteen dollars per month. Noncommissioned officers and officers were also paid at the higher engineer rate, which amounted to a difference of ten to fifteen dollars per month. One soldier wrote home, "There was a great rejoicing here yesterday . . . [and] the regiment is satisfied. There was lots of whiskey close by and you can guess whether there was a merry lot of boys or not." Another noted that "the boys seem pretty well satisfied and some of them manifested their satisfaction by partaking of something for the stomach's sake or some other sake."[20]

The men were also better fed than they had been in months because of the close proximity to Nashville and the rich agricultural resources of the area. The men "liberated" foodstuffs regularly, since foraging was now the army's policy, as outlined by Rosecrans in General Order No. 17. It regulated and organized the practice of taking food and forage from civilians, even going so far as to require that payment be made or receipt be left with loyal citizens, while those whose loyalty was even in doubt were to receive a notice that the question of reimbursement would be "settled hereafter in such manner as the government may direct."[21]

This foraging was risky. On November 24 Pvts. Amos Buck, Nathaniel Birdsall, and Alonzo Van Horn of Company C left camp unarmed and were captured only a mile away while foraging for chicken and potatoes. They were taken under guard to Gen. John Morgan's headquarters, where they were paroled and sent back. They returned to their camp the following day. The three men from Hastings were immediately placed under arrest by Innes in accordance with standing orders from Rosecrans but eventually sent back to parole camp.[22]

Two days after the incident, Innes issued an order that repeated the highlights of Rosecrans's directive that men who were captured and paroled while straggling or foraging would be arrested and tried for desertion. This problem was so widespread in the army that on November 14 Rosecrans's headquarters issued General Order No. 15, which deplored that "many soldiers have sought and allowed themselves to be captured and paroled by the enemy to escape from further military duty, and in order to be sent home."[23]

To keep the men busy and improve upon the regiment's performance, the officers drilled the men almost daily. For most, this was the first time in almost a year that drill was a regular part of the day's prescribed routine. In particular, company commanders were ordered to drill the new recruits for two hours each day and reminded that this was "imperative" and that no recruits would be excused unless released for guard duty or by the surgeon. The recruits were not the only ones who had trouble with drill: Isaac Roseberry noted sarcastically that "we done such fine drilling the other day our officers was ashamed to go out again." The men still had plenty of time to read the newspapers and novelettes that were readily available, play cards, and discuss the latest from home with comrades.[24]

The mutineers remained confined in Nashville throughout December, and the remainder of the regiment followed their plight with sympathetic interest. The first of the mutineers were brought before a general court-martial on November 24, with the men tried one company at a time. The trial was finished by early December, and the men waited for word of their sentence. Lieutenant White of Company F visited the confined men from his company and wrote Captain Sligh, "I saw some of them yesterday and they look rather down hearted and I think they are sorry that they took such a course, but I think it will be likely to teach them a lesson and for the future, let well enough alone."[25]

Back in Michigan, newspapers called for their release. In addition to a lengthy recounting of the entire controversy from the initial promises at Camp Owen to the subsequent attempts to pay the men infantry wages, the *Detroit Free Press* demanded that justice be "done to these men who are now confined in a loathsome dungeon. If they were deceived and defrauded in their enlistment, they are entitled to redress; if not, and they have actually performed the duty they intended to perform, they are entitled to their pay . . . and at this late day, because these soldiers insist upon pay according to the contract, they are seized and thrown into prison, and treated worse than felons."[26]

Several of the men were too sick to stand trial and were returned at Innes's request for judgment by the regimental provost marshal. At least seven others were acquitted of the charges and returned to the regiment. Four of them were in Company F, and one had apparently been arrested for being abusive to one of the company's noncommissioned officers during the mutiny incident.[27]

Most of the arrested men, however, were convicted and sentenced to thirty days of hard labor without pay. They were also limited to a diet of bread and water for three days. Those who had been noncommissioned officers were demoted or reduced to the ranks. They were put to work on the fortifications beginning December 31, though a few men refused any further labor on January 4 and were sent to the jail. Most of the mutineers were returned to Innes's control on February 1 and rejoined their companies working along the Nashville and Chattanooga Railroad. Upon their arrival in camp, many of the mutineers were promoted back to the noncommissioned positions they had held before the mutiny.[28]

The mutineers were confined in the Nashville Workhouse during the trial and subsequent punishment. This building was a "long brick shed on the river bluff, with a leaky roof, and a bare, muddy floor." Ventilation was poor, and the few fires were fueled by green or wet wood, which filled the area with a dense smoke leading to labeling of the building among the inmates as the "smokehouse." The confined engineers were given meager rations and were forced, ironically, to supplement them with purchases out of their own nearly empty pockets. While his men were confined, Innes was accused of withholding the mail of the mutineers, a charge that he hotly denied in a letter to the family of one.[29]

One of the ringleaders managed to evade Innes's grasp. Franklin Estabrook had been one of the organizers of pay disturbances dating back to March in Nashville. His letter to a brother was a key in General Smith's investigation the previous June. While awaiting trial for the November mutiny, Estabrook managed to get transferred to special duty, but the order was quickly rescinded, probably at the insistence of an angry Innes. Estabrook was then deemed by surgeons as too sick to be tried with the others, and Innes was still trying to get his hands on him in February. He remained accounted for as absent sick at Nashville until at least the end of May 1863.[30]

Rosecrans, under pressure from Lincoln and Halleck to engage Bragg's force near Murfreesboro, had his command moving by December 26. Innes and his men remained in the army's rear to repair the rail line running south from Nashville. The men enjoyed a pleasant Christmas Day in camp, a last day of peaceful rest. On the twenty-sixth, while the regiment prepared to move, Hunton and Captains Fox, Hannings, and Crittenton rode three miles south to inspect another railroad bridge over Mill Creek that had to be rebuilt, probably Mill Creek No. 3 near Antioch Church.[31]

The men were up early the following morning, marched the three miles to the bridge, and began work. A detail moved camp the three miles to join them at the bridge site. That night, however, Innes received new orders from Rosecrans. His men were to leave the bridge repair to civilian crews and move to the front immediately.[32]

In the morning the engineers marched west about seven miles to the Nolensville Pike. The double-arched stone pike bridge across Mill Creek had been destroyed by Confederates using picks and had to be repaired if troops and supplies could move forward to support Rosecrans's army. The nearby ford was now nearly impassable because of the heavy rains, leaving many of the wagons of General Thomas's command separated from his men. Work continued through the day, and that night Hunton and four companies remained while Innes took the balance of the regiment back to continue work on the railroad bridge. Work continued at Mill Creek until the bridge was completed on the afternoon of the twenty-ninth. Hunton and the four companies marched back to rejoin the regiment near Antioch Church.[33]

On the morning of the thirtieth the regiment was at work early getting out railroad ties and repairing the bridge. Innes, who had gone back to Nashville, returned to camp at 10 A.M. with the alarming news that twenty-five hundred Confederate cavalry under Confederate Brig. Gen. Joseph Wheeler were loose in the area. Innes ordered the regiment's wagons to be formed into a hollow square. Additional pickets were thrown out around the position, and the men who could sleep that night did so clasping their guns.[34]

That same day, Rosecrans's army was getting into position opposite Bragg's a few miles north of Murfreesboro. Both commanders were trying to consolidate their forces for an attack against the opponent's right flank, and both expected to launch their attacks on the morning of the thirty-first. Meanwhile, Confederate and Union troopers were engaged in a swirl of mounted clashes in the rear of Rosecrans's line, with the Union wagon trains on the Nashville to Murfreesboro Pike as the targets of attack and defense. Scattered units like the Michigan Engineers were being used to reinforce hard-pressed Brig. Gen. David M. Stanley's Union troopers and protect Rosecrans's line of supply from Nashville along the pike.

· 10 ·

The Fight at Lavergne

O n the last day of 1862, Gen. Braxton Bragg's left hook struck Gen. William Rosecrans's line before the planned Union attack could be launched. Confederate brigades swept parts of several divisions before them, driving back the right flank of the Union line almost ninety degrees until it was fighting for its life astride the Nashville-Murfreesboro Pike and the Stones River. Though badly bent, the Union line held. That night Bragg expected that the Army of the Cumberland would be retreating along the Nashville-Murfreesboro Pike. If it were to remain it would have to be supplied from Nashville. Whichever choice Rosecrans made, the pike between Nashville and Murfreesboro was critical for the survival of the Army of the Cumberland. Bragg ordered General Wheeler to wreak havoc along this narrow corridor with his cavalry.

In response to Wheeler's first raid on the pike on December 30, Colonel Innes had received orders from Rosecrans to move his command from Mill Creek No. 3 and take up position astride the Murfreesboro Pike to protect the wagon trains. The men were up at 5 A.M. on the thirty-first and marching by 7 A.M. The marching men reached Lavergne late in the morning, while the wagons arrived later, having had to take a longer route.[1]

The men were discouraged by what they found at Lavergne. One reported that they were met by "throngs of officers and soldiers, panic stricken and wounded, all hastening back to Nashville or some other place of safety" from the battle raging south of them. There were also the still-smoking remains of several hundred wagons destroyed by Wheeler near Lavergne on the thirtieth, and the village itself was a smoldering ruin. Innes attempted to bring order out of the chaos. He put guards on the roads, allowing none except the wounded to pass. The Michigan Engineers threatened stragglers with arrest or worse, while others were compelled to reform by appeals to their sense of duty or shame. This effort to stem the flow of panic continued until well after dark.[2]

The regiment camped on a small hill eight or ten rods east of the Murfreesboro Pike, about three-quarters of a mile south of the village of Lavergne and within half a mile of the railroad. Innes established his headquarters in a small cabin on the hill and took the precaution of forming the regimental wagons in an oblong semicircle covering the north and east sides of the camp. That night was a cold one since the men were not allowed to build fires as they camped under the stars and tried to sleep.[3]

On the first morning of the new year, the engineers rose and set about strengthening their position. The efforts were hastened by the arrival of a message from Lt. Col. Joseph Burke, who defended at nearby Stewart's Creek Bridge with his Tenth Ohio and whose outposts had rebuffed attacks by Wheeler's men. Burke sent word that Confederate cavalry was loose upon the pike and that he thought they were heading to Lavergne. The open half of the perimeter was strengthened with breastworks built of cedar brush and logs taken from the nearby woods. By about 12:30 P.M. the work was completed, and the men ate their dinner.[4]

To defend the position Innes had about four hundred men, most of whom were armed with old U.S. model 1842 pattern rifled-muskets. The newer rifles, of which there were about one hundred on hand, consisted primarily of Enfields and Springfields in Companies A and H. Only the Perryville veterans in Companies A, C, and H had ever been under concentrated enemy fire, and about one quarter of Innes's force were new recruits who had been in the service less than four months.[5]

Among the senior officers, Colonel Innes and Lieutenant Colonel Hunton were both present, as were Captains Yates, Grant, Fox, Hannings, Crittenton, and perhaps Lane. Captain Coffinberry had resigned his command of Company C days earlier but was still with the regiment and fought alongside his men. Asst. Surgeon Willoughby O'Donoughue was the only one of the regiment's medical officers present for the fight.[6]

As the men labored to strengthen their position, Union wagons slowly lumbered past, moving northward along the pike en route to Nashville. The first wagon train to pass at dawn contained hundreds of wounded soldiers and reached Nashville safely. A second, passing several hours later, included more wounded carried in ambulances and empty ammunition wagons returning to Nashville. Col. Lewis Zahm was in command of the escort and had his own Third Ohio and the Fifteenth Pennsylvania cavalry regiments. A small train of about thirty wagons trailed Zahm's with a small escort drawn from the Second Tennessee (U.S.) Cavalry and the Twenty-second Indiana Infantry. By early afternoon Zahm's force was resting at Lavergne, while the smaller one was still south of that point along the pike near the engineers' position. When his scouts detected Wheeler's approach, Zahm put his wagon train in motion and formed his command into a line of battle. As he arrived on the scene, Wheeler saw the small wagon train approaching Lavergne and sent Brig. Gen. John A. Wharton's brigade to destroy it, while he moved against Zahm farther north along the pike with his own brigade and one commanded by Brig. Gen. Abram Buford.[7]

Innes had put out picket posts around his position to give warning of approaching rebel cavalry. One such picket was a mounted patrol consisting of Capt. Marcus Grant, Sgt. Albert Vandewarker, and Pvts. Joe Hawkins and William H. Kimball on borrowed horses. They had gone only about half a mile when they heard Wheeler's command open fire on Zahm and saw Wharton's mounted men charging down upon the small wagon train. Grant's small patrol was in danger between the charging cavalry and hapless wagons, so they put spurs to horse and raced back to the safety of the regiment.[8]

Lt. James D. Robinson of Company C commanded another of these picket posts. They were cut off by the Confederate attack. Robinson was able to rejoin the regiment after the fighting had ended, having gathered up stragglers as reinforcements for the position. He also captured an enemy horse, complete with saddlebags and a full Confederate uniform.[9]

Innes heard the same firing from the north to his rear and ordered the companies to take their assigned positions around the perimeter of the barricade. Young Edwin Winters and the other drummer boys beat the long roll as the men grabbed their rifles and sprang to man the defenses. In the distance, Wharton's troopers, "dashing at full speed and yelling like blood hounds," tore into the small train, scattering it. Most of the train guards discharged their guns and fled, outpaced only by the hastily mounted teamsters. The wagons were left to the Confederates, who quickly set the entire train of about thirty wagons ablaze. Some of the men from the train apparently sought safety within Innes's lines and augmented his small force.[10]

The rout of the train guard and destruction of the wagons gave the engineers a few more minutes to prepare for the onslaught. The engineers did not open fire until a company of enemy cavalry rode over toward their position from the northwest, assuming Innes's position to be a small party of teamsters with their wagons. A full volley from Companies A and H drove the small force from the field. With the volley and hasty retreat of the cavalry company, the full attention of Wharton's entire force was brought to bear on the engineers.

Wharton formed a mounted line of at least one full regiment and threw them in an assault on the engineers' position. Again the engineers held their fire until the troopers were close and then let loose a destructive fire, emptying several saddles. The Confederate cavalry made a hasty retreat.[11]

For the next three hours, Wharton's command tried to dislodge the Michigan Engineers. Through it all, Lt. Arthur Pue Jr.'s two-gun section of Capt. B. F. White's Tennessee Battery fired into Innes's position from an elevated position too distant for return fire from the muskets and rifles of Innes's command. Small parties of rebel sharpshooters kept up a steady fire from their positions behind trees and buildings within range of the engineers. The Confederates' deliberate discharges kept a "constant fire whizzing about [their] heads," according to Captain Fox.[12]

There were several more separate charges by Wharton's cavalry, both mounted and on foot. At least one was a coordinated effort by the Fourteenth Alabama Battalion and the First (John Cox's) Confederate and Fourth (John Murray's) Tennessee regiments, attacking simultaneously from the east, north, and south. Pressed from three sides, Innes shifted Company K from its position on the west side to cover the southwest corner. Among those shifted was William L. Clark, who penned the following account of the desperate Confederate charge: "Forming behind the woods, they charged up handsomely along the road, and through the woods on the southwest corner. The main force came plunging up on the left of the company, discharging their pieces and wheeling to the left when they found our defenses so good they could not gallop their horses over them. They were an excellent mark for every musket, rifle, and revolver loaded in the company."[13]

It was during this charge that one Confederate spurred his horse through the hail of lead right up to the cedar brush wall. He deliberated aimed his carbine at Innes and demanded his surrender but was quickly shot down by Lt. Cyrus M. Curtis of Company E. The brave Confederate trooper's body was dragged away some distance by his panicked horse before tumbling to the ground. Innes's conduct under fire was described as cool and reassuring. He walked along the line, lending encouraging words and directing his men's fire.[14]

Each time Wharton sent his men forward to assault the barricades, Innes's men emerged from cover and let loose volleys of lead, driving back the rebel cavalry. Between charges, the embattled engineers remained under cover. Shells exploded among the wagons, destroying or damaging six and scattering pieces of metal and wood around the position. Of the nine men wounded, at least five were struck in the legs or feet, suggesting that they were hit while they manned the barricade and wagons from a prone position. Another, Pvt. Isaac Clifton of Company D, was fortunate that the solid shot or piece of shrapnel that hit him in the shoulder was spent, or he would not have survived. The regiment's horses and mules remained exposed in the middle of the position during the fight, and over forty were killed by enemy fire.[15]

While the shells burst overhead and among the wagons, dismounted Confederates tried to pick off the men under the wagons and behind the cedar barricade. Captain Grant narrowly escaped serious injury when a bullet hit the tree trunk he was aiming from behind, spraying his face with splinters and bark. His eyes wiped clean by the surgeon, he returned and eventually killed the sharpshooter. Pvt. Josiah Easton persisted in sticking his head above the breastwork and was fortunate to receive only a slight wound from the rifle bullet that grazed his skull. Charles Mingo, an excellent shot from Company A, stood in the open as he slowly and deliberately fired his rifle at Confederates who broke from behind cover. His bravado cost him his life; he was mortally wounded after nearly an hour of exposure.[16]

Frustrated Confederates tried various tricks to take the position. A party of rebels, dressed in captured Union overcoats, ran up on one side of the position, pleading for the men not to shoot, that they were friends. Given away by the gray pants they wore and the alertness of the engineers, the men were driven back by musket fire. Another dismounted company tried to sneak up on Company D's position on the south wall by using the stumps and fallen trees as cover. They were driven back by a well-delivered volley.[17]

At one point while under fire, Yates with one wing of the regiment prepared to rush the Confederate artillery, while the remainder of the regiment held the barricade. Realizing how outnumbered they were, the "wild scheme was abandoned as probably every man would have been killed or captured," in the words of one relieved member of the intended storming party.[18]

A colorful account of the fighting was later written for publication: "The scene was at times thrilling beyond description. The rebel horde, exasperated at the successful resistance of the little force, dashed their horses against the circular brush fence, which was only breast high, with infuriated shouts and curses. The Michigan troops were cool and determined; they loaded fast and aimed well and, as the troopers rushed on upon all sides, they were met with staggering volleys almost at the muzzle of the muskets. Horses and riders recoiled again and again until they despaired, and soon swept away through the dense forests."[19]

Hot as it was within the barricade, the Michigan Engineers outside were in the most precarious position. A small group of four new soldiers from Company C were among those sent out at daybreak on picket duty. They took position as ordered, probably southeast of Innes's position and were still there when they heard guns firing. Two of the detail crept forward and soon returned on the run with news that the regiment was under attack by rebel cavalry between them and the regiment. The men tried to get back to the regiment's position, but the bullets were flying too thick, and they were forced to take cover in some bushes. For the next three hours the men remained cut off. During one of the charges Pvt. Mathias Reiser received a slight gunshot wound in the flesh of the thigh from a lone Confederate who spotted their hiding place. After the fighting ended, the Confederates moved back through the wood where the men were hiding, forcing them to lay flat on their bellies while enemy soldiers passed within fifty steps. By 10 P.M. Pvt. John Weissert ventured to a nearby hill from where he could see the engineers' position. Returning to the woods, he convinced the men to leave their cover, and shortly they met other members of the regiment on picket duty.[20]

Not all of the men outside the barricade were able to avoid capture. Pvts. Andrew Wright and John Stanton had been sent out with an ambulance to gather forage and had gone out only a short distance when they were swept up by Wharton's men. Edgar Schermerhorn of Company A was taken prisoner while on picket duty, and at least two more probably were as well. Six men in Company H outside of the barricade took off for the woods to avoid being captured, but at least two were caught and taken south.[21]

While the fighting was in progress, Innes sent messengers scrambling to nearby Union forces, seeking reinforcements. At that time there were few Union forces within supporting distance. Zahm had part of his cavalry brigade north of Lavergne but was fighting a withdrawing action along the pike to protect his convoy of wagons and did not reach Nashville until 9 P.M. Colonel Burke and eight companies of the Tenth Ohio were still at Stewart's Creek, along with four companies of the Fourth Michigan Cavalry under Lt. Col. William H. Dickinson and a section of Battery D, First Ohio Light Artillery, under Lt. Nathaniel M. Newell. The Ohio infantrymen were veterans with an enviable combat record, currently serving as the army's provost guard. Up until now Burke's main problem was not the raiding Confederates, who had only brushed against his pickets, but the hundreds of panicked Union soldiers and teamsters driven from the Union right flank who were still streaming to the rear. Despite his own exposed position, Burke sent the troopers and guns under Dickinson and Newell to Lavergne when he first received word from Innes that he was under attack.[22]

Dickinson and his command moved north but stopped when they came into contact with some of Wharton's men, well short of Innes's barricade. Soon after, a small party Innes had sent, including two of his officers and "volunteer aide" Thomas Riley met Dickinson. The three implored Dickinson to come to their regiment's aid, but he refused. Other officers of the Fourth also begged Dickinson to move to the assistance of their fellow Wolverines, or let them take the men forward, but still he refused. Instead, he turned his command around and headed back to Stewart's Creek.[23]

Two hours after Dickinson left Stewart's Creek, Thomas Riley arrived at Burke's headquarters with the astonishing information that Dickinson and his men were on their way back to Stewart's Creek, having given up reaching Innes. Intent on saving Innes, and the trains that he believed were still near Lavergne, Burke set out with his regiment on a rapid march to where the hard-pressed engineers were still under fire. He left behind a hastily formed regiment of stragglers and casuals to guard the bridge. Strengthened by Dickinson's cavalry and artillery that he met en route, Burke and his column pressed on toward Lavergne and Innes's command.[24]

Back near Lavergne, the frustrated Wharton decided to try a new tactic at about 5 P.M. "Finding they could not dislodge us, they attempted to frighten us," reported one engineer. Lt. E. Spruel Burford, assistant adjutant general for Wheeler's corps, carried a flag of truce to Innes's position. Burford conveyed Wharton's demand for an immediate surrender and a claim that because large reinforcements were available to his command any further struggle was hopeless. Captain Grant represented Innes in the discussion with Burford. He conveyed Wharton's message to Innes, who refused the demand, declaring to Burford, "We don't surrender much." Shortly after Innes's refusal, Wharton sent in another flag of truce carried by another orderly asking for a truce to allow him to bury the dead and collect and aid the wounded. Innes answered that he would take care of any dead or wounded found within his men's range of fire and that any more flags of truce would be fired upon. At this point Wharton gave up and pulled his command back.[25]

Burke reached the scene with his tired men at about 7 P.M., after Wharton had withdrawn the bulk of his command but in time to drive off a few small parties of Confederate stragglers. What Burke found was a sea of chaos: wagons destroyed and in smoking ruins, team horses running wild, and small parties of teamsters hiding in the nearby woods. Also amid the chaos and confusion were Innes and his victorious regiment, firmly in position behind their barricade of wagons and brush.[26]

That night the engineers remained in their position, with Burke's force camped alongside. During the night more Union stragglers joined the command. Many of Innes's men who had been separated while on picket duty came into camp. Captain Grant and a small party found several Union wounded in a nearby house and brought them back to the camp.[27]

The next day was spent strengthening their position, hauling off the dead horses and mules, and burying dead Confederates. Over forty government horses and mules were killed during the fight and needed burial, as did the dead private horses of the regimental officers. The wounded engineers were sent back toward Nashville, joining the thousands already there. The men kept close to their guns throughout the day, especially after four companies of the Tenth Ohio and most of Dickinson's cavalry returned to Stewart's Creek. Burke remained with the balance of his regiment, Newell's section, and one company of the Michigan cavalry to provide reinforcements for Innes's men. All day the Union troops at Lavergne heard the heavy firing near Murfreesboro as Bragg tried unsuccessfully to drive in Rosecrans's left flank on the east bank of the Stones River. At the close of the day, the battle along the Stones River came to an end with over twenty thousand men fallen.[28]

On a rainy January 3 the two exhausted armies remained opposite each other near Murfreesboro. The same rain fell on the men at Lavergne, who remained vigilant, their weapons near them. A small detachment was sent out to repair a bridge one and one-half miles back on the pike, while others were assigned the task of burning the buildings that had sheltered Confederate sharpshooters during the fight. Wheeler attacked a large wagon train with supplies for Rosecrans at Cox's Hill, just a few miles north of Lavergne. About noon the alarm was sounded in the Michigan Engineer camp, and men came running from where they were clearing the fields of fire and scouting for Confederate cavalry. The Ninth Michigan was guarding a wagon train that was arriving in Lavergne at the same time and took position alongside the engineers for an hour. For the next three days the regiment remained vigilant while continuing work.[29]

It had been a hard fight at Lavergne but not a decisive one. The engineers failed to save any wagons. Despite later claims, they didn't save any great amount of supplies at Lavergne either. They were caught up in the fighting only because they were attacked. Losses were a mere handful among the regiment compared with the bloody fight just a few miles south of them. Yet, amid the slaughter at Fredericksburg and the near disaster at Murfreesboro, the sharp fight at Lavergne stood out as a tremendous victory all out of proportion to the numbers engaged or the results achieved. It became the single incident most associated with Innes and the Michigan Engineers.[30]

Almost immediately, Lavergne was hailed as a great victory. Within days, the *Detroit Free Press* provided an early account in large type: "The Michigan Engineers and Mechanics Attacked by Two Rebel Brigades. THE REBELS REPULSED AFTER A FIGHT OF FOUR HOURS." Within months Rosecrans was using Innes's defense at Lavergne as a measuring stick against which other Union commanders in similar situations should be judged. Early book accounts took up the same theme.[31]

There was even a poem written about the fight, "War Song: Battle of Lavergne." Its author is unknown, but the poem was in circulation within the regiment in printed form by the fall of 1864. It ends with the challenge:

Our soldiers proved themselves heroes, who battled at Lavergne,
Their valor on that bloody day, our Country's praise did earn,
And if again we meet the foe, we'll whip them as before,
And battle for our glorious cause, and make secesh give o'er.[32]

Writing shortly after the war, New York newspaperman Horace Greeley evaluated the army's poor performance in the rear along the Nashville Pike during the battle at Stones River and concluded, "The silver lining to this cloud is a most gallant defense made on the 1st by Colonel Innes's 1st Michigan Engineers and Mechanics."[33]

Part of the reason for the fight's prominent treatment was the simple fact that outnumbered Union infantry had actually stood up to and defeated Confederate cavalry. Colonel Morgan and Generals Forrest and Wheeler had struck the flanks and rear of Union troops all across the western theater for almost a year with near impunity. Even though Wheeler was not present at the fight, it was his command, and in the minds of many, the Michigan Engineers had beaten the vaunted Wheeler. Since many accounts also erroneously attributed a ten-to-one strength advantage to the Confederates, the victory seemed especially noteworthy.[34]

Most significantly, the battle came during a low point for Union hopes for victory. The senseless slaughter at Fredericksburg two weeks earlier had shaken the nation, creating "a moral crisis in the army and on the home front." The fate of Rosecrans's army near Murfreesboro was in doubt for several days while the nation waited for accurate and final reports. When they did learn the truth, it was clear that another Union army in the West had been surprised and driven back, surviving only through desperate and costly fighting. In this context, the noble stand at Lavergne loomed as a glorious victory.[35]

In very real terms, Lavergne was a great victory for the regiment. During the three hours of fighting at Lavergne, several regimental ghosts had been buried. The question of whether they would fight had been answered in the affirmative. On January 11 Innes issued General Order No. 4, which complimented the men for their coolness and valor and declared, "You have all been tried and not found wanting."[36]

Innes himself had been tested and passed. Eight months previous he had been fighting to keep his rank and command. Just two months prior he had almost resigned himself to the fact that his regiment was to be dismantled and his commission vacated. Only six weeks before over one hundred men of his command had mutinied and were still in jail at the time of the fight. It would be difficult to imagine a more difficult position to be in as a regimental commander. Innes, however, not only survived the fight with his commission and reputation intact, he was heralded as a hero. After the fighting ended, officers and men of the regiment, led by Lt. Charles T. Wooding, picked up Innes and carried him around the camp on their shoulders, shouting his response to Wharton that "we don't surrender much."[37]

The victory had its cost. John Coykendall of Company D died of a gunshot through his heart. Charles Mingo and Mathias Reiser died of their wounds, and at least four more were seriously wounded and discharged from the army. Six more were carried south to rebel prisons. Since his men were attacking an entrenched opponent, Wharton's toll was greater. Without providing details, Wharton admitted in his report that the loss "in officers and men was very considerable." Based on the various counts, the best estimate is that Wharton lost at least fifty men killed, wounded, or captured.[38]

The human toll among the engineers is evident in the letters written home by Reiser's friend and fellow recruit, John Weissert. He first reported to his wife that Reiser's wound was slight and continued to reassure her that it was only a harmless flesh wound. It was not until two weeks after Reiser's death that word reached Company C: "Yesterday I received a letter. . . . It contained very sad news. I can hardly believe that it should be possible that Reiser died. . . . I cannot help feeling terribly sorry for him. He had such a good faithful soul. There was not a single person in our company who did not love him. I can imagine what a severe blow this is for his relatives."[39]

The men in Innes's regiment were proud of the victory and zealous to guard its memory. Soon after the fighting ended at Lavergne, some confused news reports gave the credit to other units or mentioned the engineers only in passing. The proud veterans of the fight were quick to respond. Albert Graves wrote his wife to set the record straight: "I believe some of the papers state that the 10th Ohio assisted us in the fight. Now the facts are we fought the battle alone." Another declared in a letter to the *Detroit Free Press* that "the regiment received no reinforcements until after the rebels had left, the *Cincinnati Commercial* [account] to the contrary, notwithstanding." Edwin Winters's postwar account concluded, "Of course, Colonel Burke was not responsible for the obscuration of the facts but others were, including some newspaper correspondents."[40]

The men also were quick to share their opinions of Dickinson and the lack of support the engineers received from their fellow Wolverines. James M. Sligh wrote home shortly after the battle, "Lieutenant Colonel Dickinson of the 4th Mich. cavalry is the meanest coward in the service [by refusing to come to the engineers' aid] and is branded as such." Innes complained to Col. Robert Minty, commanding both the Fourth Michigan Cavalry and the brigade it was attached to, that Dickinson had refused to come to the aid of the engineers, despite the entreaties of Innes's messengers and officers of Dickinson's own regiment. Dickinson resigned six weeks later upon a surgeon's certificate of disability, though it is possible his departure was not entirely voluntary given the controversy.[41]

This strong criticism of Dickinson was in stark contrast to the high praise given to Burke and his Ohio men by the grateful engineers. Innes wrote Rosecrans, "Although he [Burke] did not arrive until the enemy had fled, too much credit cannot be given that gallant officer for his promptness in coming to my aid, which he did on double-quick." Rosecrans singled out both Innes and Burke for special praise in his official report of the campaign. The army's commander wrote, "The First Regiment of Michigan Engineers and Mechanics . . . fighting behind a slight protections of wagons and brush, gallantly repulsed a charge from more than ten times their number." He also praised the "ability and spirit" with which Burke and his Ohio men performed several valuable services in the army's rear.[42]

· 11 ·

Filling Vacant Ranks

There was a manpower pattern for most Union regiments. They were originally enlisted to the strength of around one thousand, which dropped quickly once they reached the field of operations and disease and battle took their toll. Instead of filling these regiments back up, most states recruited new ones and sent them off to war. The recruits who did arrive at the old regiments were often unwilling draftees or men consolidated from other understrength units. The Michigan Engineers, however, continued to successfully recruit throughout the war. This experience provides a window into the evolution of U.S. Army manpower efforts from the heady days of 1861 to the end of the war.

On January 28, 1862, worried regimental adjutant Clement Miller reported to Governor Blair that "our last monthly return shows a deficiency of six men in our regiment and we are anxious to keep it full." Within months any company, let alone a regiment, that was missing only six of the original men would be considered fortunate indeed. By June 30, 1863, much had changed. More than three hundred new recruits were among the ranks of the enlisted men, only one-third of the commissioned officers held the same position as at Camp Owen, and only four companies retained their original captain. The success of these changes and the recruitment effort were important for the continued success of the regiment.[1]

After August 1861 state governors had the sole authority to issue all volunteer commissions in the companies and regiments raised by their respective states. To replace vacancies among the regimental officers, Colonel Innes suggested individuals to Governor Blair, who usually complied and issued the appropriate commission. These vacancies were generally filled by promotion from within the regiment, though a small number of replacement commissions were issued to civilians.

The first company commander to leave was Capt. Baker Borden, who resigned effective February 23, 1862, for health reasons, probably the same long-term affliction with severe hemorrhoids that had led to his resignation from the Third Michigan the previous summer. The reaction was mixed. Captain Sligh wrote his wife that Innes and others thought Borden's resignation had more to do with fear than anything else. A member of Company E wrote home that Borden resigned over the way the pay issue had been handled. A member of Borden's own company noted that the men "regret[ed] his loss like that of a father for he is a model captain."[2]

Instead of promoting popular 1st Lt. John "Jack" Williamson, Innes decided to go outside the regiment and select engineer George M. Lane of Detroit to lead the company. Lane was an 1853 engineering graduate of the University of Michigan and an experienced railroad surveyor and civil engineer. He had directed the laying of railroad track from Pontiac to Owosso for what became the Detroit and Milwaukee Railroad and knew Innes from this work.[3]

Silas Canfield was the second of the original captains to leave the regiment. His resignation was submitted in April, and Innes urged General Buell to accept it "for the good of the service." His health recovered, Canfield withdrew it soon after but had a change of heart when his wife arrived in camp in July, destitute from a fire that consumed their home and possessions. His resignation was accepted July 14, 1862, and he started for Michigan three days later. Command of the company was given over to Lucius F. Mills, senior lieutenant. An Ionia County miller before the war, Mills had helped Canfield recruit the original company.[4]

In May 1862 Colonel Innes, Lieutenant Colonel Hunton, and Major Hopkins asked Governor Blair to remove Heman Palmerlee from his position commanding Company I. Though not specific, they wrote, "We do not consider him competent for the position he occupies." Innes sent two more letters to Blair in June, urging speedy approval of the request. Palmerlee's place as commander of Company I was taken by Lt. Joseph J. Rhodes, who had recruited much of the original company and was acquainted with Innes and several of the other officers before the war.[5]

Wright Coffinberry was the final original company commander to leave during the first eighteen months in the field. He was one of the most popular officers, and his departure was greeted with genuine regret. Innes told Coffinberry, "Your conduct has always been that becoming a true officer of the army and in departing you may rest assured you carry the best wishes of all and I am truly sorry to lose from my command your valuable service." Despite the fact that his resignation had been accepted effective December 26, 1862, Coffinberry remained with the regiment during the Stones River campaign and led his Company C at Lavergne before leaving for Michigan.[6]

On paper the new commander of Company C was George D. Emerson, an experienced civil engineer from Michigan's Upper Peninsula. In reality, the appointment was made with the understanding that Emerson would remain in Michigan to recruit for the regiment's two new companies and then assume command of one when it was filled. Actual command of the company rested with 1st Lt. James D. Robinson, a stone mason from Grand Rapids. His commission as captain was eventually backdated to Coffinberry's resignation date.[7]

Quartermaster Robert S. Innes also resigned, claiming, "Business of a personal nature prevents me from continuing longer in the service without great detriment." Lieutenant Innes was apparently well liked within the regiment. His comrades marked his departure with great ceremony. Young James M. Sligh declared him "the best quartermaster in the service." Lt. Henry F. Williams was detailed from Company K as acting regimental quartermaster in Innes's absence.[8]

Though he remained on the regiment's rolls, Chaplain Tracy's active service with the Michigan Engineers ended shortly after reaching Kentucky. On January 24, 1862, Tracy was kicked and seriously injured by Major Hopkins's horse. He was permitted leave to return to Michigan, but the injury to his right leg was slow to heal. After his return from Michigan, Tracy, forced to rely on crutches to get around, was stationed at Park Barracks near Louisville, a convalescent home for soldiers. He was ordered to report to Nashville on March 21, 1863, but was found to be unfit for duty there. At the same time, however, he was able to attend to Masonic and personal business in Kentucky and Michigan. This circumstance caused one army staff officer to write sarcastically, "Light duty at any station *except* Louisville does not appear to *suit* the chaplain" (emphasis in original).[9]

Innes originally asked for a replacement chaplain but later indicated that the regiment was unwilling to lose Tracy and would wait until he regained his health. When that didn't happen, Tracy's resignation was accepted in June 1863. Later that same year he was again commissioned by Blair as chaplain in the Michigan Engineers, but poor health prevented his return to active duty, and he apparently declined the commission. The position remained unfilled through the remainder of the regiment's service.[10]

At least three line lieutenants departed under a cloud of controversy. In July 1862 2nd Lt. Frederick W. Huxford of Company A was cashiered for being drunk on duty at Elk River, Tennessee. Company F's 1st Lt. Albert H. Kimball left few friends behind, was facing questions about recruiting irregularities, and didn't settle his account with the sutler when departing. One of his men wrote, "I think it is a very small loss to the company as well as the government for I believe him to be about as perfect a scoundrel as one would wish to see."[11]

Lt. Theodore Prall's resignation for "disability" on January 30, 1863, ended almost nine months of swirling controversy. He and Innes were at odds over the handling of the pay issue, and Prall made it a public matter. Prall subsequently resigned, returned when he thought Innes was on his way out, and then resigned again. He spent much of his final months in the service absent, sick, or under arrest.[12]

Two other officers were lost without rendering much service. Company H's 2nd Lt. Edson Frary resigned on January 31, 1862, for health reasons and died three months later, and 2nd Lt. Arthur Connelly of Company K left in March 1862 because of bad health.[13]

The process of Innes asking Blair for replacement commissions was slow. On August 10, 1862, Innes sent Blair a list of commissions that he wanted issued to fill eight officer vacancies in the regiment. He sent reminders in early November and in February. Innes also included nominations for additional vacancies that had occurred since the original letter was sent. While Innes was waiting for the official commissions from Blair, the designated officers generally acted in the capacity to which Innes intended to promote them. When the commissions were received, they usually had an effective date backdated to the time the vacancy first occurred, so the officers did not lose seniority or pay over the delay.[14]

While he was waiting for the missing commissions in the fall of 1862, Innes received General Order No. 177 from the War Department, outlining the organization of volunteer engineer units. Though recognized by Congress in July, no specific direction had been provided by the War Department until this order. Volunteer engineer regiments were to be organized with twelve large companies of 150 men each, including three battalions of four companies each. In addition to the extra 800 men that would be needed to fill up this structure, the act called for additional officers to lead them. The regiment was now entitled to two additional majors, an extra first lieutenant in each company, another assistant surgeon, as well as a captain and three lieutenants in each of the two new companies.[15]

When Emerson was commissioned by Governor Blair to replace Captain Coffinberry, it was with the understanding that he would recruit and then command Company L. Emerson had spent most of the previous ten years as a civil and mine engineer in the Upper Peninsula, working on the ship locks at Sault Ste. Marie and in several of the copper mines. He joined Company L in the field shortly before its June 30, 1863, formal muster-in.[16]

Command of Company M was eventually given to Edson P. Gifford, who did much of the recruiting. The Kent County millwright and township official had enlisted as sergeant in Company D in 1861 and was sent back the following year on recruiting duty. Along the way he was commissioned as lieutenant in Company L but was never with the company in the field. He received permission to formally organize Company M on September 30, 1863, and received his commission as its captain on October 5 while in Detroit. He did not actually join his new company in the field until March 1864, following more recruiting and a furlough.[17]

The lieutenancies in the new companies were filled as men were recruited. One of the first went to Thomas G. Templeton, a prewar lumberman and machinist from Lenawee County and a veteran of Col. Josiah W. Bissell's Engineer Regiment of the West. As a recruiter for Bissell's unit, Templeton had aggressively promoted engineer units as "the most desirable branch in the service for men who had rather work than suffer the fatigue of long marches and short rations." Daniel M. Moore was a sash maker and original member of the regiment. He was sent back on recruiting duty and then issued a commission. Douglas H. Nelson was the son of a prominent Isabella County farmer and judge. He enlisted in the regiment in September 1863 as sergeant and within sixty days had a commission from Governor Blair. Young Nelson's meteoric rise within the ranks of the Michigan Engineers ended with his resignation in March 1864. Surveyor and teacher Caleb A. Ensign was a private in Battery C, First Michigan Light Artillery, and a headquarters clerk when he was discharged to accept the commission in Innes's regiment. He had also briefly been a recruiter for Col. Charles V. DeLand's First Michigan Sharpshooters in the summer of 1863.[18]

The two new majorities were more problematic for Innes. On paper, each of the three majors in a volunteer engineer regiment was to command a battalion of four companies. In practice, the regiment continued to be divided as needed, with companies detached in numbers ranging from one to six. Hopkins remained as the original major until his May 1863 resignation. At that time senior captain John B. Yates was promoted in his place. The two new majorities, however, could not be filled until the regiment completed its reorganization as a volunteer engineer regiment. Company M was finally mustered in on December 1863, and the regiment was soon after considered officially reorganized as a volunteer engineer regiment. Captains Fox and Hannings, the two next senior company commanders, were promoted to fill the new majorities in February 1864, with their commissions backdated to January 1, 1864.[19]

The additional first lieutenancies in the original companies were also filled in February 1864, with commissions backdated to January 1. All ten of the new commissions were given to men who had been at Camp Owen, nine of whom were senior sergeants at the time of commissioning. Among the new commissioned officers was Sgt. James M. Sligh.[20]

The other position added to the regiment by the reorganization as a volunteer engineer regiment was an additional assistant surgeon. Innes deferred to Blair, who commissioned Willard B. Smith of Ann Arbor, an 1861 graduate of the University of Michigan's medical school and the son of a prominent physician. Smith did not reach the regiment until January, and deteriorating health caused his resignation at the end of May 1863.[21]

In a November 19, 1862, letter to Robertson detailing the regiment's activities in the previous year, Innes closed with optimistic comments about the relations among the officers. He declared that the "utmost unanimity of feeling and action has ever prevailed between the field and staff and line officers of the regiment." Remembering that Innes had been active in dumping several of the original officers and was still trying to get rid of at least one more, it is likely, however, he did feel the regiment had an officer corps in place that would be loyal to him and serve the men well.[22]

By this time Innes's greatest concern was probably not with the officer corps but with the fact that they had a dwindling number of men to command. As early as May 30, 1862, over 140 men had been lost to the regiment through death, discharge, and transfer without fighting a single engagement. Another 280 were scattered across the army's rear areas, either too sick to serve or detailed to provide support services, and another 100 were in the regimental hospital.[23]

Much of the problem was that the scores of men who had been left behind at hospitals remained absent from the regiment for months, if they ever rejoined it. While a portion did die, the majority of men recovered, only to be swallowed by a large and inefficient army bureaucracy. Innes frequently complained to officials that men of his regiment were slow to return to the regiment once they had recovered. He even sent officers to comb rear area hospitals for members of the regiment who had been left behind sick but had recovered. Many of them were being kept by surgeons desperate for stewards and attendants and remained at the rear hospitals long after their convalescence was completed and they could no longer be considered light duty men.[24]

The Regimental Descriptive Book is full of examples of men who were left behind in hospitals in early 1862 but who had not returned to the regiment a year later. Edwin R. Osband of Company H was one of them. He was left behind sick in April 1862 and sent back to a hospital in Cincinnati the next month. By the end of the year he was at Fort Wayne in Detroit, nearly recovered and detailed as a hospital attendant. He expected to return to the regiment in early 1863 and was soon fit for active duty but was kept at the hospital to help with the care of the sick and wounded until the spring of 1864.[25]

It was even harder for Innes to fill the ranks emptied by death or discharge. Convinced that the Union armies in the field were about to achieve a total victory, Secretary of War Edwin Stanton ceased all recruiting efforts in early April 1862. He ordered recruiting officers to rejoin their regiments and even instructed them to sell off the public property in their possession. Maj. Gen. George B. McClellan's constant demands for men and the casualty lists from Shiloh overcame such naive optimism. Recruiting was restored on June 6, 1862, and federal and state authorities were back in the recruiting business. The successful state efforts of 1861, however, could not be replicated simply by order from Washington, even while the situation was made more desperate by losses of hard fighting on the Peninsula.[26]

In early July 1862 President Lincoln called upon the states for another three hundred thousand men to serve for three years, followed in August by a request for a similar number of militia to serve nine months. If a state did not meet its quota, a draft would be used to fill the ranks. Hoping to get his share of these new men, Innes dispatched a recruiting party to Michigan under the command of Captain Sligh and Lt. John W. McCrath. The group left for Michigan on August 16. Upon their arrival in Detroit, Sligh's group reported to Col. Joseph R. Smith. In turn, Smith distributed them to recruit in the areas surrounding Grand Rapids, Marshall, Flint, and Jackson.[27]

Fortunately for Sligh and his men, they arrived in Michigan at a propitious time to enlist men into existing regiments. Recruits in 1862 were now eligible for about forty dollars up front at the time of enlisting. To sweeten the pot, communities were willing to offer additional bounties to avoid having to resort to a draft to meet the local quotas. This push-pull has been described by one historian as "the rod of conscription in one hand and an open purse in another." But the offer was for a limited time since a draft was scheduled for early September. Taking advantage of this pressure, Sligh's recruiters were able to quickly enlist almost 120 men, most in just four days. The most successful efforts were in Grand Rapids, Hastings, and Flint. Recruiting soon slowed, and Sligh asked for orders in November to return to the regiment.[28]

At the same time, Innes also needed an additional eight hundred men to bring the Michigan Engineers up to regulation strength as an engineer regiment. On December 10 another recruiting party left for Michigan. Innes placed Major Hopkins in charge of this party, believing that "his intimate personal acquaintance with the Governor of the state" and being "favorably known throughout the state renders him particularly fit for the recruiting service."[29]

The recruiting party reported to Colonel Smith within days. Hopkins gave Smith a letter of introduction signed by Governor Blair that emphasized that the directive to reorganize as an engineer regiment was "really creating a new regiment, nearly doubling the number of officers and men." Given the circumstances, Blair asked that Hopkins be "allowed to recruit in such places as he may find most beneficial without much restriction." At Hopkins's request, Smith combined the two recruiting parties under the major's command and gave him authority to move the men around the state as he saw fit.[30]

New regulations governing recruiting had been published by the War Department on December 2, 1862. Although similar to earlier ones, there was a greater emphasis placed on several issues that had proved to be problems. Recruiting officers were expressly forbidden to enlist minors under eighteen without parental consent. Recruits had to be submitted to a "minute and critical" medical inspection at both the state recruiting depot and upon arrival in the field. Recruits would receive only a minimum of clothing at the local rendezvous, the balance being issued after inspection at the state's recruiting depot. At the latter, training was to be rigidly enforced until the recruits "were well drilled in the infantry tactics." A published list of thirty-one different forms accompanied the orders, which also contained a great deal of precise information on how to fill them out and account for the public money to be expended.[31]

Like Sligh's group, Hopkins and his party initially benefited from timing. With a draft scheduled for sometime in January, communities were willing to add to federal bounties in order to secure local enlistments and avoid the stigma of forcing men to serve. Within days, sixty men were enrolled, most in towns paying local bounties to men credited against the quota, but it quickly ground to a standstill once the draft threat was removed and in the face of continued Union disasters. The "moral crisis in the army and on the home front," as historian James M. McPherson has termed it, brought a near halt to a manpower machine that was already moving in increasingly shorter lurches.[32]

Many of the recruiters were sent back to regiment, and those remaining in Michigan found it difficult to fill the ranks. After late

January most of the recruiting for the Michigan Engineers was focused on filling out the two new companies. A decision had been made in the fall that instead of organizing two companies in Michigan and then taking them to the South, men would be enlisted in the regiment and sent to the field, where they would select the company they wanted to serve in. Those who opted not to join one of the original ten companies were to be assigned to fill Company L first, with Company M on hold until the former was filled. The principal recruiters were Emerson, Gifford, and Templeton, though recruits were found by ones and twos, not dozens. Through their persistence, enough men were on hand by June 30, 1863, to constitute a company (L). Company M reached the minimum size in September and was mustered in by the end of 1863.[33]

Hopkins and Sligh mixed recruiting with personal business and continued to trim down the size of the recruiting party filling the original companies. Hopkins was unable to get Colonel Smith to issue orders sending them all back to the regiment. Innes's request for orders sending them back also failed. An increasingly frustrated Hopkins left for the regiment in May without any orders and submitted his resignation to Innes. Sligh and the last of the recruiting party did not return to the regiment until July. Only those recruiting for the new companies remained in Michigan.[34]

Appendix I contains comparative information on the recruits who enlisted in the Michigan Engineers between the summers of 1862 and 1863, and they are remarkably similar to the original men. An excellent example of this point is a group enlisted at Hastings in the fall of 1862. Hastings's prewar population included about one hundred men fit for military service. In the fall of 1861, almost half of the thirty Michigan Engineers recruited in Barry County were residents of Hastings. When Lieutenant McCrath's recruiting party reached Hastings in late August 1862, they were still able to quickly enlist another twenty-seven men, at least half from the village proper. The *Hastings Banner* labeled it "recruiting extraordinary." Most of the new recruits from the village were artisans or craftsmen, and all but two were married. The close-knit group of recruits from Hastings enlisted on August 30 and traveled to Detroit, where they were mustered in on September 8. Two days later they were on a train for Louisville and eventually caught up with the regiment on the last day of September.[35]

Army authorities had a year's experience in manpower acquisition by the time these 1862 Michigan Engineer recruits were entering the system. Even though the process was improved from the chaos a year earlier, much remained to be done. The replacements should have been a healthier lot because examinations were more consistent and a smaller percentage of the replacements were over forty-five. Surgeons inspected the regiment's 1862 and 1863 recruits, and many were rejected for physical disability, but there were still heavy losses during the first year of service. One in five of these replacements were lost to death or discharge in the first twelve months of service in the field. While this was better than the nearly one in four original regimental members who were gone within the first year, the improvement was just as likely a result of fewer older recruits. In fact, replacements under the age of forty died or were disabled within the first year of service at about the same rate as original members of the regiment.[36]

Again, the Hastings contingent was fairly typical of the experiences of the 1862–63 recruits for the Michigan Engineers. They were among eighty-five men recruited by Lieutenant McCrath and his sergeants in August and September. Seven of the eighty-five men were rejected by surgeons, yet of the fifty-six who can be individually identified from regimental records, thirteen were dead or discharged before one year was up, a similar rate to that experienced by the original members. Despite an inspection process that weeded out almost 10 percent, the Hastings group contained several men who were in poor health from the time they joined the regiment. Private Weissert reported on November 24, 1862, that four of his fellow townsmen had not done a day of work since joining the regiment several weeks previous and that several more were chronically sick and frequently hospitalized.[37]

Given the better organization of the Union war effort by the end of 1862, the replacements should have arrived in the field better trained than the original men. This was certainly the intention behind various orders from the War Department calling for camps of instruction and state recruiting depots. In reality, however, the regiment's replacements spent less time in the state depot than most of the original men had in Camp Owen in 1861 and were no better trained upon reaching the field than their predecessors. For example, 85 percent of the men recruited before June 1863 for whom data is available were with the regiment in the field within one month of being sworn into federal service or within five weeks of enlisting. Obviously there was barely enough time to say good-bye to friends and family, let alone pick up much drill or formation.[38]

This was similar to the experience of the recruits from Hastings. They were enlisted by September 4 at Hastings, were in Detroit by the eighth, and were on a train for Louisville two days later. They did not join the regiment until the thirtieth but only because parties of recruits were not being sent to the regiments retreating from northern Alabama. In several letters written during this period, there is not a single reference to drill or training, and they were not even issued weapons until just before September 19.[39]

Many of the 1862 recruits might have taken some consolation that they were en route to join a regiment that had avoided any hard fighting to date instead of one of the state's bloodied infantry units. Waiting for a ride to the regiment from Michigan, Private Weissert claimed the other recruits "thought like myself . . . once we are with the [Michigan Engineers] regiment there is little further danger left." Within five months of their enlistment, Weissert's two dozen comrades from Hastings had been in two hard fights and lost five men to death or medical discharge, and another two were hospitalized with maladies that would eventually disable them.[40]

· 12 ·

Forward to Murfreesboro

On January 7, 1863, the regiment, joined by Lieutenant Newell's section and a company from the Fourth Michigan Cavalry, marched five miles down the pike to Smyrna. That night Captain Grant and a detail of cavalry went out into the countryside in search of small parties of Confederate cavalry and captured four bushwhackers. In the morning, most of the regiment began work on a nearby railroad bridge, probably over Stewart's Creek, with Company H and a force of artillery and cavalry on picket duty. A detail sent to repair the telegraph, escorted by some of the troopers, returned quickly with news of an attack on a nearby train. The command was pulled from work and put in a defensive square. Back at work on the bridge early the next morning, the men were to finish it by noon and spend the rest of the day washing and resting.[1]

On the tenth Colonel Innes led his men further along the pike to the Stones River, southwest of the town. Their route took them through the recent battlefield, still filled with the piles of rotting horse corpses, makeshift graves, and the burned or destroyed buildings. One man described it as a "dreadful desolate looking country." John Weissert penned a frightful description to his wife: "It makes your hair stand on ends to see the graves, dead horses lying around, fences turned over and all the houses charred to ruins." Along the march from Nashville to Murfreesboro, through one of the most prosperous regions of Tennessee, he reported that there were not twenty houses left standing, and these were full of wounded and dying soldiers.[2]

For several days the regiment set up camp near Murfreesboro. Detachments worked on the pike bridge over Overall's Creek, cut and framed timber for another bridge, and performed some minor repair to highway and street bridges in and around the town. For most of the next two weeks, however, the men generally were able to rest, clean and repair clothing and equipment, and recover from the active campaigning.[3]

On January 28 Colonel Innes issued orders to the regiment to be ready to march at nine the next morning toward Nashville. With the pike repaired and back in operation, the Michigan Engineers and infantry working parties were shifted to repair the railroad from Nashville to Murfeesboro. Innes was placed in charge of the repair and also ordered to personally supervise the construction of duplicates for each bridge. Once a regular rail supply line could be opened and supplies accumulated at Murfreesboro, General Rosecrans was expected to move forward against General Bragg, who had retreated with his command to Shelbyville and Tullahoma.[4]

For the next several days, Lieutenant Colonel Hunton and the Michigan Engineers repaired railroad track, bridges, and culverts in the area around Lavergne. The largest one was Mill Creek No. 3 crossing, seven miles to the north at Lavergne. This was the same bridge that the regiment had been working on when they were ordered to hurry forward and protect Rosecrans's wagon trains a month earlier. Work on all of these projects was greatly delayed by the lack of railroad iron and materials to repair and replace track that had been destroyed on the bridges and in several places between the two points.[5]

Getting the iron tracks and spikes consumed most of Innes's time and energy for several days. On February 2 he reported to army headquarters that the railroad from Nashville to Lavergne would be open that day but for the lack of iron. Later that day he telegraphed John B. Anderson asking for eight carloads of railroad iron, fish bars, bolts, nuts, and spikes; the request was repeated the following day. By February 4 the bridge over Mill Creek was also rebuilt, but the nagging lack of railroad iron and spikes kept the regiment from being able to complete the job. Innes's badgering of officials in Nashville continued. Enough railroad materials trickled in on the seventh for Innes and his men to attach the rails at Mill Creek by "half bolting," and the rails were laid to within one thousand feet of the depot at Lavergne Station by the other companies. Though trains could run from Nashville almost to Lavergne, it would be necessary to fully spike and bolt the track as soon as possible to prevent accidents.[6]

Even while the regiment was finishing the work on the railroad between Nashville and Murfreesboro, Innes explored different possible future assignments for his regiment with federal authorities: the Edgefield and Kentucky ("Clarksville") Railroad, the Nashville and Northwestern line, and the rail between Nashville and Decatur. The first two were part of Rosecrans's efforts to open up multiple rail lines between points upriver and Nashville, while the third would allow for easy supply of Union troops in advanced positions near Franklin. Though Captain Yates completed initial inspection and survey work on both the Clarksville and Northwestern routes, it was decided the regiment was most needed to repair the Decatur route.[7]

By the evening of February 12 the Nashville to Murfreesboro route was completed, and the engineers were back near Nashville. They set up camp two miles south of the city on land owned by the prominent Rains family. The owner, an uncle to Confederate Gen. James E. Rains, recently killed at the Battle of Stones River, remained on his property. The Michigan Engineers set up their tents under the stately oak trees that dotted the hill encampment, giving them a panoramic view of Nashville. The guns of Fort Negley were reassuringly nearby. From this camp, work details would be sent by train on the Decatur Road to make repairs, while details remained to get out timber and frame the bents.[8]

One detachment left in the morning by rail to repair a bridge two miles south of Brentwood Station and replace some work. Before returning that night, they were able to remove this last obstruction to rail traffic between Nashville and the Little Harpeth River, twelve miles to the south. At the same time Captain Fox with three companies started work on the bridges over the Big and Little Harpeth rivers. Each day details from the three companies were loaded onto a train with prepared bridge sections and taken to the crossing where they were working, returning at night. The bridge over the Little Harpeth was completed on the fourteenth, and a train passed over to test its strength. Fox and his men then started work on the larger one six miles further south at Franklin.[9]

While Fox and his men were commuting to Franklin each day, the balance of the regiment remained near Nashville working on a variety of projects for the army. Many of the men were organized into daily parties to cut and finish timber to be used for Fox's bridge repair. The huge old oak trees on the Rains plantation, some of which were over two hundred years old, were the first to be cut down. Then the men moved farther away along the railroad. Trees were cut down, moved to the Nashville and Decatur road, and loaded onto cars for transport to camp. The daily excursions from camp and the ride on open flat cars provided a break from the routine of daily camp life. On the nineteenth so many of the men used passing dogs and rabbits as targets for rifle practice that they were threatened with arrest to restore order. By February 20 the men had cut and framed enough timber to complete the bridge at Franklin.[10]

The Big Harpeth railroad bridge at Franklin was one of the most frustrating that the regiment ever worked on, its assembly delayed by the high water, a swift current, and frequent heavy rains. It illustrates the challenges faced by the Michigan Engineers throughout the war.

On the nineteenth the men loaded the prepared bridge tampers on rail cars and went to Franklin, intending to raise them. The water was too high, and one man was almost lost when he tried to swim his horse across. They tried again the next day without success, though they were able to do some work on the foundation on the bank. On the twenty-first heavy rains stopped their work after only one bent had been raised. When they returned on the twenty-fourth, the weather had cleared and the water level was lower, but the bent raised earlier was down. The entire day was spent raising it back up, along with another three.[11]

Work continued on the twenty-fifth, hampered by an afternoon rain that soaked the ropes the engineers were working with, making it hard to raise the timbers. On the twenty-sixth heavy rains kept them in camp. On the twenty-seventh the men again arrived in Franklin to find bents knocked down by the current, and the following day rain kept them in camp. They returned again on March 2, only to discover three bents down, one of which had been destroyed. The water, however, was dropping, and the current was not as strong. For the next several days, it remained cold and cloudy, but the rains held off and the men were able to work on the bridge. Working long days in the cold water, they were able to get the bridge done on the sixth, and a train ran over it that afternoon as a test. The men also planked the bridge so that infantry and cavalry could cross over it. The exhausted men returned on the train to camp that night.[12]

After March 6 the entire regiment remained together in camp with little work to do, a welcome rest in the pleasant surroundings of the Rains plantation. Weather permitting, the officers drilled the men for a few hours each day, but there was still time to play baseball or visit the area. On rainy days the men remained in their tents, writing letters, singing, playing cards, or just talking. Many of the men took the time to improve their quarters, hoping that their stay would not be brief.[13]

A few men were detailed for special assignments. In response to heavy and illicit drinking among the men, Sergeant Vandewarker and five others of Company H were sent to search a combination grocery and "house of ill fame" for evidence of the liquor the men had obtained. William H. Kimball was part of the detail that interrogated the establishment's owner and noted that "the fellow was from Michigan and as he treated us well we were not very close in our search, but confiscated a keg of beer [and] ordered the shop closed up."[14]

On March 18 the men awoke under orders to break down the camp and prepare to move back to Murfreesboro. Begrudgingly, they left the comforts of the Rains estate. Marching once again south along the Murfreesboro Pike, they camped that night in the familiar surroundings at

Lavergne. The following day the regiment continued on to Murfreesboro, which they reached that night.[15]

For several days the men set up camp a mile from Murfreesboro
near the pike bridge over the Stones River. They traded their old large
Sibley and Bell tents for the new two-man tents, derisively called "pup"
or "dog" tents for their small size. These tents consisted of two shelter
halves made of cotton drilling buttoned together and thrown over a
guyline suspended between posts or guns thrust bayonet-first into the
ground. While in camp the Michigan Engineers also prepared their
tools for work, and many received new uniforms and weapons.[16]

Among the new uniforms were coats with trimming cords in engineer yellow. The new clothes were of mixed quality but were a general improvement. As early as November 1862 Innes had requested
new clothing and camp and garrison equipage for his men, described
as "of vital importance to the regiment," but to no avail. Subsequent
efforts were also unsuccessful until the February 1863 issue.[17]

The new weapons were part of Innes's determined efforts to replace the regiment's aged rifled-muskets with new rifles. Through a
series of successive requests and issues while at Murfreesboro, the regiment was able obtain enough of the prized Enfields for three quarters
of the men, with the balance having the reliable Springfield rifle.[18]

While in camp near Murfreesboro on March 21 the regiment was
reviewed personally by General Rosecrans and his staff. The general
complimented the men, telling them, "Do as well in the future as you
have in the past and when you return, your home state will be proud to
place your flag in the State House." One engineer officer wrote in his
diary that Rosecrans said, "We could work well, fight well, and march
well." Of greater interest to the men was the issue of pay, covering
through the end of 1862. One officer wrote, "What a difference it has
made to efficiency since the regiment received their pay, there is now
no grumbling if you ask a man to go out to work."[19]

The regiment remained in camp working on the defenses of that
place until leaving Murfreesboro at the end of June. Between January
and June 1863 Rosecrans's army built the largest enclosed earthen for-
tification constructed during the war. By the time Fortress Rosecrans
was completed, a total area of about two hundred acres north and west
of the city center was turned into a fortified encampment, including
redoubts, lunettes, and connecting earthworks. It was large enough
to protect and supply an army of fifty thousand men, with work done
under the direction of James St. Clair Morton, still chief engineer of
the Department of the Cumberland and newly promoted to brigadier
general.[20]

By the time the Michigan Engineers were assigned to the work in late March, the outer lines were largely done, but much remained to be finished in the redoubts and interior buildings. The first major project assigned to the Michigan Engineers was the construction of a warehouse 450 feet long and 36 feet wide built along the railroad and large enough to hold five million rations when completed. The men used cedar poles to floor it and roofed it with canvas. The engineers cut much of the wood for the warehouse, while other boards were obtained by details tearing down old buildings in Murfreesboro. Work on this large project did not end until early May.[21]

Another major undertaking worked concurrently with the warehouse was the main magazine, located about seven hundred yards south of the Stones River along the Nashville and Chattanooga, in the center of the fortress. Built in the shape of the letter *L*, it measured eighty feet by thirty-two feet, with a wing forty feet by thirty-two. The magazine was built in a large hole blasted by explosives from the rocky ground. It was at least nine feet high above the ground and thickly covered with timbers and planks in addition to dirt. Only the lack of proper caulking materials pushed the completion of this project into early May.[22]

Beginning in May details from the regiment also got out timbers for small magazines in Lunettes Palmer and Rousseau. In early June details from the regiment helped finish a storehouse started by the pioneers. By the end of June the regiment was working on laying gun platforms for Lunettes Negley and Crittenden. During this same period other details performed various construction and carpentry work around the fortifications, especially on gates and doorways.[23]

As work continued on Fortress Rosecrans, the Michigan Engineers became entangled in a controversy that demonstrated the sometimes-rocky relationship between regular army engineer officers and their volunteer counterparts. General Rosecrans was a successful civilian and military engineer in his own right. Shortly after taking command, he had ordered that every infantry regiment in the army detail twenty mechanics and skilled laborers for the new Pioneer Brigade. In this manner a battalion of one thousand was formed from each army corps. Morton was assigned command of the three battalions, while keeping his duties as chief engineer for the department.[24]

Morton was one of the outstanding young engineers in the antebellum Corps of Engineers and had already published several works on military fortifications by 1861. Appointed chief engineer by Buell in June 1862, Morton was bright and brash in equal parts and was considered "one of the most controversial members of the staid and conservative Corps of Engineers." Under Morton's command the Pioneer Brigade quickly established for themselves an important position in the army. The three battalions worked with the advance of the army, clearing roads and repairing bridges, as well as performing major construction projects such as that at Murfreesboro. They could also fight. During the Battle of Stones River, Morton and his men filled a key gap in the Union line on December 31, earning Morton his general's star and lavish praise for the command from a grateful Rosecrans.[25]

Morton and his Pioneer Brigade were laboring on the fortifications at Murfreesboro by March 1863. While the Michigan Engineers reported directly to the army commander, the type of work done by Morton's Pioneer Brigade and the Michigan regiment overlapped, as did the background of the men in each unit. Though he valued volunteer engineers as soldiers and sometimes as junior officers, Morton and most of the other regular army engineers believed that it was necessary to have West Point men in command of their efforts and frequently said as much.[26]

At the same time, there was a months-old concern among many of the Michigan Engineers that Morton would try to incorporate their regiment into his brigade. Companies B and F had been loaned briefly to Morton in November 1862, and though they were returned to the regiment soon after, there were many who believed the assignment was a first step toward consolidation.[27]

On March 22 Innes left camp for Michigan to both visit his family and meet with Governor Blair about the regiment's reorganization. At Governor Blair's request, Rosecrans extended the furlough from twenty to thirty days to allow Innes to visit Washington, D.C., and resolve matters still outstanding about the reorganization. With Innes gone from Murfreesboro, Morton saw his opportunity and moved quickly to absorb the Michigan Engineers.[28]

Just four days after Innes's departure, Morton sent a flurry of new demands to the Michigan Engineer regimental headquarters for morning reports, ordnance reports, quartermaster consolidated reports, and a report from the regiment's transportation officer. Morton ordered that the Michigan Engineer surgeon report to the chief surgeon of the Pioneer Brigade. He also issued an order officially designating the Michigan Engineers as the "Fourth Battalion" of his brigade, though this was withdrawn amid a howl of protest. Despite this setback, when Morton decided to drill his entire brigade from April 9 to 11, orders were sent to the Michigan Engineers assigning them a place in the review alongside the Pioneer Brigade battalions. Morton even tried to force the engineers to change their regimental banner to reflect their place in his Pioneer Brigade. The furious Michigan officers and men grew increasingly apprehensive that they would be permanently consolidated into the pioneers.[29]

Many of the Michigan Engineers believed that Morton had acted so aggressively because of Innes's absence. James Greenalch wrote his wife about the unresolved questions, stressing the significance of Innes's absence: "We shall probably know pretty soon after the colonel gets back." On April 12 Lt. George W. White wrote to an officer back in Michigan, "I think that when the Colonel returns there will be a change in the *programme*. The staff and line officers do not seem to think much of the present arrangement and are all anxious to get back and remain as we were."[30]

Innes's long-awaited return came on April 24, and the situation quickly came to a head. Morton sent Innes an order to report to the headquarters of the Pioneer Brigade "immediately." Innes met with Rosecrans on the twenty-seventh to permanently resolve the matter. On the twenty-eighth Rosecrans ordered Morton to cease efforts to attach the Michigan Engineers to his command, "as it was not intended to include the regiment in the Pioneer Brigade." With his commander's firm support, Innes was successful in stopping the "bogus brigade business." Relations between Innes and Morton, and the men of the two units, however, soured even further, and William Kimball noted that "Innes turned a cold shoulder" to Morton.[31]

The friction between Morton and Innes, and the competition between their units, continued into May and June. Innes frequently complained to Morton about the lack of support and low quality work done by Pioneer Brigade men. There were persistent rumors in camp that Innes had resigned and was to leave for home. Innes was frustrated by his conviction that the Michigan Engineers did the work but Morton and his pioneers got all the credit. In fact, Innes did submit his resignation, but Rosecrans rejected it. On June 17 he wrote Tennessee Military Governor Andrew Johnson, "After much labor on my part up to this time, I have failed to get General Rosecrans to accept my resignation." Rosecrans needed both Morton and Innes for his army's upcoming offensive.[32]

Pressure mounted on Rosecrans to lead his army against Bragg's. Pleading the lack of cavalry mounts and equipment and an inadequacy of supply levels, Rosecrans remained in place. As months passed, suggestions from the War Department and President Lincoln turned to outright threats if the inactivity continued. Finally, by mid-June it was clear that Rosecrans deemed his command fully prepared for a general advance.

On June 23 the first forward elements of Rosecrans's army moved southward. As directed, the Michigan Engineers remained behind, completing work on Fortress Rosecrans. On the twenty-seventh, Governor Blair joined with Governor Andrew Johnson on an inspection of the Michigan Engineers. That night the regiment received orders to move in the morning. After six months of inactivity, Rosecrans's Army of the Cumberland was moving against Bragg's army, and the Michigan Engineers were needed to keep the supplies moving forward.[33]

· 13 ·

Back across the Tennessee

Union forces had several routes that they could use to move against the Confederates' seventy-mile-wide position, and General Bragg had been forced to disperse his troops in order to feed them from local sources. Most important, Bragg's troops lacked confidence in his ability, and he was warring with his senior generals. His cavalry commanders were quarreling with him and with one another and demanding to serve elsewhere, and the quality and quantity of the rebel-mounted arm was at a low point. Bragg had also failed to develop a coordinated plan among his subordinates to combat any Union moves against the Confederate positions.[1]

General Rosecrans's plan took advantage of Bragg's weaknesses. He divided his army into five separate columns to facilitate movement and confuse Bragg. He intended to gather the bulk of his forces at Manchester and move against the Confederate right and rear at Tullahoma and Elk River. Bragg would then be forced to abandon his position in Middle Tennessee or be trapped against the river. Bragg, confused at first by the conflicting reports of the main Union effort, ordered counterattacks against the various Union columns but then on June 27, 1863, ordered his troops to fall back to Tullahoma. Finally realizing the danger his army was in, he decided on the thirtieth to retreat behind the Tennessee River. His rearguard was ordered to destroy the bridges over the flooded Elk River to slow the Union advance. Though Bragg's forces escaped the trap, Rosecrans's brilliant move drove the Confederates out of Middle Tennessee.[2]

The Michigan Engineers remained at work on Fortress Rosecrans during the first several days of the Tullahoma campaign, finally leaving Murfreesboro on June 29. Lieutenant Colonel Hunton and a detachment were sent by rail to inspect the Nashville and Chattanooga tracks for Confederate sabotage. On the twenty-ninth and thirtieth they were able to inspect as far south as Christiana before they found a break in the line near Bellbuckle. Leaving the gap for others to repair, they continued on to Wartrace by foot. They remained there until Innes and the rest of the regiment came up on July 1. Meanwhile, Colonel Innes and most of the men were making the trip on foot, marching from Murfreesboro to Wartrace, where they arrived in the morning of the first. The teams and exhausted teamsters, lagging behind on muddy roads, did not reach the camp until that afternoon.[3]

On July 2 the whole regiment marched several miles to the Duck River Bridge. Retreating Confederates had done a poor job of destroying it during their retreat on June 27, and the 350-foot-long bridge was not seriously damaged. The entire regiment went to work getting out timbers and replacing damaged sections. Two companies left behind completed the work the following day. The rest moved forward to near Normandy, where retreating Confederates had destroyed another bridge. The Michigan Engineers were able to repair it by early afternoon on July 4.[4]

The next day the entire regiment was back together and marched seven miles from Normandy Station to Tullahoma and encamped. Some of the men were detailed to chop out and corduroy a new road leading into Tullahoma to help Rosecrans's struggling supply wagons. Hunton and another detachment marched to near Concord on the McMinnville railroad branch and rebuilt the trestle of two bridges. Others apparently remained in camp, repairing equipment and resting.[5]

The biggest enemy during the campaign was the mud. The heavily traveled roads were a quagmire from days of rain and the tramp of men and wagons. The march on July 2 was described by James Greenalch of Company B, traveling with the wagons, as "the hardest march I have ever had since I have been with the regiment." Rosecrans blamed the "incessant rains and the impassable state of the roads" for Bragg's escape from Tullahoma, while most of the reports of corps and division commanders have similar references to the heavy rains and impassable roads.[6]

The rains came in powerful storms, creating dangerous conditions. J. Newton Crittenton, the regimental telegrapher and the son of Capt. Emery O. Crittenton, was struck by lightning on July 4 when he "carelessly rested his arm on his instrument." He was rendered senseless for about ten minutes. His injuries were severe, including temporary paralysis of the right arm and patches of burned skin across the body. Sent back to Normandy in his father's care, he eventually regained his health and was commissioned second lieutenant in Company K. The same storm spooked Dr. DeCamp's horse, which upset a hive of bees. The enraged bees attacked in turn, and "the mules and horses broke loose and stampeded over the hills lively." A bystander noted, "It was amusing to see the mules dance and caper." DeCamp's horse was stung to death.[7]

Meanwhile, Rosecrans's pursuit of Bragg's Confederates came to a halt at the Tennessee River. His men were at the end of a sorely stretched supply line back to Nashville. The region between Tullahoma and the Tennessee River was barren of forage and supply. Despite pressure from Washington to continue the advance, Rosecrans decided to repair the railroad leading back to Nashville and secure his flanks before forcing a Tennessee River crossing. Rosecrans had four significant resources with which to repair his supply line: John B. Anderson's civilian working parties, the Michigan Engineers, James St. Clair Morton and his Pioneer Brigade, and fatigue parties drawn from the infantry divisions.[8]

Elk River presented the biggest obstacle to repairing the supply line back to Nashville. There were several bridges across the flooded Elk southeast of Tullahoma, but the most important were the pike and railroad crossings, just south of the village of Estill Springs, both of which had been destroyed by Bragg's rearguard on July 1. Pursuing Union troops were slowed at the flooded Elk and did not cross in force until July 3. Eventually, falling river levels allowed some divisions to ford artillery and wagons across the Elk, but the railroad bridge had to be fixed to allow the depots at Nashville to supply Rosecrans's army.[9]

Work on the Elk River railroad bridge began almost as soon as Union troops reached the river. At least a portion of Morton's Pioneer Brigade worked on several bridges near Allisonia, including those over the Elk River, starting July 3. Company- and battalion-sized detachments cleared obstructions, cut and hewed timber for bridges, and repaired roads in the vicinity until at least the tenth, though only a small part of the brigade worked on the railroad bridge at any given time. On July 10 Hunton left Tullahoma with six companies of the Michigan Engineers and marched eight miles to the destroyed railroad bridge over the Elk. The other companies followed on the eleventh and spent part of the afternoon working on the bridge. Hunton inspected the remains and prepared an estimate of how long it would take to complete the critical bridge.[10]

On the twelfth Innes was summoned to meet with Rosecrans and decided to take Hunton with him. Morton was present and estimated that it would take four to six weeks to complete the bridge, perhaps a week less if the Michigan Engineers were directed to report to him for the project. Innes, deferring to Hunton's estimate, countered that it would take only a portion of the Michigan Engineers regiment eight to ten days but only if Morton and his pioneers were ordered away. Rosecrans accepted the regiment's challenge to Morton and ordered the Michigan Engineers to finish the bridge.[11]

Two views of the railroad bridge over Elk River built by the Michigan Engineers in July 1863. The first image shows the men at work on the vital span. The three officers in front are, from left, Surgeon William DeCamp, Capt. James W. Sligh, and Adj. Charles W. Calkins. Sligh, *Michigan Engineers.* The second image is from a different angle and provides a clearer image of the bridge's design. Archives of Michigan.

The stone piers were intact, but retreating Confederates had burned the rest of the wooden bridge, leaving a gap almost five hundred feet wide. Timber for the bents and stringers could be cut from the surrounding woods. Nails, railroad spikes and rail, and sawed planks for flooring could not be, however, and getting these materials slowed the work.[12]

Unlike for most of the bridges that were constructed during the war by the Michigan Engineers, there is clear photographic evidence of their handiwork at Elk River. In common with most military railroad bridges in the West at the time of the war, the bridge over Elk River was of the trestle type. The 470-foot-long span contained at least twenty bents and made use of the three existing stone abutments. The span was more than 50 feet high at its tallest, and the portion over the river itself was built in about 5 feet of water. The first tier of trestle was built level with the tops of the three abutments, at least 30 feet above the water and nearby valley floor.[13]

On the fourteenth, Innes reported to Rosecrans's headquarters that the bridge was ready for the planking being cut at army sawmills by Morton's men. The following day, in addition to complaining that the planking had not arrived, Innes requested that 750 feet of track of railroad iron be sent by train to Elk River, where Maj. John B. Yates was working, for use there and beyond. That same day, Innes complained to Lt. Col. J. W. Taylor, chief quartermaster of the department, that the nails that had been sent to the bridge were the wrong ones. He repeated his complaint on the sixteenth and claimed that work was "at a stand still" until the correct ones arrived. Apparently, some of both the nails and iron arrived later that day, and work resumed. By the afternoon of the seventeenth, the men were working on the last of the trestles, and enough iron arrived to complete the job.[14]

Work on the bridge was completed on the afternoon of the eighteenth, and a train ran across it while the regimental band played "Hail Columbia." Innes and other officers took the train to Decherd, where they telegraphed to Rosecrans that the bridge was completed and received a complimentary telegram in reply. According to one observer's account, the success of the Michigan Engineers at Elk River caused Rosecrans to give the department's engineer flag to the Michigan Engineers to fly at their regimental headquarters. If true, this must have been a bitter pill for Morton's men to swallow.[15]

While Innes and the bulk of the regiment rebuilt the bridge over Elk River, Yates and Companies E, K, and I repaired the Nashville and Chattanooga further south. By the thirteenth they were at Tantalon Station. Over the next few days they repaired three bridges over

Crow Creek. Work was delayed for lack of materials, as at Elk River, but Yates and his men were finishing the bridge on July 18 when a jubilant Innes arrived by train. He was escorted by several officers and the regimental band and serenaded Yates's detachment. The battalion returned by rail to Elk River on the nineteenth, while a small guard helped the wagons back over the mountain.[16]

The regimental headquarters remained at Elk River for three more months. From that point detachments of Michigan Engineers were sent out to perform various projects, mostly repairing bridges, building water towers, and getting out railroad ties along the line of the Nashville and Chattanooga and its branches. Rosecrans's army remained along the Nashville and Chattanooga between Tullahoma and the Tennessee River, waiting for Burnside to advance on Knoxville on the army's left flank and for supplies to accumulate at Stevenson, which was now being served by regular rail transportation.[17]

Hunton inspected the railroad track on the Fayetteville branch line of the Nashville and Chattanooga, and a detail from the Michigan Engineers repaired a bridge near Winchester. Others fixed the round-table and water tower at Decherd and had the branch line in operation by the twenty-eighth. Meanwhile, Hunton moved on to inspect the branch running eastward from the main line to Tracy City, and it was repaired by other working parties from the Michigan Engineers. The Michigan Engineers detachments returned to Elk River.[18]

Meanwhile, other companies were assigned various projects along the railroad. One detachment repaired the water tank at Cowan Station. Others served as train guards or continued to get out railroad ties. It was not all work, especially after the men got paid on the twenty-fifth. Several organized an impromptu show and sold tickets. In exchange for free tickets, the regimental teamsters provided wagon covers that were fashioned into a large tent to accommodate the large crowd of soldiers. The show's organizers netted $115 for their efforts. Members of Company F bought too much beer from the sutler and promptly got into a drunken brawl.[19]

On the thirty-first Companies G and H, along with a company of black soldiers, were sent to repair the bridge over Widow Creek on the railroad between Stevenson and Bridgeport, where they remained until the third. Company G and the black soldiers did the heavy work, while Company H guarded the working parties. The timber was sent down by rail from above Elk River.[20]

The summer of 1863 was the first time the Michigan Engineers had regular contact with black soldiers. Companies that were later incorporated in the Twelfth and Thirteenth infantry regiments (U.S. Colored Troops [USCT]) were initially recruited and organized by Innes and his officers. Innes even floated unsuccessfully the idea of having these companies permanently attached to his regiment. Non-commissioned officers were detailed from the engineers to help with training and drill, and many of them later sought and obtained commissions in black regiments.[21]

All of this contact between the Michigan Engineers and former slaves helped produce an evolution of opinion. Many of the Michigan Engineers began to view them as fellow warriors, serving in the same army. One measure of the confidence that the members of the Michigan Engineers had in these troops was the decision to have the black regiment provide the pickets for the camp at Elk River. Though the men in the Michigan Engineers were likely pleased to be relieved of this tedious duty, putting the safety of the camp into the hands of the newly raised Twelfth USCT reflected some confidence in their reliability.[22]

There was certainly strong racism, even among those working with the black soldiers. Lt. Bert Jewell, praised for his conduct in training the Twelfth USCT, referred to them as a "nigger regiment." Even Lt. Henry Burt from Rosecrans's headquarters, whose inspection report was filled with praise for the men of the Twelfth USCT, noted with approval that the men were "driven into the river often enough to keep them clean"—a phrase likely never used by him in reference to white troops.[23]

Most likely, however, the best assessment of the men's view of the whole idea of serving alongside the black soldiers is the fact that there was no trouble when they did so for several months. Within the letters and diary entries for this period, there are few comments about how the members of the Michigan Engineers viewed Col. Charles R. Thompson and his regiment of black troops, but those comments that were made are positive. Likewise, there is no evidence that any man in the Michigan Engineers refused to serve alongside the black troops or to be detached to train them. Apparently, most accepted it as a means to an end. Enlistment of black soldiers meant an earlier end to the war and return to their homes in Michigan. Just as the members of the regiment had previously accepted the advantages of denying rebel slaveholders (and the Confederate war machine) the labors of their slaves, so too did they come to accept the advantage of arming these same men.

Michigan Engineer companies continued to arrive and depart the Elk River area during August and early September 1863. Those who remained were often put to work cutting railroad ties from near Estill Springs, just north of the river. One detachment repaired a bridge over Mud Creek, east of Stevenson. Others built water towers and roundtables. During the month of August the regiment at Elk River produced and delivered to the railroad 11,915 feet of twelve by twelve square timber, 2,910 feet of the larger fifteen by fifteen timber, and almost twenty thousand railroad ties. Others repaired several bad places in the railroad between the tunnel and Stevenson and between Elk River and Decherd.[24]

On August 10 Innes was formally appointed military superintendent of all the railroads within the department, replacing John B. Anderson. Innes was directed to make a "thorough inspection of all the railroads now in use" and report what was "absolute necessary to keep them in running order for the present and then which will be needed prospectively." He was expected to repair and manage the railroads within the department as well as set rates for passengers and freight. He was also required to report regularly to the departmental headquarters on the operations of the railroad, including revenues and expenditures. To assist in the repair and running of the railroad, Innes retained authority to use as much of his regiment and Thompson's Twelfth USCT as needed.[25]

Innes's appointment represented a huge victory for him in the long-running dispute with Anderson. They had clashed over the use of civilian repair crews, usage of trains and equipment, and first call on replacement parts for track repair. On several occasions Innes had tried to be named Anderson's replacement, without success.[26]

By the summer of 1863 it must have been obvious to everyone that Innes sought a greater role in running the railroads in Tennessee. He even enlisted a powerful sponsor, Military Governor Andrew Johnson. In late June Innes suggested that Johnson write to the secretary of war asking for permission to have "a suitable person . . . run the roads upon the same terms and conditions as the Louisville and Nashville road is run," obviously himself. His ambition was clear to the men he commanded. James M. Sligh wrote home on the last day of July that speculation was that Innes had replaced Anderson, and "I hope it is as the Colonel was wanting the position very much."[27]

Now that he finally had the position, Innes could expect to be scrutinized with the same intensity as Anderson had been. He also labored under many of the same difficulties. For example, the resources at his disposal were a mixed assortment of civilian employees, Michigan Engineers, infantry fatigue working parties, employees of the Quartermaster Corps, and a handful of regular army engineer officers. Except for his own regiment, the other assets all reported to different people, not to Innes.[28]

This problem had been solved on a regional basis in Virginia, where experienced railroad men like Daniel McCallum and Herman Haupt built a complex and effective organization. Involving an overwhelmingly civilian force of mechanics, carpenters, and railroad specialists, the entire operation was divided into divisions for construction and repairs, with further subdivisions based on specializations necessary to run a railroad. One person controlled it all. This organization, however, took almost a year to evolve and become efficient. Furthermore, it controlled and regularly operated fewer than one hundred miles of track. By contrast, Anderson, and now Innes, had responsibility for hundreds of miles of track through hostile country and did not have the large number of experienced civilian railroad managers that were available in the East.[29]

With the army preparing its move against Chattanooga and on into the wilds of northern Georgia, the railroad resources of the department would be stretched to the maximum, and Innes would be hard-pressed to avoid the fate that befell his predecessor. Within days Innes was in trouble with Rosecrans. Apparently, he interfered with the activities of the independent military telegraph service, which drew a strong rebuke from the army commander: "You have done wrong in interfering with our operations. Hereafter all facilities you desire in telegraphing should be made known to these headquarters. All control of operations is confided to the chief, Captain Van Duzer." This must have made managing the railroads more difficult, since the telegraph was essential to the efficient and safe functioning of the railroad.[30]

After a month of prodding and threats from General Halleck, Rosecrans finally put his army in motion on August 16, 1863. Repeating the strategy of using multiple columns to confuse Bragg, Rosecrans sent Thomas Crittenden's XXI Corps southeastward on a diversion over the Cumberland Mountains and into the Sequatchie Valley north of Chattanooga. The balance of his army began crossing the Tennessee unopposed between Shellmound and Caperton's Ferry (near Stevenson) beginning on August 29. Though the Michigan Engineers did not move forward as a regiment with the army's advance, detachments quickly began to leave Elk River to aid the move against Chattanooga.[31]

On August 19 Company E and a company of contrabands were sent to Stevenson from Elk River under the command of Captain Mills, joining six companies of the Pioneer Brigade already there. Over the next two months, Mills's command built commissary storehouses to store supplies for Rosecrans's army. With the repair of the Nashville and Chattanooga through to that point by July 25, Stevenson became the forward point for supplies. Storehouses and tents full of supplies and equipment occupied every available space.[32]

Companies A, D, G, and part of L left Elk River on August 28 and arrived at Bridgeport the next day. They had been ordered to help bridge Rosecrans's army across the wide Tennessee. Both spans—the 1,232-foot span connecting the west bank and the island and that of 428 feet connecting the island with the east bank—had been destroyed by retreating Confederates. Eventually a permanent span would have to be rebuilt, but Rosecrans did not have the luxury of further delay.[33]

Rosecrans's plan for forcing the Tennessee River line had two divisions crossing at Bridgeport, along with the horse-drawn supply trains. First to cross would be Philip Sheridan's division of Alexander McCook's XX Corps, and the fiery commander was anxious to see his command on the other bank. Since the army's main pontoon train was being used at Caperton's Ferry to cross other divisions, the crossing at Bridgeport would have to be constructed using both trestle and pontoon bridging. Sheridan specifically asked for, and was given, a detail from the Michigan Engineers and a handful of pontoon boats from the army's train. In addition, several companies from the Pioneer Brigade were ordered to Bridgeport with part of their pontoon equipage, including fifty-six pontoon boats.[34]

The work was divided between Hunton's Michigan Engineers and the men of the Pioneer Brigade. Hunton's companies began work on a temporary trestle bridge between the west bank and the island on the thirtieth and by the following day were framing timbers. The timber was cut by infantry details from Sheridan's division, working in the nearby woods. Cut planks for the flooring were delivered by train to Bridgeport from army-run sawmills elsewhere, since the one at Bridgeport was "very much torn up by the enemy" upon Bragg's retreat. Additional flooring was secured by stripping barns and houses in the area. By the afternoon of the thirty-first the bents were up one-third of the distance and stringer and planks were being laid as fast as possible. The Michigan Engineers were back at work on the morning of the first and finished getting the timbers assembled. Under pressure to complete the bridge so Sheridan's division could cross, they continued laboring through the night laying flooring. Work did not stop until the bridge was completed at 11 A.M. on the second.[35]

Meanwhile, men from the Pioneer Brigade built a pontoon bridge from the island to the east bank. The pioneers might have been

This image was taken while the Michigan Engineers were spanning the river from the west bank to the island. There was an insufficient supply of pontoon boats for the entire distance, more than twelve hundred feet, so the men constructed the crossing using both bents and boats. It was one of the most difficult bridges they constructed during the war. Using this and other crossings, Rosecrans's forces were across the Tennessee by September 4. Miller, *Photographic History of the Civil War.*

motivated by doubts that Hunton expressed about their ability to complete the task by the morning of September 1. Lt. George Burroughs, supervising the engineers, noted to Capt. P. J. O'Connell of the First Ohio Infantry, temporarily commanding the Pioneer Brigade, "I have promised that our bridge shall be done by tomorrow morning. Colonel Hunton says it cannot be done. Let us prove him a poor judge of our working qualities." By mid-afternoon on the first, Burroughs was able to report to Rosecrans that the pontoon bridge was complete between the island and the bank.[36]

Hunton's combination of trestle and pontoon was only a temporary measure, but it remained standing long enough for Sheridan's infantry and artillery to cross. At about 3 P.M. on September 2, however, part of the bridge collapsed as supply wagons were crossing. Several wagons of the XIV Corps were thrown into the river, and one mule was drowned. The exhausted Michigan Engineers waded into the river, working until dark to make repairs. At 9 P.M. seven bents fell as a result of wash at the bottom of the piles, and the crossing of wagons came to a halt again. Rosecrans's headquarters suggested to Hunton that he allow the exhausted men to sleep that night before starting work again in the morning.[37]

Working through September 3, the Michigan Engineers were able to reopen the bridge and allow the balance of Sheridan's trains and those of the cavalry to cross. That night, however, as the tired men dropped off to sleep, the "general opinion [was] that it will go down again." The next morning the men were surprised to find it still standing. One trestle that had broken was replaced, and those that had leveled were braced up again to allow more of the army's wagons to cross, but the bridge remained standing long enough to cross over the brigades and wagons still waiting on the west bank.[38]

Their work done, the tired men expected to return to Elk River and rejoin the regimental headquarters. Instead, they received orders to start construction of additional pontoons to be used to replace the sagging temporary trestle and for the construction of a second crossing at Bridgeport, located parallel and close by the existing one. The pontoons were of the wooden bateaux style. Companies I and K were brought up from Elk River to speed up the construction of pontoons, arriving on September 5. Working long days in the searing heat and through several nights, the men built more than fifty pontoons at Bridgeport in one week, finishing on the eleventh.[39]

By September 4 most of the Army of the Cumberland was across the Tennessee River. The bulk of the army moved southeast through gaps in the mountain ridges toward Bragg's railroad running between Atlanta and Chattanooga. Bragg decided to abandon Chattanooga on the sixth and concentrate his army further south at La Fayette, Georgia. His plan was to attack Rosecrans's corps in detail as they emerged from the mountain passes along a forty-mile front.[40]

The shortage of rolling stock was Rosecrans's largest problem by this time. On August 20 Innes received assurances from Rosecrans's staff that one hundred cars were on order and that additional ones would be sent. Despite their assurances, Innes was forced to scour the north for additional locomotives and collect whatever extra rolling stock could be sent south. At the same time, however, it was necessary to take already scarce rail cars and convert them for the transportation of the army's sick.[41]

Innes also had to direct the efforts of his civilian employees in the continuous repair of the railroad track, worn out by constant use and inadequate maintenance. Such efforts were necessary to "prevent repetition of accidents and detention of freight and other trains." Yet the only additional labor pool he could call on, the USCT detachments that had been doing much of the fatigue labor, were needed elsewhere. His own regiment was also off-limits, needed as it was for the passage of the army across the Tennessee River.[42]

Meanwhile, Innes was ordered to transport Gordon Granger's reserve corps south by rail to the Tennessee River, where they could cross and catch up with the main part of the army. Supplies were also unloaded from railroad cars arriving in Nashville from Louisville and then shipped south along the Nashville and Chattanooga to Stevenson, where they could be loaded on wagons and dispatched to Rosecrans's distant divisions. Not only did Innes have to forward supplies and re-inforcements to Rosecrans; he also had to transport prisoners back to Nashville, where they could be collected and sent to prison camps in the rear.[43]

While Rosecrans took the long-sought prize of Chattanooga, the Michigan Engineers at Bridgeport and Elk River prepared for new assignments. Rosecrans intended to have the Michigan Engineer companies reunited, but various demands soon scattered the companies throughout the region. By September 16 the regiment was distributed as follows: four companies (C, G, H, and I) remained at Elk River, four more (A, B, F, and L) were at Nashville, another two (D and K) were en route to Chattanooga, and one (E) was at Stevenson. On that same date, the scattered corps of Rosecrans's army were marching quickly to join together and avoid a trap Bragg had set for them in the valleys of northern Georgia.[44]

After two days of bitter fighting, the Army of the Cumberland was routed and driven from positions along Chickamauga Creek in Georgia. By September 22 Rosecrans's men were back in Chattanooga, under siege by Bragg's army, which had taken the high ground south of the Tennessee River. Federal authorities, alarmed that Rosecrans might abandon Chattanooga or even surrender his command, moved quickly to reinforce that point. A great concentration of men and material was ordered to save the Army of the Cumberland. The scattered companies of the Michigan Engineers were among the forces to be used for its relief.

· 14 ·

Holding Chattanooga for the Union

Captain P. V. Fox and Companies D and K arrived at Stevenson from Bridgeport on September 12, 1863, expecting to move on to Elk River. Instead, they were ordered to Chattanooga to construct a bridge across the Tennessee River. The new span would replace the wagon bridge burned by retreating Confederates and allow for quicker supply of General Rosecrans's army. Because the large railroad bridge at Bridgeport had not yet been rebuilt, Union forces in Chattanooga relied on army wagons bringing supplies from the Stevenson depots along a winding road on the river's north bank. Brig. Gen. George D. Wagner was serving as post commander at Chattanooga, with particular orders to get supplies moving through the city and on to General Rosecrans's army. Wagner requested that men from the Michigan Engineers be sent to Chattanooga to lay a pontoon bridge across the Tennessee. Fox's small two-company command was probably selected for the assignment because they were the closest.[1]

Fox's men were delayed at Stevenson, however, because their tools and wagons had already been forwarded to Elk River, and it would take some time to get them back. The battalion and their tools finally reached Chattanooga the night of the seventeenth. Fox immediately reported his arrival to Wagner, and tents were pitched at the corner of Walnut and Sixth streets. Early the next morning, Fox's men began work on the bridge spanning the Tennessee River, near imposing Cameron Hill.[2]

Like ones constructed weeks earlier, this bridge would be a combination pontoon and trestle structure with the actual construction under the technical direction of Lieutenant Burroughs of the Corps of Engineers. He intended to build a span almost eleven hundred feet long, using over fifty pontoons. Fixed trestle was to be used where the depth of the river permitted it. On the thirteenth he submitted a large bill of timber to Wagner for the pontoon planking and urged that any captured scows, pontoons, or cut timbers left by retreating rebels be carefully collected and guarded. Companies from the Pioneer Brigade were already in Chattanooga and working on the bridge soon after,

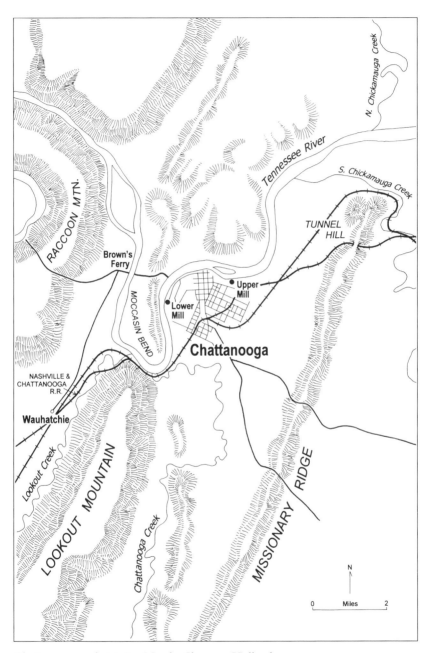

N. Chickamauga Creek

Tennessee River

S. Chickamauga Creek

RACCOON MTN.

TUNNEL
HILL

Brown's
Ferry

MOCCASIN BEND

Upper
Mill

Lower
Mill

Chattanooga

NASHVILLE &
CHATTANOOGA
R.R.

Wauhatchie

Lookout Creek

LOOKOUT MOUNTAIN

Chattanooga Creek

MISSIONARY RIDGE

N

0   Miles   2

Chattanooga and vicinity. Map by Sherman Hollander.

and on the sixteenth Wagner reported that he expected the bridge to be finished by the twentieth.[3]

Fox's men worked on the bridge alongside the pioneers for several days beginning on the eighteenth, but their work was increasingly interrupted by reports of heavy fighting along Chickamauga Creek and a stream of wounded. Detachments were pulled off the bridge-work and set to work repairing and filling water casks to be sent toward the battlefield. Later their efforts were shifted to constructing bunks for the wounded and coffins for the dead as Rosecrans's defeated divisions streamed back to Chattanooga. Other details gathered up blankets from the civilians to be used in an impromptu officers' hospital near their camp. These grim assignments delayed completion of the bridge until the twenty-third.[4]

General Bragg settled down into a semisiege following his tardy pursuit of Rosecrans. He lacked the strength to force his way into the city but was confident he could starve the Union forces out, since Rosecrans depended on a long supply line. Confederate artillery and sharpshooters stationed on the northern end of Raccoon Mountain effectively prohibited use of the direct wagon road from Bridgeport along the north bank of the Tennessee River. Instead, Rosecrans was forced to haul supplies from Bridgeport up the Sequatchie Valley to Anderson's and then over Walden's Ridge to Chattanooga. This route was through land barren of forage, with roads just wide enough for one wagon in places and in serious disrepair. Draft animals died in droves. Rosecrans's men in Chattanooga were quickly on half rations. Each day the situation grew more grave.[5]

Two major Union forces were ordered to rescue the Army of the Cumberland. Maj. Gen. William T. Sherman left Vicksburg with three divisions of the XV Corps beginning September 25, adding one division of the XVII Corps at Memphis. Continuing overland, they repaired the Memphis and Charleston Railroad on their way to Bridgeport. Meanwhile, Maj. Gen. Joseph Hooker was ordered to take the XI and XII corps from the Army of the Potomac, recovering from hard fighting at Gettysburg, and move westward to Tennessee.[6]

The movement of the XI and XII corps was one of the largest transfers of men and material during the war. Over twenty-three thousand men with their artillery and three thousand horses and mules were moved 1,157 miles by rail from Virginia to Tennessee. When Sherman's men arrived and were joined with Hooker's, there would be over forty thousand men with which to go to the aid of General Rosecrans's army inside Chattanooga. These reinforcements could be supplied at Bridgeport by the railroad leading back to Nashville and

Louisville. Supplies could also be shipped to Sherman's advancing troops via the Tennessee River from the supply base at St. Louis. All of this, however, would take time, while Rosecrans and his men had to strengthen their position, survive on the dwindling rations, and try to force open a supply line.[7]

On September 23 Rosecrans sent for Fox and directed him to build a new pontoon bridge across the Tennessee because the improvised combination pontoon and trestle bridge was in danger of being swept away by rising water. Wood was in such short supply in Chattanooga that the trestle bridge had been planked at least in part by boards torn from buildings, so by this time there was little cut timber for Fox to use on the pontoons. Scavenging in a tannery near Chattanooga Creek, however, Fox found a cache of timber left behind by retreating Confederates. The timbers had originally been cut by the enemy for use on a nearby railroad bridge and were not long enough to form pontoon boats of the standard size. Instead, Fox designed a smaller version. He reported his efforts to army headquarters on the night of the twenty-third. James Morton, recently returned from medical leave and again chief engineer in the department, ridiculed the plans. Rosecrans, himself a West Point–trained engineer and architect, was less skeptical and allowed Fox to build at least one as a test.[8]

The boats that Fox proposed to build were ungainly looking craft but could be made from the captured timber at hand. Each boat would have a triangular bow to resist the current as well as perpendicular sides so that it would settle evenly in the water when loaded. The weight of the bridge would be supported in each pontoon by a wooden brace running from bow to stern. Upon this support the balks could be locked and fastened by ropes to keep the boats in place. While different in size by necessity and varying somewhat in shape, Fox's design for the pontoons was largely of the same wooden bateaux type constructed by Colonel Innes's men the year before and Lieutenant Colonel Hunton's detachment just weeks before at Bridgeport.[9]

The following morning, the captured timber was collected and taken to the upper sawmill, where members of the Pioneer Corps cut it to the correct size. Two boats were built at river's edge, near the foot of Market Street. Rosecrans personally climbed into one and successfully tested it for buoyancy and stability. His unique boats having passed the army commander's personal inspection, Fox was ordered by Rosecrans to complete the pontoon bridge using the boats he had designed.[10]

Fox's men labored for ten days to complete enough boats to span the river. Critical materials were hard to find. Nails were brought to

Chattanooga in ten-pound shipments, stuffed in the saddlebags of army couriers. Confiscated cotton from the basement of a nearby store was used in place of scarce caulking. By October 5 fifty boats were assembled, along with balks, chess planks, and side rails. Morton's pioneers laid down most of the bridge, though the Michigan Engineers were detailed to help when progress lagged. The bridge was finally completed on the morning of the seventh, just in time since the rising river had made the other bridge impassable. The experience gained by Fox's men would be well utilized in critical operations in the weeks ahead.[11]

Pleased with the work done by Fox's men on the pontoons, Rosecrans next assigned Fox to run the two sawmills along the river, taking over from Morton's brigade. The men of the Pioneer Brigade, upset at the change in assignment, allegedly used up all the wood at one of the mills "through spite as they hated to have to leave." One account even claimed the men of the Pioneer Corps disabled the "lower mill," requiring repairs from skilled mechanics in the Michigan Engineers. While some of the Michigan Engineers worked in these mills, others from the companies were assigned to build more pontoon boats.[12]

The lower mill, operated by Company D, was a large one; it was powered by steam and included two saws, two planing machines, and other machinery to make sashes and moldings. Located near Cameron Hill, it could even be used to grind corn and wheat. Modifications were made by men in Fox's company who had run mills back in Michigan, and it was soon up and running. One of the upright saws was removed and replaced with a five-foot circular saw capable of cutting twenty-five thousand feet of lumber every twenty-four hours. This mill was powered by four boilers and included an eighteen-inch crank with a three-foot stroke from a cylinder attached to a twelve-foot flywheel on the main shaft. Most of the timber for this mill was cut by the men of the Thirteenth Michigan near their camp on Moccasin Point on the north bank. The infantrymen felled large pine trees and hauled them down to the river. From there the logs were towed individually across the river to the mill by a yawl boat made and manned by men from the Michigan Engineers. At the mill, planks two feet wide were cut by Fox's men and hauled to the boatyard upstream.[13]

Men from Companies K and C, the latter having arrived in Chattanooga from Elk River on October 8, operated the "upper mill." Less is known about this mill, which also operated at full capacity turning out cut planks for the pontoon boats and other projects within the city. The logs for this mill were cut by men from the Twenty-fourth Wisconsin from a stand of pine trees smaller than those on Moccasin Point. Operating from their camp on the north bank of the Tennessee, opposite Chattanooga Island, details from the Wisconsin regiment cut the logs and hauled them to the riverbank. They were floated across the river above the island and then to the upper mill. Since these logs were not as large as those at the other mill, they were used for balks, side rails, chess planking, bottoms, and oars.[14]

Meanwhile, the balance of the men in Fox's battalion continued their work constructing additional pontoons. Work on the boats was occasionally slowed for want of cut board. When the supply of timber at the mills grew short, the pontoon details were pulled from their work and sent out after logs. Fox himself scouted the banks of the river for suitable timber. By October 23 Fox had about fifty more pontoon boats available for use by the army.[15]

Detachments from Fox's battalion also protected the pontoon bridge they had helped build earlier. Guards were positioned in boats above the head of Chattanooga Island to spot and stop floating obstructions sent downriver by the Confederates. When they could not be safely broken up, the obstructions were towed to the upper mill boom, where they were cut at the mills or turned over to the hospitals for firewood. In addition to enemy efforts, heavy rains raised the level of the river at least twenty-two feet by October 18, threatening the pontoon bridge as great quantities of driftwood lodged against it. Besides the details from Fox's battalion, at least two hundred men from Morton's Pioneer Brigade also were at work protecting the bridge from the flotsam of the flooded river.[16]

In early October Bragg sent General Wheeler and his cavalry north to destroy the supply lines leading back from Chattanooga to Nashville. Crossing the Tennessee River east of Chattanooga on October 1, Wheeler was able to catch and destroy much of Rosecrans's supply train of five hundred wagons on Walden's Ridge. The rest of the raid, however, was less successful, as Union cavalry under Brig. Gen. George Crook blunted Wheeler's move against Murfreesboro and then drove the rebel cavalry back across the Tennessee by October 9. While in Middle Tennessee, however, Wheeler's men destroyed several Nashville and Chattanooga bridges and tore up track between the South Stones River and Wartrace, south of Murfreesboro.[17]

Innes was in charge of getting the road back in order following Wheeler's raid, and he called upon his regiment for assistance. Much of the physical work could be done by the troops of Gordon Granger's reserve corps and the XII Corps, commanded by Maj. Gen. Daniel Butterfield in General Slocum's absence. Both of these commands were already along the railroad between Nashville and Tantalon. Innes, however, needed to have the experienced bridge builders and tracklayers from his regiment working alongside these infantry regiments.

The Michigan Engineers companies at Elk River were getting out timbers for duplicate bridges when Wheeler struck the Nashville and Chattanooga. On the night of October 6 Lieutenant Colonel Hunton was telegraphed that the bridge over Garrison's Fork near Wartrace had been destroyed. Butterfield asked him to bring both men and materials to replace it. Hunton responded that he was familiar with the bridge. He also alerted Butterfield that the plates, cross-pieces, corbel ties, and stringers were already prepared and on hand for such an emergency and that he knew where posts could be found and cut in the neighboring woods at the bridge. Since the daily repair train had already passed Elk River, Lieutenant Colonel Hunton with Companies G, H, and I did not arrive until the morning of the seventh. The company wagons carrying cut timber for the bridge moved by road and did not arrive until that night. Company E from Stevenson joined them that same day.[18]

By working day and night, the four engineer companies and infantry details from the Thirteenth New Jersey and Second Massachusetts were able to finish the bridge shortly after daylight on the ninth. They were probably also assisted by two companies of Colonel Thompson's Twelfth USCT from Elk River. Butterfield's report complimented Hunton and his men, claiming the "promptness, energy and capacity displayed by this officer and his regiment were most praiseworthy." Next, Hunton and a portion of his command repaired the torn-up track back toward Murfreesboro. All repair work completed, Hunton and the three companies returned to Elk River by train on the tenth. At Elk River they continued their work of getting out duplicate bridges for use on the Nashville and Chattanooga. Company E probably returned with the other companies to Elk River but left soon after for Stevenson.[19]

Captain Sligh and Companies B, F, and L were nearby, repairing the destroyed bridge over the South Stones River. This 275-foot-long bridge south of Murfreesboro on the Nashville and Chattanooga had been destroyed during a raid by men of Brig. Gen. William T. Martin's Confederate cavalry division on the morning of the fifth. Martin's men shelled the nearby blockhouse and its garrison of men from Company D, Nineteenth Michigan. Outnumbered and under fire from rebel artillery against which the stockade provided little protection, the Michigan men were forced to lay down their arms. Their captors forced them to burn their own stockade and then destroy the nearby railroad bridge.[20]

Sligh's men had dropped their work on the Nashville and Northwestern on October 7 in response to urgent orders from Brig. Gen.

Robert B. Mitchell, commanding at Nashville. They rode by train to Nashville that day and then on to the South Stones River Bridge before dark. The company wagons left early in the morning carrying prepared timber and were able to rejoin the companies at the bridge. When Sligh's men arrived, they found Adjutant Miller and a squad from the regiment already at the site working. Working without rest, the men under Sligh and Miller completed the bridge on the ninth. After they were finished with the bridge, Sligh and Companies F and L moved to Christiana, while Company B was sent to join Company E at Stevenson. Presumably Miller and his detail moved on to other breaks in the line or returned to their assignments with the railroad.[21]

Sligh remained at Christiana with Companies F and L until he received orders on October 23 to move to Elk River by rail. The men were divided into two sections and loaded on trains for the trip, leaving late in the afternoon. Sligh and a small party were on the first train, protected by men from the regiment serving as train guard. The rest of his command was on the second, larger train. Upon reaching Tullahoma, the trains stopped, probably to take on fuel and water. While at Tullahoma, Sligh apparently decided to push ahead in the dark on the smaller train, with the intention of selecting a camp for the night. Assistant Surgeon Henry Van Ostrand, Sgt. James Cortright, and the small train guard accompanied him. About three miles below Tullahoma the train was thrown from tracks sabotaged by a party of Confederate cavalry. The engine, tender, and several cars were smashed. Sligh, riding in the locomotive, was trapped between the engine and tender, and both of his legs were crushed by the impact.[22]

While the train guard tried to drive off the enemy, Van Ostrand raced back on foot to the two companies still back at Tullahoma. He brought back enough men to drive the remaining raiders away. The men carefully cleared enough of the wreck to free their captain, and Sligh was taken back to Tullahoma under Van Ostrand's care. A nearby squad of USCT men started clearing the wrecked train, and on the twenty-fourth details from the Michigan Engineers returned from Tullahoma and finished clearing the wreckage and repaired the railroad.[23]

Sligh's condition worsened at Tullahoma while the doctors debated over whether his right leg, the most damaged, could be saved. It was amputated on November 3, but he continued to weaken. Each day, Sligh recorded his worsening condition in his diary as the doctors and his wife cared for him. On the fifteenth, a fever took hold, and he never recovered. His wife made the diary entry for the day, writing, "His spirit took its flight." His body was taken back to Grand

James W. Sligh was the only officer in the Michigan Engineers to die in the service and the original commander of Company F. His death in the fall of 1863 was mourned, both in the regiment and back home in Grand Rapids. His young son, James M. Sligh, ended the war also a captain. Son Robert, too young to serve, became the regimental historian and a fixture at postwar reunions. Bentley Historical Library, University of Michigan.

Rapids for burial. Because he was a well-respected leader in the community, Sligh's death received prominent mention from the local papers. The *Grand Rapids Eagle* eulogized, "In the death of Captain Sligh his company has lost a good officer, the government a good and loyal defender, our city a good and esteemed citizen, a worthy woman a beloved husband, and several children an exemplary and indulgent father ... may the turf be ever green over the grave of the fallen patriot."[24]

Sligh was not the only member of the regiment lost during this time. Several men from Company E were taken prisoner while traveling south from Elk River on the Nashville and Chattanooga on October 15. The train they were on was attacked by rebels and destroyed.

Company E's Franklin Hogle, left behind at Elk River as a regimental teamster, was sent out as part of a foraging expedition from Elk River in early November. Near Tullahoma Hogle left the party in search of turkeys that a local civilian told him about. He was never seen again. Some accounts state that local guerrillas, among whom he was "notorious for his petty marauding," killed him.[25]

The regimental headquarters remained at Elk River, as did at least six companies. With the damage from Wheeler's raid repaired, the men returned to getting out railroad ties and timbers for duplicate bridges. Some were detailed to distribute the ties along the line, while others went on foraging parties or worked in the camp. Others worked on rifle pits and stockades protecting the bridge over Elk River. On October 13 it was reported that only 155 men from the Michigan Engineers were at Elk River from these companies, reflecting the large number of men detailed elsewhere. These companies remained in place at Elk River until early November.[26]

Though Bridgeport was the advance position of Union troops outside Chattanooga, Stevenson was the key supply base. Its location at the intersection of the direct Nashville to Bridgeport rail line and the longer supplemental Nashville to Decatur to Bridgeport railroad made it a logical point for the accumulation of supplies and animals for the Army of the Cumberland and later its rescuers at the end of September. Captain Mills and Company E were still at Stevenson, where they had constructed a commissary warehouse. On October 2 Mills was ordered to supervise the construction of a new ordnance depot at Stevenson, presumably to help replace one that had erupted in a fiery explosion at Bridgeport two days earlier. Before it could be completed, however, Company E was ordered north along the Nashville and Chattanooga to join Hunton's force working on repairing the railroad following Wheeler's raid.[27]

After finishing the repair work, Company E returned to Stevenson. Company B also arrived in Stevenson at about the same time, following its work at the South Stones River Bridge with Sligh's battalion. Work on the ordnance depot at Stevenson was halted by an order from Thomas on November 6 because of the decision to concentrate supplies at Bridgeport. About this time, one or both of the companies were detached to repair bridges on the Memphis and Charleston, including one near Paint Rock, Alabama. On November 12 Company E left for nearby Bridgeport, and Company B left at about the same time to join Fox's detachment in Chattanooga, which it did on November 17.[28]

Bragg's army remained in position on the heights above Chattanooga, willing to let Rosecrans's army starve to death, surrender, or retreat. The Lincoln administration was concerned that Rosecrans was likely to actually allow one of these to happen. Having lost patience and becoming increasingly alarmed by Rosecrans's messages from Chattanooga, federal authorities made two important changes. Rosecrans was relieved of his command on October 18, and Thomas was promoted to command the Army of the Cumberland. Secondly, the decision was made to combine the forces in the Departments of the Cumberland, the Tennessee, and the Ohio under one command, which was given to Maj. Gen. Ulysses S. Grant.[29]

Though he is best known for his defeat at Chickamauga and subsequent plight at Chattanooga, Rosecrans's tenure with the Army of the Cumberland was important because of the development of an effective and efficient engineering force. Though hampered by the refusal of the Corps of Engineers to devote the same level of resources to the West as to the East, Rosecrans applied his formal and practical experience to a complete reorganization of his army's engineering arm. The later victories of Grant and Sherman in the West drew heavily upon the engineering personnel and ability of the Army of the Cumberland, resources that had been allowed to develop and mature under Rosecrans's interested tutelage. One exhaustive review of the Union engineering arm in the West has concluded that "under Rosecrans, the Army of the Cumberland had developed the most sophisticated engineering system of any of the armies."[30]

Innes was another casualty of the command shake-up and lost his position as military superintendent of railroads on October 19. For the ten weeks that he held the position, Innes faced several major challenges that ultimately caused his removal. Several of the same problems had previously plagued John B. Anderson and were rooted in the lack of coherent Union railroad command and policy in the West at the time. Others, however, were aggravated by Innes's knack for making enemies with the wrong people.[31]

One major difficulty facing Innes was the lack of central command over railroads running from Louisville to the army at the front. After the decision was made to send Gen. Joseph Hooker and the XI and XII corps west in late September, the responsibility for their transportation was delegated into several pieces along the line. Even though Innes remained in charge of coordinating military use of the railroads in the department, Assistant Secretary of War Thomas A. Scott was appointed to direct efforts south from Louisville. To assist him, Scott prevailed upon Secretary of War Stanton to appoint John B. Anderson as a special assistant, working primarily to secure additional rail cars and direct transportation with his old employer, the Louisville and

Nashville Railroad. Quartermaster General Montgomery C. Meigs was already in Nashville and was to coordinate the arrival and disbursement of Hooker's men. Other civilian railroad and military quartermaster officials had various supporting roles in this maze of responsibilities. The possibilities for confusion were endless. Innes and Scott both had to move men or material over the same worn-out line cursed with too few engines and cars for normal use. Innes reported directly to Rosecrans, who told him to "strain every nerve to send through Hooker's corps," while Scott answered to Stanton, and supply officials worked for Meigs, who reported in turn to Stanton.[32]

Following another dispute over use of cars, and caught between orders from Meigs and ones from army headquarters, an exasperated Innes pleaded with Rosecrans for a resolution of the problem: "It does seem to me there ought to be some understanding about this transportation, and I ought to act under orders only from the commanding general. I receive telegrams every day to send cars to the rear. Can't the Louisville road do this kind of freighting without calling upon us for cars? It is hard to keep up both ends of this thing. Please see General Meigs, and decide upon what action you desire me to take. I will, of course, cheerfully obey any instructions I may receive, but I should like them to come from department headquarters."[33]

Innes also argued with civilian railroad officials, especially President James Guthrie of the Louisville and Nashville. Innes believed that Guthrie's line shipped military material only when the higher paying civilian material was not on hand. In turn, Guthrie, former U.S. secretary of the treasury, and his ally Alfred Gaither of the Louisville and Nashville Railroad accused Innes of refusing to abide by earlier contracts negotiated between the government and the company for carrying military stores. Gaither believed that Innes requisitioned cars from his line only to turn around and use them to transport private freight in direct competition with his company. Arguments with civilian officials also erupted when Innes tried to cancel the contract with Adams Express Company without giving the necessary sixty days' notice. Though Rosecrans's headquarters backed up Innes's decision to cancel the contract, they insisted the notice requirements be met.[34]

By early October Stanton was personally involved in these disputes, ordering Quartermaster General Meigs to investigate Innes's conduct and management of the railroad. For those who disliked Innes anyway, this investigation was welcome. Scott reported to Stanton on October 9 that "your message to Innes has raised quite a commotion in that camp" and that Innes was dispatching a special messenger to

Washington to plead his case. Scott cautioned Stanton that "all statements made a connection with matters over there should be carefully
considered." Innes himself responded to Stanton that he welcomed
the investigation and asked "in justice to myself to have it done at the
earliest possible moment." Within less than a week Scott telegraphed
Stanton that he was planning to visit Nashville "and see if matters cannot be improved. From there south the evidences that reach me here
indicate that matters are in a very unsatisfactory shape." Though Innes
and Scott were able to reach some agreements on rolling stock, the
drumbeat of criticism against Innes and the department's management
of the railroad continued.[35]

War Department authorities also heard negative appraisals of
Innes from F. H. Forbes, a newspaperman and friend of Herman
Haupt who had been sent west in the spring of 1863 with blanket authorization to conduct "a general inspection of the military railroads"
in the theater with particular attention on contracts for scarce railroad
iron. For the next several months Forbes roamed throughout the rear
areas and supply points of the armies west of the Appalachian Mountains, sending scathing reports back to Haupt, which were in turn forwarded to Meigs and Stanton. Forbes accused the men running the
military railroads and supply centers of incompetence, stupidity, and
even outright corruption.[36]

At some point Innes also incurred Forbes's wrath. In scathing reports at the end of August 1863, Forbes complained to Haupt about
Innes's appointment in place of Anderson. He wrote that when he first
inspected the Nashville and Chattanooga, "The management was in the
hands of competent superintendents and efficient subordinates. From
recent events, however, the Government has been deprived of the service of Mr. J. B. Anderson." Forbes reported further that "every officer
under Anderson has left. No experienced engineer will trust himself on
the road under Innes. No train has arrived on time." Though Forbes
himself was relieved of his duties within three months, his reports to
senior officials in Washington could not have done Innes any good.[37]

Problems within his command also hindered Innes. When he
took over from Anderson, he apparently released the latter's employees,
preferring to have his own men in place. Yet the problems that had led
to Anderson's replacement did not stop. After continued accidents delayed trains, Rosecrans wrote Innes with stern advice: "I regret to learn
you have had collisions. . . . You must draw the strings of discipline
tight. Cut off heads with severity . . . and stop stealing on the road. Any
authority or orders that may be required from here will be given." Innes
was so short of trained railroad men that he received special permission

in early October to employ refugees and rebel deserters as employees on the road "as may be practicable."[38]

Finally, of course, while Innes faced all of this fire from his rear, the Confederates could be counted upon to try to cut the railroad whenever possible. While Wheeler's raid was a failure in terms of forcing Rosecrans from Chattanooga, it did close the Nashville and Chattanooga between Nashville and Bridgeport for several days. Even after the Michigan Engineers and other units repaired the damage, Confederates still regularly attacked trains and the telegraph lines the railroad depended upon. On October 16 Innes reported to Rosecrans that "obstructions have been placed on tracks near switches, throwing trains off two nights running, which together with the utter impossibility of using the telegraph line at times . . . has caused delay."[39]

Under fire from front and rear and facing an investigation by War Department authorities, Innes's tenure came to abrupt end. Anderson was recalled from his assignment with Scott and Stanton and assigned control of all military railroads in the new Military Division of the Mississippi. Though Innes's tenure had been stormy, his departure was noted with regret by at least two key figures in the Tennessee theater. Military Governor Johnson noted, "I doubt this change. Colonel Innes was making a good, efficient officer, and was not under an influence at Louisville operating to our injury." And to Lincoln he complained that Anderson's reappointment was "an unfortunate one." General Thomas agreed, writing to Johnson after learning of the change, "I sincerely hope that the new arrangement will work. Colonel Innes is an energetic and intelligent officer."[40]

Grant took over this new Military Division of the Mississippi on October 18 and was in Chattanooga by the twenty-third. When Grant arrived he found a starving army with only one day's supply of ammunition and dwindling stocks of food. Among the staff officers who briefed him on the military situation was Brig. Gen. William F. "Baldy" Smith, who had replaced Morton as the chief engineer of the Department of the Cumberland. Grant liked what the engineer had to report. Smith had developed a plan to evict Confederates from the heights overlooking the direct Chattanooga to Bridgeport road, and Thomas had approved the plan just before Grant's arrival. After personally inspecting the area the twenty-fourth, Grant gave it his approval and placed Smith in command of the entire operation. Because of the desperate position of the army, Grant ordered Smith to force the crossing on the night of October 26–27.[41]

The critical part of the plan required fifty pontoon boats, drawing primarily upon those that details from the Michigan Engineers had been constructing since finishing the first pontoon bridge. Though originally built for a second pontoon bridge to connect Chattanooga and Moccasin Point to the west, they were pressed into service by Smith for the crossing at Brown's Ferry. His plan approved by Thomas, Smith took Fox into his confidence and outlined the intention to force a crossing at Brown's Ferry. Smith and Fox personally reviewed the ground to be crossed by the pontoon wagon train and examined the area of the crossing itself.[42]

While Smith made his preparations, work continued at a feverish pace among the Michigan men. Although most of the boats had already been built and some of the balks and chess planking constructed, Fox and his men still had to finish the balance, cut and size the joists and planks for a bridge, collect the needed equipage and tools, and assemble a bridge team train. Working feverishly, Fox's men were able to finish in two days, as well as make 250 oars and rowlocks. The last of the work, the oars and rowlocks, was finished late on the night of the twenty-sixth, after the boat parties had been assembled at their pontoons along the river's edge.[43]

The pontoon boats to be used at Brown's Ferry were constructed from a design created by Fox. The pontoons utilized the availability of large pine trees on Moccasin Point and the power of the steam lower mill. Planks as long as twenty-seven feet and as wide as two feet could be cut in this manner, expediting the construction of boats larger than those used previously. The result was a boat about twenty-five feet long and about seven feet wide. All available rope was pressed into service for lashing the boats together and for use as anchor cables. Army engineer Lt. George W. Dresser scavenged train car wheels from the railroad shop, which were used as the anchors. Cotton was used as substitute caulking.[44]

Smith's plan for the evening of the twenty-sixth intended that Fox and the rest of the Michigan Engineers load the chess, balks, and other bridging equipment onto wagons in Chattanooga, cross over the river, and march across the neck of Moccasin Point to a concealed location opposite Brown's Ferry, where they would wait. All was ready to be loaded on the wagons at 3:30 P.M. on the twenty-sixth. Five small companies of the Twenty-first Michigan, totaling fewer than one hundred men, under Capt. Benton D. Fox arrived as ordered to help load and move the wagon train, but the wagons were nowhere to be seen. Engineer Capt. P. V. Fox went to army headquarters well aware that time was running out if the move was to be made before dark. Despite his prodding, however, it was not until after dusk that the wagons finally arrived. Finally loaded, the Michigan Engineers and infantry had to quickly manhandle the wagons over rough roads to the assembly point in a woods about sixty rods from where the bridge would be thrown across.[45]

Meanwhile, the picked parties from the brigades of William B. Hazen and John B. Turchin were assembled in the city and told for the first time of their mission. Each of the pontoon boats, described by one of the officers aboard them as "heavy and clumsy in the water as a square box," was loaded with twenty-five soldiers and five oarsmen. Two larger flatboats were also loaded with men, and the armada pushed off from the boatyard at about 3 A.M. and slowly moved downstream, careful that not a sound be made to alert Confederate sentries along the riverbank. Union signal fires were lit on Moccasin Point at 4:30 A.M. to orient the boats to their position, and the boats quickly made for the rebel-held shore opposite. Though shots were fired, the landing was a shock to the handful of Confederate troops on guard, and the entire landing force was quickly ashore and driving inland. The boats crossed back to Moccasin Point, loaded the balance of the two brigades, and returned to unload the reinforcements at Brown's Ferry. The boats and their tired crews then crossed back over the river to Moccasin Point, so their pontoons could be assembled into a bridge.[46]

By 8:30 A.M. Fox and the Michigan Engineers and detailed infantry from the Twenty-first Michigan had started to span the river with the pontoon bridge. Though the Confederate infantry had been driven from the opposite bank, a rebel battery on higher ground shelled Fox's men for the first hour as they worked. One piece of shell struck inside a pontoon boat, but quick-thinking Pvt. Adrian Musty stuffed his hat into the hole until the boat could be taken to shore and repaired. Another fragment almost removed Sgt. Henry Lampman's head. Working with "energy and zeal," the men finished the 870-foot-long bridge in less than eight hours. In future dispatches, the Brown's Ferry Bridge was referred to as the "Michigan Bridge" in honor of its builders.[47]

Reinforcements from Brig. Gen. Walter C. Whitaker's brigade moved across the river on the pontoon bridge to reinforce the first two Union brigades that had entrenched to protect the bridgehead. On the twenty-eighth the troops from Chattanooga linked up with Hooker's XII Corps men marching from Bridgeport. A Confederate attack on Brig. Gen. John W. Geary's division of the XII Corps that evening was repulsed at Wauhatchie. With Union troops firmly in control of the valley, supplies could once again be sent from Bridgeport to Chattanooga by steamer or wagon road.[48]

The successes at Brown's Ferry and Wauhatchie were critical to the survival of the Army of the Cumberland. Those in command, who knew just how close the army was to starvation, had high praise for those involved in the operation. Thomas singled out the troops under Smith, including Fox's engineers, for special mention, noting the "skill and cool gallantry of the officers and men . . . deserve[ed] the highest praise." In turn, Smith praised Fox's "vigorous and skillful superintendence" of the pontoon bridge. In postwar accounts Smith continued to praise Fox and his men as "a most excellent officer and splendid battalion of men" and declared that "without the zealous and efficient labors of Captain Fox . . . the bridge could not have been made or thrown." Historian James McDonough in his study of the campaign concluded that "once in a great while, and perhaps when least expected, the awful drama of war narrows to a very small focus, to a relative handful of men, and the story of a great struggle takes a decisive turn through the successful execution of a simple, daring plan—and the fearful momentum of war begins to swing from one army to the other. So it was at Brown's Ferry."[49]

The steamer *Chattanooga* arrived at Kelly's Ferry on October 30 with forty-thousand rations and forage, all of which was quickly taken by wagon to Chattanooga. The effect among the troops was electric. Lt. Col. Robert Kimberly of the Forty-first Ohio, who had been with the boat parties that stormed ashore at Brown's Ferry, remembered, "The depression which had lasted from the days at Chickamauga was gone. The troops felt as if they had been in prison, and now were free."[50]

By November 20 Grant had about seventy thousand men near Chattanooga or approaching that point. During the four weeks since the successful crossing at Brown's Ferry, Fox's battalion of Michigan Engineers, grown to four companies by the arrival on November 17 of Company B, continued to run the two sawmills and construct pontoon boats as well as maintain the two pontoon bridges already in place. Details were also ordered by Smith to cut timber for siege gun platforms and repair small bridges around the city. Preparations were underway for a general advance to clear Bragg's forces from the heights. Isaac Roseberry wrote in his diary that night, "I think the Johnies has menaced Chattanooga about as long as they can."[51]

Grant planned to have Hooker's men take Lookout Mountain and Thomas's command demonstrate against the face of Missionary Ridge, while Sherman's men were secretly transferred to the far left for the main assault against the Confederate right at the northern end of Missionary Ridge. Sherman's men would march from Bridgeport, cross over the Michigan Bridge to the north bank at Brown's Ferry, and march eastward to a jumping off position opposite the mouth of South Chickamauga Creek. From there they would be crossed in the dark on a hurriedly assembled pontoon bridge. It was critical that Sherman's divisions be moved at the last moment and without the Confederates' knowledge.[52]

Originally it was believed that two pontoon bridges were necessary to cross Sherman's force for the main assault. Dresser would command the army's regular one, gathered together from points all along the Tennessee River. The other pontoon bridge was a Michigan production. The boats had been made by the Michigan Engineers and were secretly placed in the position along North Chickamauga Creek by Captain Fox, aided by Maj. Henry S. Dean and men from his Twenty-second Michigan. From that point they could be floated down the creek to its mouth on the Tennessee east of Chattanooga and thrown across the river.[53]

On the night of November 23, the pontoons were loaded with Sherman's troops and floated the four miles down the creek to its mouth and then across the Tennessee. Sherman's men stormed ashore the next morning against minimal opposition on either side of South Chickamauga Creek and entrenched their bridgehead. The pontoon boats continued to ferry troops across, as did the steamer *Dunbar* sent from Chattanooga. Because the swollen river was much wider than originally calculated and because of the lack of Confederate opposition, it was decided that only one bridge would be laid across the river. Meanwhile, Fox and his men were ordered to take part of their boats and assemble a bridge two hundred feet in length across South Chickamauga Creek. Its completion at 12:30 P.M. allowed the divided infantry of Brig. Gen. Giles Smith's brigade to be reunited. At 3 P.M. that same day Col. Eli Long's Union cavalry brigade crossed over this bridge and began a destructive raid against the rear of Bragg's army.[54]

As soon as the Michigan Engineers finished spanning Chickamauga Creek on the twenty-fourth, Fox and his men hurried back to Chattanooga. Flood-swollen waters of the Tennessee had swept away much of the pontoon bridge spanning the river at the city on the twenty-first and damaged Fox's earlier bridge at Brown's Ferry. Some of the surplus materials from the recent crossing were used for a replacement pontoon bridge between the city and the north bank. Fox supervised this work, though much of the labor was actually done by the men of the Twenty-second Michigan. This new pontoon bridge, laid at the foot of Chestnut Street, was completed on November 25.[55]

As Fox's men were completing this new pontoon bridge, Thomas's command swept forward toward Missionary Ridge. Ordered to take the advance rifle pits and distract Bragg's attention from Sherman's sputtering assaults on the north, the men instead continued on and drove Bragg's forces from the crest of the ridge. Combined with the advance of the Union right under Hooker, the forces under Grant delivered a decisive and crippling blow to Confederate hopes. Fox's four companies of Michigan Engineers in Chattanooga, and the others strung along the railroad leading back to Nashville, had played a large role in this critical victory.

Building the Supply Net

Chattanooga and the Army of the Cumberland were saved for the Union, but merely saving Union armies or holding territory could not win the war. The main Confederate armies must be brought to battle and destroyed if victory was to be won. Just twenty-five miles south of Chattanooga was Braxton Bragg's Army of Tennessee, recovering at Dalton from the debacle astride Missionary Ridge but still the largest rebel army between the Alleghenies and the Mississippi River. Drawing by railroad from its secure supply depots at Atlanta, Bragg's army posed a threat to Union plans for a further advance southward.

General Grant's supply lines were still barely sufficient to feed and supply men and animals. If Chattanooga was to be the forward base for a move into northern Georgia and against Bragg's army, the supply line leading back along the river to Stevenson and ultimately to Nashville and Louisville had to be rebuilt and secured. Even before P. V. Fox's four-company detachment helped in efforts to pry Bragg's army from Missionary Ridge, the balance of the regiment was laboring to improve and secure this route.

By the middle of November 1863, Companies A, F, G, H, and M were working on the Nashville and Northwestern under Major Yates and Colonel Innes. Captain Fox and Companies C, D, and K, joined on the seventeenth by Company B, were finishing work on pontoons in Chattanooga. Lieutenant Colonel Hunton and Companies E, I, and L were at Bridgeport. In response to orders from Gen. "Baldy" Smith, Company M was sent from the Nashville and Northwestern to Bridgeport later in the month, joining Hunton and his three companies already there. With Innes detached to supervise the construction of the Nashville and Northwestern, Hunton assumed command of the regiment, and the regimental headquarters moved to Bridgeport with him. This latter point was a critical one for Union plans.[1]

Bridgeport was rapidly being developed as the transfer point for supplies brought from Nashville on the railroad and then taken to Chattanooga by steamer and wagon train. Huge warehouses were needed to stockpile supplies at the railhead, and transfer facilities had to be built.

General Thomas ordered Lt. Col. William G. LeDuc, quartermaster of the XI Corps, to take charge of the work at Bridgeport, and Hunton was ordered to him. LeDuc was responsible to review construction plans with Hunton and to provide the lumber and nails, while the Michigan Engineers were expected to provide the working parties. Because of previous problems with the flooding of the Tennessee River, all buildings and platforms were to be built above the high waterline.[2]

The first projects for Hunton and his men after their arrival on November 12 were a rail line and warehouse to speed the transfer of supplies from the cars of the Nashville and Chattanooga to steamers and barges. As originally constructed, the Nashville and Chattanooga crossed the Tennessee River at the island, downstream from the best point for a steamboat landing. A rail spur approximately two miles long, leading from the railroad as it neared the river to the landing had to be built. In addition, since supplies would be arriving quicker than steamers could make the trip, it was necessary to have a warehouse built at the landing to protect the supplies until they could be transferred. By November 20 the rail line needed only the iron to be completed. The storehouse, measuring as many as 450 feet long by 30 feet wide, took until January to complete. By early January the men were at work on a second, larger storehouse at the steamboat landing and then went to work on commissary and ordnance depots along the railroad spur leading to the river. Company M arrived on November 23, and the men were put to work alongside the other Michigan Engineers.[3]

Work on the buildings at Bridgeport continued seven days a week until February 17, interrupted only by bad weather or lack of cut timber. Hunton blamed LeDuc's mismanagement of the mills as the cause of the lumber shortage and claimed that adequate board was cut only after General Thomas placed their supervision in Hunton's hands. Eventually four mills were operating at full speed, cutting some forty thousand feet of oak plank per day. The mills represented the makeshift efforts required to keep up with construction demands. One was appropriated near Battle Creek east of Bridgeport, another was taken over and repaired at Bridgeport, a third was on the railroad west of Stevenson, and the fourth was purchased in Cincinnati and shipped by rail to Bridgeport. A fifth was nearing completion in February. Details from the Michigan Engineers were assigned to help operate the mills, working alongside other army details and civilian quartermaster employees.[4]

Until their departure in the spring to build blockhouses, the men in the four companies had little work to do and were able to rest. On February 22 the camp was moved into the main breastworks along the river because of rumors that Confederate cavalry was planning an assault upon the place. A few days later Maj. Gen. Henry Slocum inspected the defenses and reported to Grant, "I think you can feel perfectly safe as to this post." Within days, three of the Michigan Engineers companies at Bridgeport left this "perfectly safe" post for assignments at more vulnerable points along the railroad.[5]

The supplies reaching Bridgeport came by rail from the great depots at Nashville. As Confederate cavalry had demonstrated in the past, however, the narrow rail line into Nashville from Louisville was vulnerable to raids. Nashville was on the Cumberland River, but low water in the summer prevented all but the shallowest boats from moving as far upriver as that city. Since it was expected that Union armies would be in the field in northern Georgia in the summer of 1864, the supply line into Nashville needed to be expanded to make it less vulnerable to a single break in the line.

One of the easiest ways to create a second rail connection with Nashville was to accelerate the completion of the Nashville and Northwestern Railroad. At the war's start, twenty-eight miles of track was in place westward from Nashville and five or six miles eastward from the Tennessee River terminus near Reynoldsburg (later Johnsonville). The forty-four-mile gap had been surveyed and some grading completed. Most of the trestles along the proposed route were not over major rivers but instead designed to ease the grade through the hilly terrain. Though Confederates could tear up track and destroy bridges on this line just as they had along the Louisville and Nashville, the bridges were fewer and generally shorter. More important, there were no tunnels that could be blocked, stopping all rail traffic.[6]

Though often discussed and studied, no wartime work had been done on this line until August 1863, when Rosecrans placed its completion in the hands of Military Governor Andrew Johnson. To aid in the actual construction, Railroad Superintendent Innes was to detail engineers and furnish rolling stock, while guards were to be furnished by General Granger and Brig. Gen. Alvan C. Gillem in Nashville. On September 1 Rosecrans sent Innes a message that as much of the regiment as could be spared from its work should be sent to the Nashville and Northwestern. This was followed a week later with specific directions that four companies should be sent, as long as it would not delay the work the regiment was doing along the Nashville and Chattanooga.[7]

It was logical to assign the task of finishing the Nashville and Northwestern to Innes and his Michigan Engineers. Innes and many of his officers had constructed prewar railroads from scratch, and he was familiar with the western terminus of the line from the train-stealing expedition mounted in March 1862. Major Yates had inspected the route in the spring of 1863 and prepared a report on what was necessary to complete work on it. Innes added to the report in July.

The report identified the following work to be done to finish the railroad link between Nashville and the Tennessee River: 115,000 cubic yards of grading, 5,200 feet of trestle, 107,000 ties, and the laying of forty-three and a half miles of track, which would require some 230,000 railroad spikes and over 3,200 tons of rail. If two small bridges were constructed, the first twenty-eight miles westward from Nashville could quickly be in operation.[8]

Captain Sligh and Companies A, B, F, and L left Elk River by train on September 14 and were along the Nashville and Northwestern at the Big Harpeth River by the seventeenth. There were at least seven bridges on the Nashville and Northwestern over the Harpeth River within a stretch of about ten miles. The first two were located within a mile of each other, between thirteen and fourteen miles from Nashville. By October 5 work was nearing completion on these bridges. Two days later, Sligh and Companies F, B, and L were pulled off the Nashville and Northwestern to aid in the repair of the Nashville and Chattanooga following General Wheeler's raid. During their absence, Company A was the only portion of the Michigan Engineers still working on the Nashville and Northwestern under the command of Major Yates.[9]

Though attention was focused on Wheeler's raid along the Nashville and Chattanooga, Yates's men were also exposed to rebel attacks. Franklin Foster of Company A was riding a Nashville and Northwestern train on the night of October 18 when guerrillas killed him. Despite the long exposed road and scattered working parties, the men of the Tenth (First Middle) Tennessee and the newly formed and incomplete Thirteenth USCT provided the only available protection. The black soldiers were a regiment in name only, just six companies strong and having had little opportunity to drill or train when first assigned to the road. Their commander, Lt. Col. Theodore Trauernicht, described his regiment's position at Camp Rosecrans as "simply an outpost, constantly in danger, with no chance to improve our drill and discipline."[10]

Despite Andrew Johnson's claim that "the work is underway and progressing very well," the work on the road was behind schedule, badly hindered by the absence of all but one company of the Michigan Engineers and the inability of Trauernicht's hard-pressed regiment to detail more men for fatigue duty. Military Governor Johnson asked General Thomas for the return of as many companies of the

Michigan Engineers as possible to continue work on the Nashville and Northwestern. Thomas replied, "I deem it of vital importance that the Nashville and Northwestern be finished as soon as possible and will therefore cheerfully give you as many companies from the Michigan Engineers as can be spared." On November 3 Thomas's headquarters telegraphed Johnson that Innes and three companies were under orders to report to him for duty on the Nashville and Northwestern. Joining them would be Colonel Thompson's Twelfth USCT from Elk River, the newly raised Eighth Iowa Cavalry and the veteran First Kansas Battery. The entire force along the Nashville and Northwestern was placed under the command of General Gillem.[11]

Johnson also appointed Innes to direct the construction of the Nashville and Northwestern. The governor trusted him, and they had been close allies in disputes over railroad management. Furthermore, Innes was available to concentrate solely on the Nashville and Northwestern construction following his dismissal as military rail superintendent. Commanders of troops assigned to guard duty along the line were ordered by Johnson to "give [Innes] all assistance" and cooperate fully with his efforts.[12]

In order to ensure a steady supply of iron rail and related materials, Innes met with Quartermaster General Meigs, still in Tennessee. Though iron for the line had been purchased and delivered before the war, Union officials confiscated it and used it on other lines before work began on the Nashville and Northwestern. By the end of November Johnson was reporting to the War Department that the railroad was in "such position that we can lay down the rail as fast as delivered and in a very short time open communication to the Tennessee River."[13]

By the end of November there were four companies of the Michigan Engineers working on the Nashville and Northwestern, A, F, G, and H. Experienced railroad builder Yates took command of the battalion, while Innes continued to direct the overall effort. They had completed the work of getting out railroad ties along section thirty-one near Poplar Springs and moved forward to section thirty-eight on the twenty-third. Here they were camped beside the Twelfth and Thirteenth USCT regiments and got out more railroad ties, while the black soldiers graded and filled the route.[14]

As work progressed the engineers moved their camp forward and continued to produce thousands of railroad ties. On December 2 camp was moved to section forty-two and then to section forty-nine two weeks later. It could be dangerous work. Pvt. Ross B. Swift cut his knee badly with an ax while getting out ties and died from his injuries. He was one of at least nine Michigan Engineers whose deaths were caused by work injuries, and dozens more were seriously injured.[15]

The engineers remained along section forty-nine for two months working on the railroad and several trestles. One of the largest trestles along the entire road was located in section forty-seven, 1,067 feet long and up to 33 feet high at its tallest. Nearby trestles 837 (section fifty-two) and 442 (section forty-nine) feet long also had to be constructed. These trestles were built to ease the grade of the road through the hilly country and not to cross over any streams. While details from the regiment cut the timber for these nearby bridges, other Michigan Engineers continued to get out ties. By early February the engineers had built some 2,300 feet of trestle work and gotten out thirty thousand railroad ties since reaching section forty-nine. The men might have also worked on several buildings that were built at section fifty to house telegraph operations and provide sleeping quarters for the trainmen and trackmen to come.[16]

In general the Michigan Engineers "lived well while building this railroad." Though the region they were in was not as fertile and productive as that along the Nashville and Decatur, the men were able to steal livestock and other food from neighboring farms. In late November Yates and a detachment from the regiment were surveying in section forty-nine when they were told that parties of guerrillas were nearby. Yates, "being full of whiskey," decided they should go after them. With the help of a local Union guide, the small group searched two houses of rebel sympathizers. Failing to find the men they were searching for, the group confiscated butter and poultry as "contraband" and returned to a nearby USCT camp with their loot. The next day while Yates and most of the men finished the surveying, Captain Grant and a small detail continued the search for rebels and whiskey. Failing to find the former but locating the latter, the group rejoined the major's party and returned to camp. One participant described it as "altogether . . . one of the most pleasant time we had during the war." William H. Kimball described a pre-Christmas raid: "I captured a goose and some cabbage. The boys of our tent got fresh pork and turkeys. One of the boys chased a hen in the house and captured her while the old lady looked on in horror." Six weeks later three men in a Company H mess contrived to shoot a nearby pig, dressed it under the noses of the camp guards inquiring about the shot, and smuggled it into camp in a wheelbarrow under a sack of coffee and a load of firewood.[17]

By the end of January it could be reported to Thomas that work on the Nashville and Northwestern was progressing well. Thirty-four miles of track were in running order westward from Nashville, with another twenty miles ready for grading and iron. Working from the Tennessee River, construction crews had eighteen miles ready for iron, with only six miles yet to grade. Innes was asking for two more USCT regiments as well as three hundred civilian contract railroad men from the East. Provided these reinforcements and the iron for the track, Innes was projecting that the line would be completed within sixty days.[18]

Innes, however, did not have sixty days in which to finish the line. There was great dissatisfaction among Union authorities regarding the entire construction of the Nashville and Northwestern. Much of the criticism was directed at Military Governor Johnson, who had insisted on personally directing its construction and fought with the army over his prerogative to do so. Johnson, in turn, placed much of the blame on the military rail superintendent, John B. Anderson.[19]

Criticism of Anderson's overall performance came from other leading figures in addition to Johnson. Thomas complained to Grant on January 14, 1864, that Anderson had failed to properly run the railroads in the department, leaving the army short of rolling stock and stores. Thomas charged that Anderson, despite the shortage of trained workmen, had tried to refuse the offer of twelve hundred civilians from Daniel McCallum's military railroad force in the East, in the end grudgingly accepting only five hundred of them. The Nashville and Chattanooga was still not opened through to Chattanooga, and when it opened Thomas believed the credit should be given to McCallum and not Anderson. Frustrated with Anderson, Thomas wanted McCallum to direct the railroad in the military division, believing that "if anybody can help us out of this railroad difficulty he can." A month later, Meigs also compiled a report critical of Anderson's handling of the railroads in the department.[20]

On February 4 Grant made much of this contentious dispute moot and appointed McCallum as general manager of all railroads in the Military Division of the Mississippi, in place of Anderson. Two weeks later, Innes was relieved from his responsibilities for the Nashville and Northwestern and ordered to return to his regiment. By the same order, McCallum was directed to take charge of the construction of the Nashville and Northwestern, including those companies of the Michigan Engineers working along it. Though Innes did not come in for the strong criticism reserved for Anderson at this time, the government was clearly not happy with Johnson's and Innes's performance in directing this vital rail project. McCallum's appointment meant a clean sweep of the structure and individuals who had been running and building military railroads in the western theater.[21]

By the time Innes was replaced, the four companies of his regiment under Yates along the Nashville and Northwestern were at section fifty-five, to which point they had moved on February 16 and 17. Most of the men were working on a trestle about one thousand feet long that included seventy bents in its construction. Another portion of the battalion was in the process of distributing railroad ties along the line. Since the Missouri Engineers and Mechanics regiment was working the road beyond section fifty-seven, the Michigan men prepared to finish up their work and rejoin the rest of the regiment. They left on March 5, rested for a few days in Nashville, and then were headed south along the railroad to their next assignment.[22]

In addition to Nashville and Bridgeport, the other main point for concentration of men and supplies was Chattanooga. Once the siege was lifted and Bragg's men driven back to northwestern Georgia, Union quartermaster officers labored to turn it into an advance base for the movement into Georgia the following spring. Companies B, C, D, and K remained near Chattanooga, and with the departure of Captain Fox on recruiting service on November 30, command devolved upon senior captain Emery O. Crittenton of Company K. The four companies were officially designated as the Third Battalion, and newly promoted Maj. Garrett Hannings was assigned command of the battalion on March 1, 1864.[23]

For six months the men of this battalion worked on a wide variety of projects in and around Chattanooga. Immediately after the battle for Missionary Ridge, the men were put to work on the roads and rail line leading south. On December 1 the Michigan Engineers were relieved from duty at the mills, and Major Dean and his Twenty-second Michigan were ordered to report to Crittenton to assist with the road repair. During the following week they hewed and loaded timbers for the Chattanooga Creek pike bridge between Chattanooga and Rossville. Several more days were spent working on a nearby railroad bridge. Details from Crittenton's battalion framed the bridge timbers, while others from the regiment rebuilt them.[24]

Work continued on these and other projects during the winter. By late December details of the battalion were back running the sawmills. They also constructed several bridges over Chattanooga Creek and Lookout Creek, relayed over three miles of railroad track, built a large quantity of platforms for the protection of government stores awaiting transportation, and got out countless railroad ties. During this whole time details from the battalion worked night and day shifts in the mills to meet the army's voracious appetite for cut lumber. Frequently

Several companies were stationed in and around Chattanooga between September 1863 and the summer of 1864, as it became one of the most important Union supply depots. Pictured here is a part of their camp in the eastern part of the city, with Lookout Mountain looming in the background to the southwest. Archives of Michigan.

The four officers sitting outdoors are, from left, Lt. William Bettinghouse, Capt. Joseph Herkner, Lt. Benjamin Cotton, and Capt. George D. Emerson. The first three were from Company D. Emerson commanded Company L, but because he was one of the most experienced civil engineers in the regiment, he was detailed to Chattanooga in April or May 1864 to help oversee construction projects there. Archives of Michigan.

The men of Company D were among the first from the regiment to arrive in Chattanooga in September 1863. They remained there for more than a year and earned high praise for their work in the relief of the Army of the Cumberland. Archives of Michigan.

work was interrupted by failures at the mill, requiring the skill of the trained mechanics within the companies.[25]

In early March Hannings reported to Innes that the men were working at several sawmills, turning out lumber for various projects including the Soldiers' Home and a field hospital. Other details worked on projects at the brick railroad depot, including building or repairing platforms and erecting a fence around it. Hannings estimated that it would take at least two months for the battalion to complete the various projects it was working on.[26]

On March 23 General Thomas ordered Hannings to detail one company to Lookout Mountain for the purpose of repairing the officers' hospital and to prepare for the arrival of a portable sawmill en route from the North. Company C moved its camp to Lookout Mountain on the twenty-eighth, and by April 7 the portable saw mill was nearly assembled. The men spent the next several weeks turning out lumber for hospitals located near the prewar resort of Summertown, at the northeast end of Lookout Mountain.[27]

Lookout Mountain dominated the Chattanooga area and was a popular backdrop for wartime images. Here members of Company C join Capt. James D. Robinson for a group photo. Archives of Michigan.

In mid-April the balance of the battalion began to build defenses along local railroad spurs, including those on Hospital Hill. Hannings was placed in charge, and five hundred black soldiers were assigned to work with the Michigan Engineers companies. Hannings was a master carpenter but had no practical engineering experience, a deficiency common to all of the present officers in the four companies under his command. He requested of Innes that Capt. George D. Emerson of Company L or Lt. George W. White of Company F be ordered to Chattanooga to provide engineering and surveying direction for the work.[28]

By late April other details from the battalion were at work on a new magazine in Chattanooga. Located along the river on the northeast corner of First and Chestnut streets, it measured seventy by one hundred feet. The foundation was made from lime rock, and the superstructure was made of bricks taken from existing nearby warehouses that the Michigan Engineers pulled down. The walls were about twenty feet high, and the roof was supported by large timbers and covered with three feet of solid tamped earth. The boards for the roof were cut at a steam sawmill operated by Company D and were first planed and then grooved, serving as efficient eaves. General Thomas frequently visited the engineers, chatting with the men and viewing their work.[29]

When the building was finished, the Michigan Engineers built a railroad spur down the street to the front of the building. This was one of the most extensive buildings ever built by the Michigan Engineers, and they were justifiably proud of the accomplishment. Using the back of a broken tombstone found in one of the abandoned warehouses, Charles C. Marsh of Company C carved the following inscription: "Erected by the First Michigan Engineers, A.D. 1864." This, and a castle carved out of solid rock, was inserted in the front wall of the magazine.[30]

During this time the battalion camp remained on a hillside in Chattanooga, near General Thomas's headquarters. On several of the projects the Michigan Engineers worked alongside details drawn from the army's Engineer Brigade. This organization was formally created in January when the Eighteenth Ohio and the Thirteenth, Twenty-first and Twenty-second Michigan infantry regiments were brigaded together under Col. Timothy R. Stanley of Ohio. All of these regiments had experience on engineering-type projects at Chattanooga, and three of them had worked with details from the Michigan Engineers at one time or another. Details from the four infantry regiments cut and hauled timber to the Michigan Engineers working parties at the two mills, built steamers and barges for the supply line, constructed hospitals and other buildings, and built and operated two sawmills on the north bank of the Tennessee. They remained at work near Chattanooga on various projects until the fall of 1864.[31]

Work at the mill, operated by details from Company D, continued sporadically during May and early June. The mill was frequently broken, and the supply of timber was erratic. During down times some of the men worked on nearby bridges. By late June 1864 the work at Chattanooga had slowed, and orders were given to construct railroad defenses on the railroad leading south from Chattanooga. On June 23 Companies B, C, and K left Chattanooga for the railroad south toward Atlanta. Only Company D remained in Chattanooga, where it stayed for another four months.[32]

· 16 ·

Protecting Sherman's Supply Line

By the end of March 1864 plans were in place for the coming campaign. Ulysses S. Grant, promoted to lieutenant general and placed in command of all Union armies, went east to personally direct the operations of the forces in northern Virginia. Maj. Gen. William T. Sherman was promoted to command the Military Division of the Mississippi. Sherman's assignment was to take Atlanta and destroy the Confederate Army of Tennessee. That force, now commanded by Gen. Joseph Johnston, was still a potent fighting force over fifty thousand strong. It rested astride the route of any advance by Sherman toward Atlanta.

To accomplish this task, Sherman assembled a force of 110,000 men, divided into three armies. Maj. Gen. George H. Thomas's Army of the Cumberland was by far the largest with over 73,000 men in the IV, XIV, and new XX corps. The XI and XII corps were combined to form the XX Corps. Maj. Gen. James B. McPherson took Sherman's place as commander of the Army of the Tennessee, 24,500 men in five divisions drawn from the XV, XVI, and XVII corps. The smallest component was Maj. Gen. John M. Schofield's Army of the Ohio, consisting of only the small XXIII Corps with 13,500 men. Another 25,000 noncombatants supported the fighting men, including civilian railroad employees, teamsters, medical personnel, and laborers.[1]

This huge army would need an enormous logistical effort to keep it fed and equipped during the upcoming campaign. A planning conference in April studied the matter and concluded, "It would require one hundred and thirty railroad cars, each carrying ten tons of supplies, arriving in Chattanooga each day to provide for the army." Sherman's offensive would come to a grinding halt if the railroad were broken for any length of time, just as General Buell's had two years earlier. To prevent a repetition, authorities ordered that huge storehouses be built and filled at Chattanooga and stronger railroad defenses be constructed along its length.[2]

By trial and error, Union military authorities had settled on wood and dirt blockhouses as the best means of defending the long railroad supply lines. In January 1864 Capt. William E. Merrill, now chief engineer of the Army of the Cumberland, was ordered by Thomas to construct railroad defenses back to Nashville. In turn, Merrill called upon Lieutenant Colonel Hunton for assistance. They inspected locations and also conducted experiments upon an unused blockhouse at Lavergne. Merrill decided to modify his earlier stockade designs, and a second wall was added for strength. Roofs were also added to the plans to protect against plunging fire from surrounding elevations.[3]

Merrill's plans outlined blockhouses constructed in a square or rectangular shape, with a second story or tower set diagonal to the ground floor, providing a better field of fire against attacks from any direction. The walls of the first floor were usually a double-thickness of timber, at least forty inches combined, with twenty-inch-thick timbers erected vertically as an inner wall and another wall of twenty-inch-thick timber set horizontally to provide maximum strength. The walls of the upper level were designed with only a single thickness for better stability. The roof was made of a layer or two of logs placed side by side with earth thrown on top. Shingles of boards or battens provided waterproofing. For the comfort of the garrison of twenty or so, ventilators, cellars, watertanks, and bunks were added. As skilled engineers were available, mortises and tenons were used instead of spikes because the latter would have to be supplied along already-stretched supply lines.[4]

In general, the framing and erecting of the blockhouse was done by the engineer troops, but they often left after completing only the inner vertical wall. The outer wall, filling of earth, and finishing touches were left to the garrison, usually an infantry squad. Though the natural defensive advantages of an octagonal shape were recognized, it was decided to make the blockhouses square or rectangular to speed their construction. In practice, there was great difficulty getting all of the blockhouses fully completed because of the frequent garrison changes, the difficulty of overseeing so many scattered locations, and the lack of earnest work among the short-term troops often assigned garrison duty.[5]

These blockhouses were considered sufficient to deter Confederate raids on the vulnerable railroad bridges in Sherman's rear. Though the strong points could eventually be reduced by artillery or overrun by a mass dismounted assault, cavalry commanders were loath to spend the time necessary to concentrate the guns and men necessary to take each one by force of arms. A small squad of twenty men inside a blockhouse could hold out long enough for relief to arrive or until the attackers lost interest, as long as the garrison resisted the temptation to surrender when threatened with annihilation. Merrill recounted after

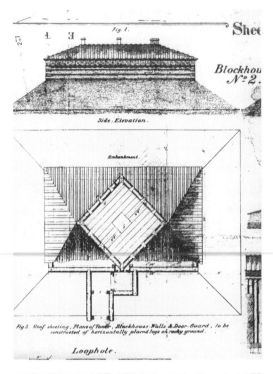

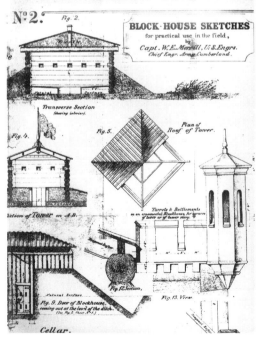

"Supplement to Blockhouse Sheets No. 1 and No. 2," April 1864. Capt. William E. Merrill was meticulous in the preparation and modification of plans for railroad defense blockhouses. Instructions and designs such as these were provided to the officers and men working on their construction. Many of the design elements resulted from March 1864 experiments carried out by Captain Merrill, with help from Lt. Col. Kinsman Hunton of the Michigan Engineers. In the rush to get them completed, most of the more frivolous elements, such as the turrets, were never constructed. Buell-Brien Papers, Tennessee State Library.

the war that few blockhouses were taken by assault. Those that were captured succumbed to immediate surrender or were evacuated in the face of overwhelming forces of infantry and artillery.[6]

As commander of the Department of the Cumberland, Thomas's responsibilities included protecting the rear areas leading back to Nashville. The eight Michigan Engineers companies not at Chattanooga were organized into two battalions, and the work was divided between them. Major Yates and a four-company battalion (A, F, G, and H) were sent to the Nashville and Decatur to construct blockhouses between Franklin and Decatur. The four companies at Bridgeport (E, I, L, and M) were placed under Hunton's command and assigned to build the Nashville and Chattanooga blockhouses. Regimental headquarters remained at Bridgeport, where it had been since the fall. The eight companies under Major Yates and Lieutenant Colonel Hunton were divided into squads of about twenty men, each under the command of a lieutenant or noncommissioned officer. In this manner, each company could work simultaneously on several blockhouses. Major Hanning's Third Battalion (Companies B, C, D, and K) remained near Chattanooga and was not involved in the initial blockhouse construction.[7]

By mid-March Yates's battalion was scattered in detachments along the railroad from Franklin to Decatur. Between these points there were at least thirty blockhouses to be built, with the greatest concentration in the ten-mile section between Columbia, Carter's Creek, and Rutherford Creek. As the companies finished their work, they were moved further south on the Decatur line.[8]

One of Yates's scattered detachments was a squad of twenty-three men from Company H under the command of Cpl. Irving Updike, assigned to build a stockade at one of the bridges over Rutherford Creek. Their work was typical of that performed along the railroad by the Michigan Engineers. The blockhouse measured fifty-three by twenty-one feet on the outside. The inner wall of the blockhouse was built with timbers twelve by eighteen inches set into the ground vertically, with timbers twelve inches square cut for the roof, which was covered with dirt to make it "bomb proof." In all, the detail cut and framed twenty-four hundred cubic feet of lumber from standing timber for the stockade.[9]

One whole day was required to set up camp, prepare the ovens, and grind the tools. The work of clearing the site and cutting timber started on March 15. The logs were framed beginning March 29 and took one week. The foundation was laid on April 4, and the sides were raised beginning two days later. The roof plates were raised the next week using greased railroad iron to put them in place. A dirt covering was added over the next few days. Some of the work was done by a USCT detachment temporarily stationed nearby as guards for the Company H working parties. Finishing work was done shortly after. The finished product was inspected and approved by Major Yates on April 28.[10]

Captain Grant and Lieutenant Chapel were both critical of the pace of Updike's detachment and made frequent visits to spur the men on. William H. Kimball's diary indicates that the men did work on the blockhouse almost every day, weather permitting, but there was plenty of time for visiting area farms on social calls and in search of fresh food to purchase. In fact, he noted that the detail "obtained the best food from the surrounding country at this camp of any while in the service." Some of the delay was caused by the lack of teams and proper tools, a problem for many of the Michigan Engineers detachments on blockhouse duty.[11]

By the end of April, Yates's work along the Nashville and Decatur was practically completed, and the men moved to construct blockhouses along the Memphis and Charleston, with the battalion headquarters at Huntsville. There were at least ten blockhouses guarding key railroad bridges between Decatur and Stevenson, where the Memphis and Charleston and Nashville and Chattanooga roads joined. After another month's labor most of these blockhouses were also nearly complete. The individual detachments of the four companies moved to Bridgeport as they completed their assigned blockhouses. All were at that point by late June.[12]

Meanwhile, Companies E, I, L, and M had been building blockhouses along the Nashville and Chattanooga. Almost half of Hunton's blockhouses were to protect the many spans over meandering Crow Creek, and Companies E and I were given that assignment. Among the Michigan working parties was a squad from Company I that started work on the first blockhouse north of Stevenson on March 3. By March 20 the hard-working detail had moved north a short distance and begun work on the blockhouses at the bridges over Crow Creek No. 3 and Crow Creek No. 4. They finished work on both of them by April 13. Since the rough terrain precluded Confederate use of artillery, the blockhouses over Crow Creek were built with only a single thickness of timber.[13]

As detachments completed work on the Crow Creek blockhouses in April, they moved east beyond Bridgeport to build four blockhouses over Running Water near Whiteside. These structures guarded the most important railroad bridge between the Tennessee crossings at Bridgeport and Chattanooga. The blockhouses were placed on the slopes of a steep ravine and commanded any approach to the 780-foot-long and 116-foot-high trestle bridge. One of the men from Company I who worked on the blockhouses at the Running Water Bridge described the terrain as "nothing but mountain and rock." After finishing the work at Running Water, these men were ordered to Bridgeport to work on its defenses.[14]

During this same time, Hunton's other two companies (L and M) worked further north along the Nashville and Chattanooga. Details constructed blockhouses near Elk River, Tullahoma, Cowan Station, Normandy, and nearby locations. As this work was completed, they were shifted to the Stevenson area.[15]

On April 18 Merrill ordered Major Fox to take charge of finishing the defenses of Stevenson. Companies L and M were ordered to report to Fox. At the same time, the other two companies of Hunton's battalion (E and I) were ordered to Bridgeport on similar duty. Colonel Innes was to assume command of the defenses at Bridgeport. Unlike the blockhouses that had been built along the railroad, the defenses of Bridgeport and Stevenson were designed to do more than delay roving bands of rebel cavalry armed with light field guns. Each point was a major link in Sherman's supply net running back to Nashville, and their defenses were priorities.[16]

Bridgeport was the site not only of extensive quartermaster buildings built by the Michigan Engineers and others but also of the critical railroad span across the Tennessee River. Merrill intended to protect against a sudden assault as well as to deny the Confederates any position from which they could rain a storm of shot and shell upon the critical crossing. Two large artillery blockhouses were planned to protect the long bridge over the river. They were located at each end of the east span, one on the island and the other on the east bank. Additional fortifications on both sides of the bridge were designed for a garrison of one thousand men and two dozen pieces of artillery.[17]

Work on these two artillery blockhouses started in late April under the personal direction of Colonel Innes, though most of the details from Companies E and I did not arrive until two weeks later. Yates's four companies working on the Memphis and Charleston blockhouses were directed to Bridgeport as they completed work, greatly speeding up Innes's construction schedule. The men working at Bridgeport also benefited from having army sawmills cut most of the timber. By the middle of June the two artillery blockhouses were nearing completion, and the men prepared for new assignments. After the war Merrill wrote that the "construction of these [artillery] blockhouses reflected great credit upon the Michigan Engineers by whom they were built."[18]

Meanwhile, Major Fox and most of Companies L and M were strengthening the defenses at Stevenson. Two redoubts and eight

The railroad bridge across Running Water in the Whiteside Valley was one of the most important between Bridgeport and Chattanooga. The Michigan Engineers did not work on the bridge, but they did construct the blockhouses seen here. In total, four blockhouses were constructed at and near the bridge for its defense. Miller, *Photographic History of the Civil War*.

This blockhouse was built by the Michigan Engineers and probably guarded the approaches to the Running Water Bridge. Notice the abundant cover for approaching enemy troops. Miller, *Photographic History of the Civil War*.

standard-sized blockhouses provided a strong defense of the critical supply point and rail junction. Lieutenant Templeton and Captain Gifford arrived with the advance detachments of their companies on May 9, with the balance of each company under orders to follow as soon as the Nashville and Chattanooga blockhouses were completed. In the meantime, Fox was provided with details from the Thirteenth Wisconsin to get out timber, but progress was delayed on the blockhouses themselves because of the small number of men available. For the next four months, Fox and Companies L and M labored on the fortifications of Stevenson. With their camp pleasantly situated in a nearby apple orchard, the men settled into a predictable daily work schedule, leading Pvt. Simeon Howe to write home that "it seems more like working by the month than going to war."[19]

With most of the army at the front with Sherman, the working parties of the Michigan Engineers were exposed to Confederate raiding parties and guerrillas. C. L. Hequembourg, chief of the courier line along these roads, warned, "The military force has been so largely withdrawn that the protection of the roads is entirely inadequate and its weakness will invite the malicious who prowl in the country." Company F's bugler was only a mile from camp near Columbia when he was spotted by guerrillas and chased back to camp under fire, receiving a slight hand wound but evading his would-be capturers. A few days later a member of Company A was taken prisoner by Confederates but managed to escape. However, on his return to camp he was fired on and wounded by the Union pickets. In early May Cpl. Absalom N. Hatch of Company F was captured near Brownsboro, Alabama, while riding from Huntsville and spent the rest of the war in Confederate prison camps.[20]

Major Fox, writing home from Stevenson in June, noted that the rebels were "quite thick about here and also quite bold," knowing that "there is nothing but green hundred day men so they are inclined to try them." He wrote about rebel incursions into the Union lines, appearing and withdrawing without loss.[21]

Another area of strong rebel activity was along the Nashville and Chattanooga just south of Tullahoma, considered "the worst place for guerrillas on the whole road" because the road ran through a dense forest with cover for bushwhackers. This area included the stretch of track where Captain Sligh had been fatally injured the previous fall. On March 16 several members of the regiment were riding on a train that was derailed and attacked midway between Estill Springs and Poor Man's Creek. Pvt. John W. McGowan was badly shot through his thigh, and Pvt. Otis Pitts was severely wounded in the thigh and groin. Lts. Ferdinand Boughton and Henry Williams were held long enough for rebel soldiers to take watches, pay, a trunk, and most of their clothes. Capt. Joseph Herkner's horse was captured and ridden off. Only the timely arrival of a company from the 123rd New York, which drove back the mounted raiders and freed most of their prisoners, prevented these officers from being led south into captivity. A harsher fate was in store for the black soldiers and civilian army employees on the train, who were killed as quickly as the Confederates could catch them.[22]

Another serious incident occurred early in the morning of May 19, when a train was derailed and attacked between Bellefonte and Stevenson on the Memphis and Charleston. A detachment from the Fifty-sixth Illinois and a handful of Michigan Engineers, men from Company H working on the nearby Mud Creek blockhouse, heard the shots and ran through the dark and the dense fog to the rescue. Among those narrowly escaping death in the train wreck was Daniel Bennett of the same company, who was serving as one of the regiment's mail couriers.[23]

This was bitter warfare, reminiscent of the regiment's service along the same railroad two years earlier. Lt. James M. Sligh wrote home approvingly that William B. Stokes's unionist Fifth Tennessee troopers were killing any Confederates that they captured: "This is the only way to deal with the prowling bands that are continually hurrying around to see who they can plunder and kill." When one man from a rebel raiding party near Cumming's Wood Yard was captured and taken to nearby Tullahoma, a member of the Michigan Engineers speculated that he was shot, since "they shoot them in Tullahoma as fast as they catch them."[24]

The work was also dangerous because of accidents. Sgt. William F. Muir of Company M was killed instantly on August 20, 1864, while working on the defenses of Stevenson. A post was being raised, and the strap holding the tackle slipped. He was a particularly close friend of Newton Fox, and Maj. P. V. Fox wrote home with the sad news: "The boy turned swinging round . . . [and] dropped on the ground just at the spot where it fell, crushing him to death instantly. He was a fine fellow and generally beloved." The work was dangerous, and at least nine men in the regiment died from construction accidents during the war, and dozens more were seriously injured.[25]

By late June the blockhouses along the railroad leading back from Chattanooga were largely completed. Meanwhile, Sherman's forces were nearing Marietta, having driven Johnston back upon his defenses near Kenesaw Mountain. Daniel McCallum's repair parties from the U.S. Military Railroad (USMRR) had moved southward along the railroad in Sherman's wake, repairing track and rebuilding bridges. These additional miles of railroad ran through hostile and rugged territory. They had to be defended to ensure a steady flow of supplies for one hundred thousand men and thirty thousand animals at the front and the evacuation of sick and wounded to the hospitals in the rear. In June Sherman created the District of the Etowah with responsibility to protect the railroad between Bridgeport and the front and placed Maj. Gen. James B. Steedman in command. Willett remained in charge of the construction of the railroad defenses within the entire department, but Innes was named superintendent of the railroad defenses along the Western and Atlantic at Thomas's direction. Infantry commands were ordered to provide working parties to assist Innes, and quartermaster and railroad officers were instructed to pass detachments of the Michigan Engineers along the railroad.[26]

One key stretch of railroad to protect included at least a dozen bridges over Chickamauga Creek between Chattanooga and Tunnel Hill. Other blockhouses were built at key locations and river crossings further south, including at Buzzard Roost Gap, Dalton, Allatoona, and Kingston. In all twenty-two were built between Chattanooga and Atlanta, all of them double-cased for maximum protection against the light artillery provided to Confederate cavalry divisions. These blockhouses also were larger than those further north, eighteen feet by thirty feet instead of the typical eighteen by eighteen or twenty-one by twenty-one.[27]

Major Hannings and Companies B, C, and K left Chattanooga on June 23, moving south along the railroad into positions at bridges over Chickamauga Creek. Company B was taken to Chickamauga Station, near three bridges over the creek of the same name. Company was K was dropped off at Graysville, near the locations for two blockhouses at the Chickamauga Creek bridges. Company C was deposited one mile south of Ringgold at another bridge site. Hannings established the battalion headquarters at Ringgold. They remained working on these and nearby blockhouses throughout the summer.[28]

More companies were en route. Most of the men in Companies A, F, G, and H left Bridgeport on June 28 and reached Ringgold that night. Along the way they stopped and unloaded additional tools for Companies B, C, and K. Early on the twenty-ninth details from Company G were dropped off at three bridges over Chickamauga Creek just south of Ringgold. Company F was dropped at the next two bridges further south. A squad from Company A was unloaded at Tilton, with other detachments from that company left at two bridges between Calhoun and Adairsville.[29]

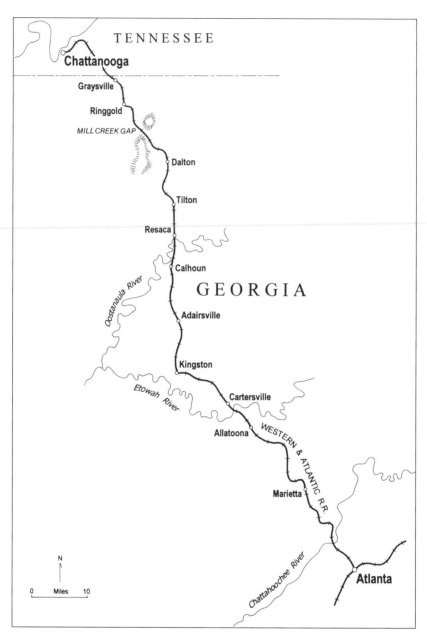

TENNESSEE

Chattanooga

Graysville

Ringgold

MILL CREEK GAP

Dalton

Tilton

Resaca

Calhoun

Oostanaula River

GEORGIA

Adairsville

Kingston

Etowah River

Cartersville

Allatoona

WESTERN & ATLANTIC R.R.

Marietta

Chattahoochee River

Atlanta

N

0   Miles   10

Chattanooga to Atlanta. Map by Sherman Hollander.

Meanwhile, Company H and the regimental headquarters continued further south on the railroad to Cartersville, eighty-nine miles from Chattanooga. In the absence of any other Union troops, Innes took command of the post and positioned his command as pickets. A makeshift headquarters was established in the depot building, and Captain Grant was appointed provost marshal. That night there was considerable firing by the pickets, but no determined attack was forthcoming. Grant, however, had to collect and arrest several drunken soldiers who had broken into a private house and caused a general alarm in the town. The next morning Innes wrote Steedman that he had decided the area was "infested with guerrillas" and that he would establish a post at Cartersville to protect the railroad. Citizens were forced to help build a barricade around the town, and Grant and his provost guard were busy rounding up officers and men who were passing through without proper authorization and sending them back to their commands. Within days Col. William W. Lowe and part of his Third Cavalry Division arrived to provide for the defense of Cartersville. The arrival of Company I, the regimental wagon train, and the balance of Company H also reinforced Innes's small command.[30]

From his new regimental headquarters, Innes tried to direct the activities of twelve companies scattered in detachments along 118 miles of track from Cartersville to Stevenson. He ordered Hunton to make a tour of inspection of the companies along this line and gave him authority to issue any instructions he thought necessary to the scattered commands. For the rest of July the men in Companies H and I drilled, performed guard duty, foraged in the country, and worked on blockhouses in the immediate vicinity of Cartersville.[31]

Meanwhile, the scattered companies north of Cartersville continued working on the blockhouses as July turned to August. Company F finished work on the blockhouses a few miles south of Ringgold in early August and marched to Tilton, twenty-one miles away. Company B moved south in August from Chickamauga Station to near Ringgold, but the others remained in the same general areas as assigned in June. Part of Company E came up from Bridgeport by early August and joined the blockhouse construction, probably north of Tunnel Hill, since they came under Major Hannings's command. At the end of July Merrill reported to Col. Richard Delafield, the new head of the Corps of Engineers, that the Michigan Engineers were engaged in building twenty-one blockhouses between Chattanooga and Marietta, with each about four-fifths finished.[32]

During June and July Confederate cavalry and guerrillas harassed the working parties and trains. On June 22 a Michigan Engineer was conductor on a train that had to brake suddenly when rebels were seen tearing up the track just north of Dalton. The train guard scrambled down from the cars and drove the Confederates off. The break in the road was quickly repaired, and the train was able to leave just in time to escape a second band of enemy cavalry. On July 5 a loaded supply train going to the front was thrown from the tracks and burned by rebel cavalry just three miles south of Dalton. On July 9 a body of rebel cavalry fired on a number of Michigan Engineers, probably from Company F, who were scattered in the woods cutting timber three or four miles south of Ringgold.[33]

But these bands were only a nuisance compared with Joseph Wheeler's raid the next month. By early August what remained of the Confederate Army of Tennessee was in the defenses surrounding Atlanta. Unable to stop Sherman's advance on that city, Johnston had been replaced on July 18 by Lt. Gen. John B. Hood. The fiery Hood immediately struck against Sherman's advancing columns, hoping to isolate and destroy them in detail. Three sorties and fifteen thousand casualties later, Hood and his command fell back within the fortifications of the city. Unable to defeat Sherman's army, Hood now hoped to force it to retreat on Chattanooga by cutting the supply line. Hood sent Wheeler on a raid against the Western and Atlantic line in Sherman's rear on August 10.[34]

Wheeler took with him over four thousand men divided into three divisions. His column struck the railroad north of Marietta, again near Cassville, and later at Calhoun, tearing up track at each place. Next his men destroyed the railroad south of Dalton and threatened that place August 14–16. He then crossed his command over the Tennessee River above Knoxville and rode into Middle Tennessee. Tearing up track on the Nashville and Chattanooga and Nashville and Decatur as he went along, Wheeler finally crossed back over the Tennessee on September 10 near Tuscumbia. Though his men caused a lot of concern and confusion, the raid was a failure that cost Wheeler half of his command and only temporarily disrupted Sherman's supply line. To the Michigan Engineers and other troops scattered along the railroad, however, these were very uncertain times.[35]

At Tilton Lt. Col. S. M. Archer of the Seventeenth Iowa formed the men of Company F into a line of battle on the night of August 14. Archer had been ordered to collect the scattered companies of his regiment and repel any Confederate attack on the railroad bridge and water tanks at Tilton. Using his men and 130 Michigan Engineers, a total of fewer than 250 men, Archer threw up breastworks and rifle pits on each side of Swamp Creek and prepared to contest the point.

Lieutenant Sligh with 30 men was sent forward to guard the crossing across the nearby Connesauga River some three hundred yards away. Eventually the rebel cavalry slipped across the river below and tore up the railroad. Archer and his small command, outnumbered and concerned for the safety of the bridge, remained in position throughout the night. Though several shots were fired at the pickets, none were wounded.[36]

On the night of August 16–17, several hundred of Wheeler's men struck near Graysville. About thirty of the men in Crittenton's Company K were sent to reinforce a nearby stockade, while the rest formed into a line of battle near their camp. Aided by about thirty men from a Kentucky regiment, the remaining engineers exchanged fire. "The balls commenced flying quite freely from both sides," but the Confederates did not press home the attack. That same night Innes's men at Cartersville remained in their defensive positions until after daylight, though no attack was made.[37]

On the seventeenth the men of Company B near the Chickamauga Station bridges were called in from chopping wood when word was received that Confederate cavalry was moving against them. On the eighteenth John W. Dunsmore of Company I was wounded in both wrists and taken prisoner while on detached duty. On the night of August 22, Sligh and thirty of his men at Tilton were up all night guarding against a threatened attack that never materialized. As late as August 27 members of the regiment leaving the convalescent camp at Chattanooga were being issued arms and sent in squads for their protection, and three days later a group of men in Company A were shot at while chopping wood. Most of the brushes were probably with the small detachments from Maj. Gen. William T. Martin's division that Wheeler left behind to slow repair efforts.[38]

Even though Wheeler never came close to Stevenson, the Union troops there were put on full alert and prepared for the worst. With most of the garrison withdrawn to form mobile pursuit columns, the defense of Stevenson fell to the Michigan Engineers in Companies L and M. The men slept within the fortifications and were assigned to support a battery if an attack was made. Regular mail service from Nashville did not resume until September 11, and details from the Michigan Engineers were still being diverted for picket duty a month later.[39]

Wheeler's raid did demonstrate the effectiveness of the blockhouses, if the garrison was willing to fight. Though sections of railroad were destroyed, Wheeler's men burned none of the bridges protected by blockhouses along the Western and Atlantic. Further north, the

115th Ohio was garrisoning several blockhouses near Murfreesboro on the Nashville and Chattanooga when Wheeler's men struck. Blockhouse No. 5 at Smyrna refused to surrender and endured a pounding from small arms and cannons but saved the nearby bridge. Neighboring Blockhouse No. 6, however, was surrendered without a fight, and the rebels burned the blockhouse and bridge. Maj. Gen. Robert H. Milroy, commanding the defenses of the Nashville and Chattanooga, commended "the efficiency of the blockhouse system for the defense of the railroad, which has been clearly demonstrated by the total failure of the raid to do any material damage."[40]

Meanwhile, railroad officials were finding it difficult to procure enough wood to fire the train engines. On August 8 orders were sent to Innes by department headquarters to have his men cut wood for the railroad as soon as they completed the work on the blockhouses. Headquarters believed that it would be necessary for the regiment to remain along the line of the railroad only ten or twelve additional days to complete the cutting of firewood and ties. By the middle of August most of the Michigan Engineers companies in northern Georgia were cutting wood for the railroad. At the same time, the blockhouses were incomplete, according to Merrill and his inspection teams. When Merrill complained about the lack of progress, Innes cited the regiment's "special duty" assignment of cutting fuel for the railroad.[41]

This special duty created one of the largest controversies involving the Michigan Engineers, and Merrill went after Innes, convinced he was involved in swindling the government. The root of the swindle according to Merrill was the contract let by the railroad to a civilian contractor, Benham and Company, who in turn hired three subcontractors with close ties to the Michigan Engineers: former adjutant Clement F. Miller, an unnamed "right-hand man" of former major Enos Hopkins, and the regiment's former sutler. The three were paid $4.50 per cord by the government, Merrill reported. In turn, they hired the Innes's men at $1.00 per cord to cut the wood and deliver it using government wagons to the railroad, where it was credited to the contractors. Merrill claimed that the balance of the money was divided as follows: $.50 per cord divided among the company officers, while part of the contractors' profit of $3.00 per cord went to pay off senior officers of the regiment, including Innes.[42]

In response to Merrill's accusations, Capt. Henry Cist, assistant adjutant general on Thomas's staff, conducted a comprehensive investigation. Cist spent several days along the railroad interviewing witnesses and taking depositions. His report verified the general arrangement between army subcontractors and the Michigan Engineers.

He found that the wood was being cut beginning July 21, even though it was not until August 8 that Innes officially received orders to have his men get out railroad ties and cordwood for the railroad. He also pointed out the inconsistencies of Innes's defense. Innes admitted knowing that the men were being paid to cut the wood but denied knowing anything about the details of payment or having anything to do with the money. Yet he maintained to Cist that he had cautioned his company commanders to be very careful in the handling of the money being paid by the subcontractors.[43]

Cist submitted his report to Maj. Gates P. Thruston, Thomas's acting judge advocate. Thruston prepared a summary dated October 10 and submitted it to Maj. Southard Hoffman, assistant adjutant general on Thomas's staff. Thruston recounted the basic facts gathered by Cist, adding only that other regiments were apparently similarly hired by Benham and Company, and then took Innes to task for his lack of judgment in the whole affair: "His failure to protest against, or object to this transaction cannot but be regarded as disloyal to the government and a connivance at fraud." Thruston recommended that the contractor's claim for payment be reduced by the amount of wood gotten out by the Michigan Engineers, almost forty-seven thousand dollars. On November 9 Thomas accepted Thruston's summary of the facts as well as his recommendations reducing the amount due Benham and Company. He further ordered that the Benham contract for providing wood to the army be annulled. He did not, however, endorse any further action against the officers or men of the Michigan Engineers. No effort was made to recover the partial payments received by the officers and men in the regiment.[44]

Despite the controversy surrounding Innes's actions, it should be noted that no one at department headquarters took up the other charges Merrill made at the time against Innes: "If the investigation could embrace the operations of Colonel Innes while in charge of the Northwestern railroad and of the Nashville and Chattanooga railroad . . . some interesting developments of rascality would be made."[45]

Perhaps the tone of the charges brought into question Merrill's motives: "Having long considered Colonel Innes an accomplished and smooth-tongued rascal I am on that account pleased to be able to point out with some certainty a method for bringing him to trial that he may receive the reward due his long course of treachery towards his government when struggling for existence. . . . I will mention in passing that the paymaster who paid the regiment at Cartersville is currently reported here to have said that he heard more treason and copperheadism in that week than ever before. It might not be amiss to examine into that."[46]

The deep personal conflict between Merrill and Innes had its origins in the dispute between the Michigan Engineers and the regular army engineer officers associated with John St. Clair Morton and the Pioneer Brigade. There was clearly a sense of competition between the Michigan Engineers and the Pioneer Brigade, at least among the officers, as to who represented the engineering leadership within the Army of the Cumberland.

In addition, Morton, Merrill, Lt. George Burroughs, and the others were members of the elite Corps of Engineers and graduates of West Point. They viewed Innes and his civilian engineer officers as useful but lacking in many of the skills needed by military engineers. Merrill summarized them the year previous in this way: "Though very good in their place [railroad work], [they] are utterly ignorant of fortifications and only second rate pontoniers." Though Merrill saw a role for civilian engineers within the military effort, it could only be in a subordinate role.[47]

In this regard, Merrill was more accepting of the civilians than some of his colleagues were. The most conservative element in the tradition-bound Corps of Engineers was represented by seventy-five-year-old chief engineer Joseph Totten, commander of the corps until his death in April 1864. When Merrill first broached the idea of using volunteer officers with engineering experience in his new Pioneer Brigade, Totten was quick to point out that such men could never be allowed to formally join the elite Corps of Engineers. As Totten lectured in his February 1863 response, the officers of professional military engineers could not be filled "from any other source than such distinguished graduates of the Military Academy as have heretofore been exclusively received into the Corps [of Engineers]." Any other suggestion would be heresy, as "this is a fundamental principal," and every officer of the Corps of Engineers was "bound now as heretofore . . . to resist every effort to introduce members from other sources."[48]

Over the next eighteen months, Morton, Merrill, Gen. Rosecrans, and others had continued to argue for the creation of regiments of volunteer engineers, commanded by regular army engineering officers and drawing upon the men of the Army of the Cumberland's Pioneer Brigade. Eventually Congress authorized the formation of one such regiment, and Thomas assigned its formation to Merrill. Most of the officers were drawn from the Pioneer Brigade or Corps of Engineers. Merrill was commissioned colonel, while commissions were also issued for Lt. Col. Henry C. Wharton and Majs. Patrick O'Connell and James R. Willett. Michigan Engineer Maj. Perrin V. Fox was eventually given the commission as senior major. The enlisted ranks were limited to men who had served with the Pioneer Brigade. No other member of the volunteer regiments in the army could enlist in this new regiment without the permission of his colonel.[49]

The creation of the Veteran Volunteer Engineers also provided a small but important footnote in the command structure of the Michigan Engineers. In August 1864 Major Fox resigned his commission in Innes's regiment to accept the senior majority in Merrill's regiment. This followed by several months of private correspondence in which Fox was offered and finally accepted the position. The final straw for Fox was probably Innes's efforts to elevate Major Hannings over him for the second-ranking majority. Fox's commission as major had been issued effective December 15, 1863, while Hannings's was dated January 1, 1864. Fox had also outranked Hannings among the original captains, commanding Companies D and G, respectively, at Camp Owen.[50]

Feelings were strong on both sides of the controversy. Lieutenant Sligh wrote his mother, "Everyone in the regiment is glad that Major Fox has left it. He did not do right when he was home on recruiting service and the colonel treated him coldly when he came back." Seventeen-year-old Newton Fox defended his father, accusing Innes and Hannings of "swearing false and another trick" to ease Fox out. He explained that Fox had protested to higher authorities, who advised him that the "chief engineer" (presumably Merrill) would make things right and predicted that Innes and Hannings would be cashiered for their trickery: "Things will all come out right and the plotters will fall into a pit their own hands had dug for another." Once Major Fox received his commission and day-to-day command of the new regiment, son Newton assured his mother that "it will make Colonel Innes feel more than mad to see Father with a larger and better command than he has got."[51]

Innes continued to clash with Fox even after his resignation. The colonel instructed Major Hannings to investigate the circumstance in which Fox had granted a disability furlough to a Private Church. Innes wanted the investigating officer to detail a case against Fox and the attending surgeon, instructing that "in your specifications be plain and concise, but at the same time make them strong—the stronger the better." Likewise, Innes sent Fox a letter a month after his departure, accusing him of losing a valuable piece of engineering equipment. Innes claimed that the piece, a leveling instrument valued at $175 and of great sentimental value, had been lost through the actions of Fox and John H. Sanford of Company A months earlier. It is not clear if Fox ever answered the letter or the charges it contained. For his part, Fox was delighted to force Innes's hand and be able to control the appointment of friend Captain Gifford to take charge of the work at Stevenson after his departure, something he thought would "call forth some tall swearing" from Innes.[52]

Though Fox could be as stubborn as Innes and had clashed previously with fellow officers and higher authorities, his service with the Michigan Engineers earned high marks. In particular, Fox demonstrated extensive ability and ingenuity in the face of true crisis while in command of the detachment at Chattanooga. The many contemporary and postwar accounts of the opening of the Tennessee River supply line to Chattanooga featured lavish praise for Fox's leadership. Likewise, the official ceremonies marking Michigan's role in the Chattanooga campaign in 1895 provided Fox a prominent role. Whatever the reason for the falling-out between Innes and Fox, after August 1864 Colonel Innes was the only man of the original group of organizers still present with the Michigan Engineers.[53]

· 17 ·

Wheeler, Elections, Atlanta, and a New Regiment

Orlando M. Poe was appointed chief engineer for the Military Division of the Mississippi in May 1864. His engineer organization included engineering officers, two volunteer engineer regiments, several infantry regiments detailed for engineering duty, and provisional pioneer formations consisting of detailed infantrymen. Most of these troops, however, were scattered along the railroads and at key supply depots in the army's rear. During the campaign for Atlanta the only engineer troops accompanying General Sherman's field army were the Fifty-eighth Indiana acting as pontoniers for the Army of the Cumberland, an "engineer battalion" of detailed men from the regiments in the Army of the Ohio, and a pontoon train and detailed pontoniers from the Army of the Tennessee.[1]

By late August Sherman was on the verge of taking Atlanta, and Poe issued orders for his scattered volunteer engineer units to report for its expected occupation. The First Missouri Engineers and Mechanics arrived on August 31 from the Nashville and Northwestern Railroad. Colonel Innes received orders on September 17 to concentrate his Michigan regiment at the Chattahoochee River crossing north of Atlanta. At the time, however, the Michigan Engineers regiment was still scattered along 130 miles of railroad. Companies L and M remained in Stevenson completing the defensive works. Company E had returned to Bridgeport from the Western and Atlantic and was also finishing fortifications. Company D was still in Chattanooga running sawmills and building fortifications. The balance of the regiment was along the Western and Atlantic south of Chattanooga, with regimental headquarters at Cartersville.[2]

Companies A, B, C, F, G, I, and K arrived in Atlanta on September 28. They marched through the city and camped on the southeastern outskirts. Company H was left at the nearby Chattahoochee River crossing to help with the pontoon bridge. Companies D and E arrived a month later, and L and M never rejoined the regiment that fall.[3]

For the first few days the Michigan Engineers in camp at Atlanta returned to a regular routine. Some set up the camp, while details were sent into the nearby woods to cut timber for the fortifications. The companies were drilled each day, and the officers inspected the men and their equipment. Innes made arrangements to have regular mail delivery from the post office in Chattanooga to the companies in Atlanta. Some of the Michigan Engineers were allowed to explore the city, noting the serious damage done during the siege. One young officer wrote, "It now looks as if every house was a pigeon coop."[4]

During this time General Hood and his Confederate army had remained in camp at Palmetto, Georgia, supplying via the railroad from Montgomery, Alabama. Hoping to lure Sherman out of the defenses of Atlanta or cut him off from his supply base at Chattanooga, Hood decided to attack the vulnerable Union-controlled Western and Atlantic Railroad. The first assault upon the iron road was at Big Shanty on October 3 and at Acworth the next day. A total of twenty-four miles of track was destroyed between Marietta and Allatoona before Hood's columns retired westward to Cedartown, Georgia. A week later, he surprised the Union command with a strike against Resaca. The commander at that place held firm, but the garrison of Dalton surrendered, and the twenty miles of track between Resaca and Tunnel Hill was soon smoldering. Sherman left Atlanta with most of his force in early October but was never able to catch the elusive Army of Tennessee. Likewise, Hood was unable to trap the pursuing Union columns before returning to Gadsen, Alabama. By October 20 Sherman and his armies, minus the XX Corps and detached troops in Atlanta, were resting near Gaylesville, Alabama, in the rich valley of the Chatooga. The Western and Atlantic was quickly back in operation.[5]

Again the Michigan Engineers–built blockhouses proved their value, as long as the garrison was willing and able to fight. Even against infantry and field artillery, a brave garrison could at least delay the enemy. During the summer Company F had built a blockhouse at the Western and Atlantic railroad bridge over Mill Creek in Buzzard Roost Gap, a break in Rocky Face Ridge between Tunnel Hill and Dalton. The gap was the best route for a force moving north along the railroad and wagon road from Dalton, and the blockhouse commanded both. Company D, 115th Illinois, held their position for hours before surrendering, even as Confederate cannon shelled them and infantry kept up a steady fire. Though half the garrison was killed or wounded, they seriously delayed the enemy's passage and destruction of the railroad line. In contrast, just weeks earlier the garrisons of several blockhouses along the Nashville and Decatur meekly surrendered when confronted by Confederate cavalry. As a result, all of the bridges and trestles along the thirty miles between Pulaski and Athens were destroyed, including the large one over Elk River.[6]

While W. W. Wright's well-trained men of the USMRR did most of the railroad repair, other troops were put to work getting out timber. Beginning October 7 Major Hannings and three hundred men from Companies C, F, and G were near Big Shanty getting out railroad ties, while civilian crews from the USMRR relayed the railroad. These ties replaced some of the estimated thirty-five thousand burned by Hood's men.[7]

Hannings's men were issued little more than hardtack because of the ruptured supply line. Foraging parties were sent out into the surrounding countryside to supplement the men's diet and find feed for the starving regimental teams. On the sixteenth two members of Company G out foraging were "gobbled" up, likely by the small parties of Confederate cavalry left behind by Hood. The next day four members of the regiment were sent to look for them, but at least two of the would-be rescuers were captured themselves. Larger search parties subsequently found the bodies of two Union soldiers from another regiment hanging from a nearby tree. The discovery left the Michigan Engineers concerned. "It is getting pretty close work here. . . . We shall have to keep close," wrote one. When the missing men did not turn up, a fellow soldier in Company G speculated that "their necks are stretched before now," though both survived their captivity. At night the men of the regiment posted a heavy guard and were up and in a line of battle long before sunrise. This routine continued until they left for Atlanta on the twentieth.[8]

When Sherman left Atlanta on October 4 in pursuit of Hood's army, he left behind General Slocum with the XX Corps and various other unattached or detached commands. New fortifications were already under construction for the city, but the uncertainty of Hood's intentions accelerated the pace of work. Sherman advised Slocum to "work day and night in perfecting those entrenchments." Most of the work was eventually done by the Michigan and Missouri engineer regiments and infantry details from the XX Corps, all working under the personal direction of Captain Poe.[9]

Poe had laid out the lines for the fortifications with help from Innes and his officers, and many of them were detailed to directly supervise work at several of the redoubts. At least seven positions were constructed under their immediate direction, including Redoubts One and Two (Capt. John Williamson), Twelve (Lt. Ferdinand Boughton), Fourteen and Fifteen (Lt. James M. Sligh), Sixteen (Lt. John Draper), and Seventeen (Lt. Thomas Fisher). Details from the regiment were assigned work in Redoubts One through Six and Thirteen through Seventeen. The enlisted men made fascines, cut wood for rifle pits and revetments, pulled down buildings in the fields of fire, and performed guard and detail duty for the regiment. On October 6 Slocum reported to Sherman that the new defensive line was nearly done and that the position was very strong.[10]

By this time the greatest threat to the Union forces in Atlanta was not rebel assault but the shortage of supplies caused by the break in the railroad leading back to Chattanooga. One especially large foraging expedition scoured the countryside from October 21 to 23 under the command of army quartermaster Capt. Moses Summers with a guard drawn from Col. Daniel Dustin's brigade. Summers commanded over 900 wagons, drawn from throughout the forces in Atlanta. Included in Summers's expedition was a group of 18 wagons from the Michigan Engineers, manned by regimental teamsters and commanded by Capt. John W. McCrath. All told, the four expeditions sent out by Slocum brought back an average of 650 wagons full of food and fodder, including almost two million pounds of shelled corn. Since the teams were also needed for the work on the fortifications, most work stopped during these expeditions. On October 13 Innes complained that his regimental teams had been worn out and requested replacements. A few days later all work came to a standstill.[11]

On October 17 the companies of Michigan Engineers at Atlanta moved their camp back into the city and within the fortifications, where the detached men of Companies C, F, and G under Major Hannings joined them on the twenty-third. This detachment was followed a week later by the arrival of Companies D and E from Chattanooga and part of Company H from the Chattahoochee crossing.[12]

The arrival of Companies D and E, followed by the balance of Company H in early November, meant that only L and M were not with Innes in Atlanta. Even though the fortifications they were building at Stevenson were nearly completed by the end of September, the two companies remained at that point. They were assigned guard duty as infantry and were the only garrison of Stevenson after the infantry was sent after Confederate cavalry late in the month. Details from the companies were also sent along the railroad to destroy any buildings or other combustibles that could be used by rebel raiders to burn the railroad and outbuildings. They remained on alert during Hood's move against Sherman's railroads in early October and subsisted on meager rations.[13]

On October 11 the men of the two companies were relieved from guard duty, and they prepared to finish their long stay at Stevenson. Many of the men expected to be ordered to Atlanta to rejoin the companies already at that point. Within the army command, however, there was a need for more work on the defenses of the Nashville and Chattanooga. On October 24 the two companies were ordered to report to Major Willett and construct blockhouses south of Murfreesboro, and some of the men were at work within days.[14]

Meanwhile, the other ten companies were still working on the defenses of Atlanta. During the last weeks of October the men constructed the redoubts and cleared fields of fire for Poe's line. One of the major landmarks to be destroyed was a large brick seminary. Poe agonized over the building's destruction, noting in his diary the "desire to save the building but fear it will be impossible." On October 13 Innes received orders from Poe to stop the destruction of the seminary, only to be countermanded a week later. Finally, on October 23 the men pulled down the building in two sections with ropes and tackles, producing "an awful crash." Other details put the finishing works on the outlying redoubts and supporting defenses.[15]

Fortifications were not the only things on the mind of the Michigan Engineers. Throughout the summer and fall of 1864 it was uncertain if Lincoln and his Union coalition would prevail in the upcoming elections. What was certain was the interest in the election among the soldiers. The opposition Democrats nominated former Maj. Gen. George B. McClellan and adopted a platform calling for an immediate end to the fighting. The major issue before the voters was whether the government would wage war until the Union was restored or begin immediate peace negotiations with the Confederates. Among those to decide the issue were the men wearing blue. In February 1864 the Michigan legislature passed a law allowing the soldiers absent from the state to vote in upcoming elections while in the field. Similar legislation was passed by eighteen other states.[16]

The soldiers were informed voters, following the debate through the newspapers that were readily available in camp. Since the major issue was the continuation of the war, they were especially interested, and the two candidates' positions were debated around the campfires in the army. Often these debates triggered straw polls among the men in the ranks. One held in Company B in July had Lincoln getting 146 votes, with 1 each for McClellan and John C. Fremont. Another straw poll among the men of Company E at Bridgeport produced only 7 or 8 McClellan votes out of one hundred men. Likewise, the men of Company H held a vote within their company on October 2, with Lincoln getting 98 of 121 votes.[17]

Many of these Lincoln supporters had not been Republicans before but were changed by their war service. Howe directed his wife to "tell your copperhead [friends] that their cursed principles play out as soon as any of them get down here. I know of a good many [Democrats] here, but I don't think there is two in the company but will vote for Old Abe." Another declared, "Some who had always been Democrats said the war had cured them of democracy."[18]

While McClellan was still personally popular in the army's ranks, the platform adopted at his convention calling for peace ahead of the restoration of the Union made it impossible for many Democrats in the army to support him. Others were offended by the addition of Ohio congressman George Pendleton as the nominee for vice president. Pendleton had been an opponent of the war effort since 1861 and was a close associate of discredited pro-southern Illinois congressman Clement L. Vallandingham. Combined, the platform and Pendleton drove many soldier Democrats to support Lincoln. One Michigan Engineer noted from Stevenson in October, "There is lots of McClellan men in our company but they won't vote for him because Pendleton is on the ticket. I think that Old Abe will be elected by a very large majority." A few days later a member of Company E at Bridgeport noted that by this point "'Little Mac' men are as scarce as hens teeth." One historian noted that many soldiers "still admired McClellan [but] they did not like the company he kept" and estimated that half of the army's Democrats voted for Lincoln.[19]

Some of those who remained McClellan supporters against the tide of soldier opinion did so because of Lincoln's public position that Union and emancipation could not be separated. For them, the core issue in the election was slavery. These Democrats argued that northern boys were dying in a crusade to free the slaves and not to preserve the Union. This message had its supporters in the regiment, including Raycide Mosher of Company A. Mosher, a soldier since December 1863, wrote his parents that he hoped Democrats would prevail since "Old Abe is for us all to go down South and fight for the nigger." Instead, Mosher wanted a president who "don't like nigger blood better than white blood."[20]

The men supporting Lincoln believed that the fundamental issue to be decided at the ballot box was whether the Union would be preserved or not. One member of the regiment, writing about Lincoln supporters, predicted, "If the soldiers don't roll up a good majority for the unconditional surrender of the rebels I miss my guess." Another wrote home noting the strong support for Lincoln in Company E and urging the "Union men of the north" to work tirelessly in his support, since "the election of George B. McClellan is equivalent to destroying this government."[21]

Lincoln won 53 percent of the popular vote in the November 1864 election but received 78 percent of the soldier vote. His Union ticket captured 76 percent of the vote among all Michigan soldiers for whom official returns exist and 78 percent of the Michigan Engineers. In Kent County, from which the largest block of Michigan Engineers hailed, Lincoln and other Republican candidates won only 53 percent of the total vote but over 75 percent of the Kent County soldier vote, which was tabulated separately.[22]

For the strong Lincoln supporters, the lopsided vote in the army was very gratifying. Howe wrote home a few days later that "Old Abe is elected all right so our country is safe for another four years and by that time this war will be all settled up." James M. Sligh wrote on November 9, "Old Abe is elected by a big majority and I for one am glad of it."[23]

Since the voting among the men of the Michigan Engineers was done in detachments, it is possible to analyze the election returns and identify patterns that were consistent with the soldier vote throughout the army. The strongest Lincoln supporters in the army were the veterans who viewed McClellan's peace platform with disdain and anger. In the Michigan Engineers the highest percentage for Lincoln was in Companies D and K, which contained a disproportionate share of the regiment's reenlisted veterans. As new companies, L and M had no reenlisted veterans in the ranks, and most of the men had been in the service less than one year. They also cast the lowest percentages for the Lincoln-Johnson ticket. Throughout the army, those least likely to support "Old Abe" were the men who had been in the ranks the shortest period of time.[24]

Besides the election, the other issue stirring the most interest among the men in the regiment was the impending muster out of the approximately 350 original men who had not reenlisted. For some time there was confusion over whether the determination of three years' service was to be measured against October 29, 1861, when most of the original men had been mustered, or December 6, 1861, when the balance took the oath. If the later date were the standard, Innes argued a "great injustice" would be done to those who had mustered on the earlier date. Likewise, the men who enlisted in August 1864 could not be added to the regimental payroll until the men they were replacing had departed. Innes also urged that the regiment be mustered out while in the field since many of the men wanted to enter

Table 3. 1864 presidential election returns (by company)

Companies	Lincoln	McClellan	Lincoln (%)
B and E	155	45	77.5
D and K	160	13	92.5
C and G	159	31	83.7
H and I	100	22	82.0
A and F	115	53	68.5
Parts L and M	79	45	63.7
Balance L	17	12	58.6
Total	785	221	78.0

into government employ in the quartermaster shops and military railroad. Innes was successful in convincing higher authorities to accept his logic in both cases.[25]

In addition to the enlisted men leaving, twenty-five officers who had joined in 1861 decided to give up their commissions and return home. Initially it was thought that only those officers who held the same commissioned rank as in 1861 were eligible. This policy brought forth howls of protest from original men promoted up from the ranks. Under these stricter criteria, the short list of eligible officers would have included only Colonel Innes, Lieutenant Colonel Hunton, Captain Crittenton, Surgeon DeCamp, and Assistant Surgeon O'Donoughue. One man wrote home that "it hardly seems fair that a man who has been promoted should be held longer than three years because his promotion only shows that he had been a good and faithful soldier and for that reason, if not other, he should be honorably discharged at the expiration of his term of enlistment."[26]

In late September the War Department rescinded the requirement and allowed officers to be mustered out at the end of three years' volunteer service, regardless of when they had been commissioned. This decision meant that at least forty-nine officers, 86 percent of the total, were eligible to leave the service and return to Michigan. Some wavered between the two options. Two for example, Lts. Harry Chapel and Jacob White, changed their minds at the last minute. Originally, they were included on a list of officers remaining, but on October 27 Innes notified department headquarters that they intended to accept the discharge. With so many of the officers openly debating leaving, the inevitable new opportunities for obtaining a commission were discussed around the regiment's campfires. Some, like Company H's William H. Kimball, were offered a commission if they remained but found the prospect of returning home too great a temptation.[27]

On October 27 the original men from Company H arrived in Atlanta from the Chattahoochee River crossing. On the twenty-eighth the last of the departing men from all ten companies were relieved from duty and turned in their equipment. Company and regimental clerks labored through the night reconciling payrolls. On the final day of the month the men were mustered out of the service at noon and received four months' pay the next day. Since the railroad between Atlanta and Chattanooga was still not safe from marauding rebels, the detachment was issued guns and accouterments for the trip to Nashville.[28]

Innes's final action before turning over command to Major Yates was to issue a farewell address to his men. He lamented that "circumstances will not admit of [his] remaining longer in the army" and then praised Yates, who would succeed him, describing him as "well qualified and able to conduct [the regiment] successfully through the campaigns which await in the future." Finally, Innes recounted the last three years of service, convinced that the men could always "look back with pride . . . [knowing] that while serving your country honestly and faithfully you were at the same time erecting for yourselves a monument which time cannot destroy."[29]

In return, Innes was given a purse of fourteen hundred dollars, raised from the officers and men in the regiment. Though not everyone was sad to see him return to Michigan, there were many in the ranks that had high praise for him. One was Lt. J. Newton Crittenton, son of Captain Crittenton. Young Crittenton wrote the *Detroit Advertiser and Tribune* that "for his many excellent qualities as a commander; his kind and sympathizing care of the men; his unostentatiousness and genial manners towards all, as well as for his patriotism and bravery, the colonel will never be forgotten. He retires to the bosom of his own family with our best wishes. He should be promoted."[30]

On a cold and stormy November 3, amid the best wishes of their comrades, the departing men were escorted to the train by the regimental band. Many of the men were forced to ride on top of freight cars carrying ammunition back from Atlanta. After delays in Chattanooga and Nashville and several close calls when the trains they were riding jumped the tracks, the men finally arrived in Detroit on November 13. They were anxious to be paid off and allowed to go home but were delayed until the paymaster could obtain enough money to pay them all.[31]

It is not clear why Innes chose to leave the regiment in October 1864, but several theories can be advanced. The controversy over the woodcutting contract had certainly caused him embarrassment and tainted his reputation among the army command. Perhaps his departure was a chance to leave gracefully, ahead of any additional recriminations. In addition, the previous year had not been kind to his ambitions. He had won, and then quickly lost, the long-sought position of military railroad superintendent, and he had been dismissed from his position constructing the Nashville and Northwestern. He was also suffering physically, the result of a two-year-old infection in his right ear that refused to heal and left him partially deaf. Innes might have also hoped to return to a more lucrative position as a civil engineer in Grand Rapids.[32]

Without any personal papers, it is difficult to form a complete analysis of Innes's three years in the army because much of what has survived was written by his critics. Clearly, Innes was an effective regimental commander. Even though his conduct was not without detractors, he certainly passed the basic test for regimental command: his regiment successfully performed the missions it was assigned. Under his direction it repaired roads and bridges, built blockhouses and storehouses, and fought when called upon. At no time did the Michigan Engineers fail to perform a mission that they were ordered to complete, even when in turmoil over pay. Unlike most other regimental commanders, Innes was even faced with fundamental questions about the legitimacy of his commission and command, questions that meant his men went without pay for over a year and threatened to tear his command apart. Though his handling of the pay controversy was at times clumsy, he refused to yield to his critics and actively sought to resolve the situation to the benefit of his men. His continued entreaties to higher authorities must be considered a factor in the eventual recognition of the regiment as volunteer engineers.

Under Innes's leadership, the Michigan Engineers proved they could fight, and the most serious combat added luster to his reputation. The engagement at Lavergne was the single action for which Innes was best known throughout the army and for which he received the most praise. Though the details of the fight became obscured by the legend that emerged, the underlying facts cannot be disputed. First and foremost, Innes refused to surrender when faced by a superior force of veteran Confederate cavalry. This alone set him apart from scores of other Union commanders. Second, by his personal example and fortitude, he inspired the men of his regiment, who were still smarting from the pay controversy and whose comrades were still confined to a jail in Nashville.

Countering these successes, however, was the increasing frequency with which Innes became embroiled in controversy while detached from his regiment command. This was particularly true in the position he sought more than any other, running the military railroads for the army. Perhaps Innes simply had problems running a railroad; his handling of railroads both before and after the war was also controversial. More likely, Innes's performance as military rail superintendent suffered from the limitations placed upon military railroad officials in the western theater: divided command, little real authority over military commanders or the military telegraph, conflict between civilian railroads and military officials, and unclear objectives. It is important to note that the problems that bedeviled Innes cost the reputations of more successful and better-respected railroad men in both the East and the West, including John B. Anderson, Thomas A. Scott, and Herman Haupt, all of whom were pushed aside by the end of 1863. Innes was unable to overcome these obstacles and shared their fate as a result.[33]

Innes might have been his own worst enemy, as evidenced by the predictability with which he became involved in disputes, usually on the losing side. During the summer and fall of 1862 Innes remained a steadfast supporter of unpopular General Buell. Buell in turn resisted pressure from the War Department to dismiss Innes over his handling of the pay controversy. After Buell's dismissal and public humiliation, Innes stood by his former commander, even testifying in his defense at the Court of Inquiry. Innes next enjoyed a good working relationship with General Rosecrans, who in turn protected the independent status of the Michigan Engineers from Morton and appointed Innes to the position of military railroad superintendent. Innes's sacking from the superintendent position happened at the same time Rosecrans was removed from his command of the department. Almost immediately, Innes was selected by Military Governor Johnson to direct the construction of the Nashville and Northwestern. In doing so, Innes gained from the time he had spent cultivating Johnson's support. He was also saddled with the baggage Johnson carried with the War Department, especially as the controversy raged over who controlled the Nashville and Northwestern. When officials became disgruntled with Johnson's management of the Nashville and Northwestern, Innes was reassigned.

Innes's problems, moreover, went beyond the dwindling influence of his patrons and supporters. Many of the men he quarreled with were individuals with access and influence within Edwin Stanton's War Department. C. P. Buckingham, a prominent civil engineer and roving trouble-shooter for Stanton, had led the charge to get Innes dismissed in 1862 over the pay controversy. Thomas A. Scott was a confidant of Stanton's and a successful railroad executive from Pennsylvania who clashed with Innes in the fall of 1863 over scarce rolling stock. Quartermaster General Montgomery Meigs had the full support of the War Department for his position during the same time period he was battling with Innes over supply priorities.

An incident near the conclusion of Innes's service reiterates the clumsiness with which he sometimes handled others. As the original members of the regiment prepared to leave, a petition was circulated among the regiment asking Innes to remain with the regiment in the field. Apparently, the petition lacked for success, and Innes's role in the petition was fairly transparent, leading one man to note that "a paper came from the Colonel in the shape of a petition which he wanted us to sign, a petition asking him to still keep charge of this regiment for the next three years." Though the failure of the petition to generate any enthusiasm within the ranks was unlikely to have caused Innes to leave in and of itself, it might have answered any lingering doubts.[34]

Innes was eventually brevetted brigadier general in the volunteer service. His brevet, issued in 1867 but effective March 1865, was for "gallant and efficient services during the war." It was one among hundreds of similar brevets issued after the war's close and a sign of respect for his overall wartime service.[35]

With the muster-out of the original men, the regiment lost valuable officers in addition to Innes. Lieutenant Colonel Hunton decided to return home because of continued health problems. In doing so, he lost out on the opportunity to replace Innes and receive a colonel's commission. Despite his frequent attacks of fever and enlargement of the liver, Hunton's service was marked with distinction. Because of Innes's frequent absences from the regiment, Hunton had commanded large parts of the regiment for long periods at a time. Likewise, his engineering work, at Elk River and Bridgeport in particular, earned him praise from higher authorities.[36]

In addition, Surgeon DeCamp and Assistant Surgeon O'Donoughue departed with the original men. O'Donoughue must have had a change of heart, since he was commissioned surgeon to replace DeCamp within days of reaching Michigan. He rejoined the regiment at Savannah in January and remained in the service until the final muster-out in September 1865.[37]

An additional twenty-one company grade officers also left, representing every company. At least one of the departing company officers left with a cloud over his reputation. Lt. Henry F. Williams had served as acting regimental quartermaster for over a year following the resignation of Lt. Robert Innes in December 1862. On April 1, 1864, Williams's permission to travel to Cincinnati to obtain engineering instruments was revoked. Two weeks later he was ordered under arrest until he was able to explain the regimental accounts. Eventually he satisfied higher authorities and was allowed to leave the service.[38]

The men who were appointed to fill the vacancies of the regiment's departing officers were not officially commissioned for two months but took over the responsibilities almost immediately. For the most part, these were the men who would lead the Michigan Engineers through the balance of the war.[39]

· 18 ·

More Men

Command of the regiment passed to Major Yates with the departure of Colonel Innes and Lieutenant Colonel Hunton. By the fall of 1864 Yates was an experienced military officer with a commendable record. He had earned the confidence of higher authorities beginning with his command of the two-company detachment assigned to General Mitchel's division in the spring of 1862. Even though he served as assistant superintendent of the military railroads under Innes and commanded the Michigan Engineers battalion working along the Nashville and Northwestern, Yates apparently avoided any of the criticism that was attached to Innes during these assignments.

Perhaps most important, Yates was being recruited by higher authorities for more prominent positions at the same time Innes was defending himself against William E. Merrill's charges of duplicity regarding the woodcutting contract. After having declined Military Governor Andrew Johnson's initial offer in June 1864 to superintend the operation of the Nashville and Northwestern, Yates received orders from Gen. George H. Thomas to report to that position. Though he received his orders on August 2, 1864, Yates was bedridden and forbidden by the surgeons to travel. During his convalescence the order was countermanded, and Yates remained with the regiment and succeeded to its command with Innes's departure.[1]

Yates had an experienced officer corps to assist him. Four men who had been with the regiment since Camp Owen eventually filled the other field officer positions. As the next senior major, Garrett Hannings became the regiment's lieutenant colonel, replacing Hunton. Hannings had recently commanded the three-hundred-man detachment repairing the railroad above Atlanta and before that had command of the four companies at Chattanooga and at the Western and Atlantic blockhouses along Chickamauga Creek. Capt. Marcus Grant of Company H frequently quarreled with other officers but seemed to have come into his own commanding the two-company detachment at Stevenson and was elevated to senior major upon Hannings's promotion. Capt. Emery O. Crittenton, the object of so much derision and abuse at Camp Owen, had proven his abilities through three years of service and was also given a majority. The junior majority was issued to Capt. Joseph J. Rhodes, originally first lieutenant and then captain of Company I. The only man to become a field officer who was not in command of a company at Camp Owen, Rhodes nonetheless had commanded Company I for over two years and was the senior captain after Crittenton by the fall of 1864.[2]

Qualified men also filled vacancies on the regimental staff. Having given up his commission as assistant surgeon, Willoughby O'Donoughue returned in January with a commission as surgeon, vice William H. DeCamp. O'Donoughue likely influenced filling his vacancy as assistant surgeon since a commission was given to a former Albion colleague, Robert H. King. King left a family and successful practice behind to enter the regiment.[3]

Given the lack of permanent staff positions for regimental adjutant and regiment quartermaster, both continued to be filled by officers detailed from their companies. Lt. Francis D. Adams of Company D was selected by Yates to take the place of departed Adjutant Calkins and remained in that position until the following spring. Yates also confirmed Lt. Albert Jewell's position as regimental quartermaster. Jewell had been acting as quartermaster since April while his embattled predecessor, Lt. Henry F. Williams, labored to rectify the accounts and clear his name. Jewell remained quartermaster through the end of the regiment's service.[4]

Yates also benefited since the two dozen company officer vacancies were filled by experienced men, most of who had been with the regiment since Camp Owen. Of the twelve men commanding companies in late 1864, all but three had been at Camp Owen and had risen through the ranks. The company commanders in late 1864 are shown in table 4.[5]

The lieutenants generally had the same level of experience as the company commanders. Of those in that rank at the end of 1864, half had joined as enlisted men at Camp Owen, and all but four of those remaining had been with the regiment more than a year. Two of these four exceptions, 1st Lt. Caleb A. Ensign and 2nd Lt. John W. Spoor, had served in the ranks in other Michigan regiments before receiving their commissions in the Michigan Engineers. The other two, wagon manufacturer Francis Adams and farmer David Skidmore, did not have any previous military experience but were well known within Kent County. A local paper even called Adams "an excellent mechanic and influential citizen . . . one of the best men in Grattan."[6]

Though they were apparently well respected back home, the appointment of men who had sat out the war so far did not set well with

Table 4. Michigan Engineers and Mechanics company commanders, late 1864

Company A *John W. Williamson, captain since May 1863. Previously first lieutenant of Company B. Cooper.

Company B *John W. McCrath, captain since May 1863. Previously second lieutenant and first lieutenant in the same company. Tinsmith.

Company C *James D. Robinson, captain since December 1862. Previously first lieutenant of same company. Stone mason.

Company D *Joseph C. Herkner, captain since January 1864. Previously first lieutenant of same company. Jeweler and watchmaker.

Company E Commanded briefly in November 1864 by 1st Lt. Thomas Templeton of Company L and then by 1st Lt. **John W. Spoor** through the war's end. Spoor served one year in the 13th Michigan before receiving a commission in the Michigan Engineers in January 1864. Harness maker.

Company F *Ferdinand Boughton, commissioned captain November 1864. Previously corporal, sergeant, second lieutenant, and first lieutenant, all in Company A. Teamster.

Company G *Daniel M. Moore, commissioned captain November 1864. Previously corporal and sergeant in Company D and first lieutenant in Company M. Sashmaker.

Company H *Andrew B. Coffinberry, captain since October 1864. Previously sergeant, sergeant major, and first lieutenant in Company C. Watchmaker.

Company I Thomas E. Templeton, captain since November 1864. Previously second lieutenant and first lieutenant in Company L. Originally served in Engineer Regiment of the West. Lumberman, blacksmith, and machinist.

Company K *Cyrus M. Curtis, captain since November 1864. Previously sergeant, first sergeant, second lieutenant, and first lieutenant, all in the same company. Carriage maker.

Company L George D. Emerson, captain since December 1862. Commissioned from civilian life. Civil engineer.

Company M *Edson P. Gifford, captain since October 1863. Previously sergeant Company D and first lieutenant in Company L. Millwright and farmer.

Note: *denotes original members of the regiment

the men in the regiment. In addition to Adams and Skidmore, two other late 1863–early 1864 commissions had been given to relative outsiders—Orsamus Eaton, a fifty-four-year-old businessman and office holder from Otsego, Allegan County, and Robert D. McCarthy, a Kent County minister. The appointment of these four brought forth a storm of criticism from the men in the regiment. One enlisted man wrote to the *Detroit Advertiser Tribune* that "there exists a dissatisfaction among the men in regard to officers being sent to fill vacancies . . . who have never seen one day of service. . . . The men who have served nearly three years in their country's service should be the first to receive such rewards." Both Eaton's and McCarthy's service lasted less than a year, and they were gone before Yates took command. Adams and Skidmore weathered the storm and served through the rest of the war, both earning promotions to first lieutenant along the way.[7]

In contrast to the experienced officers, the enlisted ranks of the regiment were filled with hundreds of men with relatively little experience, among whom were scattered a much smaller number of seasoned veterans. When Yates took over, almost four hundred of the Michigan Engineers had been in the army for less than three months, and a full two-thirds of the enlisted men had been in the army less than twelve months. As shown in table 5, the Michigan Engineers' rank and file in November 1864 had less experience than at any time since 1862.

The 1,100 men in Yates's regiment who had been in the army less than twelve months were the product of two major recruiting efforts. It should be remembered that by the summer of 1863 recruiting for the ten original companies had come to a virtual standstill, with each gaining only about one new man per month. The handful of men still recruiting in Michigan for the two new companies was only marginally more successful. By September 30, 1863, the ten companies—which should have had 150 men each—averaged just 80, including the sick and absent. New Company L was still only half-filled, and no men had yet been assigned to Company M.[8]

On October 17, 1863, President Lincoln issued a call for three hundred thousand more men to serve three years. If quotas were not met, there would be a draft. The federal bounty for first-time recruits was raised to three hundred dollars to spur enlistments. Additional local bounties, averaging between one and two hundred dollars, raised the total money available to new recruits even higher. The *Jackson Citizen* was optimistic, confident in the combination of "liberal bounties of the government for men and the certainty of this draft if the quota is not filled by volunteering."[9]

Table 5. Michigan Engineers and Mechanics military experience in the ranks

Date	Average experience	Under one year (%)
November 1, 1861	1.71 months	100.00
November 1, 1862	11.35 months	23.77
May 1, 1863	15.44 months	29.80
November 1, 1863	17.66 months	30.95
May 1, 1864	14.55 months	58.59
November 1, 1864	13.65 months	65.18

A recruiting party under Captains Fox and Grant was sent back to Michigan in late November 1863. They arrived in the middle of the rush to meet quota and avoid the draft. Within four weeks over eight hundred men were mustered into the regiment. Kent County was the largest point of recruiting for the Michigan Engineers. Over four hundred were enlisted at Grand Rapids and surrounding towns, drawn from Kent and the surrounding counties of Ionia, Barry, Allegan, and Ottawa. The *Grand Rapids Eagle* reported, "Everybody is going . . . with the almost irresistible tide which has been for some time past and is still sweeping our citizens, friends, neighbors, and everybody into the ranks of Uncle Sam's army." Their job completed, Fox's recruiting party returned to the regiment.[10]

Just six months later President Lincoln issued another call for troops—five hundred thousand men for terms of one, two, or three years. Recruits would receive a federal bounty of one hundred dollars per year of enlistment and whatever local bounties were being offered. No state bounty was available, the appropriated fund having been exhausted, but local bounties continued to increase as towns competed for a dwindling pool of willing men. A draft would be held in September 1864 if quotas were not met.[11]

The men already in the army felt cheated by the large bounties and shorter terms offered to the 1864 recruits. Though local bounties had been offered in many places since the start of the war, they reached their climax under this call. They resented the fact that these new recruits were getting about three hundred dollars in local bounty upon enlistment, while the original men had received nothing in advance and those who joined in 1862 only received twenty-five dollars of the

Levi Watkins was one of the December 1863 recruits whose enlistment meant the regiment had nearly full ranks as Sherman started the 1864 campaign. Watkins had served earlier in the Twenty-first Ohio (three months' service) and was a twenty-four-year-old carpenter from Lenawee County. He survived his service, not dying until 1909. Photo courtesy of Orrin Watkins and Bonnie Pierce Hartnett.

federal bounty up front. One fall 1862 recruit bemoaned the fact that several men he knew in Grand Rapids enlisted two years after he did and received four times the bounty yet would finish their service a week before him: "For being in one year they get enough to buy a farm."[12]

The idea that a man could pay money to avoid serving in the army, either by commutation or hiring a substitute, also did not sit well with the soldiers already in the field. Oscar Baxter, a late 1863 recruit, wrote home in August of 1864, "It is not money but men that we want to put down this infernal rebellion and I heartily wish there was no substitutes." Three weeks later another member of the regiment wrote, "I hope [the draft] will call a good many of the men out. I suppose that the copperheads will make a fuss but I hope they won't, for men we want and must have. This rebellion must be put down."[13]

Whatever the system's inequities and imperfections, the threat of a draft and the reward of the bounties worked in tandem to meet Michigan's quota. Over 12,500 men were enlisted in Michigan under the call of July 1864, and almost 400 of them joined the Michigan

Elliott F. Moore was another who stepped forward to fill the empty ranks. He certainly looks younger than the eighteen years of age he claimed in his enlistment certificate. Moore was one of five men enlisted in Company M at Hamtramck in early November 1863 by Capt. Edson Gifford. Two died in the service, another was sent home by the surgeons, and Moore and just one other remained until the regiment's service ended in October 1865. Archives of Michigan.

Engineers. Virtually all enlisted within a four-week period in August. Though regiments could send one officer back to Michigan on recruiting duty for this call, Innes suggested to Governor Blair that it was not necessary. Instead, the men were enlisted by the provost marshal in each recruiting district and subdistrict and forwarded to the regiment.[14]

It is a mistake to underestimate the importance of the 1863–64 recruits to the regiment, or to the entire army. Almost half of all Michigan men who served in the Union army enlisted after September 19, 1863. The same is true for the Michigan Engineers. Though not among the first to answer their nation's call, the war could not have been successfully concluded without these later recruits.[15]

Much has been written about the men who enlisted in 1863 and 1864, and little of it is favorable. Certainly, many of the men most eager to enlist had already done so and were already in the ranks, dead, or disabled by 1863. Likewise, there can be no doubt that the large bounties offered during the last two years of the war influenced many of the recruits. Yet the record as it applies to the Michigan Engineers does not support a blanket critical assessment of these later recruits and their motives. Appendix I demonstrates that the later recruits were very similar to those who had enlisted earlier. Though there were more recruits under twenty-one years of age, the overall average age remained about the same. It continued to be an overwhelmingly native-born group, and skilled craftsmen and artisans were present in large numbers. Many still joined in family groups. The later recruits actually had a lower rate of desertion than earlier recruits, and they also had a lower rate of overall loss to death or medical discharge in the first year.[16]

Upon their arrival with the regiment, the recruits quickly discovered the reality of a soldier's life. Walter Phillips of Company E found little of the "flowery oratory and charms which . . . politicians, trembling patriots and interested recruiting officers" had offered back in Michigan. Phillips concluded that soldiering was "hard tack, hard bacon, hard bunks, hard work, and hard fare generally."[17]

The regiment had also benefited from the 142 original men who had reenlisted for the duration of the war. Their reenlistment culminated an intense effort by the government to keep as many of these men in uniform when their original terms expired as possible. They were entitled to wear special veterans' chevrons and receive a federal bounty of $402 and the balance of $75 due from their original $100 federal bounty. Michigan would also pay them a $50 state bounty. Many of the men also collected local bounties from their own communities against whose quota they were credited. Perhaps the greatest inducement was the thirty-day furlough they were granted in early 1864. Though comprising only about 10 percent of the total men in the regiment by November 1, 1864, these veterans could be counted on to provide a steadying hand upon the new recruits. They also provided the regiment with a large pool of veteran enlisted men to draw upon as replacement officers. By war's end at least nineteen of them received commissions in the regiment, and virtually all the rest were noncommissioned officers.[18]

Yates's regiment numbered over 1,730 strong in early November 1864. They were a combination of veterans determined to finish the task that had already consumed three years of their lives and large numbers of replacements for those who had died or had their fill of the war. Ahead of them lay the hardest marching they would ever do and the greatest loss sustained in action with the enemy.

· 19 ·

Atlanta and the March to the Sea

Though he had already begun to make preparations, it was not until November 2, 1864, that General Sherman received the long-sought approval from General Grant to take the largest part of his army and strike out east through the heart of Georgia. Because his army would be traveling light, Sherman intended to first use the Western and Atlantic to evacuate the surplus equipment, animals, and men from Atlanta back to Chattanooga. Even before the railroad could be repaired, Sherman ordered his supply officers to begin evacuating surplus equipment and supplies from Atlanta and prepare the "wounded and worthless" for shipment north. With trains again running between Chattanooga and Atlanta after October 28, the pace of preparation quickened. In the following days a steady stream of ordnance, ammunition, equipment, and men flowed back northward to Chattanooga.[1]

In response to the concerns of Lincoln and Grant that General Hood would threaten the Union hold on Tennessee, Sherman agreed to leave behind General Thomas and a large enough force to contain any Confederate offensive. Thomas was given the twenty-five thousand men in the IV and XXIII corps, all of Sherman's cavalry except for one division, and thousands more serving in units along the railroad south of Nashville. Twelve thousand men of the XVI Corps were also to be sent to Tennessee from Missouri. Sherman could spare all of these commands because of the scarcity of Confederate troops left in Georgia to oppose him, and it would also relieve the difficulty of feeding a larger army on the march. With Hood's army in Alabama preparing to march north, the only rebel soldiers between Atlanta and Savannah were the troopers of General Wheeler's cavalry corps and thirty-five hundred old men and boys of the Georgia militia. Lt. Gen. William J. Hardee and other Confederate commanders were desperately gathering troops from throughout the southeast for the defense of Savannah, but they would not be able to contest Sherman until he reached the coast.[2]

To oppose this ragged band, Sherman assembled an experienced army of sixty-two thousand men. The regiments he was taking were stripped of the sick, lame, and otherwise medically unfit. Cavalrymen without horses were sent to the rear, and the baggage and personal equipment of all regiments were reduced to a minimum. Artillery was reduced to one gun per thousand men, and the army's wagon train was cut to twenty-five hundred wagons carrying reserve ammunition and supplies and six hundred ambulances. Unneeded teamsters were returned to their regiments.[3]

The bulk of Sherman's field army for the march were the infantrymen of the veteran XIV and XX corps of the Army of the Cumberland, joined by the XV and XVII corps of the Army of the Tennessee. Brig. Gen. Judson Kilpatrick's Third Division provided the only cavalry force. All of these commands were composed of experienced regiments, veterans of Shiloh, Stones River, Vicksburg, Chickamauga, or the Atlanta campaign, as well as the veterans of the Army of the Potomac within the XX Corps. The men who led the regiments were themselves veterans. Over 90 percent of the regimental commanders had been company officers, and over 50 percent of the captains had been promoted from the ranks. The enlisted men they commanded were also experienced. Eighty percent had been in the ranks since 1862, and about half were reenlisted veterans. Most important, virtually all of the noncommissioned officers had been in the ranks for at least two years.[4]

Among the sixty-two thousand were over four thousand men included as engineers, pontoniers, and pioneers for the long march. Ten companies of the Michigan Engineers, a five-company battalion of the Missouri Engineers, and the Fifty-eighth Indiana were all under Chief Engineer Poe's direct command. The Missouri and Indiana units were assigned to man the pontoon bridges of the right and left wings, respectively, while the Michigan men were available for railroad destruction and bridge repair. In addition, the thirteen infantry divisions each had a pioneer corps of varying size, averaging about one hundred detailed infantrymen. The divisional pioneer corps of the XV and XVII corps also included an average of seventy former slaves.[5]

The Michigan Engineers were included as a result of Poe's direct request of Sherman, and the men hurriedly prepared for the march. Strict orders were issued limiting the men to one overcoat, one rubber blanket, one woolen blanket, one shirt, one pair of pants, and one pair of shoes with an extra pair in their knapsacks. The only other authorized personal equipment were a haversack, canteen, rifle and accouterments, and sixty rounds in the cartridge box. Everything else was taken from the men and shipped north on the railroad under the command of Lt. E. A. York, assisted by Sgt. Ami Fields. On November 7 the entire command was lined up in parade formation and inspected. Surplus equipment that had evaded earlier searches was discarded.[6]

The regiment's equipment and tools were also sorted with an eye for the tasks that might be needed along the march. When it left Atlanta the Michigan Engineers' train had fifty wagons, twenty of which were loaded with tools. The inventory of tools included fifteen hundred axes, fifteen hundred shovels, seven hundred picks, two hundred hatchets, and a large supply of carpenters' and bridge-building tools and extra saws and augurs. The remainder of the regimental wagon train carried subsistence and quartermaster's stores. Captains were given strict orders that under no circumstances would the men be allowed to put their knapsacks in the wagons during the march, though four wagons were detailed to carry the balance of the regimental baggage, including that of the officers.[7]

In addition, the men themselves were inspected for their physical ability and fitness to withstand the rigors of a thirty-day march. During the first two weeks of November 1864, almost 170 enlisted men belonging to Companies A through K were sent back to hospitals in Chattanooga, Stevenson, and other points to the rear.[8]

Sherman also prepared the city of Atlanta for the departure of his army. Since Atlanta was of strategic value to the Union only as a base of forward movement and would thus be abandoned, Sherman was determined to leave nothing behind of value for the Confederate cause. At the urging of his staff, he entrusted command of the destruction at and near Atlanta to Chief Engineer Poe, "to prevent irregularities, he having reliable men under him."[9]

On November 7 Poe received the official word that he would command the destruction of anything in Atlanta that might later be used by returning Confederates, including "railroads, depots, steam machinery, etc." He called together the commanders of his engineer units and reviewed the details. Five days later Poe received permission from Sherman to start the destruction but was cautioned not to use fire "until the last moment." With the Missouri Engineers detailed on other assignments, the Michigan Engineers were the major engineer force at Poe's command for the destruction in and around Atlanta.[10]

The first priority for destruction were the three railroads leading into Atlanta, including the newly repaired Western and Atlantic running back north to Chattanooga. On November 12 the last northward-bound train left Atlanta for Chattanooga, passing Kingston early in the afternoon. As the train rolled northward, infantry details along the Western and Atlantic began to tear up the road in its wake. Stations were destroyed with fire, and the Etowah River Bridge was dismantled and carried to the rear for storage. That same day details from the Michigan Engineers and the XX Corps began work on the other railroads leading into the city. For the next several days the Michigan men tore up and destroyed track and buildings along the Georgia Railroad (Atlanta and Augusta Road) and line running south to East Point.[11]

By the fall of 1864 the task of destroying railroads had been honed to a fine art. Experience had taught the soldiers of both sides that rails that were removed and simply bent could be quickly straightened and put back to use. Instead, by heating the rail on a fire of ties and twisting it around a nearby tree, they ensured that the iron rail would have to be cut free and shipped to a mill to be melted down and reformed. Eighty-four miles of the Western and Atlantic between Atlanta and Resaca were destroyed in this manner, while another twenty miles of iron further north was taken up and stored in the rear. The Confederacy did not have the industrial capacity to repair or replace these miles of railroad iron, effectively denying them to the cause for the duration of the war.[12]

Enterprising officers even simplified the process of tearing up the railroad. E. C. Smeed, one of Daniel McCallum's USMRR officials, and Poe are both credited with inventing a U-shaped bar of steel that could be used to pry the rail loose, twist it, and destroy the spike heads and several feet of adjacent rail. Poe's "hook" was described by one of Sherman's staff as "simply a large iron hook, hung on a chain whose other end has a ring to insert a crow-bar or other lever. The hook is caught on the inside of the rails, but supported against the outside, at the ring end of lever. With these the heaviest rails are easily and quickly turned over."[13]

On the thirteenth Crittenton and Companies B, F, and K destroyed the Western and Atlantic Railroad within Atlanta near the Chattanooga Depot. In order to reduce the chance that the fires would spread, Crittenton was ordered by Yates to tear down all wooden frame buildings in the area. That same day Rhodes and Companies H and I tore up the Georgia Railroad track from the railroad roundhouse east for some distance. Eventually ten miles of rail was destroyed near Atlanta.[14]

As the destruction of the railroads was completed, the Michigan Engineers and other troops under Poe's command turned their attention to the public buildings within the city. Many of the buildings targeted for destruction were constructed of solid stone, and Poe developed a special battering ram to knock down the walls. The ram was constructed of a twenty-one-foot iron bar swinging on chains from a ten-foot wooden brace. If the ram was not sufficient, Poe was authorized by Sherman to use gunpowder and blow up the buildings. Poe, in turn, authorized Yates to "use powder or such other means as he may think proper in destroying depot and storehouses at Atlanta."[15]

Details were drawn from the Michigan Engineers and assigned various destruction in the city. Lt. Benjamin A. Cotton was ordered to direct the demolition of all steam chimneys along the railroad in the city. Lieutenant Spoor commanded the detail that destroyed the railroad roundhouse. Lt. Walter F. Hubert directed the destruction of a pistol factory. Lieutenant Skidmore and thirty men of his company destroyed a deserted Confederate barracks and tannery yard on November 15. Captain McCrath and some of his men from Company B burned the old Confederate field hospital. Throughout the fourteenth and fifteenth these and other details knocked down the walls of key structures, working through choking dust and smoke, crumbling masonry, and deafening noise. The most difficult building to destroy was a solid stone depot that eventually required seven hundred pounds of gunpowder to blow up. The destruction was done under the direction of Lieutenant Cotton late in the afternoon of the fifteenth. Other details remained at work tearing up railroad iron at least through the fourteenth. David P. Conyngham, a correspondent for the *New York Herald*, later wrote that in their work "everything in the way of destruction was legalized."[16]

Despite Sherman's directive that fire not be used until the very end, the destruction in Atlanta quickly spread out of control. A block of buildings burned on Decatur Street the night of the eleventh, and other parts of the city were in flames each night thereafter. By the night of the fifteenth, "the sky was bright with fires from burning buildings throughout the city," according to the regimental history. Conyngham recorded a scene drawn from Dante: "The streets were now one fierce sheet of flame; houses were falling on all sides and fiery flakes of cinder whirled about." Add to this the exploding of shells left behind in the depots by retreating Confederate quartermasters, and "the heart was burning out of beautiful Atlanta." When the last of Sherman's men finally left Atlanta the next morning, only four hundred of the city's forty-five hundred businesses and homes had escaped damage.[17]

Sgt. Allen Campbell was among a detachment of men from the regiment ordered to remain behind and torch the camp and surrounding buildings on the final day of the destruction. Though a veteran of three years' hard service and no stranger to destruction of rebel property, Campbell was moved by the plea of a small girl: "Most of the people left their houses without saying a word for they heard the cry of 'Chambersburg' and they knew it would be useless to contend with the soldiers, but as I was about to fire one place a little girl about ten years old came to me and said 'Mr. Soldier, you would not burn our house would you, if you do where are we going to live' and she looked into my face with such a pleading look that I could not have the heart to fire the place so I dropped the torch and walked away. But Chambersburg is dearly paid for."[18]

On the morning of November 16, the last of Sherman's men left a still-smoking Atlanta behind and marched eastward toward the Atlantic Ocean. In order to confuse Confederate authorities about the target of the march, Sherman moved his army in a wide path across central Georgia. Maj. Gen. Oliver O. Howard's right wing, including Kilpatrick's cavalry division and the XV and XVII corps, threatened Macon. The left wing, consisting of the XX and XIV corps under Maj. Gen. Henry Slocum, moved toward Augusta. During the march the wings were as many as fifty miles apart.[19]

For the first eleven days the Michigan Engineers marched with the troops of Maj. Gen. Jefferson C. Davis's XIV Corps as the southern prong of Slocum's left wing. Leaving Atlanta in ruins on the morning of the sixteenth, the Michigan Engineers marched eighteen miles and camped near Sherman's headquarters near Latimer's. Sherman traveled with the XIV Corps during the first few days of the march, and the Michigan Engineers' camp was often near the commander's. The men spent this first night of the march in a cornfield, under a sky "lurid with the bonfires of rail-ties."[20]

The regiment was split into two detachments in the morning of the seventeenth. Companies C, D, E, G, I, and K with three days' cooked rations left the main column and struck the Atlanta and Augusta track at Lithonia. They helped details of the XIV Corps tear up five miles of the Georgia Railroad, burning ties and twisting track. The track was lifted using hooks that the men in the Michigan Engineers had manufactured, presumably in a fashion similar to Poe's. Leaving the railroad smoldering and twisted, they next followed the infantry from the XIV Corps to Conyers and again twisted rails beyond repair. Camp was set up near that point.[21]

On the eighteenth the six companies marched along the railroad until late afternoon, when they stopped to tear up more rails. The men then left the railroad and marched three or four miles to the Eatonton Road and camped near the Olcofauhachee River. Many of the men fell out of ranks during the day on account of exhaustion and did not catch up until nightfall. That evening the six companies were joined by the balance, which had marched with the wagon trains.[22]

On the nineteenth the entire regiment moved forward with the XIV Corps, manhandling the wagons and artillery through the mud. While the first three days' march from Atlanta had been made in near perfect weather, a cold rain soaked the columns for the following three. The rain and thick Georgia mud were churned into a perfect swamp by the wagons and artillery. Muddy ruts as deep as two feet were reported, and stranded cattle, brought along as emergency rations, were shot and left behind. Wagons toppled over, spilling their contents into the sea of mud and causing more delay and cursing on the part of the struggling men. But the columns continued on.[23]

That night the Michigan Engineers camped near Sherman's headquarters on the Eatonton Factory Road between Newborn and the Shady Dale plantation. Both locations were burned that day by Union troops. On the twentieth the XIV Corps and Michigan Engineers passed Shady Dale and continued on to Eatonton Factory, near Stanfordville. After another march on slippery and muddy roads, the tired Michigan Engineers set up camp near Sherman's headquarters. A heavy rain fell all night.[24]

November 21 was another cold and rainy day, with the road the worst since leaving Atlanta. Companies A, C, D, G, and H were detailed to maneuver the wagons over the wet roads and through the thick clay. Ruts as deep as two feet continued to hamper their efforts. The wagons made only four or five miles before stopping for the night near Murder Creek, well short of the rest of Davis's corps. Though the rain began to subside, a cold wind chilled the men to the bone. Most of the XIV Corps remained in camp near Cedar Creek on November 22, while the Michigan Engineers and small infantry details labored to catch the wagon train up to the infantry. After moving the wagons across Cedar Creek by fording below a dam, the engineers set up camp in a pine grove and tried to rest.[25]

On the morning of the twenty-third, the entire corps was in motion early and marched the final dozen miles to Milledgeville by early afternoon. After halting, the Michigan Engineers (and presumably other elements of the corps) marched into the state capital with music blaring and colors flying. Though other troops camped within the city, the Michigan Engineers continued through town and across the Oconee River. Company C was sent back across the river to the west bank to destroy a section of the branch railroad, while the rest of the regiment camped in a cornfield. Though from the engineers' camp across the river the night sky was "bright with fires," Milledgeville fared better than many other towns captured by Sherman's men. The railroad depot and a bridge were burned that night, but the state capitol building remained standing, as did most of the public buildings, and only a handful of residences were destroyed or severely damaged.[26]

By reaching Milledgeville on the twenty-third, Sherman was keeping with the schedule he had established back in Atlanta. While Henry Slocum's two corps remained in the state's capital, Oliver Howard and his two corps of the right wing worked along the Georgia Central Railroad south of that point. That day Sherman issued orders to his two columns. Howard's men were to move eastward along and to the south of the railroad, breaking it up as they went along. Slocum was to march southeast toward the Georgia Central and reach it at Tennille Station (No. 13), just beyond Sandersville. They were then to destroy the road beyond that point. Meanwhile, Kilpatrick and his cavalry were sent to Millen to rescue Union soldiers held prisoner there.[27]

Also on November 24 the XIV Corps became the left flank column of Slocum's left wing. That day the Michigan Engineers marched almost ten miles on the dirt pike with the corps artillery and camped alongside Town Creek near a gristmill. The next day the Michigan Engineers were sent as part of a column with Brig. Gen. James D. Morgan's division and the Fifty-eighth Indiana pontoniers. They marched eight miles before stopping in the mid-afternoon near Long's Bridge over Buffalo River, about eight miles from Sandersville. In response to orders from corps headquarters, Colonel Yates sent Major Crittenton and Companies D, F, G, and K to corduroy the road through a nearby swamp. The detachment returned to camp after dark.[28]

The Michigan Engineers moved over this swampy ground early on the morning of the twenty-sixth. After reaching Sandersville in the early afternoon, they left the wagons behind and used pack mules for the transportation of officers' mess and tools. Long-eared animals in tow, they marched to near Tennille Station on the Georgia Central Railroad. The companies reported to different brigades of the XX Corps to twist rails and generally wreck the track between Tennille and Powers stations. After breaking up a few miles, the exhausted men camped for the night alongside Brig. Gen. John W. Geary's men of the XX Corps. Shortly after midnight the men were wakened and formed into a line of battle, but no attack was made on their position.[29]

Now assigned to Brig. Gen. Alpheus S. Williams's XX Corps, the Michigan Engineers continued working alongside infantry details destroying the Georgia Central. On November 27 the Michigan companies were parceled out to the brigades of Geary's division. They tore up and twisted four or five more miles of track beyond Tennille Station, ending at a point about seven miles east of the station. From there the companies followed the marching infantry brigades eastward along the track. Eventually the companies found one another and then marched together through the swamp to Davisboro, camping with Geary's division north of Railroad Station No. 12. Throughout the night men who had dropped out along the way rejoined the regiment.[30]

On the twenty-eighth, two companies of engineers were attached to each brigade of the First and Second divisions and ordered to destroy two miles of track. Some of the working parties came under fire near Davisboro but apparently without loss to the engineers. Details from Company D and perhaps others also tore up track around the depot, burning it and a large cotton gin. They camped again that night near Davisboro.[31]

On the morning of the twenty-ninth, Company D burned a bridge over Williamson's Swamp Creek and then rejoined the regiment in the rear of Geary's two brigades. Geary's column marched eastward along the Louisville Road for seven miles to Fleming's, turned right, and continued on southeastward eight more miles to Spier's Station (No. 11) on the Georgia Central. Upon reaching the railroad the tired men stopped for dinner and then continued on a road that roughly paralleled the Georgia Central. Six more miles of marching got them to the bank of a small creek, where they finally camped at nightfall.[32]

On the morning of November 30, Crittenton and half the regiment were sent forward to repair Ragford's Bridge over the Ogeechee. The bridge, however, had been totally destroyed, and the detachment was recalled. Instead, the brigades of General Jackson's and General Geary's divisions marched north toward Louisville on a road that roughly paralleled the Ogeechee River. South of that town they found that retreating Confederates had done a poor job of destroying Coward's Bridge. Details from the Michigan Engineers made the necessary repairs while the infantry regiments ate dinner. By late afternoon, the column was across the Ogeechee. They joined General Williams, the Third Division, and Kilpatrick's recently arrived cavalry. All of these commands had reached Louisville on the twenty-ninth. The XIV Corps was also encamped near Louisville. The engineers camped the last night of November near Williams's headquarters, south of the town itself.[33]

For the next week the men of the XX Corps marched into the narrowing peninsula between the Ogeechee and Savannah rivers on a road running roughly parallel to the Georgia Central. The road crossed several small streams, and retreating Confederates had destroyed many of the bridges. On December 1 General Geary's division and the engineers took the advance with the tool wagons alongside. The engineers built bridges over Big, Dry, Spring, and Baker's creeks before nightfall. Camp was near Williams's headquarters at the four corners between Baker's and Bark Camp Creek. The route that day covered thirteen miles.[34]

The next day the column marched through Birdville, with Geary's division and the engineers in advance. The men halted at 1 P.M. along the west bank of Buckhead Creek. Retreating Confederates had partially destroyed the bridges and left pickets behind to harass the Union column. The Twenty-ninth Ohio was ordered across the river and easily drove the Confederates from the opposite bank. With the crossing secure, the Michigan Engineers repaired two or three bridges over the swampy crossing. After they finished fixing the bridges, the column crossed and camped at nearby Buckhead Church.[35]

On December 3 the corps continued forward with the advance elements, now provided by the First Division, with Yates's men marching alongside a division battery. The advance reached the Augusta branch of the Georgia Central at noon. The engineers and the First Brigade spent two hours destroying a section of track while the rest of the column caught up. Eight companies of the Michigan Engineers (less D and K) fielded 13 officers and 742 enlisted men, who destroyed a total of 8,321 feet of track. Meanwhile Company K remained with the wagons as a train guard, and Company D was detached early in the day to repair the bridge across a nearby milldam, working in waist-deep water through the night. After dinner the column continued on, camping along the road several hours after dark. Still in the advance, the engineers and Jackson's division spent the night near the crossing of Horse Creek.[36]

In the morning the engineers were ordered to repair the sections of the road through several swampy areas just east of Crooked Creek. Because of the poor condition of the road in these flooded places, the corps wagons were stuck and could not continue on. While some details from the regiment cut small pine trees and gathered nearby fence rails, others laid them across the worst stretches of road or jostled the wagons through. Some of the men remained at work through the night again, though most of the Michigan Engineers swung into line with the wagons and made camp with Geary's division further down the road.[37]

Up early the morning of December 5, the regiment marched at 5 A.M. and overtook the First Division of the XX Corps along the road south of Sylvania. Here they were joined by the regimental wagon train and received orders to march south and join Maj. Gen. Frank Blair's XVII Corps. After dinner they marched to Hunter's Mill, arriving just in time to prevent the dams and bridges from being destroyed. After putting out the fire and repairing the bridge, the ten companies and regimental train continued south. The tired men camped for the night three miles from the railroad. Their hard work with the XX Corps earned them special praise from General Williams. Writing of his fellow Michigan men, Williams saluted the "valuable services of Major Yates and the officers and men of the First Michigan Mechanics and Engineers who . . . were indefatigable, as well as skillful, in assisting in the destruction of railroads, in constructing bridges, and repairing roads."[38]

Sherman's command was now closing in on Savannah, advancing in a southeasterly direction toward the port city. Slocum's left wing continued down the narrowing peninsula formed by the Ogeechee and Savannah rivers, with the XIV Corps on the left and the XX Corps on the right. Howard's right wing straddled the Ogeechee River and Georgia Central, with the XV on the south bank and the XVII on the north bank. Kilpatrick's cavalry was covering the left flank, while Sherman was personally moving with the XVII Corps.[39]

After marching five more miles, Yates and his men caught up with the troops of Blair's XVII Corps on the morning of December 6, tearing up track along the Georgia Central in the vicinity of Oliver's Station (No. 5). The engineers pitched in on the work, twisting railroad iron pulled from the line by infantry details. Other details destroyed the bridge over the Little Ogeechee, foraged for food, and served as the picket and train guard. Yates complained to Poe that the destruction would have been easier if the infantry had not started the work but had instead left the whole project to the Michigan Engineers.[40]

The Michigan Engineers were placed in the advance of the XVII Corps column on December 7. For seventeen miles the men cleared trees from the road. Confederate sympathizers had felled the trees across their path in hopes of slowing the march. The column finally reached a creek near Guyton and encamped. There was no rest for Yates's men, however, since they spent most of the night repairing a bridge over the creek.[41]

After snatching what sleep they could, the exhausted engineers were roused from their beds to march early on December 8. Again with the advance of the corps, they repaired the road for the passage of the column's wagons, especially through the swamps at the crossing of the Little Ogeechee River. By early afternoon they were approaching the area near Station No. 2 but were forced to halt while additional troops were sent forward to drive off rebel skirmishers. The XVII Corps and Michigan Engineers rested the balance of the day, while artillery boomed in the distance.[42]

On December 9 the Michigan Engineers were distributed along the flooded road where it crossed through a long swamp, and details were ordered to repair the road and help the corps' wagons through the morass. As the last of the column was passed over the flooded section, Yates's men loaded up their tools and joined the marching men. The tired engineers camped that night at Pooler's Station (No. 1) on the railroad.[43]

Pooler's Station was just nine miles from Savannah. Within that city the Confederate commanders were trying desperately to entrench a hastily formed and badly outnumbered collection of veterans, invalids, and militia. Originally, General Hardee had hoped to stop Sherman's army well to the west of the city, protecting the vulnerable Savannah and Charleston Railroad, the only rail link with reinforcement and supplies from further north. Sherman's men quickly outflanked that line behind Monteith Swamp, however, and drove on. Instead, Hardee's main defensive line would rely more on the geography of the western approaches to the city than upon the strength of its defenders.

Savannah had been built on the highest ground in the area, surrounded by swamps and low-lying rice fields. Hardee's defenses on the land approaches were constructed to sweep the fields along which Sherman would have to approach. In addition, the rice fields could be flooded to form a crude moat. Heavy works were constructed along the few causeways that formed the only routes into the city from the west. Artillery was removed from the seaward defenses and repositioned into these defenses, against which Sherman could use only the light field artillery he had brought from Atlanta.[44]

To man these positions, however, Hardee could count on only about ten thousand effectives, many of whom were old men and boys of the Georgia Militia. Wheeler's cavalry was screening the Union advance and then was to move north of the Savannah River into South Carolina and protect that escape route should evacuation be necessary. While Hardee had at least eighty pieces of well-served artillery along his line, the quality of infantry to protect them was uneven, and they were badly outnumbered.[45]

The Michigan Engineers marched at 7 A.M. on the morning of the tenth with the Third Division of Blair's corps. They turned off the railroad near Telfair, four miles east of Pooler's Station and five miles west of Savannah. The Michigan Engineers formed columns by companies and closed in mass while waiting for orders. Suddenly a cannon ball flew from the Confederate lines and ricocheted through the Union ranks. Pvt. Robert S. Brown of Company H was killed instantly, while Pvts. Edward B. Ingalls of Company B and Parker S. Truax of Company H were both severely wounded. The balance of the regiment scurried for cover, and the cannonading stopped soon after. Several accounts claim that the Michigan Engineers' casualties were caused by a heavy field piece mounted on a railroad car, though it might have been fired from the Confederate defenses at Battery McBeth.[46]

After a short time huddled in the trees, the regiment was ordered on to the nearby Ogeechee Canal. The canal ran northeast from the Ogeechee River to a point near the Georgia Central southwest of the city and then due east to a junction with the Savannah River on the west edge of Savannah. From the vantage point of the Michigan Engineers, the canal ran roughly parallel with and to the south of the Georgia Central and the road Blair's troops were on. Yates's regiment worked until midnight building a dam across to slow rebel efforts to flood the ground over which Union troops would have to advance.[47]

Work on the dam continued on the eleventh, and then the Michigan Engineers moved back to camp. The twelfth was spent resting in camp for six of the companies, while Companies B, C, E, and I were sent under the command of Major Hannings to destroy track on the Charleston and Savannah Railroad. The detachment was provided four days' rations and two tool wagons.[48]

Though Sherman's army emerged from the heart of Georgia with little loss, the tactics of living off the land would not serve it in fixed positions in the swamps around the city. The active campaign had also worn out the army's clothing and equipment. A large Union fleet with full store ships stood off the city but could not reach the army because the Great Ogeechee River was blocked to the navy by Confederate Fort McAllister. On the twelfth a member of the Michigan Engineers wrote in his diary, "These are starvation times, nothing but corn in ear for us to eat as our rations are played out. So it is corn or starve." Though he exaggerated the gravity of the immediate supply situation facing Sherman, the army would eventually starve if a supply link with the fleet were not established. In particular, the supply of forage for the army's animals was very limited. Sherman also needed heavy naval guns to challenge the heavy siege pieces along Hardee's defenses.[49]

Sherman understood the difficult situation he faced, and the next day a division from the XV Corps stormed Fort McAllister and opened the river to the fleet. While the Union forces were moving into position against Fort McAllister, Captain Herkner and Company D were sent along the Ogeechee Canal to the Little Ogeechee River, inspecting the lock gates that prevented further flooding of the ground closer to Fort McAllister. His men dammed the canal where it was likely the locks would not hold. With the fort's fall, supplies were quickly unloaded at King's Bridge and moved along the Ogeechee Road. For several days, the Michigan Engineers corduroyed the route to make it easier for wagons.[50]

With the supply situation under control, the Michigan Engineers destroyed more railroads as part of an overall effort under Poe's direction. At Sherman's order, the Savannah and Charleston was to be destroyed to the Savannah River, the Gulf to the Altamaha River, and the Georgia Central as far west as Station No. 1½. The efforts of the Michigan Engineers were first directed against the latter. On the sixteenth, with a guard provided by the Third Division, XIV Corps, the men destroyed part of the Georgia Central near Pooler's Station. This time the men were instructed to lift the rails off and dump the entire line down the embankment. This technique left a clear roadbed that could be used by the army as a wagon road since much of the surrounding countryside was still inundated with water except for these raised causeways. This work continued through the twentieth, when the details returned to camp on the Ogeechee Road.[51]

Hardee's command evacuated Savannah under the cover of darkness that same night. Civilian officials surrendered the city early on the twenty-first. That same morning the Michigan Engineers left their camp along the Ogeechee Road, marching south to King's Bridge. From there they moved east to the Gulf Railroad and then north along the track for three miles. Though this railroad had been thoroughly destroyed south of the Ogeechee in the previous days by Maj. Gen. Peter Osterhaus's XV Corps, the road remained intact north of that river and into the city. On the twenty-second the Michigan Engineers destroyed part of this remaining section while the army entered Savannah. Companies of the Michigan Engineers moved into Savannah as work was completed, all reaching the new camp by the twenty-fourth.[52]

With the occupation of Savannah, Sherman completed one of the greatest military campaigns of his day. His army operated for a month without a base of supply, relying solely on the resources of the enemy's heartland. The Confederate rail system through the lower South was destroyed beyond repair. Any lingering hopes of ultimate Confederate victory were crushed by the ease with which Union columns traveled across Georgia, and the campaign is still studied for its audacity.[53]

Sherman's march is also still widely debated because of the destruction that was left in its wake. A path three hundred miles long and sixty miles wide was carved through the heart of Georgia. Entire towns were burned, and the march route could be followed in many places by the twisted iron around trees and the stark chimneys of burned-out dwellings.[54]

Sherman intended to live off the land, and his men did so with a flourish. Each day foraging parties were sent out into the surrounding countryside and returned with full wagons of meat and produce to feed the hungry men in the marching columns. Though the quality of foodstuffs varied as the army crossed different agricultural regions of the state, few soldiers complained of not having enough to eat while on the march. This pillaging of the Georgia larder was official army policy as outlined by Sherman in Special Field Order No. 120, which directed that "the army will forage liberally in the country during the march." Often the foraging parties went beyond gathering provisions. Not official policy but still commonplace was the looting and destruction of private dwellings. Special Field Order No. 120 contained a prohibition that "soldiers must not enter the dwellings of the inhabitants or commit any trespass." During the march, however, the foraging parties frequently entered, looted, and even burned the private dwellings along the route. It proved to be a fine line between foraging and plunder.[55]

When the foraging turned into looting and pillaging, there was little sympathy for the victims from the men in Sherman's army, including the Michigan Engineers. Shortly after his arrival near Savannah, Sgt. Alex Campbell wrote his father that "it is a dark time for Georgia and long will she remember the time when Sherman's men marched through . . . but they have sown on the winds and now they reap of the whirlwind." Another wrote his wife back in Michigan, "Before I started out on this raid I heard the boys telling about going for things when they were out foraging. . . . I must confess that it looked rather hard to see almost the last things taken out of a house and off from the farm and see the women crying to see their things get taken . . . but then the rebels made that raid up in Pennsylvania."[56]

Some of the officers tried to contain the worst behavior among the soldiers. General Howard issued almost daily orders against the destruction, even authorizing officers to shoot on sight men who would not cease. Other officers followed suit. On November 19 orders were read in each of the Michigan Engineers companies against "entering houses and pilfering." The next day Yates called upon his company commanders to enforce "the orders against entering houses, pilfering, and shooting without orders." Though the exact content of Yates's order has not been preserved, it was probably in response to a circular published by XIV Corps headquarters on the eighteenth that decried the "indiscriminate destruction" and ordered frequent roll calls among forage parties and greater accountability among officers whose men violated "the dictates of humanity."[57]

Most of the Union soldiers reported missing or captured along the march were casualties of the bitter war fought between foraging parties and small bands of Confederate cavalry. The only Michigan Engineer lost between Atlanta and the arrival outside Savannah was Pvt. Nathan Gilman of Company B, reported captured while foraging on November 30, 1864, near Louisville, Georgia. Gilman did not survive the war, but the details of his death are not clear. Several comrades claimed in later pension proceedings that he was hung by the Confederates, and at least one claimed to have seen his body. Most of the Union soldiers that were captured near Louisville on the twenty-ninth and thirtieth were sent to rebel prisons. Union army records state that Gilman was later released by Confederate authorities and died in a Wilmington hospital in March 1865.[58]

Once Savannah was secured and his army supplied, Sherman wanted to march northward to form a junction with Grant around Richmond and Petersburg. By doing so, he would cut another track through the heart of the Confederacy and destroy its ability to continue waging war. After the capture of Savannah, Geary's Second Division of the XX Corps served as its garrison. Since Sherman wanted Geary's veterans to accompany him on the march, a division of the XIX Corps was transferred from the Shenandoah Valley to Savannah, arriving January 17–18, 1865. This force was not large enough to defend along the original lines of the Confederate fortifications but was ample enough to hold a shortened defensive perimeter.[59]

Sherman directed Poe to design and supervise the erection of a contracted line of fortifications for Savannah more consistent with the size of garrison he intended to leave. Poe incorporated existing Confederate works where possible in his design. When completed, they would form a line of defenses two and a half miles in length. The positions could be manned by a garrison of five thousand and be armed with some of the two hundred artillery pieces captured in Savannah.[60]

The actual erection of works was placed under the direction of Capt. Chauncey B. Reese, and Yates was ordered to report to Reese and furnish details as needed. The Michigan Engineers were at work on Poe's line by December 29, staking out works and preparing the materials. For the next three weeks the regiment had an average of 570 enlisted men at work every day on the defenses. They labored under the direct supervision of Poe's engineer officers and their own commanders. Hannings had general supervision of the interior works. Crittenton and Rhodes were each assigned several of the works to complete with the services of their respective wings of the regiment. In turn, the company commanders within their wings were given specific types of work to complete or instead assigned the work of constructing a position to completion.[61]

The first few days were mostly occupied with putting up battery profiles and hauling dirt. Within days the men were switched to putting up stakes and building fascine revetments. These revetments were walls that supported a soldier leaning to fire over the top of the parapet and were constructed of a variety of different materials, including fascines—tightly bound bundles of green brush. Details also put in drains to prevent the flooding of the batteries and built platforms for the large cannon. Others tore down buildings for the lumber and cleared the fields of fire. Additional men built fascines for use elsewhere in the defenses.[62]

During this time, other details from the Michigan Engineers worked on Lunettes A through G. Working alongside them were infantry details, especially from the XIV and XX corps. Sometimes these infantry working parties slowed the work instead of advancing it. On January 3 Yates complained to Poe that infantry details totaling almost twelve hundred men had reported that day to him, equipped with a grand total of eleven shovels.[63]

By early January details from Yates's regiment were also running a sawmill, providing lumber for Poe's work parties. After the middle of January increasingly larger numbers of men from the regiment were shifted to finishing each position's magazine and interior works. Others labored on the rifle pits that connected the strong points. Apparently some changes in the design of the works were necessary, since many of the details were assigned to raise and relay the platforms after the first week's work.[64]

By January 19 the Michigan Engineers were largely finished with their work on the fortifications but were driven back to camp by the heavy rains. The storm lessened in its intensity, but the rain continued to fall off and on for two more days. Though the men were able to do some work on the defenses, other details were sent to the Savannah River pontoon bridge that had to be opened so that steamers could proceed up river against the heavy flood-driven currents.[65]

The regiment prepared for the next march as work on the fortifications slowed. Again the companies were stripped down to the barest of equipment. Noncombatants were limited to five servants for the field and staff and one for each company. Each company was allowed one-third of a wagon to carry its baggage, while the field and staff were allowed only one wagon for the regimental records, reserve ammunition, and one hospital tent. The regimental quartermaster's wagons carried ten days' supply of rations and five days of forage for the animals.[66]

Yates also used the time in Savannah to finish filling officer vacancies created by the muster-out three months earlier. When the ten companies left Atlanta in November, only thirteen officers had commissions for the positions they were serving in. More than twice as many were acting in higher positions while waiting for signed commissions from Governor Blair. With communications with the North restored and commissions in hand, the new officers were mustered into their new positions on January 8.[67]

· 20 ·

With Thomas in Tennessee

While Colonel Yates and the majority of the regiment were cross-ing Georgia with General Sherman, the balance of the regi-ment was concentrated in Middle Tennessee. Though not as famous as the march to Savannah, the fighting in Tennessee helped end the war and ultimately cost the Michigan Engineers more casualties than all of Sherman's campaigns.

The roots of the fighting rested in the lack of options available to General Hood after the fall of Atlanta. On October 20, 1864, Sher-man's army was resting from a vain pursuit of Hood's army along the smoldering Western and Atlantic Railroad. Hood's tired men were camped at Gadsen, Alabama, en route for Tuscumbia. Tired of chas-ing the enemy along the railroad, Sherman took most of his army back to Atlanta and prepared to march to the Atlantic. Hood recognized he could not storm the fortifications around Atlanta but hoped that a move into Tennessee would force Sherman to abandon Atlanta in order to save his supply line. Instead, Sherman reinforced General Thomas's Department of the Cumberland and completed his own preparations to march to Savannah.[1]

While Thomas had a much larger force available to him on paper than Hood, most of the Union troopers were without mounts, many of the infantry were in new regiments or companies of convalescents and supply clerks, and the XVI Corps was still in Missouri. For immedi-ate operations, Thomas's effective force consisted only of the twenty-two thousand men of the veteran IV and XXIII corps and about three thousand mounted cavalry. Under the command of Maj. Gen. John M. Schofield, these units were posted at Columbia along the Tennessee and Alabama Railroad with orders to delay Hood. Meanwhile, rein-forcements would be gathered at Nashville and mounts found for the rest of the cavalry.[2]

Almost 450 Michigan Engineers were among the Union troops scattered throughout Thomas's department by late November. Compa-nies L and M, each numbering about 100 men, were still at Stevenson, largely idle since finishing the defenses of that post. Another 230 were sick or convalescing in rear area hospitals, and others were still detailed for various tasks in rear areas. As Sherman made his final preparations for the move to Savannah, Colonel Yates expanded Major Grant's command to include not only Companies L and M but also all of the Michigan Engineers not marching with Sherman. Grant's small battalion, officially designated as the Third, reported directly to William E. Merrill, Chief Engineer of the Department of the Cumberland.[3]

While Major Grant's headquarters and some of the men remained at Stevenson, details from the Third Battalion continued their work for Willett along the Nashville and Chattanooga, strengthening defenses between Murfreesboro and Bellbuckle. For the balance of November, details of Grant's battalion labored at these and other points along the Nashville and Chattanooga erecting and finishing blockhouses. Captain Gifford and a detail of fifty men also were ordered to repair a break in the Memphis and Charleston Railroad west of Stevenson.[4]

By the end of November, Union commands from along the Nashville and Chattanooga were being pulled back to strengthen Thomas's command at Nashville. As part of this general movement on November 29 Grant ordered his scattered detachments to withdraw to safer positions. Lts. John Earl and Caleb Ensign were directed to evacuate their detachments to Murfreesboro, moving "with the least possible delay." Gifford was ordered to remain in place at Elk River unless the garrison was withdrawn. If forced to leave, he was to use his own judgment as to the best post to fall back to. The battalion headquarters, already removed from Stevenson to Tullahoma, was moved further northward to Murfreesboro.[5]

Also on November 29, Hood's forces were nearing Franklin, having almost trapped Schofield's force along the Nashville Pike at Spring Hill. Schofield turned to fight at Franklin, while his wagons were crossed over the swollen Harpeth River. Hood's divisions were recklessly hurled against Schofield's defenses and driven back after bloody hand-to-hand fighting. While Hood's army recoiled from the loss of a dozen general officers and at least six thousand men, Schofield's men and wagons slipped northward and joined Thomas in Nashville on December 1.[6]

Having reached Nashville, Hood was powerless to do anything further. The losses he suffered at Franklin reduced his effective force to about twenty-one thousand infantry, less than half of what was now available to Thomas, and his artillery was short of ammunition. Hood could slip small parties across the Cumberland, but he was unable to sustain a move by his entire army further north than Nashville. Nor could he retreat without conceding the futility of the campaign and inability of the Confederacy to contest the war west of the Appalachians. Instead, Hood entrenched his men in a four-mile line, the longest he could man but less than half the distance across the base of the Tennessee River loop in which Nashville was located.[7]

Hood concentrated his planning against scattered Union positions south of Nashville, especially those along the Nashville and Chattanooga. In particular, he hoped that a move against Murfreesboro would draw Thomas out of the strong Nashville fortifications to go to its relief. At that point, Hood was convinced he could retake the initiative by defeating Thomas out in the open. Gen. Bedford Forrest was given two divisions of cavalry and one of infantry to destroy the railroad, surround Murfreesboro, and force Thomas to its relief. In reality, Maj. Gen. Lovell H. Rousseau's firmly entrenched Union soldiers at Murfreesboro actually outnumbered the besieging Confederates.[8]

Murfreesboro and its well-fortified garrison of eight thousand men was cut off but never really threatened with capture. The infantry in Forrest's command was roughly handled by a striking force from the Murfreesboro garrison on December 7, and the next day William Bate's Confederate infantry division was recalled to Nashville. General Buford's cavalry was ordered to picket the Cumberland River on the army's right flank, leaving Forrest with only one mounted division and a small force of infantry to invest Murfreesboro. Within days Rousseau was bragging that his men were able to forage without interference.[9]

While Forrest concentrated his efforts on the railroad between Nashville and Murfreesboro, the Michigan Engineers and the other small garrisons along the railroad further south remained exposed to attack by small parties of Confederate cavalry. From November 30 to December 22, Captain Gifford and sixty men of Company M remained isolated at Elk River, part of a garrison of only five hundred men and two pieces of artillery.[10]

In the meantime, the balance of Grant's command formed a portion of the besieged garrison at Murfreesboro. Among the men with Grant were Lieutenant Earl's Company L, Lieutenant Ensign with half of Company M, and a detail of men from the other ten companies, probably commanded by Sgt. Henry Norton of Company M. Lieutenant York was also present, originally ordered back from Atlanta with the regiment's surplus equipment but now attached to Grant's force. The engineers worked on the fortifications in case Forrest was rash enough to attack. Details from the regiment also worked on hospital buildings at the post. At one point, a detachment of twenty men from

Company L was even detailed to receive instruction as heavy artillerists, but the order was withdrawn shortly after it was given.[11]

Though the garrison was safe within the walls of Fortress Rosecrans, supplies were limited. On December 12 Rousseau sent a train south to Stevenson after rations. A heavy guard was placed on board the empty cars, including 150 men from the Sixty-first Illinois. Anticipating that the railroad had been damaged, Lieutenant Earl and 30 men from Company L were ordered to join the train with their tools. A flat car was loaded with spare rails and spikes and added to the train for their use. Lt. Col. Daniel Grass of the Illinois regiment was placed in the command of the train and its guard. Proceeding slowly and warily southward along the track, the train reached Stevenson without serious incident on the morning of the thirteenth.[12]

After reaching Stevenson, the balance of December 13 was spent loading tens of thousands of rations onto the seventeen train cars. The train guard was strengthened by the addition of thirty dismounted troopers of the Twelfth Indiana Cavalry, trying to rejoin their regiment in Murfreesboro. No doubt these reinforcements were welcomed as they hopped on board the cars.[13]

The return trip to Murfreesboro started early on the morning of December 14. The train had a difficult time ascending the steep grade on the wet iron and did not get over the mountains until early afternoon. It then picked up speed and continued without difficulty. In the fading light near Bellbuckle, however, a Confederate cavalry picket fired at the train. No one was hurt, but the engineer slowed the train for fear that the cars would be derailed in the dark by sabotaged track. Anxiously they continued on, expecting to be ambushed at any moment.[14]

Just beyond Christiana at about 2 A.M. on December 15, the train came to a screeching halt at a large break in the road. Within minutes it was under heavy small arms fire. The Illinois and Indiana men scrambled down from the train and formed into a line of battle, while the Michigan Engineers grabbed their tools and set about repairing the track. The engineers were "bully boys, understanding their business thoroughly" and quickly made the repairs. Even after the track was repaired, the men remained on foot, certain that there were more breaks in the railroad and additional enemy troopers ahead. The infantry and cavalry formed up as flank guards on either side of the railroad track, while Lieutenant Earl's Michigan men marched close by the slowly moving engine. The engineer halted the train at several points where Earl's men quickly repaired the damaged track. At one point mounted Confederates appeared across their front but were driven off by a volley from the Union ranks.[15]

During the night the command continued walking north along the railroad. As dawn approached they were within six miles of Murfreesboro. Ahead of them was the largest break yet encountered, stretching for several rods, and a deep culvert had also been destroyed. While the Michigan Engineers started repairing the break, the infantry and cavalry slumped to the ground to rest. Suddenly a volley of enemy fire erupted to their front left, coming from a heavily timbered ridge. While shots were exchanged, another party of Confederates started destroying the track in their rear out of gunshot range, effectively trapping the train. A third group of rebels began firing from a stand of willows on their right, along the banks of the Middle Fork of the Stones River. By this time the engineers had thrown down their tools, shouldered their weapons, and joined in the defense of their position. The exchange of small arms fire continued for an hour with little loss of life. Suddenly "a cannon ball screamed over [their] heads, followed by the roar of the gun." Within minutes the rebel gunners to their left and rear got the range and struck the engine with solid shot.[16]

At this point, the small train guard was under attack by three regiments of Texas cavalry of Brig. Gen. Lawrence "Sul" Ross's brigade, with artillery support from the Columbus (Georgia) Light Artillery. Union accounts state that Lieutenant Colonel Grass, believing any further attempt to save the train was hopeless, ordered the train guard to abandon its position at 8 A.M. and fight through to Murfreesboro. Confederate accounts call the Union retreat a rout.[17]

The Union soldiers ran a gauntlet of small arms fire, trying to stay together along the railroad. Individual soldiers exchanged shots with the rebels, but no organized stand was made along the track. Many of the pursuing Confederates were mounted, making it much easier to pick off the fleeing Union soldiers. After a half mile, the remnant of Grass's force came to a tributary of the Middle Fork of the Stones River. The men did not hesitate, running into the knee-deep and frigid waters. Once their prey crossed over the stream, pursuing Confederates abandoned the chase. Another half mile closer to Murfreesboro, the survivors reached Union-garrisoned Blockhouse No. 8 at the railroad bridge over the Middle Fork. Reinforcements arrived from Murfreesboro soon after, and the combined force returned to the train, only to find it ablaze.[18]

The Confederate cavalry were long gone, carrying as much of the prized coffee, food, and equipment as they could carry. Gone with them were the Union men who had fallen behind during the race from the disabled train to safety. Among the prisoners were Lieutenant Colonel Grass and over eighty others from his regiment, most of the Indiana cavalry detachment, and all of Lieutenant Earl's detachment from the Michigan Engineers. Though none of the engineers were reported killed or wounded, the fact that eight did not survive the war makes this the most deadly encounter with rebel forces the regiment experienced during the entire war.[19]

It is not clear exactly when the engineers and others were captured. Since all of the Michigan Engineers were taken, they were likely near the rear of the running column, or perhaps Earl made some attempt to delay the pursuit. Some apparently decided to take their chances hiding in the surrounding countryside and remained at large through the night, trying to make their way to safety. Young Pvt. William Simms took to the woods and spent the night huddled against a fallen log, finally falling asleep near dawn. A Confederate officer who demanded his surrender startled him awake. Simms obliged, first breaking his gun over the log and receiving a swift kick in the seat of his pants for his insolence, and was marched away.[20]

The survivors who reached Murfreesboro had nothing but praise for the conduct of Earl and his Michigan Engineers. Maj. Jerome Nulton of the Sixty-first Illinois, commanding in the absence of captured Lieutenant Colonel Grass, wrote General Rousseau, "In justice to the First Michigan Engineers, allow me to say that they behaved themselves with firmness and during the engagement they fought like veterans." One Illinois soldier, who had fought alongside the engineers but was able to escape, praised their willingness to put down their tools and "fight like tigers." Confederate General Ross reported that Grass's entire force "fought desperately." Despite his youth and lack of command experience, Earl performed well, prompting Lieutenant Sligh to write home after the fight that Earl "was a fine man, thought a good deal of by his men."[21]

There was a lot of concern for the safety of the captured engineers, given the bitter nature of the war along the railroad. Lieutenant Sligh wrote home a month later that "it almost makes my blood run cold to think of the probable fate of the thirty-one men who were captured." In the weeks following the fight, there were several messages sent between Union and Confederate authorities regarding these and other prisoners taken during the campaign. Forrest and Rousseau had been in the middle of making a deal for the exchange of men taken by each during the campaign when the sudden Confederate rout and retreat from Tennessee halted the process. Rousseau stated on December 16 that the first Union men he wanted released were the Illinois and Michigan men captured in the attack on the train the day before. Forrest later proposed to trade Grass, described by him as a "high-toned gentleman, a brave soldier, and a magnanimous foe," for Col. E. W. Rucker of his cavalry corps, who had been wounded and taken prisoner by Union forces on the second day of fighting at Nashville. Nothing came of the offers to exchange the lesser-ranked officers and men, and Lieutenant Earl and his men trudged south along with the tattered remnants of Hood's army.[22]

As the men of Lieutenant Earl's detachment were fighting for their lives along the railroad, Thomas's army emerged from its fortifications at Nashville and swept Hood's army from the field. Thomas's sledgehammer attacks on December 15 and 16 routed the Confederate forces, capturing over fifty pieces of artillery and eighty-five hundred prisoners in the attacks and subsequent pursuit. Among those engaged in the fight was Lieutenant Sligh, who had been detailed as assistant inspector of fortifications and managed to attach himself to the Second Michigan Cavalry for the battle. Other Michigan Engineers probably served in the provisional units made up of detailed and unattached men in the army's rear areas.[23]

With Hood's broken army in retreat southward toward the safety of the Tennessee River, Union positions along the Nashville and Chattanooga were freed from the threat of capture. Hood's forces had destroyed much of the railroad running south from Nashville, including blockhouses and water tanks. Detachments worked on several different repair projects, and some of the officers were detailed to supervise the work of civilian working parties. Other details got out railroad ties or were sent in search of salvageable railroad iron.[24]

By early January 1865 detachments of Major Grant's battalion were working on a wide variety of projects. Fatigue parties labored on a hospital at Murfreesboro, while others repaired tools belonging to the quartermaster department. Details from the Michigan Engineers labored alongside infantry parties rebuilding the destroyed blockhouses guarding the three Mill Creek bridges between Nashville and Murfreesboro. Other detachments were sent further south to complete work on the supplemental blockhouses at Christiana and Fosterville. Additional details returned to the task of completing the still unfinished defensive works at Cummings Wood Yard, Elk River, and other points south of Murfreesboro. Work at these points continued into February.[25]

During this whole time, Grant and Yates urged military authorities to reunite the regiment, each time unsuccessfully. Refusing to give up, Yates wrote O. M. Poe on January 10, 1865, asking yet again that

Grant and his men be ordered east. Poe endorsed the request, Sherman concurred, and it was referred to Thomas for implementation. Thomas's headquarters issued the orders on February 2, 1865. All members of the regiment within the limits of the department were to be sent to Savannah via New York. It had required the personal attention of the military division commander, but the regiment was finally to be reunited.[26]

Grant and his officers spent the balance of February making the necessary arrangements for the men to leave the department. By March 2 the men of Companies L and M were at Nashville, together with at least eighty healthy men from the other ten companies. The next morning Grant's command left Nashville on the railroad. For six days the men rode the cars through much of the North on a route taking them through Louisville, Indianapolis, Pittsburgh, Harrisburg, and Philadelphia.[27]

The battalion remained in New York City for a week while arrangements were made for the next phase of the transfer. One of Grant's priorities was to get the men paid, since they were "almost entirely destitute" from not having been paid for six months. Despite the fact that the proper paperwork was completed and the paymaster had the money, the men did not receive any pay while in New York City.[28]

After many delays, the battalion was transported by steamer to Beaufort, North Carolina, and disembarked at nearby Morehead City. From there they took the train through New Berne and on to Kinston, which they reached on March 22. They unloaded and marched to Goldsboro, where they finally caught up with Colonel Yates and the other ten companies on March 25.[29]

· 21 ·

Into the Carolinas

After several false starts and a few repair projects the preceding day, the Michigan Engineers started leaving Savannah on January 26, 1865. By the twenty-eighth, all ten companies and their equipment had moved to near Beaufort and set up camp. There they prepared for active operations. By this time, the units in General Sherman's field army were approaching their jumping off positions for the march northward through the Carolinas. As he had done for the march to Savannah, General Sherman divided his command into two wings. Henry Slocum again commanded the left with the men of the XIV and XX corps. Oliver Howard remained in command of the right wing, composed of the XV and XVII corps. Howard's wing was called the Army of the Tennessee, while Slocum's wing was styled the Army of Georgia. Judson Kilpatrick's Third Cavalry Division marched with Slocum's wing.[1]

O. M. Poe's engineer organization remained the same as in the march to Savannah. The one thousand officers and men of the First Michigan Engineers and Mechanics remained attached directly to Poe's headquarters. The five companies of the First Missouri Engineers manned the pontoon bridge of the right wing, while the Fifty-eighth Indiana Infantry served as pontoniers for the left wing. Each infantry division retained a detail of pioneers from its regiments. Though the Confederates could call upon a larger force than in Georgia to oppose the march, the main obstacles to Union passage would be the terrain and the elements. For the hard-working men in the engineer and pioneer units, the march through the Carolinas would be much more difficult than the one from Atlanta to Savannah.[2]

While Sherman's march route through the central parts of the Carolinas would avoid the worst of the coastal swamps and wide rivers, the region he intended to cross was still among the most difficult in the South. Heavy rains were common during the winter months. In such downpours, the rivers quickly flooded over their banks and turned the surrounding low ground into lakes and swamps. On the march through South Carolina it rained half of the days, and nine out of ten consecutive days at one point. Most of the "bridges" across the major rivers were in fact causeways, consisting of numerous bridges and a narrow raised roadbed. The approaches to these rivers were through swampy ground, providing little room for maneuver and flanking. So daunting were the natural obstacles, in fact, that many Confederate authorities deluded themselves and the civilian population into believing that Sherman's army would meet its doom in the Carolina swamps.[3]

In order to create even more confusion, Sherman remained elusive about his real target. Charleston, the birthplace of secession, was still in rebel hands despite Union attempts to take it. Howard's right wing was to be moved by water to Beaufort, South Carolina, and then advance northward from nearby Pocotaligo, leading the enemy to believe a drive was imminent on Charleston. Slocum's left wing was to advance from its position near Savannah, feinting northward toward Augusta, Georgia. Once these initial moves were completed, the two wings would shift axes and converge at Columbia. From there Sherman had several possible routes to Goldsboro, North Carolina. With its rail and road connections to the Union-controlled port at Morehead City, Goldsboro was an ideal destination for Sherman's army as well as viable point for supply and reinforcement. In the initial advance, the Michigan Engineers were to move with Howard and the right wing.[4]

On January 31 John B. Yates moved his regiment across a pontoon bridge spanning Port Royal River and onto the mainland. They continued on to Pocotaligo Station on the Savannah and Charleston Railroad and camped near General Sherman's headquarters. That night final preparations were made for a long march.[5]

On the first day of February, Howard's wing marched northward from its camps. The engineers moved in the rear of John Logan's XV Corps, marching with Maj. Gen. William B. Hazen's Second Division. They made about fifteen miles and camped near Hickory Hill. Mounted skirmishers from Illinois and Missouri fought throughout the day with the elusive Confederates. During this day and most that followed, the only organized Confederate opposition was from Gen. Joseph Wheeler's, and later Gen. Wade Hampton's, troopers, who fell back before Sherman's columns, destroying the bridges and crossings.[6]

The march on February 1 took them through the still-smoking remains of McPhersonville, torched by Howard's advance. McPhersonville's fate was a portent of what was to come throughout South Carolina. Lt. Alex Campbell later wrote home, "We have left a strip of ashes fifty miles in width." It was not pity, however, that the Union soldiers felt in the birthplace of secession. Sherman wrote Halleck in late December from Savannah, "The whole army is burning with an insatiable desire to wreak vengeance upon South Carolina. I almost

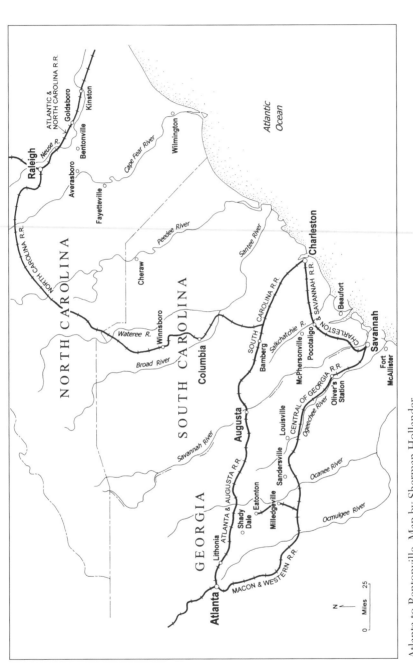

Atlanta to Bentonville. Map by Sherman Hollander.

tremble at her fate, but feel that she deserves all that seems in store for her." After making the march, James Greenalch of Company B wrote his wife, "I thought we used the country and people pretty rough coming down through Georgia, but it was but a show [compared with what was done to South Carolina]. It was the general understanding through the entire army when it left Savannah that she would be made an example of and I can say it has been carried out to the letter."[7]

On the morning of February 2, Yates's engineers moved with the advance. After a fifteen-mile march the division advance made camp at Loper's Crossroads amid the sounds of desultory firing just one-half mile to their front. The engineers camped with Sherman's headquarters at the crossroads, near the mouth of Duck Creek on the north side of the Coosewatchie Swamp. They remained in camp all day on a cloudy and rainy February 3. From their camp the men could hear firing as the skirmishing continued, and a brigade of infantry and section of artillery went past their camp on the way to force a crossing over Duck Creek.[8]

In the morning the men followed the road to the northeast and marched twelve to fifteen miles toward the South Carolina Railroad at Bamberg. An hour before sundown they camped on the road to Buford's Bridge, again near Sherman's headquarters. In the vicinity of Buford's the Big Salkehatchie River was split into a maze of channels. Retreating Confederates had destroyed at least twenty-two bridges, all scattered over a mile of swamp and averaging twenty-five feet in length. John Logan's XV Corps was under orders to cross over the river at this point, while Frank Blair's XVII crossed a few miles downstream at River's Bridge.[9]

Though the advance division of Logan's corps found the Confederate works at Buford's deserted on the fourth, the difficult crossing was not made until the following day. On the morning of the fifth, the engineers struggled through the swamps leading to the bridges before reaching the far bank. A member of Sherman's staff described the mile-wide crossing over twenty-seven separate wooden bridges at Buford's along a narrow winding causeway: "the ground always soft and muddy, the impenetrable trees and bushes on both sides standing in water and mud." Since they moved only three or four miles, the Michigan Engineers spent most of the afternoon and evening in camp, located near Logan's headquarters at Dickinson's plantation.[10]

On the sixth the engineers were ordered to move in the advance with Brig. Gen. John E. Smith's Third Division. They had marched about six miles in the rain when the mounted infantry in the advance encountered enough rebel opposition to halt the column. Smith's infantry took the advance and drove the Confederates through a swamp and across the Little Salkehatchie River. By mid-afternoon the column was moving again, and the engineers marched another three miles across the river and made camp at dusk.[11]

Logan ordered his First and Second divisions to strip down to "light fighting trim" with the minimal number of wagons. Yates's command also prepared to move light, with just one tool wagon and one ambulance. On the morning of the seventh the engineers and First and Second divisions were thrown forward in the direction of the South Carolina Railroad. Despite marching with minimal equipment and baggage, the column struggled through the mud in a "steady and detestable drizzle" for several miles before they reached the tracks of the South Carolina Railroad at Bamberg (also known as Lowry's Station). In response to direct orders from Sherman, Logan's infantry tore up the railroad but left its final destruction to the Michigan Engineers. Two of Logan's brigades lifted the iron and laid it across piles of burning ties. Following behind them, the engineers carefully lifted the red-hot rails and twisted them until rendered useless. Four or five miles of railroad were destroyed in this manner before the men made camp at Bamberg.[12]

Poe considered his Michigan Engineers to be the key to successfully destroying the railroad. On the seventh he requested that Logan provide detailed orders to his infantry on the manner in which railroad iron be prepared for the engineers to twist. By "systematizing in this way the engineer regiment can twist all the iron that can be taken up by your corps: three ties in the roadbed as they lie, one tie across these at each end, at right angles; six ties crosswise with these (right angles) with intervals to allow their being fired; then the iron laid on top, parallel with the railroad, and kindling wood and surplus ties on top of all. The piles to be fired by the infantry details, and the heated iron will then be twisted by the engineer troops. The piles should be about thirty five feet apart."[13]

Yates's men continued their work of destroying the railroad throughout the morning of the eighth, under orders to work their way westward along the railroad until joining with Slocum's left wing. Three infantry brigades drawn from the First and Second divisions of the XV Corps again tore up track and piled and fired it for the engineers to twist. In this cooperative fashion several more miles were destroyed. After dinner the engineers set up camp at nearby Lowry's Station and reported to Slocum's headquarters.[14]

Slocum had been ordered to destroy the railroad west from Blackville, while Howard finished the work of destroying it east to the Edisto. Sherman was traveling with the right wing and inspected the work done by Yates's men along the railroad, reporting that they were "twisting the iron here beautifully." The next day he examined the destruction done by Slocum's infantry and was displeased that the rail had simply been bent and not twisted. In response, Sherman ordered Yates and his men to report to Brig. Gen. A. S. Williams's XX Corps. He wrote Williams that the engineers were to be used specifically to properly twist the heated iron tracks as they had previously with Logan's men. Tearing up and piling the rails for burning was to be left to the infantry. On the ninth the regiment was up early and marching in light snow eastward along the railroad toward Graham's Station. At night they made camp at Blackville, fourteen miles west of Bamberg and reported to Williams.[15]

On the tenth Major Crittenton and several companies marched six miles westward and joined with XX Corps infantry near Post 96. Working together, they destroyed over two miles of track working westward toward Williston. Lieutenant Colonel Hannings with four companies moved through Post 96 and about four miles beyond Williston to near White Pond Station. Here they twisted over two miles of track, working with men of the Third Division. In both cases, the infantry pulled up and heated the iron, while the engineers were assigned the task of thoroughly twisting it.[16]

The regiment remained divided on the eleventh. Hannings's men returned to Williston with Brig. Gen. William T. Ward's Third Division and then turned north off the railroad and continued toward the south branch of the Edisto River. They rebuilt the main crossing at Guignard's Bridge that had been destroyed by retreating Confederates and worked through the night to get the crossing ready for the infantry but did not cross over. Meanwhile, Yates with Crittenton's four companies marched nine miles north from Blackville alongside Williams's First and Second divisions and the corps' wagons. At Duncan's Bridge, the engineers and infantry details repaired the burned bridge and corduroyed the approaches. Yates was joined by Company B at Duncan's that night, the company having made a march of about twenty miles. Company K and the thirty-one regimental wagons moved with the corps' train. The last of the wagons did not cross until after 10 P.M.[17]

On the twelfth Ward's division rejoined the rest of the XX Corps north of Duncan's Bridge, and together the corps marched northward on the main road to Columbia, accompanied by Yates and Crittenton's battalion. At noon the advance was halted by the Confederate destruction of the bridges at Jeffcoat's over the north branch of the Edisto River. The engineers were sent forward to repair the crossing but were driven off by two pieces of Confederate artillery and a small force of Alabama infantry commanded by Gen. Zachariah C. Deas. Gen. John Geary's infantry drove Deas's small force back from the north bank of the Edisto, and Yates and several companies of the Michigan Engineers returned to the bridge and labored through the night to finish it. While inspecting the crossing, Yates was nearly hit by enemy artillery fire, a piece of shell passing through the waist of his jacket, and two men of his command were slightly wounded. On the following morning the companies with Yates crossed over on their own bridge and went into camp five or six miles away with the rest of the XX Corps.[18]

For the next three days Yates and the several companies with Crittenton marched alongside the advance of Williams's XX Corps. Averaging only a little more than eight miles per day, the column moved through the Sand Hills, across Congaree Creek and then eastward toward Columbia. By the night of the sixteenth the corps was within three miles of South Carolina's capital. On the seventeenth the column marched to Zion Church, on the banks of the Saluda River, which joined with the Broad just north of the city to form the Congaree. While Williams's troops formed up to cross over the river on a pontoon bridge, Yates and his companies received orders to march southeast along the river toward the city and cross over onto the peninsula. On the morning of the eighteenth, the engineer companies with Yates continued across the peninsula and crossed over the Broad on a pontoon bridge. They marched on for another two miles to a good camp in the northern outskirts of Columbia. That night Major Hannings and the companies of the left wing joined them.[19]

Hannings and his four companies, meanwhile, had been detached from the XX Corps on February 11. After destroying track along the South Carolina as far west as Johnson's Station, they had left the railroad and marched to Columbia with the XIV Corps. The south branch of the Edisto was crossed on the thirteenth at Guigard's Bridge, using the bridge the engineers had rebuilt just days earlier. On the fourteenth the engineers were part of the advance, repairing bridges. By the seventeenth they were in the middle of the column, helping the corps wagons over the rough roads approaching Columbia. On the eighteenth Hanning's battalion left the XIV Corps and reached the regimental camp north of the city.[20]

Sherman intended to destroy anything of military value in and around Columbia and made preparations while his columns were closing in on South Carolina's capital city. On February 16 Poe ordered the two battalions of the Michigan Engineers to Sherman's headquarters for special duty. The infantrymen of Howard's right wing were to destroy public buildings and stores in Columbia and then march along, and destroy, the Charlotte and South Carolina Railroad northward to Winnsboro. Slocum's left and the cavalry were to destroy the Greenville and Columbia Railroad north from Columbia and then join the rest of the army at Winnsboro. From there the columns would strike north toward Fayetteville, North Carolina. While still at Columbia the engineers were again shifted between army wings, this time back to Howard's right.[21]

Columbia was first occupied by Union forces on February 17, hard on the heels of evacuating Confederate cavalry. That night raging fires destroyed much of the city's business district. While blame has been much debated, it is clear that the men in Sherman's army, including those in the Michigan Engineers, held little sympathy for the city's fate. Isaac Roseberry described Columbia as he marched toward it as "the nest egg of the rebellion." After its destruction, he wrote without any regret that Columbia was a "horrible looking place . . . a dozen times worse than Atlanta." Ironically, the fires on the night of the seventeenth spared many of the buildings with the most military value, which had been abandoned bulging with equipment, ammunition, and ordnance vital to the South's war effort.[22]

The two wings of the Michigan Engineers both reached Columbia on the eighteenth. The next day Major Rhodes and Companies C, F, G, and K were sent into the city to destroy military buildings spared in the earlier fires. Rhodes and his men worked under Poe's personal direction and alongside infantry details from the XV Corps. Smokestacks and buildings were smashed to rubble and then set afire. Large stores of gun-making equipment and guns were broken up and thrown into the river. Public works and railroad cars and engines were destroyed. They set fire to the state arsenal's magazine. By the time the last of the XV Corps marched out of Columbia on February 20, they left behind little with which the Confederates could wage war.[23]

Yates and the balance of the regiment, meanwhile, marched to the Columbia and Charlotte Railroad with Blair's XVII Corps. During the day they destroyed over six miles of railroad strap iron leading northward from Columbia. Continuing the division of labor, the infantry tore up the track and fired it in great pyres fueled by the ties. The Michigan Engineers followed along behind the infantry and twisted the rails beyond simple repair. Camp that night was about six miles north of Columbia, where they were rejoined by Rhodes's detachment. The regiment was now under orders to rejoin the right wing, reporting to the XVII Corps.[24]

The regiment continued northward along the railroad on the twentieth, repeating their work of the day before. About ten miles of track was heated and twisted beyond repair. Each of Blair's divisions supplied one brigade to tear up the track. In turn, Yates assigned three engineer companies to each of the three brigades. Presumably the tenth company of Yates's regiment remained with the regimental wagons that marched with the bridge wagons. Camp that night was at Doko's Station with the XVII Corps.[25]

Rebel cavalry struck at isolated bands of foragers sent out each morning. Engineer Pvt. Martin J. Cole, taken prisoner on February 15, was lucky to survive. A few days later two captured Union soldiers were found murdered, with a sign affixed that said "death to foragers." On the twenty-second the bodies of eighteen soldiers were found, two with their throats cut from ear to ear. On the twenty-fifth two more met a similar fate near a XV Corps camp. In addition, at least four more Michigan Engineers fell out of the marching column in February. All were apparently saved from capture, but two died from their illness and another never rejoined the regiment.[26]

The railroad destruction continued on February 21, and another eight or nine miles were torn up and twisted. In addition, the engineers burned fifteen thousand bales of cotton. Sherman was unwilling to leave anything of value for the rebel cause, even heavy bales of cotton alongside destroyed railroad tracks. The engineers marched fourteen miles in all and then camped at night about nine miles south of Winnsboro, near Simpson's Station.[27]

On the twenty-second the Michigan Engineers twisted more railroad iron, working nearly to Winnsboro with the infantry of the XVII Corps. As before, three companies of Yates's regiment were paired with each of the three infantry brigades ordered to tear up the road. Because the railroad north of Winnsboro had already been destroyed by Slocum's left wing, Blair's corps and the engineers turned off the railroad and marched eastward toward Cheraw, the army's next point of concentration. Camp that night was at Poplar Springs Church.[28]

Continuing on with the XVII Corps, the engineers left their camp early in the morning of the twenty-third, eventually crossing the Wateree River on pontoons at Peay's Ferry. After marching a total of fifteen miles in the rain, they camped at Liberty Hill at about

8 P.M. The engineer wagons, however, had a hard time crossing the Wateree. The pontoon bridge became increasingly slippery with the accumulated mud of the tramping divisions. During the night, one of the regiment's supply wagons tumbled off the pontoon bridge, smashing one of the pontoons. The same happened soon after to a supply wagon of Brig. Gen. Manning Force's division train, and crossing was delayed for two hours.[29]

The next day the march continued along muddy roads, and the men made only fourteen miles before setting up camp between Patterson's and Flat Rock. The engineers had to repair the roads for most of the day, corduroying over the worst places. General Force later penned a vivid description of the day's march: "The country was swimming with water. Brooks had become torrents scarcely fordable. Wood laid on the road for corduroy floated off."[30]

Despite the obstacles caused by the rain, corduroying was the best way to make the roads passable. The engineer or pioneer details laid logs across the roadway, giving the wagons a more solid footing than they had in the mud. The corduroy also distributed the weight of a wagon across a larger area, instead of just one wheel track, and made it less likely that the wheeled transport would sink into the mud. Corduroying was essential to the passage of the army through the swamps of the Carolinas, and about eight hundred miles of it was constructed by the entire command during the campaign. A description of the labor required to properly corduroy a road was written by one of Sherman's men at the conclusion of the march: "After the passage of a score or two of heavy laden wagons, the corduroying sank into a muddy chasm, and new layer of rails and trees had to be put down on the muddy surface through which the first had disappeared. It is detestable work felling trees and trimming them of limbs and bough among those boggy pines, after working knee-deep in the oozy soil. After the trees are shaped they have to be dragged through morass to the pool or mud pits where they are needed and then laid down."[31]

On the twenty-fifth the column was marching early in a cold rain. After stops to lay corduroy, the men halted near the flooded Little Lynch at Hough's Bridge. Confederates had destroyed a nearby milldam, sending a wall of water in their path and stranding a division of the XVII Corps on the far bank. After wading through water, the soaked and tired men reached camp, hopeful for supper. Instead, they were ordered into line in their wet clothes and sent back to build a bridge over the flooded crossing. The engineers worked into the rainy night in waist-deep water building a foot bridge 250 yards in length, "getting wet as rats." In the morning the tired men discovered that their labors had been unnecessary, since the water receded to its normal level, and they were ordered to remove their work.[32]

The tired engineers were allowed time for a quick breakfast and then marched at 8 A.M. in the advance with Joseph Mower's First Division. After twelve miles they halted and went into camp, though any sleep was to be short-lived. The approach road to the Young's Bridge crossing over the Big Lynch was so flooded that the column could not continue. Blair reported that the stream was two to four feet deep but that he would build a footbridge through the swamp that night. At 10 P.M. the bugle was blown, and the tired men in Yates's regiment roused themselves from the ground. They were formed up and sent forward into the swamp to their front. Working through the night in water "ass deep" they constructed a mile of footbridge along the road. The engineers completed their work just before dawn with help from infantry details.[33]

The exhausted men were then sent back to work after breakfast on the morning of the twenty-seventh. Even though the water level had dropped some, the road had to be corduroyed for the passage of the trains. The engineers finished their work by noon, and the men had a chance to get some sleep while waiting for new orders. In total, some twenty-five hundred engineers and infantry completed 850 feet of bridging and 7,000 feet of corduroying. That night, they formed into column and crossed over on their handiwork.[34]

On the last day of February, the engineers marched another fifteen miles and made camp near Black Creek. Because of the delays encountered by Slocum's left wing, Sherman had already cautioned Howard to slow his command's march to keep the two wings from becoming too far separated. In addition, because of the difficulties encountered by Logan's corps in the crossing at Kelly's Bridge, Blair received an order from Howard to proceed no further than McDonald's Crossroads. Since that point had already been passed, Blair halted his corps and selected a strong defensible position at which to entrench and camp. The engineers worked on breastworks for three hours after dark on the twenty-eighth and then were allowed to sleep around midnight.[35]

The men remained resting in camp for the next two days with very little to do. The officers took the opportunity to have an inspection of the regiment's arms and equipment. Major Rhodes, the regimental provost martial, ordered nine men tied to a pole by their thumbs for infractions along the march. Blair's men, including the Michigan Engineers, waited in entrenched positions through March 2 for Logan's XV Corps to catch up. Sherman and Howard did not want Blair moving on Cheraw unless the XV Corps was in supporting position because of reports that a large Confederate force was gathering at that point. With Logan's column nearing, Howard sent Blair orders the afternoon of March 2 to move on Cheraw in the morning.[36]

The rested Michigan Engineers marched on March 3 with the XVII Corps and went into camp after covering eleven miles. During the day they built corduroy to help the wagons over the worst places in the road and constructed a bridge over Thompson's Creek on the approach to Cheraw. Retreating Confederate cavalry burned the large bridge over the Pee Dee River at Cheraw, and Yates received orders to build pontoon boats and assemble a bridge. Construction of the pontoons started on the morning of the fourth but was stopped after only a few boats had been completed because the pontoon train of the Missouri Engineers arrived and was thrown across the river.[37]

Instead of completing more pontoons, the engineers were ordered to report to the depot and destroy captured ordnance and ammunition stores that had been left behind by retreating Confederates. A detachment of two hundred men from the regiment worked until after dark on the fourth, destroying the artillery and throwing the guns and ammunition into the river. Meanwhile, other details from the regiment repaired the road leading to the pontoon crossing and probably crossed over the river to make similar repairs on the road leading away from the distant bank.[38]

Destruction of the captured ordnance and ammunition continued on the morning of the fifth. By the time they were finished, twenty-one pieces of artillery, seven hundred stands of small arms, and thirty loads of ammunition were broken up and thrown into the river. At noon the engineers broke camp and crossed over the Pee Dee River on the Missouri pontoon bridge. Yates and his men went into camp one mile north of Cheraw.[39]

By March 6 most of Sherman's army had crossed the Pee Dee River, Howard at Cheraw and Slocum ten miles upstream at Sneedsborough. Sherman was very pleased with his army's progress so far, writing Slocum, "I feel confident that nothing can now stand before us." The army's next target was Fayetteville, on the Cape Fear River. At Fayetteville Sherman could communicate with Union commanders along the coast, using steamers on the river. A limited amount of supplies could also be dispatched upriver to Fayetteville for Sherman's ragged column. During the march to Fayetteville, the engineers remained with the XVII Corps, moving on the route of Bennettsville to Gilopolis to Fayetteville.[40]

On the sixth the regiment marched fourteen miles and camped with Blair's men near Bennetsville. Along the route the regiment built thirty or forty rods of corduroy road and repaired two small bridges. On the seventh the regiment again repaired the road for the XVII Corps as it advanced. They marched with the advance division of General Force through Bennettsville and then on for twelve miles. The designated camp between Panther Creek and Beaver Dam Creek was reached by noon. The men were formed into working parties and ordered to repair the Fayetteville Road.[41]

On the eighth the engineers again marched with Force's advance division. Force penned another vivid account of the labor throughout the day: "the worst marching for troops I ever saw; had to wade much of the time, and scramble through wet trees nearly all the time." After a day of this struggle, the engineers camped at Floral College after making about sixteen miles. On the ninth Blair split his XVII Corps along parallel roads, and the engineers worked in the rain, repairing the road for Brig. Gen. Giles A. Smith's Fourth Division. Smith's column marched on the left, or upper, road from Gilopolis to beyond Raft Swamp. At 11 P.M. the tired engineers finally made camp near Antioch.[42]

The march on the eighth took the men into North Carolina, one of the last states to leave the Union and home to many unionists. Sherman ordered the men to deal more carefully with the civilians along their route. Though not all of his men heeded his caution, and thorough foraging remained army policy, historians have noted that "a remarkable change came over the marchers. The wholesale destruction they had practiced in South Carolina ceased." Not only did Sherman hope to drive a wedge between the ardent secessionists in South Carolina and their cousins in the Tar Heel State, he also was sensing that the war was coming to an end and with it any need for accompanying devastation.[43]

On the tenth, Smith's division and Yates's men continued on toward Rock Fish Creek, struggling the entire route with deep mud and having to put down layers of corduroy for the wagons. Work continued on the following day. The engineers struggled with timbers to build a firm enough road bottom for the wagons along the twelve-mile march route and did not reach the crossing at Davis's Bridge until about 6 P.M. Early on the morning of the eleventh the engineers built a footbridge for the troops of Logan's XV Corps, who were expected to use the crossing behind them. The command was marching by late morning and continued on to Fayetteville, fixing sections of road as they advanced. Retreating Confederates destroyed the bridge over the Cape Fear River, and the XIV Corps camped one mile south while a crossing was made.[44]

Sherman's army was all in or near Fayetteville by the night of March 12, 1865. In just six weeks, he had moved his sixty thousand men from near Savannah to Fayetteville. The columns lived off the land and pushed their way through some of the worst terrain in the South, in the most difficult season for passage. Sherman reported his arrival to Secretary Stanton on March 12, bragging, "No place in the Confederacy is safe against the Army of the West."[45]

· 22 ·

Final Weeks of the War

Since he was not garrisoning the town, General Sherman decided to leave nothing behind in Fayetteville with which the rebellion might be prolonged, especially the former U.S. arsenal. During the war the Confederates had enlarged the facilities and shipped in equipment from other captured arsenals, particularly that at Harper's Ferry. The brick and stone buildings formed a hollow rectangle around the citadel, which was a three-story oblong structure. All together, they were "the handsomest collection of buildings the town could boast of."[1]

Confederates had been able to evacuate only a portion of the equipment and machinery before Sherman's men arrived on March 11, 1865. That same day, Sherman issued orders for O. M. Poe to supervise the "utter demolition of the arsenal building and everything pertaining to it." To another, Sherman stated his intention to "destroy the arsenal utterly." As a staff officer wrote, "We have just stopped here to take breath and destroy a fine Arsenal which Uncle Sam built and the rebels stole but will never steal nor use again." Poe intended to use Colonel Yates's Michigan Engineers for the task.[2]

The Michigan Engineers completed the actual destruction on March 12–14. Details used sledgehammers to wreck the machinery. Others tore down the brick walls of the arsenal buildings. Special rams were constructed from railroad iron, timber, and chains to speed this task. A small detail of men was ordered to blow up the arsenal magazine. The men stacked rosin against the door and lined the nearby alley with wood taken from abandoned houses. The fuse was lit, and the men quickly departed, confident of their work. Later that day the men began to wonder about the lack of explosion and to question the effectiveness of their work, when suddenly there was a tremendous roar from the direction of the magazine.[3]

The work was similar to what the engineers had done in Atlanta, Columbia, and Cheraw. As before, the engineers worked under the direct supervision of Captain Poe, who sent Sherman the following report of their activities: "The immense machine-shops, foundries, timber sheds, etc., were soon reduced to a heap of rubbish, and at a concerted signal fire was applied to these heaps and to all wooden buildings and piles of lumber; also to the powder trains leading to the magazines."[4]

The destruction of the Fayetteville arsenal was not without cost to the engineers. On March 14 Company B was knocking down brick walls when one collapsed onto the working party. Sgt. Joseph Kennedy was killed instantly, and two others were seriously injured. Another was standing next to Kennedy but escaped without injury by springing aside as the wall tumbled. Kennedy, an original member of the company and one of the oldest surviving men in the regiment, left a large family behind in Grand Rapids.[5]

Despite frequent skirmishing, Sherman's army on the march from Savannah to Fayetteville had faced little serious opposition, mostly delaying harassment by rebel cavalry. In late February Gen. Joseph E. Johnston was given command of all Confederate forces in the region, with General Beauregard appointed his second-in-command. At that time the forces available to Johnston numbered over twenty-four thousand but were widely scattered. Within two weeks, he was assembling his command at Smithfield, North Carolina, on the railroad between Raleigh and Goldsboro. This position allowed him to concentrate his command against a Union move on either point.[6]

Sherman intended to feint from Fayetteville toward Raleigh with several divisions of the left wing while the wagons and balance of troops moved to Goldsboro. From Goldsboro he would be able to form a junction with supplies and reinforcements moved overland from the Union-controlled port at New Berne. Then his enlarged and supplied command would march northwest toward Raleigh and a final confrontation with Johnston's forces. The plan relied on the ability of his command to move quickly and with little encumbrance. Officials sent the sick by steamer down the Cape Fear River to Wilmington and ordered that surplus equipment and animals be destroyed.[7]

Henry Slocum's left wing was divided into two columns for the upcoming march. John Geary's (Second/XX Corps) and Absalom Baird's (Third/XIV Corps) divisions would accompany the wagons of the left wing and march on a direct route toward Bentonville and Goldsboro, with Howard's wing on their right. Slocum remained with the other four divisions: Nathaniel Jackson's (First) and William Ward's (Third) of the XX Corps and William Carlin's (First) and James Morgan's (Second) of the XIV Corps. These, along with Judson Kilpatrick's cavalry, were stripped to the bare minimum of wagons and equipment and ordered to move northward to Averasboro and feint against Raleigh, drawing the enemy away from the bulk of the army en route for Goldsboro. By noon on the fourteenth, the engineers had finished their work at the arsenal. They crossed to the east bank of the Cape Fear River on a pontoon bridge and camped with the troops of A. S. Williams's XX Corps.[8]

Major Hannings and Companies C, D, F, and I reported to Geary to be part of the slower-moving column to Goldsboro. Hannings's command marched in the advance early on the fifteenth and camped that night eleven miles away, on the banks of South (or Black) River. Having been sent to the crossing ahead of the trains, the engineers cut and prepared the timbers to rebuild the bridge. Enemy rearguard forces near the crossing itself, however, delayed work on the bridge. Starting early in the morning, the engineers rebuilt the bridge by 10 A.M. on the sixteenth and crossed over the swollen stream. Continuing on with Geary and the advance brigade they corduroyed five miles of road before camping at H. T. Jackson's farm.[9]

On the seventeenth Geary's command moved forward only a short distance, halting for the passage of troops of the XV Corps. The next day they marched forward eight miles after frustrating delays. Hannings's command cleared the roads before any movement by the wagons. Instead of having the men work alongside the moving wagons, this new technique allowed the column to stay together and reach camp in a more compact manner. Camp was along Seven Mile Creek, near Rainer's Mill. On the nineteenth the routine continued, though the column had to camp at Canaan Church, some three miles from the Newton Grove Post Office. Their advance was delayed because the XV Corps had not cleared the road ahead. In addition to crossing Cohera Creek, the column had to corduroy three of the ten miles that they marched.[10]

With the fight near Bentonville raging several miles away to the west, Geary was ordered away with most of his division, and defense of the wagon train was left to Col. George W. Mindil with his Second Brigade, Hannings's four companies of the Michigan Engineers, and Lt. Col. Joseph Moore's Fifty-eighth Indiana pontoniers. This small force of fewer than two thousand men spent the twentieth entrenching their positions at Canaan Church but were then ordered to continue on to Goldsboro. That night they camped near flooded Falling Creek, described by one soldier as a "miserable man-trap." Delayed by the difficult crossing, they did not reach Grantham's Store until mid-afternoon on the twenty-first. On the following day Mindil's command marched to within a few miles of Union-held Goldsboro.[11]

It was probably during Hanning's march on the twentieth that four more men were gobbled up by roving Confederates. Charles

Warner, John Druyour, Francis Buck, and Oscar Crouch were all taken prisoner on this date, probably captured while foraging away from the main column. All four were paroled within days, but for them the war was over.[12]

On the twenty-first Sherman ordered Generals Howard and Slocum to collect all of the trains and wounded of their commands together near Goldsboro. Each wing was directed to establish a depot along the Wilmington and Goldsboro Railroad, south of the Neuse. Howard's was to be east of the railroad, Slocum's to the west. Hannings's command was among those who organized and fortified the left wing depot on the twenty-second. The depot was located near the intersection of the Everettsville and Goldsboro Road with the Dead Fields and Goldsboro Road, near or on Murphy's plantation.[13]

On the twenty-third all able men in Hannings's battalion were sent to work on railroad trestle between Goldsboro and Kinston, leaving the sick with the corps wagon train depot. While Union troops had occupied Goldsboro on March 21, the railroad leading back to the supply depots at Kinston was not yet repaired. Hannings's companies worked along the railroad leading into Goldsboro for two days and returned to camp on the twenty-fifth. This was the last railroad repair work performed during the regiment's four-year service.[14]

Meanwhile, Yates and the remaining six companies were part of Slocum's feint against Raleigh. They left camp on the fifteenth, marching between the two divisions of the XX Corps, and camped for the night at Silver Run. On the sixteenth the march order remained the same, with the engineers moving beyond Taylor's Hole Creek and on toward Averasboro. While the engineers struggled to corduroy and repair the poor roads, the First Division was rushed forward to help the Third drive Confederate infantry back from positions astride the road. That night the regiment camped on the Averasboro battlefield, amid the unburied Confederate dead. One soldier noted in his diary, "The woods was just strewn with dead rebels."[15]

On the seventeenth, Yates and his men marched to a crossing over Black River and rebuilt a bridge near Smith's Mill. Then they crossed over and marched another five or six miles through the country before camping for the night near Mingo Creek. The next day Yates's men rebuilt the bridge over Mingo Creek and then marched to Lee's Store, having repaired and corduroyed the road for much of the thirteen miles. Supper was not served to the tired and hungry men until after midnight, and many had nothing more than moldy hardtack.[16]

Johnston had decided the day before to strike Slocum's isolated wing with the forces he had concentrated near Smithfield. These included an assortment of units from throughout the embattled Confederacy: forty-five hundred survivors of Hood's army under the command of Lt. Gen. Alexander P. Stewart, Maj. Gen. Robert Hoke's division from General Bragg's Department of North Carolina, General Hardee's remnants from the evacuation of Savannah and retreat through South Carolina, and veteran troopers from General Hampton's and General Wheeler's cavalry corps. The quality of the infantry ranged from consolidated regiments of veterans to green troops of the South and North Carolina Reserves. In total, Johnston had about twenty-one thousand effectives, of which about eighteen thousand were infantry or artillery. Slocum had about the same number of men in the four divisions and attached cavalry.[17]

On March 19 foragers and cavalry in advance of the XIV Corps came under increasing pressure from enemy cavalry as they approached the direct road to Bentonville. Union infantry was sent to their assistance but proved unable to dislodge the Confederate infantry and artillery entrenched behind the rebel cavalry screen. Suddenly, at 3 P.M. the proud remnant of the Confederate Army of Tennessee swept forward against the poorly positioned Union line, driving Carlin's division back in disorder. Elements of Davis's other division and the First Division of Williams's corps were thrown into the fight and stabilized the line while reinforcements were hurried forward from further back in the column.[18]

Yates and his companies of Michigan Engineers were among the troops still struggling along the roads, marching alongside Col. Daniel Dustin's brigade of Ward's division and laying corduroy. Throughout the morning the sounds of battle were heard in the distance, but most assumed it was skirmishing between rebel cavalry and Kilpatrick's division. While halted, however, a series of couriers from Slocum requested that Ward hurry his men forward.[19]

Dustin and Yates's men led Ward's division forward on the Raleigh Road, moving at double time for several miles. As they arrived, Dustin's brigade was used to build a new line to the left and rear of the XIV Corps, taking position on the left side of the road. The Michigan Engineers were placed to expand the line further left. On Yates's left were placed the men of Col. Henry Case's brigade, and Kilpatrick's cavalry division took position on Case's left. As the Michigan Engineers took their assigned position in the line, packs of panicked mules from Carlin's division stampeded through, adding to the sense of disaster. With hard-pressed Union regiments to their front and right fighting for their lives, the men immediately started entrenching with shovels taken from the just-arriving tool wagons.[20]

The engineers "worked lively," expecting the federal line to their front to collapse. When it was reported, falsely, that a Confederate force was moving up on their left flank, tools were exchanged for rifles and Yates "exhorted his men to stand firm, declaring, 'We will whip the rebels.'" When no attack was forthcoming, the men picked their tools back up and continued to strengthen their position.[21]

By dark the last of the Confederate attacks upon the Union line sputtered to a stop. After the initial flight of most of Carlin's division, the patchwork line of blue had held against desperate assaults by the rebels. Though he failed to destroy an isolated portion of Sherman's army, Johnston remained in position opposite Slocum's force during the night, while Union reinforcements hurried forward. By morning most of Slocum's two corps were on hand in addition to the first of several divisions from Howard's right wing of the army. For the next two days there was only scattered fighting, save for a division-sized unsupported assault that nearly broke the Confederate line on the twenty-first. The Michigan Engineers remained in their defenses during the twentieth and twenty-first, and that night Johnston's army slipped away back to Smithfield.[22]

The march toward Goldsboro resumed on the twenty-second. Yates and his men served as a train guard and laid corduroy, first with the XX Corps and then with the XIV Corps. They reached Goldsboro on the twenty-third and marched through the city with flags. On the twenty-fifth they were joined by Hannings's working party from the railroad, the regiment's sick men from the army depot south of the city, and Major Grant's small battalion from Tennessee. For the first time during the war, twelve companies of the Michigan Engineers were together in one camp, with more than eleven hundred officers and men present for duty.[23]

The stay at Goldsboro was a welcome respite for the engineers after two months of continuous campaigning or, as Howard described it, "prolonged labors, perils, and privations." The Michigan Engineers had completed a "march of nearly 500 miles through the enemy's country, crossing swamps, rivers, etc., drawing most of [their] subsistence from a poor and wasted country, and defeating the enemy on his own ground." After such an arduous campaign, the engineers needed to rest and refit but looked forward to then playing a part in the "grand final overthrow of the great rebellion." They quickly set up camp, constructing huts of wood with dog tents serving as cover. With little to do, they lay around camp, resting and drawing new equipment.[24]

Uniforms and footwear to replace those worn out on the march were among the most important items to reach Goldsboro, arriving via the newly repaired railroad line from Kinston and the Atlantic port of New Berne. Like most of Sherman's army, the engineers arrived at Goldsboro with their clothing in tatters. One described the engineers as "ragged and lousy." Another wrote home that "many of the troops are without shoes and boots and many with not pants enough to hide their nakedness" and that he had been able to replace his worn-out boots only because a friend on Sherman's staff had an extra pair. One of the officers who arrived at Goldsboro with Major Grant's battalion wrote that when Yates's men reached that point they were "The roughest looking set of customers you ever saw. Half of them being dressed in rebel clothes for want of better ones and a great many barefooted."[25]

On March 27 the happy engineers eagerly received the first mail since Savannah, and many of the men took advantage of the opportunity to send letters. These letters assured families back home that they had emerged from the Carolina forests and swamps with Sherman's army, a little sore but safe. They also reported a general optimism that the war would soon be over. They tried to describe the kind of war that was being waged by Sherman's army, especially by the foragers. Wrote one, "I have been detailed a considerable [amount of the time] to forage and most of the time we lived tiptop. We have had everything almost that ever was [to] eat when it could be got and we have stood many narrow chances of our lives in getting them. The foragers are called bummers and when the history of this war is made out, the name bummer will be used quite often."[26]

After so many months of active campaign, the officers in Sherman's army tightened discipline to control the men who were confined to camps for the first time since Savannah. In Yates's camp, the engineers were drilled for a few hours each day by squad, company, or battalion, weather permitting. Yates ordered roll call four times a day in an effort to keep the men in camp. Any absent man was put on extra duty. With the end of the war in sight, this emphasis on discipline and drill "made the boys mad," and some at least talked a tough line. One wrote home, "Colonel Yates will have to look out when the war is over for some of the men will tend to him."[27]

Meanwhile, Sherman planned a resumption of the army's march northward. On March 25 he left for meetings with Grant at City Point, Virginia, not returning until the thirtieth. The day before he left to meet with Grant, Sherman ordered Schofield to organize several commands from the Department of North Carolina into two army corps that would form the reorganized Army of the Ohio. Taking form over a period of several days, this command eventually included Schofield's old XXIII Corps from Tennessee and the reorganized X Corps and was labeled as the "center wing" of Sherman's field army for the upcoming campaign. Howard's Army of the Tennessee remained as the right wing and Slocum's Army of Georgia as the left. Kilpatrick remained in command of the sole cavalry division. Sherman's combined force totaled almost ninety thousand men, most of them hardened veterans, flushed with a string of successes.[28]

Poe's engineer organization also expanded. The Missouri, Michigan, and Indiana men who had been a part of the march since Atlanta remained. They were joined by a detachment of the Fifteenth New York Engineers regiment and the engineer battalion from the Army of the Ohio, both of which were to accompany Schofield's command.[29]

By early April the army was finishing preparations for what many hoped would be its final campaign of the war. Yates and his officers inspected the men to make sure that all surplus equipment was left behind. Each man would be carrying only his rifle and accouterments and a haversack containing minimal cooking implements and spare clothing and boots or shoes. Each man carried a shelter half, which became part of a dog tent. Cooked rations would be issued to the men just before leaving, and extra rations were to be carried in the limited wheeled transport allowed each corps as well as on the hoof.[30]

On April 5 Sherman sent a confidential field order to his army and corps commanders outlining his plans for a march starting April 10. He intended to move the three columns northward across the Roanoke River and into westward-facing positions to the south of Petersburg with Norfolk as a base of supply in his rear. On the sixth, however, official word was received that Richmond was in Union hands, and two days later Grant wrote Sherman that he had Gen. Robert E. Lee's army on the run. He finished his letter with the charge "Let us see if we cannot finish the job with Lee's and Johnston's armies." At this point it was clear that Grant's army was perfectly capable of running Lee's army to ground and that Sherman's greatest contribution to ending the war would be forcing the surrender of Johnston's command. Instead of continuing preparations for a march to Virginia, Sherman ordered his commanders to put the army in motion against Johnston.[31]

At this time Johnston was at Smithfield with his men. From that point he could resist any advance on Raleigh or try to flank an expected move northward by Sherman into Virginia. While Sherman rested his army, the Confederate command labored feverishly to reinforce and reorganize Johnston's command. Most important, several thousand more men arrived from Tennessee, the last of the survivors of Hood's army to be sent east. During this time, Johnston was receiving only sketchy reports of the evacuation of Richmond and flight of Lee's army.

Still hoping for a junction with Lee, Johnston sent urgent requests for more information, not realizing how close the Southern cause was to a final collapse. On April 9 Wheeler's cavalry passed on ominous reports from local sympathizers that Sherman's army would march the next day out of Goldsboro and toward Raleigh. Johnston started his army west toward Raleigh early the next morning, hoping to form a junction with Lee. He did not know that Lee had surrendered his army to Grant.[32]

Sherman's plan was to have Slocum's army move on the direct road to Smithfield, while Howard's column would march on its right. Though labeled the "center wing," Schofield's army actually operated on the left flank during the movement to Raleigh. The engineers would march with the XX Corps of Slocum's command, moving on the southernmost of two parallel roads running west from Goldsboro toward Smithfield.[33]

Sherman's army would again be traveling light, with even less transport and baggage than upon the departures from Atlanta or Savannah. The army was short of wheeled transportation and lacked forage for any unnecessary animals. The number and type of wagons were limited as much as possible, and many were shifted between the army corps to achieve a better balance. On the eighth Yates issued orders to his regiment for a march on the tenth and placed a severe limit on the number of wagons, three to each battalion for tools and headquarters, while companies were expected to use pack mules and horses to carry equipment.[34]

A small number of wagons were loaded with rations on the night of the ninth as insurance against unsuccessful foraging, and each man was ordered to have four days' rations in his haversack. Despite these precautions, Sherman intended that his command would live off the land as they had done ever since leaving Atlanta. Yates organized his mounted foragers under the command of Capt. Cyrus M. Curtis. Each company commander was ordered to select four of the "best and most reliable" and have them report to Curtis. Yates also reminded the foragers of previously issued orders on the importance of remaining with the larger group. Foragers who went off on their own, presumably with evil intent, would be promptly dismounted and returned to the ranks. This was a serious punishment to men who enjoyed the greater freedom and easier work of foraging than the companies struggling on foot through the swamps.[35]

Early on April 10 the Michigan Engineers moved from camp at Goldsboro, marching with A. S. Williams's division of Maj. Gen. Joseph Mower's XX Corps. Mower had replaced Williams as corps commander a week previously. The column marched about thirteen miles in the rain along the Neuse River Road toward Smithfield. After Williams's infantry drove rebel skirmishers back across the swampy approaches along Moccasin Creek, the engineers were ordered out of the column to corduroy a path through the flooded route. Retreating Confederates had destroyed a nearby dam at Holt's Mill, further flooding the area between Moccasin and Raccoon creeks. At least 350 feet of road was constructed in this fashion before two battalions of the regiment were allowed to set up camp. The other four companies, working under the command of Majors Grant and Crittenton, remained at the crossing most of the night helping wagons across Moccasin Creek.[36]

The rain was gone by morning, but unseasonably hot temperatures took its place. For the next two days the men suffered badly from the heat, weather one referred to as "hot as love." Many gave out during the march because of the heat, and two suffered sunstroke. One battalion of Yates's regiment was ordered forward to march with Geary's Second Division in the corps advance. Despite noisy skirmishing, Geary's division did not suffer any losses on the eleventh. A sixty-five-foot bridge over Boorden's Creek was constructed by the engineer detachment in seventeen minutes according to an impressed Geary. The balance of the regiment marched in the column's rear with Williams's division. Mower's corps camped that night near Smithfield, on the east bank of the Neuse River. Retreating rebels burned the bridge over the river, but Slocum had two pontoon bridges across by morning. The regiment was apparently reunited in camp that night and given orders to take the advance of the entire corps in the morning.[37]

Early on the morning of April 12, Yates moved ten companies over the Neuse River and started repairing the Raleigh Road. The men fixed bad sections of the road and rebuilt at least one bridge over Swift Creek. The direct road from Smithfield to Raleigh crossed this creek just west of the Neuse River and then again about fifteen miles east of Raleigh. Meanwhile, the other two companies and regimental wagons, except those carrying tools, moved with the corps train, the engineers repairing the road for its passage. That afternoon the engineers camped with the corps just north of Swift Creek, midway between Smithfield and Raleigh.[38]

The marching on the twelfth was lightened by news of Lee's surrender, received while marching on the road to Raleigh and with plenty of "cheering and congratulating each other over the happy event." In fact, another Michigan Engineer remembered that the news "almost made the boys crazy by the way they cheered and yelled." That day Sherman issued an order to the army announcing the news and offered "all honor to our comrades in arms, toward whom we are marching." He challenged his command to swiftly complete the task, since "a little more labor, a little more toil on our part, the great race is won and our Government stands regenerated after four long years of bloody war."[39]

On the thirteenth the engineers were up early and marching with the advance. As on the previous day, the engineers worked forward of the infantry, repairing and clearing the road. When the column approached Raleigh late in the morning, it was forced to wait for the XIV Corps to clear the route ahead. Finally, another road was discovered, and the corps camped near the asylum southwest of the city. The city had been abandoned by Johnston on the thirteenth and occupied by Kilpatrick's cavalry ahead of the infantry.[40]

The engineers remained in camp at Raleigh on the fourteenth, while Sherman made arrangements for the repair of the railroad back to Goldsboro and allowed his forces to concentrate. There was still a war on, however, as two men of the Michigan Engineers found out. Pvts. Julius Taubert and Calvin L. Mann, both of Company E, were captured on April 14 near Raleigh. Even though the war's end was in sight, fighting between isolated parties of Union and Confederates soldiers remained bitter, especially for small patrols of Union soldiers caught away from the main columns. Yates and his men must have feared the worst for their two comrades, especially since a party of sick and wounded Union soldiers taken prisoner on the eleventh was widely reported to have been shot out of hand. Taubert and Mann both survived their brief captivity.[41]

Sherman issued orders on the fourteenth for his army commanders to prepare for a move southwest to Ashboro, where he hoped to cut off any retreat by Johnston along the North Carolina Railroad in the direction of Salisbury and Charlotte. Slocum prepared his command to move forward the next day. Mower's XX Corps and the engineers were encamped two miles south of Raleigh and were ordered to move southward toward Jones's, later amended to Holly Springs.[42]

Sherman's efforts on the fourteenth, however, were interrupted by news that a packet was being forwarded by Johnston. Sherman halted most of his units. Following communications delays, Sherman and Johnston met in the small farmhouse of Daniel Bennett on the seventeenth. Sherman offered Johnston the same generous terms Grant had given to Lee days earlier. Johnston, however, offered to negotiate terms for the surrender of not just his army but of all remaining Confederate forces and a permanent peace. Eager to bring an end to the bloodshed, and still concerned Johnston's army might slip away and initiate a guerrilla war, Sherman expanded the discussion to include possible terms for a settlement of political issues as well. Not able to reach any final agreement, the two men concluded to meet again on the eighteenth and returned to their respective camps that night.[43]

Sherman returned to an expectant army that was fully aware negotiations were taking place that would end the war and send them home. Sherman, however, also had sad news to convey. While leaving to meet with Johnston in the morning, he had received a telegram announcing the assassination of President Lincoln. Afraid of the reaction of his army to this shocking news, he swore the telegraph operator to secrecy and stuffed the flimsy into his pocket. That night he broke the news to his men, issuing Special Field Order No. 56 "with pain and sorrow." Sherman did try to convey his belief that "the great mass of the Confederate army would scorn to sanction such acts" but threatened "woe upon the people who seek to expend their wild passions in such a manner, for there is but one dread result."[44]

The news of Lincoln's death struck the army like a thunderbolt, "a pall upon the minds of us all." Through the years of bloodshed and service the men identified their struggle with Lincoln. They had answered his calls for troops, voted overwhelmingly for him the previous fall, and shared a deep bond of mutual respect. Lieutenant Sligh wrote his mother, "You cannot [understand] the despondency of this army at the cold blooded murder of a president so nearly worshipped as was Lincoln by the army. It came like a thunderbolt, a black cloud casting with the shade and rendering as naught the late victories won by Grant and Sherman's armies. Men who had faced the guns of the enemy many and many a time, had faced death bravely in the cause of freedom, wept over the sad news."[45]

Some harbored hope that the news was false. Pvt. Robert Leach of Company K wrote his wife on the sixteenth that "the camp is depressed today with the news of the death of President Lincoln, but we are in hopes it will be contradicted yet." When contradiction was not forthcoming, they poured out their grief in letters home. Recently promoted Cpl. James Greenalch wrote his wife, "I never have for the last three years felt the sorrow and grief that I do at present. . . . If by my staying in the service another year would place Mr. Lincoln back again I would cheerfully stay."[46]

Many of the men turned their grief to anger and vowed revenge upon the South for Lincoln's death. One believed that "the news is awful to think of, it renders the army about frantic for revenge." In another letter two days later, this same soldier noted the continuing surrender discussions and predicted that if Johnston did not surrender his army, "Woe unto the country that the army has to pass through for they are frantic for revenge for the death of our President."[47]

On the morning of April 18, Sherman returned to the Bennett farmstead and continued his discussions with Johnston, both men fearful of the consequences Lincoln's murder would bring should the campaign continue. By the end of the day agreement had been reached on terms that Sherman thought President Andrew Johnson and the cabinet would accept. Johnston, in turn, thought he could convince President Jefferson Davis to accept them.[48]

Word of a settlement quickly spread through the Union troops at Raleigh, confirmed by Sherman in a communication to his army on the nineteenth. The commander told his men that hostilities were suspended pending approval by Washington of the terms the two adversaries had negotiated in the Bennett house. The official news, coming after days of continued rumor and speculation about Johnston's impending surrender, set off a round of wild celebration. Roseberry noted in his diary that night that "a great deal of excitement is going on." The men waited to hear Washington's acceptance.[49]

With the end of the war in sight, and little in the way of activity, the men's thoughts turned to resuming their civilian lives. Simeon Howe wrote his wife that he would be coming home with over three hundred dollars in pay and bounty and planned to immediately put up a frame house to replace their pioneer cabin. Another sent home detailed instructions for the spring planting, expecting to be "at home in time to hoe it." Private Mosher wrote he would be back in time to cut the June hay for his father's sheep. For others, just coming home was enough. Robert Leach ended a letter home simply "my love to all my little children, tell them father will be home soon."[50]

The celebration and expectations, however, were brusquely cut short a few days later. At 6 A.M. on the morning of April 24, Sherman was surprised by the unannounced arrival of General Grant at his headquarters. Grant had come quietly to tell his friend that the authorities in Washington had rejected the terms negotiated by Sherman and Johnston. Sherman, somewhat warned the day before by the harsh tone of the New York newspapers that had reached camp, calmly sent two notes to Johnston. One notified him that active hostilities would resume in forty-eight hours, while the other told him that they could offer no terms different than what Lee had accepted. Sherman also notified his army commanders that the army would continue the pursuit on the twenty-sixth in the manner outlined by Special Field Order No. 55, issued ten days earlier but suspended for the negotiations.[51]

While the engineers were marching on the twenty-sixth, Sherman and Johnston were back at the Bennett farmhouse. Determined to prevent any further and needless bloodshed, Johnston knew that he had little choice but to accept the same terms as Lee. After his concerns for the feeding and transportation of his men were addressed in a side agreement, Johnston signed the instrument of surrender. Sherman returned to Raleigh and turned the document over to Grant, who approved it and left for Washington. A sympathetic Sherman spared the Confederates the humiliation of a formal surrender ceremony, and they were quietly disbanded in their camps.[52]

Word of the surrender was received in the engineer camp on the twenty-sixth, "hailed with demonstrations of joy and gladness." An engineer noted in his diary, "great joy in camp, the band played Yankee Doodle and the Star Spangled Banner." The following day the engineers marched with the XVII Corps back toward Raleigh and settled into their old camp in the pines. The merriment in the ranks continued as the good news was confirmed in an official announcement from Sherman's headquarters.[53]

· 23 ·

Homeward Bound

General Sherman met with his commanders on April 28, 1865, to discuss final details of the dispersal of Union forces around Raleigh. Generals Schofield and Kilpatrick were to remain in North Carolina with their commands and oversee the disbanding of Joseph Johnston's Confederate forces, while the four corps in General Howard's and General Slocum's armies were to march north to Washington, D.C.[1]

Final preparations were also being made at the regimental level. Capt. Thomas Templeton of Company L was ordered to move the sick and convalescent men by train to Morehead City. From that point a steamer would transport them to Alexandria, Virginia, where the regiment's camp would be established under Templeton's command. Lieutenant Henika was ordered to proceed to New Berne and Beaufort, collecting the surplus regimental equipment that had been stored and directing its transportation to Templeton's camp at Alexandria. Lt. Albert Jewell was directed to Chattanooga to turn over the regimental surplus equipment that had been sent back when they left Atlanta and to ship to Detroit any private property belonging to the regiment.[2]

Colonel Yates made his first visit back to Michigan since leaving in December 1861. With Lt. Col. Marcus Hannings still absent on a leave begun a month earlier, Major Grant assumed command of the regiment and led it on the march from Raleigh to Alexandria, Virginia.[3]

Templeton and the convalescents left on the twenty-ninth. The balance of the regiment marched from Raleigh on the thirtieth, moving across Neuse River and joining Frank Blair's XVII Corps of Howard's right wing. On the following day the engineers repaired the road in advance of Mortimer Leggett's Third Division, which led the corps, making camp near the Tar River. En route they passed through Morrisville and Forrestville, admiring the "fine college" at Wake Forest. For the next several days, the Michigan Engineers helped the Union columns make a rapid march to Richmond.[4]

One of their most important projects was a bridge over the Roanoke River at Robinson's Ferry, constructed on the third. At that point the river was 740 feet wide, about 160 feet more than the combined length of both of Howard's pontoon bridges. Four large wooden boats were found in the river and were rigged up with centerpieces and freshly cut trestle to complete the crossing. The engineers cut and finished the trestle, and probably the center pieces, from standing timber. It was completed early the next morning.[5]

The engineers finally reached Petersburg on the eighth, after crossing Swift Creek. The column marched through the city that day with bands playing and colors flying. Though not formally reviewed, the regiments shouldered arms as they passed General Howard near the Jarratt Hotel. They continued northward several miles beyond the city. On the ninth they camped at Manchester, just two miles south of Richmond. Guards were posted in the small town, and it was declared off limits to the men in Howard's army.[6]

Many of the men in the regiment moved from Raleigh to Richmond as part of the army's long supply train. Plyn Williams was one of the soldiers detailed to move with the cattle drivers. His detachment was able to obtain several horses, and the men took turns riding. Pack mules carried their equipment. The cattle herd they were driving was in such poor condition that even the army did not want them for beef, and many were sold along the route.[7]

General Sherman rejoined his army on the ninth and issued orders for the march from Richmond to Alexandria. Slocum's army was to lead the march as far as Hanover Court House, where the two armies would move onto parallel routes and continue northward with Howard's army on the right. Still marching with the XVII Corps, the engineers would be following the route of Hanover Court House to Fredericksburg to Alexandria. There were two major command changes while the men rested near Manchester. Blair turned over command of the XVII Corps to Leggett on May 8, and Howard left his army two days later to take over the Freedman's Bureau, leaving John Logan as senior officer.[8]

The Michigan Engineers finally marched from their camps and through Richmond with the XVII Corps on May 12. The route in the former rebel capital took them by Libby Prison, Castle Thunder, and the Confederate White House. At night they camped about five miles north of the city on the pike road to Fredericksburg. The march to Alexandria continued on for another week.[9]

On the evening of the nineteenth the Michigan Engineers reached a point just two miles south of Alexandria and remained there for three days, resting from the long march. Despite the good roads and lack of enemy opposition, the movement from Raleigh to Alexandria was remembered as "a very hard march." So many men fell out or took lame along the march that special provision had to be made to take some from Richmond to Alexandria by steamer. One participant, a company commander in the Twenty-first Ohio, later wrote, "The march was a foolish race between ambitious commanders and the infantry suffered severely in consequence of it."[10]

While the regiment rested at Alexandria, plans were being concluded for a final review of the veterans of the nation's largest armies. On May 18 General Grant issued orders that the review would be held on the twenty-third and twenty-fourth, the Army of the Potomac on the first day and Sherman's veterans on the second. Two days later Sherman issued detailed orders for his command. As George G. Meade's Army of the Potomac marched in review on the twenty-third, the men in the Armies of the Tennessee and of Georgia would move from Alexandria along the river to the Long Bridge over the Potomac. On the following morning the men would be roused early so that the four corps could be in position near Capitol Hill before the 9 A.M. start of the review. After moving around the Capitol, the column would march down Pennsylvania Avenue and by the reviewing stand near the White House. After the review's conclusion, the men were expected to march to new camps that would be set up by quartermaster officials during the day. The new camps were considered to be superior to those near Alexandria, rendered nearly uninhabitable by years of constant use by other troops.[11]

Sherman's headquarters decided that the Michigan Engineers and Missouri Engineers would march together during the review, taking position between the XV and XVII corps. Orders were issued to Colonel Yates to assume command of the two regiments and prepare the men for the review. Since the engineers had "not had as much experience in reviews," Yates was ordered to have his officers drill the men and review regulations for reviews. Lieutenant Colonel Hannings, back with the regiment by about May 19, commanded the combined force in Yates's absence.[12]

The crowds would inevitably draw comparisons between the eastern and western soldiers. Sherman was a little concerned about how his recently arrived men would appear in contrast to the better-supplied and -rested Army of the Potomac, but he was proud of the rough veterans of his command. He wrote Grant's chief of staff, "Troops have not been paid for eight or ten months, and clothing may be bad, but a better set of legs and arms cannot be displayed on this continent." Speaking of himself, he added, "Let some newspaper know that the vandal Sherman is encamped near the canal bridge . . . he is untamed and unconquered."[13]

The men of the Army of the Potomac marched in review on the twenty-third, while Sherman's men moved from their camps at Alexandria as planned. On the following morning the veterans of the western fighting took position around the Capitol, moving forward at the appointed hour. Sherman was at the front of his men, and Howard and the military division staff accompanied them by special invitation. The first of Sherman's armies to pass in review were the men of the Army of the Tennessee, Logan now at its head with Howard's departure. The XV Corps marched first, now led by William Hazen. Immediately behind Hazen's corps marched the Michigan and Missouri regiments of engineers, followed by the XVII Corps, with Blair back in command. Behind Blair's men were Slocum's XIV and XX corps. As the review was completed, the Michigan Engineers continued on to their new camp near Crystal Springs, a resort for the city's wealthy some three miles away.[14]

Marching past this "concourse of humanity," the Michigan Engineers were part of the largest military parade in American history. With bands playing and flags flying, the columns marched through a cheering throng that lined the streets and waved from every window. In the reviewing stand stood President Andrew Johnson and a host of military and civilian dignitaries, joined by a jubilant Sherman as he reached it. Sherman's army also added its own unique stamp to the formal review. Mixed among the marching soldiers were six ambulances for each division, representative of its baggage train. Interspersed with the ambulances were goats, cows, and mules loaded with poultry or hams, while families of freed slaves walked alongside. The black pioneers who had done so much to help move the army through the swamps and across rivers marched as units, armed with picks and spades.[15]

For six and a half hours, the men paraded down Pennsylvania Avenue, marching with a "rolling cadenced stride" that reminded the crowd of the "hundreds of miles those long, strong legs had ranged, through swamps and over mountain tops." They could not help but boast their day's review was the better of the two. One engineer noted that "there was quite a strife between the . . . armies as to which should make the best appearance [but] the general opinion is that the Western armies bore the palm." Sherman wrote later that many had looked upon his men "as a sort of mob" but that day saw an army "well organized, well commanded and disciplined." Lt. James M. Sligh, soon to be promoted to captain, wrote his mother a long account of the army's review and the crowd's reaction: "They expected to see a pretty sturdy looking set of farmers and mechanics, but not very good soldiers in

These were likely the colors that the regiment carried in the Grand Review in May 1865. Many regiments commissioned new ones after the end of the hostilities, their original flags too badly torn by battle and wear. These and other surviving Civil War flags are carefully preserved and interpreted by the staff of the Capitol Committee and the Michigan Historical Museum in Lansing. Photos courtesy of Peter Glendenning and the Capitol Committee.

point of efficiency in drill. But when the first company front of the XV Corps in the advance came in sight . . . such a cheer ascended as nearly shook the buildings—bouquets were showered in among the ranks—and handkerchiefs without number waving a welcome to 'our western heroes' as they styled us on several banners."[16]

Not all of the soldiers in Sherman's command participated in the Grand Review. In addition to the men of Schofield's and Kilpatrick's commands left behind in North Carolina, detachments of men remained in the old camps in Alexandria. As their comrades marched, they served as a camp guard and completed loading the tents and equipment for transport to the new camps. Among the Michigan Engineers left behind in camp was one who wrote his wife that he was missing the "grandest military display ever witnessed on this continent, if not the world."[17]

The regiment had many visitors in the days that followed. Republican Governor Henry Crapo of Michigan reviewed the engineers on May 25, and his flowery speech was politely received. Of greatest interest to the men, however, was the governor's prediction that they would be going home as soon as things could be settled. Three days later Colonel Innes and his wife, joined by the wife of Captain McCrath, visited the camp. Their former commander gave a speech, which was answered by three cheers "given with a will."[18]

A very welcome visitor was Miss Julia Wheelock, agent for the Michigan Soldiers' Relief Society. In addition to gracing the men with "her bright and cheering presence," Wheelock distributed a large amount of food and delicacies to supplement their standard rations. Also included in her gift were fifty bushels of potatoes, several barrels of pickles, some butter, a barrel of beer, and some tobacco. Delicacies, however, could not take the place of going home. One soldier noted, "The boys feel pretty well about [the visits by Wheelock and others], although they would feel much better to be at home at once."[19]

The regiment remained camped near Crystal Springs for two weeks following the review, and many toured the nation's capital and historic sites. The most popular attractions were the White House, patent office, Capitol, and Smithsonian, along with nearby Mt. Vernon. One engineer wrote that the Capitol was the "largest and most splendid structure" he had ever seen but did not provide a detailed description of the imposing structure "for the feeling I should certainly fail." Sherman appreciated the men's desire to see the sites, writing Grant, "I hope the good men of the command will have a few days in which to visit the Capitol and public grounds, to satisfy the natural curiosity."[20]

Since only one squad from each company was allowed to visit the city at a time, most of the men sat in camp with "not one solitary thing to do" or, as another wrote, "nothing else to do now but talk about going home and cook our grub." Increasingly, the men's thoughts turned to frustration over their delayed release from the army.[21]

Back in April most of the men had realized their release would take some time. They had been in the service long enough to know that the army moved at its own speed. In letters home they consistently cautioned their families that it would be at least a matter of weeks yet before they returned. One wrote home, "You must not look for me until you see my coming. It will take some time to get this army in a shape to discharge them." In the final assessment, "when" did not matter as much as the certainty of returning. "Some say that we will be at home in six weeks, others two months, however rest assured that I will be at home as soon as I can," wrote one.[22]

A month later, however, the men were less patient with the delay. Daniel Sterling wrote home in detail about these frequent discussions: "In the soldier's mind it is the theme of conversation in every camp and every knot of soldiers in every tent. It is the first thing in the morning and the last thing at night. The first word after salutation is 'when are you going home,' 'what is the prospect about going home,' or 'what is the news about going home.' We have all got this home on the brain, the home in the heart and home we will come. This is so if God permits."[23]

Unknown to the men in uniform, the War Department was just as interested in getting them home as the soldiers were themselves. Authorities were anxious to disband the expensive and now unnecessary regiments, and General Grant approved a detailed plan on May 11, 1865. The War Department quickly issued orders beginning the muster-out of the million men in Union blue. The first Michigan Engineers to be released were those in recruitment depots or en route to the front. According to the April 1865 Regimental Monthly Return, twenty-two recruits assigned to the regiment had not yet arrived from Michigan. Almost all enlisted in the previous August but never joined their companies for various reasons. Some never would. Pvt. Elisha O. Herrington of Company B died of typhoid fever at his home on December 3, 1864, having never even left the state, though word of his death failed to reach the regiment. Several others became sick shortly after enlisting and were scattered at hospitals between Detroit and Savannah at war's end. Others had simply disappeared within the army's vast bureaucracy.[24]

The next large group to leave the service was men who had served in the field but at war's end were sick or wounded in army hospitals. At the end of April 230 Michigan Engineers were absent from the regiment in rear area hospitals. Three days later general orders from the adjutant general ordered them discharged as soon as their health allowed it. The largest concentrations were at Alexandria (68) and New Berne (29) in the East and at Stevenson (41) and Chattanooga (51) in the West. Another 22 men were in hospitals in Michigan, primarily Detroit. Before June 30 most had recovered their health sufficiently to be discharged.[25]

Some did not recover. Pvt. Conrad Miller had taken sick soon after reaching Savannah. He was left there in the hospital when Sherman moved north. At war's end forty-four-year-old Miller was transferred to a Philadelphia hospital, where he died on June 1, 1865. At least eighteen of the regiment's sick died of disease in the hospitals after the war ended and before they could be mustered out.[26]

Recently released prisoners of war were also being discharged throughout the spring and early summer of 1865. On April 30 the regiment noted thirty-nine men last reported as being in Confederate prisoner of war camps. Formal exchanges of prisoners had broken down, but an agreement was reached in early March to release Union soldiers held in Confederate prisons on parole. They were forwarded to camps to be fed and treated by Union authorities while awaiting formal exchange and transportation north. With the sudden surrender of Lee's army and collapse of the Confederacy, any efforts at formal exchanges were scrapped. Instead, the men were transported north as quickly as their health allowed, and most of them were out of the service by mid-June.[27]

The largest group of Michigan Engineers in captivity at war's end was Lt. John Earl and his men of Company L, who had been captured on December 15, 1864. Following the difficult march south into captivity, Confederate authorities had shuttled them around. Four died while in confinement at Selma, Alabama. By March 1865 most were at Andersonville, where another died. During the final days of hostilities, most of the men were shipped by rail toward Savannah but then diverted to near Baldwin, Florida. With the collapse of the rebellion, Confederate authorities released the men, "turned loose" as a survivor remembered it. The sick and emaciated men were treated, fed, and processed by Union authorities from nearby Jacksonville. From that point, Union steamers took the survivors to hospitals and parole camps in Maryland. Those in worst health were discharged from hospitals in Annapolis, while the balance were forwarded to Camp Chase, Ohio, and subsequently discharged in June.[28]

Some of the men confined at Andersonville, however, had been sent by the Confederate authorities to Camp Fisk at Vicksburg instead of Florida. George A. Richmond and Asa Sinclair traveled north from Camp Fisk in late April, probably on the steamer *Henry Ames*. The two were discharged within weeks after treatment for chronic diarrhea at a

St. Louis hospital. At least seven of the others, however, were loaded onto the ill-fated steamer *Sultana*.[29]

The new Cincinnati-built paddle wheeler was one of several steamers at Vicksburg vying for army contracts to take the released prisoners home. The *Sultana* docked at Vicksburg on April 23, and the next day most of the remaining paroled prisoners at Camp Fisk were brought by rail and loaded onto the steamer. Among them were Lieutenant Earl, four members of his company who had been captured with him, and two other Michigan Engineers taken prisoner the previous summer in northern Alabama. When the *Sultana* nosed into the Mississippi River and started upstream at 9 P.M. on the twenty-fourth, there were nearly 2,300 soldiers, civilians, and crew members on board, a staggering number given the boat's legal capacity of 376 passengers and crew. When the boat docked at Helena, Arkansas, on April 26, the soldiers nearly swamped her when rushing to one side to be photographed from shore. Continuing northward against the heavy current of the flooded river, the *Sultana* stopped at Memphis and then eased back into the river en route to Cairo, Illinois. At about 2 A.M. on April 27, 1865, the *Sultana* exploded seven miles north of Memphis in the middle of the flooded river. While the burning boat remained afloat for several hours, most of the survivors of the explosion jumped or were thrown into the river and grabbed for debris or branches to keep from drowning. By 3:30 A.M. authorities in Memphis were aware of the tragedy and boats were sent to rescue survivors, scattered across some five thousand acres of swollen river.[30]

Lieutenant Earl, Cpl. Absalom N. Hatch, and Pvt. John W. Dunsmore all survived the explosion. Earl was slightly scalded but able to swim to within hailing distance of the steamer *Bostona*'s yawl that was pulling men from the river. An ailing Hatch jumped into the river as the burning boat disintegrated and remained afloat by hugging an oak scantling. He floated several miles downriver until pulled from the river by a boat from the steamer *Pocahontas*. Dunsmore survived by jumping overboard while tightly clutching window blinds. They kept him afloat until he could be pulled from the river by a picket guard at Fort Pickens. All were taken to Memphis hospitals for treatment of minor injuries and within a few days were loaded onto another steamer en route to Ohio. Four members of Earl's company, however, perished in the steamer's explosion or ensuing nightmare on the river. Henry Wait, Henry Johnson, Jasper Decker, and Job T. Bunn were among at least seventeen hundred victims of the largest maritime disaster in U.S. history. Bunn left a widow and six small children behind in Michigan.[31]

By late May 1865, several hundred more Michigan Engineers were preparing to leave for home, pursuant to War Department orders to release all soldiers whose enlistments expired prior to September 30, 1865. Among the Michigan Engineers camped near Washington, D.C., were over 350 men who had enlisted for three years before September 30, 1862, or for one year in August 1864. Eventually 356 of these men, "'62 men" and "yearlings" in regimental slang, were discharged from the service on June 6 and left by rail the following morning. Major Rhodes commanded the detachment on the trip home, assisted by Capt. John W. Williamson and Lts. Charles Cudney, Julius W. Smith, and Martin Canfield. The officers were to remain until the men were mustered out of the service and then rejoin the regiment.[32]

Rhodes and his group traveled by rail and Lake Erie steamer, arriving at Detroit on the tenth to a hero's welcome. In the morning they loaded onto the train for Jackson, the point at which Michigan troops were paid off and mustered out of the service. The reception was that befitting heroes. They were met at the station by the Citizen Cornet Band, a detachment from the Thirtieth Michigan, and various community leaders. Austin Blair personally addressed the men at a banquet held that night in their honor. Captain Williamson responded to the governor on behalf of the men, and his tribute to the regiment's dead caused "tears to course down the cheeks of many a veteran." After dinner the men marched to Camp Blair. Rhodes's men were paid off on the eighteenth and soon left for their homes and families throughout the state.[33]

The remainder of the regiment—reenlisted veterans and three-year recruits from 1863 and 1864—were included in orders shifting the remainder of Sherman's command to Louisville, Kentucky. It was not easy for these men to watch others being mustered out. One was starting a letter home when the 1862 men lined up to go home and wrote his wife, "I wish to God I was among the number."[34]

After several days of preparation and filling out paperwork, Colonel Yates issued the orders putting the regiment in motion westward. Men were to carry six days' rations. Each battalion commander was ordered to assign a party of officers and men to make sure no men were left at the stops along the route. The enlisted men were reminded, "We are to travel through our own country and no guards or unnecessary restraints will be imposed on the men in transit," and that Yates hoped "each and every one will conduct himself in an orderly and soldier-like manner."[35]

The regiment broke camp on the night of June 8 and marched into the city. They were loaded onto rail cars of the Baltimore and

Ohio early the next morning and reached Harper's Ferry at 9 A.M. By June 11 they were at Parkersburg, West Virginia, on the Ohio River. The next morning they loaded onto steamers and headed downriver. The trip on the river was a great lark for the men as they cheered on the racing steamers. They arrived at Louisville on the afternoon of the fourteenth and went into camp.[36]

For the next eighteen days they remained in camp near the Blind Asylum, many of the men expecting to be allowed to go home at any time. Some of the men took advantage of the relative inactivity to visit the city's sights, while others visited friends in the camps of other regiments. Most of the time, however, was spent in camp with little to do. A few inspections were held, and new clothing was issued, but little else occurred to break up the monotony. One engineer noted that after only a few days in Louisville "the time begins to drag and gets a mite tedious."[37]

There was a great deal of anger among the troops at Louisville at the delay in mustering the regiments out. This frustration was intensified because many of the men had not been paid for at least eight months and alcohol was freely available throughout the camps and in the city's bars. The result was an ongoing series of discipline problems throughout the army. Union soldiers broke into bars and threatened civilians. Tensions ran high between the soldiers and civilians, and provost guards had to be posted on the city streetcars and outside businesses. One engineer reported home that "there is some big times around town once in a while especially when some of them gets a little tight, there is a good many of them get shot by the patrol guards."[38]

The situation continued to get worse. One soldier wrote home on June 21, "I have been very discontented." A fellow engineer wrote his wife, "The boys talk mutiny very strong." One member of the regiment who had been in a Louisville hospital for several months and visited the nearby regimental camp wrote home, "There is considerable dissatisfaction among them. They think they ought to be sent home and they say they never will be taken away from this place unless it is to go to Michigan." Some blamed their officers, one writing his sister that "the officers haven't made enough yet. Damn their stinking souls. If we could go into battle once I would make some of them bite the dust. It is worse than being in prison [by] a damn sight. They get big pay, what do they care. [They have] plenty to eat and their work is done and they ride their horses and we privates can carry our loads and follow them through the streets until the sweat runs off of us like rain."[39]

The complaints written home were more than mere talk, and almost twenty men deserted when the regiment was ordered on June 29 to prepare for a move to Nashville. Another dozen left for Michigan on an approved leave of absence from which they never returned. Some of these deserters were hard cases. John Comstock of Company I was awaiting sentence of a court-martial for an earlier unsuccessful desertion when he disappeared on June 29, taking his rifle and accouterments. Lemon Coats was also awaiting sentencing. The rest of the deserters, however, were simply tired of waiting for the army's bureaucracy to send them home.[40]

The remainder of the seething men were loaded onto the cars and rolling south by sunset on June 30. They settled down for the familiar ride south along the Louisville and Nashville. Nashville was reached without serious incident at sunset on the first. The regiment set up camp on the "old Rains place" south of the city, site of their camp in early 1863.[41]

On July 3 the regiment was ordered to repair the city's defenses. For many of the men this was the last straw. Several more men deserted, and at least twenty-six members of Company I refused to follow orders and were locked up. Another eleven noncommissioned officers from various companies were reduced to the ranks for offenses ranging from "conduct unbecoming" and "absence without leave" to "seditious words and influences." Six more enlisted men deserted within the next week. Meanwhile, the rest of the regiment worked on fortifications.[42]

Yates granted furloughs to a large number of officers and men while in camp at Nashville as part of an effort to soften their anger at being held in the service. Yates even allowed the entire band to visit home, though the regiment was already over the allowed number of men on furlough. He reasoned that since the regiment was scattered among the fortifications, the band could be spared "better now than later." Many of the officers were also granted leave to attend to matters at home, and several submitted their resignations.[43]

By the middle of August, Yates could report that the regiment had completed its work on the fortifications. He explained, "Like all other volunteers we have been anxiously awaiting orders to permit us to return home." He was hopeful that the Michigan Engineers could be disbanded "if consistent with the best interest of the public service." By this time Thomas had been given the authority to muster out any regiment within his department that he believed was not needed to maintain order and protect U.S. property.[44]

On September 12 the officers received orders to complete the muster-out rolls. Three days later, Lieutenant Colonel Hannings, commanding in Yates's absence, wrote Michigan adjutant general John Robertson that the regiment expected to leave by the twenty-fifth and

Impatient to be sent home after peace was secured, Gilbert Hackett was one of several dozen Michigan Engineers who deserted in June and July 1865 after the regiment was kept in the service. His record and those of many others who had served honorably until the end of actual fighting were changed after the war to state they were discharged effective the date they left, instead of deserted. Archives of Michigan.

requested that arrangements be made for final payment of the men. The next day Hannings requested of the provost marshal that all members of the regiment confined in Nashville prisons be released so that they could be mustered out with the regiment. Hannings even requested that the sentences of any convicted men be remitted for the same purpose, affecting as many as fifty men from the regiment.[45]

On September 21 the Second Battalion, consisting of Companies C, D, F, and I, was mustered out at the Exchange Barracks. The following day the balance of the regiment broke camp and marched to Fort McCook, where it too was mustered out of the service. In total 952 officers and enlisted men were mustered out of the service, 146 of whom had been among the original members of the regiment at Camp Owen. Yates remained behind in Tennessee to help run the railroad, so he did not accompany the regiment north to Michigan and final discharge. Upon taking leave of the regiment, he boasted that the regiment "has won for itself lasting honor and each member may well be proud of having served in it." Yates also publicly thanked the men in his command

and wished them a bright future, "trusting all may enjoy the blessings of peace and prosperity for many years to come."[46]

The following morning they boarded rail cars for the ride home, but delays kept them from leaving until late afternoon. Finally, the train started the welcome journey north. For the veterans of the early campaigns in Kentucky, it would have been nearly impossible not to recall memories of previous labors and long-dead comrades as they rolled by Gallatin, Bowling Green, Munfordville, and on into Louisville. Once across the Ohio River they continued on through Indianapolis and Michigan City and then across southern Michigan to Jackson. The Michigan Engineers went into camp at the barracks in town and remained for several long days while the payrolls were completed.[47]

Finally, on October 1, 1865, the men were paid off, and their war was over. As one veteran of four years' service wrote in his diary, "We are now again citizens of this United States—the country we helped to save with lives and blood composed of the flower of the country." Isaac Roseberry was probably one of the last of the group in Jackson to reach his Ottawa County home. Left behind sick at Jackson with two comrades when the others left, Roseberry was loaded onto a sleeping berth on the night of October 3. He arrived home in Berlin the morning of the fourth, "more dead than alive."[48]

In the days following the departure from Nashville, scattered members of the regiment were mustered out from rear area hospitals and posts. The last member of the regiment to officially be discharged from the regiment was probably Walter S. Phillips of Company E. Phillips was transferred back from a Chattanooga hospital and then discharged in Detroit on October 12.[49]

On October 20, 1865, General Grant reported to Secretary of War Stanton on the reduction of the army. He noted that, despite concerns of many to the contrary, great armies had been dissolved and their men returned home without any resulting disruption or chaos: "These musters out were admirably conducted, 800,000 men passing from the Army to civil life so quietly that it was scarcely known, save by the welcomes . . . received by them."[50]

· 24 ·

Postwar Heroes

The war ended, and the men were home. But in very real terms, the story of the Michigan Engineers, and the war they fought, did not end in October 1865. Though the officers and men quickly went different routes with their lives, for many service in the Michigan Engineers was not something that simply stopped at muster-out. Instead, the "incommunicable experience of war," as Oliver Wendell Holmes Jr. later phrased it, remained with the men long after the guns fell silent.[1]

The most obvious lingering effects of their service were all too apparent on men who returned alive but forever damaged in body or mind. This was probably most true of those recently released from the privations and suffering of prison camps. Franklin Craig reached his Lenawee home in the summer of 1865 and was described by a neighbor as "a complete living skeleton from Andersonville." Another Andersonville survivor, Oliver Bamford, returned "thin and emaciated—hardly able to work." He traveled to the warm South for two years in a futile attempt to regain at least some of his vigor and remained dependent on others until his lingering death in 1921.[2]

Those fortunate enough to survive a battle wound often suffered its effects the rest of their lives. Walter F. Kimball was seriously wounded when a bullet tore through his thoracic cavity and left lung in the confused fighting at Perryville in 1862. Surgeons were unable to extract it from its lodgment between the lung and bone. Fifty years later pressure from the bullet finally ended his lifetime of suffering. Parker Truax, wounded outside Savannah by cannon fire on December 10, 1864, spent over five hundred dollars of his own money on fruitless operations to repair the damage.[3]

Even those whose injuries were caused by more mundane incidents bore the scars of service for the balance of their lives. Myron B. Hoag of Company D seriously injured his back and kidneys while destroying railroad track near Atlanta in November 1864. Though he lived until 1907, he was never again the "strong, robust man" who had answered his country's call at the age of sixteen. Instead, he was plagued by back pain, diarrhea, piles, kidney disease, and other ailments, unable to do more than a quarter of the work reasonably expected of someone his age. In recent years a descendant reviewed his thick pension file and family records, noting that "his life had been one of serious illness and disability . . . greatly limiting his ability to serve his family as provider, husband, and father." Young Hoag was not yet eighteen at the time he suffered his injuries.[4]

These men were not isolated incidents, and the pension files are full of further examples of men who, like Hoag and Kimball, bore the scars of their military service for the rest of their lives. William C. Harrison's Perryville wounds never healed properly. Ten years later it was reported that the "pain continues at all times when he is not under the influence of morphine." Thomas A. Cook never recovered from chronic diarrhea and inflammation of the lungs caused by a bridge building accident and later confinement in Confederate prisons. He died in 1870, barely twenty-five years of age. Ten years after being struck by a Confederate rifle ball, Otis Pitts was still unable to use his legs, the muscles having been severed permanently. Marcus Grant developed catarrh in his already damaged nasal passages while inspecting blockhouses in the fall of 1864. He continued to have noxious discharges, often-unbearable pain, and a loss of hearing and smell despite several medical operations and various forms of treatment. By 1894 complications had set in, and he wavered in and out of consciousness until he died two years later.[5]

For many, the effects of war service were harder to see but still very real. There was nothing in the prewar life or subsequent military service of Thomas A. Fisher to suggest any instability. He was one of the best recruiters for the regiment and was rewarded with greater responsibilities and rank during his years of service. Yet Fisher clearly couldn't settle back into life as a civilian. His pension records document a life of constant upheaval with two postwar marriages and periods in which he deserted his family for years at a time. Writing after his 1891 death in a Chicago insane asylum, his widow described him bluntly, but without any apparent malice, as "such a queer kind of person." Alphonso Bullen's mental health deteriorated between his 1861 enlistment in the Michigan Engineers and eventual discharge from the army in 1866. His brother-in-law later noted, "When he came out of the army his health was good, but his mind was not right for some reason." A veteran who had served under Bullen in the Twelfth USCT noted his spells of odd behavior that led to a pressured resignation from that unit. He continued to have spells of great excitement that could not be calmed right up until his death of a morphine overdose in 1873.[6]

Even those who survived their service sound in body and mind could not, or would not, put their experience with the Michigan Engineers behind them. Their identification with the regiment and their comrades continued long after military service ended. For many these ties continued uninterrupted by the end of hostilities. A good example is the large number of Michigan Engineers, especially former officers, who worked together in postwar Tennessee. At war's end, John Yates was appointed military superintendent of railroads in Tennessee, even before his regiment's muster-out. When the railroads were returned to civilian control on September 1, 1865, William Innes was selected to head the business of running both the Nashville and Chattanooga and Nashville and Northwestern railroads. Yates was retained as assistant superintendent, and Marcus Grant and Charles Calkins represented the railroads as agents in Nashville. Calkins later served as Innes's chief clerk. In addition, Yates reported that "a good many of my own regiment" were retained as employees by the Nashville and Chattanooga in 1865–67. Enos Hopkins set up shop as a coal merchant, doing business with mines and mining railroads in the Cumberland Mountains and was later appointed postmaster of Nashville. Garrett Hannings settled in Tullahoma in 1866 or 1867 and by 1870 was a railroad contractor along the familiar winding route of the Nashville and Chattanooga.[7]

In the fall of 1867 a bitter battle among shareholders for control of the Tennessee railroads forced Innes and Yates from the state, to be replaced with men who had served the Confederacy. Calkins, who had married the daughter of a prominent Nashville businessman, returned to Grand Rapids with Innes. Yates returned to his native New York and worked for several railroads. Also in 1867, locals upset with his Northern ties burned Edson P. Gifford's new mill in Nashville, and he returned to Michigan in frustration. Marcus Grant found work as a chief clerk in the U.S. Revenue office in Nashville, moved to Chattanooga by 1872, and eventually became a successful lumber and coal dealer. John McCrath, who had probably also worked for Innes and Yates on the railroad, did not return to Michigan until about 1894, having spent many years in business in the South. Hannings remained in Tullahoma until his death in 1893.[8]

As these officers scattered during the years following, so too did the men who had served under them. For many of them, however, the ties of former comrades were kept intact by annual regimental reunions. On October 29, 1867, six years to the day after the original muster-in, many of the former Michigan Engineers gathered together in Grand Rapids for the first postwar gathering of the Reunion Association of the First Michigan Engineers and Mechanics. This was the first of dozens of annual regimental reunions, and the old comrades continued to gather nearly as long as any lived. This first reunion differed little from subsequent ones, only the thinning ranks attesting to the passage of time. These reunions continued for at least fifty-nine years, a testament to the bond that drew these men together.[9]

After speeches of welcome by local leaders and the playing of national airs by a local band, the veterans in 1867 were treated to a banquet and more speeches. Toasts were drunk to "Gen. W. P. Innes —the long-haired Colonel who was not surrendering muchly." Somber toasts, "drunk standing and in silence," were offered to the martyred Lincoln; to the dead hometown hero Sligh, "he gave his life in his country's cause"; and "to fallen comrades—God bless them, may they rest in peace." A favorite toast, to be repeated in similar fashion at virtually every subsequent gathering, was also offered: "The Battle of Lavergne—a New Year's ball at which we gave our visitors the best we had." After more speeches, and presumably more drinking, the party finally broke up at midnight as comrades bid one other adieu until the next.[10]

There was sometimes a willingness to include former enemies in these gatherings. When the residents of Grand Rapids gathered on July 4, 1882, to celebrate their nation's independence, the featured speaker was the Reverend Spruel Burford of St. Mark's Episcopal Church. Less than two decades before, Confederate Burford had been sent by General Wharton to demand the surrender of Innes's command at Lavergne. When Burford arrived in Grand Rapids in 1880 he renewed his acquaintance with Innes on more friendly terms and was promptly named an honorary member of the regiment. Likewise, the Michigan Engineers sent regular invitations to former Confederate general Joseph Wheeler, elements of whose division they faced at Lavergne, to be their guest at regimental reunions.[11]

Another honorary member was Alexander Hamilton, Innes's wartime servant who had joined the regiment in 1863 as a nine-year-old runaway slave. He traveled to Michigan with the departing original men in 1864 and worked as a farm laborer. After two years service as a private in the Tenth U.S. Cavalry, the famous Buffalo Soldiers, Hamilton returned to Michigan and resumed his life as a laborer. He eventually put himself through Grand Rapids public schools and secured admission to the legal bar. He was made an honorary member of the Michigan Engineers veterans' association at the 1885 reunion.[12]

Many of the men also became involved in local veterans' groups. During the 1870s membership in the Grand Army of the Republic (GAR), the nation's largest veterans' organization, declined rapidly until fewer than twenty-seven thousand nationwide were counted on the rolls, and the Michigan Commandery was defunct just eight years after its founding. In the following decade, however, the GAR experienced a grand rebirth, and posts quickly sprung up in virtually every town. By 1890 there were about four hundred thousand GAR members, one-third of all Union veterans found in that year's special census.[13]

The Michigan Engineers were in the middle of this burst of recruiting and interest among the Civil War Union veterans. Innes was the first commander of Post 5 in Grand Rapids. Twelve years later, GAR Post 29 was started in Grand Rapids, and six of the charter members were veterans of the regiment. Apparently two new GAR posts in the 1890s were named after Innes: Post 408 in Grand Rapids and Post 428 in Antrim County's Central Lake. Post 281 in Petersburg, Monroe County, was named in memory of Morgan Parker, who died in 1862 as a member of Company F, Michigan Engineers.[14]

The lists of GAR officers are filled with veterans of the Michigan Engineers. Former lieutenant William H. Herbert served as the long-time chaplain of the Michigan Commandery as well as chaplain at the Soldiers' Home in Grand Rapids. Pvt. Fayette Wyckoff was a longtime secretary of the Michigan Commandery and active in various other veterans' causes. When the national GAR Encampment was held in Grand Rapids in 1885, several of the regiment's veterans were given prominent roles. Innes served as chairman of the reception committee and provided housing for Generals Rosecrans and Buell. Fox was chairman of the society's executive committee for the event.[15]

The GAR was not the only Union veterans' organization. Former officers were eligible for membership in the Military Order of the Loyal Legion of the United States, and Tracy served as chaplain of the Michigan Commandery. A Grand Rapids–based command of the GAR-rival Veterans' Union was named for Innes and included among its charter members Esquire C. Phillips of Company B. Lt. Jacob W. White was one of the organizers of the Soldiers and Sailors of Genesee County in 1879, one of many such regional organizations.[16]

One of the largest reunions of former Union troops held in the former Confederacy occurred in September 1895, when thousands traveled to Chattanooga for the dedication of monuments to the units and men who had fought in the Chickamauga and Chattanooga campaigns. A large monument was dedicated to the Michigan Engineers on September 19, complete with a bronze panel showing the construction of the pontoon across the Tennessee River at Brown's Ferry. Though the location for the monument had to be moved at the last minute from within the city of Chattanooga to nearby Orchard Knob, the regiment's veterans had a successful reunion, full of speeches by dignitaries and comrades. Col. P. V. Fox presided over the ceremonies, and among the dignitaries was Col. Henry S. Dean, who had led a detachment of the Twenty-second Michigan alongside Fox's battalion in the struggle to break the siege of Chattanooga.[17]

These trips to the Southern battlefields were important to many of the veterans. As historian Earl J. Hess has noted, "Standing on the ground; breathing Southern air; locating old landmarks, earthworks, and campsites; talking with local inhabitants; collecting souvenirs; and placing monuments all made the war physically real to them again."[18]

The monuments were visible symbols of a regiment's importance and a public measure of the value of a man's service. In 1911 more than one hundred of the regiment's surviving veterans gathered together in Marshall for their annual reunion and the fiftieth anniversary of the regiment's rendezvous at Camp Owen. The highlight of the reunion was the dedication of a monument on the grounds of the GAR Hall. A large boulder with bronze panel was placed in front of the hall, built in part by former members of the regiment in 1903. The monument and hall remain to this day, a reminder of the important role Marshall played in the regiment's formation.[19]

The ranks were much thinner at Marshall in 1911 than they had been fifty years before. Of the more than one thousand men at Camp Owen in 1861, only thirty-five were able to return fifty years later. They made an emotional visit to the fairgrounds, and some of them pointed out their former lodgings in Floral Hall. They were served bread of the same kind furnished at Camp Owen.[20]

These were no longer young men. Willoughby O'Donoughue was too feeble to make the short trip from nearby Albion. Jonathan Butler showed up with a stitched forehead, injured in a recent fall. William Hicks remained at home, nursing several broken ribs and other assorted injuries also suffered in a bad fall. As Rev. A. Watson Brown, himself a veteran's son, noted in the welcoming ceremonies, "The frosts of fifty winters have whitened your hair and sapped your strength, but you are heroes still, and this boulder is a slight evidence of the love and gratitude we have for you and your departed comrades." The veterans were driven around to the various events in citizens' automobiles to spare their energy.[21]

The monument building reached its zenith for the Michigan Engineers in 1912, when a memorial of Vermont granite was erected on the grounds of the state capitol in Lansing, one of only two representing individual Civil War regiments. The face of the monument featured a carved castle, thirty inches square. The castle design was inspired by the similar castle insignia inset into the ammunition magazine that

This monument was dedicated in 1911 and remains in front of the Grand Army of the Republic Hall in Marshall. It commemorates the fiftieth anniversary of the regimental rendezvous at Camp Owen. Sligh, *Michigan Engineers.*

Hannings's battalion built in Chattanooga in 1864. The Chattanooga stone had been saved in the 1870s by Capt. John W. McCrath when the building was torn down and stored in the basement of the Michigan state capitol building. Originally the intention had been to include the Chattanooga castle into the monument, but it was deemed too soft in composition. Several Civil War publications and newspaper stories on the regimental reunions were deposited in the hollow base of the structure. Funding was provided by a subscription of surviving members of the regiment, their family and friends, and a generous contribution from the City of Lansing.[22]

About two hundred veterans of the regiment formed a hollow square around the monument when it was formally dedicated on October 9, 1912. The monument was unveiled by six-year-old Charles R. Sligh Jr., grandson of Capt. James W. Sligh and nephew of

Only two Michigan Civil War regiments have monuments on the grounds of the Michigan state capitol building. That to the engineers was dedicated amid much fanfare in 1912 and remains in place today, a monument to their unique service and the sacrifice of more than 350 men. Sligh, *Michigan Engineers*.

Capt. James M. Sligh. Lieutenant Herbert formally presented the monument to the people of Michigan with the prediction that "this monument . . . will continue to speak to unborn generations long after the last call has been heard and the taps have been sounded for the last survivor of the First Michigan Engineers."[23]

Inclement weather forced the rest of the day's activities into the House chambers, where veterans and guests heard rousing speeches from several well-known men. Hal H. Smith, a prominent Detroit businessman and son-in-law of the late Col. John B. Yates, presented the keynote address. A banquet followed at the nearby Central Methodist Church.[24]

By this time, the men who had led the regiment were mostly dead. P. V. Fox died in 1910, the last survivor among the original company commanders, and he had been unable to attend several of the previous reunions because of declining health. Even the youngest officers were now answering the final call. Joseph Herkner went to war as a twenty-one-year-old lieutenant in 1861 and was laid to rest on March 19, 1914. The story had come full circle. His funeral was a major community event, befitting the postwar success earned by this self-made German immigrant. He married the sister of fellow engineer officer Charles W. Calkins, thus joining one of Grand Rapids' most prominent families. He founded a very successful jewelry business and rose to lieutenant colonel in the Michigan State Troops. Maj. Earl Stewart and four Grand Rapids companies of State Troops, including the "Innes Rifles," led his funeral procession. Stewart was himself the son of Charles R. Stewart, who had enlisted as a private at the age of eighteen and served for a year in the Michigan Engineers.[25]

By 1921 only forty-seven of the Michigan Engineers were able to attend the reunion in Grand Rapids. A photograph taken at the event shows a line of white-haired men, some clutching canes for support. If there were any doubts of the passage of time, it was then answered by the increasingly important role played by descendants at the reunions. The chairman of the banquet in 1921 was Charles R. Sligh Sr., son and brother of the Captains Sligh. Two of the speeches were by Colonel Stewart and Brig. Gen. Louis Covell, the sons of Pvt. Charles Stewart and Sgt. Elliot F. Covell. The ranks of the veterans were swelled by another 135 friends and family.[26]

This new generation considered themselves to be a part of the regiment, their place earned by the service of fathers, and the bond extended across generations. For many, the regiment and its record meant a great deal more. Colonel Stewart, now a respected veteran of the Great War, recounted in 1921 what it meant to be the son of a Civil War veteran: "As a tiny lad on our old farm out in Byron, through the long winter evenings, he and I marched with Sherman to the sea, and following him in the dusty furrows of our farm, he and I passed in the Grand Review up Pennsylvania Avenue. . . . His beliefs and his patriotism have been my guide and inspiration through over thirty years of military service. I am proud of his record as a soldier; I am as proud of his Regiment as I am of my own, and I only hope that I may be able to lay down the military burden some day feeling that I have been worthy of his love and trust in me."[27]

No one, however, was as tightly woven with the regiment of their fathers as Charles R. Sligh Sr. In conjunction with the 1921 reunion, Sligh published a regimental history, drawing heavily upon information from men he had first known as a young lad in Grand Rapids. Though shorter on text than most other regimental histories of the day, the account contains several stories and a valuable collection of pictures of Michigan Engineers, particularly officers. Sligh was a central figure in regimental reunions for many more years and counted many of the veterans among his closest friends. Though too young to have served, he deeply identified with their experience, declaring at

Surviving Members of the First Regiment Michigan Engineers and Mechanics Attending Reunion Sept. 28, 1921

Co. A	Co. C	James M. Hope	Myron S. Creager	Wm. H. Comstock	Co. I	Co. K
F. A. Shattuck	Marion Wilder	Harry Courtright	John W. McGowan	Hezekiah Draper	Job L. Whipple	Dennis Macomber
Hugh Johnson	John Barrett	E. R. Cottright	Miller Stocking	Wm. R. Andrews	James E. Mansfield	Ira S. Herriman
Co. B	David O. Shear	Co. D		Co. G	Wm. H. Stokes	Co. L
George R. Boyer	Robert R. Patterson	Salon Hutchins	Co. E	Hiram Corbin	Henry J. Cummings	Willis Bertram
Julius A. F. King	Eustace E. Church	Charles Miller	George W. Connor	D. F. Austin	Calvin W. Winchester	James L. Barrett
Wm. Gelock	Benjamin F. Tower	S. W. Ward	Orson McLeod	Co. H	Augustus J. Rowe	Alvin Watson
Charles C. Marsh	Benedict Tower	Ira Van Stinvell	Co. F	Mort C. Masten		Co. M
	George Brown	A. C. Huntley	N. L. Chamberlain	Alva Smith		John M. Wells

These forty-seven men were the only survivors able to attend the 1921 reunion in Grand Rapids, sixty years after the regiment was formed. Perhaps as many more still lived but were unable to attend. All would be dead within fifteen years. This is the last known group image of men who served in the Michigan Engineers and Mechanics. Sligh, *Michigan Engineers.*

the 1912 gathering that "it has been the regret of my life that I was not born ten years earlier so that I might . . . tonight hail you as comrades." Sligh was made an honorary member of the regiment for his tireless efforts on their behalf.[28]

By the 1930s there were only a handful of Michigan Engineers yet living, among them Caleb Ensign, Emery C. Morris, Phillip Afton, and Theodore Bortles. By 1936 they too were gone. What remains is the record that these three thousand men left behind. Many stepped forward as heroes; a small handful proved to be knaves and cowards. Most simply performed the patriotic task they had taken an oath to fulfill. Their unique service played an important part in the triumph of Union arms.

Appendix 1

Selected Characteristics of the Michigan Engineers and Mechanics

Researchers using Civil War official primary source documents know too well the type of errors that are commonly found. Names are misspelled, some soldiers simply drop from sight with a "no further record" annotation, and others do not appear on the rolls yet clearly served. These challenges aside, the myriad of documents compiled by the military bureaucracy provides invaluable information for understanding the men who served in the Union ranks.

Though it is an impossible task to develop a complete profile of every individual who served in the First Michigan Engineers and Mechanics during the Civil War, it is possible to draw an approximate statistical portrait of the regiment's members as a group. This statistical portrait in turn helps us to better understand who answered the nation's call and served in the Michigan Engineers.

The base for this analysis is a collection of data on the men who served in the Michigan Engineers. The information came from a variety of sources, but the following is an annotated listing of the major sources used. Together they have provided the vast majority of the information.

Record of Service of Michigan Volunteers in the Civil War. 46 vols. Kalamazoo, Mich.: Ihling Bros. and Everard, 1904. Volume 43 covers the First Michigan Engineers and Mechanics. With its short service summaries, this source served as the framework to which the other demographic data was added to fill in holes and provide more understanding of the men.

Michigan Adjutant General. Michigan Engineers and Mechanics. Regimental Service Records. RG 59-14, State Archives of Michigan. Among regimental records, the most important are the company descriptive books, which furnished most of the information on age and much of the occupation data. Of particular interest is a listing of the original 1861 recruits with marital status—one of the few sources for such information.

U.S. Bureau of the Census. Census of Population. 1850 and 1860. These are the most important sources for information on occupation of the 1861 recruits, as well as nativity for all. As any researcher knows, errors are frequently found in the census schedules, but overall they are a valuable source for a group study such as this. This researcher has failed to find any consistent patterns of error that would change the overall analysis.

Benjamin A. Gould. *Investigations in the Military and Anthropological Statistics of American Soldiers.* Vol 2. of *Sanitary Memoirs of the War of the Rebellion.* Cambridge, Mass.: Riverside Press, 1869. By far the best single statistical compilation and assessment of who served in the Union armies, it makes possible a valuable comparison between the Michigan Engineers and the overall Union soldier pool.

John Robertson. *Michigan in the War.* Rev. ed. Lansing: W. S. George, 1882. This source provides valuable information on the nativity of Michigan soldiers as a group.

Some modifications were made to the available data for purposes of this appendix. Officers were counted only in the demographic tables upon their initial entry in the regiment, either by commission or enlistment. The same is true for the original three-years men who reenlisted. The handful of men who were discharged and then rejoined the regiment, however, are each treated as two different recruits.

Many of the tables break down the regiment's members into three distinct enlistment groups. The term "1861" includes the original members of the regiment who enlisted in the fall of 1861. The label "1862–63" covers recruits who joined between January 1, 1862, and June 14, 1863. Designation of "1863–64" is given to men who enlisted in the regiment after that point, including a very small number who signed up during 1865. As noted earlier, this latter group does not include the 1861 men who reenlisted in the regiment when their original three-year term ended.

This information is not presented as a scientific sampling of the regiment as a whole. For much of the data (especially age, length of service, and reason for departure) information is available for almost everyone. Information on nativity and occupation was sought, though not found, for all. It is acknowledged that this may have resulted in underrepresentation or overrepresentation of certain characteristics. For example, the younger members of the regiment were harder to identify in the 1860 census than the established and less transient older men. This means that occupations and nativity are better known for the older recruits. The notes provide more information on the difficulty of data gathering for certain categories. In addition, universal size figures have been provided throughout the charts when data was found for less than 90 percent of the possible cases.

Table A. Summary of demographic characteristics for original commissioned officers

Age	
Average age	32.95
Youngest officer	20 (Joseph Herkner)
Oldest officer	54 (Wright Coffinberry)
Nativity (%)	
Foreign	10.53
Michigan	10.53
New York/New England	68.42
Other U.S.	10.53
Prewar occupation (%)	
Mechanic, artisan	52.63
Civil engineer or railroad	18.42
Other, mostly business	28.95

Table B. Summary of major enlistment groups by demographic characteristics

	Michigan Engineer recruits				All Michigan[a]	Total Union[b]
	1861	1862–63	1863–64	All		
	1047	327	1514	2888		
Age						
Average age[c]	28.75	28.77	27.00	27.91	25.53	25.84
Under 21	18.81	19.69	34.30	23.52	29.57	N/A
Over 40	14.24	14.15	8.41	11.10	6.59	N/A
Nativity (%)						
Foreign	15.04	16.60	21.56	18.06	25.65	24.52
Michigan	19.91	14.72	19.36	18.56	23.71	
New York/ New England	57.52	59.62	42.32	51.72		
Other U.S.	7.53	9.06	16.76	11.66		
N=	452	265	501	1218		
Occupation (%)						
Farmer/laborer[d]	34.55	30.49	50.77	43.82		
Mechanic/ Artisan	52.00	58.74	41.12	46.25		
Other	13.45	10.76	8.10	9.93		
N=	550	223	1160	1933		
Family (%)						
Family ties[e]	14.33+	7.95+	11.29+	12.01+		
Married	45.4[f]	N/A	N/A	N/A	N/A	30.00+[g]

Notes

[a] Age of Michigan soldiers includes all new recruits for new regiments through August 1864 (total 39,107). Gould, *Investigations*. Nativity of Michigan soldiers is from Robertson, *Michigan in the War*, 69–70.

[b] Age of Union soldiers is from a study done of all original recruits for new regiments, various states and times (total 1,012,273). Gould, *Investigations*.

[c] Gould, *Investigations*. To be consistent for comparison, the known age errors for Michigan Engineers have not been corrected from what is found in *Record of Service*.

[d]Includes "farmer," "farm laborer," and "laborer"; the 1860 census enumerators were inconsistent in distinguishing between the two latter categories in agrarian areas.

[e]Family ties counts men who served in the Michigan Engineers with a father, son, sibling, cousin, or uncle. These are conservative figures and are calculated from adding the total number of known cases and adding half of the probable cases that cannot be proven.

[f]"List of officers and men . . . enrolled . . . between . . . original muster and July 1, 1862," RSR. This information is not available for later recruits, and the author has not been able to find any compilation of married data on Michigan soldiers as a group.

[g]The Union estimate is from Holmes, "Such is the price we pay," 174n17. Holmes developed her estimate using a formula that utilized general marital status percentages from the 1890 U.S. Census as a whole and weighting it against the age breakdown of Civil War veterans. This estimate could be considered low, since the older (and more likely to be married) veterans would have suffered greater losses to disease during the war as well as in the twenty-five-year period between peace and the 1890 census. The author has been unable to find any other estimate of marital status of Union soldiers. Also see McPherson, *For Cause and Comrades*, 189n2, for a discussion on the lack of study of soldier marital status.

Table C. Loss of 1861 recruits to noncombat death or discharge before January 1, 1863, by age range (percent)

Age at enlistment[a]	Noncombat death[b]	Medical discharge[c]	Combined
Under 21	6.3	4.7	11.0
21–29	13.2	10.0	23.2
30–39	9.8	15.7	25.5
40 and over	13.8	28.1	41.9
Entire regiment	11.3	13.2	24.5

Notes

[a]Ages are as reported at time of enlistment. Most who lived fall within either the forty and over or under twenty-one categories, and any adjustments for actual ages would have little effect on the percentage loss by category.

[b]Died of disease or injuries only. Men who were killed in combat or died of wounds are not counted.

[c]Does not count men discharged to accept promotion or transfer unless it was to the Invalid Corps or Reserve Corps.

Table D. Loss of all enlisted men to death and discharge in first twelve months of service, by enlistment group (percent)

	1861	1862–63	1863–64	Total
Noncombat death[a]	6.78	8.26	9.84	8.55
Medical discharge[b]	15.76	11.93	2.25	8.24
Total	22.54	20.19	12.09	16.79

Note: First month of service based on when enlisted, not mustered in.

[a]Includes death from disease or injuries.

[b]Also includes transfer to the Invalid Corps or Reserve Corps.

Table E. Distribution of 1861 recruits, by company and major county

Company A	Calhoun 29, Jackson 27, Washtenaw 24
Company B	Kent 63, Genesee 24
Company C	Kent 55, Barry 23
Company D	Kent 71, Ottawa 12
Company E	Ionia 44, Clinton 10
Company F	Wayne 30, Monroe 23, Genesee 17, Kent 12
Company G	Kalamazoo 31, Van Buren 31, Genesee 17
Company H	Jackson 72
Company I	Lapeer 37, Wayne 24, Washtenaw 14, Oakland 11
Company K	Calhoun 29, Ionia 10

Note: Includes counties with ten or more recruits within each company of about one hundred men. Includes both company officers and enlisted men. Does not include field or staff officers. Except for the troubled Company K, into which most of the late recruits were added irrespective of residence, every company drew more than half of its original men from just one or two counties.

Appendix 2

Additions to *Record of Service*, Volume 43

A fairly complete roster of the men who served in the First Michigan Engineers and Mechanics appears in volume 43 of the *Record of Service of Michigan Volunteers in the Civil War*. While there are some errors, it reflects the information generally necessary to obtain a brief summary of each soldier's service in the regiment. There are some, however, who were left out and are listed below:

WILLIAM T. ANIBA, Ionia. Enlisted in Company A, Twenty-first Michigan Infantry, as first sergeant, August 1, 1862, at Ionia, for three years, age forty-one. Mustered September 3, 1862. Discharged for disability at Nashville, Tennessee, February 1863. Reentered service in Company E, Engineers and Mechanics. Enlisted December 23, 1863, at Grand Rapids, for three years. Mustered January 5, 1864. Admitted to Harper Hospital, May 26, 1865. Discharged at Detroit, Michigan, July 21, 1865. [*Record of Service*, vol. 24]

BAKER BORDEN, Grand Rapids. Entered service in Company B, Third Michigan Infantry, at organization, as captain, June 10, 1861, at Grand Rapids, for three years, age forty-seven. Commissioned to date May 13, 1861. Mustered June 10, 1861. Resigned on account of disability July 30, 1861. Reentered service in Company B, Engineers and Mechanics, at organization, as captain. Commissioned September 12, 1861. Mustered October 29, 1861. Resigned February 23, 1862. [*Record of Service*, vol. 3]

MILES W. BRAGG, Milford. Enlisted in Company I, Engineers and Mechanics, September 16, 1861, at Detroit, for three years, age forty-five. Mustered October 29, 1861. Discharged for disability August 4, 1862. Reentered service in Company C, Ninth Cavalry. Enlisted December 28, 1862, at Milford, for three years. Mustered January 22, 1863. Mustered out at Lexington, North Carolina, July 21, 1865. [*Record of Service*, vol. 39]

CALEB A. ENSIGN, Jonesville. Enlisted in Battery C, Light Artillery, October 22, 1862, at Jonesville, for three years, age twenty-four. Discharged to accept promotion December 8, 1863. Commissioned second lieutenant, Company M, Engineers and Mechanics, December 8, 1863. Mustered December 9, 1863. Commissioned first lieutenant March 11, 1864. Mustered April 6, 1864. Mustered out at Nashville, Tennessee, September 22, 1865. [*Record of Service*, vol. 42]

JOHN S. GORDON, Calhoun County. Enlisted in Company E, First Infantry, September 11, 1861, at Tekonsha, for three years, age twenty-nine. Mustered September 14, 1861. Discharged for disability at Washington, D.C., April 26, 1862. Enlisted in Company H, Engineers and Mechanics, December 31, 1863, at Spring Arbor, for three years. Mustered January 6, 1864. Corporal. Mustered out at Nashville, Tennessee, September 22, 1865. [*Record of Service*, vol. 1]

PHILLIP MOTHERSILL, Oakland County. Enlisted in Company I, Engineers and Mechanics, as sergeant, September 18, 1861, at Pontiac, for three years, age twenty-one. Mustered December 6, 1861. Promoted to first sergeant. Discharged for disability at Shiloh, Tennessee, April 21, 1862. Reentered service. Enlisted in Company A, Fifth Cavalry, as sergeant, August 14, 1862, at Pontiac, for three years. Mustered August 26, 1862. Promoted to first sergeant. Discharged to accept promotion January 4, 1863. Commissioned second lieutenant July 3, 1863. Mustered January 5, 1864. Wounded in action Hawes' Shop, Virginia, May 28, 1864. Commissioned first lieutenant, Company F, October 28, 1864. Mustered November 12, 1864. Discharged to accept promotion February 20, 1865. Commissioned captain, Company K, February 1, 1865. Mustered February 21, 1865. Brevet major, U.S. Volunteers, March 13, 1865, for gallant and meritorious services during the war. Mustered out June 22, 1865. [*Record of Service*, vol. 35]

WILLIAM MURCH, Van Buren County. Enlisted in Company G, Engineers and Mechanics, as sergeant, September 6, 1861, at Waverly, for three years, age forty-four. Mustered December 6, 1861. First sergeant. Discharged for disability at Shiloh, Tennessee, April 21, 1862. Reentered service in Company G, Thirteenth Infantry, as second lieutenant. Commissioned January 11, 1864. Mustered March 19, 1864. Resigned on account of disability May 26, 1864. [*Record of Service*, vol. 13]

SEBA D. MURPHY, Ida. Enlisted in Company F, Engineers and Mechanics, at Ida, for three years, age forty-one. [Desc. Roll: Enlisted

October 22, 1861. Mustered October 29, 1861.] Discharged for disability May 6, 1862. Reentered service in Company D, Ninth Cavalry. Enlisted November 26, 1862, at Ida for three years. Mustered January 22, 1863. Transferred to Invalid Corps, January 15, 1864. Discharged at Detroit, Michigan, August 18, 1865, from Company I, Twenty-third Regiment, Veteran Reserve Corps. [*Record of Service*, vol. 39]

DANIEL J. RANDALL, Clayton. Enlisted in Company B, Engineers and Mechanics, as corporal, September 23, 1861, at Flint, for three years, age twenty-five. Mustered October 29, 1861. Discharged for disability March 6, 1862. Reentered service in Company K, Fifth Cavalry. Enlisted August 23, 1862, at Detroit, for three years. Mustered September 2, 1862. Wounded in action and in Lincoln Hospital, Washington, D.C., August 12, 1863. Discharged at Frederick, Maryland, May 17, 1865. [*Record of Service*, vol. 35]

In addition, the following men enlisted in the Michigan Engineers in the fall of 1861 and mustered into federal service but were transferred to Battery E, First Michigan Light Artillery, in December 1861 before leaving for Kentucky. Their service information appears in *Record of Service*, vol 42:

Asa Alexander
William Amos
Newton L. Chamberlain
John P. Day
George H. Draper
Charles Durand
John H. Fields
Duncan Gilchrist
Jeptha Talady

Similarly, Johnson Prall enlisted in and mustered into federal service with the regiment but then transferred almost immediately to Company K, First Michigan Sharpshooters and served in that regiment. His service is summarized in *Record of Service*, vol. 44.

Abbreviations

CMCF Court-Martial Case Files, Records of the Judge Advocate General's Office, RG 153, NARA. All files from RG 153 are provided courtesy of Tom and Beverly Lowry, The Index Project.

CMSR Compiled Military Service Records of Union Volunteers, Records of the Adjutant General, RG 94, NARA.

COB Company Order Book, Michigan Engineers and Mechanics, Regimental Papers, Records of the Adjutant General, RG 94, NARA.

Cont. Commands Records of the U.S. Army Continental Commands, 1821–1920, RG 393-1 and RG 393-2, NARA.

CWPF Civil War Pension Files, Records of the Veterans' Administration, RG 15, NARA.

DAT *Detroit Advertiser and Tribune*

DDA *Detroit Daily Advertiser*

DDT *Detroit Daily Tribune*

Desc. Roll Regimental Descriptive Rolls, Michigan Engineers and Mechanics, Michigan Adjutant General, RG 59-14, microfilm copy, State Archives of Michigan.

DFP *Detroit Free Press*

FWC *Flint Wolverine Citizen*

GO General Order

GR Eagle *Grand Rapids Daily Eagle*

JNC Jason Newton Crittenton. His diary appears in print in both Robertson, *Michigan in the War*, and Sligh, *Michigan Engineers and Mechanics*, and letters were printed in Michigan newspapers.

JMS James May Sligh (son)

JWS James Wilson Sligh (father)

Letters Out Letters Out, Michigan Adjutant General, RG 59-14, State Archives of Michigan.

Letters RCMS Letters to the Adjutant General Relating to the Raising of Companies for Military Service, 1861–78, Michigan Adjutant General, RG 59-14, State Archives of Michigan.

LNRR 1884 Profile Louisville and Nashville Railroad, Office of the Chief Engineer, *Main Stem, Louisville and Nashville Railroad* (Louisville: Louisville and Nashville Railroad, 1884).

LR-Reg. Letters Received Register, Michigan Engineers and Mechanics, Regimental Papers, Records of the Adjutant General, RG 94, NARA.

MDE *The Marshall Democratic Expounder*

MEMRP Michigan Engineers and Mechanics, Regimental Papers, United States, Records of the Adjutant General, RG 94, NARA.

Mich. Biog. Michigan Historical Commission, *Michigan Biographies*, 2 vols. (Lansing: The Michigan Historical Commission, 1924).

Minutes SMB Minutes of the State Military Board, Michigan Adjutant General, RG 59-14, State Archives of Michigan.

Monthly Return Monthly Returns, Michigan Engineers and Mechanics, Regimental Service Records, Michigan Adjutant General, RG 59-14, State Archives of Michigan.

MS *The Marshall Statesman*

NARA National Archives and Records Administration, Washington, D.C.

OCE Records Records of the Office of the Chief of Engineers, RG 77, NARA.

O.R. U.S. War Department, *The War of the Rebellion: A Compilation of the Official Records of the Union and Confederate Armies*, 128 vols. (1880–1901; repr., Harrisburg, Pa.: National Historical Society, 1985). All references are to volumes and parts in serial 1 unless otherwise noted.

O.R.A. U.S. War Department, *Atlas to Accompany the Official Records of the Union and Confederate Armies* (Washington, D.C.: Government Printing Office, 1891–1895). All references are to plate number unless indicated.

Orders General and Special Orders, Michigan Adjutant General, RG 59-14, State Archives of Michigan.

QG Records Records of the Office of the Quartermaster General, RG 92, NARA.

RG Record Group

RLB Regimental Letter Book, Michigan Engineers and Mechanics, Regimental Papers, Records of the Adjutant General, RG 94, NARA.

ROB Regimental Order Book, Michigan Engineers and Mechanics, Regimental Papers, Records of the Adjutant General, RG 94, NARA.

ROE Record of Events, Michigan Engineers and Mechanics, Records of the Adjutant General, RG 94, Microcopy Publication 594, NARA.

ROS **43** *Record of Service of Michigan Volunteers in the Civil War.* Vol. 43. Kalamazoo, Mich.: Ihling Bros. and Everard, 1905.

RSR Regimental Service Records, Michigan Engineers and Mechanics, Michigan Adjutant General, RG 59-14, State Archives of Michigan.

SFO Special Field Order

SFP Sligh Family Papers, Bentley Historical Library, University of Michigan. Unless indicated otherwise, all letters to or from James Wilson Sligh or James May Sligh are in Sligh Family Papers.

SO Special Order

WPI William P. Innes

Yates/Burton John B. Yates Papers, Burton Historical Collection, Detroit Public Library.

Notes

Chapter 1

1. G. A. Youngberg, *History of Engineer Troops in the United States Army, 1775–1901*, No. 37, Occasional Papers, Engineer School, U.S. Army (Washington, D.C.: Press of the Engineer School, 1901), 1–5, 34–37, 76. Three accounts of the important Mexican War service of army engineers are John S. D. Eisenhower, *So Far from God: The U.S. War with Mexico, 1846–1848* (New York: Doubleday, 1989); Adrian Traas, *From the Golden Gate to Mexico City: The U.S. Army Topographical Engineers in the Mexican War, 1846–1848* (Washington, D.C.: U.S. Army Corps of Engineers, 1993); Leonne M. Hudson, ed., *Company "A" Corps of Engineers, U.S.A., 1846–1848, in the Mexican War, by Gustavus Woodson Smith* (Kent, Ohio: Kent State University Press, 2001).

2. Youngberg, *Engineer Troops*, 6–17, 39–40, 51; Philip L. Shiman, "Engineering Sherman's March: Army Engineers and the Management of Modern War, 1862–1865" (PhD diss., Duke University, 1991), 60–68.

3. Shiman, "Engineering Sherman's March," 68, 74–75; Philip M. Thienel, "Engineers in the Union Army, 1861–1865," *The Military Engineer* 47 (1955), 36–37. Thienel's estimate of twenty thousand volunteer engineers was based on authorized, not actual, strength of several of the units. A more accurate count would be about twenty-five thousand.

4. Information about the Illinois Central volunteer company is from J. Henry Haynie, *The Nineteenth Illinois: A Memoir of a Regiment of Volunteer Infantry Famous in the Civil War of Fifty Years Ago for Its Drill, Bravery, and Distinguished Services* (Chicago: M. A. Donohue, 1912), 153. The experience of David's company is found in David Lathrop, *The History of the 59th Regiment Illinois Volunteers, or a Three Years' Campaign through Missouri, Arkansas, Mississippi, Tennessee, and Kentucky, with a Description of the Country, Towns, Skirmishes, and Battles* (Indianapolis: Hall and Hutchinson, 1865), 5–7, and the *Chicago Tribune*, August 7, 8, 11, 13, 18, 27, and 30, 1861. For an example of unsuccessful 1861 efforts to raise engineer companies in Michigan, see Asst. Adj. Gen. DeGarmo Jones to P. Morey, July 29, 1861, Letters Out, Michigan Adjutant General, RG 59-14, Archives of Michigan (hereafter cited as Letters Out); and T. Woodruff Collins to Adjutant General, June 4, 1861, Letters to the Adjutant General Relating to the Raising of Companies for Military Service, 1861–78, Michigan Adjutant General, RG 59-14, Archives of Michigan (hereafter cited as Letters RCMS).

5. Shiman, "Engineering Sherman's March," 73–77.

6. There are numerous examples in 1861 Michigan newspapers of the wide range of pay offered to volunteer engineers—for example, fifty cents per day extra (*Saginaw Enterprise*, September 26, and *Detroit Free Press*, September 13); one dollar per day with "everything found" (*Detroit Daily Tribune*, September 20); seventeen

dollars per month and forty cents per day extra when assigned engineering work (*Grand Rapids Weekly Enquirer*, October 16); twenty-six dollars per month (*Hillsdale Standard*, September 17); twenty-six dollars per month "and expenses" (*Marshall Statesman*, August 28); and "higher pay" and fifty cents per day extra over other volunteers (*Allegan Journal*, September 23). In addition, it is clear that the men at the 1861 engineer rendezvous had been promised more than seventeen dollars per month. Albert Graves to wife, October 6, 1861, Graves Family Papers, Bentley Historical Library, University of Michigan (unless otherwise noted, all letters from Graves are in this collection); William H. Kimball Diary, September 26, 1861, Burton Historical Collection, Detroit Public Library (hereafter cited as Kimball Diary); Ezra Stearns Memoir, Carr Family Letters, Bentley Historical Library, University of Michigan (hereafter cited as Stearns Memoir). Examples of expectations of higher pay are also found in other states, see for example the *Chicago Tribune*, August 27, 1861, and the *New York Times*, September 8, 1861. A circular printed for use in St. Louis dated July 14, 1861, and promising extra pay for engineers is found in the file of Col. Josiah W. Bissell, Engineer Regiment of the West, in Compiled Military Service Records of Union Volunteers, Records of the Adjutant General, RG 94, NARA (hereafter cited as CMSR). Recruitment posters for the Fiftieth New York Engineers also mention the supplemental daily pay, see Ed Malles, ed., *Bridge Building in War Time: Colonel Wesley Brainerd's Memoir of the 50th New York Volunteer Engineers* (Knoxville: University of Tennessee Press, 1997), 17, 270.

7. Henry L. Scott, *Military Dictionary* (1861; repr., Denver: Fort Yuma Press, 1984), 545.

8. Henry Halleck to Joseph Totten, July 18, 1861, in U.S. War Department, *The War of the Rebellion: A Compilation of the Official Records of the Union and Confederate Armies*, 128 vols. (1880–1901; repr., Harrisburg, Pa: National Historical Society, 1985), ser. 3, 1:336–37, 617–19 (hereafter cited as O.R.; unless otherwise noted all references are to volumes and parts in serial 1). For more on the theme, see Shiman, "Engineering Sherman's March," 60–68.

9. There is a surprisingly large amount of information on the recruiting for Wilson's regiment. See the *Chicago Tribune*, August 18 and 20, 1861, for information on recruitment and the ensuing controversy (particularly issues of January 1, 4, 9, 14, 27, and 30, 1862). References to recruiting in Michigan are found in the *Detroit Free Press*, September 1, 13, and 15, 1861 (hereafter cited as DFP). Another helpful source is Illinois Military and Naval Department, *Report of the Adjutant General . . . for the years 1861–66* (Springfield, Ill.: H. W. Rokker, 1886), 1:106. Other sources include Canfield to Robertson, September 16, 1861, Letters RCMS, and James W. Sligh to Wilder D. Foster, March 10, 1862, Sligh Family Papers, Bentley Historical Library, University of Michigan. (Unless noted, all Sligh letters—of both father, James Wilson [JWS], and son, James May [JMS]—are included in the Sligh Family Papers, hereafter cited as SFP.)

10. Examples of Wilson's recruiting and higher pay are found in the *Marshall Statesman*, August 26, 1861 (hereafter cited as MS), and the *Chicago Tribune*, August 23, 1861.

11. References to Michigan companies being raised for Wilson's regiment and which later joined the Michigan Engineers are in DFP, September 1,

1861 (Albion); *DFP*, September 13 and 15 (Marshall, though incorrectly labeled "Niles"); Canfield to Robertson, September 16, 1861, Letters RCMS (Ionia); and JWS to Foster, March 10, 1862. The Kalamazoo company is suggested from information in the file of Elias Broadwell, Civil War Pension Files, Records of the Veterans' Administration, RG 15, NARA (hereafter cited as CWPF). Account of the September 10 meeting is from JWS to Foster, March 10, 1862 (including quotations), and Charles R. Sligh, *History of the Services of the First Regiment Michigan Engineers and Mechanics, During the Civil War, 1861–1865* (Grand Rapids, Mich.: White Printing, 1921), 7.

12. Sligh, *Michigan Engineers*, 7; JWS to Foster, March 10, 1862.

13. Sligh, *Michigan Engineers*, 7; John Robertson, *Michigan in the War*, rev. ed. (Lansing: W. S. George, 1882), 321. There is no record that the captaincies for Coffinberry, Sligh, Borden, and Fox were discussed at the meeting with Blair, but it is very likely. All were commissioned in that rank and recruiting their companies within days of meeting with Blair. Before the war Foster served as mayor and state senator and was a founder of the city's fire department. Michael Leeson, *History of Kent County* (Chicago: Chapman, 1881), 832–35.

14. General account from Sligh, *Michigan Engineers*, 7, and JWS to Foster, March 10, 1862. Cameron to Blair, September 10, 1861, and Blair to Cameron, September 13, 1861 ("cheerfully"), in O.R., ser. 3, 1:497, 509. Robertson's orders are in General and Special Orders, Michigan Adjutant General, RG 59-14, Archives of Michigan (hereafter cited as Orders).

15. Cameron to Blair, September 16, 1861, Letters RCMS; GO 79 in O.R., ser. 3, 1:518. For contrast of federal and state performance, see James M. McPherson in *Battle Cry of Freedom: The Civil War Era* (New York: Oxford University Press, 1988), 322.

16. War Department standards from O.R., ser. 3, 2:230.

17. Selection of Marshall is from *Marshall Democratic Expounder*, September 19, 1861 (hereafter cited as *MDE*). Description of Marshall is from George W. Hawes, *Michigan State Gazetteer and Business Directory for 1860* (Detroit: F. Raymond, 1861), 239; Marshall citizens to Michigan Engineers, n.d., 1861 ("agreement to furnish supplies, etc.") in Letters Received Register, Michigan Engineers and Mechanics, Regimental Papers, Records of the Adjutant General, RG 94, NARA (hereafter cited as LR-Reg.).

18. *MS*, August 28 and September 11, 1861; *MDE*, September 12 and 19, 1861; Stearns Memoir; Kimball Diary.

Chapter 2

1. The important role of the volunteer colonels is described in Thomas Harry Williams, *Hayes of the Twenty-Third: The Civil War Volunteer Officer* (New York: Knopf, 1965), 21–22. An excellent example of the havoc that could be caused by a bad colonel is in Robert C. Myers, "'The Worst Colonel I Ever Saw,'" *Michigan History Magazine* 80 (1996): 34–43. Some of the most outrageous examples appear in Thomas Lowry, *Tarnished Eagles: The Courts-Martial of Fifty Union Colonels and Lieutenant Colonels* (Mechanicsburg, Pa.: Stackpole Books, 1999).

2. Drawn heavily from Marvin A. Kreidburg and Merton G. Henry, *History of Military Mobilization in the United States Army, 1775–1945*, Department of the Army Pamphlet No. 20-212 (Washington, D.C.: Department of the Army, 1955), 116–17; also O.R., ser. 3, 1:69, 227–28.

3. Kreidburg and Henry, *History of Military Mobilization*, 89; Russell F. Weigley, *History of the United States Army* (New York: Macmillan, 1967), 200; Paddy Griffith, *Battle Tactics of the Civil War* (New Haven, Conn.: Yale University Press, 1987), 96.

4. The only reference to Innes's involvement in the Mexican War appears in his obituary printed in the *Grand Rapids Daily Democrat*, August 3, 1893, which states that he served in the First Michigan Infantry during the Mexican War. Service records for that regiment in both federal and state archival holdings verify that a William P. Innes (variant spellings) did serve from January 28 to March 5, 1848. This soldier is listed as twenty-six years old, from New York, and enlisted at Vera Cruz, Mexico. The age at enlistment on neither federal nor state records matches with William P. Innes's (he was only 22 in 1848), though military records often contained such errors. Broadwell's earlier military service is found in RG 98, Microcopy Publication, M233, Reel 21, Register of Enlistments in the United States Army, 1798–1914, , Records of the Adjutant General, NARA.

5. It is unclear whether either Grant was actually in the fighting along Bull Run. Charles V. Deland, *Deland's History of Jackson County* (Logansport, Ind.: Bowen, 1903), 384, notes that only thirty-two men in the Jackson company were in the fighting at Bull Run, "as many were too sick to march." Nevius's service is in Abraham Van Doren Honeyman, *Johannes Nevius . . .* (Plainfield, N.J.: Honeyman, 1900), 363 and 640; Wm. H. Beach, *The First New York (Lincoln) Cavalry . . .* (New York: Lincoln Cavalry Association, 1902), 568; and Michigan Adjutant General, *Record of Service of Michigan Volunteers in the Civil War*, 46 vols. (Kalamazoo, Mich.: Ihling Bros. and Everard, 1905), 45:133, which spells his surname as "Neviers" (hereafter cited as *ROS* and volume number). Innes specifically requested that Sergeant Nevius be allowed to accept a commission in the Michigan Engineers; William P. Innes (WPI) to Col. A. T. McReynolds, September 20, 1861, in the file of William Nevius, CMSR.

6. Innes's early railroad work in New York and Michigan is found in "Memorial Report—Kent County," *Michigan Pioneer and Historical Collection* 26 (1895): 138–40; Albert Baxter, *History of the City of Grand Rapids, Michigan* (New York: Munsell, 1891), 586–87; "Obituaries," *Engineering Record* 28 (1893), 166; Willis F. Dunbar, *All Aboard: A History of Railroads in Michigan* (Grand Rapids, Mich.: William B. Eerdmans, 1969), 77–78; *Grand Rapids Daily Democrat*, August 3, 1893; Dwight Goss, *History of Grand Rapids and Its Industries* (Chicago: C. F. Cooper, 1906), 617–21. Innes's work on the Muskegon River is described in detail in William P. Innes, *Report and Estimate of the Plan, Prospects, Character, and Advantages of the Proposed Improvement of the Muskegon River Flats, Ottawa County, Michigan* (Grand Rapids, Mich.: Grand Rapids Enquirer Printing, 1855). During the same period, Innes teamed up with his surveyor/cartographer brother-in-law J. F. Tinkham on *Innes' and Tinkham's Map of Kent County, Michigan* (Chicago: H. Acheson Lithographers, 1855) and *Map of the Muskegon River* (Chicago: Lithographic Press of Edward Mendel, [1855?]). An

excellent source to understand the confusing corporate configurations of Michigan railroads is Graydon M. Meints, *Michigan Railroads and Railroad Companies* (East Lansing: Michigan State University Press, 1992).

7. Bruce Carlson, "The Amboy, Lansing, and Traverse Bay Railroad" (master's thesis, Central Michigan University, 1972), 61–62.

8. Carlson, "Amboy, Lansing," 62–68. As late as 1865 Innes was a target of complaints and charges by those who had lost money in the endeavor. "Memorial," in Michigan House of Representatives, *Journal of the House of Representatives of the State of Michigan* (1865), 724–28. Advertisements for the AL&TB throughout the state in late 1860 and early 1861 touted the combination rail and stagecoach service between Owosso and Lansing and listed Innes as "Chief Engineer and Superintendent." For examples, see *Grand Rapids Daily Eagle*, December 12, 1860 (hereafter cited as *GR Eagle*, and *Johnston's Detroit City Directory and Advertising Gazetteer of Michigan, 1861* (Detroit: H. Barns, 1861), advertisement on back leaf.

9. U.S. Census, 1860, Calhoun County, Michigan. Also see *Detroit Daily Tribune*, January 7, 1862 (hereafter cited as *DDT*); John Fitch, *Annals of the Army of the Cumberland . . .* 5th ed. (Philadelphia: J. B. Lippincott, 1864), 196; and Daniel T. V. Huntoon, *Phillip Hunton and His Descendants* (Cambridge, Mass: J. Wilson and Son, 1881): 82.

10. U.S. Census, 1860, Jackson County, Michigan; Fitch, *Army of the Cumberland*, 197; Kimball Diary, October 2, 1861; Constance Green, *History of Naugatuck, Connecticut* (New Haven, Conn.: Yale University Press, 1949), 136; Fred Engelhardt, *Fulling Mill Brook: A Study in Industrial Evolution, 1707–1937* (Brattleboro, Vt.: Stephen Daye, 1937), 35–43; *History of Jackson County* (Chicago: Interstate, 1881), 554; Deland, *Jackson County*, 784–85. Fitch states Hopkins was in Jackson by 1854, but 1857 is a more likely date for his arrival. Innes later noted the "intimate personal acquaintance" between Hopkins and Blair in a letter to Julius P. Garesche, November 30, 1862, Regimental Letter Book, Michigan Engineers and Mechanics, Regimental Papers, Records of the Adjutant General, RG 94, NARA (hereafter cited as RLB).

11. Fitch, *Army of the Cumberland*, 197; Union College (Schenectady, New York) alumni file on John B. Yates, Class of 1852; *Engineering Record*, 40 (1899), n.p.; U.S. Census, 1860, Calhoun County, Michigan; *MDE* advertisement running August–October 1861; Letter of recommendation, John B. Yates Papers, Burton Historical Collection, Detroit Public Library (hereafter cited as Yates/Burton); *GR Eagle*, July 12, 1858.

12. R. S. Innes background is from Hawes, *Michigan State Gazetteer*, 257–58; U.S. Census, 1860, Kent County, Michigan; and Baxter, *Grand Rapids*, 277. DeCamp background is from Leeson, *Kent County*, 465–67, 697, 989–90. O'Donoughue background is from Emory Wendell, *Wendell's History of Banking . . . Michigan*, 2 vols. (Detroit: N.p., 1900), 2:169. Miller background is from *Kalamazoo Gazette* advertisements, summer and fall 1861; U.S. Census, 1860, Kalamazoo County, Michigan; Marguerite Miller, *A History of Elder Jacob Miller and Some of His Descendants* (LaPorte, Ind.: N.p., 1958). Tracy background is from Clarence M. Burton, ed. *The City of Detroit, Michigan, 1701–1922*, 5 vols. (Detroit: S. J. Clark, 1922), 5:888–92.

13. See appendix I, table A for a summary of the prewar occupations of the original Michigan Engineers officers. The only negative comment on the engineering ability of the Michigan Engineers officers is in David Noble to wife, October 12, 1861, Dorothy Keister Collection, Grand Rapids Public Library, Grand Rapids, Michigan (unless otherwise noted, all letters from Noble are from this collection). Noble wrote cryptically that "there is some of our officers that will have to resign when they come to oversee a set of carpenters, they won't know how to instruct them."

14. Fitch, *Army of the Cumberland*, 197, and Carlson, "Amboy, Lansing," 61–62.

15. Freemasons, Grand Lodge of Michigan, *Transactions of the Grand Lodge . . . Michigan* (Detroit: The Grand Lodge, 1858–64). Representatives to annual gatherings are included for each year; a listing of Masons by lodge is attached to the report for 1862. Individual Masonic records are from files of The Grand Lodge of Free and Accepted Masons of the State of Michigan, provided by Richard Amon in 1996 correspondence with the author. Hunton background is from *Loomis and Talbott's City Directory and Business Mirror for Kalamazoo, 1860–1861* (Detroit: G. W. Hawes, 1860), 86. Knights Templar background is from Knights Templar, Grand Commandery, *Proceedings of the Regular Conclave . . . Michigan* (Detroit: The Grand Commandery, 1858–1861); Samuel W. Durant, comp., *History of Kalamazoo County* (Philadelphia: Everts, 1880), 272.

16. The nine were Innes, Hunton, Hopkins, Yates, Hannings, Fox, Marcus Grant, Crittenton, and Rhodes.

17. This is based on information found in enlistment data, local histories, and the 1860 U.S. Census. See appendix I, table B, for a summary.

18. Appendix I, table B.

19. Appendix I, table B.

20. Specifics are from the 1850 and 1860 census schedules for Genesee County, Michigan.

21. Evidence that DeCamp conducted at least some inspections from Kimball Diary, October 4–5, 1861; *ROS* 43:113; Regimental Descriptive Rolls, Michigan Engineers and Mechanics, Michigan Adjutant General, RG 59-14, Microfilm copy, Archives of Michigan (hereafter cited as Desc. Roll); *DFP*, October 31, 1861. The CMSR for Eugene Noble contains a certificate of examination signed by Wm. DeCamp that he had "carefully examined" the recruit and that Noble was "free from all bodily defects and mental inferiority." Norwich and Sivey background is from H. R. Lovell to JWS, November 17, 1862, ("unsound"), and from their respective files in CMSR.

22. U.S. Census, 1860, Van Buren County, Michigan County; *ROS* 43, and Desc. Roll. *ROS* 45 includes a roster of Michigan men in the Seventieth New York.

23. Estimate is based on positive identification of thirty-six family groupings and about fifty more likely ones. Father and son estimate includes twenty-two pairings verified with another eight likely ones based on enlistment data. Other relationships include fourteen sibling and/or cousin pairs that have been verified, with at least another forty likely sets of siblings or cousins based on enlistment data.

Because of the tendency of portions of families to settle near one another, it is often difficult to separate out brothers from cousins. At the same time, many relationships are not uncovered because of different surnames or lack of identification of relationship. This could potentially double the number of men who enlisted with relatives.

24. J. Matthew Gallman, *The North Fights the Civil War: The Home Front* (Chicago: Ivan R. Dee, 1994), 15–16. This theme is also addressed in Gerald J. Prokopowicz, *All for the Regiment: The Army of the Ohio, 1861–1862* (Chapel Hill: University of North Carolina Press, 2001), 75.

Chapter 3

1. *MS*, September 25, 1861; *MDE*, September 26, 1861; Graves to wife, September 29 and October 6, 1861; Stearns Memoir; Kimball Diary, October 1 and 8, 1861; Blair to Robertson, September 30, 1861, Regimental Service Records, Michigan Engineers and Mechanics, Michigan Adjutant General, RG 59-14, Archives of Michigan (hereafter cited as RSR); Richard W. Carver, *A History of Marshall* (Virginia Beach, Va.: Donning, 1993), 168.

2. *MS*, September 25, 1861, states that the provisions were contracted to "Mssrs Greenough, Hyde, and Phelps," probably references to prominent local merchant Horace E. Phelps and members of the mercantile Hyde and Greenough families. Advertisement for "sealed bid" from *Detroit Daily Advertiser*, August 15, 1861 (hereafter cited as *DDA*). Fountain served from April 1, 1861, to March 25, 1863. Robertson, *Michigan in the War*, 5.

3. Camp Owen background is from Miller to Robertson, October 7, 1861, RSR; Graves to wife, October 6, 1861; Kimball Diary, October 8, 1861; *DFP*, October 12, 1861; *MS*, October 9, 1861. On September 30 Blair was still cutting through the state military establishment's bureaucracy to get enough tents from state resources to be used until the federal government provided them. See Blair to Robertson, September 30, 1861, RSR, and GO 20 in Orders. When the regiment reached Kentucky it was equipped with Sibley tents, which were probably the ones issued in early October. Inspection report in Charles C. Gilbert to James B. Fry, December 20, 1861, Michigan Engineers and Mechanics, Regimental Papers, United States, Records of the Adjutant General, RG 94, NARA (hereafter cited as MEMRP). Owen information is from *DDA*, October 5, 1861, and Michigan Historical Commission, *Michigan Biographies*, 2 vols. (Lansing: Michigan Historical Commission, 1924), 2:165 (hereafter cited as *Mich. Biog.*).

4. GO 10, October 3, 1861, Regimental Order Book, Michigan Engineers and Mechanics, Regimental Papers, Records of the Adjutant General, RG 94, NARA (hereinafter cited as ROB).

5. Griffith, *Battle Tactics*, 106. The importance and difficulty of this early drilling is further discussed in James I. Robertson, *Soldiers Blue and Gray* (Columbia: University of South Carolina Press, 1988), 47–53, and Bell I. Wiley, *The Life of Billy Yank* (1978; repr., Baton Rouge: Louisiana State University Press, 1987), 49–52. The several types of drills the men performed are listed in various orders in ROB.

6. *MS*, November 6, 1861; Kimball Diary, October 5, 1861; Stearns Memoir; *DDA*, October 5, 1861.

7. T. Williams, *Hayes of the Twenty-Third*, 29.

8. Stearns Memoir and Kimball Diary both contain descriptions of camp life, including the frequency of religious meetings and activity.

9. Graves to wife, October 20, 1861 ("sociable"). Also see Robertson, *Soldiers Blue and Gray*, 122–44. Guard Report Book, October 12, 1861, included in ROB.

10. Graves to wife, October 26, 1861; Stearns Memoir.

11. Guard Report Book, ROB. Aaron Decker, for example, served his punishment for desertion and then remained with the regiment throughout his three-year enlistment. Likewise, eighteen-year-old Pvt. James Lahr of Company H deserted but was caught and returned to camp in early December, serving out his three-year term without incident. Edwin R. Osband Diary, December 5, 1861, Michigan State University Archives and Historical Collections (hereafter cited as Osband Diary).

12. Account of Waldo is in Kimball Diary, November 2 and 5, 1861. Waldo served out his three-year enlistment, mustering out with the original men in October 1864.

13. Wilson's Fusileers advertisement is in *MS*, August 28, 1861. Kimball recruiting is in *DDT*, September 20, 1861. Graves to wife, October 6, 1861; Kimball Diary, September 26, 1861. Also see *DDA*, October 8, 1861, and *DDT*, November 11, 1861 ("highest"), for comments on the pay promised the recruits in Chadwick's company. The *Allegan Journal*, September 23, 1861, contains the following enticement for Chadwick's volunteers: "Men get higher pay and fifty cents per day extra over other volunteers." Chadwick's company eventually became part of Thirteenth Michigan Infantry.

14. Ruggles to Robertson and accompanying note to WPI, Letters Out. For army rates of pay, see *Revised Regulations for the Army of the United States, 1861* (Philadelphia: J. G. L. Brown, 1861, reprinted in 1980 by the National Historical Society), 351–52 and 127.

15. *MDE*, October 3, 1861; Graves to wife, October 6, 1861; Stearns Memoir; *GR Eagle*, October 16, 1861; *MS*, November 6, 1861; Sligh to Foster, March 10, 1862. Also see George C. Cullum to John Pope, December 31, 1861, MEMRP. Sligh's letter states that Innes published a telegram he had received from the War Department with this authorized rate of compensation, but it has not been located to correspond to this time period; a later written acceptance of the regiment was sent by the War Department October 12 and is noted below. Kimball indicates that at least one early recruit had removed his name from the Jackson company roster over the issue of pay even before the company moved to Camp Owen. Kimball Diary, September 26, 1861.

16. WPI to Blair, October 1, 1861, and WPI to Robertson, October 2, 1861, RLB. Reference to letter of introduction from U.S. Senator Zachariah Chandler in LR-Reg. JWS to Foster, March 10, 1862, indicates that Innes left shortly after the offer to the men to leave. The meeting with Lincoln is described in WPI to Henry R. Mizner, January 9, 1862, RLB.

17. Graves to wife, October 20, 1861; *MDE* October 24, 1861; Kimball Diary, November 7, 1861; JWS to Foster, March 10, 1862. The written authorization (including "by direction" and "a regiment") is included in a communication from Assistant Secretary of War Thomas A. Scott to WPI, October 12, 1861, a copy of which is in MEMRP.

18. Permission for Serrell's battery is in O.R., ser. 3, 1:544–45; for examples of the reporting of this fact, see *New York Times*, September 7 and 8, 1861, and on through the month.

19. Innes sent Hunton orders on November 4 to obtain two brass cannons; reference in LR-Reg. They were reported as at Marshall by November 30. Michigan Quartermaster General, *Annual Report of the Quartermaster General of the State of Michigan* (Lansing: Quartermaster General's Office, 1861), 11. Also see Minutes of the State Military Board, Michigan Adjutant General, RG 59-14, Archives of Michigan, 86, for details on the transportation of the guns (hereafter cited as Minutes SMB). *DFP*, September 15, 1861, states that Dennis had served for five years in the regular cavalry, but this cannot be confirmed.

20. The best account of the ceremony is in *DFP*, October 12, 1861. Shearman was a prominent Calhoun County newspaperman and attorney who had served previously as state superintendent of public instruction. Washington Gardner, *History of Calhoun County, Michigan* (Chicago: Lewis, 1913), 313–14.

21. Seth S. Chapin, *The Three Campaigns: Sermon Preached before the First Regiment Fusileers at Camp Owen Marshall, Michigan, October 20, 1861* (Marshall, Mich.: Mann and Noyes, 1861), 6, 11. Chapin was Rector of Marshall's Trinity Church from 1860 to 1866. Gardner, *Calhoun County*, 373–74.

22. Accounts of the hospital are from *MDE*, October 3, 1861; *DFP*, October 12, 1861; and Daniel M. Moore, CWPF. Report of Mitchell's death is from Kimball Diary, October 15, 1861; the funeral is described in *MS*, October 23, 1861. Nothing further is known about Mitchell, and since he died before the regiment was mustered into federal service, there is nothing in service records about him. Hunt information is from Kimball Diary, November 12, 1861, and *MDE*, November 14, 1861. Hunt was one of Ransom and Flavia Hunt's three sons, all of whom died of disease in the service and are buried together in the Spring Arbor, Michigan, Cemetery. According to *ROS* 43, the three who died in December were Daniel Lillis of Yates's company on December 6 (or December 8 according to Kimball Diary) and two men from Hannings's company—Henry D. Hubbard on December 14 and Parker Scott the next day. According to the *Jackson True Citizen*, December 12, 1861, John Wells of Jackson, a member of the regiment, died the day before and was buried in Jackson—though the regimental records are silent about him.

23. *DFP*, October 12 and November 24, 1861. Vaccination information is from Kimball Diary, November 1, 1861; he does not specify what the vaccinations were for.

24. Wiley, *Billy Yank*, 24–25.

25. Stearns Memoir; Graves to wife, November 2, 1861; *MDE*, November 7, 1861; *DFP*, October 31, 1861. There are conflicting accounts of how many men refused to be sworn in, but about thirty seems reasonable. Mizner's military service is summarized in Guy V. Henry, *Military Record of Civilian Appointments in the*

United States Army, 2 vols. (New York: Van Nostrand, 1873), 1:396, and Robertson, *Michigan in the War*, 890. Detailed army procedures for mustering in a regiment are found in O.R., ser. 3, 1:961–64.

26. *MS*, September 11 and November 6, 1861; *MDE*, November 7, 1861. The Tyler Fusileers had elected officers on September 10, when many were not present. Apparently Innes had respected the results of the election by selecting Crittenton to command the company. Phelps was the original captain of the Marshal Light Guard in 1858–59, with Hunton as his first lieutenant.

27. *DFP*, October 31, 1861; *MS*, October 30, 1861; *MDE*, November 7, 1861; Robertson, *Michigan in the War*, 956. The views of the Michigan military command were expressed in a letter from Michigan assistant adjutant general DeGarmo Jones to Lt. Hiram S. Warner, First Michigan, who was a resident of Marshall and on recruiting duty there at the time. Letters Out ("not considered desirable" found in vol. 174, 384). Also see *MDE*, September 12, 1861. Eventually eighteen of the thirty-one men who were drummed out of the regiment on October 29 served in the army. Three died in the service, and another nine were discharged for disabilities.

28. *MDE*, October 24, 1861. An interesting plea for a requirement that uniforms for Michigan troops be made from cloth produced by Michigan manufacturers is found in *DDA*, May 16, 1861; it is signed by "Davis and Hubbard of Milford," a manufacturer of cloth. Some regiments had trouble getting out-of-state companies to fulfill their commitment. For example, when a Philadelphia contractor failed to meet the order for uniforms for the Eleventh Michigan, Sykes and Company of Detroit was contracted to complete the order. See Leland Thornton, *When Gallantry Was Commonplace: The History of the Michigan Eleventh Volunteer Infantry, 1861–1864* (New York: P. Lang, 1991), 51.

29. Information on wagons and implements is from *DDA*, December 21, 1861, and *MDE*, November 21, 1861. Charles C. Gilbert inspection in December referenced "Utah" wagons obtained while in Michigan; MEMRP ("Utah" wagons). Also see references to equipment in LR-Reg. Shoes information is from WPI to Fish, November 5 and 12, 1861, RLB, and also referenced in LR-Reg. Full company names are from Hawes, *Michigan State Gazetteer*, 201–3. See *Jackson American Citizen*, May 12, 1861, for reference to Austin and Tomlinson's army contracts for wagons. The Withington firm was headed by Capt. William Withington, a prewar business associate of Hopkins after whom Company H had been named. Hopkins was involved in the contracting of work to these Jackson companies; see references in LR-Reg. to letters written by Hopkins to WPI on November 4 and December 4, 1861, regarding shoes and wagons, respectively.

30. Uniforms were made in Detroit according to *DFP*, October 31, 1861, and *DDA*, December 21, 1861. References to letters from various firms in LR-Reg. These firms are cited in *DDA*, July 7, October 10, and November 19, 1861, as supplying new regiments. Also see Minutes SMB for this time period. A summary of Detroit business and army contracts is found in *DDA*, October 17, 1861.

31. Notice found in *DDA*, October 14, 1861. Bids were to be submitted by October 16, but there is nothing further about who won the bid. A similar notice in found in *DDA*, October 28, 1861.

32. WPI to Capt. E. G. Owen, U.S. Quartermaster in Detroit, October 31, 1861, RLB.

33. WPI to Owen, October 31, 1861, and WPI to Don Carlos Buell, November 28, 1861, both in RLB; WPI to Chief of Engineer Dept. of Ohio and WPI to Chief of the Ordnance Dept., both October 21, 1861, RLB.

34. SO 21, October 3, 1861, and SO 30, November 23, 1861, both in Orders. Kimball Diary, October 5, 1861, includes reference to the early arrival of a limited number of arms for the regimental camp guard; the entry for October 7, 1861, states, "We were the first that had guns to use on guard and felt quite important," but it was clear that only a handful of weapons were on hand before late November. Michigan Quartermaster General, *Annual Report*, 10–12; Francis A. Lord, *Civil War Collector's Encyclopedia* (Harrisburg, Pa: Stackpole, 1965), 245 ("refuse").

35. *DDA*, December 17, 1861, states that the Michigan Engineers were issued eight hundred Prussian and two hundred French muskets, part of a large state import of three thousand muskets divided among Innes's regiment and the Tenth and Eleventh infantry regiments. Thornton, *When Gallantry Was Commonplace*, 52–53, states they were Belgian and Prussian. December 1861 inspection report of Charles C. Gilbert in MEMRP ("clumsy"); Graves to wife, December 1, 1861 (flank companies); Company A Order Book, included with ROB; Lord, *Civil War Encyclopedia*, 245 ("uneven"). See WPI to Lt. Theodore Edson, January 2, 1862, RLB, on lack of full complement of arms and Osband Diary, December 23, 1861, for issue of ammunition and first live fire practice. Griffith, *Battle Tactics*, 86–90, contains a discussion of the lack of serious weapons training among Civil War soldiers.

36. Letter in *Jackson True Citizen*, November 28, 1861 ("months"); Noble to wife, November 8, 1861 ("tear down"). Noble complained regarding the lack of stoves in an undated letter from this time.

37. Noble to wife, November 6, 1861; *DFP*, November 24, 1861; Graves to wife, November 2, November 25, and December 1, 1861; Company A listing in Company Order Book, Michigan Engineers and Mechanics, Regimental Papers, Records of the Adjutant General, RG 94, NARA (hereafter cited as COB); Kimball Diary, November 28, 1861 (includes best description); William B. Calkins to wife, November 30, 1861 ("trimmed to death"), Bentley Historical Library, University of Michigan (unless otherwise noted, all letters from Calkins are in this collection).

38. Graves to wife, December 15, 1861; Company A listing in COB.

39. *DDA*, December 21, 1861; *DFP*, January 8, 1862; Robertson, *Michigan in the War*, 744–45, 915.

40. WPI to John D. Delafield, Michigan Southern and Northern Indiana Railroad, November 23, 1861, and WPI to Rice, Michigan Central Railroad, November 17, 1861, both in RLB. LR-Reg. also includes references to letters received from railroad officials in November.

41. Stearns Memoir.

42. Noble to wife, October 10, 1861 ("flood of tears"). This theme is repeated in other letters written from Camp Owen. *ROS* 43:148.

43. *MDE*, December 5, 1861; Noble to wife, December 2, 1861.

44. WPI to Blair November 4, 1861, RLB; *MDE*, December 5, 1861; Calkins to wife, December 6, 1861; Stearns Memoir; Graves to wife, December 15, 1861 ("patience"); Noble to wife, December 2 and 7, 1861.

45. Letters from WPI to U.S. Quartermaster in Louisville, November 27, 1861, to Don C. Buell, November 28, 1861, and to John Robertson, December 2, 1861, all in RLB; GO 122 in Orders.

46. Calkins to wife, December 15, 1861; Graves to wife, December 15, 1861; Kimball Diary, December 15, 1861.

47. Stearns Memoir; Kimball Diary, December 16, 1861 ("closing").

48. Information about transfers is in GO 84, December 17, 1861, ROB. This transfer was completed without mustering the men out of their current companies first, a fact that later caused Innes administrative work and embarassment but did not remove the men from the battery. See WPI to Ely and WPI to Major Larned, both January 10, 1862, RLB. A few men also transferred from the battery to the engineers in early December, including Andrew Coffinberry, son of Capt. Wright L. Coffinberry. On December 10, 1861, it was reported that the battery included only forty-five men. Report accompanying Orders. Upon the regiment's arrival in Kentucky, the army inspector noted that only "a squad of artillerists" was attached to the regiment. Charles C. Gilbert, December 20, 1861, MEMRP.

49. Kimball Diary and Osband Diary, December 17, 1861; *MDE*, December 16, 1861; Stearns Memoir.

50. *MS*, December 18, 1861; Kimball Diary, December 17, 1861.

51. *MS*, December 18, 1861; Wm. L. Clark letter in *MS*, January 1, 1862; *MDE*, December 26, 1861; Kimball Diary, December 17, 1861. The engines were not identified, but when the Sixth Michigan left Kalamazoo in August pulled by the "two best engines" of the same line, they were identified as the *Stag Hound* and *Ranger. DFP*, August 31, 1861. Osband Diary, January 13, 1862, indicates that at least one man was left in Marshall sick (Henry Fullerton, who rejoined his company on that date).

52. John L. Rolison Diary, Archives of Michigan (hereafter cited as Rolison Diary); Kimball Diary; William C. Swaddle to friends, December 21, 1861 ("banners"), Mrs. Roy Struble Collection, Western Michigan University Archives and Regional History Collections (unless otherwise noted, all letters from Swaddle are from this collection); Nathan Robinson to family, December 18, 1861 ("men"), Nathan Robinson Letters, possession of Sharon Patton, Lansing, Michigan (unless otherwise noted, all letters from Robinson are from this collection).

53. *MDE*, December 26, 1861; Wm. L. Clark letter in *MS*, January 1, 1862; Osband Diary, December 17, 1861 ("handsome").

54. Swaddle to friends, December 21, 1861.

55. JMS to mother, December 21, 1861 ("cheered"); Stearns Memoir. Noble to wife, December 19, 1861, and Swaddle to friends, December 21, 1861, echo Sligh's comments about the march through Louisville, though Noble believed the women to be decidedly friendlier to Union troops than the men.

56. Kimball Diary; Graves to wife, December 22, 1861; *DFP*, December 27, 1861; Stearns Memoir; Wm. L. Clark letter in *MS*, January 1, 1862 (reference to liquor).

57. Stearns Memoir; Wm. L. Clark letter in *MS*, January 1, 1862; Swaddle to friends, December 21, 1861; Gilbert inspection in MEMRP; Kimball Diary, December 17 and December 22, 1861 ("gloom"); Osband Diary, December 19–25 (including reference to battery).

58. For a history of the battery, see Monthly Returns and undated letter of Peter DeVries to Henry R. Mizner, early 1862, both in Battery E, First Michigan Light Artillery, RSR. Also see Frederick H. Dyer, *A Compendium of the War of the Rebellion*, 2 vols. (Dayton, Ohio: Press of Morningside Bookshop, 1979), 2:127, and Robertson, *Michigan in the War*, 528–29. Additional information on the connection of the battery with the Michigan Engineers is found in WPI to Col. E. Backus, January 31, 1862, to Blair, January 31, 1862, and to Ely, January 20, 1863, all in RLB. Also see WPI to Ely, August 7, 1863, MEMRP. In his inspection of the regiment, Gilbert referred to the battery as a "squad," and the battery's returns for January show only one officer and seventy men present for duty.

59. Orders to split the regiment are in SO 37, cited in the Regimental Record of Events for December 1861, Record of Events, Michigan Engineers and Mechanics, Records of the Adjutant General, RG 94, Microcopy Publication 594, NARA (hereafter cited as ROE). The several detachments of the Michigan Engineers were officially labeled "divisions" and numbered in order of commander seniority. In order to avoid confusion with the divisions of Buell's army, and because of its later use, the term "battalion" or "detachment" has been substituted and the numbering has been dropped.

Chapter 4

1. Frank J. Welcher, *Union Army, 1861–1865: Organization and Operation*, 2 vols. (Bloomington: Indiana University Press, 1989–93) 2:88, 127; Herman Hattaway and Archer Jones, *How the North Won: A Military History of the Civil War* (Urbana: University of Illinois Press, 1983), 58.

2. Hattaway and Jones, *How the North Won*, 76; Benjamin F. Cooling, *Fort Donelson's Legacy: War and Society in Kentucky and Tennessee, 1862–1863* (Knoxville: University of Tennessee Press, 1997), 20.

3. Hattaway and Jones, *How the North Won*, 60–61.

4. McPherson, *Battle Cry of Freedom*, 395; James L. McDonough, *War in Kentucky: From Shiloh to Perryville* (Knoxville, University of Tennessee Press, 1994), 39–40; Hattaway and Jones, *How the North Won*, 56; James R. Chumney Jr., "Don Carlos Buell: Gentleman General" (PhD diss., Rice University, 1964), 53–54.

5. Henry Cist, *The Army of the Cumberland*, vol. 7 of *Campaigns of the Civil War* (New York: Charles Scribner's Sons, 1882), 13–14; Thomas L. Connelly, *Army of the Heartland: Army of Tennessee, 1861–1862* (Baton Rouge: Louisiana University Press, 1967), 96. A less critical account of Zollicoffer's decision to remain on the north bank is found in C. David Dalton, "Zollicoffer, Crittenden, and the Mill Spring Campaign: Some Persistent Questions," *Filson Club Historical Quarterly* 60 (1986): 463–71.

6. JWS to wife, January 4, 1862; Perrin V. Fox Diary, January 1, 1862, Ray Smith Collection, Seymour Library, Knox College (hereafter cited as Fox Diary).

Muldraugh's Hill is best described in Joseph Kleber, editor in chief, *The Kentucky Encyclopedia* (Lexington: University Press of Kentucky, 1992), 660. The marches of the various battalions of the Michigan Engineers during the winter of 1862 can best be traced by using U.S. War Department, *Atlas to Accompany the Official Records of the Union and Confederate Armies* (1891–95; repr., New York: Fairfax Press, 1978), especially plates 150 and 151 (hereafter cited as O.R.A.).

7. Fox Diary.

8. Fox Diary.

9. JWS to wife, January 17, 1862; Fox Diary; Isaac Roseberry Diary, Bentley Historical Library, University of Michigan (hereafter cited as Roseberry Diary).

10. Fox Diary; JWS to wife, January 17, 1862; Morgan Parker letter in *DDT*, February 4, 1862; Cist, *Army of the Cumberland*, 14. Hunton's men arrived with the Fourth Kentucky and Ninth Ohio.

11. Connelly, *Army of the Heartland*, 97; 488; Dalton, "Mill Spring Campaign," 468; Mark M. Boatner, *The Civil War Dictionary* (New York: David McKay, 1959), 488.

12. Fox Diary; JWS to wife, January 17, 1862 [but clearly finished after that date].

13. JWS to wife, January 17, 1862; O. J. King letter in *MS*, January 29, 1862. *ROS*, 43:170, states that Wilford Roberts of Company H was wounded in action at Mill Springs, but his Civil War Pension File establishes that he was in the battalion hospital at Camp Wickliffe, where his company was stationed.

14. Connelly, *Army of the Heartland*, 97–99; Cist, *Army of the Cumberland*, 17–20; Boatner, *Civil War Dictionary*, 488–89.

15. Morgan Parker letter in *DDT*, February 4, 1862; JWS to wife, January 17, 1862.

16. Boatner, *Civil War Dictionary*, 489; O. J. King letter in *MS*, January 29, 1862 ("sickening"); Ira Remington letter in *Flint Wolverine Citizen*, February 1, 1862 ("awful") (hereafter cited as *FWC*); Capt. John W. Free, Thirty-first Ohio, in the *Perry County (Ohio) Weekly*, February 5, 1862.

17. Fox Diary. JWS to wife, January 26, 1862, states his conversation was with a captured "Lt. Col.," and Carter was the only one with that rank taken during the battle. Cliffe information is from Fox Diary, January 21, 1862; O.R., 7:109, 565; Janet B. Hewett, ed., *The Roster of Confederate Soldiers, 1861–1865*, 16 vols. (Wilmington, N.C.: Broadfoot, 1995–), 3:459; and Joseph H. Crute, *Confederate Staff Officers, 1861–65* (Powhatan, Va.: Derwent Books, 1982), 219.

18. Cist, *Army of the Cumberland*, 20; Fox Diary; Thomas to Buell, O.R., 7:564–655; JWS to wife, January 26, 1862.

19. James Barnett, "Munfordville in the Civil War," *Register of the Kentucky Historical Society* 69 (1971): 340, 342; Maury Klein, *History of the Louisville and Nashville Railroad* (New York: Macmillan, 1972), 30; Joseph G. Kerr, *Historical Development of the Louisville and Nashville Railroad System* (Louisville: Louisville and Nashville Railroad Company, 1926), 22.

20. James Barnett, "Willich's Thirty-Second Indiana Volunteers," *Cincinnati Historical Society Bulletin* 37 (1979), 51; Barnett, "Munfordville," 342–46; Thomas

Van Horne, *History of the Army of the Cumberland, Its Organization, Campaigns, and Battles*, 2 vols. (1876; repr., Wilmington, N.C.: Broadfoot, 1992), 1:65.

21. Calkins to wife, January 6, 1862; Joseph Thompson Gibson, *History of the Seventy-Eighth Pennsylvania Infantry . . .* (Pittsburg: Pittsburg Printing, 1905), 32–33 ("vivid"). Barnett, "Willich's Thirty-Second Indiana," 52, suggests that there was a conflict between the Michigan Engineers and Willich over jurisdiction of the pontoons. Also see Kerr, *Historical Development*, 22, for completion of the bridge.

22. For descriptions of work at Green River, see Rolison Diary; Graves to wife, January 7 and 12, 1862; Calkins to wife, January 6 and 8–9, 1862; Stanard to wife, January 12, 1862; *DDT*, February 19, 1862; and *GR Eagle*, January 22, 1862. Description of Fort Innes and Mitchel crossing are from Wm. L. Clark letter to *MS*, February 26, 1862 ("Fort Innes"). "Basket Maker" of Company B described the status of earthworks on January 18 in *FWC*, February 1, 1862, but did not include "Innes" label. Other Union accounts do not use the term "Fort Innes" for any fortifications on the south bank of the river, but the unnamed enclosed stockade shown alongside the railroad on the south bank of the river crossing in O.R.A., 102, is the approximate location.

23. Balloon description is from Graves to wife, January 7, 1862; no further information has been found on Confederate balloon operations in central Kentucky at this time. January 17 scare description is from "Basket Maker," *FWC*, February 1, 1862, and Calkins to wife, January 19, 1862.

24. Graves to wife, January 12, 1862.

25. Graves to wife, January 28, 1862 ("quails"); Rolison Diary, January 26, 1862.

26. Kimball and Osband diaries; Noble to wife, December 29, 1861.

27. Location of Camp Wickliffe is from Welcher, *Union Army*, 2:195, and Ebenezer Hannaford, *The Story of a Regiment: A History of the Campaigns, and Association in the Field, of the Sixth Regiment Ohio Volunteer Infantry* (Cincinnati: Ebenezer Hannaford, 1868), 174–75. Nelson background is from Boatner, *Civil War Dictionary*, 586.

28. Kimball Diary, December 31, 1861; Osband Diary, December 30, 1861 ("cross looking"), and January 1 and 6, 1862 ("alright").

29. Ezra Stearns Diary, January 1–February 11, 1862, Carr Family Letters, Bentley Historical Library, University of Michigan (hereafter cited as Stearns Diary); Kimball and Osband diaries, January 1–February 11, 1862; Noble to wife, February 11, 1862; Hannaford, *Story of a Regiment*, 187. Despite the drilling, Noble's letters home (especially January 15, 1862) tell of a great boredom in the company.

30. Kimball, Osband, and Stearns diaries; Noble to wife, January 2, 1862; Guard Book for February 1862, in ROB. For more on the dangers armed green recruits posed to one other, see Prokopowicz, *All for the Regiment*, 50–51.

31. Description of work is from Stearns and Osband diaries, including "best soldiering" (Osband Diary, February 1, 1862); Nathan Robinson to family, January 25, 1862; James D. Robinson to wife, January 31, 1862, The Studley, Pickard, Stackhouse Collection, Washington, D.C., courtesy of Jeanette Studley (unless otherwise noted, all letters from J. D. Robinson are from this collection) ("rather").

Also see Kimball Diary for advantages of being away from Camp Wickliffe. Stearns Diary describes the general camp duties of men remaining at Camp Wickliffe.

32. Wm. L. Clark letter in *Eaton County Republican*, January 17, 1862; Boatner, *Civil War Dictionary*, 557; Welcher, *Union Army*, 2:194. Mitchel's camp at Bacon Creek was also known as Camp John Quincy Adams. The nearby Bacon Creek post office was renamed Bonneville after the war.

33. Wm. L. Clark letters in *Eaton County Republican*, January 17, 1862, *MS*, February 5, 1862, and *DFP*, February 9, 1862. The mills were probably located a short distance east of the Nolin Creek Louisville and Nashville Railroad (LNRR) station, which was just west of the village and the Elizabethtown Road bridge; see O.R.A., 150.

34. Wm. L. Clark letters in *DFP*, February 9, 1862, and *MS*, February 5, 1862 ("shed more ink").

35. Osband Diary, January 10, 1862 ("old Michigan"); Calkins to wife, January 8–9, 1862 ("felt to rejoice"). The importance of mail, and the army's attempts to deliver it, are detailed in Arthur Hecht, "Union Military Mail Service," *Filson Club Historical Quarterly* 37 (1963), 227–48. Also see Wiley, *Billy Yank*, 189–90 and Robertson, *Soldiers Blue and Gray*, 104–10.

36. Graves to wife, February 19, 1862. Also see letters from JWS to wife, February 19, 1862, and Noble to wife, January 11 and 25, 1862.

37. JWS to wife, January 17, 1862 ("ignorant"); Noble to wife, December 29, 1861 ("fifty"); Nathan Robinson to family, January 25, 1862. Also see "Basketmaker" letter in *FWC*, February 8, 1862 (particularly about the lack of schools in Kentucky), and the diary entries of Fox and Osband throughout January and February.

38. Benjamin F. Cooling, *Forts Henry and Donelson: The Key to the Confederate Heartland* (Knoxville: University of Tennessee Press, 1987).

39. Wm. L. Clark letter in *MS*, February 26, 1862; David D. Holm, *History of the Fifth Indiana Battery . . .* (N.p., n.d.), 5.

40. Wm. L. Clark letter in *MS*, March 5, 1862; John Beatty, *The Citizen-Soldier; or, Memoirs of a Volunteer* (Cincinnati: Wilstach, Baldwin, 1879), 83–84; Lucien Wulsin, *The Story of the Fourth Regiment Ohio Veteran Volunteer Cavalry*, edited by Eleanor N. Adams (Cincinnati: n.p., 1912), 20, 23 ("remarkably"), and 119 ("so active"). Wulsin identifies them as Wisconsin engineers, yet Yates's are the only men with the command who would have met the description.

41. Wm. L. Clark letter in *MS*, March 5, 1862; Cist, *Army of the Cumberland*, 24–25; Welcher, *Union Army*, 2:195; Report of A. S. Johnston, O.R., 7:418–19; Turchin to Mitchel, February 16, 1862, in Ormsby M. Mitchel Papers, RG 94, Generals' Papers, Records of the Adjutant General, NARA (hereafter cited as Generals' Papers); Report of Mitchel, O.R., 7:419–21 ("enable us to cross"); Wulsin, *Story of the Fourth*, 24.

42. Cooling, *Fort Donelson's Legacy*, 118–19; O.R., 7:623; Welcher, *Union Army*, 2:194–95, 575, 578.

43. March description is from Osband, Stearns, and Kimball diaries; Hannaford, *Story of a Regiment*, 195–97.

44. Stearns, Osband, and Kimball diaries for February 17, 1862 ("great passion," "fairly purple," and "rather blue," respectively); Nathan Robinson to family, February 18, 1862; WPI to Blair, March 12, 1862, RLB. Also see SO 63, Fourth Division, Army of the Ohio, February 16 ("not desiring"), Nelson to Fry, March 6, 1862, and Maj. Dorus M. Fox to Fry, all in MEMRP. Nelson eventually dropped the charges, though under the condition that Hopkins and Grant acknowledge they had been in the wrong. Innes takes credit in his letter to Blair for getting the "Major honorably out of his trouble." Lieutenant Robinson credits General Buell for clearing the charges with trial on March 9. James D. Robinson to wife, March 9, 1862. Hopkins and Grant had returned to their regiment on February 24, 1862, while awaiting the outcome. SO 51, Army of the Ohio, Records of the U.S. Army Continental Commands, 1821–1920, RG 393-1, ser. 890, NARA (hereafter cited as Cont. Commands).

45. Roseberry and Fox diaries; JWS to wife, February 19, 1862; Orlando P. Cutter, *Our Battery; or, a Journal of the Company B, 1st Ohio Volunteer Artillery* (Cleveland: Nevin's Book and Job Printing, 1864), 33–34; Hannaford, *Story of a Regiment*, 192–208.

46. O.R., 7:615, 623, 627, 938; Rolison Diary; Heman Lowe Diary, Burton Historical Collection, Detroit Public Library (hereafter cited as Lowe Diary); Graves to wife, February 19, 1862.

47. For work done by Michigan Engineers, see Graves to wife, February 19, 1862, and Lowe Diary. Destruction description is from Klein, *Louisville and Nashville*, 30, and Kerr, *Historical Development*, 22. For railroad repair in general, see O.R., 7:627 ("push"), 657. Bell's Tavern is near present-day Park City. Robert M. Rennick, *Kentucky Place Names* (Lexington: University Press of Kentucky, 1984), 226.

48. Klein, *Louisville and Nashville*, 48.

49. Hattaway and Jones, *How the North Won*, 76.

50. Stearns, Osband, and Kimball diaries, February 25, 1862 ("felt proud"). Additional information can be found in U.S. Navy Department, *Official Records of the Union and Confederate Navies*, 30 vols. (1896–1906; repr., Harrisburg, Pa.: National Historical Society, 1987), 22:640.

51. Stearns, Kimball, and Osband ("right side") diaries, February 27, 1862.

52. Rolison and Lowe diaries.

53. Rolison and Lowe diaries; Gibson, *Seventy-Eighth Pennsylvania*, 34–36.

54. O.R., 7:419–21, 631, 634–35; Wm. L. Clark letter in *MS*, March 26, 1862; Rolison and Lowe diaries; John B. Yates, "Military History, 1866, of John B. Yates of the 1st Michigan Engineers and Mechanics," Bentley Historical Library, University of Michigan (hereafter cited as Yates, "Military History"). Despite later claims (see for example, WPI to Robertson, November 19, 1862, RSR), there is nothing to suggest that the Michigan Engineers were among the first to enter Bowling Green, unless a small detachment was crossed over with the advance on the fourteenth.

55. Fox and Roseberry diaries; JMS to mother, March 3, 1862; JWS to wife, February 25 and March 6, 1862; Cutter, *Our Battery*, 34–39.

56. Absent sick list for February 1862 and attached list of "Absent enlisted men accounted for by name," are in Monthly Return, Michigan Engineers and Mechanics, Regimental Service Records, Michigan Adjutant General, RG 59-14, Archives of Michigan (hereafter cited as Monthly Return). Grant to "Ladies of Sandstone and Spring Arbor," in *Jackson True Citizen*, March 19, 1862. Murray's report is from Janet B. Hewett, Noah Andre Trudeau, Bryce A. Suderow, eds., *Supplement to the Official Records of the Union and Confederate Armies* (Wilmington, N.C.: Broadfoot, 1994–), part 1, 7:523–24.

57. *ROS* 43, Desc. Roll, and Monthly Return; Calkins to wife, n.d. [early April 1862].

58. George W. Adams, *Doctors in Blue: The Medical History of the Union Army in the Civil War* (New York: Shuman, 1952), 206–13.

59. Robertson, *Soldiers Blue and Gray*, 152–55. JWS to wife, February 19, 1862 ("they must take care"); James D. Robinson to wife, January 31, 1862.

60. JWS to wife, January 26, February 6, and February 9, 1862. For comments on hard marching and poor health, see Swaddle to sister, January 24, 1862, and to father July 24, 1862. Swaddle blamed his continuing poor health on sleeping on the wet ground during the January marches made by Hunton's battalion. Also see Fox Diary, February 9 and 20, 1862; "Absent enlisted men accounted for by name," RSR.

61. Tripler report in O.R., 5:81–82. See appendix I, table C for a summary of the higher losses among the oldest soldiers.

62. JWS to wife, February 25, 1862.

63. Calkins to wife, March 4, 1862. The comrade who died was probably Eli Brink of Otisco, Ionia County. He was the only Michigan Engineer who died at Munfordville in early March. Calkins reported that Brink caught a cold that settled on his lungs and proved fatal.

64. *Kalamazoo Telegraph*, April 9, 1862 ("loyal hearts").

Chapter 5

1. Various sources were consulted to place the camps of the Michigan Engineers companies around Nashville. Information about Companies B, E, I, and headquarters at Camp Andy Johnson is drawn from Calkins to wife, March 9, 1862; Rolison Diary; RLB and ROB; and Walter T. Durham, *Nashville, Occupied City* (Nashville: Tennessee Historical Society, 1985), 65. Location information for Companies A and K is from Wm. L. Clark letter in *MS*, April 16, 1862, and O.R., 10-2:292. Information about Companies C and H at Camp Andrew (or Andy) Jackson is from Kimball, Stearns, and Osband diaries. In addition, Edwin C. Bearss, "Nelson Saves the Day at Shiloh," *Register of the Kentucky Historical Society* 63 (1965), 40, states Camp Andrew Jackson was two miles southeast of Nashville on the Murfreesboro Pike and that Nelson's division was located there from February 25 to March 16, 1862. Location information for Companies D, F, and G is from JWS to wife, March 6, 1862, and Roseberry Diary. See O.R.A., 73:1, for the various pikes and features in the Nashville area.

2. Welcher, *Union Army*, 2:82; Van Horne, *Army of the Cumberland*, 1:98–100; Cooling, *Fort Donelson's Legacy*, 27.

3. Welcher, *Union Army*, 2:82, 776; Van Horne, *Army of the Cumberland*, 1:98–100; Bearss, "Nelson Saves the Day," 39–41.

4. McCallum's order is from O.R., ser. 3, 5:974; Robert E. Riegel, "Federal Operations of Southern Railroads during the Civil War," *Mississippi Valley Historical Review* 9 (1922): 128–30.

5. *Rebellion Records*, ser. 1, 16:301, as cited in Riegel, "Southern Railroads," 129; LeRoy P. Graf and Ralph W. Hasking, eds., *The Papers of Andrew Johnson*, 16 vols. (Knoxville: University of Tennessee Press, 1967–2000), 6:439ff.

6. At the time of his appointment, Smith was commanding a brigade in Crittenden's Fifth Division. For more on Smith, see Boatner, *Civil War Dictionary*, 776, and Ezra Warner, *Generals in Blue* (Baton Rouge: Louisiana State University Press, 1964), 464. Anderson assumed charge of the Nashville and Chattanooga (NCRR) and the Nashville and Decatur (NDRR) in April 1862 after Smith left with Buell on the march to Savannah. John Byars Anderson to brother, April 21, 1862, Anderson Family Papers, Kansas State Historical Society. Order to WPI from SO 1, Army of the Ohio, March 15, 1862, RG 393-1, ser. 944, Cont. Commands.

7. Jessie C. Burt, "The Nashville and Chattanooga Railroad, 1854–1872: The Era of Transition," *East Tennessee Historical Society Publications* 23 (1951): 58–60; Robert Dunnavant, *The Railroad War: N. B. Forrest's 1864 Raid through Northern Alabama and Middle Tennessee* (N.p.: Pea Ridge Press, 1994), 15–16, 102.

8. See Klein, *Louisville and Nashville*, 31, for the problems with using cars from Northern railroads. Smith background from William Sooy Smith Papers, Generals' Papers.

9. SO 1, Army of the Ohio, RG 393-1, ser. 944, Cont. Commands; Calkins to wife, March 17; WPI to Robertson, November 19, 1862, RLB; Rolison Diary. The Tennessee River terminus of the Nashville and Northwestern Railroad (NNWRR) in 1862 was located two miles upstream of Reynoldsburg, at Lucas Landing, on the southern bank of the mouth of Trace Creek. This site was named Johnsonville after Military Governor Andrew Johnson when he dedicated the completed line on May 19, 1864. Additional information can be found in "Lost City of Reynoldsburg" and related materials, Jill K. Garrett Collection, Tennessee State Library and Archives; Donald Steenburn, *Silent Echoes of Johnsonville: Rebel Cavalry and Yankee Gunboats* (Rogersville, Ala.: Elk River Press, 1994); Correspondence from Mr. John H. Whitfield to the author, Humphreys County Historian, February 10, 1998; and Graf and Hasking, *Andrew Johnson*, 6:701–2.

10. Calkins to wife, March 17, 1862; WPI to Robertson, November 19, 1862; Lowe and Rolison diaries; GO 23 and SO 28, both on March 25, 1862, ROB; WPI to M. Burns, President, NNWRR, February 25, 1863, RLB. Some accounts mistakenly refer to the steamer as *T. W. Haelman*. Charles Dana Gibson and E. Kay Gibson, *Dictionary of Transports and Combatant Vessels, Steam and Sail, Employed by the Union Army, 1861–1868, The Army's Navy Series* (Camden, Maine: Ensign Press, 1996), 170, lists her as the *J. W. Hillman*.

11. Expedition description is from WPI to Robertson, November 19, 1862, RLB; Lowe and Rolison diaries; GO 23 and SO 28, both March 25, 1862, ROB. Hopkins had all of his men and the sick at the depot by about the seventeenth. Companies A and K remained with Mitchel, and Hunton was detached with Companies D, F, and G; see below. For various detachments, see SOs 22, 23, and 27, March 15–16, 1862, ROB; Fox and Roseberry diaries; JMS to mother, March 16, 1862; and JWS to wife, March 29, 1862.

12. Wm. L. Clark letter in *MS*, April 16, 1862; F. A. Mitchel, *Ormsby MacKnight Mitchel, Astronomer and General: A Biographical Narrative* (New York: Houghton, Mifflin, 1887), 267–72; SO 3, March 17, 1862, Army of the Ohio, RG 393-1, ser. 908, Cont. Commands. The men were probably working on Mill Creek No. 2, the largest of the three bridges over that stream.

13. Haynie, *Nineteenth Illinois*, 163–64; Mitchel, *Ormsby MacKnight Mitchel*, 267–72; Wm. L. Clark letter in *MS*, April 16, 1862. Two companies of the Thirteenth Ohio were ordered by Mitchel on March 17 to report to Yates to assist in the repair of the bridges. SO 3, Army of the Ohio, March 17, 1862, ser. 944, Comp. Commands. Mitchel's personal involvement is also noted in Silas S. Canfield, *History of the Twenty-First Ohio Volunteer Infantry in the War of the Rebellion* (Toledo, Ohio: Vrooman, Anderson, and Bateman, 1893), 40–41.

14. Work details are from Kimball, Rolison, and Stearns diaries; Noble to wife, March 19, 1862; also see orders in ROB, especially SO 33, March 28, 1862. *FWC*, April 5, 1862 ("doesn't seem much"). Stearns Diary, March 25, 1862, implies that a civilian working party arrived on March 25 to help with the bridge.

15. Roseberry and Fox diaries; JMS to mother, March 16, 1862; JWS to wife, March 29, 1862; JMS to mother March 22, 1862; P. V. Fox to wife, April 13, 1862, Private Collection of John Gelderloos, Grand Rapids, Michigan (unless otherwise noted, all letters from Fox are in this collection). The men rested on the twenty-fourth at the Little Harpeth crossing.

16. Fox and Roseberry diaries; JWS to wife, March 29, 1862; ROE, March 1862.

17. JWS to wife, April 4, 1862; Fox Diary, April 3, 1862. Ebenezer Hannaford, and later Wiley Sword, suggested that "engineers and mechanics" were part of the inexperienced work force slowly repairing the Duck River bridge. This cannot be a reference to the Michigan Engineers since the repairs to that bridge were completed on March 31 and the men in Sligh's advance company did not reach Columbia until April 1. Hannaford, *Story of a Regiment*, 228, and Wiley Sword, *Shiloh: Bloody April* (1974; repr., New York: HarperCollins, 1992), 44.

18. Graves to wife, January 12, 1862; Calkins to wife, January 19, 1862.

19. WPI to Hunton, January 17 and February 8, 1862 ("in no way prejudice"), and to Palmerlee, February 6, 1862 ("whole matter"), both RLB; [Men in Companies B, E, and I] to "The honorable Gen. Buell," February 7, 1862, and "Undersigned" in Companies C and H to Buell, February 7, 1862, both in MEMRP.

20. Accounts of attempts to pay the men during this time are from Calkins to wife, Munfordville, n.d.; JMS to mother, February 28, 1862; Swaddle to brother, March 3, 1862; Kimball, Stearns, and Osband diaries; Nathan Robinson to family, January 18, 1862 ("excitement"); and James D. Robinson to wife, January 26,

1862. Examples of communications between detachments are from Kimball Diary, February 6, 1862 ("commotion"), and Stearns Diary, February 2, 1862.

21. Calkins to wife, January [probably early], 1862 ("fraud and deception"); Graves to wife, January 28, 1862 ("low ebb"). Also see Osband Diary, January 16–18, 1862, and Noble to wife, February 2 and March 18, 1862, on blaming officers. Similar charges were leveled at Colonel Serrell of the First New York Engineers and Colonel Josiah Bissell of the Engineer Regiment of the West. The regimental papers of the Fifteenth and Fiftieth New York are silent on the pay question. See RG 94, Regimental Papers, Records of the Adjutant General, NARA.

22. Nathan Robinson to family [date not recorded on loose sheet, but with letters from February 1862].

23. For Sligh's sentiments on this, see JWS to Foster, March 10, 1862, and JWS to wife March 29 and May 23, 1862.

24. For the debate over this legislation, see *Congressional Globe*, 37th Cong., 2nd sess., 1862, 32:1022–30. See also Shiman, "Engineering Sherman's March," 74–75, who points out that the twenty-five thousand volunteer engineers authorized in the defeated legislation was about the same number as eventually served.

25. WPI to Hunton January 27 and February 8, 1862, RLB.

26. Comment appended to Kimball Diary entry for October 12, 1862; Noble to wife, February 2, 1862; JWS to wife, June 22, 1862 ("hardly"); James D. Robinson to wife, March 9, 1862.

27. Gouldsbury information is from GO 13, March 4, 1862, ROB; JWS to wife, June 27, 1862 ("mutiny and rebellion"); James D. Robinson to wife, March 9, 1862. Forfeit pay is from Kimball and Osband diaries, March 6, 1862, and Noble to wife, March 19, 1862. Ban on letters is in GO 16, March 7, 1862, ROB. Sligh pointed out in his letter that Gouldsbury had actually little contact with any but Innes's three-company detachment until early March and sarcastically noted, "He must have been very industrious in that time attending to gossip to have learned so much." Robinson lamented the loss of Gouldsbury's services—he ranked him strong on his job as orderly—but criticized him for doing "his best to excite a war between the men and officers."

28. Undated news clipping in SFP, almost certainly from the *Grand Rapids Enquirer*.

29. Osband, Kimball ("groaned"), and Stearns diaries, March 6, 1862. Stearns was among those who took the pay. March 12 incident information is from Graves to wife, April 1 and 22, 1862. Graves did not accept the pay but apparently had a later change of heart; LR-Reg. All enlisted men and commissioned officers were paid higher in the engineer branch than the infantry, so all had an incentive to fight for the higher pay. The monthly difference ranged from four dollars for privates (thirteen dollars vs. seventeen dollars) to at least ten dollars for most of the officers. The largest percentage differences were among the noncommissioned officers: seventeen dollars versus twenty-four dollars for sergeants and thirteen dollars versus twenty dollars for corporals. At least thirty noncommissioned officers were later reduced in rank, temporarily in most cases, for their role in the pay controversy at Nashville. The reduction of noncommissioned officers is found in GOs 35 (April 16, 1862) and 37–40 (April 20, 1862); JMS to mother May 23, 1862; and Graves to

wife, April 22, 1862. Graves is specific that the demotions were for signing the written protest, though the orders cite the seventh article of war and contain an effective date of April 1, 1862. Also see Graves to wife and Osband Diary, both April 22, 1863, for the lack of concern among those who were demoted (including both Graves and Osband).

30. Kimball Diary, March 22 [probably March 25], 1862.

31. Company H information from Osband Diary, March 27, 1862, and Graves to wife, April 1, 1862 ("myth"). The three were John Forbes, John McDonald, and William F. Cole; see Kimball, Stearns, and Osband diaries, March 28, 1862, and the CMSR for each. Cole and Forbes were still in jail at Nashville two months later when Coffinberry requested their release, citing "no prospect of speedy trial and that men are needed in the company;" MEMRP. At least eight men were confined in Nashville during this time (four from Company C, two from Company I, and two or three from Company F), so others might have joined Cole and Forbes.

32. April 2, 1862, order to move is GO 30, April 2, 1862, ROB; Kimball, Lowe, and Osband diaries, April 1–2, 1862.

33. Calkins to wife, April 12, 1862; Graves to wife, April 22, 1862; Kimball, Lowe, and Osband diaries, April 3, 1862; JWS to wife, April 12, 1862.

34. Chumney, "Don Carlos Buell," 69–70; Bearss, "Nelson Saves the Day," 45–48; P. V. Fox to wife, April 13, 1862. Detailed maps for the march from Nashville to Savannah are lacking, but O.R.A., 144, shows the general area.

35. The best engineer accounts of the march are JWS to wife, April 12, 1862, and Osband Diary (including "awful" on April 5, 1862).

36. James L. McDonough, *Shiloh: In Hell before Night* (Knoxville: University of Tennessee Press, 1977), 183, 196.

37. Kimball, Rolison, Stearns, Osband, and Roseberry diaries; Graves to wife, April 12, 1862; JWS to wife, April 17, 1862; James D. Robinson to wife, April 12, 1862; Richard W. Barker Diary, April 12, 1862, Bentley Historical Library, University of Michigan (hereafter cited as Barker Diary).

38. Osband Diary, April 14, 1862; JWS to wife, April 17, 1862.

39. John C. Cavanagh, "The Operations of Major-General Henry W. Halleck's Union Army in the Corinth Campaign of 1862," (master's thesis, Columbia University, n.d.), 22; JWS to wife, April 17, 28, and May 3, 1862; Barker, Kimball, Stearns, Osband, Rolison, and Roseberry diaries; Graves to wife, April 22, 1862; ROE, April 1862; ROB, April 26–29, 1862.

40. McPherson, *Battle Cry of Freedom*, 415–17; Hattaway and Jones, *How the North Won*, 157–58, 170–71. Also see Peter Cozzens, *The Darkest Day of the War: The Battles of Iuka and Corinth* (Chapel Hill: University of North Carolina Press, 1997), 19, for the importance of Corinth as a rail junction.

41. Cavanagh, "Corinth Campaign," 32–34; Stephen E. Ambrose, *Halleck: Lincoln's Chief of Staff* (Baton Rouge: Louisiana State University Press, 1962), 49–52; Boatner, *Civil War Dictionary*, 176.

42. Welcher, *Union Army*, 2:559–62.

43. William B. Scott, "The Topographical Influences on the Campaigns in Middle and West Tennessee during the First Year of the Civil War" (master's

thesis, The University of Tennessee, 1953), 70; Hattaway and Jones, *How the North Won*, 171; Cozzens, *Darkest Day*, 19. Maps of the area between Pittsburg Landing and Corinth are found in O.R.A., especially plates 12:5, 13:2, 6, and 14:2, 3.

44. Roseberry, Stearns, Barker, Kimball, and Rolison diaries; JWS to wife, May 3, 1862; O.R., 10-1:672–73, 678, 705, 10-2:144.

45. Movements of Buell's divisions are from Welcher, *Union Army*, 2:561; route was matched against maps in O.R.A., plates 13:6 and 14:3. Account of marching and work is from Roseberry, Barker, Stearns, Kimball, Lowe, and Rolison diaries, and JWS to wife, May 17, 1862.

46. GOs 49 and 50 and SO 48, May 2–4, 1862, ROB.

47. Roseberry, Barker, Stearns, and Fox diaries; JWS to wife, May 17, 1862; James D. Robinson to wife, May 11, 1862.

48. Fox, Kimball, Stearns, Rolison, and Lowe diaries; JWS to wife, May 17, 1862; O.R., 10-1:678, 832–37; James D. Robinson to wife, May 11, 1862.

49. Rolison Diary, May 10, 1862; Welcher, *Union Army*, 2:561–62; O.R., 10-2:177.

50. Roseberry, Rolison, Stearns, Barker and Fox diaries; JWS to wife, May 17, 1862; JMS to mother May 15, 1862; Henry H. Bellamy to Miss Wolfe, Bellamy Letters, Bentley Historical Library, University of Michigan; GO 53, 54 and 57, May 15–17, 1862, ROB.

51. Graves to wife, May 20, 1862.

52. Welcher, *Union Army*, 2:562; JWS to wife, May 23 and 26, 1862; Graves to wife, May 20, 1862; O.R., 10-1:675.

53. See JWS to wife, May 27, 1862, and JMS to mother, May 23, 1862, on the expectation of large numbers of wounded. Additional information about construction is in Rolison, Barker, Stearns, Fox, and Kimball diaries, and Swaddle to father May 27 [?], 1862.

54. Welcher, *Union Army*, 2:654; JWS wife June 6, 1862; SO 61, May 27, 1862, ROB; Swaddle to father May 27, 1862. Sligh was more confident: see JWS to wife, May 27, 1862.

55. Barker Diary, May 30, 1862 ("defeated"); Noble to wife, May 30, 1862 ("follow").

56. O.R., 10-2:232–33.

Chapter 6

1. Buell to Mitchel, March 27, 1862, in O.R., 10-2:71–72.

2. Beatty, *Citizen-Soldier*, 91–101; Joseph W. Keiffer, *Slavery and Four Years of War* . . . (New York: G. P. Putnam's Sons, 1900), 1:266; John B. Turchin, "Huntsville, Alabama: The Seizure of It and of a Part of the Memphis and Charleston Railroad in April 1862," *War Papers, Department of Ohio, Grand Army of the Republic* (Cincinnati, Ohio: Privately printed, n.d.), 1:170; ROE, 3rd Div. for April 1862, in O.R., 10-1:642.

3. O.R., 10-1:641; ROE, 3rd Div. in O.R., 10-1:642–43; Beatty, *Citizen-Soldier*, 101–2; Turchin, "Huntsville, Alabama," 171–76; George E. Turner, *Victory Rode the Rails: The Strategic Place of the Railroads in the Civil War* (Lincoln: University

of Nebraska Press, 1992), 31–32. Mitchel's column included the infantry brigades of Joshua W. Sill and John B. Turchin, cavalry, artillery, and Yates's two-company battalion of engineers. William H. Lytle's brigade was left at Fayetteville to guard supply lines from Nashville.

4. Turchin, "Huntsville, Alabama," 174–77; O.R., 10-1:641–43. See O.R.A. 149 for Mitchel's route to Huntsville and the Memphis and Charleston Railroad (MCRR) between Corinth and Chattanooga. According to his report, Mitchel's advance force that took Huntsville by surprise included Turchin's brigade, the Fourth Ohio Cavalry, and the Fifth Indiana Battery. There is no reference to Yates's battalion in this advance force, though Yates later mentions his men as "arriving in Huntsville with the first troops"; see Yates, "Military History."

5. O.R., 10-1:641–43; Turchin, "Huntsville, Alabama," 178–79; Angus Waddle, *Three Years with the Armies of the Ohio and the Cumberland* (Chillicothe, Ohio: Scioto Gazette Book and Job Office, 1889), 14–15; Wm. L. Clark letter in *MS*, April 30, 1862. Turchin's train was engineered by two experienced railroad men detailed from the Twenty-fourth Illinois. William Vocke, "The Military Achievements of Major General Ormsby MacKnight Mitchel," *Illinois Commandery, Military Order of the Loyal Legion of the United States*, 8 vols. (Chicago: Illinois Commandery, 1891–), 4:92.

6. O.R., 10-2:619.

7. O.R., 10-2:133–34.

8. O.R., 10-2:134, 155–56, 291; Lieutenant Mason letter in *DDA*, June 2, 1862; Mitchel, *Ormsby MacKnight Mitchel*, 308–9; Vocke, "Military Achievements," 95; *Saginaw Enterprise*, May 22, 1862, reprinting account from the *Louisville Journal*. The length of the floating bridge varies in accounts from 160 to 315 feet; the former probably is the stream width and the latter the length of a railroad bridge including the measurement of bank and approaches.

9. O.R., 10-2:134, 155–56, 291; Mitchel, *Ormsby MacKnight Mitchel*, 308–9; Jeffrey N. Lash, "A Yankee in Gray: Danville Leadbetter and the Defense of Mobile Bay," *Civil War History* 37 (1991), 202. The scow, or "flatboat," had been captured by Sill's command and probably saved the Michigan Engineers the task of building another temporary cotton bridge, this time over Crow Creek; see Mitchel to Joshua W. Sill, April 28, 1862, in Mitchel Letterbook, RG 393-2, ser. 839, Cont. Commands.

10. Mitchel to Stanton in O.R., 10-2:156.

11. Mitchel reported capturing fifteen locomotives at Huntsville and another five the following day at Stevenson. On April 24 he credited the "sixteen" locomotives in possession as being the only reason he could hold such a long and exposed line. Mitchel to Buell April 24 in O.R., 10-2:124.

12. WPI to Robertson, November 19, 1862, RSR; Wm. L. Clark letter in *MS*, June 18, 1862. The depot was completed in 1860. Jim Miles, *Piercing the Heartland: A History and Tour Guide of the Tennessee and Kentucky Campaigns* (Nashville: Rutledge Hill Press, 2000), 22. For references to Union soldiers running the trains immediately after the capture of Huntsville, see Wm. L. Clark letter in *MS*, April 30, 1862, and Vocke, "Military Achievements," 92.

13. Clark writes of the activity at Huntsville in *MS*, June 4 and June 18, 1862 ("lively"). Information about Larcombe's role is from Mitchel to Larcombe, April 25, 1862, in Mitchel Letter Book, RG 393-2, ser. 839, Cont. Commands. Larcombe was let go in early July since Innes did not consider "his services adequate to the pay he receiv[ed]." WPI to Yates, July 6, 1862, RLB. A few examples of dispatches concerning Yates's operation of the railroad are found in Mitchel's Letterbook and "Memoranda" of the 3rd Div. for May 1862, both RG 393-2, ser. 839, Cont. Commands. Also see WPI to Yates, July 6, 1862, RLB.

14. Yates to Mitchel, April 18 or 19 and June 17, 1862, in Ormsby M. Mitchel Papers, Generals' Papers; Wm. L. Clark letter in *MS*, June 4, 1862. The railroad lines from Nashville and Corinth had not yet been repaired, and steamers large enough to haul locomotives and cars could not ascend the Tennessee River far enough.

15. O.R., 10-1:877; Wm. L. Clark letter in *MS*, June 4, 1862; *DDA*, June 2, 1862.

16. Wm. L. Clark letter in *MS* June 4, 1862 ("suffocated"); *DDA*, June 2, 1862; O.R., 10-1:877, 10-2:291; *ROS* 43. Details on Harvey and Bates are found in their respective Civil War Pension Files. The injuries to Harvey and Bates were so serious that both were discharged by the surgeons within months.

17. Wm. L. Clark letter in *MS*, June 4, 1862.

18. John S. Daniel Jr., "Special Warfare in Middle Tennessee and Surrounding Areas, 1861–1862" (master's thesis, University of Tennessee, 1971), 85–89; O.R., 10-1:874–76. Capture of E. M. Mitchel is in Mitchel, *Ormsby MacKnight Mitchel*, 263–65. Lieutenant Mitchel was exchanged for Col. John Morgan's younger brother, whom Mitchel had previously captured. Cooling, *Fort Donelson's Legacy*, 70–78, contains a good summary of the activities and organization of partisan rangers during the summer of 1862.

19. O.R., 10-2:165–66.

20. Wm. L. Clark letter in *MS*, May 28, 1862; Beatty, *Citizen-Soldier*, 108–9.

21. This account is from Canfield, *Twenty-First Ohio*, 45–46. Though no date is given, Canfield clearly implies that it happened early in Mitchel's occupation of northern Alabama.

22. Roy Morris Jr., "The Sack of Athens," *Civil War Times Illustrated* 25 (1986), 26–32; O.R., 10-2:290 ("cursed"). Some of the accounts of the attack at Limestone Creek mistakenly state that two men were burned alive.

23. O.R., 10-1:891–92, 10-2:178, 624; Welcher, *Union Army*, 2:196–97.

24. Interview with Lt. Lorenzo Mason, *DDA*, June 2, 1862. Further details have not been found, but Wulsin, *Story of the Fourth*, 128–29, recounts a similar incident along the Elk River on May 3 (with different troops) following the reoccupation of Athens.

25. Account of Crittenton's service is from William R. Plum, *The Military Telegraph during the Civil War in the United States*, 2 vols. (New York: Arno Press, 1974), 1:207–8; Wm. L. Clark letter in *MS*, May 28, 1862. See Plum, *Military Telegraph*, 1:106–16 for a review of the curious and confusing status of telegraph operators in the employ of the Union military during the war. Jason Newton Crittenton

generally went by Newton or J. Newton. Crittenton was captured in the fall of 1862 while on telegraph duty but was released shortly.

26. The role of the Union military telegraph in the West during this time is outlined in Plum, *Military Telegraph*, 1:207–15. Also see O.R., 10-2:620, for the vulnerability of Mitchel's couriers.

27. Accounts of the capture of the ten men vary by specific date and location. The most consistent sources, and those most relied upon, are Wm. L. Clark letter in *MS*, June 18, 1862; *DFP*, May 31, 1862; WPI to McCook, August 9, 1862, RLB; listing of paroled Michigan men at Portsmouth Grove, Rhode Island, printed in *DFP*, November 20, 1862; materials in CMSR files; James Boss to father, February 26, 1863, Boss Family Papers, Bentley Historical Library, University of Michigan (unless otherwise noted, all letters from Boss are in this collection); and CWPF. For some insight into the fate of Union prisoners taken from Mitchel's command during this time, also see O.R., 10-2:188, 585, 594, and Norman Niccum, ed., "Diary of Lieutenant Frank Hughes," *Indiana Magazine of History* 45 (1949). For more on the argument over sanctity of paroles issued by Morgan and others, see Graf and Hasking, *Andrew Johnson*, 5:399.

28. Charles Rice, *Hard Times: The Civil War in Huntsville and North Alabama* (Boaz, Ala.: Boaz Printing, 1994), 73–74, quoting the *Cincinnati Gazette* among others; O.R., 10-1:892–93, 10-2:570–71, 16-1:485, 16-2:17; Matthew C. Switlik, "Loomis' Battery: First Michigan Light Artillery, 1859–1865" (master's thesis, Wayne State University, 1975), 30–31. An account of the gunboat ambush from the Confederate side is found in John A. Wyeth, *With Sabre and Scalpel* (New York: Harper and Brothers, 1914), 171–76.

29. O.R., 10-2:282–83.

Chapter 7

1. O.R., 10-2:223–33, 237. For an excellent summary of Halleck's choices see McDonough, *War in Kentucky*, 30–42.

2. McDonough, *War in Kentucky*, 39–40.

3. Halleck to Buell June 2, 1862, in O.R., 10-2:244, 251–81, 628–33, 16-2:9.

4. Abstract from tri-monthly return, O.R., 16-2:5; McDonough, *War in Kentucky*, 68–69.

5. A good summary of the difficulties of supplying Buell's army is in Darr Testimony, O.R., 16-1:602–20. Lt. Col. Francis Darr was Buell's chief of commissary. Despite its railroad connections, Union efforts to supply Buell's forces by railroad via Corinth were largely unsuccessful due to destroyed bridges, poor management, and a lack of engines and rolling stock. For more on this theme, see testimony in O.R., 16-1 of Innes (249), Wm. S. Smith (390–91), and Darr (604, 609–10).

6. McDonough, *War in Kentucky*, 33. See Charles Dana Gibson and E. Kay Gibson, *Assault and Logistics: Union Army Coastal and River Operations, 1861–1866, The Army's Navy Series* (Camden, Maine: Ensign Press, 1995), 612–17, for a good summary of the role of the western river systems in Union movements and supply efforts.

7. O.R., 10-2:77, 237, 628. In his communication to Halleck, Buell outlined Smith's experience in railroad engineering and called him "an officer of remarkable industry and energy."

8. O.R., 10-2:633, 16-1:390, 16-2:12, 52-1:253. There is nothing to identify whether a regiment was ever detailed from Hurlbut's command. The only other reference to the composition of McPherson's engineer Brigade is in Dyer, *Compendium*, 1:486, which includes only the Missouri and Michigan regiments. Dyer erroneously states that the Michigan regiment remained attached to McPherson's brigade beyond the end of June.

9. Barker, Kimball, Stearns, Rolison, and Lowe diaries; JWS to wife, June 6, 1862; WPI to McPherson, June 30, 1862, RLB; Guy Gilbert to sister, *FWC*, July 26, 1862 ("showed"). The movements of the Michigan Engineers across northern Alabama can be followed in O.R.A., 149.

10. Barker, Stearns, Kimball, and Lowe (who was in the same eating mess as Bellamy and Coon) diaries; JWS to wife, June 6 and 13, 1862; Graves to wife, August 2, 1862. Though Confederate deserters continued to come into camp at Bear Creek throughout the next few days, only Graves's account claims that the bushwhackers were ever caught and punished.

11. The Bear Creek Bridge was destroyed by the Fourth Illinois Cavalry and Fry's brigade of Sherman's Fifth Division, Army of the Tennessee; O.R., 10-1: 644–45.

12. For a description of bridge construction in the U.S. before the Civil War see Llewellyn N. Edwards, *A Record of History and Evolution of Early American Bridges* (Orono, Maine: University Press, 1959), and American Society of Civil Engineers, *American Wooden Bridges* (New York: American Society of Civil Engineers, 1976). Two important contemporary accounts are Herman Haupt, *General Theory of Bridge Construction* (New York: D. Appleton, 1851), and Squire Whipple, *A Work on Bridge Building . . .* (Utica, N.Y.: H. H. Curtiss, 1847). Also see definition in Shiman, "Engineering Sherman's March," 697 ("natural").

13. On use of temporary bridges, see for example, Dunnavant, *Railroad War*, 16–17. Information about trestle bridge use is from Herman Haupt, *Military Bridges, with Suggestions of New Expedients and Constructions for Crossing Streams and Chasms . . .* (New York: D. Van Nostrand, 1864): 8–9 ("not required" and "preferable"). Also see George W. Cullum, *Systems of Military Bridges* (New York: D. Van Nostrand, 1863), 140–41, for conditions where a trestle bridge could be used instead of a more permanent structure: "Trestles should be simple, that any pontonier-carpenter can frame them; quickly made, for in war delays are dangerous; and solid, for accidents are serious, and trestles are the most liable of all military bridges to break down." Francis T. Miller, ed., *The Photographic History of the Civil War*, 10 vols. (New York: Review of Reviews, 1911), 5:280 ("beanpoles"). Haupt's pioneering work in Virginia is best described in Francis A. Lord, *Lincoln's Railroad Man: Herman Haupt* (Rutherford, N.J.: Farleigh Dickinson University Press, 1969).

14. General description in this and the following paragraphs are drawn from Haupt, *Military Bridges*, 9–13, 60–70; Cullum, *Military Bridges*, 141–44; and Shiman, "Engineering Sherman's March," 696 ("deck").

15. Cullum, *Military Bridges*, 140–50; Haupt, *Military Bridges*, 60–70.

16. For efforts to design simple structures, see Haupt, *Military Bridges*, 60.

17. ROE June 1862; WPI to McPherson, June 30, 1862, RLB; Lowe, Stearns, Barker, and Kimball diaries of. The Record of Events also identifies work at the small bridge over Buzzard Roost Creek, a tributary of Bear Creek, at about this time, but no other sources provide more information. The bridge would have been about midway between Bear Creek and Cherokee Station (present-day town of Buzzard Roost).

18. O.R., 16-2:11–12; Kimball, Lowe, Fox, and Stearns diaries; Calkins to wife, June 14, 1862; "E." [member of Thirteenth Michigan] letter in *DFP*, June 27, 1862; WPI to McPherson June 30, 1862, RLB.

19. Movement of the five companies is in Barker, Rolison, and Fox diaries and JWS to wife, June 16 and 22, 1863. Bridge measurements are from ROE, June 1862.

20. Discussion of bridges in general is from WPI to McPherson June 30, 1862, RLB, and Welcher, *Union Army*, 2:627. Description of Town Creek is from Kimball Diary, and Spring Creek is from Fox and Barker diaries. Mallet's Creek is mentioned in WPI to McPherson June 30, RLB, but is not among the bridges listed in ROE; it is shown on O.R.A., 149, just west of Hillsborough. Bridges over Trinity Creek and Limestone Creek are both included in ROE but not in the other sources. Trinity was located six or eight miles west of Decatur on the Memphis and Charleston; O.R., 16-1:820, 825; O.R.A., 118:1 and 24:3. There is no specific mention of a crossing named Trinity in a report of Union bridge defenses in O.R., 16-1:824–26, though Confederate accounts in O.R., 16-2:842, indicate that Union troops were fortifying "at Town Creek, Mallett's Creek, Fox's Creek and Trinity."

21. O.R., 16-2:10; dimensions of Elk River bridge are from O.R., ser. 3, 5:938–40. It should be noted that there were two important railroad bridges over the Elk. The bridge along the Nashville and Chattanooga was seventy-seven or seventy-eight miles south of Nashville between Tullahoma and Decherd. The Nashville and Decatur crossing over the Elk was ninety-two or ninety-three miles south of the city. During the war, the Michigan Engineers repaired both at various times.

22. O.R., 16-2:17–18, 133; ROE for June, July, and August 1862; Wm. L. Clark letters in *MS*, June 25 and July 16, 1862; Mitchel to Anderson, June 27, 1862, and Mitchel to Crittenton June 29, 1862, both in RG 393-2, ser. 899, Cont. Commands. Dimensions of Widow's Creek Bridge are from O.R., ser. 3, 5:935–36. There is some confusion about which Crow Creek Bridge north of Stevenson was repaired. Mitchel's order states Crow Creek Bridge "north of Stevenson," which he also states is "Crow Creek No. 2," while ROE states Crow Creek No. 1, which was actually eighteen miles north of that point and the northernmost of at least eleven railroad bridges spanning the meandering creek north of Stevenson. A listing of the bridges with dimensions is in O.R., ser. 3, 5:935–36; Crittenton's men probably worked on bridge no. 10 or 11 from this list.

23. Graves to wife, June 23, 1862; WPI to McPherson, December 2, 1862, RLB; Wells CWPF. There is no record of whether Innes's request was ever approved. Within two weeks of Innes's letter, Walker was discharged for his disabilities after several months of hospitalization. Wells recovered in Michigan

sufficiently to serve out his enlistment, eventually winning a commission as second lieutenant. Innes had also tried in August to get army-contracted civilian railroad employee pay for all of the men in his regiment who were detailed to serve under McPherson's command operating the trains; see WPI to McPherson, August 12, 1862, RLB.

24. Smith report to Buell, from *DFP*, July 13, 1862; Fox, Kimball, and Barker diaries. Reference to Smith's investigation is in *GR Eagle*, June 25, 1862. Though the engineers were under McPherson's command at this time, there is no evidence that he played any role in the pay dispute during the month. Most likely, the order to Buell to investigate the matter predated the reassignment of Innes's regiment away from the Army of the Ohio, which would also explain Smith's role. There is no evidence that Companies A and K, still attached to Mitchel's division and serving in northern Alabama, were included in the investigation.

25. WPI to Col. Stanley Mathews, March 26, 1862, RLB (Estabrook and another man turned over to Mathews by Innes); JWS to Wilder, June 22, 1862 (attached to letter of March 10, 1862). "In arrest since April in Nashville" in Monthly Return for May and June 1862. Sligh misidentified Private Estabrook as "Westover." For more on the Estabrook connection and biographical information on Joseph Estabrook, see James E. Pittman to WPI, February 11, 1862, WPI CMSR; William Booth Estabrook, *Genealogy of the Estabrook Family . . .* (Ithaca, N.Y.: Andrus and Church, 1891), 82–83; *Mich. Biog.*, 1:277.

26. For Buckingham, see Whitelaw Reid, *Ohio in the War: Her Statesman, Her Generals, and Soldiers,* 2 vols. (New York: Moore, Wilstach, and Baldwin, 1868), 1:887–89, and Boatner, *Civil War Dictionary,* 95. Warner, *Generals in Blue,* 50, and Boatner date rank as brigadier general from July 1862, while Reid says April 1862. Buckingham's efforts against Innes are found in Buckingham to Buell May 17, 1862, and officer's casualty sheet with endorsement, both in WPI CMSR; SFO 75, Department of the Mississippi, May 26, 1862, RSR. Buell's quote, which Innes claimed was told to him by Fry, appears dramatized but is consistent with Buell's support for Innes; see WPI to Patterson, June 29, 1862, RLB. For example of rumors, see *MDE*, June 5, 1862 (citing information from the *Grand Haven Clarion*), and *Allegan Journal*, June 16, 1862.

27. Smith report to Buell, in *DFP*, July 13, 1862.

28. Smith report to Buell, in *DFP*, July 13, 1862.

29. Smith report to Buell, in *DFP*, July 13, 1862. On July 2 Smith succeeded Mitchel in command of the Third Division and then on July 11 was also assigned command of all guards on the NDRR, NCRR, and MCRR; Welcher, *Union Army,* 2:627.

30. WPI to Blair, June 29, 1862, RLB.

31. WPI to *DFP*, June 29, 1862, RLB; there is no indication that the letter was ever printed, though a copy of the report was published by the *DFP* on July 13, 1862, under the headline "Col. Innes Vindicated." Patterson information is from Baxter, *Grand Rapids,* 754.

32. JWS to wife, June 22, 1862.

33. Undated news clipping from the *Grand Rapids Weekly Enquirer*, probably late July, in SFP.

34. *Allegan Journal*, June 16, 1862. This account is not found elsewhere, but even if embellished it is indicative of the strong partisan overtones found throughout much of the controversy. Also see the *Allegan Journal*, July 21, 1862, which reviewed the men's grievances and concluded, "certainly just cause for complaint."

35. Withey to Robertson, RSR; *Mich. Biog.*, 2:464; *Allegan Journal*, June 16, 1862 ("Governor").

36. Mitchel to Buell, June 25, 1862, and Mitchel to Crittenton, June 29, 1862, both in Mitchel Letterbook, Ormsby M. Mitchel Papers, Generals' Papers. Mitchel was replaced on July 2, and there is no further record of Buell's response to Mitchel nor whether the men were actually paid the higher rate. In general, there was less agitation in Companies A and K over the pay issue than in the other companies. Wm. L. Clark letter in *MS*, June 25, 1862, stated that the two companies had received thirteen dollars per month recently. Though he shared his disappointment at the lesser amount, he did not indicate any mass refusal to accept the infantry pay.

37. SFO 136, Department of the Mississippi, July 1, 1862, in MEMRP; Fry to Wood, June 24, 1862, in O.R., 16-2:57–58. For Buell's efforts, see O.R., 16-2:67; Buell to Halleck and response, O.R., 16-2:76–77. McPherson remained in control of railroad repair around Corinth, including the MCRR to Decatur; see O.R., 17-2:78. For arrival at Huntsville, see Wm. L. Clark letter in *MS*, July 16, 1862. Order about Companies A and K is from SO 93, July 5, 1862, RG 393-1, ser. 944, Cont. Commands. This order gave Innes the discretion to keep the two companies on the same work but now under his control.

38. McDonough, *War in Kentucky*, 43–45; O.R., 16-2:903.

39. O.R., 16-1:248, 16-2:90; ROE, July 1862; Kimball, Stearns, and Rolison diaries. The Nashville and Decatur crossed Richland Creek four times in less than twenty miles, the three northernmost near Reynold's Station and within a length of track little more than three miles long. These three were probably all rebuilt by the Michigan Engineers, though sources refer to "Richland Creek #1," "Richland Creek #2," and "Reynold's Station bridge." Anderson testimony in O.R., 16-1:297, suggests that his civilian repair crews repaired Robertson's Fork and the Richland Creek bridge north of Reynold's Station. Buell had earlier ordered that civilian contractors be allowed to inspect and bid on repairing the bridges on the NDRR; see O.R. 10-2:628. The Richland Creek dimensions given in ROE and Innes are about double the length of any of the Richland Creek bridges listed in O.R., ser. 3, 5:938–40; the differences are unclear. Description of Columbia Duck River Bridge work is found in J. B. Anderson to Buell in O.R., 16-2:194 (bridge over Duck River washed out July 17) and WPI testimony (248), though Innes was not specific as to which two companies repaired the bridge over Duck River. Help from infantry details is in O.R. 16-1:90, 172.

40. Bridge descriptions are from ROE, July 1862; Wm. L. Clark letter in *MS*, August 13, 1862; and O.R., 16-1:248, 602. Information about work at the bridge and arrival and departure of companies is from Barker, Stearns, Kimball, and Fox diaries.

41. Rolison Diary; JWS to wife, July 13, 1862; Graves to wife, July 23, 1862. Innes later stated he had charge of work at Cowan Station Bridge; O.R., 16-1:248.

42. The debate over route and control is found in O.R., 16-2:4, 10–17. Also see letter dated June 20, 1862, in Anderson Family Papers. References to Yates's position in late July are found in SO 113 (July 25) and SO 117 (July 29), Army of the Ohio, RG 393-1, ser. 944, Cont. Commands. Also see Yates, "Military History."

43. Stearns, Kimball, and Fox diaries for July 1, 1862, all contain comments about the mystery, which were appended later. Court-Martial Case Files, Records of the Judge Advocate General's Office, RG 153, File LL110, NARA, courtesy of The Index Project (hereafter cited as CMCF).

44. McDonough, *War in Kentucky*, 48–53; O.R., 16-1:607.

45. Information about Clark is from CMSR, which states the attack was along the MCRR, and Desc. Roll, which states it was along the NCRR. Clark was discharged in October as the result of his wounds. Information about Glover is from CMSR; Kimball and Stearns diaries, August 18, 1862; SO 74, August 16, 1862, ROB; CSPF. Glover remained in the hospital until his discharge for disability in December 1862 (Desc. Roll). Also see O.R., 17-2:184, for more on the frequent Confederate attacks on the MCRR in northern Alabama.

46. Guy Gilbert letter in *FWC*, July 26, 1862 ("protect").

47. "By an officer [not identified]" in *DFP*, July 30, 1862. An excellent description of the evolution of the soldiers' opinion of Buell is found in Mark Grimsley, *The Hard Hand of War: Union Military Policy Toward Southern Civilians, 1861–1865* (Cambridge: University Press, 1995), especially 61–66 and 79–85. Also see Stephen Engle, "Don Carlos Buell: Military Philosophy and Command Problems in the West," *Civil War History* 41 (1995): 89–115, and Prokopowicz, *All for the Regiment*, 123.

48. Graves to wife, August 2, 1862 ("miserable"); JWS to wife, July 13, 1862 ("blunder"). Sligh stated the Ohio regiment in question was the First. Also see "By an officer" in *DFP*, July 30, 1862, who is similarly critical of providing guards for the property of civilians who attacked Union troops by night.

49. JWS to wife, January 4 and July 27, 1862. Sligh does not name Hunton and the others; rather he uses the phrase "colonel and captains," indicating Lieutenant Colonel Hunton who commanded the battalion and the three company commanders. Other similar comments from Michigan Engineers appear in *FWC*, April 19, 1862, and *MS*, March 26, 1862. For views of Union soldiers in general, see Wiley, *Billy Yank*, 109–19, and Prokopowicz, *All for the Regiment*, 123–25.

50. Graves to wife, August 2, 1862.

51. Helpful reviews of pontoon bridges prewar and in the first years of the war include Shiman, "Engineering Sherman's March," 120–21, 151–53; M. J. McDonough and P. S. Bond, *Use and Development of the Ponton Equipage*, vol. 6 in *Professional Memoirs, Corps of Engineers, United States Army and Engineer Department at Large* (Washington, D.C.: Engineer School, 1914); Haupt, *Military Bridges;* J. C. Duane, *Manual for Engineer Troops* (New York: D. Van Nostrand, 1863), 17–33; and an article written by Barton S. Alexander that appeared in the *New York Herald* and is reprinted in Malles, *Bridge Building*, 289–93. Cullum, *Military Bridges*, contains a description of the India rubber pontoon bridge designed for the Mexican War as well as a review of the various means of crossing rivers that were under

consideration by the professional military engineers. Also see James C. Duane, Henry L. Abbot, and William E. Merrill, eds., *Organization of the Bridge Equipage of the United States Army . . .* (Washington, D.C.: Government Printing Office, 1870). This summary of Civil War experiences and lessons was written by three regulars who played prominent roles in wartime military engineering.

52. Morton testimony is in O.R., 16-1:722. Also see Morton to Totten, July 10, 1862, Records of the Office of the Chief of Engineers, RG 77, ser. 18, NARA (hereafter cited as OCE Records).

53. Arrival of companies is in Fox, Kimball, Stearns, Rolison, and Barker diaries. Innes's arrival in Stevenson is uncertain.

54. Test of Yates is described in O.R., 16-1:486–92. LR-Reg. mentions report by Yates on lumber for pontoons. In addition to the Michigan Engineers, Yates testified that men of the Tenth Wisconsin were detailed to run local mills. References to waiting for cut lumber are found in Stearns and Fox diaries and Yates testimony. Innes testified, "There was only one mill that could cut the long timber needed for the pontoons," but he might have been omitting the sporadic operation of the Paint Rock Mill; O.R., 16-1:248. Captain Mills of Company E faced a similar challenge one year later, and his report contains a great deal of detail on civilian-owned and -operated mills in the area; ser. 925, RG 393-1, Cont. Commands.

55. McDonough, *War in Kentucky*, 54–55; Fry to Capt. J. D. Bingham and response, O.R., 16-2:302. LR-Reg. has references to oakum and nails for pontoons. Buell to WPI, O.R., 16-2: 287 ("surprised"). Apparently the men did not start the actual assembly of the boats until August 11; see Stearns, Fox, and Barker diaries.

56. O.R., 16-2:317; SO 85, August 11, 1862, ROB. By August 18 one hundred pontoon boats had been assembled, lacking only the corking and floorboards, which could be done with two hours' notice. JMS to mother, August 18, 1862.

57. McDonough, *War in Kentucky*, 57–59, 100–101.

58. JMS to mother, August 18, 1862; Kimball Diary, August 17, 1862; O.R., 16-1:487; Michael Shoemaker, "The Michigan Thirteenth," *Michigan Pioneer and Historical Collection* 4 (1883), 146. Captured Michigan Engineers were Benjamin R. Rice of Company I and Daniel W. Moore of Company A. They were taken south, paroled at Vicksburg on September 1, and then sent north for formal exchange. CMSR, *ROS* 43, and Desc. Roll for Rice and Moore. Both Rice and Moore eventually rejoined their companies in the spring and served until the end of their three-year enlistments.

59. McDonough, *War in Kentucky*, 70–83; McPherson, *Battle Cry of Freedom*, 517; Kenneth Noe, *Perryville: This Grand Havoc of Battle* (Lexington: University Press of Kentucky, 2001), 31–36.

60. Welcher, *Union Army*, 2:629–30.

61. Location of Innes and five companies is from O.R., 16-2:376. These companies left Stevenson on August 22. Information about Company A is from O.R., 16-2:356; Fox Diary, August 18 and 21, 1862; and Kimball Diary, August 21, 1862. Information from Company E is from Fox Diary, August 19, 1862, and Lowe Diary, August 12–September 13, 1862 (single entry).

62. O.R., 16-1:142–47, 243. Morton's report for operations is in July 1862, ser. 18, OCE Records. Harker's brigade (Twentieth/Sixth Division) consisted

of the Sixty-fourth and Sixty-fifth Ohio, Thirteenth Michigan, and Fifty-first Indiana.

63. Shoemaker, "Michigan Thirteenth," 148–50, and O.R., 16-2:420. Description of destruction on the twenty-fourth is in Nevius to JWS, August 27, 1862. Evacuation of Fort McCook is from O.R., 16-1:887–89. Retention of two companies is from O.R., 16-2:432, 438, and Shoemaker, "Michigan Thirteenth," 153.

64. GO 107, August 28, 1865, ROB; Rolison Diary; Shoemaker, "Michigan Thirteenth," 154–55.

65. Plum, *Military Telegraph*, 1:282–85 ("orderly" on page 284). Crittenton reached Nashville safely but was captured on September 22 while under orders to report to General Buell. Plum, *Military Telegraph*, 1:291, and Wm. L. Clark letter in *MS*, October 8, 1862. He was paroled a few days later and returned to Union lines.

66. O.R., 16-2:451–52; Shoemaker, "Michigan Thirteenth," 153–60; JMS to JWS, September 11, 1862.

67. JMS to JWS, September 11, 1862; Shoemaker, "Michigan Thirteenth," 160–63. Sligh maintains that at least some of the pontoons had not been destroyed earlier and that the engineers were sent to finish the job on the August 31. Shoemaker is silent about the pontoons at this late date. Confederate accounts are equally unclear. See, for example, O.R., 16-2:783, 793, and O.R., Supplemental 3:256–59.

68. Shoemaker, "Michigan Thirteenth," 160–63; Calkins to wife, September 7, 1862; testimony of John C. Hagan in U.S. Congress, House, 40th Cong., 2nd sess., H. Rep. 3, serial 1357, 80–81 (hereafter cited as 40th Cong., H. Rep. 3).

69. JMS to JWS, September 11, 1862, and Shoemaker, "Michigan Thirteenth," 160–63.

70. Lowe Diary; Fox and Barker diaries, September 5, 1862. It is almost certain that Company E of the Michigan Engineers was among the troops who were evacuated on the morning of August 31 after destroying anything that might be of military value; see O.R., 16-2:477. Mills was in command of the company because Canfield had resigned and returned to Michigan in July. Fox Diary, July 17, 1862, and Desc. Roll; Monthly Return for August 1862, which lists Company E in Huntsville under Lieutenant Mills. Account of men left behind is from CMSR for Bishop and Wilcox and Bishop CWPF. Both were paroled and inside Union lines at Nashville within three weeks.

71. Controversy still rages about why Buell failed. While Halleck later denied requiring Buell to be supplied by the MCRR, he did not relieve Buell from the duty of repairing it between Corinth and Decatur until June 30; O.R., 16-1:12, 16-2:75. A sympathetic account of Halleck's actions is found in Ambrose, *Halleck*, 55–57, and Hattaway and Jones, *How the North Won*, 214–16. Among those critical of Buell is Kenneth P. Williams, *Lincoln Finds a General: A Military History of the Civil War*, 5 vols. (New York: Macmillan, 1949–59), 4:25–51. Most of Buell's decisions are strongly and logically defended in McDonough, *War in Kentucky*, 102–4; Chumney, "Don Carlos Buell," 98–101; and Noe, *Perryville*, 24–26. A thorough discussion of Buell's "rosewater" policy is found in McDonough, *War in Kentucky*, 97–99. Buell's own defense is found throughout the commission proceedings; see

O.R., 16-1:5–726, especially his statements found on pages 22–60. A recent study of Buell's record as army commander and his relationship with Halleck is found in Engle, "Don Carlos Buell," 90–115.

72. This argument draws largely from Shiman, "Engineering Sherman's March," 106–21, including "failure of engineering" (113) and "valiantly" (120).

73. Shiman, "Engineering Sherman's March," 106–21, including "little support" (108). In the Peninsular campaign, the Army of the Potomac had eighteen regular engineer officers, the battalion of regular army engineers, two New York regiments of volunteer engineers, and seven pontoon bridges with over fifteen hundred feet of bridging. As Shiman points out, at the same time in the West the combined Union Armies of the Ohio, the Tennessee, and the Mississippi had no regular engineer troops and only a small handful of regular engineer officers, two regiments and one company of volunteer engineers, and no pontoon equipage (106–8).

74. Wm. L. Clark letter in *MS*, December 10, 1862.

Chapter 8

1. Thorough assessments of Buell's decision not to contest south of Nashville are found in McDonough, *War in Kentucky*, 109–13, and Noe, *Perryville*, 50–59. Also see Welcher, *Union Army*, 2:630–31.

2. Kimball, Stearns, Fox, and Barker diaries; O.R., 16-1:249, 300. Engineers working at Manscoe Bridge account is from Innes test in O.R., 16-1:249; Anderson test in O.R., 16-1:300; Kerr, *Historical Development*, 28; Barker, Stearns, Kimball, and Fox diaries; and Graves to wife, August 25, 1862. Innes refers to the crossing as "Therman Cove Creek," a term not found elsewhere and inconsistent with the many other sources. There is some confusion about the proper name for the second bridge, since Innes refers to it as "Pilot Knob Bridge" and Anderson as "bridge over Station Camp Creek at Pilot Knob." A valuable source is Louisville and Nashville Railroad, Office of the Chief Engineer, *Main Stem, Louisville and Nashville Railroad* (Louisville: Louisville and Nashville Railroad, 1884) (hereafter cited as LNRR 1884 Profile). A copy of this rare title is in the possession of the Elkstrom Library, University of Louisville, and was brought to the author's attention by railroad historian Charles B. Castner. This profile of the road has bridges over Station Camp Creek Nos. 1, 2, and 3 over a seven-mile stretch: No. 1 two miles north of Gallatin, No. 2 two miles south of Gallatin, and No. 3 another three miles further south at "Pilot Knobs." This is consistent with the crossings for "East Station Camp Creek" as outlined in O.R.A., 150, though Pilot Knob is not identified on this O.R.A. map. According to LNRR 1884 Profile, Station Camp 3 at Pilot Knob was nine miles north of Manscoe and two miles north of Saundersville, consistent with the various Michigan Engineer accounts for the work done September 5–8.

3. Lowe, Rolison, and Fox diaries; Shoemaker, "Michigan Thirteenth," 163–65; ROE-regiment for August 1862; Allen Campbell to brother, September 8, 1862, Campbell Family Papers, Michigan State University Archives and Historical Collections (unless otherwise noted, all Campbell letters—of both Allen and Alex—are in this collection); WPI to Robertson, November 19, 1862.

4. O.R., 16-1:249; Rolison, Stearns, Fox, and Kimball diaries; Allen Campbell to brother, September 8, 1862; Welcher, *Union Army*, 2:631, and Kenneth Hafendorfer, *Perryville: Battle for Kentucky* (Utica, Ky.: McDowell, 1981), 23. Innes used the label "Alexander Creek" for the bridge location, a term not found in any other accounts or on contemporary maps. Other Michigan Engineer sources do not include any name identification for this bridge. It was almost certainly the crossing identified in LNRR 1884 Profile as Station Camp Creek No. 2. The profile locates Station Camp No. 2 three miles north of Station Camp No. 3 and a little more than two miles south of Gallatin, consistent with this location.

5. Kimball, Stearns, Barker, and especially Fox diaries; O.R., 16-1:159–60.

6. JMS to mother, September 11, 1862. Sligh had remained at Stevenson with Companies C and K until its evacuation.

7. Work at Bowling Green description is from SO 83, 85, and 86, September 12–14, 1862, ROB; Barker, Stearns, Lowe, Kimball, and Fox diaries; Alex Campbell to brother Arthur, September 12, 1862; and O.R., 16-1:250.

8. McDonough, *War in Kentucky*, 157; Noe, *Perryville*, 68–70; Welcher, *Union Army*, 2:631.

9. McDonough, *War in Kentucky*, 158–81. Discussion of Michigan Engineers at Munfordville drawn from *ROS* 43 and Desc. Roll; Fox Diary, September 19, 1862; Nevius to JWS, October 16, 1862; CMSR. Fox and Barker diaries for September 19, 1862, noted the passing of the paroled men.

10. McDonough, *War in Kentucky*, 172; Noe, *Perryville*, 71–74; Hafendorfer, *Perryville*, 41.

11. The argument that Buell moved from Bowling Green with the intention of bringing Bragg's army to battle and not to slip by to Louisville is convincingly developed in Hafendorfer, *Perryville*, 23, 32.

12. SO 87, September 16, 1862, ROB. For difficulties along the march, see particularly Fox Diary, September 17, and Kimball Diary, September 18, 1862.

13. O.R., 16-1:48, 101, 208.

14. Bragg's choices are discussed in detail in McDonough, *War in Kentucky*, 184–90, and Hafendorfer, *Perryville*, 40–45. Bragg is roundly condemned in Stanley F. Horn, *The Army of Tennessee* (Norman: University of Oklahoma Press, 1953), 169–72, who declared it "probably" the "greatest moral crisis" of the war. A recent backhanded slap of Buell is in Steven E. Woodworth, *Jefferson Davis and His Generals: The Failure of Confederate Command in the West* (Lawrence: University Press of Kansas, 2000): "All that was required of Buell was to do nothing, and that was something Buell did very well" (146). Contemporary criticism of Buell is found throughout the questioning of the Buell Commission in O.R., 16-1, while a contemporary defense of Buell is in Cist, *Army of the Cumberland*, 73–77.

15. O.R., 16-1:48–49; McDonough, *War in Kentucky*, 187; Hafendorfer, *Perryville*, 47, 51, 57–58. McDonough makes a compelling argument that Louisville had never been an objective of Bragg's move into Kentucky and that his decision to unite with Smith was a reflection on the problems of the divided Confederate command and not a failure of Bragg to complete his objectives.

16. Fox and Kimball diaries; Wm. L. Clark letter in *MS*, October 8, 1862.

17. JMS to mother, October 7, 1862; Lowe Diary; O.R., 16-1:514, 16-2:567–68.

18. Wm. L. Clark letter in *MS*, October 8, 1862; Graves to wife, September 26, 1862; Fox, Barker, and Kimball diaries.

19. Welcher, *Union Army*, 2:204–5, 639–40; Boatner, *Civil War Dictionary*, 642–43.

20. McDonough, *War in Kentucky*, 191, 196–97; Noe, *Perryville*, 93; Hafendorfer, *Perryville*, 58, 63–65; Alex Campbell to father, September 30, 1862.

21. Welcher, *Union Army*, 2:632; Robertson, *Michigan in the War*, 496.

22. McDonough, *War in Kentucky*, 200; Hafendorfer, *Perryville*, 81–83; Noe, *Perryville*, 125–27; Welcher, *Union Army*, 2:632.

23. Hafendorfer, *Perryville*, 85–88.

24. Fox and Barker diaries; George White to JWS, October 17, 1862; O.R., 16-2:578, 602; Noe, *Perryville*, 124–25.

25. Rolison Diary and Wm. L. Clark letter in *MS*, October 15, 1862; O.R., 16-2:560–61.

26. Stearns and Kimball diaries.

27. Welcher, *Union Army*, 2:633.

28. Hafendorfer, *Perryville*, 93; McDonough, *War in Kentucky*, 216. For example, on October 2 McCook reported to Thomas that his command had to move to a point five miles off his intended route in search for water; see O.R., 16-2:565. Crittenden's corps was delayed in arriving near Perryville on the eighth because it had been forced to move off course in pursuit of water.

29. McDonough, *War in Kentucky*, 219–23, 227–33.

30. McDonough, *War in Kentucky*, 240–46.

31. McDonough, *War in Kentucky*, 236–37; Kimball Diary, October 8, 1862. Kimball states that the companies were in support of an "Indiana battery." Simonson's Indiana battery was present and actively engaged for most of the battle. Kimball might have been referring to a brief early assignment or, less likely, confused the Indiana gunners with those of Loomis's Michigan battery.

32. Welcher, *Union Army*, 2:636–37; O.R., 16-1:1040–41, 1045–47.

33. Welcher, *Union Army*, 2:636–37; O.R., 16-1:1040–41, 1045–47. Also see "General's Tour Guide," *Blue and Gray* 1, no. 2 (1997): 40, for the important role of the Russell house and high ground.

34. Welcher, *Union Army*, 2:636–37, O.R., 16-1:1040–41, 1045–47.

35. The most important accounts for understanding the role of Hopkins's battalion in the fighting are the reports in O.R., 16-1:1038–49; Testimony of Lt. Harry J. Chapel of Company H in Harris's court-martial file, CMCF; JMS to JWS, October 17, 1862; and Hafendorfer, *Perryville*, especially maps at pages 299, 313, and 333. Additional information is found in Yates, "Military History," and Kimball and Stearns diaries. There are no reports from Hopkins or Loomis in O.R., 16-2, but those by Cols. George Humphrey and Michael Gooding provide some helpful information on time and place. Chapel's account uniquely states the Michigan Engineers were ordered forward for the purposes of saving wounded Union soldiers being treated in the Russell house. James M. Sligh was not present at the battle but got his account from officers and men of the three companies.

The account of Rousseau with his hat on his sword is from Wm. L. Clark letter in *MS*, November 19, 1862. Clark was not present at the fight, but a similar account appears in J. J. Polk, *Autobiography of Doctor J. J. Polk*, quoted in Hafendorfer, *Perryville*, 311: "Rousseau at this point [after ordering Loomis's battery to open fire with canister] is reported to have ridden forward in front of his line and putting his hat on the sword point, held it high in the air and shouted to his men, 'my brave boys, I know you will never desert me in the day and hour of danger.'" The account is also included in William McDowell, "Reminiscences of Perryville" (Filson Club Historical Library), cited in Hafendorfer, *Perryville*, 311.

36. Of those struck on a specific side, all were hit on the left, suggesting that they may have been in the process of firing or loading when hit. At least three others were struck by projectiles from the back, suggesting they were moving to the rear when hit as the Union line fell apart. Details of wounded are from CWPF, and an incomplete list of wounded is found in *DFP*, October 18, 1862.

37. Hafendorfer, *Perryville*, 331–32, 336–41, 345–53.

38. O.R., 16-1:1033–34, 1042. The officers were Jackson, Terrill, and Webster killed, Lytle wounded and captured, and Gooding captured.

39. Monthly Return dated September 30, 1862, includes a total of 8 officers and 138 men present for duty in these companies, with another 62 left behind sick at various places including Louisville. The companies received replacements on October 1, but after accounting for those detailed, sick, etc., on October 8, the estimate of 150 seems reasonable. The only officer not present from the three companies was Capt. Marcus Grant of Company H, who was sick and rejoined October 15 according to Kimball and Stearns diaries. Lt. Solon E. Grant commanded Company H at Perryville; see testimony of Lt. Harry J. Chapel of Company H in Harris's court-martial file, CMCF. The Monthly Return for October 1862 shows the other officers in the three companies present for duty on September 30. Losses reported in O.R., 16-1:1034, are fourteen wounded and three captured. A list published in *DFP*, October 18, 1862, includes fourteen casualties by name, though two are in conflict with other sources. Regimental records suggest that the tally of fourteen wounded and three captured is accurate. Accounts of the night after the fight are from Kimball and Stearns diaries.

40. O.R., 16-1:489. Position is from Yates, "Military History," and map is in Hafendorfer, *Perryville*, 349. McDonough, *War in Kentucky*, 304–5.

41. The Monthly Returns for September and October are incomplete on the arrival of the new recruits. Only Companies A, recipient of eighteen recruits in September, and H, with twenty during October, are noted in the records. Other sources, however, provide a more complete picture. For example, the information in the Harris court-martial file suggests that the Company H recruits joined at Louisville on October 1. Company C reported only one recruit in each of the two months, yet the information in the John Weissert letters (Bentley Historical Library, University of Michigan; unless otherwise noted, all Weissert letters are in this collection) and CMSR for the Hastings recruits makes it clear that most of the twenty-some September Hastings recruits for that company were in the ranks at Perryville. For more on the arrival of new recruits while at Louisville, see Fox Diary, September 30 and October 3, 1862. Harris information is from CMCF and

Kimball Diary, August 16, 1864. Harris unsuccessfully appealed the life sentence; MEMRP, with documents dated February and March 1865. His captain opposed the appeal, stating, "I know of no man so worthy and well adapted to a life sentence on Dry Tortugas."

42. Noble and Eddy details are from CMSR. Kimball, Conley, and Harrison details are from CWPF. Grosevenor details are from *The City of Grand Rapids and Kent County, Michigan* (Logansport, Ind.: Bowen, 1900), 724–25.

43. Weissert to wife, October 17, 1862.

44. McDonough, *War in Kentucky*, 305–9; Hafendorfer, *Perryville*, 369–79; Stearns and Kimball diaries.

45. Stearns, Rolison, Fox, and Kimball diaries.

46. Account of captured men is from *ROS* 43 and Desc. Roll. Background on Lawrenceburg area October 8 and 9 is from George White to JWS, October 17, 1862, and reports and correspondence in O.R., 16-1:1134–36 ("presume" on 1134) and 16-2:601, 923–27. The four might have later been among several former POWs from the regiment who were unwilling to rejoin it. According to one account, they "demanded of the military authorities at Louisville to show them the papers that they were exchanged and they being unable to do it, refused to take arms and were accordingly sent to Camp Chase." JWS to Joseph R. Smith, January 30, 1863, in MEMRP.

47. Fox, Kimball, Barker, and Rolison diaries; George White to JWS, October 17, 1862.

48. Welcher, *Union Army*, 2:641.

49. Fox, Kimball, Stearns, Rolison, and Barker diaries; JMS to mother October 26, 1862; James Greenalch to wife, October 23, 1862, in Mellon Knox Jr., ed. "Letters of James Greenalch," *Michigan History* 44 (1960): 194–95 (unless otherwise noted, all letters from Greenalch are from this source).

50. Graves to wife, November 1, 1862.

51. O.R., 16-2:621–27, 636–39; Welcher, *Union Army*, 2:20, 377; Fox and Kimball diaries, November 2, 1862; Boatner, *Civil War Dictionary*, 708.

52. Barker, Stearns, Kimball, Fox, and Rolison diaries. Mitchellville description is from Rosecrans to Halleck, O.R., 20-2:9; Walter T. Durham, *Rebellion Revisited: A History of Sumner County, Tennessee, from 1861 to 1870* (Gallatin, Tenn.: Sumner County Museum Association, 1982), 109 ("unparalleled activity"); and Azra Bartholomew (Twenty-first Michigan) to wife, November 6, 1862, Christman Collection, Archives of Michigan. The town of Mitchellville was a short distance west of the railroad station of the same name, along the main Bowling Green to Nashville road; see O.R.A., 30:2. November 5 incident account is from O.R., 20-2:5–7, 12–13.

Chapter 9

1. Halleck to Rosecrans, O.R., 16-2:640–41.

2. Welcher, *Union Army*, 2:807–8.

3. Welcher, *Union Army*, 2:807–8.

4. O.R., 20-2:5–6, 9, 14; Albert Fink, *Chief Engineer's Report, Louisville and Nashville Railroad, 1862–63*, 31. Charles Castner, railroad historian with the University of Louisville's Elkstrom Library, brought this and other valuable railroad sources to the author's attention.

5. "An Act to define the Pay and Emoluments of Certain Officers of the Army, and for other Purposes" in Statutes at Large, 37th Congress, 2nd session, chapter 200. Section 20 specifically addressed volunteer engineers. The House Military Affairs Committee added language about volunteer engineers to an existing Senate bill on army pay, and the full House accepted the amendment without dissent on June 11, 1862. The Senate adopted the bill on July 17, 1862. See *Congressional Globe, 1861–62*, 2663.

6. Larned to Goddard, November 25, 1862, and attached Larned to Lorenzo Thomas, October 17, 1862, with endorsements, in MEMRP. Graves to wife, September 16, 1862; WPI to McCook, November 11, 1862, RLB; Graves to wife, October 13, 1862 ("disappointed"). Fox Diary, September 29, 1862, states "paymaster is waiting for special instructions about paying our regiment."

7. WPI to Stanton October 13, 1862, RLB; Petition (unsigned) to McCook, November 9, 1862, RLB.

8. Reprinted in *DFP*, November 7, 1862. It is not clear when the *Journal* published the letter or who signed it.

9. JWS to Blair, November 8, 1862, JWS to "Congressman [Kellogg]" on about the same date, Paymaster General to Honorable Kellogg, November 18, 1862, all in SFP. Sligh's letters appear to be drafts, but the latter one is referenced in the paymaster's response to Kellogg's. Presumably the one to Blair was also sent, but even if not, it reflects the frustration felt among the officers and their belief that only intervention by political figures could force the War Department to take action.

10. Stearns Diary, November 8, 1862 ("excitement" and "strike"); Weissert to wife, November 11, 1862; JMS to father, November 16 and 26, 1862; George White to JWS, December 9, 1862; Nevius to JWS, November 28, 1862; Graves to wife, November 28, 1862. Most accounts place the number of mutineers at between 110 and 120, while the Fox and Stearns diaries claim 134 and 200, respectively. The Monthly Return for December 1862, in a list entitled "Absent Enlisted Men Accounted for by Name," identifies 101 men as arrested on November 10 and still in confinement. At least 7 others were tried and acquitted and are named in WPI to Col. John A. Martin, December 26, 1862, RLB. Martin, commander of the Eighth Kansas, was serving as provost marshal in Nashville.

11. This summary is based largely on the itemized list of mutineers.

12. Review of Prall's Company I recruits is from descriptive rolls for that company. At least four more of the original Prall recruits were still on the rolls but absent in hospitals at the time of the mutiny.

13. Fox's account is from his diary for November 9, 1862.

14. Data from *ROS* 43 contrasted with listing in Monthly Return, December 1862.

15. Ibid.

16. WPI to McCook, November 11, 1862, RLB. At this time McCook was commanding the right wing of the army, and the regiment might have been formally attached to it. Perhaps Innes was merely drawing upon his acquaintance with McCook, dating back to the regiment's first weeks in Kentucky. A frustrated Colonel Serrell of the First New York made an almost identical comment to his commander six months earlier: "Either we must be paid or disbanded." See Serrell to Quincy Gillmore, March 6, 1862, RG 94, Regimental Letter Book, First New York Engineers, Regimental Papers, Records of the Adjutant General, NARA.

17. ROE states there were "three bridges" but gives no names. WPI to Robertson, November 19, 1862, RSR, states the Michigan Engineers repaired five bridges at this time. Also see Kerr, *Historical Development*, 30–34, for background on Confederate destruction on this section of the road built earlier by Buell's men and the difficulty of operating the line even after the bridges and tunnel had been repaired. Fox Diary; JMS to father, November 16, 1862; Graves to wife, November 16, 1862; Weissert to wife, November 11 and 16, 1862. There is confusion about the proper names for the two bridges over Station Camp Creek. The first one worked on is described by James M. Sligh as "first bridge this side of Pilot Knob." The second is labeled "West Station Camp Creek" by Fox and stated by Graves to be three miles from Gallatin and the same bridge they were working on September 9 when ordered to Bowling Green. These descriptions, and the other information in the accounts, make it clear that they were working on two crossings over Station Camp Creek.

18. Kimball, Stearns, and Fox diaries; Nevius to JWS, November 28, 1862. Numbers vary from fifteen (Kimball) up to forty (Nevius).

19. Specific reference to Mill Creek No. 2 is in ROE, November 1862. Account of work is from Stearns Diary and Abram F. Conant to wife, November 23 and 29, 1862, Abram F. Conant Letters, Library of Congress (unless otherwise noted, all letters from Conant are in this collection). Information on the crossing is from O.R.A., 30:2, 31:2, and Wright's report in O.R., ser. 3, 5:935–36. For railroad ties, see WPI to JB Anderson, January 5, 1863, RLB. The LNRR was constructed with about twenty-seven hundred ties to the mile.

20. Specific location of camp is from ROE, December 1862; WPI to Garesche, December 11, 1862, RLB. Orders had actually been received to move on December 11, but the wagons were out in search of forage. Pay information is from Kimball, Fox, and Roseberry (who alone says the seventh) diaries; *Revised Regulations*, 524–26; Conant to wife, December 9, 1862 ("great rejoicing"); Stearns Diary, December 8, 1862 ("manifested"). The officers were also paid up through August, see Fox Diary, December 8, 1862. Fox received $831.70. The *DFP* reported optimistically on December 20, 1862, that with the pay issue resolved, "Innes was beloved by his whole command." The paper was reporting on the arrival of Lt. Clement F. Miller in that city and was probably basing its assessment on his opinion.

21. JMS to mother, November 26, 1862; Greenalch to unidentified, December 23, 1862; Conant to wife, November 29, 1862; GO 17 in O.R., 20-2:61–62. Rosecrans's order was consistent with directions received from Halleck upon taking command; O.R., 16-2:641. See Grimsley, *Hard Hand of War*, 101–5, for the change in policy following Rosecrans's replacement of Buell.

22. Account of the November 24 incident is from JMS to father, November 26, and to mother, December 14, 1862; Stearns Diary, November 26, 1862; Weissert to wife, December 9, 1862; Conant to wife, November 29, 1862; *ROS* 43; and Desc. Roll. There is no record that the men were punished for the incident. Van Horn [or Vanhorn] and Birdsall returned to the regiment from parole camp in 1863 and were discharged in June 1865; Buck deserted in December 1862 from the parole camp. CMSR for these three men indicate that they were taken between December 25, 1862, and January 10, 1863, near Murfreesboro, but this is contradicted by contemporaneous accounts by other soldiers.

23. O.R., 20-2:49. Innes's order is from GO 112, November 26, 1862, ROB.

24. Greenalch to unidentified, December 23, 1862; Graves to wife, December 25, 1862; Weissert to wife, December 17, 1862; Conant to wife, December 21, 1862; Kimball and Roseberry ("such fine drilling") diaries, December 20, 1862; GO 131, December 15, 1862, ROB. The exceptions to this stay in camp were Companies F and B, who in response to orders had moved from Mill Creek to Nashville on the twenty-third. The two-company detachment was assigned to guard the headquarters and black working parties of the Department's Pioneer Brigade laboring on the fortifications of Nashville.

25. Trial and waiting for sentence account is from JMS to JWS, November 26, 1862; WPI to JWS, November 17, 1862; JMS to mother, December 14, 1862; and George H. White to JWS, December 9, 1862 ("down hearted").

26. *DFP*, December 9, 1862. This Democratic newspaper laid most of the blame at the feet of the all-Republican Michigan congressional delegation, though the paper did note that legislation passed in July seemed to authorize pay for volunteer engineers.

27. Information about those too sick to stand trial is from WPI to McCook, December 26, 1862, WPI to Martin, January 24, 1862, and WPI to Lt. R. H. Long, commanding Barracks No. 2, February 21 and 27, 1863, all in RLB. It is not clear what eventually happened to these men. Information on acquittal is from WPI to Martin, December 24 and 26, 1862, and WPI to James Flynn, January 21, 1863, all in RLB; GO 139, December 26, 1862, ROB.

28. WPI to Provost Marshall, Nashville, January 21, 1863, RLB; response January 24, 1863, in MEMRP; Rolison Diary; WPI to Joseph Steg, January 31, 1863, RLB; *DFP*, February 4, 1863 (based on interview with Captain George Lane). A review of the CMSR for the men identified as mutineers shows most were back with the regiment by February 5, 1863. Not all of those reduced in rank were reinstated, but the reason for the difference is not clear. Likewise, some men were recorded as in arrest in November after the mutiny but remained present with the regiment while the mutineers were confined in Nashville. Fox claimed that all the mutineers, save those too sick to leave Nashville, were back with the regiment by February 10; Fox to wife, February 10, 1863.

29. John B. Williams, *Leaves from a Soldier's Diary* (Philadelphia: Privately printed, 1869), 102 ("leaky," "filled," and "smokehouse"), and Rolison Diary. The Nashville provost marshal reported that in early January there were 110 Michigan Engineers and over 300 of the Pennsylvania troopers in the workhouse; see Martin to Major Davis, O.R., 20-2:362–63. The men from the Fifteenth Pennsylvania

("Anderson Troop") Cavalry were confined following a late December mutiny. Also see Charles H. Kirk, *History of the Fifteenth Pennsylvania Volunteer Cavalry . . .* (Philadelphia: N.p., 1906), 178–81. Withholding mail denial is in WPI to A. O. Currier, January 15, 1863, RLB.

30. WPI to Lt. R. H. Long, commanding Barracks No. 2, February 21 and 27, 1863, RLB; also see JMS to JWS, November 26, 1862. Estabrook eventually returned to the regiment and was discharged at the expiration of his three-year enlistment. Regimental records are silent about anything further on Estabrook and the trial.

31. Christmas Day description is from Conant to wife, December 25, 1862; Graves to wife, December 25, 1862. Bridge repair information is from RG 393-1, ser. 908, Cont. Commands, and Fox Diary. The timber was already prepared according to GO 140, December 27, 1862, ROB.

32. GO 140, December 27, 1862, ROB; Fox, Kimball, and Roseberry diaries; Garesche to WPI, RG 393-1, ser. 908, Cont. Commands.

33. O.R., 20-2:256–58, 272; Fox, Roseberry, and Kimball diaries. P. V. Fox states that the four companies that stayed with Hunton were D, E, G, and K; Roseberry (D) states that his company remained with Hunton.

34. Kimball, Stearns, and Fox diaries; Weissert to wife, December 28 and 29, 1862.

Chapter 10

1. JMS to mother and father, January 6, 1863; Fox and Stearns diaries; letter from "An Engineer," in *FWC*, February 7, 1863; Wm. L. Clark letter in *MS*, January 21, 1863; O.R., 20-1:651; Edwin E. Winters account in *Grand Army Sentinel* (Nashville, Tennessee), January 5, 1886 (hereafter cited as Winters, *Grand Army Sentinel*). In general, when accounts conflict, Innes's report published in the O.R. has been considered the most accurate; almost identical versions of his report are also found in *DFP*, January 16, 1863, and in the RLB. The three accounts written by "An Engineer," Winters, and Clark are the most complete, including detail not found elsewhere. Since Winters's account was written nearly twenty-five years later, and because it contains some quotes that stretch credibility, it has been used primarily to verify information found elsewhere, expand on incidents suggested in other accounts, and to further establish the position of the regiment and the direction of the Confederate attacks. When in conflict with the other two accounts, it has not been relied upon. The area between Nashville and Murfreesboro is outlined in maps accompanying the opposing commanders' reports; see O.R.A., 30:2, 31:2.

2. *DFP*, January 27, 1863 ("throngs"); Winters, *Grand Army Sentinel;* Wm. L. Clark letter in *MS*, January 21, 1863; Weissert to wife, [January 1863]; Fox Diary; Conant to wife, January 9, 1863; O.R., 20-1:959.

3. Winters, *Grand Army Sentinel;* Wm. L. Clark letter in *MS*, January 21, 1863; *FWC*, February 7, 1863; Graves to wife, January 9, 1863; Conant to wife, January 9, 1863. The best map reference is O.R.A., 31:2.

4. JMS to mother and father, January 6, 1863; Conant to wife, January 9, 1863; Graves to wife, January 9, 1863; Winters, *Grand Army Sentinel; FWC*, February 7, 1863; Wm. L. Clark letter in *MS*, January 21, 1863.

5. O.R., 20-1:651; Winters, *Grand Army Sentinel;* Wm. L. Clark letter in *MS*, January 21, 1863; Fox Diary; Sligh, *Michigan Engineers*, 14; James G. Genco, *Arming Michigan's Regiments, 1862–1864.* (N.p.: J. G. Genco, 1982), 73. The Monthly Return for December 31, 1862, lists twenty-six officers and 443 men present for duty, but Innes stated he took only 391 effectives into the fight. Presence of the army teamsters is reported in Roseberry Diary; Winters, *Grand Army Sentinel;* and Clark letter in *MS*, January 21, 1863. Fox Diary includes the estimate that 100 "stragglers" joined the engineers behind the barricades and that four of them were wounded in the fight. Monthly Returns for September through December and Desc. Rolls indicate that at least 150 recruits were sent to the regiment within the four months preceding the fight at Lavergne, but many were delayed en route and others were sent back to rear area hospitals shortly after their arrival. It is reasonable to estimate that about 100 of the 1862 recruits were with Innes at Lavergne on January 1, 1862.

6. *ROS* 43; Desc. Roll; JMS to mother and father, January 6, 1863; reference to report on casualties by O'Donoughue, January 6, 1863, in LR-Reg. 493. According to regimental records, Major Hopkins and Captains Sligh, Mills (acting), and Lane were in Michigan, the first three on recruiting duty, the latter convalescing; *DFP*, January 6, 1863, however, includes a telegram from Lane dated January 3, 1863, from "Lagrange" [*sic*], which suggests he was not in Michigan. It is not clear who was commanding the few men from Company I in the fighting. Lieutenant Rhodes had been commanding Company I since July, vice Palmerlee, but was reported sick in Nashville as late as December 31, 1862. Surgeon DeCamp remained on assignment at Harrodsburg, Kentucky, and newly commissioned Asst. Surgeon Willard B. Smith was on his way from Michigan.

7. Edwin C. Bearss, "Cavalry Operations in the Battle of Stones River," *Tennessee Historical Quarterly* 19 (1960): 130–31; O.R., 20-1:643, 654–56.

8. Kimball Diary, January 1, 1863.

9. James D. Robinson to wife, January 6, 1863. His letter contains few details on the fight, leaving it to Captain Coffinberry to provide a full account when he reached Grand Rapids.

10. Conant to wife, January 9, 1863 ("dashing"); "B" letter in *DFP*, January 27; Winters, *Grand Army Sentinel; Monroe Evening Chronicle*, October 4, 1912; Wm. L. Clark letter in *MS*, January 21, 1863. Fox and Roseberry diaries estimate that the Confederate attacks on the wagon occurred at 2:00 P.M., as does Sligh in a letter to his parents, January 6, 1863.

11. JMS to mother and father, January 6, 1863; Conant to wife, January 9, 1863; Graves to wife, January 9, 1863, with reference to first mounted attempt after company was driven back.

12. O.R., 20-1:968; Fox Diary, January 1, 1863 ("whizzing"); Winters, *Grand Army Sentinel;* Wm. L. Clark letter in *MS*, January 21, 1863. The various accounts suggest that Pue was firing both shells and solid shot. Wharton's report indicates

that his mounted men had traded in their shotguns and "irregular" weapons just two days before for captured Union firearms "of a more approved nature," presumably rifled muskets or rifles that would have considerably improved their ability to inflict casualties on Innes's men from a safer distance.

13. O.R., 20-1: 968; Wm. L. Clark letter in *MS*, January 21, 1863 ("forming behind"); *FWC*, February 7, 1863; Winters, *Grand Army Sentinel*. The First Confederate included men from Kentucky, Tennessee, and Alabama. Wharton's assault might have also included the Fifty-first Alabama Partisan Rangers, detached from Wheeler's brigade; O.R., 20-1:964.

14. Winters, *Grand Army Sentinel*; Wm. L. Clark letter in *MS*, January 21, 1863; Conant to wife, January 9, 1863; JMS to mother and father, January 6, 1863.

15. JMS to mother and father, January 6, 1863; O.R., 20-1:651; Winters, *Grand Army Sentinel*; *FWC*, February 7, 1863; Graves to wife, January 9, 1863; Conant to wife, January 9, 1863; *DFP*, January 27, 1863. The loss of animals was reported in O.R., 20-1:228, 651. Details on the wounded are from *DFP*, January 16, 1863. Account of Clifton's close call is from Fox Diary, January 1, 1863; Clifton is not listed as wounded in the *DFP* account.

16. Winters, *Grand Army Sentinel*. Also see Kimball Diary, January 1, 1863, which reports that Mingo claimed before he died that Lieutenant Colonel Hunton shot him in the back during the fight because the private had sworn vengeance against the officer for "punishing him severely" for stealing whiskey from the sutler. There is nothing to verify this claim, though Mingo did die from a gunshot wound to the back (*DFP*, January 16, 1863, and CMSR). Charges had been leveled three weeks before that Mingo "did kick, strike, and abuse a team" (CMSR), though there is nothing further about the charges in general court-martial records and no mention of whiskey or theft.

17. Account of Confederates in Union overcoats is from Kimball Diary, January 1, 1863. Account of attack on Company D is from Winters, *Grand Army Sentinel*.

18. Kimball Diary, January 1, 1863.

19. Account is quoted in Robertson, *Michigan in the War*, 324. It is not clear who wrote the description (Robertson calls him a "correspondent"), and there is nothing in Robertson's archived notes to identify him.

20. Weissert to wife, January 1863, and January 4, 1863. The four men were Pvts. John Weissert, James and Watson Woodruff, and Mathias Reiser. Weissert's account places the picket some distance from regiment's position.

21. Account of Wright and Stanton is from WPI to Mrs. A. C. Wright, January 31, 1863, and WPI to Mr. H. H. Stanton, February 12, 1863, both in RLB. Wright died in captivity at Richmond on January 28, 1863, but Stanton returned to the regiment and served out his three-year term. Schermerhorn and others from *ROS* 43 and Desc. Roll. Company H men information is from Kimball Diary; the men taken prisoner were apparently Alva D. Welling and Alva Smith.

22. O.R., 20-1:65, 623–24, 634, 654–56; Bearss, "Cavalry Operations," 133–34. Dickinson's name is spelled in various forms, but this spelling is based on his clear signature on documents in his CMSR.

23. WPI to Minty, January 20, 1863, RLB; reports in O.R., 20-1:622, 628–29, 654–56. Dickinson and Newell state that they fought their way to Innes, omitting any repulse, return to Stewart's Creek, or later contact with Burke. Based on the greater detail in Burke's report, the strong opinions of Innes and other engineers against Dickinson, and Burke's overall performance, I have generally accepted Burke's report when there was conflict between his and those by Dickinson and Newell. Innes's letter to Minty identifies the party he sent for help as Riley and "my adjutant and quartermaster." Lieutenant Calkins was acting adjutant in the absence of Lt. Clement F. Miller on recruiting duty, and Lt. Henry F. Williams was probably already acting as quartermaster following the departure of R. S. Innes. Burke's account makes no mention of anyone but Riley.

24. O.R., 20-1:654–56, and WPI to Minty, January 20, 1863, RLB. Burke spells it "Reilly," but I have accepted Innes's spelling of "Riley." These two accounts are the only known information about the civilian Thomas Riley, who has proved elusive in further establishing his identity or background. Also see WPI report in O.R., 20-1:651, for reference to an unnamed messenger being sent to Burke for help and JMS to mother and father, January 6, 1863, for reference to an unnamed messenger making three trips to Burke. Riley might not have remained much longer, since six weeks later Innes obtained the services of local guide Joseph A. Fuller; letter of February 19, 1863, RLB.

25. *DFP*, January 17, 1863 ("frighten"). In general, Michigan Engineer accounts claim the defense of their position at Lavergne started a little after 2:00 P.M. and lasted for at least three hours. Various accounts of the demand for surrender and Innes's response are found in WPI report in O.R., 20-1:651; Wm. L. Clark letter in *MS*, January 21, 1863; Sligh, *Michigan Engineers*, 14; Graves to wife, January 9, 1863; Roseberry, Kimball (who claims four separate flags of truce were sent by Wharton), and Fox diaries; JMS to parents, January 6, 1863 (who also mentions that Innes asked for time to consider the demand and to give reinforcements more time to reach Lavergne); Conant to wife, January 9, 1863; Winters, *Grand Army Sentinel* (who places the flags apart, separated by several Confederate charges); *FWC*, February 7, 1863 (which has two flags coming twenty minutes apart before the third one with the request to bury the dead and rescue the wounded). Burford's role and name are from O.R., 20-1:982; undated [c. November 1885] newspaper clipping with Calkins Papers; *Grand Rapids Democrat*, August 3, 1893; and undated newspaper clipping with Kimball Diary. Spelling of Burford's first name is from Crute, *Confederate Staff Officers*, 206.

26. Account of arrival of Burke's men is from O.R., 20-1:654–56; Fox Dairy; and *FWC*, February 7, 1863. Winters's account contains a dubious claim that the relief of the engineers was led by Maj. Horace D. Grant of the Fourth Michigan cavalry, the brother of engineer Capt. Marcus Grant, but Major Grant was not with the Fourth Michigan Cavalry troopers who were present. *FWC*, February 7, 1863, claims that a company of the Fourth Michigan reached the barricade while the fighting was underway, but this is the only account of reinforcements reaching the regiment while still under fire and is confused with the troopers' later arrival.

27. Kimball Diary, January 1, 1863.

28. JMS letters to mother and father, January 6 and 26, 1863; Kimball Diary, January 2, 1863; Weissert to wife, January 4, 1863; Fox Diary, January 2, 1863; O.R., 20-1:656.

29. JMS to mother, January 26, 1863; Weissert to wife, January 4, 1863; Wm. L. Clark in *MS*, January 21, 1863; Fox, Stearns, and Kimball diaries; Charles W. Bennett, *Historical Sketches of the Ninth Michigan Infantry* (Coldwater, Mich.: Daily Courier Print, 1913), 29.

30. Bearss, "Cavalry Operations," 132, gives Innes credit for helping to save the larger wagon train that Zahm defended so valiantly farther north along the pike: "The presence of Col. Innes's command . . . at Lavergne probably saved Zahm's convoy" by keeping Wharton occupied while Wheeler fruitlessly tried to get through or around Zahm.

31. *DFP*, January 6, 1863 ("repulsed"), with capitalization as printed; this account was based on a telegram Captain Lane sent the paper dated January 3, 1863, which is included under the headline. In a later letter to Lorenzo Thomas, Rosecrans contrasted the defense of Lavergne with the "feeble" resistance offered at Brentwood Station in March 1863; O.R., 23-1:1117. Also see W. D. Bickham, *Rosecrans' Campaign with the Fourteenth Army Corps* (Cincinnati: Moore, Wilstach, Keys, 1863), 300–301; Fitch, *Army of the Cumberland*, 411–12; and James Gilmore [writing as Edmund Kirke], *Down in Tennessee and Back by Way of Richmond* (New York: Carleton, 1864), 39–43.

32. "Battle of Lavergne," Dr. and Mrs. Delmar Firme Collection, Western Michigan University Archives and Regional History Collections, Kalamazoo, Michigan. It is also found as a newspaper clipping with the Stearns Letters and contains the penciled notation "I was there."

33. Horace Greeley, *The American Conflict: A History of the Great Rebellion*, 2 vols. (Hartford, Conn.: O. D. Chase 1867), 2:281.

34. The surviving Michigan Engineers even invited Wheeler to their postwar reunions; see letters of J. D. Butler and Wheeler from 1898 and 1900 reprinted in unidentified news clippings found in Kimball Papers. Actual strength disparity was about three to one. Wharton's most powerful advantage was the two-gun section of artillery, not overwhelming numbers; O.R., 20-1:661, 674, 968.

35. McPherson, *Battle Cry of Freedom*, 574 ("moral crisis").

36. GO 4, January 11, 1863, ROB.

37. Sligh, *Michigan Engineers*, 16. His reported comment that "We don't surrender much" was simple and quotable. One post–World War II account of the Lavergne fighting even compared it with that given by Gen. Anthony McAuliffe at Bastogne ("Nuts"); see Jesse A. Remington, "Combat Engineers: Lavergne, Tennessee, 1863," *The Military Engineer* 52 (1960): 291.

38. O.R., 20-1:651, 969 ("considerable"); *FWC*, February 7, 1863; JMS to parents, January 6, 1863. In addition, Roseberry reported in his diary that "about fifty" dead Confederates were outside the barricade, with another eight (including one captain) captured. The Fifty-first Alabama, presumably detached from Wheeler's brigade and present at Lavergne, reported one killed and eleven wounded; O.R., 20-1:964. There are no casualty reports for the three regiments/battalions and one battery clearly identified by Wharton as being in the fight from his brigade.

39. Reiser incident account is from Weissert to wife, January 4, 7, 10, 28, and February 9, 1863 ("yesterday"). Information on casualties was gathered from *ROS* 43 and Desc. Roll, as well as various accounts cited earlier. *FWC*, February 7, 1863, and the official Union Return of Casualties in O.R., 20-1:215, report the loss as two dead, nine wounded, and five missing. *DFP*, January 16, 1863, includes a listing of the casualties by name with Innes's report, an attachment omitted from other accounts. According to information in *ROS* 43 and Desc. Roll, the wounded Michigan Engineers were evacuated to Nashville and Cincinnati within days. An interesting imprisonment account written by a member of the Fifteenth Pennsylvania Cavalry who was captured in the fighting near Lavergne is M. B. Colton, "Story of a Typical Capture, Imprisonment, and Exchange" in Kirk, *Fifteenth Pennsylvania*, 121–28. Colton's travels are similar to what is known of the imprisonment of the captured Michigan Engineers.

40. Graves to wife, January 24, 1863; *DFP*, January 27, 1863; Wm. L. Clark letter in *MS*, January 21, 1863; Winters, *Grand Army Sentinal*. Also see *DFP*, February 4, 1863, which attempts to explain the minor role played by the Ohio soldiers.

41. JMS to mother and father, January 6, 1863; WPI to Minty, January 20, 1863, RLB; Fox Diary, January 1, 1863. Account of Dickinson's resignation based on information in CMSR and Robertson, *Michigan in the War*, 813. Dickinson was a Grand Rapids native, so one can imagine the impact of letters written home by Sligh and others roundly criticizing his conduct.

42. O.R., 20-1:198 ("gallantly" and "ability"), 651 ("credit").

Chapter 11

1. Miller to Governor Blair, January 28, 1862, RSR. The recruits had been offered by Wesley Vincent of Lapeer but did not join the regiment. This was probably the same Wesley Vincent of Lapeer who later served during the war as assistant surgeon (11th Michigan) and later surgeon (102nd USCT); see Robertson, *Michigan in the War*, 954. Vincent's offer is referenced in LR-Reg.

2. JWS to wife, March 29, 1862; Calkins to unknown, n.d. [February 1862]; Graves to brother, February 9, 1862; Baker Borden CMSR, Third Michigan. Nothing has been found to verify Sligh's claim. Borden's resignation from the Third Michigan citing severe hemorrhoids was certified in writing by the assistant surgeon, who deemed him "incapable of performing military duty" because the problem had been aggravated by active campaigning; see resignation dated July 29, 1861, and endorsement in Baker Borden CMSR, Third Michigan. According to the Desc. Roll, Third Michigan, Borden resigned because of "disability incurred in service." Furthermore, there is nothing in regimental or service records to suggest that Borden's departure from the Michigan Engineers was related to anything but his health, though Private Calkins of Company E wrote home that Borden resigned because the men had been deceived as to their pay. It is not clear why Innes overlooked Williamson, who was apparently well liked by his men. Perhaps Lane's several years of engineering experience tipped the scales over Williamson's relatively short period of military service. Williamson was later

promoted to captain of Company A in May 1863 and served ably in that position throughout the war.

3. WPI to Lane, March 10 and 27, 1863, and WPI to Blair, March 12, 1862, RLB; *DFP*, February 4, 1863; Paul Leake, *History of Detroit: A Chronicle of Its Progress, Its Industries, Its Institutions, and the People of the Fair City of the Straits* (Chicago: Lewis, 1912), 662–64; CMSR and Desc. Roll. Connection is from Michael Leeson, *History of Macomb County* (Chicago: M. A. Leeson, 1882), 637.

4. Canfield information is from WPI to Fry, April 22, 1862, RLB; Fox Diary, July 17, 1862; CMSR. Mills information is from Desc. Roll and U.S. Census, 1860, Ionia County, Michigan.

5. WPI, Hunton, and Hopkins to Blair, May 22, 1862, and WPI to Blair, June 21 and 29, 1862, all in RLB. Sligh had kinder comments about Palmerlee; see JWS to wife, June 29, 1862.

6. WPI to Coffinberry, January 5, 1863, RLB ("conduct"). Coffinberry's resignation letter cited "old age and failing sight"; see CMSR. Departure of Coffinberry for Michigan found in Fox Diary, January 6, 1863. Innes later wrote to Provost General James B. Fry urging Coffinberry's appointment in the Invalid Corps; WPI to Fry, June 20, 1863, RLB. C. H. Scribner and other men in the company wrote Innes, asking him to appoint Robinson in Coffinberry's place; see WPI to Scribner, January 21, 1863, RLB.

7. For Emerson's activities, see later discussion of the organization and recruitment of Companies L and M. Robinson's commission as captain was dated December 25, 1862, but he was not actually mustered in to that position until November 1863.

8. Letter of resignation in CMSR. Letter from officers to R. S. Innes, December 12, 1862, and letter from teamsters and quartermasters to R. S. Innes, December 13, 1862, both in Robert S. Innes Papers, Bentley Historical Library, University of Michigan. Also see JMS to JWS, November 3, 1862 ("best"); JMS to mother, December 14, 1862; Fox Diary, December 12, 1862. Information about future activities as a civilian contractor in Tennessee from Headquarters, Department of the Cumberland to R. S. Innes, March 20, 1863, RG 393-1, ser. 908, Cont. Commands; copy of telegram from WPI to "Captain" R. S. Innes, February 21, 1863, RLB.

9. Details on the injury, subsequent leave, service in hospitals, and resignation are from CMSR; CWPF; Margaret B. McMillan, *The Methodist Episcopal Church in Michigan during the Civil War* (Lansing: Michigan Civil War Centennial Commission, 1965), 46; Stearns Diary, January 24, 1862; SFO 77, Department of the Cumberland, March 21, 1862, RG 393-1 ser. 950, Cont. Commands. Also see WPI to Reverend Smith, April 25, 1863, RLB; WPI to Goddard, May 4, 1863, RLB; Tracy resignation letter, May 20, 1863, LR-Reg. Innes recommended in June 1863 that Tracy's resignation be accepted, claiming that he had not "been fit for duty in over one year." Criticism from Capt. H. Thrall, Assistant Adjutant General, Department of the Cumberland, note of April 24, 1863, in CMSR ("light duty"). Thrall's comments may have had some merit. In January 1863 Lt. John McCrath found Chaplain and Mrs. Tracy boarding in Louisville on Jefferson Street, next door to the Masonic Temple; John W. McCrath Diary, January 25, 1863,

Private Collection of John Gelderloos, Grand Rapids, Michigan (hereafter cited as McCrath Diary). Despite his crippling injuries, Tracy was able to regularly attend Masonic gatherings, including annual assemblies of Michigan Masons both in June 1862 and a year later; see Freemasons, Michigan Royal and Select Masters, Grand Council, *History of Cryptic Masonry* (N.p., 1958), 12–14. Similarly, see Royal Arch Masons, Grand Chapter (Michigan), *Proceedings of the Grand Chapter of Royal Arch Masons of the State of Michigan, 1862* (Detroit: N.p., 1862). Thrall's comments also came shortly after Tracy's March 1863 visit to Murfreesboro to confer Scottish Degrees Fourth to Thirty-second upon former Quartermaster R. S. Innes; see Charles Fey to Robert M. Warner, September 8, 1868, with R. S. Innes Papers.

10. Late 1863 correspondence about Tracy's return includes reference to an application for the position dated August 4 in LR-Reg.; telegram, September 16, 1863; endorsement note from Blair to Robertson to "issue commission to Mr. Tracy as chaplain," RSR; obituary notice dated May 8, 1906, pasted in Desc. Roll book, which states that Tracy was "again commissioned as chaplain in the same regiment but was unable to rejoin his command." Burton, *City of Detroit*, 5:888–92, and Methodist Episcopal Church, Detroit Conference, *Minutes of the 1906 Annual Session* (Detroit: The Conference, 1906), 306–8, both claim that Tracy remained in government employment in western hospitals into 1864.

11. Huxford file LL3264, CMCF. Kimball information is from JWS to wife, March 30, 1862, and George White to JWS, August 23, 1862 ("small loss"); LR-Reg., August 8, 1862; and JWS to Col. J. R. Smith, August 29, 1862, in Kimball CMSR.

12. Both resignation letters are in CMSR. Also see Innes to Blair, April 22, 1862, RLB; Draper to Blair, June 7, 1862, and Blair to Robertson, June 20, 1862, both in RSR; Desc. Roll and Monthly Returns; SO 7, January 19, 1863, and SO 12, January 26, 1863, ROB.

13. Frary information is from *ROS*, 43:72; Desc. Roll; *Jackson Weekly Citizen*, May 7, 1862; U.S. Census, 1860, Jackson County, Michigan; Osband Diary, January 3, 1862 (indicates that Frary was already "quite unwell" and considering resigning); Osband Diary, February 6, 1862 (Frary's departure); CMSR (says Frary still at Louisville, February 15, 1862). Connelly information is from *ROS* 43 and Desc. Roll. Kimball Diary, March 8, 1862, states that Connelly had consumption "and was never with us [Company H]." Crittenton later claimed that Connelly suffered an attack of typhoid fever while working on the bridge over Nolin Creek in January and remained in hospitals the rest of his service; CWPF. Connelly never recovered his health and died on October 5, 1862, at home in Grand Rapids, leaving a young widow and ten-month-old infant.

14. WPI to Blair, August 10 and November 1, 1862, and February 1, 1863, all in RLB.

15. O.R., ser. 3, 2:705.

16. Recruiting description is from Yates to Lorenzo Thomas, August 31, 1865, RSR; Desc. Roll; Geo. D. Emerson to J. R. Smith, June 20, 1863, MEMRP; Monthly Returns for 1863. Biographical information on Emerson is from The Caleb Emerson Family Papers, The Western Reserve Historical Society; Clair V. Mann Papers, University of Missouri–Rolla Archives; James K. Jamison, *Families*

of Ontonagon County (Ontonagon, Mich.: N.p., 1950), 55–56; Charles Willman, *Ontonagon County in the Civil War* (N.p., 1961), 3; Thomas J. Summers, *History of Marietta* (Marietta, Ohio: Leader, 1903), 130–33, 164; Johnston, *Detroit City Directory, 1857*, 169.

17. For the details of Gifford's service see *ROS* 43; Desc. Roll. Additional references to his recruiting in Michigan are from *DFP*, September 17, 1863, and February 13, 1864; Simeon Howe to wife, December 19 and 30, 1863, and March 10, 1864, Howe Family Papers, Michigan State University Archives and Historical Collections (unless otherwise noted, all letters from Howe are in this collection); certificate signed by J. R. Smith, September 30, 1863, Battery E, First Michigan Light Artillery, RSR; JWS Diary, July 3, 1863 (which states Gifford had just returned to Grand Rapids from the regiment).

18. Templeton CMSR; Desc. Roll; *Adrian Daily Watchtower*, January 2, 1863, advertisement ("desirable"). Moore reference is from U.S. Census, 1860, Kent County, Michigan, and *ROS*, 43:142. Nelson reference is from Isaac A. Fancher, *Past and Present of Isabella County, Michigan* (Indianapolis: Bowen, 1911), 324, 541, 546–47, and 561; U.S. Census, 1860, Isabella County, Michigan; Desc. Roll. Ensign reference is from *Record of the Descendants of James Ensign*, 3 vols. (Moline, Ill.: 1939), 1:274; Robertson, *Michigan in the War*, 1823; *Record of Service of Michigan Volunteers in the Civil War*, 46 vols. (Kalamazoo, Mich.: Ihling Bros. and Everard, 1905), 42:51; and Raymond Herek, *These Men Have Seen Hard Service: The First Michigan Sharpshooters in the Civil War* (Detroit: Wayne State University Press, 1998), 33.

19. See *ROS* 43 and Desc. Roll for dates and ranks. December 15, 1863, was considered the date on which Company M's completion finalized the regiment's reorganization as a volunteer engineer regiment in some sources; see WPI to Blair, January 25, 1864, RSR. The use of the January 1, 1864, date for commissions for the final new major and first lieutenancies suggests that date as the official date recognized by Governor Blair and the War Department. The jockeying for the majorities was in full swing by February 1863. P. V. Fox actively sought the third majority, considering himself junior only to Hopkins and Yates, while at least James M. Sligh thought that Adjutant Miller would be considered; see JMS to mother, February 9 and 28, 1863.

20. Desc. Roll and *ROS* 43.

21. WPI to Blair, November 1, 1862, RLB. Innes was short of medical officers since Surgeon DeCamp was detached after the Battle of Perryville, leaving only O'Donoughue and the hospital stewards to staff the regimental hospital. DeCamp earned high marks for his performance as post medical director at Harrodsburg and did not return to the regiment until late January or early February 1863; see WPI to Swift, January 23, 1863, RLB; Robertson, *Michigan in the War*, 77; Baxter, *Grand Rapids*, 702–3. Smith reference is from *Portrait and Biographical Album of Washtenaw County, Michigan* (Chicago: Biographical Publishing, 1891), 221–22; Monthly Return, January 1863; WPI to Blair, May 30, 1863, RLB.

22. WPI to Robertson, November 19, 1862, located in both RLB and RSR.

23. Information was compiled from *ROS* 43, Desc. Roll, and Monthly Return, May 1862. During April and May 1862, 40 percent of the enlisted men in

Michigan Engineers were reported as too sick for duty, either in regimental or base hospitals. The situation was little different from other regiments in the Union army; see Benjamin A. Gould, *Investigations in the Military and Anthropological Statistics of American Soldiers, Sanitary Memoirs of the War of the Rebellion*, 2 vols. (Cambridge, Mass.: Riverside Press, 1869), 2:588–89. Gould's Table III presents the results of a study done of 147 Union regiments by U.S. Sanitary Commission agents during this time. The average regiment in the West at the end of May—including many more recently raised than the Michigan Engineers—had about 775 men on the books, of whom 170 were sick. An average regiment lost 20 men to death or discharge in the month of May 1862; that same month the Michigan Engineers lost 40 men to death or discharge.

24. WPI to J. B. Fry, April 18, 1862, RLB; WPI to Headquarters, Army of the Ohio, May 22, 1862, RG 393-1, ser. 920, Cont. Commands; WPI to Garesche, December 8, 1862, RLB. In the meantime, Innes even tried negotiating directly with hospital directors and rear area commanders; for example, see WPI to Colonel Ray, commanding city barracks at Nashville, September 8, 1862, RLB.

25. Osband Diary, December 1862–February 1863; Desc. Roll.

26. O.R., ser. 3, 2:2–3, 109.

27. WPI to Fry, August 15, 1862, RLB; SO 133, Army of the Ohio, August 14, 1862, SFP. Departure reference is in Barker, JWS, and Fox diaries; JMS to mother, August 18, 1862; WPI to Goddard, January 14, 1863, RLB; WPI to JWS, November 17, 1862, RLB ("offer"). Unnumbered order was by J. R. Smith, August 23, 1862, SFP. The rest of the recruiting party included Sgts. Charles Cudney, David Albro, Zophar Scidmore, Edson P. Gifford, David A. Jewel, Alphonzo H. Bullen, David A. Shumway, David Ingersoll, and Cyrus K. Wilder and Pvt. Ebenezer Costin.

28. Fred A. Shannon, *The Organization and Administration of the Union Army, 1861–1865*, 2 vols. (Cleveland: Arthur H. Clark, 1928), 1:282–91, 2:49–59 ("rod" on 2:49); James W. Geary, *We Need Men: The Union Draft in the Civil War* (DeKalb: Northern Illinois University Press, 1991), 14–17; Eugene Murdock, *One Million Men: The Civil War Draft in the North* (Madison: State Historical Society of Wisconsin, 1971), 12–18; O.R., ser. 3, 2:206–7, 380–81; Desc. Roll; McCrath to JWS, October 29 and November 21, 1862; Jewell to JWS, November 21, 1862; request to return from JWS to WPI, November 15, 1862, LR-Reg.

29. O.R., ser. 3, 2:705; Fox and Kimball diaries; Conant to wife, December 9, 1862; WPI to Garesche, November 30, 1862, RLB.

30. Blair to J. R. Smith, December 16, 1862, Hopkins CMSR; Hopkins to J. R. Smith, December 17, 1862, MEMRP; Order 162 by J. R. Smith, December 18, 1862, SFP. It is not clear when Hopkins's party reached Detroit, but Cotton, Mills, and Miller were among those included in a listing of hotel quests in *DFP*, December 13, 1862, and Sligh traveled from Grand Rapids to Detroit to meet with Hopkins on December 15, 1862; *DFP*, December 17, 1862, and JWS Diary.

31. O.R., ser. 3, 1:914–33.

32. Hopkins to J. R. Smith, December 25, 1862, MEMRP; Hopkins to JWS, December 27, 1862, and January 1 and 3, 1863; McPherson, *Battle Cry of Freedom*, 574.

33. Recruitment of Companies L and M is explained in Yates to Lorenzo Thomas, August 31, 1865, RSR. Also see the Monthly Returns for June–December 1863; "Return of clothing . . . transferred . . . to Company L," August 31, 1863, Emerson Papers. O. A. Brown appears as the recruiter for many of the recruits, but he was the notary public in Lenawee County and probably just signed the documents of enlistment; see Wm. M. Maloney CMSR, for example.

34. Hopkins to JWS, March 13 and 26, April 6, and May 7, 11, and 25, 1863. Captain Sligh complained in his diary on March 4 that he was unable to get orders from Smith for his return and then was detailed to sit on a court-martial in Detroit. JWS to wife, May 6, 9, 14, 17, 18, 27, 28, and 29 and June 2, 1863. Also see WPI to Goddard May 4, 1863, to C. F. Miller, May 31 and June 5, 1863, and to Goddard, June 15, 1863, all in RLB; *Detroit Advertiser and Tribune*, July 8, 1863 (hereafter cited as *DAT*); JWS to wife, July 10 and 13, 1863; JMS to mother, July 14, 1863; JWS Diary.

35. *Hastings Banner*, September 3, 1862, also noted that a "large proportion [of the recruits] are taken from among the mechanics of this village." See Weissert to wife, September 14, 16, and 19, 1862.

36. See appendix I, table D, for the actual comparison of loss rates among different groups of recruits.

37. McCrath to JWS, October 15, 1862, SFP; Desc. Roll; *ROS* 43; Weissert to wife, November 24 and December 9 and 20, 1862.

38. Drawn from information in Desc. Roll and *ROS* 43. A summary of U.S. policy on the training of recruits is in Armin Rappaport, "The Replacement System during the Civil War," in *Military Analysis of the Civil War: An Anthology by the Editors of Military Affairs* (Millwood, N.Y.: KTO Press, 1977), 124–26.

39. Weissert to wife, September 14, 16, 19, and October 3, 1862; Desc. Roll; Miller to JWS, September 30, 1862, SFP.

40. Weissert to wife, September 20, 1862.

Chapter 12

1. ROE, January 1863; Fox, Roseberry, and Stearns diaries; Goddard to WPI, January 7, 1863, RG 393-1, ser. 908, Cont. Commands; Conant to wife, January 9, 1863; WPI to Stanley, January 9, 1863, RLB; JMS to mother, January 26, 1863; WPI to Goddard, January 9, 1863, RLB; WPI to Headquarters, Department of the Cumberland, January 9, 1863, RG 393-1, ser. 925, Cont. Commands. Stewart's Creek is the only stream near Smyrna according to O.R.A., 30:2.

2. Roseberry Diary; Conant to wife, January 13, 1863 ("desolate"); Weissert to wife, January 10, 1863 ("makes").

3. ROE, January 1863; Kimball, Stearns, and Roseberry diaries; JMS to brother and sisters, January 12, 1863; Conant to wife, January 13, 1863; Weissert to wife, January 28, 1863; WPI to Goddard, January 24, 1863, RLB; orders to Michigan Engineers, January 15, 1863, RG 393-1, ser. 908, Cont. Commands. See O.R.A., 112:3, for a detailed map of some of Murfreesboro and its nearby river crossings.

4. Cist, *Army of the Cumberland*, 137; GO 6, January 28, 1863, ROB; SFO 25, Department of the Cumberland, January 28, 1863, RG 393-1, ser. 950, Cont. Commands.

5. ROE, January 1863; Stearns and McCrath diaries; Wm. L. Clark letter in *MS*, February 25, 1863; WPI to Hannings at Lavergne, February 2, 1863, RLB; Fox to wife, February 10, 1863; WPI to Goddard, February 2, 1863, RLB. Problems with iron reference is from WPI to R. B. Mitchell, January 31, 1863, RLB.

6. Telegrams, RLB; WPI to Goddard, February 4, 1863, MEMRP; WPI to Goddard, February 7, 1863, RLB; Hannings letter of February 7, 1863, LR-Reg.

7. Edgefield and Kentucky references are from WPI to Goddard, February 1, 1863, and Yates to WPI, February 6, 1863, both in RLB, and Weissert to wife, February 11 and 18, 1863. Nashville and Northwestern information is from reference to report from Yates in February in LR-Reg.; WPI to Captain Stewart, U.S. Corps of Engineers, February 12, 1863, and WPI to Captain Webster, U.S. Corps of Engineers, March 6, both in RLB; Yates's report and Michael Burns to WPI, February 14, 1863, both in U.S. Congress, House, *Affairs of Southern Railroads*, 39th Cong., 2nd sess., H. Rep. 34, serial 1306, 284–85 (hereafter cited as 39th Cong., *Affairs*); WPI to Garfield, July 24, 1863, RG 393-1, ser. 925, Cont. Commands. Decatur route reference is from WPI to Goddard, February 3, 1863, RLB.

8. Kimball Diary; Wm. L. Clark letter in *MS*, March 11, 1863; Weissert to wife, February 18, 1863; JMS to JWS, February 18, 1863; Boss to father, February 26, 1863; O.R., 23-2:59. Weissert, February 11, 1863, includes reference to work party being six miles south of Mill Creek, while Roseberry Diary, February 12–14, 1863, positively states that the men working below rejoined the regiment in camp prior to leaving, as discussed earlier. Roseberry Diary for February consistently refers to the camp on the Rains plantation as "Camp Andrew Johnson," but there is nothing to link it with the large camp of the same name used by Buell's army the previous year. The 1863 camp was probably located on what was referred to during the Civil War as Rains Hill, located between the Nolensville Pike and the Tennessee and Alabama Railroad and southeast of Fort Negley; see O.R.A., 73:1. ROE, February 1863, refers to their camp as "two miles from Nashville" along the NCRR, but this location is almost certainly in error, given the other contemporary sources.

9. Fox and Kimball diaries; WPI to Goddard February 13, 1863, RLB; SO 25, February 15, 1863, ROB; Weissert to wife, February 19, 1863; Boss to father, February 26, 1863.

10. Wm. L. Clark letter in *MS*, March 11, 1863; McCrath Diary; WPI to Goddard, February 20, 1863, RLB; Stearns Diary, February 19, 1863 (which includes the account of shooting from the train).

11. WPI to Goddard, February 20 and 24, 1863, RLB; Weissert to wife, February 19, 1863; Kimball and Stearns diaries. Sketch of area is in O.R.A., 115:3.

12. Roseberry, Stearns, and Kimball diaries; WPI to Garfield, March 5, 1863, RLB.

13. Wm. L. Clark letter in *MS*, March 11, 1863; McCrath Diary; Weissert to wife, March 12, 1863; Allen Campbell to father, March 17, 1863; Kimball and Stearns diaries.

14. Kimball Diary, March 11, 1863; WPI to Col. J. A. Martin, March 11, 1863, RLB.

15. Kimball and Stearns diaries; Wm. L. Clark letter in *MS*, April 8, 1863; Orders, March 17, 1863, RG 393-1, ser. 908, Cont. Commands.

16. Wm. L. Clark letter in *MS*, April 8, 1863; Kimball and Stearns diaries; O.R., 23-2:234; Lord, *Civil War Encyclopedia*, 279.

17. Wm. L. Clark letter in *MS*, February 25, 1863; Stearns Diary, February 6, 1863; H. F. Williams to WPI, December 24, 1862, in Williams CMSR.

18. Kimball and Roseberry diaries, March 15, 1863; WPI to Lieutenant Porter, Chief of Ordnance at Nashville, March 16 and 17 and April 2, 1863, RLB; Genco, *Arming Michigan's Regiments*, 73.

19. Stearns Diary; Kimball Diary, March 21, 1863 ("thereon"); Wm. L. Clark letter in *MS*, April 8, 1863; George White to JWS, February 11, 1863 ("difference"); McCrath Diary ("work").

20. Leonard Brown, "Fortress Rosecrans: A History, 1865–1990," *Tennessee Historical Quarterly* 50 (1991): 135–38; O.R., 49-2:502–3; O.R.A., 112:3. Since first joining Buell's Department of the Ohio staff, Morton had spent most of his time improving the defenses of Nashville and along the railroads; Paul H. Beasley and C. Buford Gotto, "Fortress Nashville," *Civil War Times Illustrated* 3 (1964): 25–26.

21. O.R., 23-2:154; Wm. L. Clark letter in *MS*, May 6, 1863; Kimball Diary, March 30–April 4, 1863; Stearns Diary, March 30–May 2, 1863; Fitch, *Army of the Cumberland*, 195. *DAT*, April 21, 1863, citing a letter "from Murfreesboro," says the warehouse was eight hundred by fifty feet.

22. O.R.A., 112:3; Wm. L. Clark letter in *MS*, May 6, 1863; Roseberry, Kimball, and Stearns diaries, April 13–28, 1863; WPI to Morton, April 28, 29, and 30, 1863, RLB.

23. Kimball, Stearns, and Roseberry diaries, May and June, 1863; JMS to JWS, May 15 and June 13, 1863; JMS to mother, May 13, 1863; P. V. Fox to wife, June 2, 1863.

24. Shiman, "Engineering Sherman's March," 126–33, 142–47, 165–68; Fitch, *Army of the Cumberland*, 186–87; Henry V. Freeman, "Recollections," in *Illinois Commandery, Military Order of the Loyal Legion of the United States*, 8 vols. (Chicago: Illinois Commandery, 1891), 3:228–29. A fourth battalion was later organized by Capt. William E. Merrill from troops at Franklin; Merrill to Totten, May 10, 1863, ser. 908, OCE Records. Shiman's account includes a favorable view of Rosecrans's role in developing a successful engineering force within his command. Shiman has also written a more recent summary of his praise for Rosecrans's engineering activities; see Philip L. Shiman, "Engineering and Command: The Case of General William S. Rosecrans, 1862–1863," in *The Art of Command in the Civil War* (Lincoln: University of Nebraska Press, 1998), 84–117.

25. Morton reference is from Shiman, "Engineering Sherman's March," 126–30, 147–48 ("controversial," page 129); Boatner, *Civil War Dictionary*, 570–71; Fitch, *Army of the Cumberland*, 186–91; Warner, *Generals in Blue*, 336.

26. See Shiman, "Engineering Sherman's March," 159–63, for analysis and underlying documents from ser. 908, OCE Records, particularly Morton's letters to Totten on February 16 and March 15, 1863.

27. Nevius to JWS, November 28, 1862, SFP; Graves to wife, November 28 and December 9, 1862; Alex Campbell to brother, December 4, 1862; George White to JWS, December 9, 1862. The two companies were ordered to relieve two companies of the Fiftieth Indiana on November 22, 1863; RG 393-1, ser. 908, Cont. Commands. Greenalch to wife, December 23, 1863, indicates that the two companies were back with the regiment three or four days previously.

28. After leaving Michigan, Innes journeyed to Washington, D.C., with Col. Cyrus O. Loomis of the First Michigan Light Artillery, joining with Major Hopkins en route; WPI to Goddard, March 20, 1863, RLB; orders in WPI CMSR. Also see Kimball Diary, March 22, 1863; Weissert to family, March 22, 1863, and to wife, April 17, 1863; Blair to Rosecrans, April 3, 1863, WPI CMSR; Hopkins to JWS, April and May 7, 1863, SFP; Greenalch to wife, April 11, 1863. Return to regiment account is from Roseberry, Kimball, and Stearns diaries, April 24, 1863.

29. Orders from Morton in Pioneer Brigade Headquarters to Hunton, April 8, 1863, RG 393-2, ser. 823, Cont. Commands. Also see Roseberry, McCrath, and Kimball diaries, April 9–11, 1863; GO 33, Pioneer Brigade, RG 393-2, ser. 793, Cont. Commands; Greenalch to wife, April 20, 1863.

30. Roseberry Diary, April 11, 1863 ("shirk"); Greenalch to wife, April 20, 1863 ("probably"); and George White to JMS, April 12, 1863.

31. Morton to WPI, April 26, 1863, RG 393-2, ser. 823, Cont. Commands; Rosecrans to Morton, April 28, 1863, RG 393-1, ser. 908, Cont. Commands; SFO 114, Department of the Cumberland, April 27, 1863, RG 393-1, ser. 950, Cont. Commands. Also see Roseberry ("bogus") and Kimball diaries, April 27, 1863; Weissert to wife, n.d. [late April]. Innes's victory did not mean that the proposed consolidation was forgotten. Within weeks, Capt. William E. Merrill, Buell's new chief topographical engineer, proposed that a permanent brigade of volunteer engineers be organized to include the Michigan Engineers and three new regiments formed from the Pioneer Brigade battalions. Months later, Capt. P. O'Connell, acting commander of the Pioneer Brigade, tried unsuccessfully to have several companies of Michigan Engineers at Bridgeport attached to the force. See Merrill to Totten May 10, 1863, Letters Received, OCE Records; Merrill to O'Connell, September 7, 1863, RG 393-1, ser. 1040, Cont. Commands.

32. WPI to Morton, May 26 and June 2, 14, and 17, 1863, all in RLB; JMS to mother, June 15 and 22, and to father, June 28, 1863; WPI to Johnson, June 17, 1863 ("labor"); Andrew Johnson Papers, Presidential Papers Microfilm, 55 reels (Washington, D.C.: Library of Congress, 1960), reel 7, Library of Congress (hereafter cited as Johnson Papers).

33. SFO 171, Department of the Cumberland, June 23, Ser. 950, RG 393-1, Cont. Commands. Visit and orders account is from JMS to JWS, June 28, 163; Rolison, McCrath, Kimball, and Stearns diaries. Blair's visit was reported in the *Nashville Union*, June 27, 1863, and *Hillsdale Standard*, July 21, 1863.

Chapter 13

1. Thomas L. Connelly, *Autumn of Glory: The Army of Tennessee, 1862–1865* (Baton Rouge: Louisiana State University Press, 1971), 112–25.

2. Robert S. Brandt, "Lightning and Rain in Middle Tennessee," *Tennessee Historical Quarterly* 52 (1993): 158–69. Also see Boatner, *Civil War Dictionary*, 850–51; William M. Lamers, *The Edge of Glory: A Biography of General William S. Rosecrans, U.S.A.* (New York: Harcourt, Brace, and World, 1961), 277; O.R.A., plates 34 and 35.

3. O.R., 23-2:476–77, 480; Department of the Cumberland Headquarters to WPI, June 28, 1863, RG 393-1, ser. 908, Cont. Commands; Kimball, Stearns, McCrath, and Rolison diaries; O.R., 23-1:582–83; JMS to mother, July 7, 1863.

4. Kimball, McCrath, Rolison, and Stearns diaries; Weissert to family, July 5, 1863; Greenalch to wife, July 2, 1863; JMS to mother, July 7, 1863; ROE, July 1863; WPI to Department of the Cumberland, July 2 and 4, 1863, RG 393-1, ser. 925, Cont. Commands.

5. O.R., 23-1:582–83; Kimball, Stearns, McCrath, and Rolison diaries; Weissert to family, July 5 and 9, 1863; JMS to mother, July 7, 1863; Greenalch to wife, July 2, 1863; ROE, July 1863. LR-Reg. contains a reference to July 6 report from Hunton about the railroad bridge at Concord. Map of Tullahoma region is in O.R.A., 35:3.

6. Greenalch to wife, July 2, 1863; JMS to mother, July 17, 1863; Rosecrans to Stanton, O.R., 23-1:403. Examples include Thomas and McCook in O.R., 23-1:433 and 469.

7. Kimball Diary, July 4, 1863 ("carelessly," "skin," "lively," and "caper"); JMS to mother, July 7, 1863 ("senseless"); Bert Jewell to Albert Graves, July 18, 1863, in Graves Family Papers. Crittenton's injuries were also noted in the Stearns Diary, July 4, 1863, and Greenalch to wife, July 2–4, 1863.

8. Hattaway and Jones, *How the North Won*, 403–4, 446–47; Welcher, *Union Army*, 2:526. A sympathetic review of Rosecrans's decision to halt at the Tennessee River is included in Van Horne, *Army of the Cumberland*, 1:310–12. Also see the recent study of Rosecrans in William J. Wood, *Civil War Generalship: The Art of Command* (Westport, Conn.: Praeger, 1997), 103–7.

9. O.R., 23-1:407, 460–61; Connelly, *Autumn of Glory*, 129–34; O.R., 23-1: 408, 429, 435–36; Welcher, *Union Army*, 2:838. Morton estimate is in letter to Totten dated July 10, 1863, ser. 18, OCE Records. The best Civil War maps of the area around the Elk River crossing are in O.R.A., 35-1. The crossing is sometimes referred to as "at Allisonia," a small village and rail station located on a bluff on the south bank of the river. Valuable information has been provided to the author by Mr. Howard "Pete" Hannah, Franklin County Historian. In particular, Mr. Hannah has clarified the relative positions of Estill Springs Resort, the station of the same name, the railroad bridge crossing, and Allisonia station. The actual crossing is now part of Tims Ford Lake, a flooding of the Elk River by the Tennessee Valley Authority. Also see Charles B. Thorne, "The Watering Spas of Middle Tennessee," *Tennessee Historical Quarterly* 29 (1970), 345–46.

10. Pioneer Brigade work reference is from O.R. 23-1:581–82; correspondence RG 393-2, ser. 823, and report dated July 6, 1863, RG 393-2, ser. 812, both in Cont. Commands. March information is from Kimball, Stearns, and Rolison diaries. Hunton reference is from William D. Travis manuscript, dated July 1863, "Bridge Building in Tennessee," James S. Schoff Civil War Collection, William L.

Clements Library, University of Michigan, Ann Arbor, (hereafter cited as Travis MS). Travis was probably William D. Travis, Company I, Twenty-second Illinois.

11. Travis MS; Kimball Diary, July 12, 1863; JMS to mother, July 20, 1863. Travis states Hunton offered to build the bridge with only four companies of the Michigan Engineers; see below for detachment of Yates and three companies for other work on the twelfth.

12. See Kimball and Roseberry diaries for getting out timber from woods. Bridge dimensions vary: ROE, July 1863, has 460 feet long by 60 feet high; JMS to mother, July 14, 1863, has 470 feet long. Also see Jewell to Graves, July 18, 1863, Graves Family Papers.

13. The best description of the Elk River railroad bridge is in JWS Diary for July 17, 1863. There are two surviving photographs of the bridge. See Sligh, *Michigan Engineers*, 51, and the image from the Michigan State Archives reproduced here.

14. RLB includes letters from WPI to Goddard on July 14 and 15, 1863, to Taylor on July 15 and 17, 1863, to Garfield on July 17, 1863, and to Yates on July 17, 1863. There are also letters from WPI to Stewart on July 15, 1863, to Goddard on July 16, 1863, and to Taylor on July 16, 1863, all included with miscellaneous materials from July and August 1863 in the ROB.

15. Kimball and Roseberry diaries, July 18, 1863; JMS to mother, July 20, 1863. Flag incident reference is from Travis MS; the flag is described in O.R., 23-2:276.

16. SO 59, July 12, 1863, ROB; WPI to Goddard, July 14 and 17, 1863, RLB; letter from A.B.C., *DFP*, July 31, 1863; *Chicago Tribune*, July 29, 1863. For accounts of the work see Wm. L. Clark letter in *MS*, August 5, 1863; Roseberry Diary, July 13, 1863 (gives Cowan Station as destination); Jewell to Graves, July 18, 1863; and JMS to mother, July 14 and 20, 1863. Also see the following letters included in the RLB: WPI to Yates, July 17, 1863; WPI to Taylor, July 18, 1863; WPI to Garfield, July 18, 1863. The *Chicago Tribune*, July 29, 1863, quotes Armstrong letter of July 21.

17. ROE, July–October 1863; Van Horne, *Army of the Cumberland*, 2:310; Welcher, *Union Army*, 2:526.

18. For Hunton and trips see Regimental Headquarters to WPI, July 20, 1863, Hunton to Taylor, July 23, 1863, and Hunton to WPI, July 22, 1863, all in RLB. Also see WPI to Department of the Cumberland, July 23 and 28, 1863, both in RG 393-1, ser. 925, Cont. Commands. Detail on repairs reference is from ROE, July 1863. References to Hunton's inspection reports are found in LR-Reg.

19. Roseberry, Kimball, and Stearns diaries; JMS to mother, July 22, 1863.

20. Information about companies and work is from Stearns Diary; Hunton to Drouillard, August 1, 1863, RLB. Reference to Anderson and bridge is from O.R., 23-2: 907, 923, 943; it is not clear if this party or another were the ones who destroyed the bridge. Stearns Diary, July 31, 1863, says the bridge had been destroyed "a few days ago."

21. References to Innes's recruiting are in letters he wrote dated July 20, 23, and 25, 1863, LR-Reg.; WPI to Goddard, July 15, 1863, RLB; O.R., 23-2:564–65; WPI to Maj. Wm. M. Wiles, August 10, 1863, RLB; WPI to Kellogg, August 4,

1863, RLB. Information about integration of black companies into the regiment is from JMS to mother, February 18 and 28, 1863; Anonymous letter in *DAT*, May 18, 1863. Reference to detached noncommissioned officers is from SO (no number) dated July 14, 1863, referencing Jewell in charge of contrabands, COB; WPI to Garfield August 4, 1863, RLB; GO 38, SO 87 and 115, August 5–September 13, 1863, ROB; Wm. L. Clark letter in *MS*, September 2, 1863; July 28 report from Jewell in LR-Reg. Also see RG 94, Twelfth United States Colored Troops, Regimental Papers, Records of the Adjutant General, NARA, as well as "Records of Musters of USCT," RG 393-1, ser. 1019, Cont. Commands.

22. Regiment Headquarters to Hunton, August 30, 1864, and Regiment Headquarters to Commanding Officer, First USCT, September 7, 1863, both RLB. Also see Wm. L. Clark letter in *MS*, September 23, 1863.

23. Jewell to Graves July 18, 1863, Graves Family Papers; Seymour Burt to Inspector's Office, Department of the Cumberland, August 14, 1863, MEMRP.

24. JMS to mother, August 4, 1863; Kimball and Stearns diaries; WPI to W. Mansfield, August 6, 1863, WPI to Rosecrans, August 7 and 9, 1863, Hunton to Yates, August 9, 1863, and Regimental Headquarters to "Beggs," August 5 and 7, 1863, all in RLB; SO 74 and 80, August 5–7, 1863, ROB; ROE, August 1863.

25. O.R., 52-1:435; Anderson Family Papers ("absolute" and "thorough"). Apparently relations between Anderson and key military officers had soured in advance of Innes's appointment. In early July Rosecrans wrote Anderson, censoring him "for slowness in making repairs of track" and asking for a statement of the accounts of the railroads under his control. Anderson responded with a detailed defense, ending with his view that "I regret the tone of your dispatches and desire that the relations between us be harmonious or that they cease to exist." A month later he was defending his mail agents and baggage handlers from accusations by Col. John G. Parkhurst, provost marshal of the XIV Corps. A lengthy response was sent to Rosecrans, which also included a denial of additional charges of dishonesty that Major General Thomas had apparently made against Anderson. Anderson to Rosecrans, July 9 and August 4, 1863, John B. Anderson Papers, Records of the Office of the Quartermaster General, RG 92, ser. 1665, NARA (hereafter cited as QG Records).

26. Information on conflict between the two is from WPI to Yates July 6, 1863, RLB. For evidence of efforts to supplant Anderson, see WPI to Rosecrans, December 27, 1862, RLB; Garesche to WPI, December 28, 1862, RG 393-1, ser. 908, Cont. Commands; JMS to mother, February 9 and July 30, 1863; George White to JWS, February 11, 1863, SFP; JMS to JWS, February 18, 1863; WPI to Johnson, in Graf and Hasking, *Andrew Johnson*, 4:279; Jewell to Graves, July 18, 1863, Graves Family Papers.

27. WPI to Johnson, June 29, 1863, in Graf and Hasking, *Andrew Johnson*, 4:279; JMS to mother, July 30, 1863; Jewell to Graves, July 18, 1863, Graves Family Papers.

28. O.R., ser. 3, 5:1000; O.R., 20-2:5–6.

29. O.R., ser. 3, 5:974–81. Also see Lord, *Lincoln's Railroad Man*.

30. O.R., 30-3:33.

31. Welcher, *Union Army*, 2:526–30; Boatner, *Civil War Dictionary*, 150.

32. Company E reference is from Stearns Diary, August 19, 1863; ROE, August–September 1863; O.R., 30-1:50.

33. O.R., 23-2:900, 30-3:32–33, 68, 75; SO 96, August 17, 1863, ROB.

34. SO 103 and 105, August 26–27, 1863, ROB; Roseberry Diary, August 29, 1863; O.R., 30-1:52, 30-3:187, 203, 235; Philip Sheridan, *Personal Memoirs of P. H. Sheridan, General United States Army*, 2 vols. (New York: Charles L. Webster 1888), 1:272; Burroughs to O'Connell and Merrill to O'Connell, both August 28, 1863, RG 393-1 ser. 1040, Cont. Commands. Sheridan says only "four or five" pontoons were used at his crossing, yet the evidence is strong that at least fifty Pioneer Brigade pontoons were used to cross over his division. The army's pontoons were still of the wooden bateaux type. Though experiments with a collapsible wooden frame and canvas hull were successful in the summer of 1863, it was not until the following year that the Army of the Cumberland adopted the more mobile form of pontoon. Shiman, "Engineering Sherman's March," 151–53.

35. Sheridan, *Memoirs*, 1:273; Roseberry Diary; O.R., 30-3:220, 234; O.R.A., 112-1. Innes had been ordered on August 13 to use the mills at Anderson to produce cut timber for the bridge at Bridgeport; O.R., 30-3:19. The lumber might have also come from a captured sawmill at Scottsboro that the Pioneers were running, about twenty-eight miles to the west of Bridgeport; Lucius F. Mills to Rosecrans, August 25, 1863, RG 393-1, ser. 925, Cont. Commands ("very much"). Mills's report identifies the substantial damage done to the sawmill at Bridgeport, enough to require that parts be shipped from Nashville and Cincinnati. Greenalch to wife, September 30 and October 8, 1863, suggest that at least one detail from Company B was assigned to run a sawmill along the Memphis and Charleston but provide few details, and nothing further has been found.

36. Burroughs to O'Connell, August 31, 1863, RG 393-1, ser. 1040, Cont. Commands ("promised"); O.R., 30-3:280, 285. Morton had been relieved from duty on account of disability in August and did not return until early September. In his absence, O'Connell, as senior captain, took over command of the brigade, while Morton's place as chief engineer of the Department of the Cumberland was taken by Merrill; see Morton to Totten, September 9, 1863, ser. 18, OCE Records; Pioneer Brigade GO 50, RG 393-2, ser. 816, Cont. Commands; O.R., 30-3:112, 701.

37. Roseberry Diary; O.R., 30-3:299, 304, 326.

38. Roseberry Diary; O.R., 30-3:346.

39. Roseberry and Rolison diaries; O.R., 30-3:507; Burroughs to O'Connell, September 11, 1863, and Merrill to O'Connell, September 5, 1863, RG 393-1, ser. 1040, Cont. Commands. The pontoons built by the Michigan Engineers were probably among those that Hooker found at Bridgeport and used to cross the Tennessee during his part in the opening of the supply route to Chattanooga six weeks later. O.R., 30-4:24, 111–12.

40. Welcher, *Union Army*, 2:526–30; Boatner, *Civil War Dictionary*, 150.

41. O.R., 30-3:84, 171.

42. O.R., 30-3:248, 310.

43. O.R., 30-3:351, 342, 480.

44. Hunton to WPI, September 5, 1863, RLB; ROE, September 1863; JWS to wife, September 13, 1863; JMS to mother, September 16, 1863; Roseberry, Stearns, Kimball, and Rolison diaries.

Chapter 14

1. O.R., 30-3:562, 582–83 ("superintend"); Fox to wife, September 13, 1863. There is nothing to indicate why the orders for one company grew to include both companies, though in strength Fox's small command was only about as large as a regulation company.

2. Roseberry Diary; O.R., 30-3:651; Francis F. McKinney, "The First Regiment of Michigan Engineers and Mechanics," *Michigan Alumni Quarterly Review* 46 (1959): 147.

3. "Engineer instructions" signed by Burroughs September 12, 1863, and Burroughs to Wagner, September 13 and 14, 1863, RG 393-1, ser. 1040, Cont. Commands; O.R., 30-3:688. It appears that Burroughs did not at first expect to have any of the Michigan Engineers to use on the bridge construction but intended from the beginning to utilize Hunton's trestle design from Bridgeport where possible.

4. Roseberry Diary; McKinney, "Michigan Engineers and Mechanics," 147; Charles E. Belknap, *History of the Michigan Organizations at Chickamauga, Chattanooga, and Missionary Ridge* (Lansing: R. Smith Printing, 1897), 156, 261; *GR Eagle*, September 30, 1863.

5. James L. McDonough, *Chattanooga: A Death Grip on the Confederacy* (Knoxville: University of Tennessee Press, 1984), 24–25, 45–49.

6. Welcher, *Union Army*, 2:166–67, 224. Sherman was bringing the First, Second, and Fourth divisions of the XV Corps and the Second Division of the XVII Corps overland.

7. Welcher, *Union Army*, 2:166, 246–49; Boatner, *Civil War Dictionary*, 142–44.

8. Roseberry Diary; Belknap, *Michigan Organizations*, 156–57, 261–62. Morton returned from leave and soon after was replaced as Department of the Cumberland chief engineer by William F. Smith effective October 3, though Smith had arrived on September 29 or 30.

9. Description of pontoon is from Belknap, *Michigan Organizations*, 156, and sketch in unidentified newspaper clipping, c. September 1895, in Kimball Papers. This sketch accompanies an identical copy of Fox's address from Belknap, *Michigan Organizations*, which alludes to an attached sketch ("see copy herewith"), but it has been found only in the newspaper clipping.

10. Belknap, *Michigan Organizations*, 156–57, 261–62.

11. Roseberry Diary; Belknap, *Michigan Organizations*, 156–57, 262; O.R., 30-4:101, 123; Department of the Cumberland to Arthur Edwards, October 4, 1863, RG 393-1, ser. 908, Cont. Commands; Sligh, *Michigan Engineers*, 78–80. The original trestle/pontoon bridge was dismantled shortly after and used in the construction of a "flying bridge" further upriver. October 14 and 16 activity is described in Pioneer Brigade records, RG 393-2, ser. 823, Cont. Commands. For pontoon operations in

the West, see Shiman, "Engineering Sherman's March," 151–54. The state of pontoon engineering in 1863 is well summarized in Cullum, *Military Bridges*. The lessons drawn from the Civil War are summarized in Duane, Abbot, and Merrill, *Bridge Equipage*. Also see McDonough and Bond, *Ponton Equipage*.

12. Roseberry Diary ("satisfaction" from entry of October 10, 1863). The charges against the Pioneers are in Belknap, *Michigan Organizations*, 158. Even if the incident involving Pioneer activities is not true, it reflects the hard feelings still existing between the organizations years after the war.

13. Belknap, *Michigan Organizations*, 262, and the photograph in Sligh, *Michigan Engineers*, 79, make it clear that the lower mill was located west of Cameron Hill, across the river from the east bank of Moccasin Point; see also William F. Smith, *The Re-opening of the Tennessee River near Chattanooga, October 1863* (Wilmington: Press of Mercantile Printing, n.d.), map pasted in cover. There were several prewar sawmills joined with Smith and McCallie's lumberyard behind Cameron Hill. Charles Stuart McGehee, "Wake of the Flood: A Southern City in the Civil War, Chattanooga, 1836–1873" (PhD diss., University of Virginia, 1985), 27. Details from the work at the lower mill are found in Belknap, *Michigan Organizations*, and Roseberry Diary. The nearby boatyard was on the river at the foot of Cameron Hill and is shown in James A. Hoobler, *Cities under the Guns: Images of Occupied Nashville and Chattanooga* (Nashville: Rutledge Hill Press, 1986), 196.

14. The upper mill was almost certainly located on the south bank of the river, across from Chattanooga Island. This would make it the same mill used by P. V. Fox to turn out pontoons in September; Belknap, *Michigan Organizations*, 158, 261–62. For general maps of the Chattanooga area, see O.R.A., 49, 50. Description of activity at the mill is from Roseberry Diary; Weissert to family, October 10 and 14, 1863; and Belknap, *Michigan Organizations*. On September 29 Rosecrans sent Innes a message: "Let me know how soon . . . those two companies of engineers. We need them very much"; O.R., 30-3:928.

15. Belknap, *Michigan Organizations*, 157–58; Henry S. Dean, "The Relief of Chattanooga," no. 5, *War Papers* (Detroit: Winn and Hammond, 1893), 5.

16. Belknap, *Michigan Organizations*, 262; O.R., 30-4:388, 417, 455. About eight hundred of the brigade's twenty-five hundred men were in Chattanooga at this time, employed on a variety of projects, see O.R., 30-4:438. Duane, Abbot, and Merrill, *Bridge Equipage*, 47, describes the importance of posting a guard in boats one thousand yards above any pontoon bridge, armed with chains and grapnels to grab the floating obstructions and anchors to secure those too large to be immediately towed to the nearest bank.

17. Boatner, *Civil War Dictionary*, 910–11; McDonough, *Death Grip*, 68–71.

18. Kimball, Stearns, and Rolison diaries; ROE, October 1863; O.R., 30-2:715, 30-3:814, 846, 903, 30-4:140.

19. O.R., 30-2:715 ("promptness"), 30-4:136, 164, 228; JMS to mother, October 13, 1863; Stearns and Kimball diaries. Information about the presence of black soldiers is from JWS to wife, October 8, 1863; O.R., 30-4:140; and Kimball Diary. Return to Elk River description is from ROE, October 1863, and Stearns and Kimball diaries. Information on duplicate bridges is found in O.R., 30-3:814, 846, 903; ROE, October 1863.

20. O.R., 30-2:719–20, 30-4:157–58; William M. Anderson, *They Died to Make Men Free*, 2nd ed. (Dayton, Ohio: Morningside Books, 1994), 240–45. Anderson's account includes both a graphic description of the garrison's experience inside the blockhouse and an accompanying photo of the effects of a shell explosion on one of the garrisons.

21. Greenalch to wife, October 8, 1863; JWS to wife, October 8, 1863; ROE, October 1863; Miller, March 1864 resignation in CMSR. Col. J. Coburn at Duck River reported on October 6 that "mechanics" were at work on the bridge, perhaps a reference to Miller and his men. O.R., 30-4:136.

22. Sligh, *Michigan Engineers*, 18; JWS and Stearns diaries. Stearns had been detailed as a train guard to Christiana and was returning to Elk River with Sligh's companies.

23. Stearns, Rolison, and JWS diaries; O.R., 31-1:715.

24. *GR Eagle*, November 20, 1863. JWS Diary; the diary entries are made in the first person and are in Sligh's writing through the fourteenth. His wife noted his death on the fifteenth.

25. Kimball and Stearns diaries; Howe to wife, November 6, 1863; *ROS* 43. The harshest assessment of Hogle, including "notorious," is from "List of Mich. Engineers who have died in the hands of the rebels . . . ," written in response to GO 38, Department of the Cumberland, 1865, and found in MEMRP. There is nothing to indicate with certainty what Hogle's fate was, though no postwar reference to him has been found. His father initiated a pension claim following the war, but it was abandoned for lack of conclusive information.

26. Rolison, Kimball, and Stearns diaries; ROE, September 1863; O.R., 30-4:345, 400. Command at Elk River was in the hands of Col. William Hawley of the 3rd Wisconsin with detachments of several understrength regiments of the XII corps (3rd Wisconsin, 2nd Massachusetts, 107th New York, 102nd Ohio, 33rd Indiana) as well as Thompson's 12th USCT, the Michigan Engineers detachment, and the 2nd Kentucky battery that had been there since July.

27. Rolison and Stearns diaries; ROE, September 1863; O.R., 30-3:947, 30-4:42.

28. ROE, October–November 1863. Information about work on ordnance building is from William G. LeDuc, *Recollections of a Civil War Quartermaster: The Autobiography of William G. LeDuc* (St Paul: North Central, 1963), 105. It is not clear if the Michigan Engineers returned to work on the ordnance building before they were ordered to the MCRR. Paint Rock reference is from SO 28, Chief Engineer, Department of the Cumberland, November 5, 1863, RG 393-1, ser. 1041, Cont. Commands; O.R., 31-1:671–72, 826. Neither source identifies the company or companies from the Michigan Engineers involved, but the clear location of the others and the above information eliminate all but these two companies.

29. Welcher, *Union Army*, 2:166–67.

30. This analysis draws heavily from Shiman, "Engineering and Command," which includes "sophisticated."

31. The only summary found of Innes's tenure is in McKinney, "Michigan Engineers and Mechanics," 145–46, which, though lacking footnotes, is a sympathetic account relying heavily on many of the O.R. and other sources cited later.

According to the regimental descriptive roll, Yates served as assistant superintendent under Innes for at least August and September before work started on the
Nashville and Northwestern. Stanton's order for Anderson to take charge again is
dated October 19, 1863, and is found in Anderson Family Papers; also see Meigs to
Anderson, October 29, in the same collection.

32. Turner, *Victory Rode the Rails*, 290; Samuel R. Kamm, "The Civil War
Career of Thomas A. Scott" (PhD diss., University of Pennsylvania, 1940), 167–70;
Thomas Weber, *The Northern Railroads in the Civil War, 1861–1865* (Westport,
Conn.: Greenwood Press, 1952), 185; Stanton to Anderson, September 28, 1863,
Anderson Family Papers. "Strain" reference is from Rosecrans to WPI, O.R., 30-
3:928. Even Scott, at the center of the chaotic railroad administration in the West,
concluded a month after Innes was replaced that the work of directing both the
Nashville and Chattanooga and the repair of the Nashville and Decatur was too
much for Anderson: "There is some reason to fear that it will be practically impossible for one man to conduct the business of both roads, no matter how great his
ability." O.R., 39-2:61.

33. O.R., 30-4:32–33, 175, 208, 334–35; Kamm, "Thomas A. Scott," 177–80.

34. Kamm, "Thomas A. Scott," 177–81; Turner, *Victory Rode the Rails*, 185;
O.R., 30-3:84, 30-4:166–67; Klein, *Louisville and Nashville*, 39–40; Roger Pickenpaugh, *Rescue by Rail: Troop Transfer and the Civil War in the West, 1863* (Lincoln:
University of Nebraska Press, 1998), 136–38. Information about cancellation of
contract is also in Department of the Cumberland to WPI, August 20, 1863, RG
393-1, ser. 1102, Cont. Commands.

35. O.R., 30-4: 141–42, 167, 207, 333 ("evidences"); Kamm, "Thomas A.
Scott," 179–82; Pickenpaugh, *Rescue by Rail*, 138–39.

36. Herman Haupt, *Reminiscences of General Herman Haupt* (Milwaukee:
Wright and Joys, 1901), 189, 277; SO 18, Quartermaster General's Office, August
8, 1863, ser. 1528, QG Records; Weber, *Northern Railroads*, 180; Kamm, "Thomas
A. Scott," 180; Eva Swantner, "Military Railroads during the Civil War," *Military
Engineer* 22 (1930): 19–20.

37. Forbes to Haupt, August 31, 1863, ser. 1528, QG Records ("deprived");
Forbes qtd. in Swantner, "Military Railroads," 20 ("no train"); Forbes to McCallum, September 1, 1863, ser. 1528, QG Records. Forbes also alludes to a report of
Innes's that was submitted to McCallum August 28, 1863, but which has not been
found. Forbes was relieved by Meigs in late October but was still arguing his case a
month later to War Department officials; Meigs to Forbes, October 19, 1863, attached to Forbes to Col. Charles Thomas, November 23, 1863, ser. 1528, QG Records. At the time he was relieved, Forbes was also quarreling with Anderson and
Thomas A. Scott; Forbes to Haupt, October 20, 1863, ser. 1528, QG Records.

38. Forbes to Haupt, September 9, 1863, ser. 1528, QG Records; O.R., 30-
4:456; Department of the Cumberland to WPI, n.d., RG 393-1, ser. 908, Cont.
Commands. For more on Anderson's men leaving when he was replaced, see
Anderson to Rosecrans, August 8, 1863, ser. 1665, QG Records, and Department
of the Cumberland to Anderson, August 11, 1863, RG 393-1, ser. 1076, Cont.
Commands.

39. O.R., 30-4:416.

NOTES TO CHAPTER 14

40. O.R., 31-1:729, 744 ("energetic"), 31-3:14; O.R., ser. 3, 4:942–44. Several of the men who had been most critical of Innes did not remain long in the region. Scott, his presence made redundant by the arrival of Stanton in Tennessee, retired from his position on October 22. Stanton forced Haupt out in September in favor of McCallum. Forbes, without Haupt as a sponsor, was gone shortly after Innes. Kamm, "Thomas A. Scott," 182–83; Forbes to Col. Charles Thomas, November 23, 1863, ser. 1528, QG Records.

41. Rosecrans later claimed credit for the plan, but it was clearly Smith's proposal. See Ulysses S. Grant, *Personal Memoirs of U. S. Grant* (1885–1886; repr., New York: DaCapo Press, 1982), 314–17; Wiley Sword, *Mountains Touched with Fire: Chattanooga Besieged, 1863* (New York: St. Martin's Press, 1995), 114; McDonough, *Death Grip*, 54–58.

42. Sword, *Mountains Touched with Fire*, 59; Belknap, *Michigan Organizations*, 262–63; P. V. Fox to Smith, June 1, 1895, in Smith, *Re-opening of the Tennessee River*, 29–30.

43. Report of P. V. Fox, November 5, 1863, MEMRP; Belknap, *Michigan Organizations*, 158–59; McKinney, "Michigan Engineers and Mechanics," 148–49; O.R., 31-1:79. At least one account suggests that some of the oars on the twenty-sixth came from the pontoon equipage of the Pioneer Brigade; see Smith to O'Connell, October 26, 1863, RG 393-1, ser. 1041, Cont. Commands.

44. Belknap, *Michigan Organizations*, 158, 262; Robert L. Kimberly, *The Forty-first Ohio Veteran Volunteer Infantry in the War of the Rebellion, 1861–1865* (Cleveland: W. R. Smellie, 1897), 64; report of P. V. Fox, November 5, 1863, MEMRP.

45. McKinney, "Michigan Engineers and Mechanics," 148–49; Belknap, *Michigan Organizations*, 158–59; Dean, "Relief of Chattanooga," 7; Belknap, *Michigan Organizations*, 159, 263. Fox's account in Belknap is not always consistent with his wartime report and postwar accounts. Report of P. V. Fox, November 5, 1863, MEMRP, states fifty wagons were furnished "on the morning of the 26th" and that the pontoon train (less the boats) crossed to the north bank by 4:00 P.M. His more dramatic account of waiting for the wagons until later that night is from his postwar address in Belknap, *Michigan Organizations*. Capts. Benton Fox and Perrin V. Fox were not brothers but did appear to be relatives of some sort with prewar Grand Rapids connections.

46. McDonough, *Death Grip*, 76–83; quote from Kimberly, *Forty-first Ohio*, 60.

47. Many sources include Belknap, *Michigan Organizations*, 159, 263; McKinney, "Michigan Engineers and Mechanics," 149; Dean, "Relief of Chattanooga," 8; O.R., 31-1:78; report of P. V. Fox, November 5, 1863, MEMRP (including "energy"); Lampman account in *City of Grand Rapids*, 828–29. Though the various accounts differ, Fox's total force included about 150 men, two-thirds of whom were from the Twenty-first Michigan; Fox's report identifies the strength of the entire bridging party as 144, with the Michigan Engineers as 40 men under Lieutenant Herkner. Some accounts state the bridge took eight hours (particularly Roseberry Diary and *DAT*, November 12, 1863), but this likely included the time to move the wagons from Chattanooga. Likewise, accounts that implied the bridge

was built amid a storm of rebel lead exaggerate the number of projectiles aimed at the detachment. P. V. Fox himself states that the CSA artillery was silenced shortly after starting, "having done but little harm"; Belknap, *Michigan Organizations*, 263. The term "Michigan Bridge" appears in W. F. Smith correspondence, October 29 and 30, 1863, RG 393-1, ser. 1041, Cont. Commands.

48. McDonough, *Death Grip*, 83–93; Dean, "Relief of Chattanooga," 8.

49. O.R., 31-1:68, 78; Smith, *Re-opening of the Tennessee River*, 25; Dean, "The Relief of Chattanooga," 18–19; McDonough, *Death Grip*, 76. Smith notes that his staff officer Capt. G. W. Dresser, U.S. Army Corps of Engineers, assisted P. V. Fox. The pontoon bridge remained in place throughout the campaign. It was taken down in January 1864 by men of the Twenty-first Michigan under Maj. Benton D. Fox; Smith to B. D. Fox, January 12, 1864, RG 393-1, ser. 1041, Cont. Commands.

50. Kimberly, *The Forty-first Ohio*, 63. The *Chattanooga* was the first of several steamers built at Bridgeport by quartermaster officials for the supply run to Kelly's Ferry. Another early supply transport was the *Paint Rock*, one of five captured river craft refloated and repaired, which at least one account erroneously credits to the Michigan Engineers. According to Wm. F. Smith, the steamer had been disabled and left behind by the Confederates when they evacuated Chattanooga, but Fox was directed to the concealed missing parts by a friendly civilian. William F. Smith, "Operations around Chattanooga, Tennessee," *Military Historical Society of Massachusetts* (Boston: Military Historical Society of Massachusetts, 1881–1918), 8:161.

51. The strength of Grant's force is drawn from O.R., 39-2:12–14, less those commands not available for the upcoming fight. Also see Belknap, *Michigan Organizations*, 159–60, 261, and Smith to P. V. Fox, November 9 and 10, 1863, RG 393-1, ser. 1041, Cont. Commands. Another Michigan Engineers company was ordered to Chattanooga by Smith on November 13, 1863, reference in LR-Reg. Roseberry Diary ("menaced").

52. Sword, *Mountains Touched with Fire*, 188–89.

53. Dean, "Relief of Chattanooga," 10–11; Sword, *Mountains Touched with Fire*, 192–93 (claims that all 116 pontoons were in place by the twentieth).

54. McDonough, *Death Grip*, 118–20 (though he mistakenly gives credit to Dan McCook for constructing all of the pontoons, page 118). Sword, *Mountains Touched by Fire*, 192–93, explains that McCook's men were used to cut three miles of road to help the wagons get to the creek. See Sword, 193–97; Dean, "Relief of Chattanooga," 12–14; Belknap, *Michigan Organizations*, 264; O.R., 31-2:73, 560, 573; McDonough and Bond, *Ponton Equipage*, 721–23.

55. Dean, "Relief of Chattanooga," 14; Belknap, *Michigan Organizations*, 160, 264; McDonough and Bond, *Ponton Equipage*, 723.

Chapter 15

1. Movements and stations of companies are from ROE, November 1863; Kimball Diary, November 8, 1863; Rolison Diary, November 8 and 9, 1863. Headquarters location at Bridgeport is from ROE, November 1863 to May 1864, and *DFP*, February 13, 1864. It is not clear why orders were changed after

November 5. On November 18 Smith wrote that Innes had one too many com-panies on the NNWRR and one too few at Bridgeport and ordered that the error be corrected; Smith to JJ Reynolds, November 18, 1863, MEMRP. Company M stayed on the NNWRR less than two weeks before moving to Bridgeport and probably had been intended to be one of the three companies Smith ordered Hunton to take to that point.

2. Smith to Hunton, November 13 and 18, 1863, RG 393-1, ser. 1041, Cont. Commands.

3. Rolison Diary; *DFP*, January 23 and February 13, 1864; Leduc, *Recollections of a Civil War Quartermaster*, 107, 113; Howe to wife, December 6, 1863; Hunton to WPI, January 19, 1864, RLB; *DAT*, January 22, 1864. Howe and Hunton both claim that the storehouse was over 900 feet long, yet a report in the O.R. (32-1:20) of buildings erected at Bridgeport up to May 1, 1864, gives the length of the two upper landing warehouses as 450 and 315 feet, while LeDuc says they were 500 and 300 feet long, respectively. Company M arrival reference is from Howe to wife, November 24, 1863, and John T. Swigart to parents, November 26, 1863, John T. Swigart Letters, Bentley Historical Library, University of Michigan, Ann Arbor, Michigan (unless otherwise noted, all letters from Swigart are in this collection).

4. Rolison Diary; Hunton to WPI, January 19, 1864, RLB; LeDuc, *Recollec-tions*, 109–13; *DFP*, February 13, 1864.

5. Rolison Diary; Howe to wife, February 28, 1864; O.R., 32-2:439–40, 485.

6. Edwin T. Hardison, "In the Toils of War: Andrew Johnson and the Fed-eral Occupation of Tennessee, 1862–1865," (PhD diss., University of Tennessee, 1981), 241–42; Jesse C. Burt, "Sherman's Logistics and Andrew Johnson," *Tennes-see Historical Quarterly* 15 (1956): 199–201; Duncan K. Major, *Supply of Sherman's Army during the Atlanta Campaign* (Ft. Leavenworth, Kans.: Army Service Schools, 1911), 8–9; O.R., 30-3:891; report in O.R., ser. 3, 5:946–47; *Nashville City and Busi-ness Directory, 1860–61* (Nashville: L. P. Williams, 1860), 53–54; O.R., 23-2:20–23. Also see Innes testimony in 40th Cong., H. Rep. 3, 65; Yates's report and Michael Burns to WPI, February 14, 1863, both in 39th Cong., *Affairs*, 284–85.

7. O.R., 30-3:67, 74, 184–85, 280, 480. Johnson's role in the building of the NNWRR needs a fuller modern examination than has been done to date. The most detailed appears to be Hardison, "In the Toils of War." Hans Trefouse, *Andrew Johnson: A Biography* (New York: W. W. Norton, 1989), contains no mention of the railroad, nor does Turner, *Victory Rode the Rails*, while Weber, *Northern Railroads*, gives it only one sentence. Of the somewhat dated accounts, a critical review of Johnson's effort appears in Burt, "Sherman's Logistics," while a favorable one is in Clifton R. Hall, *Andrew Johnson, Military Governor of Tennessee* (Princeton: Prince-ton University Press, 1916).

8. WPI to Captain Steward, February 12, 1864, and WPI to Captain Web-ster, March 6, 1864, both in RLB. WPI to Regimental Headquarters, September 14, 1863, LR-Reg.; 39th Cong., *Affairs*, 284–85; WPI report July 24, 1863, to Gar-field, RG 393-1, ser. 925, Cont. Commands.

9. SO 115, September 13, 1863, ROB; JWS to wife, September 13, 17, and 25, 1863. Wright's report is in O.R., ser. 3, 5:946–47; Henry C. Wharton, "1863 Operational Map of the Countryside South of Nashville," Tennessee State Library

and Archives. Wright's report lists the dimensions for nine spans over the Harpeth, though both contemporary and modern maps suggest that the railroad crossed the stream seven times; Wright apparently includes two spans each at Harpeth No. 6 and Harpeth No. 7. Engineer work information is from JWS to wife, September 25 and October 5, 1863; Alex Campbell to brother, September 20, 1863; Greenalch to wife, September 30, 1863. Account of departure of Sligh and Companies F, B, and L is from JWS to wife, October 8, 1863.

10. Reference to Foster's death is from Kimball and Stearns diaries; *ROS*, 43:70; Franklin Foster CMSR. Defenses of NNWRR information is from O.R., 31-3:28, 109; F. Dyer, *Compendium*, 1:467, 2:1163, 1640–41, 1647, 1185; O.R., 30-4:308, 482; and Peter Maslowski, *Treason Must Be Made Odious* (New York: KTO Press, 1978), 106ff.

11. O.R., 31-1:728–29, 744 ("vital"), 31-3:14. Troops along the railroad reference is from O.R., 31-3:28, 558, 32-3:292; F. Dyer, *Compendium*, 2:1163, 1640–41, 1647, 1185; and Madison M. Walden, *A Brief History of the Eighth Iowa Volunteer Cavalry* (Des Moines: Register and Leader, 1909), 5–7.

12. Graf and Hasking, *Andrew Johnson*, 6:460–61. Many of the black laborers along the railroad had been forcibly impressed by Union authorities in Nashville, even at gunpoint; Maslowski, *Treason*, 100.

13. Graf and Hasking, *Andrew Johnson*, 6:494–95 ("position"); 39th Cong., *Affairs*, 286. Also see Anderson to Gilman Trafton, April 25, 1863, Goddard to Anderson, June 8, 1863, and "Statement," all in Letterbook, J. B. Anderson Papers, QG Records.

14. Kimball and Stearns diaries; Alex Campbell to brother, November 9, 1863. Poplar Springs reference is from Howe to wife, November 15, 1863.

15. Stearns and Kimball diaries; ROE, December 1863 and January 1864; *DFP*, February 13, 1864. Account of Swift's injury is from Kimball Diary, November 26, 1863. Losses to work accidents reference is from *ROS* 43, Desc. Roll, and CWPF.

16. Stearns and Kimball diaries; ROE, December 1863 and January 1864; O.R., ser. 3, 5:946–47.

17. The account of the November foraging is from Kimball Diary for November 24 and 25, 1863 ("full of whiskey" and "pleasant"); Kimball was with both the Yates and Grant detachments. Also see Kimball Diary, December 23, 1863 ("captured a goose"), January 3, 1864 ("lived well"), and February 7, 1864; SO 1, Detachment, Captain Sligh commanding, September 22, 1863, COB.

18. O.R., 32-2:43, 53, 89, 269–70.

19. A good summary of the conflict between Johnson and the army command is in Burt, "Sherman's Logistics," 195–215. Also see Graf and Hasking, *Andrew Johnson*, 6:486 ("feared"); SO 20 (November 30) and SO 28 (December 24), RG 393-1, ser. 2491, Cont. Commands.

20. O.R., 32-2:88–89 ("anybody"), 436–39. Anderson was also accused of favoring the LNRR, his previous employer, in business arrangements; see Klein, *Louisville and Nashville*, 40.

21. O.R., 32-2:329, 32-3:420. In postwar testimony, Innes stated that he remained in charge of the construction of the Nashville and Northwestern until

relieved at his request so that he could accompany Sherman's advance on Atlanta, but this is inconsistent with any other account. 40th Cong., H. Rep. 3, 65. Johnson remained deeply involved in the construction of the railroad until it was almost literally pried from his hands by Sherman after its completion in May 1864; Hardison, "In the Toils of War," 245–48.

22. Alex Campbell to brother, February 25, 1864; O.R., ser. 3, 5:947; Raycide Mosher to father and mother, February 22, 1864, Raycide Mosher Letters, Bentley Historical Library, University of Michigan (unless otherwise noted, all letters from Mosher are in this collection); Alex Campbell to brother, February 25, 1864; Hamilton letter in *DAT*, March 9, 1864; Kimball Diary.

23. Hunton to Crittenton, December 23, 1863, and Calkins to Hannings, March 4, 1864, both in RLB.

24. Roseberry Diary; Smith to Dean, November 29, 1863, RG 393-1, ser. 1041, Cont. Commands.

25. *DFP*, February 13, 1864; *DAT*, March 25, 1864; Roseberry Diary.

26. Hannings to WPI, March 8, 1864, RLB. Hannings was responding to a query from Innes about sending one of the companies at Chattanooga to help with blockhouses on the railroad to Bridgeport. None were sent, probably because of the large amount of work to be done in the city. Also see Benjamin F. Tower to sister, March 10, 1864, Permelia Jenkins Papers, Bentley Historical Library, University of Michigan (unless otherwise noted, all letters from Tower are in this collection).

27. Hannings to Whipple, March 23, 1864, in Hannings CMSR; *DAT*, April 9, 1864; WPI to W. E. Merrill, April 4, 1864, RLB; Tower to sister, April 7, 1864.

28. Hannings to WPI, April 14, 1864, RLB. White was listed in the 1860 Census as an "engineer." U.S. Census, 1860, Kent County, Michigan.

29. J. W. McCrath account, October 1887, RSR; Daniel Sterling to wife, April 4 and May 25, 1864, Daniel Sterling Letters, Civil War Times Illustrated Collection, U.S. Military History Institute (unless otherwise noted, all letters from Sterling are in this collection); Roseberry Diary, April 21–23, 1864. Company D did some additional work on the magazine doors and windows in late June 1864; see Hoffman to McMichael, June 24, 1864, MEMRP.

30. J. W. McCrath account, October 1887, RSR; *Lansing State Journal*, October 9, 1912.

31. *DAT*, March 30, 1864; O.R., 32-1:40; Welcher, *Union Army*, 2:28; Belknap, *Michigan Organizations*, 198–201. In late November 1863 Smith had over fifteen hundred engineer troops present for duty and under his command, including the four detailed infantry regiments, Michigan Engineers, and three battalions of Col. George P. Buell's Pioneer Brigade; O.R., 31-2:13, 21.

32. Roseberry Diary; John Bettis to friend, June 10, 1864, Buck Family Papers, Bentley Historical Library, University of Michigan.

Chapter 16

1. Castel, *Decision in the West*, 112–13.
2. The importance of the railroads in Sherman's campaign for Atlanta is fully discussed in James J. Cooke, *Feeding Sherman's Army*, vol. 1 of *The Campaign*

for Atlanta (Campbell, Calif.: Savas Woodbury, 1994), 97–114. Also see Shiman, "Engineering Sherman's March," 468–71; O.R., ser. 3, 4:881.

3. NCRR defenses in January 1864 are outlined in the report of Brig. Gen. Joseph Knipe, O.R., 32-2:65–66. Development of blockhouse design and locations are from Merrill, "The Engineer Service in the Army of the Cumberland," in Van Horne, *Army of the Cumberland*, 440–44; William E. Merrill, Manuscript, Fortifications Map File, Drawer 160, RG 77, NARA II (hereafter cited as Merrill MS), 13; Merrill to Whipple, February 25, 1864, RG 393-1, ser. 925, Cont. Commands; Thomas to Grant, February 28, 1864, in O.R., 32-2:489. Dates on experiments are from "Supplement to Blockhouse Sheets No. 1 and No. 2" in Buell-Brien Papers, Tennessee State Library and Archives; Shiman, "Engineering Sherman's March," 512–19; Merrill to Totten, April 6, 1864, ser. 18, OCE Records. In April alone, Merrill sent at least five communications to the Michigan Engineers providing additional detail and direction; see references in LR-Reg.

4. James R. Willett, *Rambling Recollections of a Military Engineer* (Chicago: John Morris, 1888), 5; Merrill, "Engineer Service," 445–46; Merrill MS, 14–15; Shiman, "Engineering Sherman's March," 513–14. The forty inches was deemed by Merrill to be the thickness "as practicable," but it varied in practice.

5. Willett, *Rambling Recollections*, 5; Merrill, "Engineer Service," 445–46; Merrill MS, 14–15; Shiman, "Engineering Sherman's March," 520. The blockhouse in the railroad yard is pictured in O.R.A., 123:6; also see Merrill report in O.R., 49-2:434. For an example of the use of infantry to finish blockhouses, see WPI to Lieutenant Colonel Rogers, April 2, 1864, RLB. For the problems completing the work with infantry details, see a report dated October 16, 1864, RG 393-1, ser. 925, Cont. Commands; though this report is about the LNRR, the same problems were often present farther south. Also see Willett, *Rambling Recollections*, 7, on the same theme.

6. Merrill, "Engineer Service," 448–54; Willett, *Rambling Recollections*, 6–8; SO 35, Military Division of the Mississippi, April 25, 1864, in O.R., 32-3:497; Merrill MS, 7. Morton expressed a similar assessment of the value of blockhouses in August 1862; Operations for July [1862], Morton to Totten, ser. 18, OCE Records.

7. O.R., 32-1:14; Jason Newton Crittenton (JNC) letter in *DAT*, March 30, 1864; SFO 60, Department of the Cumberland, February 2, 1864, MEMRP.

8. JMS to mother, March 14, 1864; ROE, March and April 1864. Yates, "Military History," says that his four companies built all of the blockhouses between Nashville and Decatur and Decatur and Stevenson between March and June, but it is more likely that at least some were constructed by other details. A report by Lieutenant Burroughs, Acting Chief Engineer of the Department of the Cumberland, June 29, 1864, stated there were thirty-six blockhouses (all single thickness) in place by that date; O.R., 38-4:639–40. Based on the surviving regimental records and soldier letters and diaries, it is not likely that Yates's battalion completed this many blockhouses in March and April.

9. Kimball Diary, March 15–April 28, 1864. If the vertical timbers were set with eighteen inches as the depth of the wall, a similar outer wall would have provided close to the forty inches of thickness that Merrill had outlined in his sketches.

10. Kimball Diary, March 15–April 28, 1864.

11. Kimball Diary, March 15–April 28, 1864 ("obtained" in entry of March 27). Delays are referenced in Calkins to Hannings April 2, 1864, RLB; WPI to Capt. W. E. Merrill, April 4, 1864, RLB; Department of the Cumberland SFO 84 revoking permission for Lt. H. F. Williams and instead directing Hunton, MEMRP. Teams and men on NDRR information is from WPI to Polk, Assistant Adjutant General, District of Nashville, April 9, 1864, RLB.

12. O.R., 32-2:331–32; JMS to mother, April 24 and May 1, 1864; Kimball Diary. In mid-May a squad from Company H was still working on a blockhouse at Pigeon Roost Creek, twenty-seven miles south of Columbia on the NDRR; Kimball Diary, May 13, 1864. Work along MCRR account is from Mosher to family, May 10, 19, and 21, 1864; Kimball Diary; ROE, May 1864; JMS to mother, May 31 and June 11, 1864; JNC letter in DAT, June 28, 1864. Mosher and his detachment from Company A reached Bridgeport from their work at Tiney Creek, Alabama, on May 28; Mosher to family, May 28, 1864. A detachment from Company H reached Bridgeport from Paint Rock Blockhouse on June 5; SO 58, June 4, 1864, COB. Kimball and his squad from Company H worked on stockades at Mud and later Crow Creek along the MCRR, not finishing until July 5; Kimball Diary.

13. O.R., 32-3:290; O.R., ser. 3, 5:935; Merrill, "Engineer Service," 452; Rolison Diary; William F. Helle Diary, Bentley Historical Library, University of Michigan (hereafter cited as Helle Diary); Baxter to sister, March 24, 1864, with references to Crow Creek and Tantalon, Larry Martin Collection, Western Michigan University Archives and Regional History Collections. Also see William D. Niles to "Papa," June 20, 1864 ("rocky"), Niles Family Papers, The Lilly Library, Indiana University.

14. O.R., 49-2:392; Merrill MS, 17; Rolison and Helle diaries, April 15–May 16, 1864 ("mountain" in Helle entry of April 18). The men were aided by details from the Sixty-eighth New York. Movement to Bridgeport reference is from Rolison Diary, May 15, 1864.

15. Howe to wife, March 27, April 11, 19, and 24, 1864; O.R., 32-3:471. See O.R.A., 35:3, for likely location and information on the blockhouse near Tullahoma.

16. Reference in LR-Reg. to April 18, 1864, letter from Merrill; SO 36, May 7, 1864, ROB; ROE. May and June 1864; N. P. Fox to mother, April 17, 1864, Fox Family Papers; Howe to wife, May 17, 1864; JNC letter in DAT, June 4, 1864; Helle and Rolison diaries. Also see LR-Reg. with May 3, 1864, reference to "Eng. Order 26."

17. Merrill, "Engineer Service," 446; Merrill to Thomas, May 3, 1864, RG 393-1, ser. 925, Cont. Commands; Merrill MS, 15–16; O.R., 49-2:499; sketches in Buell-Brien Papers. Walter Phillips to brother and sister, May 29, 1864, states the blockhouses measured "seventy feet each way"; Larry Martin Collection, Western Michigan University Archives and Regional History Collections (unless otherwise noted, all letters from Phillips are in this collection).

18. WPI at Bridgeport from Engineer Order No. 26, referenced in LR-Reg. Blockhouse work information is from WPI to Capt. Ira Seymour, April 29, 1864, RLB. The Helle Diary has Company I working on a big stockade at Bridgeport

as early as May 16. For an example of cutting of timber, see WPI to Assistant Quartermaster at Bridgeport, May n.d., June 6, 8, and 15, 1864, all in RLB; O.R. 38-4:374, 627; JMS to mother, June 11, 1864; William B. Stanard to brother and sister, June 12, 1864, Stanard Family Papers, Bentley Historical Library, University of Michigan (unless otherwise noted, all letters from Stanard are in this collection); Phillips to sister Helen, July 19 [June 19], 1864; Baxter to brother and sister, June 21, 1864; Merrill, "Engineer Service," 446.

19. O.R., 49-2:500–501, and accompanying sketches in O.R.A., 112:2. Since this report was written in March 1865, it reflects all fortifications done up until that time. Robertson, *Michigan in the War*, 329, and Howe to wife, May 19, 1864, mention eight blockhouses, but there is no evidence that more than seven were built. LR-Reg., April 18, 1864; N. P. Fox to mother, April 17 and June 21, 1864; Howe to wife, May 17 and June 8 ("by the month"), 1864; JNC letter in *DAT*, June 4, 1864; ROE, May 1864; O.R., 38-4:167–68.

20. JMS to mother, March 25, 27, April 24, and May 10, 1864; O.R., 39-2:21 ("malicious"); Kimball Diary, especially March 28, 1864; *ROS* 43. The first two men are not named in the accounts.

21. P. V. Fox to wife, June 6, 1864.

22. O.R., 32-1:28, 56, 499–501, 32-3:290 ("worst"); James T. Siburt, "Colonel John M. Hughs: Brigade Commander and Confederate Guerrilla," *Tennessee Historical Quarterly* 51 (1992), 87–95; JMS to mother, March 20, 1864; Henry C. Morhouse, *Reminiscences of the 123rd New York* (Greenwich, N.Y.: People's Journal Book and Job Office, 1879), 82–83; Desc. Roll; Pitts CWPF; John McGowan CMSR. The attacking Confederates were members of the Twentieth Tennessee Infantry who had been cut off behind the lines the previous fall and spent several months waging a private war against Union soldiers and installations before crossing the Tennessee in April, commanded by Lt. Col. John M. Hughs; O.R., 32-1:56.

23. Kimball Diary, May 18, 1864 [the incident actually occurred on the night of the 18/19]; O.R., 38-4:259.

24. JMS to mother, March 25, 1864; Howe to wife, May 19, 1864. For Stokes's refusal to take prisoners, also see Siburt, "Col. John M. Hughs," 89.

25. Muir death account is from P. V. Fox to wife, August 21, 1864. Losses to work accidents information is from *ROS* 43, Desc. Roll, and CWPF.

26. Major, *Supply of Sherman's Army*, 41–42; Welcher, *Union Army*, 2:23; Willett, *Rambling Recollections*, 6–9; O.R., 38-1:128; Merrill to Major McMichael, June 20, 1864, and WPI to Steedman, July 1, 1864, both in MEMRP.

27. O.R., ser. 3, 5:935. See O.R.A., 149, for Chickamauga Creek detail and O.R.A., 101, for maps of points along the Western and Atlantic Railroad (WARR). Merrill, "Engineering Service," 453.

28. ROE, June 1864; JNC letter in *DAT*, July 15, 1864; O.R., 38-4:640.

29. Trip and Company A, F, and G dispositions are from ROE, June 1864; SO 66, June 27, 1864, ROB; JNC letter in *DAT*, July 15, 1864; and JMS to mother July 1, 1864. The *DAT* account states Company F was left at Tilton, but this is at odds with detailed information to the contrary.

30. Company H reference is from JNC letter in *DAT*, July 15, 1864, and Kimball Diary (though his detachment remained along the NCRR). GO 66 had

called for Company H to be deposited near Kingston and Cassville, but they were not. Guerrillas are referred to in both WPI to Steedman, July 1, 1864, RLB, and WPI to Department of the Cumberland July 1, RG 393-2, ser. 2651, Cont. Commands. Also see WPI to "Colonel," July 2, 1864, RLB; JNC letter in *DAT*, July 23, 1864; *DAT*, July 23, 1864; O.R., 38-1:154; and Helle and Kimball diaries.

31. SO 72, July 10, 1864, ROB; Kimball and Helle diaries, July 1864.

32. JMS to mother, July 29 and August 12–16, 1864; ROE, July and August 1864; Merrill report for week ending July 30, 1864, RG 393-1, ser. 925, Cont. Commands.

33. O.R., 38-3:268–69, 38-5:101.

34. John P. Dyer, *"Fightin' Joe" Wheeler* (Baton Rouge: Louisiana State University Press, 1941), 187–89; Hattaway and Jones, *How the North Won*, 610.

35. Boatner, *Civil War Dictionary*, 911; Dyer, *"Fightin' Joe" Wheeler*, 189–95; James L. McDonough and James P. Jones, *War So Terrible: Sherman and Atlanta* (New York: W. W. Norton, 1987), 285–88; Albert Castle, *Decision in the West: The Atlanta Campaign of 1864* (Lawrence: University Press of Kansas, 1992), 490.

36. JMS to mother, August 12–16, 1864; O.R., 38-3:274–75. Though Archer does not name Sligh, Nevius, or Company F, his reference to a "company of engineers" and Sligh's account fit perfectly. The *DAT* went so far as to state that Wheeler's men avoided attacking at Tilton specifically because it was defended by men of the Michigan Engineers, but there is nothing to support this improbable story; *DAT*, September 2, 1864.

37. Graysville account is from JNC letter in *DAT*, September 2, 1864, Steedman report in O.R., 38-2:496, and Wells Knapp to Mariette Hutchins, August 21, 1864, Mariette Hutchins Letters, Private Collection of John Gelderloos, Grand Rapids, Michigan. Cartersville reference is from Kimball Diary.

38. Greenalch to wife, August 17, 1864; JMS to mother, August 25, 1864; Mosher letter, August 27 and 30, 1864. There is confusion about the date Dunsmore was captured, ranging from August 8 (Desc. Roll and *ROS*, 43:61) to August 25 (CWPF); August 18 is most likely. Martin's raiding parties are referenced in Lewis Lawson, *Wheeler's Last Raid* (Greenwood, Fla.: Penkevill, 1986), 134–35.

39. Stevenson information is from Howe to wife, September 10, 1864. Merrill's reports indicate the continued use of the two companies as infantry instead of engineering troops; in particular, see reports dated September 12, 14, 24 and October 3 and 15, 1864, RG 393-1, ser. 925, Cont. Commands. Mann's portion of Company E at Bridgeport probably had the same scare. Mills and the balance of Company E returned to Bridgeport from the WARR in early September.

40. Shiman, "Engineering Sherman's March," 530; O.R., 38-3:276–77, 493, 506–8. Also see Shiman, "Engineering Sherman's March," 532–33, on the importance of garrisons willing to defy long odds and defend their positions as opposed to those that exhibited "weaknesses which were less technical than human."

41. Taylor to WPI, July 16, 1864, with endorsements, Yates CMSR; Whipple to WPI, August 8, 1864, attached to Cist Report, MEMRP. For example, Grant was ordered on July 30 to detail sixty men from his company to get out firewood for the railroad between Cartersville and Cass Station; see SO (not numbered), July 30, 1864, COB. The men from Grant's company started the work on the following day;

Kimball Diary, August 1, 1864. The Company C squad that Weissert was assigned to started getting out timber on August 7. Taylor served as general superintendent of the WARR from July 1, 1864, to September 1, 1865; James G. Bogle, "Western and Atlantic Railroad—1864," *Atlanta Historical Journal* 25 (1976): 60.

42. Merrill to Whipple, August 25, 1864, RG 393-1, ser. 925, Cont. Commands; Merrill to G. H. Thomas, September 4, 1864, in WPI CMSR. This is the only time Hopkins's name has been linked to this controversy, though he was an army contractor following his resignation, providing lumber to the government during the building of the Nashville and Northwestern. 40th Cong., H. Rep. 3, 83–84. Asa B. Ayres was the original regimental sutler, but Fox reported at this time that former adjutant Miller was now sutler; P. V. Fox to wife, April 1, 1864. Miller's associates—identified later as "Captain Wells" and "Lewis Benham"—cannot be further identified. "Higgins" was probably Thomas Higgins, identified as a contractor in charge of getting wood for the USMRR near Huntsville in June 1864; O.R., 38-4:383, 440.

43. Cist Report and attachments; WPI note, August 25, 1864, on Crittenton request for furlough in MEMRP.

44. Thruston to Hoffman, with Thomas endorsement and comments, November 9, 1864, MEMRP.

45. Merrill to Thomas, September 4, 1864, WPI CMSR.

46. Merrill to Thomas, September 4, 1864, WPI CMSR.

47. Merrill to Totten, September 1, 1863, ser. 18, OCE Records.

48. Totten to Merrill, February 25, 1863, Chief Engineer, Letters Sent to Engineering Officers, 1813–1869, Microfilm Publication T1255, roll 18, vol. 35, pp. 60–61, NARA. Merrill did not suggest the inclusion of civilian engineers into the corps, but Totten's strong response points out how concerned he was about the possibility of such a development.

49. Merrill to Totten, September 1, 1863, and May 10, 1864, and Morton to Totten, February 16, March 16, 1864, both in ser. 18, OCE Records. Rosecrans to Totten, August 29, 1863, and response in O.R., 30-3:213, 245; communications between Rosecrans and Halleck, various dates, in O.R., 30-4:102, 207, 244, 307, 361, 415, 435. Shiman, "Engineering Sherman's March," 159–64, includes a summary of efforts to form a volunteer engineer regiment from the Pioneer Brigade. Also see SFO 152, Department of the Cumberland, June 4, 1864, O.R., 38-4:407; Merrill's circular, June 20, 1864, and SO 231, Adjutant General's Office, July 8, 1864, both in Buell-Brien Papers; U.S. Adjutant General's Office, *Official Army Register of the Volunteer Force of the United States Army for the Years 1861, '62, '63, '64, '65.* 8 vols. (Gaithersburg, Md.: Olde Soldier Books, 1987), 8:120. Wharton was not with the regiment for some time, serving as acting chief engineer of the Army of the Cumberland at the front while Merrill was organizing the regiment at Chattanooga. This left Fox in command much of the time.

50. Three sources of Fox letters contain relevant correspondence. The Fox Family Papers in the Bentley Historical Library, University of Michigan, include Newton P. Fox to mother, June 21, 1864. The Gelderloos collection of Fox materials includes letters from P. V. Fox to wife dated April 1 and July 24, 1864, H. C. Wharton to P. V. Fox, May 27, 1864, and P. V. Fox to Lieutenant Merrill, June 8,

1864. Another important letter is P. V. Fox to wife, May 29, 1864, in the possession of the Stevenson Railroad Museum Depot, Stevenson, Alabama. Also see JMS to mother, August 30, 1864.

51. JMS to mother, August 30, 1864; N. P. Fox to mother, June 21, 1864, Fox Family Papers; N. P. Fox to mother, July 31, 1864, Gelderloos Collection. N. P. Fox to mother, July 24, 1864, suggests that Innes tried belatedly to clear up the Fox and Hannings rank issue, but it was too late (Gelderloos Collection).

52. WPI to "Major" [perhaps Hannings], August 31, 1864, RLB ("specifications"); WPI to P. V. Fox, September 20, 1864, RLB. Also see Hannings to WPI, August 29 and 30, 1864, MEMRP. Hannings was complaining that P. V. Fox had let soldiers go home on furlough too often. Stevenson appointment reference is from P. V. Fox to wife, August 21, 1864.

53. Fox's departure information is from LR-Reg. (citing Engineer Order No. 71) and Desc. Roll. For examples of Fox's conflict with other officers, see his diary for October 29 and 31 and November 15, 1862, which contain references to an ongoing dispute between P. V. Fox and Major Hopkins.

Chapter 17

1. O.R., 38-1:127–36; Shiman, "Engineering Sherman's March," 267–80.

2. O.R., 38-1:138; orders cited in WPI to Whipple, September 27, 1864, RLB; "Engineer Report[s] of Operations . . . week[s] ending October 10, 1864, [and] October 22 [*sic*]," Emerson Papers. For positions, see ROE, September 1864.

3. JNC letter in *DAT*, November 15, 1864; Helle and Kimball diaries; Stanard to brother and sister, October 2, 1864; WPI to Whipple, September 27, 1864, RLB.

4. Calkins to Herkner, October 1, 1864, RLB; Martin A. Westcott Diary, Mason Family (Van Buren County) Papers, Bentley Historical Library, University of Michigan, Ann Arbor (hereafter cited as Westcott Diary).

5. Wiley Sword, *Embrace an Angry Wind: The South's Last Hurrah: Spring Hill, Franklin, and Nashville* (New York: HarperCollins, 1992), 53–62; Boatner, *Civil War Dictionary*, 306; O.R., 39-1:582–83.

6. Merrill, "Engineer Service," 448–51; Jacob D. Cox, *Atlanta*, vol. 9 of *Campaigns of the Civil War* (New York: Charles Scribner's Sons, 1882), 236; O.R., 39-1:826–27. A detailed account from a defender's perspective is in Isaac H. C. Royse, *History of the 115th Regiment Illinois Volunteer Infantry* (Terre Haute, Ind.: Privately published, 1900), 220–21. References to previous surrender of blockhouses are in O.R., 39-1:507–49.

7. Kimball and Westcott diaries; Alex Campbell to brother, October 16, 1864; JNC letter in *DAT*, November 15, 1864; O.R., 39-3:134–35. LR-Reg. lists an October 6, 1864, order from Slocum to send three hundred men to a point beyond Marietta.

8. The capture and subsequent fate of Frederick Grovenburg and Miel Cory of the Company G men is drawn from several conflicting sources: Westcott Diary, October 17 and 18, 1864 (including quotes); list of "absent men accounted

for by name" attached to Monthly Return, October 1864; Cory and Grovenburg CMSR. No other Company G men were captured in October 1864 according to Desc. Roll and *ROS* 43. The only reference to the capture of the rescue party is in Westcott Diary, October 17, 1864.

9. O.R., 38-1:138, 39-1:581, 649, 655–59, 679–80, 39-3:43, 69.

10. WPI to Wharton, October 10, 1864, and to Poe, October 13 and October 17, 1864, all in RLB. Also see Orlando M. Poe Diary, Library of Congress (hereafter cited as Poe Diary).

11. O.R., 39-1:649–50, 681–84; O.R., ser. 3, 5:399; WPI to Colonel McKay, October 13, 1864, and unidentified "Lt. Col." to Wharton, October 18, 1864, both in RLB. Innes's teams had probably been "in the harness for four days" while on a foraging expedition; see O.R., 39-1:663–64, and Edwin E. Bryant, *History of the Third Regiment of Wisconsin Veteran Volunteer Infantry, 1861–1865* (Madison: Veteran Association of the Regiment, 1891), 273.

12. Helle, Kimball, and Westcott diaries. The balance of Company H rejoined the regiment in Atlanta on November 3. Also see Poe to Merrill, October 1, 1864, Orlando M. Poe Papers, Library of Congress (unless otherwise noted, all letters from Poe are in this collection).

13. Howe to wife, September 11 and 27, 1864; O.R., 39-2:523, 380.

14. Howe to wife, October 28, 1864; Yates to Grant, November 3 and 10, 1864, RLB.

15. Poe Diary, October 9, 1864; letters from Poe. October 13 and 19, 1864, LR-Reg.; Westcott Diary ("awful" in entry of October 23, 1864).

16. Robertson, *Michigan in the War*, 79–80. There are several excellent sources for the 1864 election and Union soldiers. Joseph T. Glatthaar, *The March to the Sea and Beyond: Sherman's Troops in the Savannah and Carolinas Campaigns* (New York: New York University Press, 1985), 46–50, addresses the matter as it directly affected Sherman's army. General background and important additional information is also found in McPherson, *Battle Cry of Freedom*, 803–5; James M. McPherson, *For Cause and Country: Why Men Fought in the Civil War* (New York: Oxford University Press), 176–77; David E. Long, *The Jewell of Liberty: Abraham Lincoln's Re-Election and the End of Slavery* (Mechanicsburg, Pa.: Stackpole Books, 1997), 50–51, 60–63, 215–34; and John C. Waugh, *Reelecting Lincoln: The Battle for the 1864 Presidency* (New York: Crown, 1998), 338–43. Only the states of Illinois, Indiana, and New Jersey (all with Democratic-controlled legislatures) did not extend soldiers the right to vote in their camps. In 1865 the Michigan Supreme Court struck down the soldier vote legislation, but the legislature went ahead and seated the contested Republican winners of several close legislative races in which the soldiers had tipped the balance; Willis F. Dunbar, *Michigan: A History of the Wolverine State*. 3rd rev. ed. by George S. May (Grand Rapids, Mich.: William B. Eerdmans, 1995), 389.

17. Glatthaar, *March to the Sea*, 46–47; Baxter to sister, September 21, 1864; Osband Diary, October 2, 1864.

18. Howe to wife, March 2, 1864; Kimball Diary, October 2, 1864.

19. Long, *Jewel of Liberty*, 224–25; McPherson, *Battle Cry of Freedom*, 771–72, and *For Cause and Country*, 176–77 ("admired"); Howe to wife, October 11, 1864 ("lots").

20. This Democrat theme is discussed in detail in McPherson, *Battle Cry of Freedom*, 768–71. Quote is from Mosher to parents, August 27, 1864; in a letter to his parents ten days earlier Mosher supported Vallandingham by name.

21. Howe to wife, April 12, 1864 ("good majority"); Baxter to sister, September 21, 1864 ("equivalent").

22. Robertson, *Michigan in the War*, 79–80; Glatthaar, *March to the Sea*, 46–50, 200–202; McPherson, *Battle Cry of Freedom*, 803–5. Also see Edward McPherson, *The Political History of the United States of America during the Great Rebellion* (Washington, D.C.: Phip and Solomons, 1865), 623. Kent County results are from Leeson, *Kent County*, 334.

23. Howe, November 19–20, 1864; JMS to mother, November 9, 1864.

24. Glatthaar, *March to the Sea*, 46–50, 200–202; McPherson, *Battle Cry of Freedom*, 803–5.

25. WPI to Whipple, October 4, 1864, RLB. It is not clear exactly how many men were mustered out at Atlanta, but the best estimate is 334 enlisted men and 25 officers; see quarterly supplement with Monthly Return for December 1864.

26. JMS to mother, September 6, 1864; Sligh ended up remaining in the army and finished as captain of Company E. As late as October 4, Innes believed that only himself, Hunton, DeCamp, and O'Donoughue were eligible to go home from the officer corps; WPI to Whipple, October 4, 1864, RLB.

27. O.R., ser. 3, 4:254, 566–67, 740–41. Chapel and White information is from WPI to Southard Hoffman October 27, 1864, RLB; Kimball Diary, October 24, 1864. Some of the departing enlisted men also had offers to remain and collect the substantial recruitment bounties. For example, Martin Westcott of Company G briefly considered an offer of five hundred dollars to muster out and then enlist and take the place of one of the new recruits; Westcott Diary, October 25, 1864. Others returned home briefly before rejoining the army. Herbert Titus of Company C presumably received a large bounty when he enlisted in the Tenth Michigan Cavalry in February 1865, serving through November; see *Record of Service*, 40:139.

28. Kimball, Osband, and Westcott diaries.

29. GO 47, n.d. [late October], ROB. Innes did not elaborate on the circumstances that did not permit him to remain.

30. *GR Eagle*, November 16, 1864; JNC letter in *DAT*, November 15, 1864.

31. Kimball, Osband, and Westcott diaries.

32. Innes's ear problems had apparently started in the fall of 1862, when he was forced to sleep on the ground and a foreign object, most likely a bug, crawled into his ear. As late as the summer of 1864, the ear was infected and filled with puss according to later testimony by Surgeon DeCamp; WPI CWPF.

33. Part of the problem in evaluating Innes's role in running the military railroads is that so much of the existing information was written or collected by McCallum and his supporters, to the detriment or exclusion of everyone else. For example, McCallum's voluminous report after the war on the role of military railroads does not even mention Haupt, yet he was the man who more than any other developed the concept of a civilian railroad construction and repair force and who

had the greatest success in the early years of the war in keeping the railroads working in the East. Likewise, most accounts of military railroads in the West focus on the period after February 1864, when McCallum came west to take command, and ignore the contributions of Anderson, Innes, and others in keeping the army fed and reinforced before that time.

34. Westcott Diary, October 16, 1864, and Osband Diary, October 14, 1864; both refused to sign the petition. Innes's intention to leave was apparent as early as October 4, 1864; WPI to Whipple, October 4, 1864, RLB. In an earlier letter to Blair (August 4, 1864, RLB) Innes stated that the regiment would soon be left "like a church without a bishop" at the muster-out of the original men, suggesting that he would be going with them.

35. A brevet rank was an honorary one, granting the holder the title but not the pay, rank, or precedence. Background on brevet rank in the Union army is found in Boatner, *Civil War Dictionary*, 84, and Roger D. Hunt and Jack R. Brown, *Brevet Brigadier Generals in Blue* (Gaithersburg, Md.: Olde Soldier Books, 1990), v–xx. In keeping with common use, Innes was referred to as General Innes after the war.

36. Hunton's health problems are documented in his CMSR and CWPF. The problems originated on the march from Nashville to Savannah, Tennessee, in April 1862. There may have been other reasons why he left with Innes. P. V. Fox suggests in an April 1, 1864, letter to his wife that Hunton was at odds with Governor Blair ("I heard in Michigan that the Governor would not promote Hunton"); see Fox Letters, Gelderloos Collection.

37. *ROS* 43; Desc. Roll. O'Donoughue's commission as surgeon was signed by Blair on November 17, 1864, and he finally rejoined the regiment on January 7, 1865, at Savannah; Roseberry Diary.

38. Williams CMSR.

39. The Roseberry Diary, November 6, 1865, states that the newly commissioned officers were notified of their new commissions on that date. Most of these men were officially mustered out of their old positions and into the new ranks on January 7 or 8, 1865, while at Savannah. Presumably the new commission did not arrive from Michigan until after Sherman's men had left on their march to the sea.

Chapter 18

1. WPI to Captain Stockdale, October 29, 1862, RLB; M. Burns to Johnson, June 14, 1864, and Yates to Johnson, August 22, 1864, both in Johnson Papers. O.R., 39-2:210, includes a letter from Johnson to Thomas, asking for Yates's services: "The services of Major Yates at this time are important and I hope he can be spared, which will not interfere with Colonel McCallum in any way."

2. Crittenton and Hannings were not mustered out as captains and in as majors until January 7, 1865. A month previous, they were designated acting majors and given the responsibilities of that rank while still commanding their companies. GO 5, December 7, 1864, ROB.

3. Desc. Roll; Roseberry Diary, January 7, 1865. O'Donoughue's commission was signed November 17, 1864, by Governor Blair to rank from November 3,

1864. U.S. Census, 1860, Calhoun County, Michigan. King reached the regiment on February 1, 1865, near Hickory Hill, South Carolina.

4. Adams, an experienced millwright and wagon manufacturer from Kent County, had been commissioned directly from civilian life in January 1864. In late March 1865 he was replaced by Lt. James M. Sligh, followed shortly after by Lt. Caleb Ensign, and served with his company until his resignation in August. Lt. Bert Jewell had enlisted as sergeant in 1861 and risen through the ranks. Previous to April 1864 he served as quartermaster of Hannings's battalion at Chattanooga.

5. Dates in table 4 are from commissions when most actually began to act in that capacity instead of the dates they actually received the commissions and were mustered in.

6. Information on overall experience is from Desc. Roll, 1860 census, and local historical sources.

7. *GR Eagle*, December 16, 1863 ("excellent"); *DAT*, February 2, 1864 ("exists"). Eaton and McCarthy came in for especially harsh criticism, see Kimball Diary, February 1, 1864, and C. B. Aylworth (Battery E) letter in *GR Eagle*, February 23, 1864. McCarthy resigned in May following a sawmill accident, and Eaton went home with the original men in October 1864. An interesting account of what happened in another regiment when outsiders were commissioned is Mark H. Dunkleman, "'A Just Right to Select Our Own Officers': Reactions in a Union Regiment to Officers Commissioned from Outside Its Ranks," *Civil War History* 44 (1998): 24–34.

8. Numbers from Desc. Roll and *ROS* 43.

9. *Jackson Citizen*, December 23, 1863 ("liberal").

10. SFO 318, Department of the Cumberland, November 22, 1863, MEMRP; Hill to Denison, December 23, 1864, and P. V. Fox to G. H. Thomas, January 16, 1864, both in MEMRP; Baxter, *Grand Rapids*, 158; *GR Eagle*, January 6, 1864.

11. Charles Lanham, *The Red Book of Michigan* (Detroit: E. B. Smith, 1871), 178–79.

12. Letters written during this period contain requests for updates on how recruiting is going and who is enlisting or being drafted. Greenalch to wife, June 28 and July 12, 1864; Peel to wife, August 28, 1864, Charles Peel Correspondence, Bentley Historical Library, University of Michigan (unless otherwise noted, all letters from Peel are in this collection); Baxter to sister, August 4, 1864. Bounties are discussed in Shannon, *Organization and Administration*, 2:79–80, 92 ("climax"), and Eugene C. Murdock, *Patriotism Limited, 1862–1865: The Civil War Draft in the North* (Madison: State Historical Society of Wisconsin, 1971), 27–30. Local bounties in Michigan were averaging $275 to $325 in August 1864. O.R., ser. 3, 5:746. Communities in Kent County were paying $300 in bounty for each recruit in August 1864. *GR Eagle*, August 3 and 7, 1864. Peel to wife, September 21, 1864 ("enough"); in fact, Peel was discharged in June 1865 with the other 1862 three-year recruits, as were the 1864 one-year recruits.

13. Baxter to sister, August 4, 1864; Peel to wife, August 28, 1864.

14. O.R., ser. 3, 4:515, 558; Frederick Phisterer, *Statistical Record of the Armies of the United States* (New York: Scribner's Sons, 1883), 8; WPI to Blair, August 4, 1864, RLB.

15. Michigan Adjutant General, *Annual Report of the Adjutant General of the State of Michigan for the Year 1866*, (Lansing: John A. Kerr, 1866), 33–34. After adjusting for reenlisted veterans, about thirty-nine thousand of the state's ninety thousand recruits were enlisted before September 19, 1863.

16. For an example of harsh remarks on the later recruits, see Robertson, *Soldiers Blue and Gray*, 37–40. See appendix I, tables B and D for a comparison of recruit groups.

17. Phillips to sister, May 29, 1864.

18. Geary, *We Need Men*, 112–13; Lanham, *Red Book*, 178; Shannon, *Organization and Administration*, 2:68–69, 262–63; O.R., ser. 3, 3:414–16, 5:892; Castel, *Decision in the West*, 9–11. *ROS* 43 and Desc. Roll identify 142 veteran volunteers, though Michigan Adjutant General, *Annual Report 1864*, 64, states 148.

Chapter 19

1. Grant, *Personal Memoirs*, 166; Lee B. Kennett, *Marching through Georgia: The Story of Soldiers and Civilians During Sherman's Campaign* (New York: Harper-Collins, 1995), 226–27.

2. Boatner, *Civil War Dictionary*, 509, estimates Wheeler had about ten thousand men, though Wheeler claimed to have had no more than thirty-five hundred. John F. Marszalek, *Sherman: A Soldier's Passion for Order* (New York: Free Press, 1993), 300–301, estimates that the combined strength of Smith and Wheeler was about eight thousand.

3. Glatthaar, *March to the Sea*, 18; John M. Gibson, *Those 163 Days: A Southern Account of Sherman's March from Atlanta to Raleigh* (New York: Coward-McCann, 1961), 24.

4. The XIV and XX corps were detached from the Department of the Cumberland for the march and were collectively known as the Army of Georgia while on the march. Information about experience is drawn from Glatthaar, *March to the Sea*, 21, 27–28, 187–95.

5. Poe report in O.R., 44:59, lists 4,575 men in the three regiments and pioneer detachments, but see Shiman, "Engineering Sherman's March," 559–60. The Missouri Engineers were the 500 men of the regiment consolidated into a five-company battalion after the muster-out of the nonveteran original men. William A. Neal, *An Illustrated History of the Missouri Engineers and the 25th Infantry Regiment* (Chicago: Donohue and Henneberry, 1889), 179; Shiman, "Engineering Sherman's March," 554–55. Though Poe reports the Michigan Engineers strength as 1,500, only about 1,000 men from Companies A through K made the march. Sligh, *Michigan Engineers*, 24–26; Yates, "Military History."

6. Yates cites his request in "Military History," and Poe's request was granted by Sherman on November 1. Poe to Yates, November 1, 1864, MEMRP. Preparations information is from JNC letter in *DAT*, November 21, 1864, and Roseberry Diary, November 4 and 5, 1864. Detachment of York and Fields reference is from SO 7, November 7, 1864, ROB. York was not able to rejoin the regiment before it left for Savannah and remained in the West until March 1865.

7. Roseberry Diary, November 5, 1864; SO 6, November 6, 1864, ROB; Poe's report in O.R., 44:59.

8. Monthly Return, December 1864.

9. O.R., 39-3:681; Henry Hitchcock, *Marching with Sherman* (New Haven, Conn.: Yale University Press, 1927), 56.

10. O.R., 39-3:741 and 44:59–60; Poe to Yates, November 3, 1864, Yates/Burton. The Missouri Engineers drilled with their pontoon train, tore up some railroad track in the surrounding area, and worked on the new Union defensive works. Neal, *Illustrated History*, 155; Shiman, "Engineering Sherman's March," 553–54. They were little engaged in the destruction within Atlanta, despite more exaggerated claims in Daniel Baker, *A Soldier's Experience in the Civil War* (Long Beach, Calif.: Graves and Hersey, 1914), 39. The Fifty-eighth Indiana Pontoniers did not reach Atlanta until November 14 and were not engaged in the destruction. John J. Hight, *History . . . Fifty-Eighth Indiana Regiment*, compiled by Gilbert R. Stormont (Princeton, Ind.: Press of the Clarion, 1895), 406–7.

11. Kennett, *Marching through Georgia*, 233; James G. Bogle, "The Western and Atlantic Railroad in the Campaign for Atlanta," in *The Campaign for Atlanta*, vol. 2 (Campbell, Calif: Savas Woodbury, 1994), 337; Roseberry Diary, November 12–14, 1864; Sligh, *Michigan Engineers*, 26. At East Point the road split into the Atlanta and Western (also known from that point on as the Atlanta and Alabama) and the Macon and Western. See O.R.A., 60:2.

12. Clyde Ward, "Twisting Confederate Iron," *Civil War Times Illustrated* 25 (December 1986): 24–27; Bogle, "Campaign for Atlanta," 337.

13. Smeed's claim appears in Ward, "Twisting Confederate Iron," 25. Poe's role is more substantiated, included in Hitchcock, *Marching with Sherman*, 58 ("simply"); Poe's own report in O.R., 44:60; and William T. Sherman, *Memoirs of General William T. Sherman* (Bloomington: Indiana University Press, 1957), 180 (though he does not refer to them as "hooks"). Shiman, "Engineering Sherman's March," 661–62, credits Poe with the invention of a "cant hook" and special wrench used for twisting heated rail.

14. SO 10, November 13, 1864, ROB; O.R., 44:60.

15. Adolph A. Hoehling, *Last Train from Atlanta* (New York: T Yoseloff, 1958), 534; Jim Miles, *To the Sea: A History and Tour Guide of Sherman's March* (Nashville: Rutledge Hill Press, 1989), 20; Poe to Yates, November 3, 1865 [1864], Yates/Burton.

16. Sligh, *Michigan Engineers*, 26; Roseberry Diary; work details, MEMRP; SO 10, 12, 13, and 14, November 13–15, 1864, ROB; Kennett, *Marching through Georgia*, 239–40; David P. Conyngham, *Sherman's March through the South, with Sketches and Incidents of the Campaign* (New York: Sheldon, 1865), 237.

17. Gibson, *Those 163 Days*, 29; Sligh, *Michigan Engineers*, 26 ("sky was bright"); Conyngham, *Sherman's March*, 238 ("fierce sheet of flame" and "heart was burning"); O.R., 44:56.

18. Allen Campbell to father, December 18, 1864. All condemned tents and surplus equipment were to be piled in the company streets of the camp and prepared for burning in the morning. SO 15, November 15, 1864, ROB. Most of the city of Chambersburg, Pennsylvania, had been burned by Confederate troops on

July 30, 1864, in retaliation for the burning of private property in Virginia. Boatner, *Civil War Dictionary*, 136.

19. Boatner, *Civil War Dictionary*, 509–12; Welcher, *Union Army*, 2:1000–1004.

20. Roseberry Diary. An account of the march from the diary of Jason Newton Crittenton (JNC), then serving as first lieutenant in Company G, appears in Robertson, *Michigan in the War*, and Sligh, *Michigan Engineers*. Sherman, *Memoirs*, 2:180 ("lurid"). Hitchcock, *Marching with Sherman*, 61, describes Latimer's as a "very good frame house on the roadside, with cabins, barns, outhouses,—evidently well to do."

21. JNC and Roseberry diaries.

22. Reference to detachment from JNC and Roseberry diaries; also see Poe Diary. The march order for the main column had the balance of the regiment and the regimental train following the Sherman's headquarters train, corps trains, and artillery. O.R., 44:490. The Olcofauhachee River was also known as the Alcovy.

23. Weather and march details are from Kennett, *Marching through Georgia*, 253–54; Hitchcock, *Marching with Sherman*, 73–81; and Roseberry Diary. Sherman, *Memoirs*, 2:176–77, states that each corps wagon train contained about eight hundred wagons and occupied about five miles or more of road.

24. March details are from JNC and Roseberry. Shady Dale reference is from Miles, *To the Sea*, 63, and Hitchcock, *Marching with Sherman*, 73. Shady Dale and Newborn are both shown on O.R.A., 144.

25. JNC and Roseberry diaries; Hitchcock, *Marching with Sherman*, 80–81; O.R., 44:180, 183, 514.

26. JNC Diary, October 23, 1864 ("sky was bright"). Destruction in Milledgeville account is from Hitchcock, *Marching with Sherman*, 86, and Sherman, *Memoirs*, 190.

27. Welcher, *Union Army*, 1:1003–4; O.R., 44:527.

28. JNC and Roseberry diaries; O.R., 44:541–45. The same gristmill along Town Creek is mentioned in the report of Col. Cyrus Briant, Eighty-eighth Indiana, in O.R., 44:171–72. JNC says they camped near Hebron on the twenty-fifth, yet march orders have them moving via Long's Bridge; perhaps they moved in detachments.

29. JNC and Roseberry diaries; O.R., 44:214, 272; Poe Diary. Roseberry calls it Powers Station; O.R.A., 144, and reports label it Tennille Station or Station No. 13. According to Geary (O.R., 44:273), the railroad track that they tore up on November 26 and the two following days ran through a "continuous morass," known locally as Williamson's Swamp. A stream of that name ran through it and parallel to the railroad until flowing into the Ogeechee River.

30. JNC and Roseberry diaries; O.R., 44:214, 272, 552; O.R.A., 71:6.

31. JNC and Roseberry diaries both make reference to working at Davisboro or west of it. Also see O.R., 44:214, 563, and O.R.A., 71:6. There were only five XX Corps brigades working on the destruction because the Third Division moved with the XIV Corps during this period, and Geary's Second Brigade was detached on November 28 to guard the headquarters train.

32. JNC (says camped near Bethel) and Roseberry (says camped four miles off the railroad) diaries; O.R., 44:214, 273; O.R.A., 71:6. Only the First and Third

brigades of Geary's division were with the Michigan Engineers; the Second was destroying the railroad between Spier's and the Ogeechee.

33. Roseberry and JNC diaries; O.R., 44:214–15, 217, 273, 283–325, passim; O.R.A., 71:6, 7. Williams ordered Geary to march the Michigan Engineers "at the head of the column so as to reach the Ogeechee River as soon as possible" on the thirtieth, yet there is nothing to indicate this was done unless Crittenton's movement to the river while the infantry remained in camp is what is referred to. O.R., 44:578.

34. JNC and Roseberry diaries; O.R., 44:215, 274; O.R.A., 71:7.

35. JNC and Roseberry diaries; O.R., 44:215, 274, 284, 288; O.R.A., 71:7.

36. JNC and Roseberry diaries; O.R., 44:215, 217, 256, 610; O.R.A., 71:8. The detached men from Company D rejoined the regiment the next day.

37. JNC and Roseberry diaries; O.R., 44:215, 275, 619; O.R.A., 71:8.

38. JNC and Roseberry diaries; O.R., 44:212 ("valuable").

39. Miles, *To the Sea*, 102; Welcher, *Union Army*, 1:1004–5.

40. JNC and Roseberry diaries. The XVII Corps route is shown on O.R.A., 69:7.

41. JNC and Roseberry diaries; Hitchcock, *Marching with Sherman*, 152. The XVII Corps route is shown on O.R.A., 69:7. Guyton, located near the railroad northeast of the road the column was marching on, had been established in 1838 as a resort for Savannah's wealthy who sought to escape yellow fever in the summer. Miles, *To the Sea*, 192. The pioneer detail was probably that of the Fourth Division, commanded throughout the campaign by Capt. John H. Davis of the Forty-first Illinois. O.R., 44:154, 608, 746.

42. JNC and Roseberry diaries; O.R., 44:651; Hitchcock, *Marching with Sherman*, 156–57. The road the Michigan Engineers were on crossed to the south side of the railroad near the Little Ogeechee River and then ran east into Savannah. See O.R.A., 69:5.

43. JNC and Roseberry diaries; O.R., 44:659. Pooler's was the first station along the railroad west of Savannah and was also known as Station No. 1.

44. Charles C. Jones Jr., *Siege of Savannah, 1864* (1874; repr., Jonesboro, Ga.: Freedom Hill Press, 1988); N.C. Hughes, "Hardee's Defense of Savannah," *Georgia Historical Quarterly* 47 (1963): 43–67.

45. Jones, *Siege of Savannah*; Hughes, "Hardee's Defense of Savannah."

46. JNC and Roseberry diaries; ROS 43; Desc. Roll; *Portrait and Biographical Album of Kalamazoo, Allegan, and Van Buren Counties, Michigan* (Chicago, Chapman, 1892), 901–2. Regimental and compiled service records are silent on the injuries to Truax and Ingalls. The exact location of the Michigan Engineers when they came under fire is not certain, so an approximation has been reconstructed from the available sources. See, for example, Poe's claim that the XVII Corps reached a point about five miles from the city on the tenth (O.R., 44:57) and the fact that Sherman's headquarters was also five miles from Savannah along the Louisville road and was in a nearby railroad cut when a battery eight hundred yards to the front opened fire on his party (Sherman, *Memoirs*: 194–95). Telfair's Station was located on the south side of the Georgia Central track, four and a half miles west of Savannah, according to the commander of the Tenth Michigan, who camped

there on December 12. O.R., 44:188. McLaw's headquarters on December 12 was at Telfair Place. See O.R., 44:952. Reference to "Daly farm, or Telfair swamp" is found in Jones, *Siege of Savannah*, 133. Daly Farm was on the left flank of McLaw's line, just south of the Georgia Central.

47. JNC and Roseberry diaries; O.R., 44:149–51; O.R.A., 70:2.

48. Information about Hannings and B, C, E, and I (Second Battalion) is from JNC and Roseberry diaries and SO 18, 19, and 20, all December 10, 1864, ROB. The Charleston and Savannah was one of three railroads into Savannah. The Georgia Central ran to the west and then across the state and had been largely destroyed by Sherman's men. About five miles west of Savannah, the Savannah and Charleston separated from the Georgia Central and circled north and then northeast over the Savannah River, which separated Georgia from South Carolina. Retreating Confederates destroyed the rail bridge over the Savannah River, cutting the city's only rail connection with supplies and reinforcements to the North. The remaining rail line was the Atlantic and Gulf, which ran southwest out of the city, crossed the Ogeechee, and continued on to Thomasville, Georgia. See O.R.A., 70.

49. Roseberry Diary, December 12 ("starvation") and 13, 1864; Welcher, *Union Army*, 1:1006; Hitchcock, *Marching with Sherman*, 176.

50. SO 21, December 13, 1864, ROB; Roseberry Diary, December 13–16, 1864; O.R.A., 70.

51. O.R., 44:729–30, 738; Roseberry Diary; Yates to Poe, December 17, 1864, RLB. The regiment's camp moved on the fifteenth with Sherman's headquarters from its position at Louisville Road and Georgia Central near where Brown had been killed to a location further south on the Ogeechee Road. Roseberry Diary and O.R.A., 70.

52. Welcher, *Union Army*, 1:1007; O.R., 44:685, 729–32; Roseberry and JNC diaries; SO 23 and GO 8, both December 23, 1864, ROB; Poe to Yates, December 19, 1864.

53. The importance of Sherman's march is assessed in Charles E. Vetter, *Sherman: Merchant of Terror, Advocate of Peace* (Gretna, La.: Pelican, 1992), 260–62. Sherman's own assessment is in *Memoirs*, 2:220–21.

54. Recent contributions to the debate include Kennett, *Marching through Georgia*, 262–87; Glatthaar, *The March to the Sea*, 134–55; Marszalek, *Sherman*, 302–3; and Vetter, *Sherman*, 245–68. Kennett argues that the destruction was not much different than earlier in the war but that the widespread foraging increased the incidents of contact between soldier and civilian and thus the opportunities (277). Glatthaar suggests that Sherman implemented a different strategy from that used previously—one calculated to destroy the will of the South to resist. Marszalek stresses that Sherman "was putting into practice his long-held view of collective responsibility" (303). Among the most interesting defenses of the behavior of his army is by Sherman. He admits that "no doubt, many acts of pillage, robbery, and violence, were committed by these parties of foragers" but claims that "these acts were exceptional and incidental." Sherman, *Memoirs*, 182–85.

55. SFO 120 in O.R., 39-3:713.

56. Allen Campbell to father, December 18, 1864; Greenalch to wife, December 26, 1864. Glatthaar, *March to the Sea*, 135, concludes that the men wanted

to convince the rebels that the cost of making war against the Union was more unbearable "than life within the Union." Kennett, *Marching through Georgia*, 276–86, suggests that many of the soldiers went from being looters to vandals, destroying even though they knew the plunder would be abandoned along the route.

57. Kennett, *Marching through Georgia*, 281; JNC Diary, November 19–20, 1864; Circular, XIV Corps, November 18, 1864, O.R., 44:489–90.

58. Kennett, *Marching through Georgia*, 263–64; O.R., 44:406, 411, 922. Gilman details are from *ROS* 43; CWPF; and Monthly Returns, March–May, 1865.

59. Mark L. Bradley, *Last Stand in the Carolinas: The Battle of Bentonville* (Campbell, Calif.: Savas Woodbury, 1996), 1–2; Welcher, *Union Army*, 1:638–39.

60. O.R., 44:12, 58, 811–12; Sherman, *Memoirs*, 2:237; Roseberry Diary; Engineer Order No. 6, December 29, 1864, Buell-Brien Papers; O.R.A., 70:2.

61. GO 10, January 2, 1865, ROB. Crittenton and Rhodes were both acting majors while waiting for their commissions to arrive. Other details from the regiment continued to be assigned tasks other than work on the fortifications. For example, on January 2 two hundred Michigan Engineers from Companies C, F, and G were sent with Major Rhodes to build a wharf four miles down the river for the unloading of supplies. See "Documents Received," MEMRP; SO 28, January 3, 1865, ROB.

62. Roseberry Diary. Description of field works with terms is in Scott, *Military Dictionary*, 283–85, 504–5, and Shiman, "Engineering Sherman's March," 692–96.

63. O.R., 44:114, 118, 128, 47-2:9; Neal, *Illustrated History*, 165; Baker, *Soldier's Experience*, 41; Roseberry Diary, December 31, 1864.

64. Roseberry Diary; Poe to Yates, January 9, 17, and 22, 1865; SO 28, January 3, 1865, ROB.

65. Roseberry Diary; Jacob D. Carpenter Diary, typescript in author's collection, courtesy of Nancy L. Obermayer, Grosse Ile, Michigan (hereafter cited as Carpenter Diary); O.R., 47-2:95–102, 110–11; John G. Barrett, *The Civil War in North Carolina* (Chapel Hill: University of North Carolina Press, 1963), 44–46; Poe to Yates, January 20, 1865.

66. GO 3, January 21, 1865, ROB; Mark L. Bradley, *This Astounding Close: The Road to Bennett Place* (Chapel Hill: University of North Carolina Press), 4–5.

67. See Desc. Roll. The commissions were probably brought from Michigan by former Assistant Surgeon O'Donoughue, who rejoined the regiment on January 7, bearing a commission as surgeon. See Roseberry Diary, January 7, 1865, and Desc. Roll. Three more officers (Lieutenants Beers, Henika, and Sigler) received commissions for positions in Companies L and M (detached in Tennessee) but remained with their old companies on "special duty."

Chapter 20

1. For a complete account of Hood's campaign and the Battles of Franklin and Nashville, see Sword, *Embrace an Angry Wind*. James L. McDonough and Thomas Connelley, *Five Tragic Hours: The Battle of Franklin* (Knoxville: University

of Tennessee Press, 1983), thoroughly describes the campaign preceding the battle of Nashville.

2. Sword, *Embrace an Angry Wind*, 83.

3. Estimates of numbers of Michigan Engineers left in Tennessee and Alabama are drawn from Monthly Returns for October–December 1864 and Fox to Lorenzo Hoffman, December 27, 1864, RLB. For Grant's assignment, see Yates to Grant, November 3 and 10, 1864, RLB; he arrived and formally assumed command on November 18 (GO 1, Third Battalion, November 18, 1864, ROB). As commander of the two-company battalion, Grant replaced Captain Gifford of Company M, who had been in charge as senior captain since the departure of Major Fox in August. N. P. Fox to mother, August 16, 1864, and reference August 24 in LR-Reg. Gifford was detailed away for a short period of time in late August and early September (references in LR-Reg.), but it is not clear who commanded during his brief absence.

4. Willett's report is revealing of the problems associated with leaving the finishing of the blockhouses to garrisons without a commitment to closely supervise the work. RG 393-1, ser. 925, Cont. Commands. The work of the Michigan Engineers is drawn from SO 23, November 15, 1864, COB; SO 1, 6, 7, and 8, Third Battalion, November 18–29, 1864, ROB; Howe to wife, October 28 and November 2 and 19, 1864.

5. SO 8, Third Battalion, November 29, 1864, ROB.

6. Sword, *Embrace an Angry Wind*, 269–77. On December 6 the XVI Corps was discontinued and Smith's men were referred to as Detachment, Army of the Tennessee.

7. Sword, *Embrace an Angry Wind*, 279–81.

8. Sword, *Embrace an Angry Wind*, 281–82.

9. Forrest and Murfreesboro details are drawn from Sword, *Embrace an Angry Wind*, 293–99. At its largest on December 6, Forrest's command near Murfreesboro included his divisions of Brig. William H. "Red" Jackson and Brig. Gen. Abraham Buford, the sixteen hundred men of Maj. Gen. William Bates's infantry division, and the two small infantry brigades of Brig. Gen. Claudius Sears (of French's division) and Col. Joseph B. Palmer (of Stevenson's division). Within two days Bates and Buford were gone, replaced only by an infantry brigade under Col. Charles H. Olmstead.

10. O.R., 45-1:1192. Warner states the strength of Gifford's detachment as one hundred men, but sixty is more realistic.

11. Arrival is mentioned in SO 8, Third Battalion, November 29, ROB. With Captain Emerson detailed on engineering duty in Chattanooga and senior 1st Lt. Thomas Templeton temporarily commanding Company I with Yates, Earl was the senior officer present with Company L. The formation of the provisional detail is included in SO 6, Third Battalion, November 17, 1864, ROB, and they presumably had remained with Grant and the battalion headquarters. Work details are from SO 9, 10, 15, 18, and 19, Third Battalion, December 1–13, 1864, ROB, and Grant to Lt. J. D. Williams, February 26, 1865, RLB. A helpful sketch of Fortress Rosecrans is in O.R.A., 112:3.

12. The best contemporary accounts of Grass's detachment are reports by Maj. Jerome Nulton of the Sixty-first Illinois and Brig. Gen. Lawrence S. Ross, CSA; O.R., 45-1:620–21, 768–72. The best postwar account is Leander Stillwell, *Story of a Common Soldier of Army Life in the Civil War, 1861–1865* (1920; repr., Alexandria, Va.: Time-Life Books, 1983). From the Confederate perspective, important additional information is found in Homer L. Kerr, ed., *Fighting with Ross' Texas Cavalry: The Diary of George L. Griscom, Adjutant, 9th Texas Cavalry Regiment* (Hillsboro, Tex.: Hill Jr. College Press, 1976), and W. A. Callaway, "Hard Times with Ross' Cavalry," *Confederate Veteran* 28 (1920): 447–48. The various accounts are also well presented in William Forbes II, *Haulin' Brass: Captain Croft's Flying Artillery Battery Columbus Georgia* (Dayton, Ohio: Morningside, 1993), and David Hale, *The Third Texas Cavalry in the Civil War* (Norman: Oklahoma University Press, 1993). Forrest's report for the campaign makes only a brief mention of the engagement (O.R., 45-1:756) and incorrectly dates it as December 13. SO 16, Third Battalion, December 12, 1864, ROB, makes it clear that Earl's men were included with the intention of repairing the railroad and not just as additional train guard.

13. O.R., 45-1:621; Stillwell, *Diary of a Common Soldier*, 247–48. Forrest claims that seventeen cars were loaded with sixty thousand rations, while Ross states two hundred thousand rations were destroyed by his men. O.R. 45-1:756, 771. Union accounts are silent on the size or contents of the train. Andrew Nelson Lytle, *Bedford Forrest and His Critter Company*, rev. ed. (New York: McDowell, Obolensky, 1960), 361, accepts the two hundred thousand number. Information about the role of Twelfth Indiana is from Dyer, *Compendium*, 2:1110.

14. O.R., 45-1:621; Stillwell, *Diary of a Common Soldier*, 248. Nulton says they were warned by the garrison at Bell Buckle but not fired upon. Stillwell claims the single shot struck near him.

15. O.R., 45-1:621; Stillwell, *Diary of a Common Soldier*, 248–49 (including "bully boys").

16. O.R., 45-1:621; Stillwell, *Diary of a Common Soldier*, 249–50.

17. O.R., 45-1:621, 771; Stillwell, *Diary of a Common Soldier*, 250–51; Kerr, *Ross' Texas Cavalry*, 195; Forbes, *Haulin' Brass*, 237; Hale, *Third Texas Cavalry*, 263. Confederate accounts disagree which regiment(s) made the charge and whether it was on foot or mounted. It is not clear who was commanding the artillery or exactly how many pieces were brought to bear on Grass's command. Ross's brigade was part of Brig. Gen. William H. "Red" Jackson's division; the Twenty-ninth Texas was also under Ross's command but was not present during the fighting. During the entire campaign, Ross's command suffered seventy-seven casualties and brought off 550 Union prisoners. O.R., 45-1:772.

18. O.R., 45-1:621; Stillwell, *Diary of a Common Soldier*, 250–51, 254–55; Kerr, *Ross' Texas Cavalry*, 195; Forbes, *Haulin' Brass*, 237–38; Hale, *Third Texas Cavalry*, 263. DeLorme Mapping, *Tennessee Atlas and Gazetteer* (Freeport, Maine: DeLorme Mapping, 1995), 38, and Tennessee Department of Transportation, *Rutherford County*, Tennessee Department of Transportation Map, 1991, show the geography along the route of the retreat. The blockhouse garrison was a company from the 115th Ohio. O.R., 45-1:631–34.

19. O.R., 45-1:621, 771; Stillwell, *Diary of a Common Soldier*, 253. *ROS* 43 and Desc. Roll include the names of Earl and 30 men as captured. Ross's account reasonably estimates that 150 of the 200 Union soldiers guarding the train were captured.

20. Simms information is from CMSR; Thomas Lowry, "Time Lapse," *Civil War Times Illustrated*, 25 (February 1987): 29; and family papers and correspondence provided by Tom Lowry, a great-grandson of Simms. Stillwell, *Diary of a Common Soldier*, 252, suggests that the "heavy set" and "fleshy" Grass lagged behind, stumbled, and was picked up by pursuing Confederates. This comment along with the large loss of men suggest that the race from the train to safety was not as organized or disciplined as claimed by Stillwell in his account and that pursuing Confederates were close behind. Total Confederate casualties were a "half dozen killed" and several wounded according to Kerr, *Ross' Texas Cavalry*, 196.

21. O.R., 45-1:62, 771; Stillwell, *Diary of a Common Soldier*, 248; JMS to mother, January 9, 1865 ("fine man").

22. JMS to mother, January 9, 1865; O.R., ser. 2, 7:1233–34; O.R., ser. 2, 8:31–32, 48-1:498. Forrest released Grass on parole to affect his own exchange. Immediately following the fight, the captured Union soldiers were taken under guard by the Ninth Texas to Salem along with the brigade wagons. Kerr, *Ross' Texas Cavalry*, 195–96.

23. JMS to mother, January 9, 1865.

24. SO 20 and 21, Third Battalion, December 18–19, 1864, ROB.

25. JMS to mother, January 9 and February 5, 1865; Howe to wife, January 31, 1865; report on other working parties from SOs 15 and 17, Third Battalion, December 12, 1864, ROB; Engineer Report for Third Battalion, week ending January 7, 1865, MEMRP; Merrill's report for February 1865, ser. 18, OCE Records. By the end of January Company M was divided into four detachments, stationed at Cummings Wood Yard, Murfreesboro, Smyrna, and Elk River, where Gifford established his headquarters. Lieutenant Sligh and what remained of Company L were at work on the large blockhouse at Christiana.

26. Description of unsuccessful efforts is drawn from Grant to Maj. Southard Hoffman, December 27, 1864, RLB; Yates to Grant, December 28, 1864 (with a January 15, 1865, endorsement to Merrill), RLB; and Yates to Grant, December 21, 1864 (with a January 20, 1865, endorsement by Grant and comments by Willett), RLB. Chain of correspondence is in MEMRP. Order to move is found in O.R., 49-1:629. According to the Monthly Return for December 1864, Companies A through K reported over 200 men absent sick, most of whom were presumably in Tennessee. Companies L and M had 170 present for duty and half again as many absent sick or detailed.

27. Grant to Sligh, February 18, 1865, RLB; GO 5, Third Battalion, February 24, 1865, ROB. Since at least 180 of the 450 Michigan Engineers within the department remained hospitalized or detailed, Grant actually took only an estimated 270 men with him on the trip to North Carolina, based on calculations from the Monthly Return. This includes some 190 men from Companies L and M and 80 more from the other ten companies. Newly promoted Capt. D. M. Moore (G) and Lt. Herman Perkins (D) also traveled east with Grant's battalion. JMS to mother,

March 10, 1865. Details of trip are from Howe to wife, March 5 and 9, 1865; JMS to mother, March 10 and 20, 1865; and ROE, March and April 1865. ROE states the command left on March 2, 1865.

28. Pay information is from Grant to Chief Paymaster, USA, March 11, 1865, RLB. Neither Howe nor Sligh make any mention of pay. See JMS to mother, March 10, 1865, for visit to Barnum's.

29. JMS to mother, March 10, 20, and 30, 1865; Howe to wife, March 5, 9, and 31, 1865; ROE, March and April 1865.

Chapter 21

1. JNC, Carpenter, and Roseberry diaries; ROE and Monthly Return, January 1865.

2. O.R., 47-1:169. The strength of the regiment leaving Atlanta had been about 970, but 7 died at Savannah and 63 were left there sick (3 of whom also later died). See Desc. Roll; *ROS* 43; and Monthly Return, January 1865.

3. Barrett, *Civil War in North Carolina*, 100; Glatthaar, *March to the Sea*, 108–9, 112–15. Shiman, "Engineering Sherman's March," 583–85, summarizes many of the obstacles that were in Sherman's path. A good firsthand account of the experiences of the army along the route is found in Alpheus S. Williams, *From the Cannons Mouth: The Civil War Letters of General Alpheus Williams*, edited by Milo M. Quaife (Detroit: Wayne State University Press, 1959), 373–75.

4. Welcher, *Union Army*, 1:639; Barrett, *Civil War in North Carolina*, 39. On leaving for Charleston, see, for example, Mosher to parents, January 29, 1865, and Cyrus A. Babbitt to wife, January 29, 1865, Cyrus A. Babbitt Letters, Mrs. Ann Coffee Collection, Western Michigan University Archives and Regional History Collections (unless otherwise noted, all letters from Babbitt are in this collection). Maps of the march of Sherman's forces from Savannah to Fayetteville are found in O.R.A., particularly plates 76, 79, 80, 86, and 120.

5. Roseberry, Carpenter, and JNC diaries; ROE and Monthly Return, January 1865; Hitchcock, *Marching with Sherman*, 234; Harold Frey and Wilda Babcock, *From the Diary of Thomas Marks* (N.p.: Privately published, 2000), 1. Pocotaligo Station was about two miles west of the small village of the same name. Hitchcock, *Marching with Sherman*, 229.

6. Roseberry, Carpenter, and JNC diaries; ROE and Monthly Return, February 1865; O.R., 47-1:222, 272, 47-2:196; Hitchcock, *Marching with Sherman*, 236–38. Hickory Hills is modern-day Hampton, South Carolina. Richard Harwell and P. N. Racine, eds., *The Fiery Trail: A Union Officer's Account of Sherman's Last Campaign* (Knoxville: University of Tennessee Press, 1986), 90.

7. Alex Campbell to brother, March 28, 1865 ("strip of ashes"); Sherman, *Memoirs*, 2:227–28 ("almost tremble"), 254; Greenalch to wife, March 21, 1865 ("to the letter"); Barrett, *Civil War in North Carolina*, 38–40.

8. JNC, Roseberry, and Carpenter diaries; ROE and Monthly Return, February 1865 (Duck "Branch"); Hitchcock, *Marching with Sherman*, 239–50; O.R., 47-1:222, 272, 278, 286; Sherman, *Memoirs*, 2:273.

9. JNC, Carpenter, and Roseberry diaries; O.R., 47-1:194, 222–23; Hitchcock, *Marching with Sherman*, 254.

10. JNC, Carpenter, and Roseberry diaries; ROE and Monthly Return, February 1865; Hitchcock, *Marching with Sherman*, 254; O.R., 47-2:308.

11. JNC, Roseberry, and Carpenter diaries; ROE and Monthly Return, February 1865 ("Springtown" as site of camp); O.R., 47-1:223, 316–17; Hitchcock, *Marching with Sherman*, 259.

12. JNC, Carpenter, and Roseberry diaries; ROE and Monthly Return, February 1865; O.R., 47-1:19, 224, 245, 272, 47-2:318; Hitchcock, *Marching with Sherman*, 260 ("steady"), 261; Poe Diary, February 7, 1865.

13. O.R., 47-2:331. A description of the process of destroying the rail is in Barrett, *Civil War in North Carolina*, 51, and Henry W. Slocum, "Sherman's March from Savannah to Bentonville," *Battles and Leaders of the Civil War*, 4 vols. (1887–88; repr., Secaucus, N.J.: Castle, 1982), 4:685–86.

14. JNC, Carpenter, and Roseberry diaries; Frey, *Diary of Thomas Marks*, 2; O.R., 47-1:224, 245, 272; Oliver O. Howard, *Autobiography of Oliver Otis Howard, Major General, United States Army*, 2 vols. (New York: Baker and Taylor, 1907), 2:108; Poe to Yates, February 8, 1865; Poe Diary, February 8, 1865.

15. JNC, Carpenter, and Roseberry diaries; Frey, *Diary of Thomas Marks*, 2; ROE and Monthly Return, February 1865; O.R., 47-1:592, 47-2:349 ("beautifully"), 343, 364; Shiman, "Engineering Sherman's March," 668–69. There are detailed position maps for the XX Corps in O.R.A., 80 and 86. Mileage for places along the South Carolina Railroad can be found in a printed table for 1869 in Samuel Melanchthon Derrick, *Centennial History of the South Carolina Railroad* (Columbia, S.C.: State Company, 1930).

16. JNC, Roseberry, and Carpenter diaries; Frey, *Diary of Thomas Marks*, 2; O.R., 47-1:660, 822; SO 16, February 10, 1865, ROB; O.R.A., 80:3. Crittenton's commanded included Companies A, D, E, and I, while Hannings had Companies B, C, G, and H. Company K and the regimental wagons were with the main wagon train, as probably was Company F. That night, Company B was ordered to march with the colors to join Yates at Blackville, while Company F went to join Hannings.

17. Guignard's Bridge reference is from from O.R., 47-1:598, 783, 788, 804, 831; JNC Diary; and Frey, *Diary of Thomas Marks*, 2. Duncan's Bridge information is from Carpenter Diary; O.R., 47-1:609; and O.R. ser. 3, 5:425. At both Guignard's and Duncan's, the crossing actually consisted of a series of short bridges located on a causeway through the flooded approaches. Also see O.R.A., 80:3.

18. O.R., 47-1:420, 583, 685, 706, 731, 1101, 1106, 1124–45, 1147, 47-2:409; JNC, Roseberry, and Carpenter diaries; Frey, *Diary of Thomas Marks*, 2; ROE and Monthly Return, February 1865.

19. JNC and Carpenter diaries; ROE and Monthly Return, February 1865; O.R., 47-1:593, 47-2:423; O.R.A., 80:3.

20. O.R. 47-1:430, 445, 482, 489, 47-2:409–10, 422, 449; Hight, *Fifty-Eighth Indiana*, 476.

21. O.R., 47-2:444–45; Poe to Yates, February 16, 1865; Poe Diary, February 16, 1865; Welcher, *Union Army*, 1:641.

22. Roseberry Diary, February 16 and 18, 1865. The best account of the burning of Columbia is in Marion B. Lucas, *Sherman and the Burning of Columbia* (College Station: Texas A&M University Press, 1976). Also see Vetter, *Sherman*, 277–280.

23. SO 19, February 18, 1865, ROB; JNC Diary; ROE and Monthly Return, February 1865; Frey, *Diary of Thomas Marks*, 2; O.R., 47-1:171, 199, 243–44, 318, 332, 47-2:475, 476, 503; Lucas, *Burning of Columbia*, 122–24.

24. JNC, Carpenter, and Roseberry diaries; ROE and Monthly Return, February 1865; O.R., 47-1:171, 379, 47-2:456, 461.

25. JNC, Roseberry, and Carpenter diaries; Frey, *Diary of Thomas Marks*, 3; ROE and Monthly Return, February 1865; O.R., 47-1:379, 47-2:487, 506–7; Poe Diary, February 20, 1865.

26. Monthly Return, March 1865; Martin Cole, Benjamin Lee, William Mc-Millan, Lyman Henderson, and George Jarmey CMSR. See also O.R., 47-2:566; Barrett, *Civil War in North Carolina*, 104; Howard, *Autobiography*, 2:130. Benjamin Lee fell out during the march and was left behind near the Saluda River on February 17. William McMillan fell out from lameness on February 21, and Lyman Henderson left the ranks near Winnsboro on February 25. George Jarmey was sick and fell behind during the march on February 20 and was later "supposed to have died" (CMSR). Henderson did not survive his illness, Lee was discharged early by the surgeons, and only McMillan remained until muster-out.

27. JNC, Carpenter, and Roseberry diaries; ROE and Monthly Return, February 1865; O.R., 47-2:1224.

28. Welcher, *Union Army*, 1:641–42; JNC, Carpenter, and Roseberry diaries; ROE and Monthly Return, February 1865. See O.R.A., 79:3, for route of XVII Corps in the Carolinas campaign.

29. JNC, Carpenter, and Roseberry diaries; Frey, *Diary of Thomas Marks*, 3; ROE and Monthly Return, February 1865; orders in O.R., 47-2:531; Manning F. Force, "Marching across Carolina," in *Sketches of War History, Papers Prepared for the Ohio Commandery of the Military Order of the Loyal Legion of the United States* (Cincinnati: Robert Clarke, 1888), 1:6; Neal, *Illustrated History*, 169. Liberty Hill reference is from Barrett, *Civil War in North Carolina*, 101; Force to Blair, O.R., 47-2:552; Harwell and Racine, *Fiery Trail*, 144. Liberty Hill was an attractive village consisting of about twenty residences of wealthy planters from the surrounding countryside.

30. JNC, Roseberry, and Carpenter diaries; ROE and Monthly Return, February 1865 (camped at "Copeland Roads"); Force, "Marching across Carolina," 6.

31. O.R., 47-2:945; Glatthaar, *March to the Sea*, 109–10; Shiman, "Engineering Sherman's March," 624–29. Description is from *New Bern (N.C.) Times*, April 25, 1865, as quoted in Barrett, *Civil War in North Carolina*, 36 ("detestable work"). An especially vivid account of the difficulties of moving even over corduroyed road on this advance is found in Hitchcock, *Marching with Sherman*, 251–52.

32. JNC, Roseberry, and Carpenter diaries; Frey, *Diary of Thomas Marks*, 3; Greenalch to wife, March 21, 1865 ("rats"); ROE and Monthly Return, February 1865; O.R., 47-1:380, 47-2:541–42, 550–52.

33. JNC, Roseberry, and Carpenter ("ass deep") diaries; Greenalch to wife, March 21, 1865; ROE and Monthly Return, February 1865; O.R., 47-1:380, 47-2:572, 583, 587–88; O.R.A., 79:3 and 143.

34. JNC, Carpenter, and Roseberry diaries; Frey, *Diary of Thomas Marks*, 3; ROE and Monthly Return, February 1865; O.R., 47-1:380–81, 47-2:597, 608. Force, in "Marching across Carolina," 7, states he started to move the corps' trains across at 11 p.m. and was moving infantry by 6:30 a.m. This is at odds with other accounts.

35. O.R., 47-1:681, 47-2:547, 565, 582, 598–99, 609; JNC, Roseberry, and Carpenter diaries; Frey, *Diary of Thomas Marks*, 3; ROE and Monthly Return, February 1865; O.R.A., 143.

36. JNC, Carpenter, and Roseberry diaries; Frey, *Diary of Thomas Marks*, 4; ROE and Monthly Return, March 1865; O.R., 47-1:201–2, 381, 47-2:631–32, 649–50, 661–62.

37. JNC, Roseberry, and Carpenter diaries; Frey, *Diary of Thomas Marks*, 4; ROE and Monthly Return, March 1865; Barrett, *Civil War in North Carolina*, 108; Neal, *Illustrated History*, 170–71; Howard, *Autobiography*, 2:134.

38. Barrett, *Civil War in North Carolina*, 109; JNC, Roseberry, and Carpenter diaries; ROE and Monthly Return, March 1865; Reese to Yates, March 4, 1865, MEMRP; O.R., 47-1:171, 381, 666; O.R.A., 79:3; Poe to Yates, March 4, 1865; Poe Diary, March 5, 1865. The Carpenter Diary, ROE, and Monthly Return contain references to the Michigan Engineers crossing over on the fourth, but they are probably references to working parties and not the regiment as a whole.

39. JNC, Roseberry, and Carpenter diaries; Frey, *Diary of Thomas Marks*, 4; ROE and Monthly Return, March 1865; Yates to Poe March 5, 1865, Yates/Burton. An account of the explosion is found in O.R., 47-2:701.

40. Welcher, *Union Army*, 1:642; O.R., 47-2:690 ("confident").

41. Carpenter Diary, March 7, 1865 ("Pretty"); Roseberry Diaries; Frey, *Diary of Thomas Marks*, 4; ROE and Monthly Return, March 1865; Yates to Poe, March 6 and 7, 1865, Yates/Burton; O.R. 47-1:98, 382, 47-2:690, 703. During the march from Cheraw to Fayetteville the regimental wagon train moved with the trains of the division they were attached to, while the tool wagons and ambulances remained with the companies.

42. Yates to Poe, March 8 and 9, 1865, Yates/Burton; ROE and Monthly Return, March 1865; Roseberry and Carpenter diaries; O.R. 47-1:98, 382, 47-2:718–19, 727–31, 1344–45, 1352; Force, "Marching across Carolina," 8 (states that the descriptions were drawn from his wartime journal); O.R.A., 79:3. Antioch is referred to as Antioch Church in O.R. 47-2:1345, 1352, and was on the road between the Lumber River and Davis's Bridge over Rock Fish.

43. Marszalek, *Sherman*, 327 ("remarkable change"); Barrett, *Civil War in North Carolina*, 120–21. Blair also made the same point in a letter to Howard. O.R. 47-2:717.

44. Yates to Poe, March 10 and 11, 1865, Yates/Burton; Roseberry and Carpenter diaries; Frey, *Diary of Thomas Marks*, 4; ROE and Monthly Return, March

1865; O.R., 47-1:203–4, 382, 47-2:740, 754–55, 759–60, 783–84, 1345–48; Bradley, *Last Stand*, 108–9; O.R.A., 79:3; Neal, *Illustrated History*, 172.

    45. O.R., 47-2:793 ("no place").

Chapter 22

    1. O.R., 47-2:793–95; E. B. Long, *The Civil War Day by Day: An Almanac, 1861–1865* (Garden City, N.Y.: Doubleday, 1971), 64; Eliza Stinson, "Taking of the Arsenal" ("handsomest") in United Daughters of the Confederacy, J. E. B. Stuart Chapter, *War Days in Fayetteville, North Carolina: Reminiscences of 1861 to 1865* (Fayetteville, N.C.: Judge Printing, 1910), 7–27, quote on p. 8.

    2. O.R., 47-2:779, 790, 1303 ("utter"), 1289 ("destroy"); Hitchcock, *Marching with Sherman*, 270 ("stopped").

    3. *National Tribune*, May 18, 1916; Roseberry, JNC, and Carpenter diaries; Frey, *Diary of Thomas Marks*, 5; O.R., 47-1:171–72; United Daughters of the Confederacy, *War Days in Fayetteville*, 51–52.

    4. O.R., 47-1:23, 171–72.

    5. Greenalch to wife, March 21, 1865; Roseberry Diary (with incorrect date of March 13, 1865); Frey, *Diary of Thomas Marks*, 5; Carpenter Diary. Background on Kennedy is from *ROS* 43; Desc. Roll; and U.S. Census, 1860, Kent County, Michigan. None of the accounts identify the two men who were injured.

    6. Welcher, *Union Army*, 1:643–44; Boatner, *Civil War Dictionary*, 126; Barrett, *Civil War in North Carolina*, 112–13; O.R., 47-2:1050–51.

    7. Bradley, *Last Stand*, 112–13; Welcher, *Union Army*, 1:644; Barrett, *Civil War in North Carolina*, 149. According to the Monthly Return, March 1865, twelve men were in Wilmington hospitals and had presumably been sent there from Fayetteville.

    8. Welcher, *Union Army*, 1:644; JNC and Roseberry diaries; ROE and Monthly Return, March 1865; O.R. 47-1:422–23, 551, 691. March route of XX Corps and Michigan Engineers to Goldsboro is referenced in O.R.A., 80:8, 9.

    9. ROE and Monthly Return, March 1865; Roseberry; O.R. 47-1:691–92, 753; O.R., ser. 3, 5:428; O.R.A., 86:7. Jackson's farm might be the same location identified in O.R.A., 80:9, as "Jackson's Store."

    10. Roseberry Diary; O.R. 47-1:693–94, 729–33; O.R., ser. 3, 5:429; O.R.A., 80:9, 86:7.

    11. Roseberry Diary; O.R. 47-1:588, 693–94, 729–33, 735–44, 47-2:907–8; O.R.A., 86:7; Hight, *Fifty-Eighth Indiana*, 502 ("man-trap"). Falling Creek Church was also known as Dead Fields. Harwell and Racine, *Fiery Trail*, 192.

    12. All four were taken prisoner on the twentieth and paroled on the thirtieth at Cox's Wharf, Virginia, on the James River. They were eventually sent to Camp Chase, Ohio, with other released Union prisoners and were discharged together on June 19, 1865. See *ROS* 43, CMSR, and Desc. Roll. The notations in CMSR state that they were taken "near Bentonville," but there is nothing to connect them with the battle there and nothing further in regimental records. Three belonged to the companies with Hannings, and the other was a teamster with the wagon train.

13. O.R., 47-1:426–28, 47-2:930; O.R., ser. 3, 5:429; Roseberry Diary; O.R.A., 80:9, 86:7, 138; Hight, *Fifty-Eighth Indiana*, 501–2. More on the depots is found in O.R., 47-2:931, 937, 940.

14. The best review of the rebuilding of the railroad from Kinston to Goldsboro is found in Charles L. Price, "The United States Military Railroads in North Carolina, 1862–1865," *The North Carolina Historical Review* 53 (1976): 243–64. O.R., 47-2:951 ("pay any price"), 47-3:7; O.R., ser. 3, 5:29–37, 589.

15. JNC Diary; Frey, *Diary of Thomas Marks*, 5 ("woods"); ROE and Monthly Return, March 1865; O.R. 47-1:423, 585–86, 595, 599–600; Poe to Yates, March 16, 1865; O.R.A., 80:8; Welcher, *Union Army*, 1:644–45; Bradley, *Last Stand*, 114–33; Barrett, *Civil War in North Carolina*, 150–55. Bradley states that the Black River was actually a northern extension of South River (141).

16. JNC and Carpenter diaries; Frey, *Diary of Thomas Marks*, 6 ("mouldy"); ROE and Monthly Return, March 1865; O.R., 47-1:586, 595, 47-2:885; O.R.A., 80:9, 83:1; Poe Diary, March 17 and 18, 1865. The exact location of Lee's Store is not clear. O.R.A., 86:3 shows two Lee's Stores in the general area, while O.R., 47-2:891, identifies Blackman Lee's Store as twenty-six miles from Goldsboro. Confederates reported Union troops camped around Blackman Lee's Store on March 18 (O.R., 47-2:1435), while Harwell and Racine, *Fiery Trail*, 190, says camp was at "Lee's Store" twenty-six miles from Goldsboro.

17. Boatner, *Civil War Dictionary*, 61; O.R., 47-2:1426. Johnston failed to concentrate all of his forces; see Connelly, *Autumn of Glory*, 524–25.

18. Barrett, *Civil War in North Carolina*, 162–72; Bradley, *Last Stand*, 153–231, passim; O.R., 47-1:586–88.

19. JNC Diary; O.R., 47-1:784–85, 808–9; Frey, *Diary of Thomas Marks*, 6; Bradley, *Last Stand*, 275–86; Welcher, *Union Army*, 1:648–94.

20. Bradley, *Last Stand*, 287; O.R., 47-1:808–9; JNC Diary. The position of the Michigan Engineers at Bentonville is shown in Bradley, *Last Stand*, 281, 291, 299, 336, and O.R.A., 79:4, 80:10, 133:2. The JNC Diary implies that the regiment held a temporary position closer to the road before moving to the left flank, though Bradley's account and reports in O.R., 47-1, do not support this.

21. Bradley, *Last Stand*, 287; JNC Diary.

22. JNC Diary; O.R., 47-1:784–85, 790, 808–9; Bradley, *Last Stand*, 287; Welcher, *Union Army*, 1:648–49.

23. Bradley, *Last Stand*, 407; JNC, Carpenter, and Roseberry diaries; ROE and Monthly Return, March 1865; O.R., 47-1:424, 436, 588, 595–96, 47-2:957–59. Williams states his camp at Goldsboro was near the XIV and XVII corps and located on the north side, two miles distance and across the Weldon Railroad. Strength information is from Monthly Return, March 1865.

24. Howard, *Autobiography*, 2:153 ("prolonged labors"); Greenalch to wife, March 26, 1865; Mosher to parents, March 25, 27, and April 6, 1865; JNC Diary, March 23, 1865 ("defeating the enemy" and "final overthrow").

25. O.R., 47-2:795, 799–800, 835; Mosher to parents, March 25, 1865 ("lousy"); Greenalch to wife, March 21, 1865 ("nakedness"); JMS to mother, March 30, 1865 ("roughest"). Issues of clothing and equipment are also mentioned in the

Roseberry and Carpenter diaries. For other comments on the ragged condition of Sherman's army upon reaching Goldsboro, see Harwell and Racine, *Fiery Trail*, 202–3; Glatthaar, *March to the Sea*, 114–17; Williams, *From the Cannon's Mouth*, 376–77; and Bradley, *This Astounding Close*, 30–31.

26. Roseberry Diary, March 27, 1865; Barrett, *Civil War in North Carolina*, 192; Bradley, *This Astounding Close*, 40. Examples of the letters sent upon arriving at Goldsboro include Mosher to parents, March 25, 1865; Alex Campbell to brother, March 28, 1865; and Greenalch to wife, March 21, 1865 ("tip top"). By this time, Sherman's command had two officers and twelve enlisted detailed exclusively to collect and distribute soldier mail. Hecht, "Union Military Mail Service," 244.

27. Barrett, *Civil War in North Carolina*, 192–94; Frey, *Diary of Thomas Marks*, 7–8; O.R., 47-3:45–46; Roseberry Diary, March 31, 1865 ("mad"); Carpenter Diary; Mosher to mother, April 6, 1865 ("Yates").

28. Welcher, *Union Army*, 1:653–54; Boatner, *Civil War Dictionary*, 127; Sherman, *Memoirs*, 2:334. The XXIII Corps had traveled from Tennessee to North Carolina in January and February following the defeat of Hood's invasion of Tennessee. Slocum's designation of the Army of Georgia, dating back to the Atlanta campaign, was made official and severed the ties linking the XIV and XX corps with Thomas's Department and Army of the Cumberland.

29. O.R., 47-1:56, 175; F. Dyer, *Compendium*, 2:1404. The organization of the Army of the Ohio's engineer and pioneer battalion during 1864–65 is detailed in Shiman, "Engineering Sherman's March," 278–79, 679–80, as well as in O.R., 45-2:561, 47-1:57.

30. Mosher to mother, April 6 and 24, 1865; Babbitt to unknown, April 9, 1865.

31. O.R., 47-3:102–3, 109, 111; Carpenter Diary, April 2 and 6, 1865; Roseberry Diary, March 30 and April 3 and 6, 1865; Mosher to mother, April 6, 1865; Barrett, *Civil War in North Carolina*, 199. Change of plan is from Sherman, *Memoirs*, 2:343; O.R. 47-1:30, 47-3:99–100 ("let us see"), 118–23; Welcher, *Union Army*, 1:654.

32. Barrett, *Civil War in North Carolina*, 200–202; Connelly, *Autumn of Glory*, 530–32.

33. O.R., 47-1:30; Welcher, *Union Army*, 1:654–55.

34. O.R., 47-3:83, 113; GO 30, April 8, 1865, ROB.

35. SO 24 and GO 30, April 3 and 8, 1865, ROB; Babbitt to unknown, April 9, 1865; Poe to Yates, April 8, 1865.

36. Carpenter and Roseberry diaries; JNC letter in *DAT*, May 12, 1865; Frey, *Diary of Thomas Marks*, 8; Howe to wife, April 22; JMS to family, April 21, 1865; O.R. 47-1:603, 47-3:132, 155–57; Barrett, *Civil War in North Carolina*, 203–4; O.R.A., 80:9; Bradley, *This Astounding Close*, 85.

37. Carpenter ("hot as love," April 12, 1865) and Roseberry diaries; Robert Leach to wife, April 17, 1865, C. C. Wheeler Collection, Western Michigan University Archives and Regional History Collections (unless otherwise noted, all letters from Leach are in this collection); O.R., 47-1:699–700; Barrett, *Civil War in North Carolina*, 204–5; JNC letter in *DAT*, May 12, 1865. The detachment was probably only two companies strong.

38. Yates to Poe, April 12, 1865, Yates/Burton; Carpenter and Roseberry diaries; JNC letter in *DAT*, May 12, 1865; JMS to family, April 21, 1865; O.R., 47-3:171, 185; O.R.A., 86:8.

39. JMS to family, April 21, 1865 ("congratulating"); Greenalch to wife, April 19, 1865 ("crazy"); Frey, *Diary of Thomas Marks*, 9; JNC letter in *DAT*, May 12, 1865; O.R., 47-3:177, 180 ("all honour"). General accounts of the response by Sherman's army are also found in Barrett, *Civil War in North Carolina*, 207–9; Bradley, *This Astounding Close*, 103–5; and Hitchcock, *Marching with Sherman*, 296 ("billows").

40. Carpenter and Roseberry diaries; JNC letter in *DAT*, May 12, 1865; JMS to family, April 21, 1865; O.R., 47-3:185; O.R.A., 86:8; Welcher, *Union Army*, 1:655.

41. Roseberry Diary; Taubert and Mann CMSR. Both were paroled at Durham Station on April 29 and eventually sent to Camp Chase, Ohio, and discharged on June 12, 1865. Accounts of the capture of other Union soldiers are from O.R., 47-1:269–71, and Barrett, *Civil War in North Carolina*, 205–6.

42. O.R., 47-1:31, 47-3:208–9, 213; Barrett, *Civil War in North Carolina*, 226–27.

43. Barrett, *Civil War in North Carolina*, 228–34; Bradley, *This Astounding Close*, 159–61.

44. Barrett, *Civil War in North Carolina*, 230–31; Bradley, *This Astounding Close*, 157–58; Marszalek, *Sherman*: 341–44; O.R., 47-3:238–39.

45. JNC letter in *DAT*, May 12, 1865 ("pall"); JMS to family, April 21, 1865 ("wept"); Barrett, *Civil War in North Carolina*, 235–36; Noah Trudeau, *Out of the Storm: The End of the Civil War, April–June 1865* (New York: Little, Brown, 1994), 239; Sherman, *Memoirs*, 2:350–51; Hitchcock, *Marching with Sherman*, 306–7.

46. Leach to wife, April 17, 1865; Greenalch to wife, April 19, 1865.

47. Howe to wife, April 18 and 20, 1865.

48. Barrett, *Civil War in North Carolina*, 237–40; Bradley, *This Astounding Close*, 169–76.

49. O.R., 47-3:250–51; Roseberry Diary ("excitement," April 19, 1865); Leach to wife, April 17, 1865; Greenalch to wife, April 19, 1865.

50. Howe to wife, April 20, 1865; Sterling to wife, April 23, 1865 ("hoe"); Mosher to family, April 24, 1865; Leach to wife, April 17, 1865.

51. Barrett, *Civil War in North Carolina*, 241–44, 267–68, 273–77; Bradley, *This Astounding Close*, 210–13; O.R., 47-3:293, 295; Marszalek, Sherman, 342–51; Vetter, *Sherman*, 283–85.

52. Barrett, *Civil War in North Carolina*, 267–71; Bradley, *This Astounding Close*, 215–17; Connelly: *Autumn of Glory*, 534–35.

53. JNC letter in *DAT*, May 16, 1865 ("demonstrations"); Frey, *Diary of Thomas Marks*, 10 ("joy"); O.R., 47-3:314, 316; Carpenter and Roseberry diaries.

Chapter 23

1. Barrett, *Civil War in North Carolina*, 277; Welcher, *Union Army*, 1:655–56; Sherman, *Memoirs*, 2:368–69.

2. SO 67, April 28, 1865, ROB.

3. JNC letter in *DAT*, May 16 and June 12, 1865. Grant is referred to as commanding in O.R., 47-3:479, 496, 501, 518, 527, and Yates, "Military History." Hannings returned on May 19, Yates on May 28. Hannings was granted a leave because he had postponed his veteran furlough a year earlier because of the "press of business," SFO 14, Army of the Ohio, May 30, 1865, MEMRP.

4. ROE, May 1865; Roseberry and Carpenter diaries; Frey, *Diary of Thomas Marks*, 12; JNC letter in *DAT*, June 12, 1865.

5. O.R., 47-1:211; O.R., ser. 3, 5:199; ROE, May 1865; Frey, *Diary of Thomas Marks*, 11.

6. Roseberry and Carpenter diaries; ROE, May 1865; O.R., 47-3:423, 469.

7. Plyn Williams to wife, May 10, 1865, copy in possession of the author, courtesy of Ron Thinnes.

8. O.R., 47-3:421, 437, 455, 477.

9. Carpenter and Roseberry diaries; Frey, *Diary of Thomas Marks*, 12–13; Babbitt to family, May 20, 1865; JNC letter in *DAT*, June 12, 1865.

10. Roseberry and Carpenter diaries; ROE, May 1865; Mosher to parents, May 28, 1865 ("very hard"); Babbitt to family, May 20, 1865; O.R., 47-3:423, 437, 456; Canfield, *Twenty-First Ohio*, 189 ("foolish").

11. O.R., 47-3:526, 539–40.

12. Hannings to MDM, May 20, 1865, and MDM to Yates, May 21, 22, and 23, 1865, all in MEMRP; Hannings to Lieutenant Colonel Tweedale, May 23, 1865, RLB.

13. Sherman to Rawlins, May 19, 1865, O.R., 47-3:531.

14. Noah Brooks, *Washington, D.C., in Lincoln's Time* (Chicago: Quadrangle Books, 1971), 270–84; Margaret Leech, *Reveille in Washington, 1860–1865* (New York: Harper and Brothers, 1941), 414–17. Though describing the same general area, primary source documents are widely inconsistent in exactly where the regimental camp was located. It was variously reported as at Crystal Springs (JMS to mother, May 29, 1865), Tenallytown (Roseberry Diary and letter from "AC" in *DAT*, May 31, 1865), "three miles northwest of the city" ("AC" letter in *DAT*, June 8, 1865), "two miles from city on a rolling hill" (*DAT*, June 21, 1865), and Georgetown (ROE).

15. Sherman, *Memoirs*, 2:378; Brooks, *Washington, D.C.*, and Leech, *Reveille in Washington*, both mention the review in passing; O.R., 47-3:554–55; Roseberry Diary, April 24, 1865 ("concourse"); Mosher to parents, May 27, 1865.

16. Leech, *Reveille in Washington*, 471 ("rolling" and "strong legs"); "AC" letter in *DAT*, June 8, 1865 ("quite a strife"); Sherman, *Memoirs*, 2:378 ("well organized"); JMS to mother, May 29, 1865 ("never professed"). Sligh was probably commanding Company E in the review and was officially mustered in as captain on May 29. More on the comparisons between the two armies is found in Barrett, *Civil War in North Carolina*, 179–82; Brooks, *Washington, D.C.*, 280; and Leech, *Reveille in Washington*, 416.

17. Sterling to wife, May 5, 1865 ("grandest"); O.R., 47-3:555; Brooks, *Washington, D.C.*, 278–79.

18. Roseberry Diary; Mosher to parents, May 27, 1865; JMS to mother, May 29, 1865 ("with a will"); JNC letters in *DAT*, June 8 and 12, 1865. On May 25 Governor Crapo also visited the Second, Seventeenth, Twentieth, Fifteenth, and Twenty-seventh infantry regiments as well as the First Sharpshooters. As the Republican nominee in the November elections, Crapo had received strong support from the soldiers voting in the field. Despite the previous controversies, the Michigan Engineers gave generally favorable reviews of Innes's lengthy speech.

19. AC letter in *DAT*, June 8, 1865; Sterling to wife, June 1, 1865 ("pretty well"); Julia Susan (Wheelock) Freeman, *The Boys in White: The Experience of a Hospital Agent in and around Washington* (New York: Lange and Hillman, 1870). A recent account of Wheelock's war service is found in Weldon Petz, "Michigan's Florence Nightingale," *Michigan History* 82 (1998): 67–74.

20. Carpenter Diary, May 31, 1865; Roseberry Diary, June 2, 1865; "AC" letter in *DAT*, June 8, 1865; Sterling to wife, June 1, 1865 ("fail"); Sherman to Grant, O.R., 47-3:582 ("hope").

21. Roseberry Diary, May 25, 1865 ("solitary"); Babbitt to wife, June 3, 1865 ("grub").

22. Babbitt to wife, April 19, 1865 ("see me coming"); Sterling to wife, April 23, 1865 ("rest assured"); Leach to wife, April 17, 1865; Greenalch to wife, April 28, 1865.

23. Sterling to wife, May 25, 1865.

24. O.R., ser. 3, 5:113, 516; comparison of list attached to Monthly Return, May and August 1865, with Desc. Roll and *ROS* 43. An excellent description of the Union plan for demobilization is found in William B. Holberton, *Homeward Bound: The Demobilization of the Union and Confederate Armies, 1865–66* (Mechanicsburg, Pa.: Stackpole Books, 2001), 7–15.

25. O.R., ser. 3, 5:4–5, 516. At the end of June, the regimental rolls still carried at least twenty-three men as absent in hospital. Monthly Return, June 1865.

26. Account of Miller is from Desc. Roll and Albert E. Cowles, *Past and Present of the City of Lansing and Ingham County, Michigan* (Lansing: Michigan Historical Publishing, 1905), 547–49. Losses are from a comparison of list attached to Monthly Return, April 1865, with Desc. Roll and *ROS* 43.

27. Monthly Return, April 1865; Gene E. Salecker, *Disaster on the Mississippi: The* Sultana *Explosion, April 27, 1865* (Annapolis: Naval Institute Press, 1996), 17–24. The handful of Michigan Engineers who had been captured during the march through the Carolinas were paroled and back in Union hands within weeks.

28. Account of Company L is from a review of information on the thirty-one men in CWPF, Desc. Roll, and CMSR records. Also see CWPF of Willis Bertram ("turned loose") and Holberton, *Homeward Bound*, 101.

29. Richmond and Sinclair information is from CMSR and *DAT*, April 29, 1865. Their arrival in St. Louis from Vicksburg on the twenty-fourth or twenty-fifth suggests that they were passengers on the steamer *Henry Ames* and missed riding with most other paroled prisoners from Michigan on the *Sultana*.

30. The best accounts of the *Sultana* tragedy are Salecker, *Disaster*; Chester D. Berry, *Loss of the* Sultana *and Reminiscences of Survivors* (Lansing: Darius D.

Thorp, 1896); Jerry O. Potter, *The* Sultana *Tragedy: America's Greatest Maritime Disaster* (Gretna, La.: Pelican, 1992); and James W. Elliot, *Transport to Disaster* (New York: Holt, Rinehart, and Winston, 1962).

31. Lists of survivors are in *DFP*, May 4, 1865; Berry, *Loss of the* Sultana, 63, 67, 94; and Salecker, *Disaster*, 248. Accounts of the three after the explosion are from Salecker, *Disaster*, 104–5, 138–39; Berry, *Loss of the* Sultana, 109–10, 168–69; and Elliot, *Transport to Disaster*, 111, 180, 191–94. Earl, Hatch, and Dunsmore were discharged in May, June, and August, respectively. Information about deaths is drawn from CWPF, CMSR, *ROS* 43, and Desc. Roll records. The list of fatalities in Salecker, *Disaster*, 248, also includes three men identified as members of the Michigan Engineers but for whom there is no evidence of their membership in the regiment: J. L. Bremer, Edward H. Ives, and William F. Johnson. The lack of records on the exact number of people on the boat and uncertainty as to the number of survivors makes it impossible to know exactly how many died, but Salecker, *Disaster*, 206, provides a well-reasoned estimate of 1,700–1,750.

32. Roseberry Diary; "AC" letter in *DAT*, June 8, 1865; JNC letter in *DAT*, June 12, 1865; *DFP*, June 11, 1865; O.R., 47-3:588–91, 599; O.R. ser. 3, 5:25, 56, 131, 516; Yates to L. Thomas, June 7, 1865, RLB. Reference to discharge on June 7 is from Roseberry Diary, June 6 and 7, 1865; SO 82, June 3, 1865, ROB.

33. O.R., ser. 3, 5:24, 303; *DFP*, June 11, 1865; Capt. E. M. Clift to J. H. Knight, June 13, 1865, MEMRP; *Jackson Daily Citizen*, June 12 and 19, 1865.

34. Howe to wife, June 7, 1865.

35. GO 53, June 8, 1865, ROB; SO 65, Military Division of the Mississippi, May 30, 1865, MEMRP.

36. Carpenter and Roseberry diaries; GO 53, June 8, 1865, ROB. The trip west to Louisville by Sherman's men is described in James P. Jones, "Farewell to Arms: Union Troops Muster Out at Louisville, June–August, 1865," *The Filson Club Historical Quarterly* 36 (1962): 272–74.

37. Jones, "Farewell to Arms," 274–81; Carpenter and Roseberry ("drag," June 19, 1865) diaries; *DAT*, June 18, 1865; Yates to Assistant Adjutant General, Louisville, June 14, 1865, MEMRP.

38. Jones, "Farewell to Arms," 274–81 (drawn heavily from local newspapers); O.R., 49-2:1007; Carpenter and Roseberry diaries; Swigart to parents, June 25, 1865 ("big times"); Yates to Assistant Adjutant General, Louisville, June 19, 1865, RLB.

39. Sterling to wife, June 21, 1865 ("veiled"); Howe to wife, June 15, 1865 ("mutiny"); Swigart to parents, June 25, 1865 ("never will be taken from this place"); Mosher to sister, June 17, 1865 ("stinking souls"). Mosher repeated many of his assertions in a letter to friends dated August 18, 1865.

40. GO 60, June 29, 1865, ROB (including "approbation"); O.R., 49-2:1023. *ROS* 43 and Desc. Roll list eighteen as deserting on June 29–July 1 at Louisville, while another eleven are noted as "discharged to date" from those dates. Examples of men not returning are found in CMSR and *ROS* 43 (see Seeley Clark and George Collar). Many of the deserters eventually had their records cleared by the language of postwar congressional action.

41. See Roseberry and Carpenter diaries for the move to Nashville.

42. Yates to Hill telegram, July 3, 1865, MEMRP ("look out"); Carpenter and Roseberry diaries; Mosher to sister, July 7, 1865; GO 61, July 4, 1865, ROB. List attached to Monthly Return, August 1865, includes twenty-six men from Company I who were confined July 3 and another twelve from Company C who were confined July 4, presumably for the same reason.

43. Furlough notes are contained in LR-Reg. Davis allowed his division commanders to approve short furloughs for men in their regiment as long as no more than 20 percent of the men were gone at one time. O.R., 49-2:1018. Troops of the XV Corps were allowed to visit home, up to 12 percent of each regiment. O.R., 49-2:1055.

44. Yates to unknown, August 15, 1865, RLB; Carpenter and Roseberry diaries, mid-August 1865; Howe to wife, August 18, 1865; Mosher to mother, August 18, 1865; O.R., 49-2:1100–1112.

45. Roseberry Diary, September 4, 1865; *DFP*, September 13, 1865; "Lieutenant Colonel Commanding" to Robertson, September 15, 1865, RLB; Sterling to wife, September 17, 1865; "Lieutenant Colonel Commanding" to Military Department of the Tennessee, September 16, 1865, RLB; Monthly Return, August 1865.

46. Carpenter and Roseberry diaries; GO (unnumbered), September 23, 1865, printed in *DFP*, October 7, 1865. Presumably Lieutenant Colonel Hannings commanded the regiment on the trip home, though there is nothing specific to verify it.

47. GO 84, September 22, 1865, ROB; Roseberry and Carpenter diaries.

48. Roseberry Diary ("again citizens").

49. Phillips from Desc. Roll and *ROS* 43. Phillips regained his health and lived for another thirty years.

50. O.R., ser. 3, 5:126.

Chapter 24

1. Oliver Wendell Holmes Jr., Memorial Day Address, Harvard University, May 30, 1895.

2. Franklin Craig and Craig Bamford CWPF.

3. Walter F. Kimball CWPF. Truax information is from *Portrait and Biographical Album of Kalamazoo*, 901–2, and CWPF.

4. Hoag information is from Kenneth R. Beardslee, *The Burtis and Phebe Hoag Family Tree (with Hill, Clabaugh, and Beardslee Branches), 1795–1985* (Spring Arbor, Mich.: Kenneth R. Beardslee, 1985), 85.

5. William C. Harrison, Thomas A. Cook, Otis Pitts, and Marcus Grant CWPF.

6. Thomas Fisher and Alphonso Bullen CWPF.

7. Tennessee railroads were ordered turned over to civilian owners. O.R., ser. 3, 5:355–56. Railroad activities of Innes, Yates, and Hopkins's business endeavors, are documented in 40th Cong., H. Rep. 3, 66–69, 72 ("good many"), 83–85. For more on Hopkins, see U.S. Census, 1870, Davidson County, Tennessee; "Hist of Officers" in RSR; *King's Nashville City Directory* (Nashville: E. D. King, 1866) for 1866 has Hopkins and his son Robert boarding at the same location as Innes. After

leaving Nashville in the mid 1870s, Hopkins spent twenty years further developing his business interests along the East Coast before his death in New York City in 1896. *ROS* 43 and David B. Tracy CWPF. Additional information on Innes and Grant is from *Traveler's Official Railway Guide of the US and Canada* (1868), 216. A biography of Innes is in *Michigan Pioneer and Historical Collections*, 26 (1897), 138–40. Calkins reference is from Leeson, *Kent County*, 967–68, and *City of Grand Rapids*, 88–90. Hannings information is from CWPF and U.S. Census, 1870, Coffee County, Tennessee. Grant's activities in Tennessee are found in U.S. Census, 1870, Davidson County, Tennessee; *Chattanooga General and Business Directory, 1876–77* (Chattanooga, Tenn.: T. M. Haddock, 1877), 48; *Chattanooga City Directory, 1880* (Chattanooga, Tenn.: Norwood, Klene, 1880), 146; and Grant CWPF.

8. The best information on Innes's and Yates's postwar Tennessee railroad experience is in 40th Cong., H. Rep. 3, particularly their testimony on pages 65–73. Gifford information is from *Portrait and Biographical Album of Ionia and Montcalm Counties, Michigan* (Chicago: Chapman, 1891), 680–81. McCrath details are from Masonic and CWPF records and personal communications with John Gelderloos. Grant and Hannings information is from CWPF. Winters, *Grand Army Sentinel*; *Marshall Evening Chronicle*, October 4–5, 1912; CWPF.

9. *GR Eagle*, October 30, 1867, states that the association had been formed in August 1864 but that this was its first gathering. In 1868 it was referred to as the "Regimental Association." Designation in published accounts varies over the years. The last reunion account found to date is from the fifty-ninth in 1924, though there were almost certainly ones for a few more years. *Grand Rapids Press*, September 18, 1924.

10. See *GR Eagle*, October 30, 1867 for the first reunion. Examples of accounts from later reunions include *Kalamazoo Telegraph*, September 14, 1868; *DFP*, October 30, 1869; *Grand Rapids Daily Democrat*, September 15–18, 1885; *Lansing State Journal*, October 12, 1888; *Jackson Daily Citizen*, October 20–21, 1892; *Kalamazoo Telegraph*, October 18, 1900; *Charlotte Republican*, October 17, 1901; *Grand Rapids Daily News*, October 3, 1910; *Grand Rapids Press*, September 18, 1924.

11. Burford information is from undated clipping in Kimball papers; Baxter, *Grand Rapids*, 170; *Grand Rapids Daily Democrat*, August 3, 1893. Also see account of 1885 regimental reunion written by Edwin E. Winters, printed in an unidentified veterans' publication and included with the Calkins Letters.

12. *Grand Rapids Democrat*, December 6, 1885; *Grand Rapids Evening Leader*, July 4, 1891; *Grand Rapids Evening Press*, July 31, 1894; CMSR, U.S. Regular Army, vol. 69, p. 22, entry 842.

13. An excellent recent review of the GAR is found in Stuart McConnell, *Glorious Contentment: The Grand Army of the Republic, 1865–1900* (Chapel Hill: University of North Carolina Press, 1992). Also see Mary Dearing, *Veterans in Politics: The Story of the G.A.R.* (Baton Rouge: Louisiana State University Press, 1952). McConnell points out the powerful position eventually reached by the resurgent GAR—in 1890 one in ten eligible American voters was a member, and by 1900 Americans had elected only one postwar president who was not a member.

14. Post Records, Grand Army of the Republic, Michigan Commandery, RG 63-19, Archives of Michigan.

15. *Grand Rapids Daily Democrat*, September 15 and 16, 1885.

16. Tracy obituary is in Methodist Episcopal Church, *Minutes*, 307. Reference to "William P. Innes command, Union Veterans Union" is from *City of Grand Rapids*, 93, 348. White reference is from Edwin O. Wood, *History of Genesee County, Michigan*, 2 vols. (Indianapolis: Federal, 1916), 1:699.

17. An account of the Orchard Knob dedication, including Fox's speech, is found in Belknap, *Michigan Organizations*, 260–65.

18. Earl J. Hess, *The Union Soldier in Battle: Enduring the Ordeal of Combat* (Lawrence: University Press of Kansas, 1997), 185–86.

19. *Marshall Evening Chronicle*, October 4–5, 1912. GAR Hall reference is from Carver, *History of Marshall*, 98.

20. *Marshall Evening Chronicle*, October 4–5, 1912.

21. *Marshall Evening Chronicle*, October 4–5, 1912.

22. *Lansing State Journal*, October 9 and 10, 1912; Sligh, *Michigan Engineers*, 52; McCrath account, October 1887, RSR.

23. *Lansing State Journal*, October 10, 1912.

24. *Lansing State Journal*, October 10, 1912. Smith reference is from Clarence M. Burton, ed., *History of Wayne County and the City of Detroit, Michigan*, 4 vols. (Detroit: S. J. Clarke, 1930), 3:973.

25. *Grand Rapids Daily News*, February 21, 1910; Sligh, *Michigan Engineers*, 86; Ernest B. Fisher, ed., *Grand Rapids and Kent County* (Chicago: Robert O. Law, 1918), 2:164–66.

26. Sligh, *Michigan Engineers*, unnumbered section following page 90. According to Sligh, *Michigan Engineers*, 5, there were only about three officers and one hundred men still living that had served in the regiment.

27. Stewart quote is from Sligh, *Michigan Engineers*, 86. Stewart commanded a Michigan regiment in the famous Thirty-second U.S. "Red Arrow" Division.

28. *Marshall Evening Chronicle*, October 5, 1912.

Bibliography

Newspapers

Unless noted, all newspapers were published in Michigan.

Adrian Daily Watchtower
Allegan Journal
Charlotte Republican
Chicago Tribune (Chicago, Illinois)
Cincinnati Gazette (Cincinnati, Ohio)
Detroit Advertiser and Tribune
Detroit Daily Advertiser
Detroit Daily Tribune
Detroit Free Press
Eaton County Republican
Flint Wolverine Citizen
Grand Army Sentinel (Nashville, Tennessee)
Grand Haven Clarion
Grand Rapids Daily Democrat
Grand Rapids Daily Eagle
Grand Rapids Daily News
Grand Rapids Evening Leader
Grand Rapids Evening Press
Grand Rapids Press
Grand Rapids Weekly Enquirer
Hastings Banner
Hillsdale Standard
Jackson Citizen (known successively as *American Citizen*, *True Citizen*, and *Weekly Citizen* during the war)
Jackson Daily Citizen
Kalamazoo Telegraph
Kalamazoo Gazette
Lansing State Journal
Louisville Journal (Louisville, Kentucky)
Marshall Democratic Expounder
Marshall Evening Chronicle
Marshall Statesman
Monroe Evening Chronicle
Nashville Union (Nashville, Tennessee)
National Tribune (Washington, D.C.)
New York Times (New York, New York)

Perry County Weekly (Ohio)
Saginaw Enterprise

Unpublished Sources

Archives of Michigan, Lansing.
 Christman Collection.
  Azra Bartholomew Jr. Letter.
 Grand Army of the Republic, Michigan Commandery.
  Post Records. RG 63-19.
 Michigan Adjutant General.
  Battery E, First Michigan Light Artillery, Regimental Service Records. RG 59-14.
  Descriptive Rolls, Michigan Militia, 1838–61. RG 59-14.
  General and Special Orders. RG 59-14.
  Letters Out. RG 59-14.
  Letters to the Adjutant General Relating to the Raising of Companies for Military Service, 1861–78. RG 59-14.
  Michigan Engineers and Mechanics, Regimental Descriptive Rolls. Microfilm copy, RG 59-14.
  Michigan Engineers and Mechanics, Regimental Service Records. RG 59-14.
  Monthly Return.
  Minutes of the State Military Board. RG 59-14.
 John L. Rolison. Diary.
Bentley Historical Library, University of Michigan, Ann Arbor.
 Richard Watson Barker. Diary.
 Henry H. Bellamy. Letters.
 Buck Family Papers.
  John Bettis. Letter.
 Boss Family Papers.
  James Boss. Letters.
 William B. Calkins. Letters.
 Carr Family Letters.
  Ezra Stearns. Diary, Memoir.
 Fox Family Papers.
  Perrin V. Fox. Letters.
  Newton P. Fox. Letters.
 Graves Family Papers.
  Albert Graves. Letters.
 William F. Helle. Translation and typescript diary.
 Robert S. Innes Family Papers.
  Kinsman A. Hunton. Letter.
  Robert S. Innes Papers.
 Permelia Jenkins Papers.

     Benjamin F. Tower. Letters.
   Mason Family (Van Buren County) Papers.
     Martin A. Westcott. Diary.
   Raycide Mosher. Letters.
   Charles Peel. Correspondence.
   Isaac Roseberry. Diary.
   Sligh Family Papers.
     Enos Hopkins. Letters.
     William P. Innes. Letters.
     James Irvine. Letter.
     Albert Jewell. Letter.
     John W. McCrath. Letters.
     Clement F. Miller. Letters.
     William S. Nevius. Letters.
     James May Sligh. Correspondence and papers.
     James Wilson Sligh. Correspondence and papers.
     James Wilson Sligh. Diary.
     John R. Smith. Letters and papers.
     George White. Letters.
   Stanard Family Papers.
   John T. Swigart. Letters.
   John Weissert. Letters.
   John B. Yates. Manuscript, "Military History, 1866, of John B. Yates of the 1st Michigan Engineers and Mechanics."
Burton Historical Collection, Detroit Public Library, Detroit, Michigan.
   William H. Kimball. Diary.
   Heman Lowe. Diary.
   John B. Yates Papers.
Elkstrom Library, University of Louisville, Louisville, Kentucky.
   Louisville and Nashville Railroad. *Main Stem, Louisville and Nashville Railroad* (N.p.: LNRR Engineer's Office, 1884).
Grand Rapids Public Library, Grand Rapids, Michigan.
   Coffinberry Family Collection.
     Wright L. Coffinberry Papers.
   Dorothy Keister Collection.
     David Noble. Letters.
Kansas State Historical Society, Topeka.
   Anderson Family Papers.
Library of Congress, Washington, D.C.
   Abram F. Conant. Letters.
   Andrew Johnson Papers.
   Orlando M. Poe. Diary and papers.
The Lilly Library, Indiana University, Bloomington, Indiana.
   Niles Family Papers.
     William D. Niles. Letters.

Michigan State University Archives and Historical Collections, East Lansing.
    Campbell Family Papers.
        Alexander Campbell. Letters.
        Allen Campbell. Letters.
    Howe Family Papers.
        Simeon Howe. Letters.
    Edwin R. Osband. Diary.
National Archives and Records Administration, Washington, D.C.
    Chief Engineer.
        Letters Sent to Engineering Officers, 1813–69. Microfilm Publication T1255.
    Records of the Adjutant General.
        Compiled Military Service Records of Union Volunteers. RG 94.
        First New York Engineers. Regimental Papers. RG 94.
        Fifteenth New York. Regimental Papers. RG 94.
        Fiftieth New York. Regimental Papers. RG 94.
        Generals' Papers. RG 94.
        Michigan Engineers and Mechanics. Record of Events. Microcopy Publication 594. RG 94.
        Michigan Engineers and Mechanics. Regimental Papers. RG 94.
        Company Order Book.
            Letters Received Register.
        Regimental Letter Book.
        Register of Enlistments in the U.S. Army, 1798–1914. Microcopy Publication M233, Reel 21. RG 98.
        Twelfth United States Colored Troops. Regimental Papers. RG 94.
    Records of the Judge Advocate General's Office.
        Court-Martial Case Files. RG 153. All copies of files from RG 153 were provided courtesy of Tom and Beverly Lowry, The Index Project.
    Records of the Office of the Chief of Engineers. RG 77.
    Records of the Office of the Quartermaster General. RG 92.
    Records of the U.S. Army Commands, Regular Army Regiments. RG 98.
    Records of the U.S. Army Continental Commands, 1821–1920. RG 393-1 and RG 393-2.
    Records of the Veterans' Administration.
        Civil War Pension Files. RG 15.
National Archives and Record Administration II, College Park, Maryland.
    William E. Merrill. Manuscript. Fortifications Map File, Drawer 160, RG 77.
Private Collection of John Gelderloos, Grand Rapids, Michigan.
    Perrin V. Fox and Newton P. Fox. Letters. First reviewed through the generosity of previous owner, Tom Jones, Medina, Ohio.
    Mariette Hutchins. Letters.

John W. McCrath. Diary.
Private Collection of Mark Hoffman, Mason, Michigan.
 Jacob D. Carpenter. Typescript diary. Courtesy of Nancy L. Ober-
  mayer, Grosse Ile, Michigan.
 Plyn Williams. Letter. Copy courtesy of Ron Thinnes.
Private Collection of Sharon Patton, Lansing, Michigan.
 Nathan Robinson. Letters.
Seymour Library, Knox College, Galesburg, Illinois.
 Ray Smith Collection.
  Perrin V. Fox. Diary.
Special Collections, Duke University, Durham, North Carolina.
  Eugene Marshall. Diary.
Stevenson Railroad Museum Depot, Stevenson, Alabama.
  Perrin V. Fox. Letter.
The Studley, Pickard, Stackhouse Collection, Washington, D.C. Courtesy of
  Jeanette Studley.
 James D. Robinson. Letters.
Tennessee State Library and Archives, Nashville.
 Buell-Brien Papers.
 Jill K. Garrett Collection.
  Manuscript, "Lost City of Reynoldsburg" and related materials.
 Henry C. Wharton. "1863 Operational Map of the Countryside South
  of Nashville."
Union College, Schenectady, New York.
 John B. Yates. Alumni file, Class of 1852.
University of Missouri–Rolla Archives, Rolla.
 George D. Emerson. Miscellaneous papers.
 Clair V. Mann Papers.
U.S. Military History Institute, Carlisle Barracks, Pennsylvania.
 Civil War Times Illustrated Collection.
  Daniel Sterling. Letters.
Western Michigan University Archives and Regional History Collections,
  Kalamazoo.
 Mrs. Ann Coffee Collection.
  Cyrus A. Babbitt. Letters.
 Dr. and Mrs. Delmar Firme Collection.
  "Battle of Lavergne." Song sheet.
 Larry Martin Collection.
  Oscar Baxter. Letters.
  Walter Phillips. Letters.
 Mrs. Roy Struble Collection.
  William C. Swaddle. Letters.
 C. C. Wheeler Collection.
  Robert Leach. Letter.
  John C. Wheeler. Letters.

The Western Reserve Historical Society Library, Cleveland, Ohio.
    Caleb Emerson Family Papers.
        George D. Emerson. Letters and miscellaneous papers.
William L. Clements Library, University of Michigan, Ann Arbor.
    James S. Schoff Civil War Collection.
        William D. Travis. Manuscript, "Bridge Building in Tennessee."

Published Works

Adams, George W. *Doctors in Blue: The Medical History of the Union Army in the Civil War.* New York: Shuman, 1952.

Ambrose, Stephen. *Halleck: Lincoln's Chief of Staff.* Baton Rouge: Louisiana State University Press, 1962.

American Society of Civil Engineers. *American Wooden Bridges.* New York: American Society of Civil Engineers, 1976.

Anderson, William M. *They Died to Make Men Free.* 2nd ed. Dayton, Ohio: Morningside Books, 1994.

Baker, Daniel. *A Soldier's Experience in the Civil War.* Long Beach, Calif.: Graves and Hersey, 1914.

Barnett, James. "Munfordville in the Civil War." *Register of the Kentucky Historical Society* 69 (1971): 340–49.

———. "Willich's Thirty-Second Indiana Volunteers." *Cincinnati Historical Society Bulletin* 37 (1979): 48–70.

Barrett, John G. *The Civil War in North Carolina.* Chapel Hill: University of North Carolina Press, 1963.

Baxter, Albert. *History of the City of Grand Rapids, Michigan.* New York: Munsell, 1891.

Beach, Wm. H. *The First New York (Lincoln) Cavalry . . .* New York: Lincoln Cavalry Association, 1902.

Beardslee, Kenneth R. *The Burtis and Phebe Hoag Family Tree (with Hill, Clabaugh, and Beardslee Branches), 1795–1985.* Spring Arbor, Mich.: Kenneth R. Beardslee, 1985.

Bearss, Edwin C. "Cavalry Operations in the Battle of Stones River." *Tennessee Historical Quarterly* 19 (1960): 25–53, 110–44.

———. "Nelson Saves the Day at Shiloh." *Register of the Kentucky Historical Society* 63 (1965): 39–69.

Beasley, Paul H., and C. Buford Gotto. "Fortress Nashville." *Civil War Times Illustrated* 3 (1964): 25–26.

Beatty, John. *The Citizen-Soldier; or, Memoirs of a Volunteer.* Cincinnati: Wilstach, Baldwin, 1879.

Belknap, Charles E. *History of the Michigan Organizations at Chickamauga, Chattanooga, and Missionary Ridge.* Lansing: R. Smith Printing, 1897.

Bennett, Charles W. *Historical Sketches of the Ninth Michigan Infantry.* Coldwater, Mich.: Daily Courier Print, 1913.

Berry, Chester D. *Loss of the* Sultana *and Reminiscences of Survivors.* Lansing: Darius D. Thorp, 1896.

Bibliography

Bickham, W. D. *Rosecrans' Campaign with the Fourteenth Army Corps.* Cincinnati: Moore, Wilstach, Keys, 1863.

Boatner, Mark M. *The Civil War Dictionary.* New York: David McKay, 1959.

Bogle, James G. "The Western and Atlantic Railroad in the Campaign for Atlanta." In *The Campaign for Atlanta.* Campbell, Calif.: Savas Woodbury, 1994. 313–40.

———. "Western and Atlantic Railroad—1864." *Atlanta Historical Journal* 25 (1976): 45–72.

Bradley, Mark L. *Last Stand in the Carolinas: The Battle of Bentonville.* Campbell, Calif.: Savas Woodbury, 1996.

———. *This Astounding Close: The Road to Bennett Place.* Chapel Hill: University of North Carolina Press, 2000.

Brandt, Robert S. "Lightning and Rain in Middle Tennessee." *Tennessee Historical Quarterly* 52 (1993): 158–69.

Brooks, Noah. *Washington, D.C. in Lincoln's Time.* Chicago: Quadrangle Books, 1971.

Brown, Leonard. "Fortress Rosecrans: A History, 1865–1990." *Tennessee Historical Quarterly* 50 (1991): 135–41.

Bryant, Edwin. *History of the Third Regiment of Wisconsin Veteran Volunteer Infantry, 1861–1865.* Madison: Veteran Association of the Regiment, 1891.

Burt, Jessie C. "The Nashville and Chattanooga Railroad, 1854–1872: The Era of Transition." *East Tennessee Historical Society Publications* 23 (1951): 58–76.

———. "Sherman's Logistics and Andrew Johnson." *Tennessee Historical Quarterly* 15 (1956): 195–215.

Burton, Clarence M., ed. *The City of Detroit, Michigan, 1701–1922,* 5 vols. Detroit: S. J. Clark, 1922.

———, ed. *History of Wayne County and the City of Detroit, Michigan.* 4 vols. Detroit: S. J. Clarke, 1930.

Callaway, W. A. "Hard Times with Ross' Cavalry." *Confederate Veteran* 28 (1920): 447–48.

Canfield, Silas S. *History of the Twenty-First Ohio Volunteer Infantry in the War of the Rebellion.* Toledo, Ohio: Vrooman, Anderson, and Bateman, 1893.

Carlson, Bruce. "The Amboy, Lansing, and Traverse Bay Railroad." Master's thesis, Central Michigan University, 1972.

Carver, Richard W. *A History of Marshall.* Virginia Beach, Va.: Donning, 1993.

Castle, Albert. *Decision in The West: The Atlanta Campaign of 1864.* Lawrence: University Press of Kansas, 1992.

Cavanagh, John C. "The Operations of Major-General Henry W. Halleck's Union Army in the Corinth Campaign of 1862." Master's thesis, Columbia University, n.d.

Chapin, Seth S. *The Three Campaigns: Sermon Preached before the First Regiment Fusileers at Camp Owen Marshall, Michigan, October 20, 1861.* Marshall, Mich.: Mann and Noyes, 1861.

Chattanooga City Directory, 1880. Chattanooga, Tenn.: Norwood, Klene, 1880.

Chattanooga General and Business Directory, 1876–77. Chattanooga, Tenn.: T. M. Haddock, 1877.

Chumney, James R., Jr. "Don Carlos Buell: Gentleman General." PhD diss., Rice University, 1964.

Cist, Henry. *The Army of the Cumberland.* Vol 7. of *Campaigns of the Civil War.* New York: Charles Scribner's Sons, 1882.

The City of Grand Rapids and Kent County, Michigan. Logansport, Ind.: Bowen, 1900.

Congressional Globe. 46 vols. Washington, D.C., 1834–73.

Connelly, Thomas L. *Army of the Heartland: Army of Tennessee, 1861–1862.* Baton Rouge: Louisiana State University Press, 1967.

———. *Autumn of Glory: The Army of Tennessee, 1862–1865.* Baton Rouge: Louisiana State University Press, 1971.

Conyngham, David P. *Sherman's March through the South, with Sketches and Incidents of the Campaign.* New York: Sheldon, 1865.

Cooke, James J. "Feeding Sherman's Army." In *The Campaign for Atlanta.* Campbell, Calif.: Savas and Woodbury, 1994. 97–114.

Cooling, Benjamin F. *Fort Donelson's Legacy: War and Society in Kentucky and Tennessee, 1862–1863.* Knoxville: University of Tennessee Press, 1997.

———. *Forts Henry and Donelson: The Key to the Confederate Heartland.* Knoxville: University of Tennessee Press, 1987.

Cowles, Albert E. *Past and Present of the City of Lansing and Ingham County, Michigan.* Lansing: Michigan Historical Publishing, 1905.

Cox, Jacob D. *Atlanta.* Vol. 9 of *Campaigns of the Civil War.* New York: Charles Scribner's Sons, 1882.

Cozzens, Peter. *The Darkest Day of the War: The Battles of Iuka and Corinth.* Chapel Hill: University of North Carolina Press, 1997.

Crute, Joseph H. *Confederate Staff Officers, 1861–1865.* Powhatan, Va.: Derwent Books, 1982.

Cullum, George W. *Systems of Military Bridges.* New York: D. Van Nostrand, 1863.

Cutter, Orlando P. *Our Battery; or, a Journal of the Company B, 1st Ohio Volunteer Artillery.* Cleveland: Nevin's Book and Job Printing, 1864.

Dalton, C. David. "Zollicoffer, Crittenden, and the Mill Spring Campaign: Some Persistent Questions." *Filson Club Historical Quarterly* 60 (1986): 463–71.

Daniel, John S., Jr. "Special Warfare in Middle Tennessee and Surrounding Areas, 1861–1862." Master's thesis, University of Tennessee, 1971.

Dean, Henry S. "The Relief of Chattanooga." No. 5, *War Papers.* Detroit: Winn and Hammond, 1893.

Dearing, Mary. *Veterans in Politics: The Story of the G.A.R.* Baton Rouge: Louisiana State University Press, 1952.

DeLand, Charles V. *DeLand's History of Jackson County.* Logansport, Ind.: Bowen, 1903.

DeLorme Mapping. *Tennessee Atlas and Gazetteer.* Freeport, Maine: DeLorme Mapping, 1995.

Derrick, Samuel Melanchthon. *Centennial History of the South Carolina Railroad.* Columbia, S.C.: State Company, 1930.

Duane, James C. *Manual for Engineer Troops.* New York: D. Van Nostrand, 1863.

Bibliography

Duane, James C., Henry L. Abbot, and William E. Merrill, *Organization of the Bridge Equipage of the United States Army*. Washington, D.C.: Government Printing Office, 1870.

Dunbar, Willis F. *All Aboard: A History of Railroads in Michigan*. Grand Rapids, Mich.: William B. Eerdmans, 1969.

———. *Michigan: A History of the Wolverine State*. 3rd rev. ed. by George S. May. Grand Rapids, Mich.: William Eerdmans, 1995.

Dunkleman, Mark H. "'A Just Right to Select Our Own Officers': Reactions in a Union Regiment to Officers Commissioned from Outside Its Ranks." *Civil War History* 44 (1998): 24–34.

Dunnavant, Robert. *The Railroad War: N. B. Forrest's 1864 Raid through Northern Alabama and Middle Tennessee*. N.p.: Pea Ridge Press, 1994.

Durant, Samuel W., comp. *History of Kalamazoo County*. Philadelphia: Everts, 1880.

Durham, Walter T. *Nashville, Occupied City*. Nashville: The Tennessee Historical Society, 1985.

———. *Rebellion Revisited: A History of Sumner County, Tennessee from 1861 to 1870*. Gallatin, Tenn.: Sumner County Museum Association, 1982.

Dyer, John P. *"Fightin' Joe" Wheeler*. Baton Rouge: Louisiana State University Press, 1941.

Dyer, Frederick H. *A Compendium of the War of the Rebellion*. 2 vols. Dayton, Ohio: Morningside Books, 1979.

Edwards, Llewellyn N. *A Record of History and Evolution of Early American Bridges*. Orono, Maine: University Press, 1959.

Eisenhower, John S. D. *So Far from God: The U.S. War with Mexico, 1846–1848*. New York: Doubleday, 1989.

Elliot, James W. *Transport to Disaster*. New York: Holt, Rinehart, and Winston, 1962.

Engelhardt, Fred. *Fulling Mill Brook: A Study in Industrial Evolution, 1707–1937*. Brattleboro, Vt.: Stephen Daye, 1937.

Engle, Stephen. "Don Carlos Buell: Military Philosophy and Command Problems in the West." *Civil War History* 41 (1995): 89–115.

Estabrook, William Booth. *Genealogy of the Estabrook Family* . . . Ithaca, N.Y.: Andrus and Church, 1891.

Fancher, Isaac A. *Past and Present of Isabella County, Michigan*. Indianapolis: Bowen, 1911.

Fink, Albert. *Chief Engineer's Report, Louisville and Nashville Railroad, 1862–63*. Louisville: Louisville and Nashville Railroad, n.d.

Fisher, Ernest B., ed. *Grand Rapids and Kent County*. 2 vols. Chicago: Robert O. Law, 1918.

Fitch, John. *Annals of the Army of the Cumberland* . . . 5th ed. Philadelphia: J. B. Lippincott, 1864.

Forbes, William, II. *Haulin' Brass: Captain Croft's Flying Artillery Battery Columbus Georgia*. Dayton, Ohio: Morningside Press, 1993.

Force, Manning F. "Marching across Carolina." Vol. 1. *Sketches of War History . . . Papers Prepared For the Ohio Commandery of the Military Order of the Loyal Legion of the United States.* Cincinnati: Robert Clarke, 1888.

Freeman, Henry V. "Recollections." In *Illinois Commandery, Military Order of the Loyal Legion of the United States.* 8 vols. Chicago: Illinois Commandery, 1891. 3:227–46.

Freeman, Julia Susan (Wheelock). *The Boys in White: The Experience of a Hospital Agent in and around Washington.* New York: Lange and Hillman, 1870.

Freemasons. Michigan Royal and Select Masters. Grand Council. *History of Cryptic Masonry.* N.p., 1958.

———. Grand Lodge of Michigan. *Transactions of the Grand Lodge . . . Michigan.* Detroit: The Grand Lodge, 1858–1864.

Frey, Harold, and Wilda Babcock. *From the Diary of Thomas Marks.* N.p.: Privately published, 2000.

Gallman, J. Matthew. *The North Fights the Civil War: The Home Front.* Chicago: Ivan R. Dee, 1994.

Gardner, Washington. *History of Calhoun County, Michigan.* Chicago: Lewis, 1913.

Geary, James W. *We Need Men: The Union Draft in the Civil War.* DeKalb, Ill.: Northern Illinois University Press, 1991.

Genco, James G. *Arming Michigan's Regiments, 1862–1864.* N.p.: J. G. Genco, 1982.

"General's Tour Guide." *Blue and Gray.* Vol. 1, no. 2 (1997): 21–44.

Gibson, Charles Dana, and E. Kay Gibson. *Assault and Logistics: Union Army Coastal and River Operations, 1861–1866.* The Army's Navy Series. Camden, Maine: Ensign Press, 1995.

———. *Dictionary of Transports and Combatant Vessels, Steam and Sail, Employed by the Union Army, 1861–1868.* The Army's Navy Series. Camden, Maine: Ensign Press, 1996.

Gibson, John M. *Those 163 Days: A Southern Account of Sherman's March from Atlanta to Raleigh.* New York: Coward-McCann, 1961.

Gibson, Joseph Thompson. *History of the Seventy-Eighth Pennsylvania Infantry . . .* Pittsburg: Pittsburg Printing Company, 1905.

Gilmore, James [writing as Edmund Kirke]. *Down in Tennessee and Back by Way of Richmond.* New York: Carleton, 1864.

Glatthaar, Joseph T. *The March to the Sea and Beyond: Sherman's Troops in the Savannah and Carolinas Campaigns.* New York: New York University Press, 1985.

Goss, Dwight. *History of Grand Rapids and Its Industries.* Chicago: C. F. Cooper, 1906.

Gould, Benjamin A. *Investigations in the Military and Anthropological Statistics of American Soldiers. Sanitary Memoirs of the War of the Rebellion.* 2 vols. Cambridge, Mass.: Riverside Press, 1869.

Graf, LeRoy P., and Ralph W. Hasking, eds. *The Papers of Andrew Johnson.* 16 vols. Knoxville: University of Tennessee Press, 1967–2000.

Grant, Ulysses S. *Personal Memoirs of U. S. Grant.* 1885–1886. Reprint, New York: DaCapo Press, 1982.

Greeley, Horace. *The American Conflict: A History of the Great Rebellion.* 2 vols. Hartford, Conn.: O. D. Chase, 1867.

Bibliography

Green, Constance. *History of Naugatuck, Connecticut.* New Haven, Conn.: Yale University Press, 1949.

Griffith, Paddy. *Battle Tactics of the Civil War.* New Haven, Conn.: Yale University Press, 1987.

Grimsley, Mark. *The Hard Hand of War: Union Military Policy Toward Southern Civilians, 1861–1865.* Cambridge, Mass: University Press, 1995.

Hafendorfer, Kenneth. *Perryville: Battle for Kentucky.* Utica, Ky.: McDowell, 1981.

Hale, David. *The Third Texas Cavalry in the Civil War.* Norman: Oklahoma University Press, 1993.

Hall, Clifton R. *Andrew Johnson, Military Governor of Tennessee.* Princeton, N.J.: Princeton University Press, 1916.

Hannaford, Ebenezer. *The Story of a Regiment: A History of the Campaigns, and Association in the Field, of the Sixth Regiment Ohio Volunteer Infantry.* Cincinnati: Ebenezer Hannaford, 1868.

Hardison, Edwin T. "In the Toils of War: Andrew Johnson and the Federal Occupation of Tennessee, 1862–1865." PhD diss., University of Tennessee, 1981.

Harwell, Richard, and P. N. Racine, eds. *The Fiery Trail: A Union Officer's Account of Sherman's Last Campaign.* Knoxville: University of Tennessee Press, 1986.

Hattaway, Herman, and Archer Jones. *How the North Won: A Military History of the Civil War.* Urbana: University of Illinois Press, 1983.

Haupt, Herman. *General Theory of Bridge Construction.* New York: D. Appleton, 1851.

———. *Military Bridges, with Suggestions of New Expedients and Constructions for Crossing Streams and Chasms.* New York: D. Van Nostrand, 1864.

———. *Reminiscences of General Herman Haupt.* Milwaukee: Wright and Joys, 1901.

Hawes, George W. *Michigan State Gazetteer and Business Directory for 1860.* Detroit: F. Raymond, 1861.

Haynie, J. Henry. *The Nineteenth Illinois: A Memoir of a Regiment of Volunteer Infantry Famous in the Civil War of Fifty Years Ago for Its Drill, Bravery, and Distinguished Services.* Chicago: M. A. Donohue, 1912.

Hecht, Arthur. "Union Military Mail Service." *Filson Club Historical Quarterly* 37 (1963): 227–48.

Heitman, Francis B. *Historical Register and Dictionary of the United States Army . . .* 2 vols. 1903. Reprint, Urbana: University of Illinois Press, 1965.

Henry, Guy V. *Military Record of Civilian Appointments in the United States Army.* 2 vols. New York: Van Nostrand, 1873.

Herek, Raymond. *These Men Have Seen Hard Service: The First Michigan Sharpshooters in the Civil War.* Detroit: Wayne State University Press, 1998.

Hess, Earl J. *The Union Soldier in Battle: Enduring the Ordeal of Combat.* Lawrence: University Press of Kansas, 1997.

Hewett, Janet B., ed. *The Roster of Confederate Soldiers, 1861–1865.* 16 vols. Wilmington, N.C.: Broadfoot, 1995–.

Hewett, Janet B., Noah Andre Trudeau, and Bryce A. Suderow, eds. *Supplement to the Official Records of the Union and Confederate Armies.* Wilmington, N.C.: Broadfoot, 1994–.

Hight, John J. *History . . . Fifty-Eighth Indiana Regiment.* Compiled by Gilbert R. Stormont. Princeton, Ind.: Press of the Clarion, 1895.

History of Jackson County. Chicago: Interstate, 1881.

Hitchcock, Henry. *Marching with Sherman.* New Haven, Conn.: Yale University Press, 1927.

Hoehling, Adolph A. *Last Train from Atlanta.* New York: T. Yoseloff, 1958.

Holberton, William B. *Homeward Bound: The Demobilization of the Union and Confederate Armies, 1865–66.* Mechanicsburg, Pa.: Stackpole Books, 2001.

Holm, David D. *History of the Fifth Indiana Battery . . .* N.p., n.d.

Holmes, Amy E. "'Such is the price we pay': American Widows and the Civil War Pension System," in Maris Vinovskis, ed. *Toward A Social History of the Civil War.* Cambridge, England: Cambridge University Press, 1990.

Honeyman, Abraham Van Doren. *Johannes Nevius . . .* Plainfield, N.J.: Honeyman, 1900.

Hoobler, James A. *Cities under the Guns: Images of Occupied Nashville and Chattanooga.* Nashville: Rutledge Hill Press, 1986.

Horn, Stanley F. *The Army of Tennessee.* Norman: University of Oklahoma Press, 1953.

Howard, Oliver O. *Autobiography of Oliver Otis Howard, Major General, United States Army.* 2 vols. New York: Baker and Taylor, 1907.

Hudson, Leonne M., ed. *Company "A" Corps of Engineers, U.S.A., 1846–1848, in the Mexican War, by Gustavus Woodson Smith.* Kent, Ohio: Kent State University Press, 2001.

Hughes, N. C. "Hardee's Defense of Savannah." *Georgia Historical Quarterly* 47 (1963): 43–67.

Hunt, Roger D., and Jack R. Brown. *Brevet Brigadier Generals in Blue.* Gaithersburg, Md.: Olde Soldier Books, 1990.

Huntoon, Daniel T. V. *Phillip Hunton and His Descendants.* Cambridge, Mass.: J. Wilson and Son, 1881.

Illinois Military and Naval Department. *Report of the Adjutant General . . . for the Years 1861–66.* 8 vols. Springfield, Ill.: H. W. Rokker, 1886.

Innes, William P. *Report and Estimate of the Plan, Prospects, Character, and Advantages of the Proposed Improvement of the Muskegon River Flats, Ottawa County, Michigan.* Grand Rapids, Mich.: Grand Rapids Enquirer Printing, 1855.

Innes, William P., and J. F. Tinkham. *Innes' and Tinkham's Map of Kent County, Michigan.* Chicago: H. Acheson Lithographers, 1855.

———. *Map of the Muskegon River.* Chicago: Lithographic Press of Edward Mendel, [1855?].

Jamison, James K. *Families of Ontonagon County.* Ontonagon, Mich.: N.p., 1950.

Johnston, James Dale. *Johnston's Detroit City Directory and Advertising Gazetteer of Michigan.* Detroit: J. D. Johnston, 1857, 1861.

Jones, Charles C., Jr. *Siege of Savannah, 1864.* 1874. Reprint, Jonesboro, Ga.: Freedom Hill Press, 1988.

Jones, James P. "Farewell to Arms: Union Troops Muster Out at Louisville, June–August, 1865." *Filson Club Historical Quarterly* 36 (1962): 272–82.

Kamm, Samuel R. "The Civil War Career of Thomas A. Scott." PhD diss., University of Pennsylvania, 1940.

Keiffer, Joseph W. *Slavery and Four Years of War* . . . 2 vols. New York: G. P. Putnam's Sons, 1900.

Kennett, Lee B. *Marching through Georgia: The Story of Soldiers and Civilians during Sherman's Campaign.* New York: HarperCollins, 1995.

Kerr, Homer L., ed. *Fighting with Ross' Texas Cavalry: The Diary of George L. Griscom, Adjutant, 9th Texas Cavalry Regiment.* Hillsboro, Tex.: Hill Junior College Press, 1976.

Kerr, Joseph G. *Historical Development of the Louisville and Nashville Railroad System.* Louisville: Louisville and Nashville Railroad Company, 1926.

Kimberly, Robert L. *The Forty-first Ohio Veteran Volunteer Infantry in the War of the Rebellion, 1861–1865.* Cleveland: W. R. Smellie, 1897.

King's Nashville City Directory. Nashville: E. D. King, 1866.

Kirk, Charles H. *History of the Fifteenth Pennsylvania Volunteer Cavalry.* Philadelphia: N.p., 1906.

Kleber, Joseph, editor in chief. *The Kentucky Encyclopedia.* Lexington: University Press of Kentucky, 1992.

Klein, Maury. *History of the Louisville and Nashville Railroad.* New York: Macmillan, 1972.

Knights Templar. Grand Commandery. *Proceedings of the Regular Conclave . . . Michigan.* Detroit: Grand Commandery, 1858–61.

Knox, Mellon, Jr., ed. "Letters of James Greenalch." *Michigan History,* 44 (1960): 188–240.

Kreidburg, Marvin A., and Merton G. Henry. *History of Military Mobilization in the United States Army, 1775–1945.* Department of the Army Pamphlet No. 20-212. Washington, D.C.: Department of the Army, 1955.

Lamers, William M. *The Edge of Glory: A Biography of General William S. Rosecrans, U.S.A.* New York: Harcourt, Brace, and World, 1961.

Lanham, Charles. *The Red Book of Michigan.* Detroit: E. B. Smith, 1871.

Lash, Jeffrey N., "A Yankee in Gray: Danville Leadbetter and the Defense of Mobile Bay," *Civil War History* 37 (1991): 197–218.

Lathrop, David. *The History of the 59th Regiment Illinois Volunteers, or a Three Years' Campaign through Missouri, Arkansas, Mississippi, Tennessee, and Kentucky, with a Description of the Country, Towns, Skirmishes, and Battles.* Indianapolis: Hall and Hutchinson, 1865.

Lawson, Lewis. *Wheeler's Last Raid.* Greenwood, Fla.: Penkevill, 1986.

Leake, Paul. *History of Detroit: A Chronicle of Its Progress, Its Industries, Its Institutions, and the People of the Fair City of the Straits.* Chicago: Lewis, 1912.

LeDuc, William G. *Recollections of a Civil War Quartermaster: The Autobiography of William G. LeDuc.* St. Paul: North Central, 1963.

Leech, Margaret. *Reveille in Washington, 1860–1865.* New York: Harper and Brothers, 1941.

Leeson, Michael. *History of Kent County.* Chicago: Chapman, 1881.

———. *History of Macomb County.* Chicago: M. A. Leeson, 1882.

Long, David E. *The Jewell of Liberty: Abraham Lincoln's Re-Election and the End of Slavery.* Mechanicsburg, Pa.: Stackpole Books, 1997.

Long, E. B. *The Civil War Day by Day: An Almanac, 1861–1865.* Garden City, N.Y.: Doubleday, 1971.

Lord, Francis A. *Civil War Collector's Encyclopedia.* Harrisburg, Pa.: Stackpole, 1963.

———. *Lincoln's Railroad Man: Herman Haupt.* Rutherford, N.J.: Farleigh Dickinson University Press, 1969.

Loomis and Talbott's City Directory and Business Mirror for Kalamazoo, 1860–1861. Detroit: G. W. Hawes, 1860.

Louisville and Nashville Railroad. Office of the Chief Engineer. *Main Stem, Louisville and Nashville Railroad.* Louisville: Louisville and Nashville Railroad, 1884.

Lowry, Thomas. *Tarnished Eagles: The Courts-Martial of Fifty Union Colonels and Lieutenant Colonels.* Mechanicsburg, Pa.: Stackpole Books, 1997.

———. "Time Lapse." *Civil War Times Illustrated* 25 (February 1987): 29.

Lucas, Marion Brunson. *Sherman and the Burning of Columbia.* College Station: Texas A&M University Press, 1976.

Lytle, Andrew Nelson. *Bedford Forrest and His Critter Company.* Rev. ed. New York: McDowell, Obolensky, 1960.

Major, Duncan K. *Supply of Sherman's Army during the Atlanta Campaign.* Ft. Leavenworth, Kans.: Army Service Schools, 1911.

Malles, Ed, ed. *Bridge Building in War Time: Colonel Wesley Brainerd's Memoir of the 50th New York Volunteer Engineers.* Knoxville: University of Tennessee Press, 1997.

Marszalek, John F. *Sherman: A Soldier's Passion for Order.* New York: Free Press, 1993.

Maslowski, Peter. *Treason Must Be Made Odious.* New York: KTO Press, 1978.

McConnell, Stuart. *Glorious Contentment: The Grand Army of the Republic, 1865–1900.* Chapel Hill: University of North Carolina Press, 1992.

McDonough, James L. *Chattanooga: A Death Grip on the Confederacy.* Knoxville: University of Tennessee Press, 1984.

———. *Shiloh: In Hell before Night.* Knoxville: University of Tennessee Press, 1977.

———. *Stones River: Bloody Winter in Tennessee.* Knoxville: University of Tennessee Press, 1980.

———. *War in Kentucky: From Shiloh to Perryville.* Knoxville: University of Tennessee Press, 1994.

McDonough, James L., and James P. Jones. *War So Terrible: Sherman and Atlanta.* New York: W. W. Norton, 1987.

McDonough, James L., and Thomas Connelley. *Five Tragic Hours: The Battle of Franklin.* Knoxville: University of Tennessee Press, 1983.

McDonough, M. J., and P. S. Bond. *Use and Development of the Ponton Equipage.* Vol. 6 in *Professional Memoirs, Corps of Engineers, United States Army and Engineer Department at Large.* Washington, D.C.: Engineer School, 1914.

McGehee, Charles Stuart. "Wake of the Flood: A Southern City in the Civil War, Chattanooga, 1836–1873." PhD diss., University of Virginia, 1985.

McKinney, Francis F. "The First Regiment of Michigan Engineers and Mechanics." *Michigan Alumni Quarterly Review* 46 (1959): 140–50.

McMillan, Margaret B. *The Methodist Episcopal Church in Michigan during the Civil War.* Lansing: Michigan Civil War Centennial Commission, 1965.

McPherson, Edward. *The Political History of the United States of America during the Great Rebellion.* Washington, D.C.: Phip and Solomons, 1865.

McPherson, James M. *Battle Cry of Freedom.* New York: Oxford University Press, 1988.

———. *For Cause and Country: Why Men Fought in the Civil War.* New York: Oxford University Press, 1997.

Meints, Graydon M. *Michigan Railroads and Railroad Companies.* East Lansing: Michigan State University Press, 1992.

Merrill, William E. "The Engineer Service in Army of the Cumberland." In Van Horne, *Army of the Cumberland,* 2:439–58.

Methodist Episcopal Church, Detroit Conference. *Minutes of the 1906 Annual Session.* Detroit: The Conference, 1906.

Michigan Adjutant General. *Annual Report of the Adjutant General of the State of Michigan for the Year . . .* Lansing: John A. Kerr, 1855–66.

———. *Record of Service of Michigan Volunteers in the Civil War.* 46 vols. Kalamazoo, Mich.: Ihling Bros. and Everard, 1905.

Michigan Historical Commission. *Michigan Biographies.* 2 vols. Lansing: The Michigan Historical Commission, 1924.

Michigan House of Representatives. *Journal of the House of Representatives of the State of Michigan.* Lansing: John A. Kerr, 1865.

Michigan Quartermaster General. *Annual Report of the Quartermaster General of the State of Michigan.* Lansing: Quartermaster General's Office, 1861.

Miles, Jim. *Piercing the Heartland: A History and Tour Guide of the Tennessee and Kentucky Campaigns.* Nashville: Rutledge Hill Press, 2000.

———. *To the Sea: A History and Tour Guide of Sherman's March.* Nashville: Rutledge Hill Press, 1989.

Miller, Francis T., ed. *The Photographic History of the Civil War.* 10 vols. New York: Review of Reviews, 1911.

Miller, Marguerite. *A History of Elder Jacob Miller and Some of His Descendants.* LaPorte, Ind.: N.p., 1958.

Mitchel, F. A. *Ormsby MacKnight Mitchel, Astronomer and General: A Biographical Narrative.* New York: Houghton, Mifflin, 1887.

Morhouse, Henry C. *Reminiscences of the 123rd New York.* Greenwich, N.Y.: People's Journal Book and Job Office, 1879.

Morris, Roy, Jr. "The Sack of Athens" *Civil War Times Illustrated* 25 (1986): 26–32.

Murdock, Eugene C. *One Million Men: The Civil War Draft in the North.* Madison: State Historical Society of Wisconsin, 1971.

———. *Patriotism Limited, 1862–1865: The Civil War Draft and the Bounty System.* Kent, Ohio: Kent State University Press, 1967.

Myers, Robert C. "The Worst Colonel I Ever Saw." *Michigan History* 80 (1996): 34–43.

Nashville City and Business Directory, 1860–61. Nashville: L. P. Williams, 1860.

Neal, William A. *An Illustrated History of the Missouri Engineers and the 25th Infantry Regiment.* Chicago: Donohue and Henneberry, 1889.

Niccum, Norman, ed. "Diary of Lieutenant Frank Hughes." *Indiana Magazine of History* 45 (1949): 274–84.

Noe, Kenneth. *Perryville: This Grand Havoc of Battle.* Lexington: University Press of Kentucky, 2001.

"Obituaries." *Engineering Record* 28 (1893): 166.

Petz, Weldon. "Michigan's Florence Nightingale." *Michigan History* 82 (1998): 67–74.

Phisterer, Frederick. *Statistical Record of the Armies of the United States.* New York: Scribner's Sons, 1883.

Pickenpaugh, Roger. *Rescue by Rail: Troop Transfer and the Civil War in the West, 1863.* Lincoln: University of Nebraska Press, 1998.

Plum, William R. *The Military Telegraph during the Civil War in the United States.* 2 vols. New York: Arno Press, 1974.

Portrait and Biographical Album of Ionia and Montcalm Counties, Michigan. Chicago: Chapman, 1891.

Portrait and Biographical Album of Kalamazoo, Allegan, and Van Buren Counties, Michigan. Chicago, Chapman, 1892.

Portrait and Biographical Album of Washtenaw County, Michigan. Chicago: Biographical Publishing, 1891.

Potter, Jerry O. *The* Sultana *Tragedy: America's Greatest Maritime Disaster.* Gretna, La.: Pelican, 1992.

Price, Charles L. "The United States Military Railroads in North Carolina, 1862–1865." *The North Carolina Historical Review* 53 (1976): 243–64.

Prokopowicz, Gerald J. *All for the Regiment: The Army of the Ohio, 1861–1862.* Chapel Hill: University of North Carolina Press, 2001.

Rappaport, Armin. "The Replacement System during the Civil War." In *Military Analysis of the Civil War: An Anthology by the Editors of Military Affairs.* Millwood, N.Y.: KTO Press, 1977. 115–26.

Record of Service of Michigan Volunteers in the Civil War. 46 vols. Kalamazoo, Mich: Ihling Bros. and Everard, 1905.

Record of the Descendants of James Ensign. 3 vols. Moline, Ill.: n.p., 1939.

Remington, Jesse A. "Combat Engineers: Lavergne, Tennessee, 1863." *The Military Engineer* 52 (1960): 291.

Rennick, Robert M. *Kentucky Place Names.* Lexington: University Press of Kentucky, 1984.

Revised Regulations for the Army of the United States, 1861. 1861. Reprint, Harrisburg, Pa.: National Historical Society, 1980.

Reid, Whitelaw. *Ohio in the War: Her Statesman, Her Generals, and Soldiers.* 2 vols. New York: Moore, Wilstach, and Baldwin, 1868.

Rice, Charles. *Hard Times: The Civil War in Huntsville and North Alabama.* Boaz, Ala.: Boaz Printing, 1994.

Riegel, Robert E. "Federal Operations of Southern Railroads during the Civil War." *Mississippi Valley Historical Review* 9 (1922): 126–38.

Robertson, James I. *Soldiers Blue and Gray.* Columbia: University of South Carolina Press, 1988.

Robertson, John. *Michigan in the War.* Rev. ed. Lansing: W. S. George, 1882.

Bibliography

Royal Arch Masons, Grand Chapter (Michigan). *Proceedings of the Grand Chapter of Royal Arch Masons of the State of Michigan, 1862.* Detroit: N.p., 1862.

Royse, Isaac H. C. *History of the 115th Regiment Illinois Volunteer Infantry.* Terre Haute, Ind.: Privately printed, 1900.

Salecker, Gene E. *Disaster on the Mississippi: The* Sultana *Explosion, April 27, 1865.* Annapolis: Naval Institute Press, 1996.

Scott, Henry L. *Military Dictionary.* 1861. Reprint, Denver: Fort Yuma Press, 1984.

Scott, William B. "The Topographical Influences on the Campaigns in Middle and West Tennessee during the First Year of the Civil War." Master's thesis, University of Tennessee, 1953.

Shannon, Fred A. Shannon. *The Organization and Administration of the Union Army, 1861–1865.* 2 vols. Cleveland: Arthur H. Clark, 1928.

Sheridan, Philip. *Personal Memoirs of P. H. Sheridan, General United States Army.* 2 vols. New York: Charles L. Webster, 1888.

Sherman, William T. *Memoirs of General William T. Sherman.* Bloomington: Indiana University Press, 1957.

Shoemaker, Michael. "The Michigan Thirteenth." *Michigan Pioneer and Historical Collection* 4 (1883): 133–68.

Shiman, Philip L. "Engineering and Command: The Case of General William S. Rosecrans, 1862–1863." In *The Art of Command in the Civil War.* Ed. Steven E. Woodworth. Lincoln: University of Nebraska Press, 1998. 84–117.

———. "Engineering Sherman's March: Army Engineers and the Management of Modern War, 1862–1865." PhD diss., Duke University, 1991.

Siburt, James T. "Colonel John M. Hughs: Brigade Commander and Confederate Guerrilla." *Tennessee Historical Quarterly* 51 (1992): 87–95.

Sligh, Charles R. *History of the Services of the First Regiment Michigan Engineers and Mechanics, During the Civil War, 1861–1865.* Grand Rapids, Mich.: White Printing, 1921.

Slocum, Henry W. "Sherman's March from Savannah to Bentonville." In *Battles and Leaders of the Civil War,* vol. 4. 1887–88. Reprint, Secaucus, N.J.: Castle, 1982. 681–95.

Smith, William F. "Operations around Chattanooga, Tennessee." In *Papers, Military Historical Society of Massachusetts,* vol. 8. Boston: Military Historical Society of Massachusetts, 1910. 149–247.

———. *The Re-opening of the Tennessee River near Chattanooga, October 1863.* Wilmington: Press of Mercantile Printing, n.d.

Steenburn, Donald. *Silent Echoes of Johnsonville: Rebel Cavalry and Yankee Gunboats.* Rogersville, Ala.: Elk River Press, 1994.

Stillwell, Leander. *Story of a Common Soldier of Army Life in the Civil War, 1861–1865.* 1920. Reprint, Alexandria, Va.: Time-Life Books, 1983.

Summers, Thomas J. *History of Marietta.* Marietta, Ohio: Leader, 1903.

Swantner, Eva. "Military Railroads during the Civil War." *Military Engineer* 22 (1930): 13–21.

Switlik, Matthew C. "Loomis' Battery: First Michigan Light Artillery, 1859–1865." Master's thesis, Wayne State University, Detroit, 1975.

Sword, Wiley. *Embrace an Angry Wind, The Confederacy's Last Hurrah: Spring Hill, Franklin, and Nashville.* New York: HarperCollins, 1992.

———. *Mountains Touched with Fire: Chattanooga Besieged, 1863.* New York: St. Martin's Press, 1995.

———. *Shiloh: Bloody April.* New York: Morrow, 1974.

Tennessee Department of Transportation. *Rutherford County.* Tennessee Department of Transportation Map, 1991.

Thienel, Philip M. "Engineers in the Union Army, 1861–1865." *The Military Engineer* 47 (1955): 36–41.

Thorne, Charles B. "The Watering Spas of Middle Tennessee." *Tennessee Historical Quarterly* 29 (1970): 345–46.

Thornton, Leland. *When Gallantry Was Commonplace: The History of the Michigan Eleventh Volunteer Infantry, 1861–1864.* New York: P. Lang, 1991.

Traas, Adrian. *From the Golden Gate to Mexico City: The U.S. Army Topographical Engineers in the Mexican War, 1846–1848.* Washington, D.C.: U.S. Army Corps of Engineers, 1993.

Traveler's Official Railway Guide of the US and Canada. N.p., 1868.

Trefouse, Hans. *Andrew Johnson: A Biography.* New York: W. W. Norton, 1989.

Trudeau, Noah. *Out of the Storm: The End of the Civil War, April–June 1865.* New York: Little, Brown, 1994.

Turchin, John B. "Huntsville, Alabama: The Seizure of It and of a Part of the Memphis and Charleston Railroad in April, 1862." Vol. 1. *War Papers, Department of Ohio, Grand Army of the Republic.* Cincinnati: Privately printed, n.d.

Turner, George E. *Victory Rode the Rails: The Strategic Place of the Railroads in the Civil War.* Lincoln: University of Nebraska Press, 1992.

United Daughters of the Confederacy, J. E. B. Stuart Chapter. *War Days in Fayetteville, North Carolina: Reminiscences of 1861 to 1865.* Fayetteville, N.C.: Judge Printing, 1910.

U.S. Adjutant General's Office. *Official Army Register of the Volunteer Force of the United States Army for the Years 1861, '62, '63, '64, '65.* 8 vols. Gaithersburg, Md.: Olde Soldier Books, 1987.

U.S. Bureau of the Census. Census of Population. 1850, 1860.

U.S. Congress. House. *Affairs of Southern Railroads.* 39th Cong., 2nd sess. H. Rep. 34, serial 1306.

U.S. Congress. House. 40th Cong., 2nd sess. H. Rep. 3, serial 1357.

U.S. Navy Department. *Official Records of the Union and Confederate Navies.* 30 vols. 1896–1906. Reprint, Harrisburg, Pa.: National Historical Society, 1987.

U.S. War Department. *Atlas to Accompany the Official Records of the Union and Confederate Armies.* 1891–95. Reprint, New York: Fairfax Press, 1978.

———. *The War of the Rebellion: A Compilation of the Official Records of the Union and Confederate Armies.* 128 vols. 1880–1901. Reprint, Harrisburg, Pa.: National Historical Society, 1985.

Van Horne, Thomas. *History of the Army of the Cumberland, Its Organization, Campaigns, and Battles.* 2 vols. 1876. Reprint, Wilmington, N.C.: Broadfoot, 1992.

Vetter, Charles E. *Sherman: Merchant of Terror, Advocate of Peace.* Gretna, La.: Pelican, 1992.

Bibliography

Vocke, William. "The Military Achievements of Major General Ormsby Mac-Knight Mitchel." In *Illinois Commandery, Military Order of the Loyal Legion of the United States*, vol. 4. Chicago: Commandery, 1891. 85–95.

Waddle, Angus. *Three Years with the Armies of the Ohio and the Cumberland*. Chillicothe, Ohio: Scioto Gazette Book and Job Office, 1889.

Walden, Madison M. *A Brief History of the Eighth Iowa Volunteer Cavalry*. Des Moines: Register and Leader, 1909.

Ward, Clyde. "Twisting Confederate Iron." *Civil War Times Illustrated* 25 (December 1986): 24–27.

Warner, Ezra. *Generals in Blue*. Baton Rouge: Louisiana State University Press, 1964.

Waugh, John C. *Reelecting Lincoln: The Battle for the 1864 Presidency*. New York: Crown, 1998.

Weber, Thomas. *The Northern Railroads in the Civil War, 1861–1865*. Westport, Conn.: Greenwood Press, 1952.

Weigley, Russell F. *History of the United States Army*. New York: Macmillan, 1967.

Welcher, Frank J. *The Union Army, 1861–1865: Organization and Operation*. 2 vols. Bloomington: Indiana University Press, 1989–93.

Wendell, Emory. *Wendell's History of Banking . . . Michigan*. 2 vols. Detroit: N.p., 1900.

Whipple, Squire. *A Work on Bridge Building . . .* Utica, N.Y.: H. H. Curtiss, 1847.

Wiley, Bell I. *The Life of Billy Yank*. 1978. Reprint, Baton Rouge: Louisiana State University Press, 1987.

Williams, Alpheus S. *From the Cannons Mouth: The Civil War Letters of General Alpheus Williams*, edited by Milo M. Quaife. Detroit: Wayne State University Press, 1959.

Williams, John B. *Leaves from a Soldier's Diary*. Philadelphia: Privately printed, 1869.

Williams, Kenneth P. *Lincoln Finds a General: A Military History of the Civil War*. 5 vols. New York: Macmillan, 1949–59.

Williams, Thomas Harry. *Hayes of the Twenty-Third: The Civil War Volunteer Officer*. New York: Knopf, 1965.

Willett, James R. *Rambling Recollections of a Military Engineer*. Chicago: John Morris, 1888.

Willman, Charles. *Ontonagon County in the Civil War*. N.p., 1961.

Wood, Edwin O. *History of Genesee County, Michigan*. 2 vols. Indianapolis: Federal, 1916.

Wood, William J. *Civil War Generalship: The Art of Command*. Westport, Conn.: Praeger, 1997.

Woodworth, Steven E. *Jefferson Davis and His Generals: The Failure of Confederate Command in the West*. Lawrence: University Press of Kansas, 2000.

Wulsin, Lucien. *The Story of the Fourth Regiment Ohio Veteran Volunteer Cavalry*. Edited by Eleanor N. Adams. Cincinnati: N.p., 1912.

Wyeth, John A. *With Sabre and Scalpel*. New York: Harper and Brothers, 1914.

Youngberg, G. A. *History of Engineer Troops in the United States Army, 1775–1901*. No. 37, Occasional Papers, Engineer School, U.S. Army. Washington, D.C.: Press of the Engineer School, 1901.

Index

Index